The Annual of Scientific Discovery: Or, Year-Book of Facts in Science and Art

by David Ames Wells

Address:
HardPress
8345 NW 66TH ST #2561
MIAMI FL 33166-2626
USA
Email: info@hardpress.net

Annual of scientific discovery

David Ames Wells, George Bliss, Samuel Kneeland,
John Trowbridge, William Ripley Nichols, Charles ...

Q. A. Gillmore

Eng. for the Annual of Scientific Discovery 1864

Gould and Lincoln Boston

ANNUAL

OF

SCIENTIFIC DISCOVERY:

OR,

YEAR-BOOK OF FACTS IN SCIENCE AND ART

FOR 1864.

EXHIBITING THE

MOST IMPORTANT DISCOVERIES AND IMPROVEMENTS

IN

MECHANICS, USEFUL ARTS, NATURAL PHILOSOPHY, CHEMISTRY,
ASTRONOMY, GEOLOGY, ZOOLOGY, BOTANY, MINERALOGY,
METEOROLOGY, GEOGRAPHY, ANTIQUITIES, ETC.

TOGETHER WITH

NOTES ON THE PROGRESS OF SCIENCE DURING THE YEAR 1863; A LIST
OF RECENT SCIENTIFIC PUBLICATIONS; OBITUARIES OF
EMINENT SCIENTIFIC MEN, ETC.

EDITED BY

DAVID A. WELLS, A.M., M.D.,

AUTHOR OF PRINCIPLES OF NATURAL PHILOSOPHY, PRINCIPLES OF CHEMISTRY,
FIRST PRINCIPLES OF GEOLOGY, ETC.

BOSTON:
GOULD AND LINCOLN,
59 WASHINGTON STREET.
NEW YORK: SHELDON AND COMPANY.
CINCINNATI: GEORGE S. BLANCHARD.
LONDON: TRUBNER & CO.
1867.

NOTES BY THE EDITOR

ON THE

PROGRESS OF SCIENCE FOR THE YEAR 1863.

THE thirty-third annual meeting of the British Association for the Advancement of Science was held at Newcastle-on-Tyne, Sir William Armstrong (the gun-maker) being in the chair. The meeting was above the average, as respects the numbers in attendance and the interest of the papers brought forward. Sir Charles Lyell was selected as the President for 1864.

From the annual address of the President, reviewing the recent progress of Science, we make the following extracts. Referring to the district of Newcastle as the birth-place of Stephenson, and of locomotives and railways, he said, " The history of railways shows what grand results may have their origin in small beginnings. When coal was first conveyed in this neighborhood from the pit to the shipping-place on the Tyne, the pack-horse, carrying a burden of three hundred-weight, was the only mode of transport employed. As soon as roads suitable for wheeled carriages were formed, carts were introduced, and this first step in mechanical appliance to facilitate transport had the effect of increasing the load which the horse was enabled to carry, from three hundred-weight to seventeen hundred-weight. The next improvement consisted in laying wooden bars or rails for the wheels of carts to run upon, and this was followed by the substitution of the four-wheeled wagon for the two-wheeled cart. By this further application of mechanical principles the original horse-load of three hundred-weight was augmented to forty-two hundred-weight. These were important results, and they were not obtained without the shipwreck of the fortunes of some men whose ideas were in advance of the times in which they lived. The next step in the progress of railways was the attachment of slips of iron to the wooden rails. Then came the iron tramway, consisting of cast-iron bars of an angular section; in this arrangement,

III

the upright flange of the bar acted as a guide to keep the wheel on the track. The next advance was an important one, and consisted in transferring the guiding-flange from the rail to the wheel; this improvement enabled cast-iron edge-rails to be used. Finally, in 1820, after the lapse of about 200 years from the first employment of wooden bars, wrought-iron rails, rolled in long lengths, and of suitable section, were made, and eventually superseded all other forms of railway. Thus, the railway system, like all other large inventions, has risen to its present importance by a series of steps; and so gradual has been its progress that Europe finds itself committed to a gauge fortuitously determined by the distance between the wheels of the carts for which wooden rails were originally laid down.

Last of all came the locomotive engine, that crowning achievement of mechanical science, which enables us to convey a load of 200 tons at a cost of fuel scarcely exceeding that of the corn and hay which the original pack-horse consumed in conveying its load of three hundredweight an equal distance.

In thus glancing at the history of railways, we may observe how promptly the inventive faculty of man supplies the device which the circumstances of the moment require. No sooner is a road formed fit for wheeled carriages to pass along than the cart takes the place of the pack-saddle: no sooner is the wooden railway provided than the wagon is substituted for the cart: and no sooner is an iron railway formed, capable of carrying heavy loads, than the locomotive engine is found ready to commence its career. As in the vegetable kingdom fit conditions of soil and climate quickly cause the appearance of suitable plants, so in the intellectual world fitness of time and circumstance promptly calls forth appropriate devices. The seeds of invention exist, as it were, in the air, ready to germinate whenever suitable conditions arise, and no legislative interference is needed to insure their growth in proper season."

Necessity for a New System of Writing. — "The facility now given to the transmission of intelligence and the interchange of thought is one of the most remarkable features of the present age. Cheap and rapid postage to all parts of the world, — paper and printing reduced to the lowest cost, — electric telegraphs between nation and nation, town and town, all contribute to aid that commerce of ideas by which wealth and knowledge are augmented. But while so much facility is given to mental communications by new measures and new inventions, the fundamental art of expressing thought by written symbols remains as imperfect now as it has been for centuries past. It seems strange that while we actually possess a system of short-hand by which words can be recorded as rapidly as they can be spoken, we should persist in writing a slow and laborious long-hand. It is intelligible that grown-up persons who have acquired the present conventional art of writing should be reluctant to incur the labor of mastering a better system; but there can be no reason why the rising generation should not be instructed in a method of writing more in accordance with the activity of mind which now prevails. Even without going so far as to adopt for ordinary use a complete system of stenography, which it is not easy to acquire, we might greatly abridge the time and labor of writing by the recognition of a few simple signs to express the syllables which are of most frequent occurrence in our language. Our words are in a great measure made up of such syllables as *com, con, tion, ing, able, ain, ent, est, ance,* etc. These we are now obliged to write out over and over again, as if time and labor expended in what may be termed visual speech were of no importance. Neither has our written character the advantage of distinctness to recommend it — it is only necessary to write such a word as *minimum* or *ammunition* to become aware of the want of sufficient difference between the letters we employ."

National Uniformity of Weights and Measures. — " Another subject of a social character which demands our consideration is the much-debated question of weights and measures. Whatever difference of opinion there may be as to the comparative merits of decimal and duodecimal division, there can, at all events, be none as to the importance of assimilating the systems of measurement in different countries. Science suffers by the want of uniformity, because valuable observations made in one country are in a great measure lost to another from the labor required to convert a series of quantities into new denominations. International commerce is also impeded by the same cause, which is productive of constant inconvenience and frequent mistake. It is much to be regretted that two standards of measure so nearly alike as the English yard and the French mètre should not be made absolutely identical. The metric system has already been adopted by other nations besides France, and is the only one which has any chance of becoming universal. We in England, therefore, have no alternative but to conform with France, if we desire general uniformity. The change might easily be introduced in scientific literature, and in that case it would probably extend itself by degrees amongst the commercial classes without much legislative pressure. Besides the advantage which would thus be gained in regard to uniformity, I am convinced that the adoption of the decimal division of the French scale would be attended with

1*

great convenience, both in science and commerce. I can speak from personal experience of the superiority of decimal measurement in all cases where accuracy is required in mechanical construction. In the Elswick Works [where the Armstrong guns are made. ED.], as well as in some other large establishments of the same description, the inch is adopted as the unit, and all fractional parts are expressed in decimals. No difficulty has been experienced in habituating the workmen to the use of this method, and it has greatly contributed to precision of workmanship. The inch, however, is too small a unit, and it would be advantageous to substitute the mètre if general concurrence could be obtained. As to our thermometric scale, it was originally founded in error; it is also most inconvenient in division, and ought at once to be abandoned in favor of the centigrade scale. The recognition of the metric system and of the centigrade scale by the numerous men of science composing the British Association, would be a most important step toward effecting that universal adoption of the French standards in this country which, sooner or later, will inevitably take place; and the Association in its collective capacity might take the lead in this good work, by excluding in future all other standards from their published Proceedings."

In this connection it may be interesting to add that a commission of scientists has recently been convened in Germany, to consider what measures may be best adopted there, to secure uniformity of weights and measures, and the various continental Governments have been called upon to examine the practicability of those which have been recommended. The Bavarian Government states its readiness to adopt the decimal system for weight and long measure, but in surface and cubic measure can only promise to have tables of reduction prepared and circulated. The land-tax, as it exists in Bavaria, is the chief obstacle to any simplification of the surface scale, while the fact that there are different measures for fire-wood, for timber, for earth and for stone would cause great confusion if any reform of cubic measure were to be introduced.

Accuracy of Modern Astronomical Investigations. — In another part of the present volume, attention is called to the discrepancy which exists in the estimates of astronomers respecting the solar parallax. This has usually been represented by eight seconds and a half; but according to the recent calculations of Hansen, the German astronomer, *four-tenths of a second* should be added, which reduces the distance of the earth from the sun about four millions of miles. At a recent meeting of the Royal Astronomical Society (G. B.), Mr. Pritchard thus represented the difference : " Take a hair and measure it, and you will find that the correction of the distance amounts to this, — that we have to look at the hair at a distance of 125 feet. This is the correction that astronomers have made : or, let us look at a sovereign at a distance of eight miles ; it amounts to about the same thing. We ought to be thankful that we are able to calculate and correct such inappreciable quantities."

Astronomical Memoranda. — The Lalande prize of the French Academy has been awarded to Mr. Alvan Clark, of Cambridgeport, Mass., for his discovery of the companion star of Sirius, the great object-glass (18 inches in diameter), with which this most interesting discovery was made, was Mr. Clark's own manufacture, and was intended for the observatory of the University of Mississippi. In consequence, however, of the breaking out of the civil war, this glass was never delivered, and has since been sold to the Astronomical Association of Chicago for 11,000 dollars. It is highly creditable to the West that such a purchase should have been made for its busiest trading city, and we may anticipate that the observatory of Chicago, which has already done good work, will achieve a reputation in the higher branches of astronomy.

At a meeting of the Royal Asiatic Society held March, 1863, Dr. Kern produced a translation of a portion of the works of Aryabhatta, a celebrated Hindoo mathematician of antiquity, which seemed to prove conclusively that the sphericity and diurnal rotation of the earth had been correctly apprehended by that early Indian writer, who flourished at an epoch variously estimated by different investigators, but which must have been prior to A. D. 600, and has been placed as far back as B. C. 100.

Extension of Telegraphic Communication.—During the year 1863, communication by electric telegraph has taken place between London and Turnen, in Siberia, a distance of 4039 miles. It was anticipated that an extension of the wires will be made to Nikolaievski, on the Pacific, by the end of 1863, and that telegraphic communication with New York, *via* Siberia and California, will be established by the end of 1865.

Meteorological Science. — The most important contributions to Meteorological Science of the year have been made through the balloon ascensions of Mr. James Glaisher, under the auspices of the British Association. The observations of the meteorologist show that the decrease of temperature with elevation does not follow the law previously assumed of 1° in 300 feet, and that in fact it follows no definite law at all. Mr. Glaisher appears also to have ascertained the interesting fact that rain is only precipitated when cloud exists in a double layer. Raindrops, he has found, diminish in size with elevation, merging into wet mist, and ultimately into dry frog. Mr. Glaisher met with snow for a mile in thickness below rain, which is at variance with our preconceived ideas.

Cinchona Bark from India. — The gradual but certain destruction of the Cinchona forests of America, which has been viewed with so much anxiety by all who know how indispensable quinine is to the existence of Europeans in many of the tropical parts of the world, may for the future be considered of minor importance, inasmuch as the successful cultivation of the Cinchonas in India has been demonstrated the past year. At a meeting of the Linnean Society, London, June, 1863, the first specimens of Cinchona bark sent from India to Europe were exhibited. It was stated that these had been found to yield a percentage of quinine, and the other febrifuge alkaloids, fully equal to that furnished by the bark of the same species when grown in South America ; and it had also been ascertained that quinine might be obtained in small quantities from the leaves. The successful culture of the Cinchona plants in India must be regarded as a subject of the highest importance, not merely to the prosperity of India, but indirectly to the whole world ; as the exploration and civilization of many tropical countries by Europeans is absolutely dependent on a reliable supply of quinine.

Acclimatizing Efforts in Australia. — The work of acclimatizing European animals in Australia, under the direction of proper authorities, is being pursued vigorously, and with great success. Mr. Edward Wilson, of Melbourne, Australia, in a report on the subject, states that the English skylark and the thrush were breeding freely in a wild state, and " not only making various neighborhoods vocal, but absolutely, by force of example, compelling the native birds to improve their song-notes." A number of fallow deer had been turned out, and taken readily to bush life. Several kinds of English pond fish had been safely brought over, and transferred to the native waters. A collection of birds, amongst others the Indian curassow, gold, silver, and common pheasants, Ceylon peafowl, American and other waterfowl, were being prepared in the Botanic Gardens for transfer to wild land, and it was thought that all would eventually thrive. The lama has been acclimatized and its wool has become one of the products of Australia.

Steam Cultivation. — A " General Steam Cultivation Company " has been started in London, with a capital of over a million dollars, whose object is announced to be to purchase, keep on hand, and rent or let

to farmers, at reasonable rates, every kind of steam agricultural implement. The prospectus suggests that many farmers would gladly use
steam in ploughing and otherwise working their soil, but cannot afford
to invest several thousand dollars in the needful machinery. To these
this company proposes to be helpful. It is asserted that applications
are already received for renting machinery to the value of quarter of
a million of dollars. A Mr. Smith, of Woolston, England, who has especially exerted himself during the last few years to promote "steam
culture," has recently published a *resumé* of his personal experience in
this matter. He states, that the cost of preparing land for roots was,
with steam, $2.88; with horses, $10.03; for barley two years, $2.16
with steam against $5.05 by horse power; four years for wheat, $50.20
by steam against the same for horse power, and foots up a total for a
number of other articles, which shows a gain of 200 per cent. in favor
of steam. The writer says also that besides the economy of the plan,
he had much better crops.

Novelty in Architectural Construction. — A novelty in architectural
construction has been brought out during the past year in the construction of a building designed for a school of art at Nottingham, England.
The dome of the tower is to be covered, and some panels in the front
filled in with Minton's encaustic tiles, patterned in bright colors. The
London *Athenæum* commenting on this peculiarity says, "We cannot
understand why, considering the exigencies of our town life and atmosphere, the whole exterior of a building could not be covered with ceram-
ics, comprising bands in bold relief richly moulded and colored, dec-
orated heads for windows, and friezes of figures, either relieved, or,
preferably, drawn on the flat, in an architectonic character and soberly
toned in color, either on a white or a bright-hued ground. Glazed surfaces are obviously the only ones fit for exterior decoration in modern
towns. Let any one look at the waste of labor on the carvings of St.
Paul's, what a stained and smeared great structure it is, or at the
Houses of Parliament, and see how the sooty streams trail over the
costly waste of mouldings and figures, and not only hide but eat them
away; then let him consider what the latter building will be a century
hence, judging by what he sees of the piebald state of the former. Do
we not make glazed earthenware for half the planet, and can we not
cover our own houses with it?"

Recent Progress of Chemical Science. — During the past year,
through the aid of the process of spectral analysis, another new body,
Indium, has been added to the list of the elements. Bessemer's process
of manufacturing iron and steel may now be considered as having

passed out from the domain of theory, into the province of actual and practical fact. The contributions made to our knowledge by Professor Graham respecting the molecular constitution and properties of gases, should also be included among the important novelties of the year in inorganic chemistry. The recent advances in organic chemistry are thus detailed by a writer in the London *Pharmaceutical Journal*, — Dr. MacAdam. He says, "Not only does the manufacturing chemistry of the day transform starch and sugar into alcohol by fermentation, as in brewing operations; sawdust into oxalic acid by the action of soda and nitre; starch or sawdust into grape-sugar by the aid of sulphuric acid; wood and coal into paraffin and paraffin oils by the process of destructive distillation; coal into aniline and the coal-tar colors; and guano into a magnificent color, rivalling that from the cochineal insect; but the organic chemistry of the day has proceeded to produce artificially many alcohols and ethers, including jargonelle pear essence and pine-apple essence; and to construct many alkaloids resembling quinine, strychnine and morphine in their composition and chemical properties, encouraging the hope that we may soon be in possession of the means of preparing by artificial processes these powerful medicines, and possibly others equally efficacious. And more than that, and principally through the researches of Berthelot, dead mineral matter has been worked up by stages into organic compounds. Thus Berthelot, taking carbon and sulphur, combines these into bisulphide of carbon, a mobile, ethereal liquid; and therefore, by the mutual reaction of copper, hydrosulphuric acid, and the bisulphide of carbon, he obtains olefiant gas. The latter is absorbed by sulphuric acid (oil of vitrol) to the extent of 120 volumes of the gas in one of the acid, and thereafter by dilution with water and distillation, the acid mixture yields alcohol of the same composition and properties as that obtained from ordinary grain. Strecker takes the olefiant gas in solution in sulphuric acid, and by adding water, neutralizing with ammonia, evaporating and heating, obtains crystals of taurine, one of the constituents of bile. Wöhler combines the simple elements, nitrogen and oxygen, by electric discharges, into nitric acid, and then by the successive mutual reaction of this nitric acid with tin, hydrochloric acid, and black lead, and lime (or oxide of lead), he obtains a complicated organic substance, called the hydrocyanate of ammonia. The latter may also be prepared by passing a mixture of the gases ammonia and carbonic oxide through a red-hot tube. The hydrocyanate of ammonia may then be employed in yielding cyanogen, hydrocyanic acid (prussic acid), oxalic acid, and urea; also formic acid, paracyanogen, cyanuric acid, sulphocyanogen, and mellon.

" When cast-iron (which contains carbon) is dissolved in dilute sulphuric or hydrochloric acid, there is evolved a volatile oil resembling turpentine, and there is left in the vessel a small quantity of graphite, and a brown mould resembling vegetable mould. Ordinary carbonate of soda (washing soda) can have carbon extracted from it, and if the latter is acted upon by dilute nitric acid, and the solution evaporated, an artificial tannin is obtained, which has the property of precipitating gelatine or glue from its solution, like ordinary tannin obtained from gall nuts or oak bark. Berthelot has taken carbonic oxide and caustic potash, and compelled them to produce formic acid (yielded naturally by red ants) ; and with a single link of the chain awanting, he has manufactured glycerine, which is the base of fatty substances, and combining it with the fatty acids, he has prepared artificially the oils and fats generally obtained from the plant and the animal, and many more new oils and fats not known in nature. Berthelot has acted upon glycerine by putrefying animal matter, and obtained artificially grape sugar ; and has converted oil of turpentine into ordinary camphor and Borneo camphor ; whilst, in conjunction with De Luca, he has prepared artificially one of the chief constituents of oil of mustard (sulphocyanide of allyl).

" These researches in organic chemistry may appear, at this, the moment of their birth, to have little influence on the arts and manufactures and on mankind in general. But are they not researches into the deep mysteries of nature ? and who can predict the influence which they may yet have on the prosperity of the human race ? "

Change of Color in Stars. — It is more than suspected by some of the European astronomers that an example of a star successively changing its color may now exist in the stellar body known as *ninety-five Herculis*. Mr. Higgins, in his observation on Spectra of Stars, has had occasion to notice the phenomena, and he describes the change as observable, even after intervals so brief as three or four nights.

The so-called Spiritual Phenomena. — A recognition of the *reality of many* of the phenomena — physical or physiological — which are popularily classified under the term " *Spiritual* " appears to be gradually gaining ground among the scientific men of the United States and Europe. Among the names of note *who are reported* during the past year as having extended such a recognition, we find that of Prof. De Morgan, who is confessedly one of the most distinguished of living British physicists and mathematicians. The position which this gentleman and others assume is probably well expressed in the following extracts of a letter recently published in the *London Athenæum*. This observer says : —

" I divide, for brevity sake, all the phenomena into *physical* and *metaphysical*, — a division which, if not strictly philosophical, will be sufficiently understood by those who have been present at any so-called sitting. My testimony, then, is this : — I have seen and felt physical facts wholly and utterly inexplicable, as I believe, by any known and generally received physical laws. I unhesitatingly reject the theory which considers such facts to be produced by means familiar to the best professors of legerdemain. I have witnessed also many *very surprising and extraordinary* metaphysical manifestations. But I cannot say that *any* of those have been such as *wholly* to exclude the possibility of their being deceptive, and indeed, to use the honest word required by the circumstances, fraudulent. This is my testimony reduced to its briefest possible expression.

" If it be asked what impression, on the whole, has been left on my mind by all that I have witnessed in this matter, I answer, one of perplexed doubt, shaping itself into only one conviction that deserves the name of an opinion, namely, that quite sufficient cause has been shown to demand further patient and careful inquiry from those who have the opportunity and the qualifications needed for prosecuting it ; that the facts alleged, and the number and character of the persons testifying to them, are such that real seekers for truth cannot satisfy themselves by merely pooh-poohing them."

Interesting Report on Fisheries. — An interesting instance of a governmental inquiry, under scientific auspices, into a branch of natural industry, has been presented to us during the past year, in a report to the British Parliament, of a commission appointed to consider and investigate the subject of the herring fishery, particularly as it is connected with British interests. This commission consisted of Col. Maxwell, Dr. Lyon Playfair, and Mr. T. Huxley ; and the following is a *resumé* of the more important features of the report in question. The conclusion is arrived at, that the herring does not, as some naturalists have affirmed, migrate to the seas within the Arctic circle, but, probably, on disappearing from the shores of the British Islands, passes into deep water near them. The herring is found under four different conditions : — 1st, Fry or Sill ; 2d, Maties, or Fat Herring ; 3d, Full Herring ; 4th, Shotten, or Spent Herring. It is extremely difficult to obtain satisfactory evidence as to the length of time which the herring requires to pass from the embryonic to the adult or full condition. The commissioners, after considering all the evidence obtainable, are of the opinion, that the herring attains to full size and maturity in about eighteen months. It is also probable that this fish arrives at its spawning condition in one year, and that the eggs are hatched in, at most, two to three weeks after deposition, and that in six or seven weeks more the young have attained three inches in length. The maties, or fat herring, feed, develop their reproductive organs, and become full herrings in about three or four months. The herrings then aggregate in prodigious numbers for about a fortnight in localities favorable for the reception of their ova. Here they lie in tiers, covering square miles of sea bottom, and so close to the ground that the fishermen have to practise a peculiar mode of fishing in order to take them, while every net and line used in the fishing is thickly covered with the adhesive spawn which they are busily engaged in shedding. So intent are the fish on this great necessity of their existence that they are not easily driven from their spawning ground; but when once their object has been attained, and they have become spent fish, the shoal rapidly disappears, withdrawing in all probability into deep water at no great distance from the coast. There is no positive evidence as to the ultimate fate of the spent herrings; but there is much to be said in favor of the current belief, that after a sojourn of more or less duration in deep water, they return as maties to the shallows and lochs, there to run through the same changes as before. The commissioners were unable to gain any information respecting the time which one and the same herring may pass through the cycle. The enemies of this fish are, however, too numerous and active to render it at all likely that the existence of any one fish is prolonged beyond two or three reproductive epochs. Great difference of opinion has been held respecting the spawning season of the herrings. The commissioners' conclusion is, that the herring spawns twice annually, in the spring and in the autumn. It is not, however, at all likely that the same fish spawn twice in the year; on the contrary, the spring and the autumn shoals are most likely perfectly distinct; and if the herring, as is probable, comes to maturity in a year, the shoals of each spawning season would be the fry of the twelvemonth before.

The food of the herring consists of crustacea, varying in size from microscopic dimensions to those of a shrimp, and of small fish, particularly sand-eels.

The commissioners ascribe the remarkable variableness in the annual visits of shoals of herrings to the British coasts to the varying quantity of food of the fish, and to the number and force of the destructive agencies at work. Any circumstance which increases or decreases the quantity of crustacea and sand-eels must exercise great influence on herring-shoals; but these are even more acted upon by their great destroyers. The latter may be ranged under the heads of fish, birds, marine animals, and man. Of these, by far the greatest destroyers are fish and marine animals, as porpoises and other cetacea. It is estimated that the total annual take of herrings by British fishermen is 900,000,000; a prodigious number; but great as this is, it sinks into comparative insignificance when compared with the destruction effected by other agencies. Cod alone destroy ten times as great a number as are captured by all our fishermen. It is a very common thing to find a cod-fish with six or seven large herrings in his stomach. When it is further considered that the conger and dog-fish do as much mischief as the cod and ling, that the gulls and gannets slay their millions, and that porpoises and grampuses destroy additional countless multitudes, it will be evident that fishing operations, extensive as they are, do not destroy five per cent. of the total number of full herrings that are destroyed every year by other causes. These facts, which cannot be controverted, prepare us for the conclusions arrived at by the commissioners with reference to the legislative enactments relating to the herring fishery.

They recommend that all prohibitory or restrictive laws bearing on the herring fishery be repealed, and that the fishermen be allowed to follow their business in any manner they may think proper. In conclusion they add: "If legislation could regulate the appetites of cod, conger, and porpoise, it might be useful to pass laws regarding them; but to prevent fishermen catching one or two per cent. of herring in any way they please, seems, in the opinion of the Commissioners, a wasteful employment of the force of law."

We present to the readers of the *Annual of Scientific Discovery* for 1864, the portrait of Major-General Q. A. GILLMORE, U. S. A., best known in science for his investigations and researches respecting "limes, mortars, and cements," and for the brilliant military engineering displayed by him in the reduction of Forts Pulaski, Sumter, and Wagner.

ANNUAL OF SCIENTIFIC DISCOVERY.

MECHANICS AND USEFUL ARTS.

THE SEWERS OF PARIS.

THE present system of sewerage in Paris, decreed by the Emperor Napoleon III. in 1852, consists of six main galleries, called collectors, fifteen secondary ones opening into the former, and themselves fed by a vast number of smaller ones intersecting the city in every direction. Three of the collectors are located upon the right bank of the Seine, and three upon the left bank. The united length of the former is 8.600 metres; of the latter, 9.200 metres.

The ratio of the section to be given to the various sewers has been fixed, as experience required, at from two to three square metres of wet surface for every 100 hectares. On this principle, twelve different sizes have been chosen, the smallest having a section of 2.15 metres in height by 1.15 in breadth, and the largest one of 4.40 metres in height by 5.60 in breadth. The former is of an ovoid shape, and offers ample space for a man and a wheelbarrow. The largest sewer or collector has a circular segment for its section; its breadth is divided into three parts, the two lateral ones being foot pavements, and the middle one a gutter or drain 1.20 metres broad. On each foot pavement, a series of iron forks support a water pipe, varying in diameter from 1.10 metres to 0.80. In some of the galleries there is but one water-pipe. To cleanse the drain a small cart, running on iron rails laid along the bottom, is pushed forward by two men; the front of this cart is provided with a drop-plank, acting like a sort of sluice, which, when down, exactly closes the section of the gutter, and pushes all the mud before it as the cart advances. By the sewers above described, all the foul waters of the right bank are easily brought to the Place de la Concorde, where a general collector receives them and carries them off to Asnieres. But what was to be done with the sewerage of the left bank, which, according to the system adopted, was also to be poured into the

15

general collector. After much reflection, it was decided that the waters of the left bank should be carried over by a siphon passing under the bed of the Seine ; and this singular engineering feat has actually been accomplished. An enormous pipe of wrought iron having an interior diameter of one metre, and about 200 metres in length, is sunk, a little above the Pont de la Concorde, two metres below the low-water mark, and thus the desired communication is established. As to the general collector, it is the most stupendous work of the kind in existence. It is 5 metres in height by 5.61 in breadth, with a length of about five kilometres and a half, in nearly a right line, except a turn under the Place de la Madeleine. The foot pavements are 1.90 metres on each side, the central drain is 3.60 metres in breadth, with a depth of 1.35 ; so large, in fact, that a well sized boat is kept afloat on it for the purpose of cleansing. This boat is also provided with a drop-plank in front; this is let down to a distance of 15 centimetres from the bottom, while the boat advances, whereby such a head of water is obtained in front as to drive all the sedimentary matter — nay, even stones — to a distance of 100 metres. There the boat finds it again as it advances, and drives it further and further, till the orifice of the emissary is reached. Four boats perform this work, and it takes sixteen days to cleanse the whole length. Ventilation is provided for by air-traps at certain distances, and the gallery is lighted with oil lamps. The execution of this immense system of sewers has cost fifty millions of francs. M. Dezobry, comparing this gallery with the far-famed Cloaca Maxima of Rome, shows that it is infinitely superior to it in size, not to mention the improvements in construction, of which the Romans had no idea. The Cloaca Maxima is two metres in height, and only 4.48 broad, and is supposed never to have exceeded a length of 900 metres. The dimensions we have given abundantly show how vastly superior the modern French construction is to the ancient Roman one.

THE NEW SEWERS OF LONDON.

It is well known to our readers (See *Annual Sci. Dis.*, 1859–60) that for the last few years, there has been in the course of construction in London, a system of sewage, of such magnitude as to form one of the marvels of modern engineering, and of such cost, as but few cities could afford to pay for. The object of the scheme is to do away with the present plan, whereby all the enormous drainage of London is discharged into the Thames ; — a plan which has latterly converted the river itself into one vast sewer, to the great annoyance and sanitary detriment of the vast population contiguous to its waters. "At the very first glance," says the London *Times :* — " This arrangement seems bad enough, though it is infinitely worse when we come to examine how it was arranged to work. On both sides of the river the banks are very little above high-water mark, while the average level of the ground immediately behind them is much below it; half Lambeth and Rotherhithe being six feet below high-water level. Of course, when this is the level of the ground, the sewers are much lower still, and their outlets so completely tide-locked that it is only at dead low-water that they can empty themselves at all. Thus, for nearly eighteen hours out of the twenty-four, the sewage on both sides of London is to an immense extent, pent up, giving off its miasma into every street and house. As

we have said, it could only escape at dead low water, when the returning tide immediately churned it *up* the river, keeping all its abomina-
ble 'flotsam and jetsam' above bridge till the tide ebbed out, finding
200,000 or 300,000 gallons of filth to be operated upon in a similar
manner on its return. This was the arrangement twelve years ago,
and is almost entirely so still; but, even bad as this was, it was capable of being made worse, and worse accordingly it was made. In
1849, most of the houses in London had cesspools attached to them,
and a very large proportion were without any drains at all. The
alarming nature of this evil showed itself slowly but surely in the Bills
of Mortality, and the then Commissioners of Sewers, who were feebly
battling with the evils of the drainage system, set to work to mitigate
the cesspool danger by drainage, making the Thames, as usual, the
general receptacle. From that time to the present some 700 or 800
miles of new drains have been made, and all cesspools made to drain
at once into the river. By this 'improved' drainage some 200,000
additional gallons of sewage were daily added to the Thames at low
water, containing no less than 300 tons of 'organic matter,' which in
this case is the scientific term of filth. The result, as a matter of
course, has been that in the summer months the stench from the river
has occasionally been intolerable. In 1857, great quantities of lime
and chloride of lime were put in daily; in 1858, the same expedient
had to be resorted to again; and in 1859, the dose had to be increased
into 110 tons of lime and 12 tons of chloride of lime, costing 1,500*l.*
per week. Even in a pecuniary point of view, however, this was not
the only evil of the system. The Thames in hot weather runs short
of water; and when there is no rain, the collections of refuse in the
sewers have to be flushed into the river by artificial means. This
flushing alone during summer costs 20.000*l.* a year to get the poison
into the Thames, where 20.000*l.* more is generally required to keep it
from breeding a plague." To obviate these difficulties, an immense
new sewage system was devised, and for the last few years has been in
the course of construction, whereby London will be effectually drained,
and the Thames purified. As may easily be imagined, it is impossible,
in an article like the present, to give more than an outline of this great
plan, which may best be briefly described as consisting of three gigantic main tunnels or sewers on each side of the river. These completely
divide underground London, from west to east, and cutting all existing
sewers at right angles intercept their flow to the Thames, and carry
every gallon of London sewage under certain conditions into the river
at a point far below the city limits and not far distant from the sea.
" These main drains are called the High, Middle, and Low Level sewers, according to the height of the localities which each respectively
drains. The High Level, on the north side, is about eight miles in
length, and runs from Hampstead to Bow, being at its rise only four
feet six inches in diameter, and thence increasing in circumference, as
the waters of the sewers it intercepts require a wider course, to five
feet, six feet, seven feet, ten feet six inches, eleven feet six inches,
and at its termination to twelve feet six inches in diameter. This
drain is now entirely finished, and in full work. Its *minimum* fall is
twelve feet in the mile; its *maximum* at the beginning nearly fifty
feet a mile. It is laid at a depth of from twenty to twenty-six feet be-

2*

low the ground, and drains an area of fourteen square miles. The Middle Level, as being lower in the valley on the slope of which London is built, is laid at a greater depth, varying from thirty to thirty-six feet, and even more below the surface. This is nearly complete, and extends from Kensal Green to Bow. The Low Level will extend from Cremorne to Abby Mills, on the marshes, near Stratford. At Bow, the Low Level waters will be raised, by powerful engines, at a pumping station, to the junction of the High and Middle Level ducts, thence descending by their own gravity through three tunnels to the main reservoir and final outfall. These three tunnels are each nine feet six inches in diameter, and nearly four miles long. Great engineering difficulties existed in the construction of these main arteries, as, from the height at which they all meet, it was necessary to take them above the level of the marshes leading to Barking. For a mile and a half the embankment which encloses the three tunnels is carried on brick arches, the piers going eighteen feet below the surface, and being based on solid concrete. In the marshes at Barking, a reservoir for the reception of the sewage of the north side has been formed. This reservoir is a mile and a half long by one hundred feet wide, and twenty-one feet deep. It is made of this great length in proportion to width to allow of its being roofed with brick arches, which are again covered with earth to a considerable thickness, so that not the slightest smell or escape of miasma can take place. This is capable of containing more than three times the amount of sewage which can enter it while the pipes are shut, and thus, when all is complete, the works will not only be large enough to take off all London's sewage now, but its sewage when London is double its present size.

"While the sewage is in the reservoir we have spoken of, it will be completely deodorized by an admixture of lime. When the tide is at its height the sluices which pass from the bottom of the reservoir far out into the bed of the river will be opened, and the whole allowed to flow away. It takes two hours thus to empty the reservoir, by which time the tide will be flowing down strongly, and will carry its very last gallon a distance of thirteen miles below Barking, which, being itself thirteen miles below London, will place the contents of the sewers, every twelve hours, twenty-six or more miles distant from the metropolis. Thus, instead of letting loose the rankest of this great city's abominations in the very midst of London, and leaving it to stagnate, or, still worse, to be agitated backwards and forwards in a small body of water, it will all be carried away a distance of thirteen miles, then deodorized, then suffered to escape into a body of water more than a hundred times greater than that into which it now crawls, and thus disinfected and diluted, so as to be without either taste or smell, swept still further down the stream, till every trace of it is lost.

" On the south side, the three great sewer arteries are constructed on similar plans, — the High Level, from Dulwich to Deptford; the Middle, from Clapham to Deptford; and the Low Level, from Putney to Deptford. At this point is a pumping station, which raises the water from the low to the high level, whence it flows away through a ten feet tunnel to Crossness Point. One part of this tunnel, passing under Woolwich, is a mile and a half in length, without a single break, and driven at a depth of eighty feet from the surface. At the outfall will be another pumping station, to lift the water to the reservoir. The southern reservoir is only five acres in extent; that on the north is fourteen. In the reservoir it will be deodorized and discharged in a similar way to that we have already described.

" The pumping stations will each consist of an engine-house, containing ten boilers calculated to work up to five hundred horse-power nominal. This power, working through eight pumps of seven feet diameter and four feet stroke, will daily raise 119,000,000 cubic feet of sewage from nineteen feet below low water to the level of the outfall; but, in case of necessity, the pumps can raise 250,000,000 cubic feet per day. The reservoir into which it will all flow is not yet finished, but when roofed in with brick will hold 20,000,000 gallons of sewage.

" The total length of the three rows of intercepting sewers, the course of which we have sketched on each side of the river, will be fifty miles, and before all the works are completed 800,000 cubic yards of concrete will be consumed, upwards of 300,000,000 of bricks, and 4,000,000 cubic yards of earthwork."

During the past year, a part of this great work has been so far completed, that a portion of the sewage of London has been diverted from its old channels.

UNSINKABLE TIMBER SHIPS.

At the last meeting of the British Association, Admiral Belcher stated that many years since, Mr. Walters, an architect, tried to render ships for mercantile purposes unsinkable, by introducing copper cylinders between the timbers, the hold-beams, and, indeed, every opening where the cargo did not prevent; and he calculated that these displacements or cells would about compensate for difference of specific gravity between cargo, vessel, and gear, so as to simply reduce her to the state of a water-logged craft, to save crew, vessel, and such portions of cargo as might be secured in air-tight vessels.

Latterly, the pneumatic trough had suggested itself to his (Admiral Belcher's) mind the propriety of close-ceiling the holds, or under-planking the hold-beams, and saving those spaces between them for the storage of light dry-goods above that deck (which was generally lost), and placing loose planks (indeed, as we were in the habit of hatching many of our brigs of 386 tons and under) as a temporary deck. Now, in the event of a dangerous leak, or even a large hole being stove in the bows or bottom of a ship, he proposed securing the hatches from beneath to hatches above, screwed firmly in opposition to each other, and filled in by pitch from the upper or open hatch. Now, it would be apparent that if the ship was air-tight, the water could only enter so long as the air was compressible, and by inverting the pump-boxes and rendering them air-pumps, the leak would not only be stopped, but, by the continued action of the air, it would be expelled by the very orifice by which it entered. Therefore, the customary and continued labor and wear of the powers of the crew would not be required to such an extent, if at all, when once the necessary quantity of air had been forced in. He came now to the use of iron plates in forming air-tight cellular vessels, and he hoped to be able to show that, by pursuing this mode of construction, a vessel would not only be very much less liable to injury by collision with a ram, but if carefully and scientifically fitted, might be overrun by an adversary, and come up on the other side. He claimed the introduction into the navy of the air-tight compartments, by constructing a vessel upon the plan of a ship within a ship — the outer, sectional compartments each independent *per se* for coals or stores ; the inner to contain compartments and accommodation, if necessity demanded, for the crew. The oval form would secure the means of withstanding, externally, any compression ; it would facilitate the delivery of coals from the bunkers, and if any one of those bunkers was perforated or stove, you possessed the engine-power, to be exerted from within, of expelling the water, by forcing in air, making every such valve self-acting from the interior.

STEERING SCREW FOR STEAMERS.

Some experiments have recently been made by the British Admiralty on a new arrangement of that screw propeller which has for its object steering, as well as the propulsion of a vessel. The peculiarity of the screw is that a universal joint is placed within the hollow boss of the screw, which is thereby connected with the main shaft, the centre of gravity of the screw and the centre line of the rudder intersecting the centre line of the main shaft, so that the entire weight of the screw is borne by the shaft ; and by means of a tail or spindle to the screw, projecting from the boss working in the rudder, or an iron carrier in lieu of rudder, whatever may be the movement of the tiller or wheel, it communicates an equal movement to the screw, which becomes not only the propelling but also the guiding power of the ship. One of these screws, fitted to a naval steamer of sixty-horse power, has been tried upon the Thames, and the result is reported in the London *Post*, as unequivocally satisfactory, — " clearly demonstrating that it is no longer needful to apply double screws, hydraulic steering apparatus, or add any other extra complications to the machinery of a steamer, when by a wave of her own screw, her motion can be directed and controlled at will."

RAILWAY TUNNELS IN GREAT BRITAIN.

At a recent meeting of the Institution of Civil Engineers, Mr. J. S. Fraser stated that the aggregate length of the tunnels, now daily traversed by railway trains in the united kingdom, amounts to eighty miles ; and, supposing their cost to have been on an average fifteen pounds per lineal yard, their construction must have caused the expenditure of six and a half millions sterling.

STEEP RAILWAY INCLINE.

The Bhore Ghaut Incline of the Great Peninsular Railway of India has occupied more than seven years in construction, and during the greater part of that time there have been 45,000 workmen daily employed upon it. The incline is a series of tunnels through mountains of rock, and viaducts stretching across valleys, alternating with each other ; each part a triumph of modern science and skill.

The incline reaches at one long lift the height of 1,832 feet, the highest elevation yet attained by any railway incline. It is 15½ miles long, and its average gradient consequently 1 in 46.39. The highest gradient is one in 37, and the sharpest curve 15 chains radius. The tunnels are twenty-five in number, the greatest length of any of them being 341½ yards. There are eight viaducts, one consisting of eight arches of 50 feet and being 129 feet high, and another, of a like number of arches, with a maximum height of 143 feet. The quantity of cutting amounts to 2,067,738 cubic yards, and of embankments to 2,452,308 cubic yards. There are twenty-two bridges of various spans, and seventy-four culverts. The total cost of the works has been £1,100,000, or £68,750 a mile.

STEAM BOILER EXPLOSIONS.

With reference to these destructive accidents, Dr. Joule, at a recent meeting of the Philosophical Society, of Manchester, England, stated his belief that, in nearly every instance, rupture took place simply because the iron, by wear or otherwise, had become unable to withstand the ordinary working pressure. Various hypotheses, set up to account for explosions, were worse than useless because they diverted attention from the real source of danger. He believed that one of these hypotheses — that which attributed explosions to the introduction of water into a boiler, the plates of which were heated in consequence of deficiency of water — was quite inadequate to account for the facts; although weak boilers might be exploded at the moment of starting the engine, in consequence of the swelling of the water through renewed ebullition throwing hot water over the heated plates. The absolute necessity of employing the hydraulic test periodically had been pointed out so frequently that he considered that the neglect of it was highly criminal.

UTILIZATION OF THE TIDES.

Let us suppose (says a writer in the *Chemical News*) that by the action of the tides, the difference of level of the surface of the ocean at a certain spot is twenty-one feet between high and low water. Omitting for the present all consideration of the power of the subjacent liquid, what is the mechanical value of a space of one hundred yards square of this water? One hundred yards square by twenty-one feet deep, equal 70,000 cubic yards of water, which is lifted to a height of twenty-one feet, or to 1,470,000 cubic yards lifted to a height of one foot. Now, since one cubic yard of water weighs about 1683 pounds, 1,470,000 cubic yards weigh 2,474,010,000 pounds, which is lifted in six hours. This is equivalent to lifting a weight of 412,335,000 foot pounds in one hour; and since one-horse power is considered equivalent to raising 1,800,000 foot pounds per hour, we have, locked up in every one hundred yards square of sea surface, a power equal to a two hundred and thirty horse power steam-engine; acting, be it remembered, day and night to the end of time; requiring no supervision; and costing nothing after the first outlay but the wear and tear of machinery. By means of appropriate machinery connected with this tidal movement, any kind of work could be performed readily.

THE PNEUMATIC DESPATCH.

In the *Annual of Sci. Dis.* 1863, p. 43, the application of the principle of forcing packages through tubes by atmospheric pressure to the conveyance of mail-bags in London, to and from the District Post

Office and the Euston Street Railway station (a distance of 1800 feet) was described as about to be put in practical operation. A recent report of the Pneumatic Despatch Company now states, — "That since the 20th of February, 1863, the authorities have discontinued their street conveyances, and intrusted the company with the transmission of the mails, and that the service of the district had since been entirely performed by the company. Thirty trains per diem (Sundays excepted) have been despatched with perfect regularity, and upwards of 4,000 trains have run without impediment or delay. The time occupied in the transmission has not exceeded seventy seconds. The daily cost of working has averaged £1. 4s. 5d. ; and five times the number of trains could have been conveyed without any appreciable increase of expense."

The successful result of these experiments has induced the company to proceed to the laying of an additional line of pipe for further post-office accommodation, which will be 2½ miles in length and 54 inches in diameter, at an estimated total cost of £65,000. It is confidently predicted that, in the course of a few years, the entire transmission of the London mails throughout the city will be accomplished by atmospheric pressure.

IMITATION RUSSIA SHEET IRON.

At a recent meeting of the Franklin Institute, Prof. Fleury presented specimens of imitated Russia sheet iron, made under the patent of Mr. Wm. Riesz from ordinary rolled iron, the original cost of which was 5 cents per pound; the expense of the process was 2½ cents, making the total cost of the iron in its present condition, 7½ cents per pound. He stated that "the inventor, who was for a number of years director of a large iron manufacturing establishment in Germany, had made it his particular study to examine theoretically and practically the manufacture of the iron which was imported in large quantities from Russia. By repeated analyses of the iron, and also through noticing its beautiful, smooth, and incorrodible surface (by scraping off the surface from a large number of sheets), he came to the curious conclusion that the Russia iron was not, as he had thought, and as the general impression among iron manufacturers still seems to be, covered by *a film of carburet of iron*, but that the smooth surface consisted of *an atomic accumulation of a peculiar substance, a* NITRIDE *of iron combined with about 20 per cent. of carbon:* the nitro-carburetted iron of Fremy. The quantity of carbon and nitrogen diminished gradually towards the centre, where the iron was nearly pure and very flexible. After years of experiments, he has finally succeeded in producing from ordinary sheet iron the best imitation of Russia sheet iron which, in my opinion, can be made."

"Though the process is very simple, it requires considerable skill; but once learned, by short practice under the guidance of the inventor, it can be carried on in the most regular manner. The iron is cleaned in a sulphuric acid bath, then washed with an alkali and water, and placed in a peculiar mixture described in the patent, which prevents oxidation; it is then rolled with the before-named coating, and, after being re-heated, placed under the hammer to receive the required temper and smoothness."

PROTECTION OF IRON FROM RUST.

At a recent meeting of the Society of Arts, London, the question of preserving iron from rusting formed a subject of conversation. It was stated that galvanized iron wire for telegraphs was not affected with rust in passing through the rural districts of England; but that the coating of zinc on the iron afforded no protection to wires in cities. The acid gas generated by the combustion of fuel attacked the coating and decomposed it. A new substitute for covering telegraphic wire was desirable.

With respect to paints for coating iron, such as the plates of iron vessels, machinery, &c., Mr. John Braithwaite stated that pure red lead was the best. His experience dated as far back as 1806, with the use of red lead, and for fifty years he had used it with success. White lead was more injurious than beneficial as a paint for iron. In April last, he inspected a well, two hundred feet deep, a short distance out of London, where he had put up an engine forty-five years ago; the long iron rods which had been placed in it had been painted with red lead, and the metal had remained unchanged in all that period. The same preservative effects of red lead paint on iron, he had witnessed upon other iron-work which had been many years in use.

ALUMINUM BRONZE.

It has long been an object with scientific inquirers to reduce the weight of the philosophical instruments which they have to employ. Especially is this the case with magnetical and astronomical instruments used in the triangulation of a country for a survey, or the highly important operation of measuring an arc of the meridian. Aluminum bronze supplies the long-sought desideratum. This metal is produced from a mixture of ten per cent. of aluminum with pure copper; and a most remarkable metal it is. Col. Strange, in a recent communication to the Royal Astronomical Society, thus enumerates some of its properties: Good gun-metal will break with a strain of 35,000 lbs. to the square inch; aluminum bronze requires 73,000 lbs to the square inch to break it. It resists compression equally well; it is malleable when heated; can be easily cast, and behaves well under the file. "It does not clog the file; and in the lathe and planing-machine, the tool removes long elastic shavings, leaving a fine, bright, smooth surface." Moreover, "it can be worked with much less difficulty than steel; tarnishes less readily than any metal usually employed for astronomical instruments, and is less affected by changes of temperature than either gun-metal or brass." This latter quality is especially important in instruments used for surveying in the tropics, as expansion by heat would very much impair their accuracy. It is remarkably well fitted to receive graduation, as it takes a fine division, which is pure and equable, surpassing any other *cast* metal in this respect. Col. Strange remarks that in its elasticity it is said to surpass even steel, and it would therefore appear to be the most proper material for the suspension strings of clock pendulums.

C. Tissier, Director of the Aluminum Works at Rouen, shows that one per cent. of aluminum in copper makes the latter more fusible, giving it the property of filling the mould in casting, at the same time preventing it from rising in the mould. The action of chemical agents upon it is also weakened, and the copper gains in hardness and tenacity without losing its malleability, thus producing an alloy which has the malleability of brass, with the hardness of bronze.

Aluminum bronze has been selected by Col. Strange as the most appropriate metal for the construction of the large theodolite for the use of the Trigonometrical Survey of India. The horizontal circle of this theodolite is three feet in diameter, and the effect of using this alloy will be to keep the weight of the instrument within reasonable limits, notwithstanding its possession of means and appliances not hitherto bestowed on such instruments. In the manufacture of the alloy, Col. Strange says that extremely pure copper must be used; electrotype copper is best, and Lake Superior copper stands next, giving an alloy of excellent quality. The ordinary coppers of commerce generally fail, owing, it is said, to the presence of iron, which appears to be specially prejudicial. Further, the alloy must be melted two or three times, as that obtained from the first melting is excessively brittle. "Each successive melting, up to a certain point, determined by the working, and particularly the forging properties of the metal, improves its tenacity and strength." The present price of English-made 10 per cent. aluminum bronze is 6 shillings 6 pence per lb. This is four or five times that of gun-metal.

MALLEABLE IRON NAILS.

There is a description of nails of cast malleable iron coming into use for fixing slates on to the roofs of factories and similar buildings. They oxidize much less in damp air than common iron nails, or even copper ones. To manufacture them, very hot metal is run into ordinary sand moulds. These malleable iron nails are very brittle before being placed in the annealing furnace. Their sojourn in the furnace renders them very ductile. They are then put into polishing barrels, in which they are cleaned, whereupon they are thrown into a zinc bath to obtain a coating.—*London Mechanics' Magazine.*

IMPROVEMENT IN STEEL WORKING.

Mr. Anderson, Assistant Superintendent of Woolwich Arsenal, announces the discovery of a simple process by which steel is rendered as tough as wrought-iron without losing its hardness. This change is effected in a few minutes by heating the metal and plunging it in oil, after which the steel can be bent, but scarcely broken. The value of this discovery will be at once appreciated by those who are aware of the difficulties hitherto experienced in obtaining a suitable material for the interior tubes of built-up guns.

FILES MADE BY MACHINERY.

The manufacture of files by machinery is said to have been successfully commenced in Birmingham, England. The blanks are forged by machinery, and they are then cut with the French machine of M. Bernot. The machine, which is very compact, resembles a small steam-hammer in its general appearance. It is provided with a vertical slide, carrying a chisel on the lower end. The top of this slide is pressed by a flat spring, which is governed by a cam mounted upon a shaft, and actuated by a ratchet wheel and pawl; and thus the strength of the blow of the chisel is regulated to the varying breadth of the file. A projection at the other end of the slide comes in contact with a cam upon the driving shaft of the machine, and so sets the machine in motion. The blank to be cut is placed upon a travelling slide, resting upon a semicircular bed, which is mounted in trunnions resting upon swivelling journals, so that the surface of the blank can be presented at the desired angle to the chisel. The blank is held parallel to the edge of the chisel by means of a weighted "leveller." All being ready, the file is fixed in the bed, the machine is set in motion, and presently the file runs out cut. The chisel makes from 800 to 1,500 cuts per minute, and will produce about five or six times the amount of work which can be supplied by hand-cutting. A comparison of the two modes of cutting — hand and machinery, — shows that, while a machine, to cut fourteen-inch hard files, makes 1,000 cuts per minute, or 600,000 cuts per day, a good file-cutter, upon the same size and description, could only make 140 cuts per minute, or 84,000 per day.

COPPER PAINT.

A paint prepared by M. Oudry, of Paris, from electrotype copper reduced to an impalpable powder (by the aid of a steam-hammer), and diffused in varnish, is, undoubtedly, a most important industrial discovery. The preparation of the color is not difficult and not expensive. It is stated to be susceptible of easy application to wood, plaster, cement, brass, or iron, and also to the hulls of ships. It forms a perfect covering, dries rapidly, and takes an agreeable lustre susceptible of receiving, by means of chemical agents, the tone of bronze, bright or dark, verd-antique, or Florence green, which has never before been communicated to pure copper. Ornaments in brass or statues in plaster, when painted in this manner, lose none of their most delicate details, and they assume completely the appearance of objects in bronze. Even statues in plaster appear to resist remarkably inclement conditions of the atmosphere. By mixing the powder of galvanoplastic copper with certain fatty oils, Oudry obtained very beautiful greens of varied hues.

REPAIRING THE SILVERING OF LOOKING-GLASSES.

The repairing of the silvering on the backs of looking-glasses has hitherto been considered a very difficult operation. A new and very simple method, however, has been described before the Polytechnic Society of Leipsic. It is as follows: — Clean the bare portion of the glass by rubbing it gently with fine cotton, taking care to remove every trace of dust and grease. If this cleaning be not done very carefully, defects will appear around the place repaired. With the point of a knife cut upon the back of another looking-glass, around a portion of the silvering of the required form, but a little larger. Upon it place a small drop of mercury: a drop the size of a pin's head will be sufficient for a surface equal to the size of the nail. The mercury spreads immediately, penetrates the amalgam to where it was cut off with the knife, and the required piece may now be lifted and removed to the place to be repaired. This is the most difficult part of the operation. Then press lightly the renewed portion with cotton: it hardens almost imme-

3

diately, and the glass presents the same appearance as a new one. — *Builder*.

CEMENT FOR ROOMS.

A recent invention by M. Sorel, of Paris, is described to consist in the discovery of a property possessed by oxychloride of zinc, which renders it superior to the plaster of Paris for coating the walls of rooms. It is applied in the following manner: — A coat of oxide of zinc mixed with size, made up like a wash, is first laid on the wall, ceiling, or wainscot, and over that a coat of chloride of zinc applied, being prepared in the same way as the first wash. The oxide and chloride effect an immediate combination, and form a kind of cement, smooth and polished as glass, and possessing the advantages of oil paint, without its disadvantages of smell.

WIRE LATHING FOR WELLS.

W. E. Gedge, of London, England, has secured a patent for the employment of iron wires as a substitute for wood laths used on the walls of rooms that require plastering. The wires are stretched and crossed on the studs and joists and then secured in screw rings. The wires are fixed at such a distance apart that the priming coat of thick plaster mixed with hair will adhere to them perfectly. These wires do not shrink nor warp like laths, and on this account they are said to be superior for plastered walls.

PREVENTION OF FIRE ACCIDENTS.

An English architect proposes to construct buildings in an improved manner by economizing the space which the staircases usually occupy, and to render them fire-proof by dividing or insulating the staircases from the building of which they form part. This he proposes to accomplish by arranging the stairs (which are to be made of incombustible materials), in a recess formed in the outer wall of a building; which recess is to extend from the foundation to the roof, and have no opening whatever on its inner side; but it is to be provided, where necessary, with openings or doorways on its outer face, leading to balconies (which are also to be formed of incombustible materials) fixed at the level of, and giving access to, each of the floors or flats of the building. By means of this arrangement of staircase and balconies, each floor will be rendered totally distinct from, and independent of, that one below or above it, so far as regards any internal communication therewith or therefrom.

WATER-PROOF WALKS.

The following new method of path-making is recommended by the *London Gardener's Magazine*, for its excellence, permanence, and economy. Instead of making the walk of loose material, on the old fashion, concreting is resorted to, by which the appearance of gravel is retained with all its freshness and beauty of contrast to grass and flowers, and the walk itself is rendered as dry and durable as the best pavement. The *modus operandi* is as follows: — Procure a sufficient quantity of the best Portland cement; then, with the help of a laborer, turn up the path with a pick, and have all the old gravel screened, so as to separate the loam and surface weeds from it, and to every six parts of the gravel add three parts of gritty sand of any kind,— but soft pit sand is unsuitable,— and one part, by measure, of Portland cement. When these are well mixed together in a dry state, add sufficient water to make the whole into a moderately stiff working consistence, and lay it down quickly two inches thick on a hard bottom. A common spade is the best tool with which to spread it; it must be at once spread, as it is to remain forever, and a slight convexity given to the surface. In forty-eight hours it becomes as hard as a rock; not a drop of rain will go through it, and if a drop lodges on it, blame yourself for not having made the surface even; but a moderate fall is sufficient with such an impenetrable material. Not a weed will ever grow on a path so formed; not a worm will ever work through it; a birch broom will keep the surface clean and bright, and of course it never requires rolling. It is necessary to be very particular as to the quality of the cement. For the flooring of a green-house, fowl-house, or barn, this is the best and cheapest that can be had,— always clean, hard, and dry, and never requiring repairs of any kind if carefully put down in the first instance.

HOW MUSKET BARRELS ARE STRAIGHTENED.

A curious and interesting part of the operation of manufacturing muskets is the straightening of the barrel. This straightening takes place continually in every stage of the work, from the time the barrel first emerges from the chaotic mass produced by heating the scalp, until it reaches the assembling-room, where the various parts of the musket are put together. As you enter the boring and turning rooms of the Springfield armory, you are struck with surprise at observing hundreds of workmen standing with musket-barrels in their hands, one end held up to their eyes, and the other pointing to some one of the innumerable windows of the apartment. Watching them a few moments, however, you will observe, that, after looking through the barrel for half a minute, and turning it around in their fingers, they lay it down upon a small anvil standing at their side, and strike upon it a gentle blow with a hammer, and then raise it again to the eye. This is the process of straightening.

In former times, a very slender line, a hair or some similiar substance, was passed through the barrel. This line was then drawn tight, and the workman, looking through, turned the barrel round so as to bring the line into coincidence successively with every portion of the inner surface. If there existed any concavity in any part of this surface, the line would show it by the distance which would there appear between the line itself and its reflection in the metal. This method has not, however, been in use for over thirty years. It gave place to a system which, with a slight modification, is still in practice. This method consisted in placing a small mirror upon the floor near the anvil of the straightener, which reflected a diagonal line drawn across a pane of glass in a window. The workman then placed the barrel of the musket upon a rest in such a position that the reflected line in the mirror could be again reflected, through the bore of the barrel, to his eye,— the inner surface of the barrel being in a brilliantly polished condition from the boring. When the barrel is placed at the proper angle, which practice enables the person performing this duty to accomplish at once, there are two parallel shadows thrown upon opposite sides of the inner surface, which, by another deflection, can be made to come to a point at the lower end. The appearance which these shadows assume determines the question whether the barrel is straight or not, and if not, where it requires straightening. Although this method is so easy and plain to the experienced workman, to the uninitiated it is perfectly incomprehensible, the bore of the barrel presenting to his eye only a succession of concentric rings, forming a spectacle of dazzling brilliancy, and leaving the reflected line in as profound a mystery after the observation as before.

At present, the mirror is discarded, and the workman holds the barrel up directly to the pane of glass, which is furnished with a transparent slate, having two parallel lines drawn across it. The only purpose subserved by the mirror was that of rendering the operation of holding the barrel less tiresome, — it being easier to keep the end of the musket presented to the line pointing downwards than upwards. Formerly this means of detecting the faults, or want of straightness in the barrel, was the secret of one man, and he would impart it to no one for love or money. He was watched with the most intense interest, but no clue could be obtained to his secret. They gazed into the barrel for hours, but what he saw they could not see. Finally, some fortunate individual stumbled upon the wonderful secret, — discovered the marvellous lines, — and ever since it has been common property in the shop. — *Atlantic Monthly.*

SMITH'S AIR-LIGHT.

A highly successful and economical application of the oxy-hydrogen lime light has recently been made by Dr. G. H. Smith, of Rochester, New York; — atmospheric air being substituted in the place of oxygen gas, and carburetted hydrogen, or common gas, in the place of hydrogen. The rendering of these substitutes applicable for the production of the oxy-hydrogen light — a project which at first seems chimerical — is explained by the inventor as follows: "Common air contains one part of oxygen and about three parts of nitrogen gas; hence it would require four parts of air to give the amount of oxygen required for illuminating purposes; i. e. to obtain one part of oxygen four feet of air would be needed, as three feet would be nitrogen. Now, the great difficulty in using air as a substitute for pure oxygen, in the production of the lime light, is due to the fact (and to this solely) that when four parts of air are combined with one of common gas, the gas is so greatly diluted as to prevent its burning readily, and, what is still worse, if combustion was complete, the nitrogen, not being combustible, would fly off unconsumed, and carry away the heat generated to such a degree as to render the luminosity of the cylinder of lime (against which the ignited jets of the combined gases are directed) of no practical value. But if an amount of heat, from any source, is applied to the current of air previous to ignition, sufficient to supply the loss of heat abstracted by the inert nitrogen, at the time of combustion, no heat is lost upon the lime, and the whole power of the oxygen is obtained as though no nitrogen was present. Hence, by supplying a current of preheated air to one of common gas, ignited, an ample supply of oxygen is afforded, and all the heat generated is saved and concentrated upon the lime." Herein is the principal feature of Dr. Smith's invention. The invention is practically carried out for railway (locomotive) lights — the purpose for which it has thus far been applied — as follows: The burner is composed of four compound jet tubes encircling a small cylinder of lime. A current of atmospheric air, and one of coal-gas, is conveyed to each jet, and the two allowed to mingle after leaving their respective jet orifices. The tube conveying the stream of air, passes over several small gas burners, which heat the air-tube to a high degree of heat, at a point near the orifice of the tube, and by this device, the air current is intensely heated before it reaches the jet and mingles with the jet of coal-gas. The effect is, to produce the dazzling whiteness of the lime, peculiar to the oxy-hydrogen light. When placed in the focus of a parabolic reflector, such as are in present use upon locomotive engines, it is increased to a ball of light twenty inches in diameter, or to the size of the mirror. The flow of air and gas is reliably and simply controlled by durable regulators and stop-cocks, within the lamp. Two gas-holders containing air and coal-gas, respectively, under pressure, placed under the engine, and communicating with the lamp by a small pipe for each, carry twice or three times the requirements of a trip. These receive their charge at the engine-houses, before starting, from two stationary holders of larger dimensions, which are kept filled by a small pump driven by the local power employed at those places. To fill the holders on each locomotive occupies its engineer only from three to four minutes — very much less time than is required for filling and trimming an oil lamp.

This light has within the past year been introduced upon the locomotive engines of the New York Central Railroad, and its efficacy and great economy has been so fully demonstrated that the invention may without doubt be ranked among the most useful and novel of the year.

IMPROVEMENTS IN TYPE-SETTING.

Mr. Thomas Rooker has lately introduced into the Tribune office, N. Y., type-cases with movable bottoms. In these cases, the bottoms may always be kept conveniently full in composition, and in distribution the bottoms may be lowered so as to receive a large quantity of type. Mr. J. H. Tobitt, of New York, and Mr. A. H. Bailey, of Boston, have also recently interested themselves, to introduce composite type, or the plan of uniting two or more letters upon one body, so that by one lift two or three letters are set up instead of one. Mr. Bailey's system of combinations is calculated to save from twenty to forty per cent. in composition. When it is considered that the word *the* forms six per cent. of the language, and *and* about four, while many others exceed about two per cent. the advantage of a combination system is evident. The difficulty in the matter is as to how many and what combinations may be used with profit.

SCENE PAINTING.

M. Foucault proposes to remedy certain defects in scenic arrangements by the following means. At present, our mountains, towns, and

3*

villages are of one piece with the back-scene; and while nature presents objects to us through a cone of visual rays drawn from the eye, the stage represents them in an exactly inverted position — that is, we see them through the base, instead of through the vertex of the cone. By M. Foucault's ingenious and artistical plan, all these inconveniences are obviated. The sky being so often required, he has made the upper part of it fixed, of a dome-like shape, as in nature; the lower or perpendicular part is of canvas stretched on frames, and arranged cylindrically, so as to form a panorama, the end of which cannot be perceived from any point of the house. His mountains or towns of the background are independent of the sky, and stand forth in real relief; so do his trees or shrubs, which are made to rise from or descend below the floor. As for those objects which are nearer the foreground, they are made of two pieces, the lower one to sink down, the upper one, a fly, to be drawn upward when a change of scene is required. His views of the sea or of interminable plains display a vast expanse never yet seen on a stage; rich architecture is also cut out, and shows beautifully on the fixed sky of the background, which, however, is so contrived that all the phenomena of storms, sunset, approaching night, travelling clouds, with varying illuminations, etc., are imitated with surprising fidelity.

SQUARING THE CIRCLE.

M. Robinet has presented to the French Academy a series of equations laboriously worked out and represented as having a remarkable approximation to accuracy. The proportion of various multiples and fractions of the diameter to the circumference is given, and it is stated that " the side of a square equivalent to a circle of a diameter equal to unity $= \frac{1 4 4}{1 6 7} - 0.000,0006 = 0.8862269$."

A NEW SLOPE-LEVEL, BY M. RIBOT.

This instrument is designed to solve practically either of the following inverse problems, namely, to find the slope per metre of a given line; or, to set a line to a given slope per metre (or per yard). The instrument is so simple as scarcely to need description. The horizontal distance between the feet or points of support is exactly one metre (or yard). The right hand foot of the figure is capable of protrusion by a screw, and is provided with a scale to measure the amount of this protrusion. When the two feet are on a level, the index is at the zero of the scale. If you want to determine a given slope, project the foot until the instrument stands on the slope; the protrusion measured on the scale gives the slope in terms of the distance apart of the feet (metres or yards). If you want to establish a given slope, set the foot to the indicated point of the scale, and adjust your plane to the instrument. The lower bar of the instrument may be graduated so that the plummet shall read angles of slope. — *Bull. Soc. d' Encour. pour l' Indus. Nationale.*

A NEW MODE OF CONSTRUCTING CASKS.

A new method of constructing casks has been recently patented by John Connolly, of Boston. It consists in making the heads of the cask of iron, or other metal, so arranged that the iron head serves at once as a head, a cap for oozing staves, and as a head-hoop, all combined in one. The head may be screwed on, the flanch or hoop part of the head having a female screw cut on it which cuts a worm for itself, and embeds in the stave as it goes on ; or it may be barbed with concentric rings, and driven on with a hammer. This latter method, the patentee considers as generally preferable. The advantages of this improvement for preventing leakage and furthering the durability of the casks are considered to be very great.

Mr. Connolly also recommends the construction of casks of iron in the place of wood, with heads applied in accordance with his improvement. The body of the cask might be rolled out in one piece, or it might be of two, three, or more pieces, which, being ground at joints, or rebated, or tongued and grooved and put together in any way with packing, would insure a tight joint, if well bound, as at present, with hoops. A cask so constructed, of boiler-iron, could be more readily "shooked" and "set up" than a wooden one. If dented, it could be beaten out. No more shrinkage, with its consequent leakage and labor, would then occur. Such casks would last for generations.

A NEW BRICK AND MORTAR ELEVATOR.

There is no operation in all the arts in which the waste of labor is more palpable than that of carrying up brick and mortar in erecting buildings. In order to raise forty or fifty pounds, the hod-carrier is required to exert muscular effort to raise his own weight (some one hundred and fifty pounds) in addition, thus involving a waste of about three-fourths of the power expended. An invention to economize the power required in this operation, devised by Mr. T. F. Christman, of Wilson, North Carolina, is substantially as follows: An endless chain, formed of iron links, passes around two pulleys, one at the ground, and the other at the top of the wall. The pulleys have spurs which take into holes in the belt, to prevent slipping, and the upper pulley is furnished with a crank for turning it. Hoppers are secured upon the upper side of the belt for receiving the brick, and as the wall rises, the belt is lengthened by the insertion of additional links, which are furnished with hooks so that this may be readily done.— *Scientific American.*

NEW MATERIAL APPLIED TO THE ARTS.

At the great London Exhibition, 1862, a new material applied to the manufacture of fancy articles, such as picture-frames, canes, inlaid-work, &c., attracted considerable attention. It is obtained from several species of marine plants, washed up on the shores in the vicinity of the Cape of Good Hope, South Africa, but principally from the *laminaria buccinalis.* It is of a dark color, and when fresh, it is thick and fleshy, but when it is dried it becomes compact and its surface looks like a beautifully-grained deer's horn. After it becomes dry and hard it can be rendered soft again by steeping in water, and in this condition it may be stretched and formed into various shapes. When dry it can also be reduced to powder, then made plastic by soaking in water, and in this condition it may be struck into almost any shape in a die press. It comes out of the moulds like articles formed of gutta percha. The discoverer of the use of this substance prepares the plant by cleaning it first with weak caustic alkali, and then with dilute sulphuric acid, after which it is washed, and before it is quite dry it may be pressed into sheets or any other form. It then may be rendered very hard by steeping it in a hot solution of alum, after which it is removed to a hot room where it is dried, and retains its shape afterward. Reduced to powder it may also be mixed with various substances, like india rubber, and moulded into a great variety of articles. When it is bleached, by treating it first with a warm alkaline solution, and afterward with sulphurous acid gas, it resembles ivory and may be used as a substitute for that material.

MANUFACTURE OF STRINGS FOR MUSICAL INSTRUMENTS, AND OTHER USES, OF GUT AND SINEW.

The London Mechanics' Magazine publishes the following interesting article on the above subject : —

A manufacture, of which comparatively little is known, is the preparation of the substance usually termed catgut, though for the most part made from the dried, twisted, peritoneal coverings of the intestines of sheep. Catgut cord is used for a variety of purposes where strength and tension are required, as for the strings of musical instruments, for suspending clock-weights, bow-strings for hatters' use, and for archers' bows.

The manufacture of musical strings requires a great amount of care and skill, both in the choice of materials and in the manufacturing processes, in order to obtain strings combining the two qualities of resistance to a given tension and sonority. Until the beginning of the last century, Italy had the entire monopoly of this trade, and they were imported under the names of harplings, catlings, lute-strings, &c.; but the trade is now carried out, with more or less success, in every part of Europe. However, in the opinion of musicians, Naples still maintains the reputation of making the best small violin strings, because the Italian sheep, from their leanness, afford the most suitable material; it being a well ascertained fact, that the membranes of lean animals are much tougher than those of high condition. The smallest violin strings are formed by the union of three guts of a lamb (not over one year old), spun together.

The chief difficulty in this manufacture is in finding guts having the qualities before mentioned, namely, to resist tension, and giving also good vibrating sounds. It is far more easy to arrive at the proper point in the making of harp, double-bass, and other musical strings, and the manufacturer is not so much circumscribed in the choice of the proper material. The tension upon the smallest string of the violin, which is made of only three guts, is nearly double that on the second string, formed by the reunion of six guts of the same size.

In the preparation, the sheep's guts, well washed and scoured, are steeped in a weak solution of carbonate of potash, and then scraped by means of a reed cut into the shape of a knife. This operation is repeated twice a day, and during three or four days, the guts being every time put into a fresh solution of carbonate of potash, prepared to the proper strength. In order to have good musical strings, it is indispensable to avoid putrid fermentation ; and as soon as the guts rise to the surface of the water, and bubbles of gas begin to be evolved from them, they are immediately spun.

In spinning, the guts are chosen according to their size; combined with three or more, according to the volume of the string required, they are fastened upon a frame, and then alternately put in connexion with the spinning-wheel, and submitted to the required torsion. This operation performed, the strings, left upon the frame, are exposed for some hours to the vapor of sulphur, rubbed with a horse-hair glove, submitted to a new torsion, sulphured again, further rubbed, and dried.

The dried strings, rolled upon a cylinder and tied, are rubbed with fine olive oil, to which one per cent. of laurel oil has been previously added. The oil of laurel is supposed to keep the olive oil from becoming rancid.

The gut-strings employed by turners, grinders, and for cleaning cotton, &c., are made with the intestines of oxen, horses, and other animals. These, cleared by putrefaction of the mucous and peritoneal membranes, and treated by a solution of carbonate of potash, are cut into straps by means of a peculiar knife, and spun in the same way as the musical strings. The uses of bladders and gut for holding lard, for covering gallipots and jars with preserves, as cases for sausages, polonies, &c., and other domestic purposes, are well known. Lately, however, the vegetable parchment, as it is termed (which is ordinary paper steeped in sulphuric acid), has come into extensive use for this purpose.

Insufflated, or inflated guts, are chiefly employed for the preservation of alimentary food. They have to pass through a long series of modifications and processes, before becoming fit for use. The end of these preparations is, to free the muscular membrane of the intestine from the two other membranes covering it, the peritoneal and the mucous.

The first operation of scouring consists in freeing, by means of a knife, the gut from the grease attached to it, and also of the greatest part of the peritoneal membrane. The scoured guts are washed and turned inside out, then tied together, put into a vat without any more water than that adhering to them, and left in this state to undergo a putrid fermentation. The time required for this operation will be from five to eight days in winter, and two or three days only in summer. If the fermentation were pushed too far, the guts would be disorganized: to avoid this inconvenience, the workmen are often obliged to add some vinegar, in order to neutralize the ammoniacal compounds formed, and also because fermentation is slow in the presence of acids. After this fermentation, the mucous membrane is completely decomposed, and the remaining portions of the peritoneal membrane are easily taken off. The guts are then well washed, and insufflated (inflated).

This operation is performed in the same way as swelling a bladder, with this difference, that the extremity of the gut is tied by a ligature, serving also to join a new gut insufflated (inflated) in the same way. During this operation, the guts exhale the most noxious smell, and workmen employed at such work could not blow or insufflate many days in succession without having their health affected.

In order to prevent that inconvenient, unhealthy process of manufacture, the *Société d'Encouragement* of Paris proposed a premium for a chemical process enabling the manufacturers of these articles to dispense with putrid fermentation. The process suggested by Mons. Labarraque, the successful candidate, is remarkable for its cheapness and the facility of its application. In following the method recommended by this chemist, these animal matters can be worked more easily, and kept for a longer time without evolving any noxious smell.

The guts, previously scoured, are put into a vat containing, for every forty guts, four gallons of water, to which 1½ pounds oxychloride of sodium, marking 13° on the areometer of Beaumé, is added. After twelve hours of maceration, the mucous membrane is easily detached, and the guts are free from any bad smell; by this method, the process of insufflation is more easily performed.

The insufflated guts are suspended in a dry room until the desiccation is complete; and, once dried, the extremities by which they were tied together are cut, and, in pressing the hand over the length of the insufflated (inflated) gut, the air inside is completely taken out. The guts are then submitted to fumigation by sulphur, in order to bleach and to preserve them from the attacks of insects. After this last operation, the guts are fit for use.

Besides a large home supply of bladders, England imports several hundred thousand a year, packed in salt and pickle, from America and the Continent; and the aggregate value of the bladders used in Great Britain, is stated at £40,000 or £50,000.

NEW METHOD OF PREPARING GUNPOWDER.

Mr. W. Bennett, of England, has invented a new method of manufacturing gunpowder, the ingredients consisting of lime, nitre, sulphur, and charcoal; the lime is dissolved in a sufficient quantity of water to bring the other elements into a paste. The lime, after having been made into a solution, is strained through a fine sieve; this solution is then added to the other ingredients, and the whole is put into a mill, and ground until it becomes a paste; it is then taken out of the mill, and passed between two rollers, one grooved and the other plain. The paste, by passing between the rollers, is formed into long strips of a triangular shape; it is then carried on an endless web or canvas over some hot tubes, which are heated by steam, hot water, or any other artificial heat which may be applied; by this means, the strips are easily broken into grains. This mode of manufacture prevents a great deal of danger, as the powder is pulverized and brought into grain while in a wet state. The lime makes a firm grain, resists the damp, and gives it a degree of lightness which increases the bulk 25 per cent. over ordinary gunpowder, — a great advantage for blasting purposes. Plaster of Paris, Roman or Portland cement, or other strong cementing substance, may be used as a substitute for lime. And the patentee finds that for blasting purposes the following proportions answer well, — that is to say, nitre, 65 lbs.; charcoal, 18 lbs.; sulphur, 10 lbs.; and lime, 7 lbs.; but the proportions may be varied according to the strength required.

THE CONSTRUCTION OF SAFES.

The following is an abstract of a series of highly interesting and important researches recently made by Prof. E. N. Horsford, of Cambridge, Mass., on the " *Construction of Safes,*" *intended for protection against fire, dampness, rust, and frost :* —

Protection against Fire.—The experience of the last few years has practically demonstrated, what might have been foreseen, that *protection against fire can be relative only, not absolute.* Fire-proof buildings, so called, yield, when stored with combustible materials and for a long time surrounded by flame. The best of fire-proof safes are destroyed, when exposed to heat sufficiently intense and prolonged. This being admitted, how shall the largest practical measure of protection against fire be secured? First. By placing the books, papers, etc., to be preserved, in an incombustible enclosure, as of iron. Second. By surrounding the books, etc., by a *non-conductor of heat.* Third, and chiefly, by interposing between the incombustible enclosure, or outer iron shell, and the wooden case containing the valuables, a substance which on the approach of fire, is *converted into vapor, absorbing the heat and carrying it away.*

If the second and third be omitted, the contents of the safe will be destroyed as soon as the iron enclosure has become sufficiently hot to set them on fire. If the third only has been omitted, the power of preservation will be proportioned to the thickness of the layer of non-conducting material; and this, at the best, is relatively but for a brief period. If the second, only, has been omitted, since the protection arising from vaporization is due to the absorption of heat in converting liquid or solid substances into vapor, it will obviously be proportioned to the quantity of substance so converted into vapor. A hundred pounds of water will absorb twice as much heat in passing off in the form of steam, as fifty pounds will; and a safe that contains one hundred pounds of water to be evaporated, will preserve its contents in safety, through a fire in which a safe containing but fifty pounds would be destroyed. A safe will then, manifestly, be a better protection against fire, in proportion as it unites within it, an incombustible shell, the best non-conductor, with the largest amount of liquid or solid to be converted into vapor, at a temperature not dangerous to the contents of the safe.

Dampness. — Injuries from dampness in safes are not unfrequently of a most serious character; such as the mildew, and disintegration of papers, writings, &c. These injuries arise from the transmission of water from the fire-resisting composition, through cracks imperfectly closed at the time of manufacture, or made subsequently by rusting; or through the pores of the wooden case; or by the freezing of the water of the composition, by the expansion of which the walls are separated from each other, and communication established between the filling and the chamber of the safe. They may be prevented by so constructing the safe as absolutely to prevent any communication of water or vapor between the filling of the safe and the books and papers.

In a climate like ours, a safe may be exposed occasionally to temperatures below freezing. Any of the safes, as at present constructed, cannot contain any considerable quantity of water above that in chemical combination, without the danger of bursting by cold. This opening of the seams of the safe at once exposes the contents of the case to the exhalation of moisture from the filling. The protection against this kind of injury manifestly lies in such construction of the safe as will provide for the expansion consequent on freezing, without opening the joints or seams of the various parts.

Rust. — This is one of the agencies by which communication between the filling and the chamber of the safe is effected after the lapse of time ; and by which the contents of the chamber become damp. It may be prevented by consuming the oxygen of the air which would otherwise act on the iron. Chemical compositions are prepared which will, by absorbing the oxygen, perfectly protect the iron from corrosion or rust, even in the presence of air and water.

Varieties of Safes in use. — The safes at present in use differ from each other in various respects, but chiefly in the capacity of the composition employed, to yield vapor.

The earliest safes were designed chiefly to protect treasure against burglary, and were distinguished for their strength. Next came safes having non-conducting walls as protection against fire. In 1840, a safe appeared which took advantage of the principle of vaporization of water as protection against fire. The alum safe, upon the same principle was devised in 1843. The gypsum safe, also on the same principle, has long been in use. The cement safe, in which hydraulic cement is substituted for gypsum, has been many years in use. In the English safe of Milner, invented in 1840, the space between the iron shell and wooden case is occupied with closed tubes containing water, these tubes being imbedded in saw dust. On exposure to fire, the tubes burst, and the water, flowing into the sawdust, is converted into vapor, and escapes through the joints of the iron shell.

In the alum safe, invented by Messrs. Tann, of England, and a modification of which is produced in this country, the vapor is derived from the water of crystallization of the alum. Twenty per cent. of the weight of the alum is converted into vapor at 212°, and eighteen more at 250°. The remainder is given up only at a heat destructive to the contents of the safe.

In the ordinary gypsum safes, the surplus water added in the mixing, if it does not remain to do injury by charging the case and books with dampness, or by freezing, is in process of time exhaled until there remains only what has entered into chemical combination. This latter amounts to twenty per cent. Of this, ten per cent. is given up at 212°, and half of the remainder below 300°. The cement safes, as they are usually prepared, contain, after setting, and after time for giving up the surplus water, about six per cent. of water. Of this, one per cent. goes out at 212°. As the Alum safes are prepared in this country, the alum is mixed with pipe clay, and this mixture with fragments of brick, the former to absorb the water as the alum melts and to facilitate the vaporization ; the latter to give support and prevent the composition from falling when the alum melts. The proportion of alum is about one quarter of the whole. This would give of water from the composition, at 212°, only five per cent., and at 250°, four and a half per cent. more, or only nine and a half in all. If the alum were raised to the proportion of one half of the whole mixture, it would give up but ten per cent. of water at 212°, and nine more at 250°, or only nineteen per cent. at temperatures not dangerous to the contents of the safe.

In most fires the exposure is for so brief a period that the protection in some of the best safes is adequate; but there is the constant possibility that the fire may be too powerful and too protracted for the composition employed, and the protection consequently inadequate.

Can this protection against fires be increased?—The incombustible inclosure is of wrought iron, and nothing could be better than this. The points, therefore, remaining for consideration are, What is the best practicable non-conductor? and, What is the best composition for keeping down heat for vaporization?

In answer to the first question, experiments were made, among other materials, with *Infusorial Earth; a mixture of Sal Soda and Gypsum; a mixture of Glaubers Salt and Gypsum; set Cement; Alum and dry Cement; Gypsum with Gelatine.*

A wrought-iron cup, containing about eight ounces of water, was filled with each substance in its turn, and the bulb of a thermometer imbedded to the same distance from the bottom in all. The vessel and its contents were then subjected to the same degree of heat. The conducting power, or the facility of heating throughout, was measured by the number of degrees swept over by the ascending column of mercury in successive minutes. The range of heat was from 220° to 572°.

Infusorial earth was heated 27° in one minute.

Sal soda and gypsum taken in equal parts, 14° in one minute.,

Glaubers salt and gypsum, taken in equal parts, 12° in one minute.

Cement, set and dried, 11° in one minute.

Potash alum, 3 oz. ⎫ 5° per minute, from 220° to 300°.
Dry cement, 6 oz. ⎭ 4° per minute, from 300° to 572°.

Gypsum, 6 oz., and water, 6 oz., ⎫ 2° per min. from 220° to 300°.
   with 3 per cent of gelatine, ⎭ 4° per min. from 300° to 572°.

From each, the water due to a temperature of 212°, had, as already intimated, been driven out. In the cement, alum, and gypsum, there remained water in combination. The infusorial earth proved the best conductor, and would of course be the poorest substance for filling a safe. Of all, the gypsum and gelatine, as prepared for this experiment, throughout the range in which the contents of the safe are secure against fire, namely, below 300°, affords the best protection, so far as conduction is concerned. It is, indeed, difficult to conceive of a substance better suited for non-conduction than this mass of set plaster and gelatine, after the surplus water alternating with every particle of gypsum has been driven out, leaving behind an infinity of minute cavities, rendering the whole porous and non-conducting to the last degree.

How shall this quality be combined most advantageously with the second requisite mentioned above, that of supplying matter to be vaporized, thereby carrying the heat away?

Two sets of experiments were undertaken to determine this point. The first on a small scale, the second on a large and more practical scale. The first was conducted at the same time with the series already detailed, and employing the same apparatus. The wrought-iron cup was filled with each mixture in turn, supported at a constant altitude over a flame of uniform height, and the thermometer imbedded to the same depth in all.

4

The results showed, that, as regards protection to be afforded by vaporization from 212° to 220°, the following substances ranked in value in the order stated :— Gypsum, gelatine, and water; Cement; Glaubers salt and gypsum; Sal soda and gypsum ; Alum.

The question of using a composition which should give up vapor at a temperature above 212° only, was tested in the use of a mixture of sulphate of ammonia and common salt, diluted with powdered coke, which, on the application of heat, yielded sal ammoniac. Experiments were also made with a mixture of ammonia-alum and common salt, diluted, like the above, with coke. This yielded water in addition to sal ammoniac. Clay and powdered brick were substituted for coke. They gave results inferior to all except the potash-alum.

In addition to these laboratory experiments, a series were undertaken on a scale of such magnitude as to render the results of more direct practical value. As the object was to determine the relative excellence of different kinds of safes in which all the circumstances of exposure were the same, it was conducted with great attention to details, and was, on many accounts, the most important ever made of which any record has been preserved.

Experiments in Reverberatory Furnaces.—Five wrought-iron safes were constructed, each of one cubic foot capacity. For each, a small wooden box four inches in the clear, and three-quarters of an inch in thickness, was prepared to represent the inside case. When in place, there was a space for composition of three inches thickness on every side of the box. In each wooden box was placed a piece of parchment, some white writing paper, cotton batting, a piece of sealing-wax, a self-registering thermometer ranging to 600°, and a series of small thermometers bursting at given temperatures.

No. 1 contained sulphate of ammonia, 15.5 lbs. ; common salt, 15.5 lbs.; powdered coke, 24 lbs. ; wooden box, 2 lbs.; iron shell, 27 lbs. Total, 84 lbs.

No. 2 contained potash-alum, 26 lbs.; pipe-clay, 26 lbs. ; brick, 28¾ lbs. ; dry cement, to fill, ¾ lbs. ; wooden box, 2 lbs.; iron shell, 28¾ lbs. Total, 112¼ lbs.

No. 3 contained ammonia-alum, 26¼ lbs. ; common salt, 13¼ lbs. ; coke, 16 lbs. ; wooden box 2 lbs.; iron shell, 29¼ lbs. Total, 87¼ lbs.

No. 4 contained cement, 60 lbs. ; water, 19¾ lbs. ; soapstone front, 9 lbs. ; wooden box, 2 lbs. ; iron shell, 30 lbs. Total, 120¾ lbs.

No. 5 contained plaster of Paris, 50 lbs.; water, 21 lbs. ; dry cement, to fill, 9 lbs. ; wooden box, 2 lbs. ; iron shell, 28 lbs. Total, 110 lbs.

These safes were carefully introduced into a reverberatory furnace from which a discharge of twenty thousand pounds of molten iron had just taken place, and when the walls were nearly at the temperature of melted iron. The safes were placed on the bottom of the furnace, the door closed, and after adjusting the draft so as to permit the furnace to cool slowly down in the usual way, the safes were left from five o'clock in the afternoon till ten the next morning.

On taking the safes from the furnace, they were first weighed. No. 1 had lost 8¼ lbs. ; No. 2,[1] 15¾ ; No. 3,[2] 16¾ ; No. 4, 13 ; No. 5, 16.

[1] This is the common alum safe, except that one-third of alum was employed instead of one-quarter.
[2] One pound of this, and of each of the preceding two, is due to the charring of the wooden box.

The temperature of No. 1 had been above 600°. The paper, cotton batting, and box were charred; the parchment and sealing-wax were destroyed.

The temperature of No. 2 had been as high as 580°. The paper, cotton, and box were charred. The parchment and sealing-wax were destroyed.

The temperature of No. 3 had been 350°. Contents were much less injured than those of No. 1 and No. 2, but were still greatly discolored. The box was partially charred.

The temperature of No. 4 was 287°. The paper and cotton were discolored. The box thoroughly dried and shrunken somewhat, but not charred. The parchment was shrivelled and the sealing-wax melted.

The temperature of No. 5 had been 212°. The parchment was somewhat shrivelled, and sealing-wax melted; but the paper, cotton batting, and box were uninjured.

In the safes filled with potash-alum, clay, and brick, — with ammonia-alum, salt and coke, — and with sulphate of ammonia, salt, and coke, a coarse porous wall around the interior wooden case was preserved after the volatile matters had been driven out. In the cement safe, the cement retained about one-third of its water and the form perfectly. In the gypsum and water safe, the plaster retained its form. It had parted with about four-fifths of its water. (Strictly $\frac{16}{21}$.)

From the foregoing, it is evident that in keeping the temperature down a given time, $7\frac{1}{4}$ lbs. of sal-ammoniac are inferior to $14\frac{3}{4}$ lbs. of water from potash-alum; and these inferior to $15\frac{3}{4}$ lbs. of water and sal-ammoniac, from ammonia-alum and salt; and these inferior to 13 lbs. of water from the cement safe; and these inferior to 16 lbs. of water from the plaster and water safe.

In the gypsum and water safe, 5 pounds of water were fixed in the setting, and 16 pounds were held by capillary attraction. These 16 were driven out at 212°. There remained 5 in combination, at the close of the experiment, to be driven out at the same temperature. In the cement safe, 6 pounds were fixed in the setting, and $13\frac{3}{4}$ pounds were held by capillary attraction. Of these $13\frac{3}{4}$, 13 were driven out at 212°. There remained but $\frac{3}{4}$ of a pound to be driven out at 212°. In the alum safe, there were but 8 lbs. expelled at 212°.

In summary—the gypsum and water safe lost 16 lbs. at 212°; the cement and water safe, 13 lbs.; the alum safe, [1]8 lbs.

The water remaining to be expelled, at 212°, from the gypsum and water safe, was 5 lbs.; from the cement safe, was $\frac{3}{4}$ lb.; from the alum safe, was 0.

Not only was there no water to be driven out at 212°, but $6\frac{3}{4}$ lbs. had been driven out at much higher temperatures, the last at 580°.

A cement safe, as ordinarily made, set and dried, of these dimensions, contains a little more than half a pound of water to be driven out at 212°. In a plaster safe, set and dried, there would have been but 5 lbs. to be driven out at 212°. In an ordinary alum safe, there would have been less than 8; while in the gypsum and water safe, as here prepared, there were 21 lbs., which, by the process already described, might have been increased to 50 lbs.

[1] A part of this loss was evidently due to the moisture in the clay.

The potash-alum safe lost altogether within 1¼ lbs. as much water as the plaster and water safe, but nearly one-half went out at temperatures from 212° to 580°, a range destructive to books and papers. The ammonia-alum and salt safe lost about 20 per cent. more of water and sal-ammoniac than the cement safe of water alone, and yet did not afford the same degree of protection, for the cement safe was heated only to 287°,[1] while the ammonia safe was heated to 350°.

Experiment in a Furnace at a White Heat. — Another experiment was undertaken with four safes of the capacity of one cubic foot each. Each contained a wooden box, enclosing a series of thermometers constructed to burst at given temperatures.

No. 1 contained cement, 64 lbs.; water, 3¾ lbs. This is cement containing the quantity of water which remains after the filling is set and dried.

No. 2 contained plaster, 62½ lbs.; water, 12 lbs. This is a plaster of Paris safe, containing twenty-five per cent. more than the quantity of water due to plaster set and dried.

No. 3 contained alum, 33 lbs.; pipe-clay, 33 lbs.; brick, 19½ lbs. This safe, with a smaller proportion of alum, is in extensive use in this country.

No. 4 contained plaster, 28 lbs.; gelatine,[2] 1½ lbs.; water, 43 lbs.

These safes were placed in the same reverberatory furnace in which the preceding experiment was conducted. There was this difference between the experiments: The first was conducted with a constantly falling temperature. This with a temperature carried from freezing up to a white heat, and there maintained for thirty minutes; and then permitted to cool down. At the end of the first half hour, Nos. 1 and 2, which were least exposed, were red hot; No. 3 was at low red, and No. 4 was dark.

At forty minutes, the condition was the same. At forty-two minutes, pronounced melting heat by the workmen, Nos. 1, 2 and 3 were red, but 4 still dark equally. At fifty minutes, No. 4 became low red, and No. 3 was burnt through and melted away at points nearest the fire. At 60 minutes, No. 3 was at a white heat, and No. 4 was red.

This white heat was maintained for thirty minutes, when the furnace was opened and cooled down sufficiently to examine the condition of the safes.

No. 4 was burned so as to crack a little on one side, but was not melted in any part. No. 3 was melted away from the top, front, and two sides. The side farthest from the fire, and bottom, were alone whole. · No. 2 was scarcely less injured. The melting did not, however, extend so far down the sides. No. 1, which was further from the fire and sheltered by the other safes, was burned but not melted.

The fire was again raised to the melting point, the furnace closed, and the safes left in this heated chamber, slowly cooling down, from five o'clock in the afternoon till ten o'clock the next morning.

---

[1] This elevated temperature, while there was still water in the cement, is manifestly due to the conducting power of the soapstone upon which the wooden box rested.

[2] I employ the term gelatine as expressing in a single word the substance obtained by the action of boiling water from gelatinizable substances, like sea-weed, of the variety known as Iceland moss, or potato starch, or animal membranes, or from other similar vegetable and animal substances.

On opening the furnace, the appearances of the safes had not apparently changed since the examination at the close of the first experiment. The wooden boxes in Nos. 1, 2, and 3, had been destroyed. The temperature in No. 2 had been above 600°, and in Nos. 1 and 3, above 300°, but not to 600°, though probably not far below.

The wooden box in No. 4 was as fresh as when put in. The thermometer bursting at 150° was destroyed, but that bursting at 212° was sound. The heat had not attained to that of boiling water. It will be borne in mind that No. 1 is the ordinary cement safe, No. 2 is the ordinary plaster of Paris safe, No. 3 is the alum safe, and No. 4 the new safe. The first three were destroyed, while the temperature in No. 4 was, at the utmost, entirely within the range of safety to the books and papers.

Conclusions. — 1st. It is evident that the protection against fire is mainly *proportioned to the quantity of water the safe can give up to be carried away as steam, and not to the non-conducting quality of its filling.*

2d. It is evident, further, that the protection against fire is not simply as the quantity of water that may be present in the composition for filling, but as the quantity of water that may be parted with *unrestrained by chemical affinity, or* WATER AS SUCH. The more powerful the chemical affinity resisting the escape of vapor, the more elevated must be the temperature at which it will leave, while the capacity of the escaping vapor to render heat latent or to absorb and carry it away will remain unchanged. The same quantity of water in combination in alum is not so serviceable in keeping down the temperature as when free.

3d. It is evident, further, that while the water, in its uncombined or natural state, must constitute a large part of the filling of a safe in order to make its protection against fire in the highest degree available, this water must be held in *solid form* so as to give strength to the safe ; and the safe must be so constructed as to prevent the water from passing off by leakage or as vapor, to the injury of the books and papers, or to the lessening of the fire-proof qualities of the safe ; and yet be so constructed as to allow, on the application of high heat, the most free escape of vapor from those points to which the heat is applied, without endangering the strength of the safe, or driving the vapor into the interior chamber of the safe ; and withal so arranged as to permit freezing, without injury to the safe or its contents.

In a safe made in the light of the foregoing experiments, from 70 to 80 per cent. of the space appropriated to filling was occupied by water, and yet was exposed for a day and two nights to a temperature of zero without injury.

On exposure to fire the water is resolved into vapor first at the outer surface of the filling, and leaves the best non-conductor, according to the results of foregoing experiments between the water which remains and the heated metal of the exterior shell. At length, when all the water has been driven out as vapor, there remains the non-conductor of the whole thickness of the filling, to protect, as long as it may, the contents of the case.

THE GREAT BOSTON ORGAN.

During the past year there has been erected in the Music Hall, of the city of Boston, Massachusetts, an organ, which for absolute power and compass ranks among the three or four mightiest instruments ever built; and in the perfection of all its parts, and in its whole arrangements, challenges comparison with any the world can show. The instrument in question was built by E. F. Walcker, of Ludwigksburg, in the kingdom of Würtemburg, and was upwards of six years in the course of construction. Its cost was upwards of $50,000, and the case alone cost $15,000.

In itself, this organ may be described as really comprising five distinct organs, or systems of pipes, which are capable of being played on alone, or in connection with each other. Four of these are played upon by manuals or hand key-boards, and the other by pedals or a foot key-board. The lowest of the former controls the swell organ, the pipes of which, as in other instruments, are enclosed in a box (in this case, itself as large as many complete organs), and so arranged that it may be open or perfectly tight at the will of the performer, thus giving opportunity for light and shade in endless variety. This organ contains 18 registers or stops, with which are drawn on or shut off an equal number of ranks or series of pipes, all of which, or any of them separately or in combination, may be made to speak through the swell manual. Next above this is placed the key-board of the "great organ," as it is technically called. Here we have 25 registers, all of which connect with pipes on a large scale, and are the loudest voiced pipes in the whole organ. Here are the grand diapasons which form the foundation of the whole sound-superstructure, and the immense trumpets and clarions which ring out like a call to battle. Above the great organ manual comes that of the choir organ, which has 15 registers, and is in many respects the "great organ" on a softer scale, but without the harsher reed stops. The last and upper manual belongs to the solo organ, which also answers for the echo organ, containing 11 stops, and among them the famous vox humana, the qualities of which have not yet been publicly tested. The pedals are the only remaining key-board, and in connection with them are 20 distinct stops, 15 loud and the rest soft, some of the former being monster reeds and a close imitation of orchestral instruments. We have then a total of 89 speaking stops, which may all be combined, and a grand total of 5474 pipes. The largest of these pipes measure thirty-two feet in length, and are sufficiently capacious in diameter to allow men to crawl through them, while the finest tubes "are too small for a baby's whistle." The breath to these pipes, "to be poured forth in music," is furnished by twelve pairs of bellows, moved by water-power derived from the Cochituate reservoirs.

But this great instrument does not differ from other organs merely in size and wonderful variety of stops, but it excels them in almost every detail which can be mentioned. The principal diapasons are made of the purest English tin which is consistent with stability, and the pipes in the swell organ, although they are always hidden from view, are finished with the most scrupulous nicety. The dip of the keys of ordinary organs is three-eighths, or at the most three-eighths and a sixteenth of an inch, while the keys of this organ dip no less than five-eighths of an inch, presenting a considerable obstable to players unused to such great depth.   But the difficulties which would arise from such a vast amount of mechanism connecting with the keys, asking of an organist's finger the strength of a blacksmith's arm, are overcome by a delicate pneumatic action, which is called too easy rather than otherwise.   The arrangement of the stops is controlled to a great extent by the feet, there being twelve separate pedals for this purpose, so that the most beautiful and changeful effects can be made without removing either hand from the key-board.   There is also a pedal by which all the stops of the organ may be gradually, one by one or instantaneously, drawn on or shut off, thus producing the most magnificent crescendo and diminuendo, as well as explosive effects.   Thus a tone which is scarcely heard at first can be augmented by degrees until it makes the air quiver with its thunders, and then slowly sink again to hushed repose; or the crash can come without warning and with almost deafening power, and as suddenly sink into music of which the listener can catch but the slightest murmurs.   The value of such immense power under perfect control will be easily appreciated.

This great instrument, enclosed in a case of black walnut covered with carved statues, busts, faces and figures in bold relief, is placed upon a low platform, the outlines of which are in accordance with its own.   Its whole height is about sixty feet, its breadth forty-eight feet, and its average depth twenty-four feet.

MANUFACTURE OF BOOTS AND SHOES BY MACHINERY.

The old system of making boots and shoes entirely by hand labor is rapidly yielding to the march of improvement, and will soon, to all appearances, be numbered with the relics of the past.   This change in the character of the manufacture of a great staple industrial product, although slowly progressing for the last eight or ten years in the United States under the spur of competition, has been rapidly consummated within the last two years under the influences growing out of the present civil war; hand labor having proved entirely inadequate to supply the immense demand for boots and shoes required by government for its armies. Machines, therefore, have been invented, and are now in use, executing the different operations necessary to the manufacture of such articles, and with a rapidity and accuracy of action which far excel the efforts of hand labor.

The following interesting account of a manufactory in New York city, in which boots and shoes are made upon an extensive scale by machinery, we derive from a recent number of the *Scientific American:*

Three large apartments are occupied by the operatives, mechanism, and goods.   The skins for the uppers are first spread out, examined, and selected according to the purposes for which they are required. Different cutters then cut out the respective parts according to the size and form required, and these are all arranged and classified.   After this these separate parts are given out in lots to be sewed by machines, and those uppers which are intended for boots are crimped, and the whole made ready for receiving the soles.   The more heavy operations of punching, sewing, pegging the soles and finishing the articles, are next executed. The sole-leather, in hides, is first steeped in a tank of water to soften it, then it is thoroughly dipped, and afterwards cut by a machine into measured lengths of a certain breadth, according to the size of sole wanted. After having become sufficiently dry, these cut strips of leather are run between rollers, and also submitted to severe pressure under plates in a press, so as to effect as complete a compression of the fibres as is attained according to the old mode by beating with a hammer upon a lapstone. From these compressed strips, soles of the different sizes are punched out at a single blow by a machine, the cutter of which is of the size and form required, and it turns round so as to cut a right and left sole alternately. Heel pieces are also cut out by hollow punches at a single blow. The edges of the soles and heels are next smoothed and polished in a small rotating machine, and another machine then makes the channels in the soles for the rows of stitching. After this the under soles and uppers are fitted upon lasts and made ready for sewing. This operation is executed by Mackay's peculiar machine, adapted for this specific purpose. The waxed thread is wound upon a vertical spool, and is conducted through a guide situated on the top of an elbow secured on a swivel joint capable of turning under the needle, and conducting the thread into the crease around the sole. The needle operates vertically above the sole, and the waxed thread is fed into the interior of the boot or shoe by the guide, the needle descending through the sole, drawing through the thread and forming the stitches, which are pressed down close into the crease by a tracer-foot, upon which great pressure is exerted. In this manner the sole and upper are united firmly and neatly together in a few seconds without employing a welt. Hand sewing cannot be compared with such machine-work for accuracy and rapidity. Another machine is employed for putting on double soles with copper pegs. A thin strip of copper is fed in at one side, and the holes are punched in the sole, the pegs cut and put into the holes, and then driven down at one continuous operation, with a speed corresponding to that of sewing the soles. The crossing of the half sole at the instep is pegged, and also fastened with a screw at each side by hand; the heels are also pegged down. The edges of the heels are neatly trimmed by a small rotating machine, and the soles are also rubbed down by a machine; so that nearly all the operations connected with the manufacture of boots and shoes in this establishment are performed by machines designed especially for the purpose. The legs of the boots are stretched and the wrinkles removed by new boot-trees secured to benches, and are expanded in an instant from the interior by pressing on a treadle with the foot. These boot-trees are altogether superior to the clumsy old wedge kind. The materials used in the manufacture of these articles appear to be of a superior quality, the machines not being adapted for operating on inferior patch leather.

The accurate operations of these machines, and the rapidity of their action, place them in a highly advantageous position for manufacturing boots and shoes. The price of hand labor had become so high and workmen so scarce that such machines became a necessity, and the change effected by their use is equal to four times the quantity of work executed by hand labor; that is, one hundred men will turn out with these machines as much work as four hundred men without them. The saving of labor to the country is therefore immense. About five hundred pairs can be turned out daily in this establishment. Perhaps no labor connected with boot-making is so severe as that bestowed upon burnishing the heel with a warm iron. This work is still executed by hand, but a machine is now being set up to accomplish this finishing operation, and it will soon be at work. For centuries, no improvement seems to have been made upon the old system of boot and shoe making; when, all at once, as it were, — within the space of two short years, — the whole art has been revolutionized.

CULINARY IMPROVEMENTS.

New Mode of Preserving Provisions. — A patent has been applied for by A. H. Remond, of London, for preserving provisions by passing a current of electricity through the cans or cases containing what are called "preserved provisions," after they are sealed up. The electric fluid is made to pass through the case on a fine iron wire; the wire is caused to become red-hot by the intensity of the current, and thus the oxygen in the can is said to be consumed, because it will unite with the hot iron wire and form an oxide.

Roasting Coffee. — In order to prevent the loss of aroma, W. Symington, of London, roasts coffee in a close vessel, which has a funnel that conveys the volatile oil, which contains the aroma, into a receptacle containing cold ground coffee, and where the aroma is absorbed. All the roasted coffee, after it is ground and becomes cold, is exposed for a short period in the absorbing chamber. — *Scientific American.*

ARTIFICIAL IVORY.

Patents have been taken by Dr. R. Havemann, of New Brunswick, N. J., for an imitation of ivory, produced by the action of chlorine on India rubber or allied gums. By his process, solid lumps of India rubber or gutta percha are dissolved in one of the well-known solvents used for the purpose; and this solution is brought in contact with chlorine by passing streams of gaseous chlorine into the same. When the combination of the gum with the chlorine is perfected, the solvent is removed by evaporation at a low temperature. After removing the liquid by filtering or evaporation, the composition of gum and chlorine is well washed with alcohol and then pressed and dried, when it forms a white, hard mass, similar to ivory in appearance and elasticity. We have seen billiard balls made of it, but we think they lacked the weight necessary to render them equal to ivory; for many purposes, however, it is an excellent substitute for ivory. — *Scientific American.*

SIEMANS'S REGENERATIVE GAS FURNACE.

A brief description of the construction and use of this furnace was given in the *Annual of Scientific Discovery* for 1863, p. 32. Since its first introduction, we understand that the principle of heating involved has been extensively applied in England, France, Germany, and other countries, to glass-houses, for heating gas retorts and muffles for metallurgical purposes, for melting steel, and for puddling and welding iron. At the meeting of the British Association for 1863, Mr. Siemans was present and exhibited the plan for a furnace for welding and working

iron, and the gas generator connected with it.   The heated chamber
is of the usual form, but instead of a fireplace there are four passages
(two at each end of the chamber) leading downwards into four regenerators or chambers filled with loosely piled firebricks.   The lower extremities of these four regenerator chambers communicate with two
cast-iron reversing valves.   The gas arriving from the producer through
a pipe is directed by the valve into one regenerator or other, according
to the position of the valve.   The gas then ascends through the one
regenerator, where it takes up the heat previously deposited in the
brickwork, and issues into the furnace at a point where it meets with a
current of heated air arising from the second regenerator to effect its
combustion.   The products of combustion pass away through the opposite regenerator and the reversing valves into the chimney flue.   The
last-named regenerators receive at this time the waste heat of the furnace, becoming heated at their upper extremity to the temperature
nearly of the furnace itself, but remaining comparatively cool towards
the bottom.   Every hour or half-hour the direction of the currents is
reversed by a change of the valve lever, the heat before deposited in
the one pair of regenerators is now communicated to the air and gas
coming in, while the waste heat replenishes the second pair of regenerators.   The gas producer consists of two inclined planes upon which
the fuel descends, being gradually deprived in heating of its gaseous
constituents, and finally burnt to carbonic oxide by the air entering
through the grate at the bottom of the inclines.   Water admitted at
the bottom also assists in the decomposition of the ignited coke at the
bottom, converting the same into carbonic oxide and hydrogen gas.
The saving of fuel which has been effected by this arrangement
amounts to from forty to fifty per cent.   In the application to re-heating and puddling furnaces, a saving of iron has been effected, owing to
the mildness of the gas flame, of from three to four per cent. of the entire quantity put in; the iron also welds more perfectly than it does in
the ordinary furnaces.   Smoke is entirely obviated.   By another arrangement the regenerative principle has been applied also to coke
ovens, the result being that the separation of the coke from its gaseous
constituents is effected without losing the latter.   In placing the coke
ovens, constructed on this plan, near the works where the iron is puddled and re-heated, the latter operation may be entirely effected by the
gas generated in producing the coke necessary for the blast furnace in
producing the pig iron.   The gas resulting from the regenerative coke
oven may be used to heat the blast and boilers connected with the
blast furnace.   These latter improvements are now in course of being
carried into effect on a large scale.   The gas produced from the last-named producers is of a very illuminating character, and may, it is reported, be used for that purpose in preference to the hydrocarbon now
manufactured for that purpose by a much more expensive process.

American manufacturers desirous of acquainting themselves in detail
with the principles of Siemans's furnace will find a descriptive paper by
the inventor in the *Proceedings of the Society of Mechanical Engineers*,
London.

IMPROVEMENTS IN THE SCIENCE OF WAR.

In accordance with the plan pursued during the last two years, we give under the above head a summary of such inventions, discoveries, and applications relative to the science of war, brought before the public during the past year, as have seemed to the editor as most worthy of notice.

IMPROVEMENTS IN GUN-COTTON.

At the British Association meetings of 1862, a joint committee of chemists and physicists was appointed to inquire into and report on the so-called "*Austrian Gun-Cotton.*" At the last meeting of the Association, a chemical report was submitted by Dr. Gladstone, and a report on the mechanical portion of the question by Mr. J. Scott Russell. We present first an abstract of Dr. Gladstone's report.

Chemical Report. — Since the discovery of gun-cotton by Schönbein, its application to war purposes has been frequently thought of; and many experiments, with a view of using it, have been made, especially by the French. Such serious difficulties have, however, presented themselves, that the idea gradually came to be abandoned everywhere but in Austria. Here experimentation was kept up, and it having been reported on good authority that the experimenters had succeeded in overcoming many of the difficulties encountered elsewhere, the committee of the Association applied to the Austrian government for information, which was furnished them. The following is a summary of the more important facts elicited. In the first place, the gun-cotton prepared by Baron Von Lenk, the inventor of the Austrian system, differs from the gun-cotton generally made in its complete conversion into a uniform chemical compound. It is well known to chemists that if cotton is treated with mixtures of strong nitric and sulphuric acids, compounds may be obtained varying considerably in composition, though they all contain elements of the nitric acid, and are all explosive. The most complete combination (or product of substitution) is that described as $C_{36} H_{21} (9 NO_4) O_{30}$, which is identical with that termed by the Austrian chemists trinitrocellulose, $C_{12} H_7 (3 NO_4) O_{10}$. This is of no use whatever for the making of collodion ; but it is Von Lenk's gun-cotton, and he secures its production by several precautions, of which the most important are the cleansing and perfect dessiccation of the cotton as a preliminary to its immersion in the acids, — the employment of the strongest acids attainable in commerce, — the steeping of the cotton in a fresh strong mixture of the acids after its first immersion and consequentim perfect conversion into gun-cotton, — the continuance of this steeping for forty-eight hours. Equally necessary is the thorough purification of the gun-cotton so produced from every trace of free acid. This is secured exclusively by its being washed in a stream of water for several weeks. These prolonged processes are absolutely necessary. It seems mainly from the want of these precautions that the French were not successful. From the evidence before the committee it appears that this nitro compound, when thoroughly free from acid, is not liable to some of the objections which have been urged against that compound usually experimented upon as gun-cotton. It seems to have a marked advantage in stability over all other forms of gun-cotton that have been proposed. It has been kept unaltered for fifteen years; it does not become ignited till raised to a temperature of 136° C. (277° Fahr.); it is but slightly hygroscopic, and when exploded in a confined space, is almost entirely free from ash. There is one part of the process not yet alluded to, and the value of which is more open to doubt, — the treatment of the gun-cotton with a solution of silicate of potash commonly called water-glass. Some Austrian chemists think lightly of it; but Von Lenk considers that the amount of silica set free on the cotton by the carbonic acid of the atmosphere is really of service in retarding the combustion. He adds, that some of the gun-cotton made at the Imperial factory has not been silicated at all, and some imperfectly; but when the process has been thoroughly performed, he finds that the gun-cotton has increased permanently about 3 per cent. in weight. Much apprehension has been felt about the effect of the gases produced by the explosion of gun-cotton upon those exposed to its action. It has been stated that both nitrous fumes and prussic acid are among these gases, and that the one would corrode the gun and the other poison the artilleryman. Now, though it is true that from some kinds of gun-cotton, or by some methods of decomposition, one or both of these gases may be produced, the results of the explosion of the Austrian gun-cotton without access of air are found to contain neither of them, but to consist of nitrogen, carbonic acid, carbonic oxide, water, and a little hydrogen and light carburetted hydrogen. These are comparatively innocuous, and this weight of evidence is, that the gun is less injured by repeated charges of gun-cotton than of gunpowder, and that the men in casemates suffer less from its fumes. It seems a disadvantage of this material, as compared with gunpowder, that it explodes at a temperature of 277° Fahr.; but against the greater liability to accidents from this cause may be set the almost impossibility of explosion during the process of manufacture, since the gun-cotton is always immersed in liquid, except in the final drying.[1] Again, if it should be considered advisable at any time, it may be stored in water, and only dried in small quantities as required for use. The fact that gun-cotton is not injured by damp like gunpowder is, indeed, one of its recommendations, while a still more important chemical advantage which it possesses arises from its being perfectly resolved into gases on explosion; so that there is no smoke to obscure the sight of the soldier who is firing or to point out his position to the enemy, and no residuum left in the gun to be got rid of before another charge can be introduced.

Physical Report. — Mr. Russell stated, that greater effects are produced by gases generated from gun-cotton than by gases from gunpowder, and it was only after long and careful examination that the committee were able to reconcile this fact with the low temperature at which the mechanical force is obtained. The great waste of force in gunpowder constitutes an important difference between it and gun-cotton, in which

[1] In ten years' experience it is proved that this temperature is sufficiently high to insure safety of manipulation; 277° Fahr. is an artificial temperature, and artificial temperatures accidentally produced are generally high enough to ignite gunpowder. The greater liability to accident from this cause can, therefore, scarcely be admitted.

there is no waste. The waste in gunpowder is sixty-eight per cent. of its own weight, and only thirty-two per cent. is useful. This sixty-eight per cent. is not only waste in itself, but it wastes the power of the remaining thirty-two per cent. It wastes it mechanically, by using up a large portion of the mechanical force of the useful gases. The waste of gunpowder issues from the gun with much higher velocity than the projectile; and if it be remembered that in one hundred pounds of useful gunpowder this is sixty-eight pounds, it will appear that thirty-two pounds of useful gunpowder gas is wasted in impelling a sixty-eight pound shot composed of the refuse of gunpowder itself. There is yet another peculiar feature of gun-cotton. It can be exploded in any quantity instantaneously. This was once considered its great fault; but it was only a fault when we were ignorant of the means to make that velocity anything we pleased. Baron Von Lenk has discovered the means of giving gun-cotton any velocity of explosion that is required by merely the mechanical arrangements under which it is used. Gun-cotton, in his hands, has any speed of explosion, from one foot per second to one foot in $\frac{1}{1000}$ of a second, or to instantaneity. The instantaneous explosion of a large quantity of gun-cotton is made use of when it is required to produce destructive effects on the surrounding material. The slow combustion is made use of when it is required to produce manageable power, as in the case of gunnery. It is plain, therefore, that, if we can explode a large mass instantaneously, we get out of the gases so exploded the greatest possible power, because all the gas is generated before motion commences, and this is the condition of maximum effect. It is found that the condition necessary to produce instantaneous and complete explosion is the absolute perfection of closeness of the chamber containing the gun-cotton. The reason of it is, that the first ignited gases must penetrate the whole mass of the cotton, and this they do, and create complete ignition throughout, only under pressure. This pressure need not be great. For example, a barrel of gun-cotton will produce little effect and very slow combustion when out of the barrel, but instantaneous and powerful explosion when shut up within it. On the other hand, if we desire gun-cotton to produce mechanical work, and not destruction of materials, we must provide for its slower combustion. It must be distributed and opened out mechanically, so as to occupy a larger space, and in this state it can be made to act even more slowly than gunpowder; and the exact limit for purposes of artillery Von Lenk has found by critical experiments. In general, it is found that the proportion of eleven pounds of gun-cotton, occupying one cubic foot of space, produces a greater force than gunpowder, of which from fifty to sixty pounds occupies the same space, and a force of the nature required for ordinary artillery. But each gun and each kind of projectile requires a certain density of cartridge. Practically, gun-cotton is most effective in guns when used as $\frac{1}{4}$ to $\frac{1}{3}$ weight of powder, and occupying a space of $1\frac{1}{10}$th of the length of the powder-cartridge. The mechanical structure of the cartridge is of importance as affecting its ignition. The cartridge is formed of a mechanical arrangement of spun cords, and the distribution of these, the place and manner of ignition, the form and proportion of the cartridge, all affect the time of complete ignition. It is by the complete mastery he has gained over all these minute points that Von Lenk is enabled to give to the action of gun-

5

cotton on the projectile any law of force he pleases.   Its cost of production is considerably less than that of gunpowder, the price of quantities which will produce equal effects being compared.   Gun-cotton is
used for artillery in the form of a gun-cotton thread or spun yarn.   In
this simple form it will conduct combustion slowly in the open air, at a
rate of not more than one foot per second.   This thread is woven into
a texture or circular web.   These webs are made of various diameters, and it is out of these webs that common rifle cartridges are made,
merely by cutting them into the proper lengths, and inclosing them in
stiff cylinders of pasteboard, which form the cartridges.   (In this shape
its combustion in the open air takes place at a speed of ten feet per
second.)   In these cylindrical webs it is also used to fill explosive
shells, as it can be conveniently employed in this shape to pass in
through the neck of the shell.   Gun-cotton thread is spun into ropes in
the usual way up to two inches diameter, hollow in the centre.   This
is the form used for blasting and mining purposes; it combines great
density with speedy explosion.   The gun-cotton yarn is used directly
to form cartridges for large guns by being wound round a bobbin so as
to form a spindle like that used in spinning-mills.   The bobbin is a hollow tube of paper or wood, the object of the wooden rod is to secure in
all cases the necessary length of chamber in the gun required for the
most effective explosion.   The gun-cotton circular web is inclosed in
close tubes of India-rubber cloth, to form a match line, in which form it
is most convenient, and travels with speed and certainty.   In large
quantities, for the explosion of mines, it is used in the form of rope, and
in this form it is conveniently coiled in casks and stowed in boxes.   As
regards conveyance and storage of gun-cotton: it results from the foregoing facts, that one pound of gun-cotton produces an effect exceeding
three pounds of gunpowder in artillery.   This is a material advantage,
whether it be carried by men, by horses, or in wagons.   It may be
placed in store, and preserved with great safety.   The danger from
explosion does not arise until it is confined.   It may become damp and
even perfectly wet without injury, and may be dried by mere exposure
to the air.   This is of great value in ships of war, and in case of danger
from fire, the magazine may be submerged without injury.   As regards
its practical use in artillery, it is easy to gather from the foregoing general facts how gun-cotton keeps the gun clean and requires less windage, and therefore performs much better in continuous firing.   In gunpowder there is sixty-eight per cent. of refuse, or the matter of fouling.
In gun-cotton there is no residuum, and therefore no fouling.   Experiments made by the Austrian committee proved that one hundred
rounds could be fired with gun-cotton, against thirty rounds of gunpowder.   From the low temperature produced by gun-cotton, the gun
does not heat.   Experiments showed that one hundred rounds were
fired with a six-pounder in thirty-four minutes, and the gun was raised
by gun-cotton to only 122° Fahrenheit, whilst one hundred rounds
with gunpowder took one hundred minutes, and raised the temperature
to such a degree that water was instantly evaporated.   The firing with
the gunpowder was, therefore, discontinued; but the rapid firing with
the gun-cotton was continued up to one hundred and eighty rounds
without any inconvenience.   The absence of fouling allows all the
mechanism of a gun to have much more exactness than where allow-

ance is made for fouling. The absence of smoke promotes rapid firing and exact aim. There are no poisonous gases, and the men suffer less inconvenience from firing in casemates, under hatches, or in closed chambers. The fact of smaller recoil from a gun charged with gun-cotton is established by direct experiment. Its value is ⅔ of the recoil from gunpowder, projectile effect being equal. To understand this may not be easy. The waste of the solids of gunpowder accounts for one part of the saving, as in one hundred pounds of gunpowder sixty-eight pounds have to be projected in addition to the shot, and at a much higher speed. The remainder Von Lenk attributes to the different law of combustion. But the fact is established. The comparative advantages of gun-cotton and gunpowder for producing high velocities are shown in the following experiment with a Krupp's cast-steel gun, six-pounder. With ordinary charge thirty ounces of powder produced 1,338 feet per second. With charge of thirteen and one-half ounces, gun-cotton produced 1,563 ft. The comparative advantages in shortness of gun are shown in the following experiments, twelve-pounder : —

	Calibers.	Charge.								Velocity feet per second.
Cotton, length 10 .	.	15.9 oz.	.	.	.	.	.	.	.	1,426
Powder, " 13½ .	.	49 (normal powder charge)		.	.	.	.	.	.	1,400
Cotton, " 9 .	.	17	.	.	.	.	.	.	.	1,402

As to advantage in weight of gun, the fact of the recoil being less in the ratio of 2 : 3 enables a less weight of gun to be employed, as well as a shorter gun, without the disadvantage to practice arising from lightness of gun. As regards durance of gun, bronze and cast-iron guns have been fired 1,000 rounds without in the least affecting the endurance of the gun. As regards its practical application to destructive explosions of shells, it appears that from a difference in the law of expansion, arising probably from the pressure of water in intensely-heated steam, there is an extraordinary difference of result, namely, that the same shell is exploded by the same volume of gas into more than double the number of pieces. This is to be accounted for by the greater velocity of explosion when the gun-cotton is confined very closely in very small spaces. It is also a peculiarity that the stronger the shell, the smaller the fragments into which it is broken. As regards mining uses, the fact that the action of gun-cotton is violent and rapid in exact proportion to the resistance it encounters, tells us the secret of its far higher efficacy in mining than gunpowder. The stronger the rock, the less gun-cotton, comparatively with gunpowder, is necessary for the effect ; so much so that while gun-cotton is stronger than powder as three to one in artillery, it is stronger in the proportion of 6.274 to 1 in a strong and solid rock, weight for weight. It is the hollow-rope form which is used for blasting. Its power of splitting up the material is regulated exactly as wished. As regards military and submarine explosion, it is a well known fact, that a bag of gunpowder nailed on the gates of a city will blow them open. In this case gun-cotton would fail. A bag of gun-cotton exploded in the same way is powerless. If one ounce of gunpowder is exploded in scales, the balance is thrown down ; with an equal force of gun-cotton, nothing happens. To blow up the gates of a city, a very few pounds of gun-cotton, carried in the hand of a single man, will be sufficient, only he must know its nature. In a bag it is harmless; exploded in a box it will shatter the gates to atoms. Against the palisades of a fortification: a small square box containing twenty-five pounds, merely flung down close to it, will open a passage for troops; in actual experience on palisades a foot diameter and eight feet high, piled in the ground, backed by a second row of eight inches diameter, a box of twenty-five pounds cut a clean opening nine feet wide. To this three times the weight of gunpowder produced no effect whatever, except to blacken the piles. Against bridges: a strong bridge of oak, twenty-four feet span, was shattered to atoms by a small box of twenty-five pounds laid on its centre; the bridge was not broken, it was shivered. As to its effects under water: in the case of two tiers of piles, in water thirteen feet deep, ten inches apart, with stones between them, a barrel of one hundred pounds gun-cotton, placed three feet from the face and eight feet under water, made a clean sweep through a radius of fifteen feet, and raised the water two hundred feet. In Venice, a barrel of four hundred pounds placed near a sloop in ten feet water, at eighteen feet distance, threw it in atoms to a height of four hundred feet. All experiments made by the Austrian Artillery Committee were conducted on a grand scale, — thirty-six batteries, six and twelve pounders (gun-cotton) having been constructed, and practised with that material. The reports of the Austrian Commissioners are all based on trials with ordnance, from six-pounders to forty-eight-pounders, smooth bore and rifled cannon. The trials with small fire-arms have been comparatively few, and are not reported on. The trials for blasting and mining purposes were also made on a large scale by the Imperial Engineers' Committee.

Sir William Armstrong said it was impossible to listen to the report which had been read without being very much impressed with the great promise there was of gun-cotton's becoming a substitute for gunpowder; but at the same time there were certain peculiar anomalies about it which he certainly should like to have cleared up, and until they were, they could not feel that perfect confidence in the results that they wished to do. In the first place, with regard to the heat evolved, they were told that, with such a quantity of gun-cotton as would produce a given quantity of gas, a certain initial velocity was imparted to the projectile, and that the heating effect upon the gun was much less than when a similar velocity was produced by an equivalent quantity of gunpowder. The absence of heat in the gun implied an absence of heat in the gas. Where was the projectile force to come from, if there was no heat in the gas? He could not, for his part, conceive how it was possible of explanation. The next point that occurred to him was with regard to the recoil. It was stated that the recoil was very much less. That was ascribed to the absence of solid inert matter in the charge, which, in gun-cotton, was next to nothing. If the recoil was only two-thirds that of gunpowder, it would require, in order to account for that difference, a much larger quantity of solid matter than there really was in the case of gunpowder. The report stated that the use of gun-cotton enabled them to reduce the length of the gun. It was quite certain, however, that with a short gun they could not get an equal initial velocity as with a long gun. If the initial velocity were increased, there was more danger of bursting the gun than with gunpowder. Because, if they got any velocity, or an equal velocity with the shorter gun, it must be concluded that it was done by virtue of a greater initial pressure and an earlier action upon the shot. That necessarily implied a greater strain upon the gun at the first explosion, and that would necessitate the employment of stronger guns. He should have expected a smaller velocity by a shorter gun, for the action of the gas was necessarily shorter than in a longer gun. The heat question, however, was to him the greatest puzzle of all. How they could have the propelling power without heat in the gas, and if they heated the gas, how they escaped heating the gun, he could not understand. Prof. Pole said he was quite unable to give any explanation of the difference of recoil. If the shot left the gun with the same velocity as when fired with gunpowder, it was natural to suppose that there must be the same quantity of recoil. Mr. Siemans, having briefly spoken on the dynamical question involved in the matter, suggested that the greater heat imparted to the gun in the case of gunpowder might be owing to the greater amount of solid matter, which, taking up the great heat of the gases under a pressure of some four hundred atmospheres, imparted a portion of the same by radiation to the side of the gun, while in the case of gun-cotton gases only were produced, which could only impart heat to the gun by the slower process of conduction, and left a larger margin of heat to be developed in force by expansion. Admiral Sir E. Belcher thought that the reason the gun was not heated by an explosion of gun-cotton might be because the gases had not time to heat the gun, owing to the rapidity of the explosion, which was slower in the case of gunpowder; or that it might arise from the greater amount of fouling in the case of gunpowder. Mr. Scott Russell then said he would endeavor to clear away the many difficulties which attended this very difficult subject. How was it that in gunpowder and in gun-cotton, where there were equal quantities of gas put in, the gas in the case of gunpowder was raised to an enormously high temperature, and came out at an enormously high pressure, showing that they had gas enormously expanded by heat; whereas in the case of gun-cotton the gas came out quite cool, so that you might put your hand upon it, and the gun itself was quite cool? He (Mr. Russell) had a theory. Steam was a gas, and steam expanded just by the same laws as other gases did. A great deal of the gas of gun-cotton happened to be steam. Let them conceive one hundred pounds of gun-cotton shut up in a chamber that just held it. They had got there all the gases that had been spoken of, but they had also got twenty-five pounds of solid water — about one-third of a cubic foot of water — in that chamber. What did they do with it? They put fuel, they put fire to it. They heated the whole remaining pounds of patent fuel. If, then, they considered the gun-cotton gun as the steam-gun, they got rid of two difficulties. They would have, first, the enormous elasticity of steam; and secondly, they would get the coolness of it. They all knew that if they put their hand to expanded high pressure steam, it had swallowed up all the heat and came out quite cool. He believed that the gun-cotton gun was neither more nor less than Perkins's old steam-gun, with only this difference, that you bottled up the fuel and water, and let them fight it out with each other. They did their work, and came out quite cool. He hoped, however, that it was understood that he did not dogmatize. He put all he had said with a note of interrogation upon it. Prof. Tyndall

5*

said he thought that a note of interrogation ought to be put to what Mr. Russell had said.

The subject was considered of so much importance that the Association not only reappointed the joint committee to continue the investigations, but passed a resolution requesting the government to investigate the matter separately.

Submarine Batteries, or Torpedoes. — M. F. Maury, formerly an officer in the United States service, who was present, remarked in the course of the above discussion, that Mr. Russell's report "was important as affording an element of security by giving the preponderance on the side of defence. Ever since steam had been applied to purposes of naval warfare, it had been considered a matter of very great doubt by many professional men how far ordinary steamers and men-of-war, where forts were to be passed at the mouth of a river, were capable of sustaining the fire of such forts and passing up the river. And to show that there was ample time for them to do so, they had only to recollect the fact of steamers having fought forts for several hours. In the Crimea and at Charleston, the steamers had remained under fire for several hours, — a much longer time than was necessary to enable them to pass the forts and go higher up the river into a place of safety, where they could do damage to the enemy. Iron-clads had rendered this much more easy than it had previously been. If, then, their principal defences failed them at the mouth of a river in this way, the question was whether they should not have recourse to mining for the destruction of the invading vessels? *He himself had been engaged upon the subject.* He found this difficulty in employing gunpowder, that in order to be sure of destroying the vessel as she passed in a given line by means of gunpowder, the magazines must be in actual contact, or very nearly in actual contact, with the side of the vessel; otherwise, the probability was that the vessel would not be destroyed. Recently they had the intelligence of a vessel having had a mine exploded under her on the James River. That magazine contained several thousands of pounds of powder. The vessel did not know that the mine was there; but the mine did not destroy the vessel. It merely threw up a column of water, which washed some of the men overboard. His own conclusion was that to make sure of destroying a vessel after she had passed the forts, they must mine the channel in such a manner that the vessel must come in contact with one or other of the mines. It was found that wooden vessels to contain the powder would not do. They would not confine the powder long enough to produce a sufficient force. It was necessary to make them of stout boiler-iron. It would not do to leave the magazines on the top of the water, and it would not do to put them at the bottom, for then there would be a cushion of water between the bottom of the ship to be destroyed and the magazine, which would protect the vessel. In short, they had to anchor them beneath the surface with short buoy-ropes, at a depth proportioned to the kind of vessel expected to come up. But when they made the magazine of boiler-iron, they had to have buoys to float it so large that they were always in danger of being carried away by the vessels crossing the line of magazine. The plan was to place those magazines in a ring in such a position that the vessel in passing would have to come in contact with at least one and probably two of them. It was necessary to place those magazines of powder so that when you saw the vessel in that range you had only to bring the two poles of the galvanic battery together and make the explosion. There was, as already stated, a difficulty in using gunpowder. But since gun-cotton had the remarkable effect of destroying a vessel — he did not know her strength — at a distance of eighteen feet, and that not vertically, but laterally, the question arose whether they might not fortify and protect those channel ways by placing a ring of gun-cotton magazines along the bottom; but, at any rate, if that was not necessary, they could float them at any depth, and out of reach of the vessels generally using the channel. That appeared to him to be one of the most important uses of gun-cotton, and it was one which would give safety to cities which were some distance from the mouths of navigable rivers. Admiral Belcher stated that the explosion of powder under water was once done under one of his own vessels to clear away ice. He placed it upon the ground, thinking that its explosion would blow the ice clear of her bows without touching the vessel. There was, however, sufficient water to form a cushion, and when the explosion took place it only produced a great wave upon which the vessel rose.

EXPERIMENTS AND RESULTS IN RELATION TO GUNS, ARMOR, AND PROJECTILES.

Armor for Ships of War. — Ever since iron-clad ships were invented, there has been a conflict of opinions upon the subject of their armor. The proper thickness, the mode of fastening it, whether single plates or a number of thin ones are the best, with wood backing or without, — these are only a few of the questions bearing upon the subject which have received attention. That some one plan has not been universally adopted is owing to obvious natural causes. Each person or government thinks himself or itself best qualified to judge where his or its immediate interest is at stake.

 In this country, we have more generally adopted the series of thin plates in preference to heavy single ones; although there are some exceptions to this statement. In Europe, the reverse is true. Thus far we have had more practical experience with iron-clad ships than any other people. The last to adopt these engines of war, we have been the first to put them into actual service, and our success has been wholly with the combinations of thin plating. The gunboats on the Western rivers — *Conestoga* and *Lexington* — were plated with solid iron 2½ inches in thickness, yet they were completely riddled in the attack on Fort Henry by the ordinary guns at that point; so also was the *Essex* before her reconstruction. The Ericsson batteries are all armored on the principle of many layers of thin plates, and they have proved themselves impregnable, so far, to every assault. The arguments in favor of thin plates may be summed up in the following list: — It is claimed that they are stronger for a given weight of metal than thicker forged armor, by reason of the " scale " or cuticle being preserved intact, as well as by the intimate relations of the fibers which occur when small quantities of the metal are subjected to intense pressure; for this reason it is apparent that the structure of thin plates must be, *ceteris paribus*, more reliable than forged ones. By the same reasoning, however, some may assert, that if the requisite machinery existed in this country for giving the same proportionate tenacity and tensile strength to heavy single plates, as good results would be produced. This sequence, although a natural one, is not, it seems by experience, a correct one. A combination of thin plates is said to be more effective in resisting the impact of a heavy shot than a single plate of the same thickness, by reason of their elasticity or reaction after the instant of percussion. All experience goes to prove this assertion; where heavy plates have been shattered to fragments, the thin ones have been displaced and bent, but not destroyed, and the injuries to them rarely extend through a whole section of armor. The heavy plates, when smashed, require much time and expense for their renewal, and are at best a poor substitute for thinner coats in many layers.

Recent improvements have rendered the thin plates still more effectual. The gunboat *Essex*, after her misadventure at Fort Henry, on the Cumberland river, was taken to St. Louis and there re-clad on the forward casemate with iron plates only one inch thick; under these were placed India-rubber sheets one inch thick, the whole being inclined at an angle of 45° upon a wooden backing of oak 16 inches through. Thus defended, the ship went into service.

"In the action between this gunboat, commanded (at that time) by Commodore W. D. Porter, and the batteries at Vicksburg, Port Hudson, and other points on the lower Mississippi River, the forward casemates were struck repeatedly by solid shots, varying from 32 to 128 pounds, some of which were fired from rifled guns at short range. None of those shots penetrated the forward casemate, but some of the larger ones indented the armor plates, started the wood-work, and broke in pieces, showing that the force of the shot was entirely spent. The after-casemates, covered with iron of the same thickness, and made by the same manufacturers, but without india-rubber, were penetrated in several places by shots fired from the same batteries and similar guns; in all, over 125 shots struck this vessel at about the same range, proving that this thickness of iron affords no protection when placed immediately upon a solid timber support." — *Scientific American.*

Corrugated Armor Plates. — The following is an abstract of a paper on the above subject, read to the British Association, 1863, by Mr. George Bedford. The principle of protecting ships by thick plates of iron against projectiles of steel or homogeneous iron, hardened and tempered, would appear to be erroneous, for the following reasons, namely, that iron plates must always be softer than the projectile, while the latter has an almost unlimited advantage in the force which can be given to it by strengthening guns so as to bear very large charges, and thus gain increase of velocity with increased weight of shot. Still more is this the case if flat-headed projectiles, hardened and tempered as the Whitworth shell and shot, are to be provided against. The method which I propose is founded upon two principles of strength, — cohesive strength and mechanical strength. The plates being made of steel, hardened and tempered as nearly as possible up to the cohesive strength of the Whitworth shot and shell, are of two kinds, — one thick and corrugated, the other thinner and plain. The steel corrugated plates, which are three inches thick, are placed upon the thinner plates of one inch, also tempered, and bolted through the skin of the ship to the ribs in the iron ship, or to the timbers in a wooden one. If iron plates of the corrugated form were backed with an inch plate of steel, hardened and tempered, they would, I think, prove impenetrable ; and even smooth iron plates of 4 inches thus laid upon steel would be more effective than iron plates even of 7 inches thick, backed by timber. In explaining the mode in which I conceive this kind of compound armor-plating to act, it is necessary to consider to what the great force of flat-headed projectiles is due. It will be admitted that this is not to be attributed to the velocity of the shot, but to its flat form and great cohesive strength ; because spherical and conical projectiles sent with higher velocity do not pierce iron plates. The rationale of the punching action may not yet be quite clearly understood, but this much seems to be established, that a flat-headed shot pierces because its whole force is applied equally in one direction, and free from the lateral resistance which the conical and round shot meet with. I venture also to state that the suddenness of the impact of such a body has much to do with the effect ; it would seem that time is an important element in the consideration, and therefore if this perfect impact can be delayed, and still more, if it can be prevented altogether, the piercing of the plate will not be effected. As an illustration of the difference between force applied with time and force without it, may be pointed out the simple experiment of striking an anvil with a small hammer, and placing the same force in weight gradually, or with time. In the first case, the force is not conducted away into the mass of the anvil, but is spent in repelling the hammer, and possibly in breaking it into fragments. This is also exemplified in the smashing of round shot against an iron target of proper thickness. In the case of the hammer's being pressed upon the anvil, no effect is produced upon either the one or the other. Another familiar illustration is in the effect of soft materials, such as gun wads or tallow candle, being sent at high velocity through wooden planks, and, as frequently occurred, killing persons struck by them. Velocity, then, may be described as force with the least possible element of time ; the best example, perhaps, of which is electric force in the form of lightning. The analogue of this force is seen in the flash of flame which occurs when a shot strikes at high velocity upon an iron plate. Now, the object of the steel plates, being hardened and tempered, is to delay the shot by its cohesive strength, and to prevent, by the corrugated surface, the whole area of the flat-head projectile bearing upon the plate at the same moment of impact. The shot is delayed partly by this means, and partly by meeting with a metal as hard and tough as itself, and thus time is allowed for the conduction of the force away into the surrounding metal without fracture and penetration ; the objects which I consider most important being, first, to prevent penetration of the outer plate, and to oppose a shot which did pierce it, when it has expended its force, by covering the skin of the ship with a thin steel plate, in preference to increasing the thickness of the outer plating. The mechanical strength of this arrangement of plates consists in the double arch form combined with a certain amount of " play " and elasticity, obtained by fixing the corrugated plate upon a flat one. The flat action of the projectile is also prevented by, as it were, converting it into a round head or a hollow head before it reaches the inner plate. The space between the corrugations being about four and a half inches, a flat-head shot of five inches diameter would begin to bear upon less than one square inch of plate if it struck across a furrow, while if it struck upon a corrugation, the surface pressed upon, even with a seven-inch shot, would be seven square inches instead of thirty-nine, which is the area of impact of a shot of this diameter upon a flat surface. In a large proportion of hits the shot would have to cut through in an oblique direction about six inches of metal before reaching the plain plate. The advantages of the plan proposed are, besides the protection of the ships, the reduction of the weight of armor much below that contemplated for the new ships of war. The saving of at least one inch in thickness of plates would give a reduction of 100 tuns; and if it should be found that timber backing can with this armor be dispensed with, — a point now so much the subject of inquiry, — the reduction of weight would be about 250 tuns in a ship of the *Warrior* class. The extra cost would be to a great extent met by the saving in the thickness of plates and the timber backing.

Interesting English Experiments with Iron-targets, Whitworth and Armstrong guns. — Some interesting experiments with guns and armor-plates, made under the direction of the British ordnance board, have been reported during the past year. The following account of trials on the 3d and 17th of March, at Shoeburyness, will be found especially worthy of notice. Upon the first named date, four guns were tried, viz: — One of Whitworth's, of 7½-inch bore, with hexagonal rifled grooves; one Armstrong 9-inch smooth-bore, and one 10¼-inch bore, rifled; also one of Thomas's rib-rifled 7-inch bore. The target consisted of several iron plates, 5, 6, 7 and 8 inches in thickness, 20 inches in width, and 8 feet in length. It was 11 feet in width and 8 feet high, with an embrasure of 3½ by 2½ feet. The plates were fastened to huge bars of iron, placed vertically and crosswise, secured with 3-inch through bolts, screwed up behind. This target represented the strongest experimental gun-shield which has yet been constructed. The first experiment was made with Whitworth's 7-inch muzzle-loading rifled gun, weighing 7½ tuns, and nominally throwing a 120-pounder shot, though in reality made for projectiles of the weight of 150 lbs. and upward. This was loaded with 25 lbs. of powder and a flat-headed hardened projectile, weighing 137 lbs. It struck on the left side of the target with terrific force, emitting, at the moment of contact, a sheet of flame as broad and vivid as if another cannon had been fired from the mark in reply. The massive bar frame of 12 inches solid iron behind the plates was dislodged, and an 8-inch plate was cracked. The impact velocity of the shot was 1,240 feet per second. The next shot was from the Armstrong 9-inch smooth-bore, with a 100-pound round shot of wrought-iron, and a charge of powder of 25 lbs. The missile struck full upon the thick side of the target with a velocity of 1,470 feet per second, inflicting a tremendous circular dent 2¼ inches deep, cracking one of the inner plates of the target, and knocking off one of the massive bolt-heads. The target was roughly shaken, but not pierced.

A new bolt was screwed into it and the third shot was fired from the 10¼-inch Armstrong shunt-rifled gun. This piece of ordnance weighs 11¾ tuns. It is rifled with 10 deep grooves on the shunt principle — the shot enters freely by the muzzle down one series of grooves, but it is regularly shunted into another series, along which it comes out when the gun is fired, and the grooves for exit being shallower than those for entrance, they, as it were, squeeze the shot with sufficient force to make it take the form of rifling, and give it the rotation on its axis. It was loaded with a hollow-headed conical-shaped shot, 19¼ inches in length, weighing 230 lbs., with a 45-lb. charge of powder behind it. It sent the shot with a velocity of 1,405 feet per second full on the thick part of the target, inflicting a broad damaging indent, shaking the whole structure a good deal, and cracking an outer upper plate; but still there was no through penetration.

The next shot was by Thomas's 7-inch muzzle-loader. This gun was 11 feet 6 inches long, rifled on a new plan, somewhat in appearance like the *canon rayé* of the French, but with this difference, that instead of three grooves it has three ridges projecting nearly an inch into the bore; the elongated projectiles, 2¼ diameters long, fitting into and between the ridges. The shot fired was a wrought-iron one of 151 lbs. weight, with a charge of 25 lbs. of powder. It was the first time the gun had ever been fired, and it hit the white spot aimed at so truly as quite to obliterate the mark, doubling up the shot itself into the form of a huge cauliflower, and making an indent almost as severe as that of the 100-pounder smooth-bore. Its velocity was 1,215 feet per second when it struck. The target appeared much shaken, but was still unpenetrated.

Mr. Whitworth's gun was then again fired, at the same range and with the same charge of powder and shot. The shot was aimed at the untouched plates, below the embrasure, and so close to the ground that the projectile struck the earth first, making a deep furrow; and, of course, considerably diminishing the force of its blow. For this reason it made but a very slight impression, and did no injury to the target that was worth speaking of.

The 10-inch Armstrong gun was again fired, with a charge of 45 lbs. of powder, and a wrought-iron shot of 230 lbs. This tremendous missile injured the target considerably, and sent fragments of it flying through the air in all directions, with a hoarse roar that was terrible to hear. The force of this blow broke some of the plates in fresh places, knocked the head off one of the bolts, and drove out another like a rocket.

Thomas's gun was again fired, with 27½ lbs. of powder, and a steel bolt weighing 133 lbs. Its maker stated he was afraid of his gun, as it was too deeply bored; and it was, therefore, fired with electricity, from a battery some distance off. When the charge was ignited, the gun burst into fragments! The explosion was so complete that the masses were scattered in every direction, one piece weighing nearly a ton being thrown to a distance of 140 yards. The experiments were then terminated for the day. This gun had a steel interior tube, and an iron breech banded with a shrunk hoop 13 inches in width and 3 inches thick. The total diameter where it burst at the breech was 29 inches. It was claimed that the victory remained with the target.

On the 17th of March following, the experimentation commenced on the third was continued. The target used on this occasion was 12 feet square, formed of three great plates of the best rolled iron; the upper one being 5¼ inches thick, the middle one 7¼ inches, and the lower one 6¼ inches. One-half of the target was backed with teak-wood planking 10 inches in thickness, and the wood was backed with inside plates of iron 2¼ inches in thickness. The other half of the target had the outside plates bolted to strong vertical iron ribs, but had no teak backing or inner skin plates. Six feet square of the target, therefore, were formed of 10, 9, and 8 inches in thickness of iron and 10 inches of teak. The quality of the plates was superior to any ever tested in a target. The firing was at a distance of 200 yards; and the guns tried consisted of the old smooth 68-pounder, Armstrong's 110-pounder service gun (with special steel shot cut down at the base to reduce them to 65 lbs. weight), Armstrong's 300-pounder muzzle-loading rifled shunt gun, Whitworth's muzzle-loading 150-pounder or 7-inch gun, and Thomas's 9-inch or 300-pounder rifled muzzle-loading gun. Both these latter were made by Colonel Anderson, at Woolwich, on the built-up coil principle adopted by Armstrong; both were admirable specimens of workmanship, though, before the experiments commenced, Whitworth's gun was found to have a crack or flaw in the centre steel tube round which the coils of wrought-iron are wound and welded in the course of manufacture. This defect prevented its being used in the course of the experiments except for one discharge with a line-shell. Thomas's gun was an enormous piece of ordnance, nearly 18 feet long, weighing 16 tons, and with a thickness of 17 inches of metal around the powder chamber at the breech. Though nominally a 300-pounder, this gun is claimed to be capable of throwing projectiles of various forms and weight, from 250 lbs. up to 410 lbs. Armstrong's 300-pounder weighs less than 12 tons.

. The first shots, three in number, were fired from the old smooth-bore 68-pounder, with the usual service charge of 16 lbs. of powder; these were directed against the 5½, 6½ and 7½-inch plates, and were immediately followed by three shots from Armstrong's 110-pounder, loaded with special steel projectiles weighing 65 lbs., and fired with the same service charge as the smooth-bore 68-pounder. Where the 68-pounder had struck, the indentation varied from 2¼ inches to 3 inches in depth; where the steel shot of Armstrong's had hit, the mark was in one case deeper, and the plate showed a perceptible crack about 8 inches long, though apparently of very trifling depth. But the most careful examination failed to discover any mark on the back of the target to show that it had been hit at all.

The next shot was fired from Armstrong's 300-pounder, loaded with a conical steel shot of 296 lbs. weight, and fired with 45 lbs. of powder. This tremendous missile struck, with a velocity of 1,298 feet per second, full upon the centre of the 7½-inch plate, where it was backed, driving in a circular piece of iron 10 inches in diameter quite through the plate, bending in the whole plate itself to the depth of an inch and a half, and buckling its ends outwards more than an inch. The massive wrought iron girder which crossed the whole back of the target horizontally was bent out and broken in several places, as were also the inner ribs; the 2½-inch skin was bulged and cracked, the rivet heads loosened, and many knocked off altogether. The examination showed that the target had received a most serious shake, though, from the wonderfully good quality of the iron, there was little of actual fracture, except in the spot on which the shot itself had struck. Had the object struck been a ship's side, the damage would have caused a most serious leakage. It is hardly possible, however, to institute comparisons between any armor-clads yet known and this target, as no sea-going vessel could possibly carry the masses of iron that were here fired at, although a floating battery might. This last steel shot rebounded from the target, and, when examined, showed little signs of damage. All competing artillerists at Shoeburyness seem to agree that the range for testing the powers of rifled guns should not be less than 1,000 yards, at which distance the force of smooth-bore projectiles would be reduced one-half, while the rifled shot would be flying at nearly their greatest impetus.

The next shot was from Sir William's 300-pounder, loaded with a cast-iron shell weighing 286 lbs., and charged with 11 lbs. of powder. This was fired with the usual 45 lbs. charge, and struck full in the centre of the 5½-inch backed plate with a velocity of 1,330 feet per second. It shattered its way completely through it, leaving a rough hole about 10 inches in diameter, and then burst in the inside, blowing the teak to minute fragments, setting it on fire, breaking off many of the rivet heads, and tearing the inner skins of iron, 2½ inches thick, into rough shredded gaps, as if they had been so much cardboard. When water had been procured and the fire in the wood extinguished, it was seen at a glance that the question of the resistance which the strongest British iron frigates would be able to offer to such ordnance was settled in the most unpleasant manner. By the side of the target was a powerful partition of wooden beams, and an examination of this, after the shell had exploded, gave terrible proofs of its destructive powers. There was scarcely a square inch of its whole surface that was not deeply penetrated with fragments of the shell of all shapes and sizes, from one pound weight to ragged particles as minute as small shot.

Mr. Whitworth's 150-pounder was next tried, loaded with a steel flat-headed shell of 156 lbs. weight, with a bursting charge of 6 lbs. of powder, and fired from the gun with 25 lbs. of powder. This shell struck within about five inches of the spot where Sir William's had struck, burst and destroyed the teak backing. The Whitworth shell passed quite through the plate and burst among the *debris* of splinters behind. The hole in the plate was of the small, clean-cut, punched kind. It was claimed that the result was equal to what had been accomplished by Armstrong's gun, with a 286 lb. shell and 45 lbs. of powder. Owing to the flaw in its breech no further trials were made with this gun.

Thomas's gun was the next competitor. Unfortunately the gun was not well pointed, and its first 330 lb. shot missed the target altogether. The next shot, weighing 307 lbs., and fired with a 50 lb. charge of powder, struck the hollow part of the target, where it was 7½ inches thick, and bent the plate. The third shot was more successful. It was a steel projectile of 330 lbs. weight, fired with the same charge. It struck on the edge of the 7½-inch plate, and made a broken indentation to the depth of 10½ inches, sufficient to establish the most alarming leak in the side of any vessel. The terminal velocities of both these last shots were lower than any fired, which was attributed to what is believed to be the excessive pitch in the mode of ribbed rifling adopted by Mr. Thomas.

Sir William Armstrong then fired his 300-pounder with an ordinary cast-iron round shot, weighing 144 lbs., with a charge of 45 lbs. of powder. The terminal velocity with which this struck the 7½-inch plate on the unbacked portion was the highest attained — no less than 1,636 feet a second — and almost in exact proportion to its velocity was the damage it inflicted. Not only was it indented larger and deeper than any shot that had gone before, but on the inner side it broke the plate both vertically and horizontally, leaving a cruciform tear nearly two inches wide at the openings, besides shaking the target to its very foundations.

The massive target was now so much damaged, both in plates and fastenings, that further experiments became almost useless. The iron, even where most torn, held together in a manner that was really wonderful; but Mr. Thomas had knocked off several of the massive screw bolt heads, and the effect of the entire day's work had been so to bend the plates and destroy the backing that there was really no part left that afforded the means of a fair test of resistance.

The practical results elicited by the day's experiments seem to be these — first, that iron plates of 7½ inches, or greater thickness, can be produced with as much perfection, as to quality and strength, as those of 4 inches; secondly, that there are guns the fire of which the strongest armor-clads could not face and float for ten minutes.

Perhaps the most remarkable fact connected with these experiments was the smashing of the target with a cast-iron shell. From previous experiments it had been concluded that all cast-iron shot would break in pieces in striking thick wrought-iron plates.

The Armstrong Gun. — Confidence in the Armstrong gun in Great Britain has been greatly diminished during the past year, both from the public discussion of its merits in the public prints, and through the publication of the report of a government committee appointed to inquire into the whole subject.

According to the *Western Morning Mail*, Mr. Armstrong has, since the commencement of his appointment of government gun-founder, "constructed not less than ten different kinds of guns; that of each kind he made and put into the government's hands a considerable number, and was paid for them, and that not one of all these cannon has proved serviceable without great and expensive alterations. He made 110-pounders, 120-pounders, both muzzle and breech loading; 150-pounders, 300-pounders, 200-pounders, 12-pounders, 40-pounders, 100-pounders; and the only guns of all these which are even claimed to be successful are the 12-pounders. But of these we read that they have been returned and are now having twelve inches cut off the muzzle to make them safe. They will, consequently, when 'fixed,' be only 9-pounders, with a diminished range."

There are a number of Armstrong guns now in use in the British navy, 110-pounders for the most part, but the committee report that "although useful as chase guns, they ought not to be introduced as broadside guns." The report adds that they are "not sufficiently powerful to penetrate iron-plated ships, and are imperfect for general naval service, owing to the difficulty of managing and manufacturing the vent pieces." The Duke of Somerset testified that "the Admiralty had a report that the Armstrong gun had the greatest range and the greatest power of penetration of any gun tried ; but that when they came to try it themselves, they found that the report was not confirmed by the facts. For naval purposes at two hundred yards it certainly had not the greatest power ; our old 68-pounder is a more powerful gun than the Armstrong 100-pounder."

Captain Wainwright of the iron-clad frigate *Black Prince*, in examination before the committee, stated that in a sea-way, the practice with the Armstrong guns was very unsatisfactory, particularly in ricochet practice, the smooth-bores beating them in accuracy. An attempt at explanation was made, on the ground that the shot was delayed in the Armstrong gun after the trigger was pulled, longer than in the old smooth-bore guns, consequently the aim, in a rolling sea-way, must be less accurate. Captain Wainwright stated that the *Black Prince*, which he commanded, being armor-clad, had very small ports, and that the smothering sensation from the black smoke produced by these guns was hardly endurable ; this he imagined to be from something in the wad ; he had no other conjecture to hazard.

19-inch Rifled Steel Guns. — Krupp, the celebrated cast-steel manufacturer of Germany has recently furnished to the Russian Government a number of 19-inch rifled cast-steel guns, designed to throw a 300-pound shell, or a 450-pound solid shot. The *London Times* gives an account of some experimental firing with one of their guns, at St. Petersburg, with a view of testing certain shell, and the quality of a large lot of 4½-inch armor-plates, manufactured for the Russian government at Sheffield, England. It says : — " First, a series of cast-iron shells, 300 pounds each, were fired at different ranges, and then shells made by Krupp were fired at the 4½-inch armor-plates. The first shell, of hard cast-steel, was 22½-inches long (two and a half diameters), with a flat end 4 inches in diameter. Fired with 50 pounds of powder at 700 feet distance, it passed through the plate, oak and teak backing, and broke into many pieces, although filled with sand only. The second and third shells were also of Krupp's steel, the same length, but with 6½-inch ends. These shells pierced plates, wood, etc., and also went to pieces, although only filled with sand. The fourth shell was made of puddled steel the same dimensions as the second and third, went through iron, teak, etc., but was only bulged up from 9 inches to 12 inches, and the end flattened ; not a single crack being visible in the shell. The fifth shell, the same as the fourth, passed through iron, teak, and a second target, and went at least a mile beyond. The sixth and seventh were from Krupp, and were charged with powder ; they were quite flattened, 9 inches in diameter. One exploded in the plate, the other in the wood. The eighth and ninth shells were of cast-iron, and, although they passed through the plates, were of course destroyed. The results on the plates were highly satisfactory. In a space of 4 feet 6 inches by 3 feet 6 inches, eight holes were made without any crack of the slightest description."

Resisting qualities of Hogs-hair Targets. — The U. S. Bureau of Ordnance, Navy Department, have recently published the results of some made of 5 bales of hogs-hair, faced and backed with pine plank 4 in ches thick, and fastened with 28 wrought-iron bolts. Two of the bales had been subjected to one and the same amount of compression, and two others were compressed alike but differing in degree from the former, and the remaining bale, as stated by the inventor, was but slightly compressed. The bales were bound with iron hoops. The target was backed with 4 feet of solid clay.

Dimensions of Target. — Eleven feet, three inches long; four feet wide; three feet, three and a half inches thick.

The gun used was a rifled 50-pounder; charge $3\frac{1}{2}$ lbs. cannon powder; weight of projectile 38 lbs. The result of the firing was unsatisfactory; the shot passing entirely through the bales and the clay backing, and embedding themselves in a bank of earth 18 feet in the rear of the target.

Wire-Rope Target. — Experiments have been made at the Washington Navy Yard with a target devised by Mr. Hodge, consisting of three thicknesses of half-inch plate iron, backed by a *tissue of wire-ropes* fourteen inches thick. The target was mounted on timber nine inches thick, consisting, first, of two one-inch boards (one horizontal and one vertical) and then of two layers of timber three and one-half inches thick, disposed of vertically and horizontally. The dimensions, of the target were as follows: Length, sixty-seven and one-half inches; width, fifty and one-half inches; iron thickness, fifteen and one-half inches; timber, nine inches. Two shots were fired at this target from a eleven-inch gun, distance eighty-three feet. The first shot, a wrought iron projectile weighing one hundred and fifty-six pounds, with a charge of twenty-five pounds of powder, hit direct and passed clear through the target. Shot No. two, cast-iron, weight one hundred sixty-five pounds, charge of powder fifteen pounds, hit direct, and, passing clean through the target, buried itself in an earth-bank to a depth of nine feet six inches.

On the Results of Experiments in Gunnery with Iron Targets. — In a discussion on this subject, before the British Association, 1863, Mr. Galvin stated that the earlier experiments showed that four and one-half inch plates at least were necessary to resist shot. This thickness of iron still left the plate liable to be hurt or fractured, and knocked off even when not directly penetrated, and the extent to which it would thus suffer would in some degree be regulated by the backing. The plan adopted in the Warrior was simply that suggested by the idea of bolting a plate of iron to the sides of a wooden ship. The iron skin of the Warrior is covered with two layers of teak planking, each nine inches in thickness, the one horizontal, the other vertical, and outside of those is the armor-plate, four and one-half inches thick, secured by bolts, screwed up with nuts inside of the ship. The wood backing was to prevent the injuries sustained by the plate from being communicated immediately to the ship, but it afforded no effectual support to the plate itself. The results of experiments with iron targets having a rigid backing, composed wholly of iron, had demonstrated that this plan was not desirable. The arrangement required for the armor-plating of a ship was a strong front plate, in which deflection under blows should be prevented, but which should have some cushion behind to prevent the full concussion of the blow being communicated to the side of the ship. Mr. J. Nasmyth expressed his opinion that for armor-plates to answer the end for which they were designed, they must be backed by some elastic substance, and, in his opinion, that best adapted to give the requisite elasticity was compressed wool. As Mr. Maury was present, he should like to have his opinion on the subject of cotton, and whether it had been found to answer so far as his experience went.

Mr. M. F. Maury, late an officer in the U. S. Navy, said he had not had an opportunity of gaining a great deal of experience on this subject, nor had he had an opportunity of witnessing the experiments that had been made upon cotton. There had been experiments to test the capability of cotton to resist cannon-balls, but the results had by no means been satisfactory. He thought that cotton had got a false reputation. In the early days of the American difficulty, they thought that cotton could resist balls successfully; but when it came to the test, they found the bales did not answer the purpose. Mr. J. Scott Russell said the whole course of experience had been to show that they must arrest and shatter the shot at the earliest possible moment, and in the shortest space of time when it struck the armor.

New Vent-holes for Artillery. — A series of experiments have been made during the past year at Shoeburyness, Eng., by the British Ordnance Committee, to ascertain how far a method now rather in favor among French artillerists, by which a series of holes, about an inch in diameter, are bored through the substance of the cannon near its muzzle, in order, by permitting a quick escape of gas, to diminish its recoil, affects the service of the piece as to range and accuracy. The experiments were made with two brass 9-pounder ordinary smooth-bore fieldpieces, which were loaded with the usual service charges, and spherical shot. Five rounds were fired from each gun in succession, the recoil of both being carefully measured after each discharge. They were then shifted, so that each occupied the platform which had been used by the other, when again more rounds were fired. The general merits of the performances of each gun were exactly what were anticipated before a shot was fired. The recoil of the ordinary gun was, in round numbers, just twice as great as that which had the holes bored round the muzzle, while the range and accuracy of the latter were scarcely more than half as good as those of the common piece. The lateral escape of gas and flame through the side holes of the French gun, if we may so call it, was very great indeed, so much so as to prove at once that even if the gun otherwise possessed the most transient merits, it could never be used either on shipboard, in casemates, or even at embrasures. In the open air the trigger had to be pulled by a lanyard nearly twenty yards long. One half of the force of the explosion evidently escaped through the side holes before the force of the powder was expended on the shot, and virtually, therefore, the barrel of the gun is shortened by as much of its length as is thus perforated. As a general rule, the recoil of the gun is always in exact proportion to the force it exerts in propelling the shot, and anything which takes off from this recoil, by allowing the gas generated by the explosion to escape before it has done its work, just diminishes by so much the range, and therefore the accuracy, of its fire. The results obtained with this curiously-bored gun were enough to satisfy the Ordnance Committee that the device in question was of no value.

India Rubber Breech Piece for Cannon. — Numerous patents have recently been taken, both in this country and Europe, for devices to lessen the strain and liability of explosion in ordnance by the use of vulcanized India-rubber or gutta-percha applied in the breech to confine the air, against which the exploded powder will act, whereby the sides of the bore are relieved from the immense strain of the ignited charge. The objects of these inventions are to lessen the danger of explosion and enable the gun to give a greatly-increased velocity to the shot by using a larger charge of powder than is allowed or deemed safe in the old kind of guns. A device recently patented by Horace H. Day, of New York, consists essentially in inserting into the bottom of the bore of the gun an India-rubber breech piece, or cushion, having a conical recess at its base. Upon the top of this the charge and projectile are inserted in the usual manner. It was claimed that the effect of this elastic cushion is to impart a gradual movement at the moment of explosion, which starts the bolt gently from its seat ; the gases then follow it up and expel it with as much force as the powder is capable of exerting. During the past year, a series of experiments to test this invention have been made under the direction of the U. S. Ordnance Bureau ; — the gun employed, in part, being a 130-pounder, filled with a vulcanized rubber breech-piece, 8 inches in length, .2 of an inch smaller in diameter than the bore of the gun, with its rear shaped to fit the bottom of the bore. Its weight was 22 lbs. The projectile was a solid shot, weighing 126 lbs., fired into a bank of earth at 85 feet distance. The following is the official record of three firings : — " 1. Rubber breech-piece was blown out and struck the bank. 2. Rubber breech-piece started forward 50½ inches. While sponging the gun out, several small pieces of rubber were found. On examining the breech, found it badly torn. 3. The rubber breech-piece was blown out, and fell fifty feet to the front of the muzzle of the gun. Finding it so badly damaged, the trial was discontinued." The results with a 32-pounder were nearly as unsatisfactory, no increase in the accuracy of fire being obtained.

Experiments with Rifled Small Arms. — A series of valuable experiments with rifled small arms have lately been conducted by the Ordnance Committee of the British Government. Rifles of different calibers and systems of rifling were tested. As it regards the effect of the number of grooves in the Enfield rifle, it was found that five were better than three — the friction in loading and firing being less and the shooting more accurate with the five grooves. To test the effect of the pitch in rifling, two Enfield rifles were tested, the one having a revolution in sixty-three inches and the other in forty-eight inches, but both of uniform twist. In calm weather the slow pitch of sixty-three inches was equal to the other at ranges up to 1,000 yards, but beyond this it was not so accurate ; and in windy weather the more rapid twist was uniformly more effective at all ranges, but the barrel fouled more rapidly with the residue of the powder. The caliber of these rifles is 0.577 of an inch, and they were tried against a Lancaster rifle of 0.55 inch caliber, elliptical bore, the twist commencing with one revolution in 36 inches at the breech, increasing to one turn in 33 inches at the muzzle. At all ranges beyond 500 yards the Lancaster rifle surpassed the Enfield in accuracy, and it was not so liable to foul.

The same kind of cartridges was used for both rifles. As it respects the quality of these rifles for army purposes, the report of the Ordnance Committee is strongly in favor of the Lancaster rifle; the report says:—" Having carefully considered the advantages of the Enfield and Lancaster systems, as applied to rifles of large calibers and adapted to the same ammunition, the committee came to the conclusion that the Lancaster system has the advantage as regards precision and non-tendency to accumulate fouling, also in simplicity of management (a smooth-bore being more easily cleaned than a grooved one), initial velocity, and flat trajectory. As it relates to rapidity of fire and cost of manufacture, the two rifles are about equal."

Experiments were also made with smaller bore rifles, the caliber of which was .45 of an inch; the barrels heavier, but stocks lighter than the Enfield service rifles. Four rifles of this caliber were tested, viz., Whitworth's, with a hexagonal bore and rapid regular twist; Lancaster's, with a smooth elliptical bore and an increasing twist; Westley Richard's breech-loader, with a Whitworth barrel; and an Enfield rifle of five grooves and regular twist of one turn in forty-three inches. No less than 1,000 rounds were fired from each rifle without cleaning. After the seventh round it became difficult to load the Enfield, and before the conclusion the bullet had to be driven down with a mallet. The Lancaster did not foul so much, still the mallet had to be used occasionally, but from first to last the Whitworth was loaded with perfect freedom. As it regards precision, the smaller bore rifles surpassed the larger bores which were first tried, at all ranges exceeding six hundred yards. The convenience in charging the breech-loader was considerable, and this advantage was fully appreciated.

As the result of these experiments, the Ordnance Committee's report states that the introduction into the army of a weapon of greater precision at long ranges would materially increase the efficiency of infantry, and this advantage would be secured in substituting a smaller bore of rifle for the Enfield service rifle of large bore now in use. But as the smaller bore rifles wear out faster than those of larger caliber, their partial introduction into the army only is recommended for the present. The Whitworth rifle is admitted to have surpassed all the others for accuracy at long ranges; but as it requires very peculiar long cartridges, it was thought these would be inconvenient for army purposes. The breech-loaders of Westley Richards were recommended for the cavalry—the only apparent obstacle to their introduction for infantry is their great cost—the price being about fifty dollars each. The Lancaster system of rifling the barrels is recommended strongly by the Ordnance Committee to supersede the present method of rifling the Enfields, which latter has been copied from the American (Springfield) rifles. — *Scientific American.*

Extraordinary Range of Artillery. — During the siege of Charleston, S. C., carried on during the past year by the United States forces under Gen. Q. A. Gilmore, some results have been attained to in artillery practice which are without parallel in the history of warfare. Fort Sumter, a modern-built, casemated fort, of the best brick masonry, with walls from six to nine feet in thickness, has been battered into an irregular heap of ruins and completely destroyed by artillery placed without elevation on Morris Island, at a distance of 3,500 yards. From batteries situated upon the same island projectiles weighing from two hundred to three hundred pounds have been also sent into the city of Charleston itself, a distance of *ten thousand five hundred and sixty yards* (or six miles) and the place successfully bombarded.   In 1861, pending the preliminary operations of the Confederate army before Fort Sumter, the question was asked by letter of one of the best authorities in gunnery in this country, whether it would be possible for the Federal commander of the fort to bombard the city of Charleston in the event of an attack being made upon him.   (The armament of Fort Sumter at that time consisted of the ordinary smooth-bored thirty-two and twenty-four pounder siege guns, a few eight and ten inch columbiads, and mortars.)   The following was the reply to the interrogatory : —

WASHINGTON, Jan. 28, 1861.

Yours of the 25th instant has been received.   I am unable to enter into the reasons on which the opinion is based, but believe that a bombardment of Charleston from Fort Sumter by any ordnance now there is out of the question.

Thus it will be seen, that since the commencement of the American civil war in 1861, a most remarkable progress has been made in the character of the ordnance used in military operations, and results have been attained to, which the most sanguine of experts would have hesitated to predict.

English and American Views Respecting Heavy Artillery. — The London *Saturday Review* says, — " On the question of the best mode of constructing heavy artillery, it is possible that we may also have something to learn from the Americans. All the experiments tried in this country have pointed at one broad conclusion : that the penetrating power of a shot depends mainly on the charge of powder, and that it makes comparatively little difference whether the powder is utilized by impressing a very high velocity on a moderate-sized bolt, or a lower speed upon such masses of metal as are hurled from the Dahlgren guns.   The shot, after all, is only a means of carrying the force of the powder from the cannon's mouth to the target ; and it is not surprising that the resulting effect should depend more on the amount of the original impulse than on the means employed for its transmission.   Still, there must be certain proportions between the charge and the shot which will produce the greatest effect ; and upon this point English and American views have long been divergent.   Our artillerists have thought more of increasing velocity, while the Americans have attached the greatest importance to the bulk of the cannon-ball.   It may deserve consideration whether (especially for long-range firing) the Americans have not come nearer than ourselves to the best model."

The London *Army and Navy Gazette* also in commenting on the reduction of Fort Sumter by the batteries established by Gen. Gilmore on Morris Island, at a distance of 3,500 yards, says, —

" It may be concluded as certain that the guns used by Gilmore were Parrott's rifled ordnance.   Their work has been effectually done.   Had such guns been available in the trenches before Sebastopol, the allies would have made short work, not only of the Redan and Malakoff, and *bastion du mat*, but of the shipping and of the forts at the other side of the harbor.   It must not be supposed that Sumter was a flimsy, gingerbread fort. It was constructed of a peculiar kind of hard, close brick, six and seven feet thick; the arches of the casemates and the supporting pillars were of eight and nine feet in thickness. The faces presented to the breaching batteries must have subtended at 3,500 yards, an exceedingly small angle, and the elevation of the fort was low. But so great was the accuracy of the fire that a vast proportion of the shots struck it; so great the penetration that the brickwork was perforated 'like a rotten cheese;' so low the trajectory that the shot, instead of plunging into, passed through the fort, and made clean breaches through both walls. Now, the guns that did this work cost, we believe, just one-fourth of our ordnance, cwt. for cwt.; they are light and very easily handled. The gun itself is finely rifled, with grooves varying from four and five in number for small calibers, to six and seven for the larger; but, as Mr. Parrott is still 'experimenting,' no settled plan has been arrived at, and all we know is that the pitch is not so sharp as is the case in our rifled guns. The projectile is like the conical Armstrong, and has a leaden sabot and coating,—at least it is coated and based with some soft metal. The Americans have constructed cannon of calibers which to us are known only as of theoretical and probable attainment, and they have armed batteries hundreds of miles from their arsenals, with the most powerful guns ever used in war, which have been carried by sea and in stormy waters to the enemy's shores. Before such projectiles as these guns carry, the breaching of masonry, whether of brick or stone, is a question of short time. And, in face of these facts, we are obliged to record that our scientific officers are of opinion that our 'best gun for breaching purposes is the old sixty-eight pounder!' Why, we know what that can do! We know that at 3,500 yards its fire would be about as effectual as that of Mons Meg. These trials at two hundred yards are perfectly fatuous, if no other results than these, or such as these, be gained by them. It is of no use saying Sumter was of brick; it was at least as good a work as most of our existing fortifications, and infinitely less easy 'to splinter up' than a work of granite or rubble masonry. In substance it resembled very much our martello towers on the beach at Hythe. Have we any gun which could breach one of these at 3,500 yards? . . . . The authorities have had no experience of the effect of such shot as the Dahlgrens and Parrotts propel. They have not got the guns to discharge them. When next the ordnance officers and gentlemen meet, let them apply their minds to the little experiments the Americans have been making for their benefit at Sumter. It is astounding to see what progress has been made in artillery since the Crimean war."

The Material of a Great War. — From the report of the U. S. Secretary of War, December 1863, we obtain the following statement of the amount of war material issued to the armies of the United States from the commencement of hostilities in April 1861, to June 30th, 1863, a period of 26¼ months:— of siege and sea-coast artillery, 2,088 pieces; of field artillery, 2,481 pieces; firearms for infantry, 1,550,-576; do. for cavalry, 327,170; sabres, 271,817; cannon-balls and shells, 1,745,586; lead and lead bullets in pounds, 50,045,515; cartridges for artillery, 2,274,490; cartridges for small-arms, 378,584,104; percussion caps, 715,036,470; gunpowder in pounds, 13,071,073; accoutrements for infantry, 1,680,220 sets; do. for cavalry, 196,298;

equipments for cavalry horses, 211,670 sets; artillery harnesses, (double) 17,485. And yet, notwithstanding this immense consumption, to which should also be added an immense stock on hand awaiting requisition and use, the Secretary states, " That the resources of the country for the production of arms and munitions of war have only commenced their development. At the beginning of the war," he continues, " we were compelled to rely upon foreign countries for the supply of nearly all our arms and munitions. Now, all these things are manufactured at home, and we are independent of foreign countries, not only for the manufacture, but also for the materials of which they are composed. The excellency of the arms and munitions of war of American manufacture, which have been supplied by the Ordnance Department to the army, has been so obvious that our soldiers are no longer willing to use those which have been imported from other countries. The efforts made during the war to extend and improve the manufacture of arms and munitions have resulted in discoveries of great importance to the country, in peace as well as war. Among the arts thus improved is the manufacture of wrought-iron, now rivalling the qualities of iron of Sweden, Norway, and England. This country, until the present year, has relied upon those countries for material to make gun-barrels, bridle-bits, car-wheel tires and other articles requiring iron of fine quality. Iron of our own production is now superior to that obtained abroad."

One interesting feature of the military operations of the present civil war, is the extent to which telegraphic communication has been resorted to as a means of facilitating and directing operations. It appears that since the commencement of the war there has been constructed, and is now in operation, 5,326 miles of land and submarine military telegraph; a length sufficient to girdle more than one-fifth of the circumference of the globe. Over these lines there were sent during the year, ending June 30th, 1863, at least 1,200,000 telegrams, varying in length from ten to one thousand words.

IRON-CLAD SHIPS AND BATTERIES.

Number and Strength of the American Iron-Clad Fleet. — From the report of the Secretary of the Navy, communicated to Congress, December 1863, it would appear that the U. S. Government is now in possession of a larger number of iron-clad steamers than any other naval power. The whole number afloat, or approaching completion, is seventy-five; of which forty-six, carrying 150 guns, and having an aggregate tonnage of 62,513, are intended for coast service; and twenty-nine, carrying 152 guns and a tonnage of 20,784, are for inland service. Of the iron-clads launched during the past year, or now in the process of construction, the following are especially worthy of notice: —

The Onondaga is an iron-turreted steamer, though not of the Ericsson (monitor) model, but was built after a design furnished by her constructor, Mr. George Quintard, of New York. She is constructed wholly of iron. The hull is 226 feet in length and forty-eight feet in width. The frames are of angle-iron five inches by three, riveted to a central plate at the bottom. There is no keel, properly speaking, but a ribbed or arched plating in the place of it, to which all the frames are joined. There are no projecting armor shelves on the sides, but the vessel is protected from shot by single plates four and a half inches in thickness with the additional protection of a layer of nine-inch locust and three-inch oak timber, covered again with two-inch solid plates of iron, thus making the mail in reality 18½ inches thick, 6½ of which are iron. The draught of the ship will be ten feet.

There are two propellers or screws, one on each side under the stern, each propeller being driven by two engines. The turrets are the same as those upon all the monitors; eleven inches thick in the walls, nine feet high and twenty-one feet in diameter inside. There are two fifteen-inch guns in each turret. Neither the bow nor stern of the Onondaga overhangs the hull, the stern projecting only enough to cover the screws and protect them from damage by shot. There are thirteen transverse water-tight compartments, and the coal bunkers surround the boilers in addition to the protection afforded by the iron plating.

The Dictator. — This name has been given to an iron-clad war-ship constructed during the past year in New York, from designs by Erics-son, based on the principles of the first monitor, but superior, so far as relates to size, speed, sea-worthiness, and impenetrability, to any armor-clad vessel hitherto constructed in the United States. The following statement of the points and dimensions involved in her construction we copy from the *Scientific American:* "The extreme length of the vessel over all, is 314 feet; its aft overhang being thirty-one feet, and forward overhang thirteen, leaving 260 feet between perpendiculars; extreme breadth fifty, and depth 22½ feet. The hull, in sides and frame, is constructed of iron. The armor shelf extends outside of the hull four feet on each side, and is prodigiously strong. Some idea of its impenetrable character will be derived from the following account of its construction. The outside is covered with six one-inch plates of iron fastened in the most substantial manner, and inside of this are three feet of oak timber and an armor lining formed of 4½ inch bars extending all around. The armor shelf therefore consists of 10½ inches in thickness of iron, and three feet of timber, and between the metal and timber is interspersed a thick layer of felting. No gun yet fabri-cated can project a shot that will pierce this armor-jacket.

The keel-plate of the *Dictator* is of one-inch plate, the side plates ⅞th inch, and the frame of double angle-iron, six by four inches. The in-terior is divided into several water-tight compartments by plate bulk-heads, and the space forward of the third bulk-head below will be used for coal bunkers, through the middle of which will be a railway to carry the fuel to the boilers. The deck beams are of kyanized oak. Two engines, each having a cylinder of one hundred inches in diame-ter and four feet stroke, will be employed to drive the screw, which is four-bladed, 21½ feet in diameter, and of thirty-four feet pitch. Six boilers, capable of furnishing 5000 horse-power to the engines, supply the motive force. The boilers have fifty-six furnaces and an aggregate grate surface of 1,000,100 feet; and allowing twelve pounds of coal per square foot of grate surface, the vessel will require, at the least, 175 tons of coal per day of twenty-four hours, steaming at full speed.

As the *Dictator* is furnished with a strong bow, its speed, strength, and mass will render it a most efficient marine ram. It is provided with one revolving turret, capable of carrying two heavy guns, which is believed to be impenetrable against any projectile hitherto experimented with. The following are its dimensions. The diameter of the inside turret is twenty-four feet. The turret itself being formed of six thicknesses of inch-plate riveted together. Over and outside of this is another turret forming a sleeve, consisting of seven thicknesses of inch-plates riveted, while between the two are additional shields of iron hoops or bars, having an aggregate of five inches; so that the whole forms one great revolving iron tower eighteen inches in thickness, twenty-seven feet in diameter, and weighing about two hundred tons. A companion vessel to the *Dictator*, named the *Puritan* is also in the course of construction.

The Dunderberg. — This name has been given to a vessel now in the course of construction, at New York, which combines the features of a ram and an iron-clad monitor. Her length is 378 feet, width sixty-eight feet, and depth of hold thirty-two feet. The model is peculiar; the floor is dead flat, at an angle with the sides, except at the forward end, where it is nearly vertical. The hull is divided into water-tight compartments. The sides below the main deck are $6\frac{1}{2}$ feet thick, and on the casemates there are three feet of solid timber firmly bolted. The iron plating is $4\frac{1}{2}$ inches thick on the sides and $3\frac{1}{2}$ inches on the casemate. This vessel is 7000 tons burthen. Her deck is bomb-proof, and she will be rigged half-mast with yards and sails, which will enable her to cruise without the aid of her engines.

The whole forward part of the vessel, for a distance of fifty feet, is solid wood-work, covered on the sides and edge with the iron armor, constituting the ram, which has the profile of an axe edge. Should this ram be knocked away, which is improbable, the hull will still remain water-tight. The engines are of 6,000 horse-power.

The *Dunderberg* is to be furnished with two revolving turrets, twenty-one feet in diameter inside, and nine feet high, placed fore and aft. The hull is pierced for three broadside guns on each side, as well as one fore and one aft for bow and stern chasers. The draught of water of the *Dunderberg* when loaded will be twenty-one feet.

New Iron-Clads of the Monitor pattern. — The iron-clad turreted vessels, of the so-called Monitor pattern, introduced by Ericsson, having proved eminently efficient and suitable for harbor attack and defence, the U. S. Navy Department has continued their construction, and has already a large fleet of them afloat, or on the stocks. Although in the chief points of their structure there is great similarity between the new vessels and the original Monitor, there is nevertheless a considerable difference in their details, which, as showing a progress in this department of naval architecture, is worthy of notice. The following table shows the peculiarities of the original Monitor; of the Passaic, one of a second series of nine built subsequently; and of the Tecumseh, one of a third series of nine, built during the past year (1863.)

	Original Monitor.	Passaic.	Tecumseh.
Length	190 ft.	200 ft.	235 ft.
Width	30 "	40 "	46 "
Depth of hold	9 "	$9\frac{1}{4}$ "	14 "
Draft of water	9 "	10 "	14 "
Armor of sides	$4\frac{1}{2}$ in.	$4\frac{1}{2}$ in.	9 in.
Thickness of turret	11 "	11 "	11 "

	Original Monitor.	Passaic.	Tecumseh.
Diameter of turret	21 ft.	21 ft.	21 ft.
Number of turrets	1	1	1
Dimensions of cylinders	30 in.	35 in.	40 in.
Armament	2 11-in. guns.	11 and 15-in. guns.	2 13-in. guns.
Tonnage	800	844	1,400

It will be observed that the most important differences between the power of the first Monitor and the Tecumseh consist in the armor and armament — the offensive and defensive attributes. · Instead of four and one-half inches we have nine inches of iron, and instead of one eleven and one fifteen-inch guns, the Tecumseh will have two thirteen-inch guns, which, however, will be able to burn more powder than the old fifteen-inch guns. It was impossible when adding more weight of armor to the ship to make the draft of water as light as in the Monitor, if that were even desirable, which is a matter not decided on. One of the peculiarities of the Tecumseh is this, that she has sponsons which tighten the frame to the vessel, as it were. In the original Monitor this sponson was left out, and the consequence was that the overhang was said to have been the cause of the loss of that celebrated little vessel.

The accident that happened to one of the monitors during Dupont's attack on Charleston, which resulted in the temporary crippling of the turret, cannot happen to the Tecumseh, because an immense band of iron, several inches thick, perfectly solid and massive, covers the whole external base of the turret, rendering it absolutely impossible for any shot or shell to pierce it. This will insure the freedom of the turret, so far as its revolving powers are concerned. The propeller is driven by two powerful engines, with cylinders of forty inches in diameter and twenty-eight inch stroke of piston; and it will be observed that the speed of the Tecumseh will, in the natural course of things, be much greater than that of the original monitors, as the dimensions of her cylinders are nearly ten inches greater than those of the other ships. The monitors of the Passaic series have not realized the speed expected of them, but it is hoped that the Tecumseh series will do better.

In still less important matters there are some points of difference; in keeping the anchor, for instance, an arrangement is now made by which two holes are placed on each side of the bow, while in the other monitors it was directly in the centre. In fastening, the armor-rivets are substituted for bolts, as the latter give way and fly about when struck by heavy projectiles in a severe engagement. In the arrangement of the machinery, the air and circulating pumps and the surface-condensers are independent of the main engines, and can thus be operated when the main engines are standing still, maintaining constantly a vacuum, and being able to keep up the condensation of steam, instead of blowing it off into the atmosphere, which every naval officer will appreciate, because it has been one of the most intolerable nuisances of the introduction of steam in the navy that when orders are given upon the deck the blowing of the steam rendered them inaudible, and it could not be silenced without danger of boiler explosions.

New pattern Monitors. — Several vessels of the Monitor pattern, building in Boston, and intended for the defence of Massachusetts harbors, have some marked differences of construction from the monitors

7

described above, and constructed for the U. S. Navy. These peculiarities or improvements are thus described in the *Boston Herald :*— " One of them is a water-tight compartment two feet in width, extending around the whole body of the vessel. The water is pumped out of this compartment when the monitor is at sea. This lightens her, and; having less surface exposed to the water, she can move more rapidly. If the monitor is preparing for action, the compartment is filled. This sinks her deeper into the water, so that little of the vessel, if any, excepting the turret, is visible. Outside of the water-tight division is to be four feet of wood, and outside of the wood five inches of iron-plate. To obviate the foul bottoms to which iron ships are liable, an oak bottom is to be bolted on the iron one, and to be coppered like those of ordinary wooden vessels. They carry propellers and are provided with two screws, one under each counter, by which they can be turned in a smaller circle and in much less time than by a single screw."

The Comanche. — This vessel is one of the Ericsson monitors, and the circumstance particularly noticeable about her is, that she was constructed in Jersey City, N. J., put together perfectly upon the stocks ; and then taken apart and conveyed to San Francisco, California, where she will be reconstructed. This feat of taking apart a ship of the size of the Comanche (200 feet) has never been attempted before, and was eminently successful in this case, every bolt being put in its place before a single particle of the hull was taken down. The armor-plating of the Comanche is composed of five courses of plates, having an aggregate of five inches thickness.

Sheathing for Iron-Clads. — Some very interesting practical experience has lately been gained in England in the use of paints for iron-clad vessels; also in the use of brass sheathing to prevent their bottoms from becoming foul. The large armor-frigate, *Black Prince*, after having been five months in the water, was recently docked at Devonport and her bottom examined. It had been coated on one side with a paint chiefly composed of oxide of copper, and on the other with one partly composed of the sulphate of copper. Both sides were corroded, but the sulphate of copper was the cleanest ; still there were thousands of barnacles adhering to the plates on both sides. The *Resistance,* another smaller armor-frigate, was docked at the same time, but it had not been in service quite so long. One of its sides had been covered with the oxide of copper paint, and the other with another paint, the composition of which has not been published ; along the bottom also several patches had been covered with thin porcelain plates cemented with marine glue. It was found that most of these plates had dropped off, the glue not being capable of holding them, and the rest of the bottom was nearly as foul as that of the *Black Prince*. But the most remarkable case was that of the *Royal Oak*, which was also docked at the same time. This was a wooden vessel which had been originally designed for a line-of-battle ship, but was afterwards plated with iron. A band of lead was then run around the whole vessel below the deep-load line, below which the vessel was sheathed with Muntz metal, — the common brass sheathing, containing about sixty per cent. of copper to forty of zinc. The iron plates were painted with red lead ; and it was supposed that the intermediate lead band, coated with paint, would prevent contact and galvanic action between the iron and the sheathing. The latter was perfectly clean, but astonishment was caused by the galvanic action which had been induced between the iron and the sheathing. The lower tier of iron plates — each fifteen feet in length, three feet two inches in breadth, and four and one-half inches in thickness — were perfectly honey-combed, the holes varying in depth from one-fourth to five-eighths of an inch. Judging from the rate at which the corrosion had proceeded, the plates would have been entirely dissolved, had the vessel remained in the water many months longer. It had been supposed that wooden vessels could be built with iron plating descending below the water-line, and that their bottoms could be sheathed with copper, and thus remain as clean as copper-bottomed wooden vessels. Indeed, this very mode of constructing war vessels has been advocated by a French naval architect as being superior to all others, and several French and Italian armor-clads have been built upon such ideas. The practical and expensive experiment made with the *Royal Oak* affords us evidence that copper, or copper alloys, cannot be employed with safety connected by sea-water with iron on a vessel. The connection of these two metals forms a galvanic battery leading to the rapid decomposition of the positive metal. — *Scientific American.*

Conflict between the Weehawken (Monitor) and Atlanta, Iron-Clads. — Some important information respecting the offensive and defensive powers of iron-clad vessels and their improved armaments has been derived during the past year from the conflict between the *Weehawken,* one of Ericsson's monitor iron-clad vessels, and the iron-clad Confederate steamer *Atlanta,* which resulted in the surrender of the latter. The *Atlanta* was originally a sea-going steamer, — the *Fingal,* — remodelled and iron-plated. Her armor is described as follows: First and on the outside were wrought-iron bars, six inches wide by two inches thick, running perpendicularly with her side, and properly secured, both above and below, by rivets and bolts. Across these bars, horizontally, and on the inside, ran bars of like material and pattern, fastened to the outside layer by the strongest rivets. Within this layer, and fastened to it, were two thicknesses of live oak two-inch plank, also running perpendicularly and horizontally, and again, within these, were two more similar thicknesses of Georgia pine plank, forming the last series of her armor. The thickness of the *Atlanta's* armor, therefore, was twelve inches, — four of iron, four of live oak, and four of pine planking. Her pilot-house is also thus described: Forward of the smoke-stack was an elevation on the top deck, to all appearance like a cone; upon this cone was a small, square lookout, just large enough on the inside to allow a man's head to turn with freedom. On each side of this lookout were two small apertures, in the shape of parallelograms, slanting toward the interior, and presenting to the pilot's optics, in the lookout, two lookouts, an inch and a half long by an inch wide. This look-out was of wrought iron, four inches thick, and the cone upon which it stood was the same thickness, with this additional strength, however, that the interior of the pilot-house being square, the interstices between the sides of the upper part of the pilot-house and the concave surface of the cone were filled with eight-inch, square, live-oak blocks. From the top of the lookout to the base of the cone was but two feet and a half.

The action commenced by the *Atlanta* firing three shots. The *Wee-hawken* then replied with her fifteen-inch gun, throwing a solid shot of 440 pounds; and the first shot virtually decided the action, for the terrible missile tore through the *Atlanta's* iron-plating and timber-backing, as if it were stubble, and prostrated about forty of her crew, — some by splinters, but the most part by the mere concussion.

The second shot struck one of the *Atlanta's* port-stoppers, which were protected by four inches of wrought iron, knocking it into fragments, and wounding seventeen men. The third shot smashed the top of the pilot-house, wounding two of the pilots, and stunned the two men at the wheel, prostrating the whole four on the floor of the pilot-house. The fourth shot struck her on the knuckle, that is, where the iron casemate joins at a sharp angle the iron plating of the side; and the fifth shot went through her smoke-stack. After the fifth shot, the *Atlanta* surrendered; the whole action, from the firing of the first gun, being over in fifteen minutes. The U. S. Secretary of the Navy, in commenting on this engagement in his report to Congress, Dec. 1863, says: "This battle was to test not only the vessels but the new fifteen-inch ordnance, then for the first time brought into naval warfare, and concerning which there had been, as well as with respect to the vessels themselves, some variety of opinion. The conflict was so brief and decisive that only one of the two monitor vessels present, though not widely separated, and each eager for the fight, was able to participate in the engagement. The *Nahant*, having no pilot, followed in the wake of the *Weehawken*, but before she could get into action the contest was over. Such was the brevity of the fight that the *Weehawken*, in about fifteen minutes, and with only five shots from her heavy guns, overpowered and captured her formidable antagonist before the *Nahant*, which was hastening to the work, could discharge a single shot at the *Atlanta*. This remarkable result was an additional testimony in favor of the monitor class of vessels for harbor defence and coast service against any naval vessels that have been or are likely to be constructed to visit our shores."

Other trials of Iron-Clads in Action. — But the most severe and practical test to which iron-clad vessels have as yet been subjected occurred on the 7th of April, 1863, in the attack made by the U. S. fleet upon the forts and earthworks commanding the harbor of Charleston, S. C. On that occasion nine iron-clads, — including seven vessels of the Monitor pattern, the *Ironsides*, an iron-clad broadside steamer, and the *Keokuk*, an iron-clad of a peculiar and novel construction, (see *Annual of Sci. Dis.* 1863, p. 63), — taking a position where they were exposed, at comparatively short range, to the concentric and cross-fire of two regularly-constructed forts, and some half-dozen earthworks mounting heavy, and in part rifled ordnance, assailed Fort Sumter, a fortress of modern construction and of great strength. The result was, that after a contest of a little less than two hours, in which the vessels engaged sustained the most fearful and concentrated fire on record, — the forts and batteries using the heaviest and most improved projectiles (including the Armstrong and Whitworth patterns), — the fleet was withdrawn. Upon the monitors and the *Ironsides*, although all these vessels were struck repeatedly (the *Ironsides* alone some ninety times) no person was killed, or even seriously injured; while the efficiency of these vessels was not permanently impaired : the most serious injury, perhaps, occurred to the *Passaic* (monitor), which was disabled by being struck at the base of its turret by a heavy shot, which so jammed the contiguous plating as to prevent the tower from rotating. The *Keokuk*, however, was more unfortunate. This vessel was smaller than any of the monitors engaged, being plated with one and three-fourths-inch plates on a four-inch backing of iron and wood ; the plates being inclined at an angle which, amidships, was equal to 36°, with a view of deflecting shot striking against them. The unfitness of such armor for defensive purposes was illustrated in a very few minutes after the *Keokuk* came under fire. The armor was riddled with shot in every direction ; a considerable number of her crew were wounded, and one killed, while the vessel herself sunk some twelve hours after the conclusion of the fight.[1]

The *Ironsides*,—a non-turreted broadside steamer, plated with four and one-half inch solid armor, backed by from twenty-four to thirty inches of oak, — which took part in the above noticed attack, and in several other subsequent actions, appears to be the most effective and invulnerable of all the iron-plated vessels as yet constructed and sent into service by the United States ; some even claiming that she is equivalent to any six vessels of the monitor pattern. In the various actions in Charleston Harbor in which the *Ironsides* participated, from April to September, she is reported to have been struck by shot and shell, *two hundred and thirteen times*, none of which have caused serious injury to life or limb of her crew, or essentially injured the vessel. The water-line of the *Ironsides* alone bears the imprint of ten ten-inch solid shot, while the most serious damage resulted from two shots striking the same plate, within a foot of each other, and within a foot of the end of the plate. The result was the partial cracking of the plate, bending it, and forcing it about an inch into the wood-work. It occasioned no leak in the vessel. Several ten-inch solid shot, and one eleven-inch, have passed through the unprotected part of the bow and stern ; but so much of their momentum was lost in the passage, that they did not reach the wrought-iron bulkheads that cross the ship forward and aft, and which would have effectually stopped their further progress.

The method of fastening the plating to the sides of the *Ironsides* has proved very effective. It consists of common wood-screws, put through the plates from the outside, and tapped into the wood, having cylin-

---

[1] All vessels with inclined armor are supposed to be so constructed that the shot will glance from them without doing any damage. If we conclude, for the purpose of argument, that the enemy will fire a round shot at a very low velocity, on a line with the horizon, then the assumption may be correct. The fact of the matter is, however, that inclined sides simply present to barbette guns the fairest target they could desire, and the supposed efficiency of the angle is utterly neutralized. The *Galena*, at Drury's Bluff, and other gunboats on the western rivers, which were constructed with inclined armor, have been repeatedly pierced by guns fired from elevations. Inclining the armor simply increases the thickness of the plating to be pierced when the shot is fired on a line with the horizon. A plunging fire is received by inclined plating fair and square, and there are no instances on record where acutely-inclined armor has resisted the impact of the heaviest rifled shot at a fair range. The Parrott 300-pounder is said to have pierced nine inches of iron inclined at an angle of 45°, and the Stafford projectile is known to have penetrated seven one-inch plates, heavily backed up with timber, at the same inclination. Inclined sides, with inadequate armor, are simply a delusion and a snare. — *Scientific American.*

drical heads countersunk into the plating and flush with the outside.
Several of these screw-bolts have been struck directly on the head without causing any damage ; whereas, if the ordinary plan of using through
bolts or rivets had been adopted, it is very probable that some persons
would have been injured by fragments of the bolts being projected
inside the ship.   In the case of the monitors, the most serious accidents that have occurred on board them have arisen from the displacement and breaking of the bolts that hold together the plates of their
turrets, through the impact of heavy shot.   An idea of the fighting
capabilities of the *Ironsides* may be formed from the circumstance that
she threw, in the various attacks in which she participated from April
to September, upwards of 4,400 shells.

It is understood that one result of the attack on the fortifications of
Charleston, by the U. S. iron-clad fleet, has been the withdrawal from
the monitors of the fifteen-inch guns, with which their turrets were
armed, and the substitution of thirteen-inch guns in place.

New Port-Closer for Vessels of War. — An ingenious device for
closing the ports of iron-clads and other vessels of war has recently
been patented by Mr. W. S. Auchincloss, of New York City.   The
nature of the invention will be readily understood from the following
clause of the patent: — The employment or use for a port-hole closer
of two rollers, each being made to rotate independently of the other,
and provided with a cavity, so that by turning the rollers to the proper
position an opening is obtained which allows of giving to the gun any
desired elevation, or of training the same to an angle of 45° or more.

NATURAL PHILOSOPHY.

THE PHILOSOPHY OF TO-DAY.

"THE natural philosopher of to-day may dwell amid conceptions which beggar those of Milton. So great and grand are they, that in the contemplation of them a certain force of character is requisite to preserve us from bewilderment. Look at the integral energies of our world ; the stored power of our coal-fields, our winds and rivers, our fleets, armies, and guns. What are they? They are all generated by a portion of the sun's energy, which does not amount to $\frac{1}{2,300,000,000,000}$ of the whole ! This, in fact, is the entire portion of the sun's force intercepted by the earth, and in reality we convert but a small portion of this fraction into mechanical energy. Multiplying all our powers by millions of millions, we do not reach the sun's expenditure. And still, notwithstanding this enormous drain, in the lapse of human history, we are unable to detect a diminution of his store. Measured by our largest terrestrial standards, such a reservoir of power is infinite ; but it is our privilege to rise above these standards, and to regard the sun himself as a speck in infinite extension ; a mere drop in the universal sea. We analyze the space in which he is immersed, and which is the vehicle of his power. We pass to other systems and other suns, each pouring forth energy like our own, but still without infringement of the law, which reveals immutability in the midst of change, which recognizes incessant transference and conversion, but neither find gain nor loss. This law generalizes the aphorism of Solomon, that there is nothing new under the sun, by teaching us to detect everywhere, under its infinite variety of appearances, the same primeval force. To nature nothing can be added ; from nature nothing can be taken away ; the source of her energies is constant, and the utmost man can do, in the pursuit of physical truth, or in the application of physical knowledge, is to shift the constituents of the never-varying total, and out of one of them to form another. The law of conservation rigidly excludes both creation and annihilation. Waves may change to ripples, and ripples to waves ; magnitude may be substituted for number, and number for magnitude ; asteroids may aggregate to suns, suns may revolve themselves into floræ and faunæ and floræ and faunæ melt in air ; the flux of power is eternally the same. It rolls in music through the ages, and all terrestrial energy, the manifestations of life, as well as the display of phenomena, are but the modulations of its rhythm."— *Prof Tyndall.*

THE NATURE OF FORCE.

The following is an extract of a lecture recently delivered before the Royal Institution, London, by Prof. Tyndall, on the above subject.

" Standing upon one of the London bridges, we observe the current of the Thames reversed, and the water poured upwards twice a day. The water thus moved rubs against the river's bed and sides, and heat is the consequence of this friction. The heat thus generated is in part radiated into space, and then lost, as far as the earth is concerned. What is it that supplies this incessant loss? The earth's rotation. Let us look a little more closely at the matter. Imagine the moon fixed, and the earth turning like a wheel from west to east in its diurnal rotation. Suppose a high mountain on the earth's surface; on approaching the moon's meridian, that mountain is, as it were, laid hold of by the moon, and forms a kind of handle by which the earth is pulled more quickly round. But when the meridian is passed, the pull of the moon on the mountain would be in the opposite direction; it now tends to diminish the velocity of rotation as much as it previously augmented it; and thus the action of all fixed bodies on the earth's surface is neutralized. But suppose the mountain to lie always to the east of the moon's meridian, the pull then would be always exerted against the earth's rotation, the velocity of which would be diminished in a degree corresponding to the strength of the pull. *The tidal-wave occupies this position;* it lies always to the east of the moon's meridian, and thus the waters of the ocean are in part dragged as a brake along the surface of the earth; and as a brake they must diminish the velocity of the earth's rotation. The diminution, though inevitable, is, however, too small to make itself felt within the period over which observations on the subject extend. Supposing then that we turn a mill by the action of the tide, and produce heat by the friction of the millstones; that heat has an origin totally different from the heat produced by another mill which is turned by a mountain stream. The former is produced at the expense of the earth's rotation, the latter at the expense of the sun's radiation.

" The sun, by the act of vaporization, lifts mechanically all the moisture of our air. It condenses and falls in the form of rain; it freezes and falls as snow. In this solid form, it is piled upon the Alpine heights, and furnishes materials for the glaciers of the Alps. But the sun again interposes, liberates the solidified liquid and permits it to roll by gravity to the sea. The mechanical force of every river in the world, as it rolls toward the ocean, is drawn from the heat of the sun. No streamlet glides to a lower level, without having been first lifted to the elevation from which it springs by the mighty power of the sun. The energy of winds is also due entirely to the sun; but there is still another work which he performs, and his connection with which is not so obvious. Trees and vegetables grow upon the earth, and when burned they give rise to heat, and hence to mechanical energy. Whence is this power derived? You see this oxide of iron, produced by the falling together of the atoms of iron and oxygen; here also is a transparent gas which you cannot now see, — carbonic acid gas, — which is formed by the falling together of carbon and oxygen. These atoms thus in close union resemble our lead weight while resting on the earth; but I can wind up the weight and prepare it for another fall, and so these atoms can be wound up, separated from each other, and thus enabled to repeat the process of combination. In the building of plants, carbonic acid is the material from which the carbon of the plant is derived; and the solar beam is the agent which tears the atoms asunder, setting the oxygen free, and allowing the carbon to aggregate in woody fibre. Let the solar rays fall upon a surface of sand; the sand is heated, and finally radiates away as much heat as it receives; let the same beams fall upon a forest, the quantity of heat given back is less than the forest receives, for the energy of a portion of the sunbeams is invested in building up the trees in the manner indicated. Without the sun the reduction of the carbonic acid cannot be effected, and an amount of sunlight is consumed exactly equivalent to the molecular work done. Thus trees are formed; thus cotton is formed. I ignite this cotton and it flames; the oxygen again unites with its beloved carbon; but an amount of heat equal to that which you see produced by its combustion was sacrificed by the sun to form that bit of cotton.

" But we cannot stop at vegetable life, for this is the source, mediate or immediate, of all animal life. The sun severs the carbon from its oxygen; the animal consumes the vegetable thus formed, and in its arteries a reunion of the several elements takes place, and produces animal heat. Thus, strictly speaking, the process of building a vegetable is one of winding up; the process of building an animal is one of running down. The warmth of our bodies, and every mechanical energy which we exert, trace their lineage directly to the sun. The fight of a pair of pugilists, the motion of an army, or the lifting of his own body up mountain slopes by an Alpine climber, are all cases of mechanical energy drawn from the sun. Not, therefore, in a poetical, but in a purely mechanical sense, are we children of the sun. Without food, we should soon oxidize our own bodies. A man weighing 150 pounds has sixty-four pounds of muscle; but these, when dried, reduce themselves to fifteen pounds. Doing an ordinary day's work for eighty days, this mass of muscle would be wholly oxidized. Special organs which do more work would be more quickly oxidized; the heart, for example, if entirely unsustained, would be oxidized in about a week. Take the amount of heat due to the direct oxidation of a given amount of food; a less amount of heat is developed by this food, in the working animal frame, and the missing quantity is the exact equivalent of the mechanical work which the body accomplishes.

" I might extend these considerations,—the work, indeed, is done to my hand,—but I am warned that I have kept you already too long. To whom then, are we indebted for the striking generalizations of this discourse? All that I have laid before you is the work of a man of whom you have scarcely ever heard. All that I have brought before you has been taken from the labors of a German physician, named Mayer. Without external stimulus, and pursuing his profession as town physician in Heilbronn, this man was the first to raise the conception of the interaction of natural forces to clearness in his own mind. And yet he is scarcely ever heard of in scientific lectures, and even to scientific men his merits are but partially known. Led by his own beautiful researches, and quite independent of Mayer, Mr. Joule published his first paper on the ' Mechanical Value of Heat ' in 1843; but in 1842 Mayer had actually calculated the mechanical equivalent of heat from data which a man of rare originality alone could turn to account. From the velocity of sound in air, Mayer determined the mechanical equivalent of heat. In 1845, he published his Memoir on 'Organic Motion,' and applied the mechanical theory of heat in the most fearless and precise manner to vital processes. He also embraced the other natural agents in his chain of conservation.

" When we consider the circumstances of Mayer's life, and the period at which he wrote, we cannot fail to be struck with astonishment at what he has accomplished. Here was a man of genius working in silence, animated solely by a love of his subject, and arriving at the most important results some time in advance of those whose lives were entirely devoted to Natural Philosophy. It was the accident of bleeding a feverish patient at Java, in 1840, that led Mayer to speculate on these subjects. He noticed that the venous blood in the tropics was of a much brighter red than in colder latitudes, and his reasoning on this fact led him into the laboratory of natural forces, where he has worked with such signal ability and success. Well, you will desire to know what has become of this man. His mind gave way; he became insane, and he was sent to a lunatic asylum. In a biographical dictionary of his country it is stated that he died there; but this is incorrect. He recovered, and, I believe, is at this moment a cultivator of vineyards in Heilbronn."

EFFECTS OF THE EARTH'S ROTATION.

M. Foucault's beautiful experiment, by which, through the medium of a pendulum, the rotation of the earth on its axis may be said to have been rendered palpable to our senses, has had the effect of calling attention to a great many other phenomena going on on its surface, into which it enters as a modifying cause. To say nothing of those great and general facts of the oblateness of its figure, and the trade-winds which Newton and Hadley explained on this principle, we have seen the phenomena of Cyclones reduced to a dependence on this cause, combined with local disturbances of temperature; and, tracing the same cause into its still more local, and, so to speak, miniature sphere of action, it is recognized that the influence of the earth's rotation cannot be left out of consideration in the accurate pointing of long-range artillery, inasmuch as in a flight of five miles, occupying twenty-five seconds of time, it would carry a projectile pointed northwards, about forty-five feet to the east, and southwards as much to the west, (*i. e. in both cases toward the right hand*) of its line of fire. Pursuing the action of this cause into geographical inquiries, it has been argued that the action of a river flowing directly northwards or southwards, or indeed in any direction considerably inclined to the parallel, cannot be equal on its right and left banks; and that in either case (and indeed, whatever be the direction of the stream, if at all so inclined), in the northern hemisphere, the rotatory motion of the earth will have the effect of driving the water against the *right* bank of the river, and thus causing it to exert a greater erosive action on that than on the opposite side; and *vice versâ* in the southern hemisphere; the effect in both being more powerful the higher the latitude; and *nil* on the equator. On the other hand, it has been contended, that although, theoretically speaking, this is a real cause, (a *vera causa*), yet the amount of erosion thence arising must be far too small to produce any sensible tendency in rivers to shift their courses to the right, or to eat away their right banks perceptibly more than their left ; and this opinion seems to have found currency among the French academicians, whenever the subject has been discussed at the meeting of the Institute.

Regarding this question as one of fact rather than of opinion, M. Von Baer, in an elaborate memoir, read before the Imperial Academy of St. Petersburg, and lately published in the bulletins of that body, has brought together so large a mass of instances, drawn from observation of the courses of almost all the rivers of any note, both in European and Asiatic Russia as to justify this enumeration as a general feature (not of course, without local exceptions, owing to the natural inequalities of ground), over the whole of that vast region, that the right bank of a river is higher and steeper ; the left the flatter and more alluvial one, and more subject to inundation, — the law being so general, that over vast tracts of country, it may be predicted, almost without risk of failure, from the aspect of a stream in this respect, in which direction it runs. It deserves remark, that this general tendency has already been noticed by more than one geologist of eminence, without any suspicion of its cause. Thus, even so long ago as 1847, Major Waugenheim von Qualen had announced it as a general feature of the Russian River system, in the bulletins of the Society of Naturalists of Moscow ; and besides giving the result of his own observations in the region to the south and west of the Ural (where, from the absence of any considerable mountain system, and the general flatness of the country, the action of this cause would be little liable to be masked by local inequalities of a geological origin), cites the authority of M. Blöde, as having observed the same thing in southern, M. Bouiller in central, and Baron Wrangell in northern Russia ; Tschichatscheff, in central Siberia ; and Blasins, and other geologists, in many other parts of Russia, — adding that a feature so uniform, and prevailing over so vast an extent of territory, must evidently be due to some uniform and general cause. This cause he seeks, accordingly, in geological upheavals and dislocations, though evidently at a loss to perceive how such upheavals should have affected always the *right* bank of the river, without regard to the point of the compass toward which the water flows.

The same cause which throws the water of a river preferentially against its right bank must act of course in every case where masses of matter are in motion along definite lines of route, and therefore on railways, wherever there is a double line of rail for up and down traffic. For in such the right-hand rail on each line will be most worn ; and, in all cases, the flanges of the right-hand wheels of the carriages will suffer most by abrasion, and a greater probability (though in a very slight ratio) will exist of running off the rail to the right than to the left side of the line of travel, especially in lines running due north and south.

CURIOUS DEVIATIONS OF THE PLUMB-LINE.

The deviations of the plumb-line at different points of the earth's surface from the general law of perpendicularity to the surface of a spheroid, is usually considered as owing to the lateral attraction of mountain masses drawing it toward them ; but a singular case of a quite contrary nature has been brought to notice in the immediate vicinity of Moscow, where the operations of the Russian geologists, confirmed by the subsequent and more recent researches of M.

Schweizer, Director of the Imperial Observatory of that city, have established the existence of a local deviation to the extraordinary amount of nineteen seconds, within a very short distance of that metropolis. At Moscow, the plumb-line is found to deviate eight seconds from the spheroidical perpendicular toward the north. At twenty Russian versts (thirteen English miles) to the northward of Moscow, this deviation ceases. It does so, also, at twelve versts (eight miles) to the south of the city; but on going farther south, it recommences in a contrary direction, and at twenty-five versts to the south of Moscow is converted into a southern deviation of eleven seconds. Proceeding from Moscow in either an easterly or westerly direction, similar phenomena are observed. As there is nothing deserving the name of a mountain in the neighborhood of Moscow, it follows, as a necessary consequence, from these facts, either, — 1st. That there exist beneath Moscow enormous cavities, occupied by air, or perhaps by water. 2d. That strata of some substance of very weak specific gravity exist beneath that city. Or, 3d, that there extends over the whole of the country surrounding it a generally loose, unconsolidated mass of geological material to a depth hopelessly beyond what human labor can ever expect to penetrate. The interest of the observation does not terminate with the particular case of Moscow, but seems to indicate that henceforth in all instrumental determinations depending on the level or the plumb line, attention must be given to the lithological character of the place of observation. Here, again, is a point of contact between the two antithetical sciences of astronomy and geology.

DEFLECTION OF THE PLUMMET CAUSED BY THE SUN'S AND MOON'S ATTRACTION.

Mr. Edward Sang, in a paper read to the Royal Society of Edinburgh, shows that the attraction of the sun causes a deflection of the plummet, having its maximum about the 240th part of a second, and proportional to twice the size of the sun's zenith distance; the deflection is at its maximum when the sun is 45° above or below the horizon, and occurs in the vertical plane passing through the attracting body. The deflection due to the moon has its maximum about the 60th part of a second, and follows the same law; it is toward or from the attracting body according as the zenith distance is less or more than 90°. Upon the cross-level of a transit instrument, the joint effect is to cause a semi-diurnal oscillation, small at the quarters and rising to the 24th part of a second at new and full moon; while the influence upon meridian observations is sufficient to cause a disagreement between the greatest inclination of the moon's orbit, as observed at St. Petersburg and Madras, amounting to the fiftieth of a second.

The general conclusion drawn was, that we cannot determine the positions of the heavenly bodies true to the one hundredth part of a second, without having made allowance for this source of disturbance.

MEAN DENSITY OF THE EARTH.

In a memoir on this subject, by M. Faye, read at a recent meeting of the French Academy, the following valuations, from pendulum experiments, are given: 4.39 by Carlini and Plana, at Mount Cenis; 4.71 by Maskelyne, Hutton, and Playfair, at Scheballien, in Scotland;

5.44 by Reich, 5.43 by Cavendish, and 5.56 by Baily, by means of the torsion balance; and 6.55 by Airy, at the summit and bottom of a coal-mine.

ATTRACTION AND ADHESION.

The phenomena of attraction and adhesion, as exhibited in solid bodies, films, liquid globules, etc., have been investigated by Mr. Richard Norris, whose paper on the subject appears in the *Proceedings of the Royal Society*, from which we extract a few experiments. These Mr. Norris prefaces by reminding his readers that it has long been observed that solid bodies floating on liquids modify the figure of the surface of the liquid; pieces of tinfoil or greased bodies depress the liquid around them, whilst other bodies elevate it, giving rise to small mounds of liquid bounded by concave lines; likes attract likes, and repel unlikes, etc. He states that the following experiments are arranged to show that these effects of attraction are not peculiar to floating bodies, and that the only requirement is that the liquid should be associated with the bodies in which the movement occurs. 1. Let two balls of sealing-wax, or other material of greater specific gravity than water, be suspended by hairs in such a manner that they will both be partially immersed in water to an equal extent, the points of suspension being at a little distance apart, and the suspending hairs consequently parallel. When brought within the proper range, they will attract each other in the same manner as the floating bodies. In doing so they necessarily describe a small arc of a circle, of which the suspending hair is the radius, and have, therefore, not simply moved toward each other in a horizontal line, but have been raised to a higher level. 2. Suspend movably, by means of a thread passing over a pulley and a counterbalancing weight, a horizontal cork disc, from the under surface of which a drop of water is hanging. On a support beneath, formed by three upright pins, place a small piece of paper or thin glass, on the surface of which there is also a drop of water. On depressing the disc until the two drops of water touch each other, the paper or plate will be instantly drawn up to it; or, if the plate at the bottom be heavier than the disc, the latter will be drawn down. 3. When a soap-bubble is allowed to fall on an irregular surface, such as a piece of lint or flannel, it maintains its spherical shape; but if a smooth surface, such as a sheet of glass, be brought into slight contact with it, the wall of the bubble will be immediately attracted and flattened out upon it. In like manner, when two bubbles come in contact by their convex surfaces and cohere, the cohering surfaces become flattened, and the bubbles in a group cohere by plane surfaces.

STEAM BOILER EXPLOSIONS.

The following novel ideas respecting the explosion of steam-boilers were given to the British Association, 1863, by Mr. Airy, the Astronomer Royal. He said, that in considering the cause of the extensive mischief done by the bursting of a high-pressure boiler, it is evident that the small quantity of steam contained in the steam-chamber has very little to do with it. That steam may immediately produce the rupture; but as soon as the rupture is made, and some steam escapes, and the pressure on the water is diminished, a portion of the water is

8

immediately converted into steam at a slightly lower temperature and lower pressure, and this, in the same way, is followed by other steam at still lower temperature and pressure, and so on till the temperature is reduced to 212° Fahr. and the pressure to 0. Then there remains in the boiler a portion of water at the boiling point, the other portion having gone off in the shape of steam of continually diminishing pressure. From this it is evident that the destructive energy of the steam, when a certain pressure is shown by the steam-gauge, is proportional to the quantity of water in the boiler. By the assistance of Prof. Miller and George Biddell, Esq., the author has been able to obtain a result which he believes to be worthy of every confidence. He first stated, as the immediate result of Mr. Biddell's experiments, that when there were in the boiler of a small locomotive twenty-two cubic feet of water, at the pressure of sixty pounds per square inch, and the fire was raked out, and the steam was allowed gently to escape, with perfect security against priming, the quantity of water which passed off before the pressure was reduced to 0 was $2\frac{3}{4}$ cubic feet, or one eighth of the whole. In regard to the use made of Prof. Miller's theory, Prof. Miller had succeeded in obtaining a numerical expression for the pressure of steam at twelve different measures of the volume occupied by water and steam, which expression the author had succeeded in integrating accurately and had thus obtained an accurate numerical expression for the destructive energy of steam. In regard to the use of General Didion's experiments, these experiments gave the velocity of the ball, in cannon of different sizes, produced by different charges of powder. The author found, by trial with the formula $\dfrac{Wv^2}{2g \times \text{weight of powder}}$, which of these experiments exhibits the greatest energy per kilogramme of powder, and had adopted it in the comparison. The result is as follows: the destructive energy of one cubic foot of water, at sixty pounds pressure, per square inch, is equal to the destructive energy of two English pounds of gunpowder in General Didion's cannon experiments. General Didion's experiments were made, as the author understood, with smooth-bored cannon. It cannot be doubted that much energy is lost in the windage; some also from the circumstance that the propelling power ceases at the muzzle of the gun, before all the energy is expended; and some from the coolness of the metal. If we suppose that, from all causes, one-half of the energy is lost, then we have this simple result: the gauge-pressure being sixty pounds per square inch, one cubic foot of water is as destructive as one pound of gunpowder. In one of Mr. Biddell's experiments, the steam-valve was opened rather suddenly, and the steam escaped instantly with a report like that of a very heavy piece of ordnance. This is not to be wondered at; it appears from the comparison above that the effect was the same as that of firing a cannon whose charge is forty-four pounds of powder.

ILLUSTRATION OF THE ACTION OF THE SO-CALLED "GIFFARD'S INJECTOR."

The paradoxical and apparently impossible action of Giffard's injector, employed instead of a feed pump in charging steam-engine boilers, was illustrated in a remarkable manner by the Abbé Moigno, at the last meeting of the British Association, by means of a new instrument invented by M. Bourdon, of Paris, and called the "Injector of Solids."

Giffard's injector consists of three tubes united at one point : one of these brings the supply of water for the boiler from any convenient source ; the second is for the purpose of conveying the water into the boiler, and opens below the level of the liquid in that vessel ; the third brings a jet of steam from the upper part of the boiler. This jet of steam has the power of injecting a constant supply of water into the boiler, and so obviating altogether the necessity for a feed pump, and, apparently impossible as it may appear, not only has the steam power to inject water into its own boiler, but is capable of feeding another boiler in which the steam has a much higher pressure than itself.

M. Bourdon's Injector of Solids, which is capable of rendering this action visible by means of solid bodies, consists of two air vessels, with a communicating tube capable of being opened or closed at the will of the experimenter. One of these vessels is made of glass, and furnished with an aperture closed by a valve opening inwards. The other has a small air-gun proceeding from it, the barrel of which is directed against the opening in the first vessel. On condensing air into the two receivers, it is found that, even when four atmospheres are condensed into the glass vessel, and only two in that connected with the air-gun, the bullet driven by the latter has power to open the valve closed by the pressure of four atmospheres and enter the glass receiver.

ESTIMATION OF DISTANCES AND SPEED.

Many people hear of distances in thousands of yards—a usual measure of artillery distances,—and have very little power of reducing them at once to miles. Now, four miles are ten yards for each mile above 7,000 yards, whence the following rule: the number of thousands multiplied by four and divided by seven gives miles and sevenths for quotient and remainder, with only at the rate of ten yards to a mile in excess. Thus 12,000 yards is $\frac{48}{7}$ of a mile, or $6\frac{6}{7}$ miles; not 70 yards too great. Again, people measure speed by miles per hour, the mile and the hour being too long for the judgment of distance and time. Take half as much again as the number of miles per hour, and· you have the number of feet per second, too great by one in thirty. Thus 16 miles an hour is 16+8, or 24 feet per second, too much by $\frac{4}{5}$ of a foot.—*London Athenæum.*

POWER OF WAVES.

The Paris *Cosmos*, in describing the effects of a stormy period in January, 1863, on the coast of France, gives instances where "blocks of stone weighing thirteen tons were hurled to a distance of more than thirty feet, and blocks of three tons to more than one hundred yards. The outer harbor of Fécamp was destroyed, and the mass of earth torn from the north side of Cape la Hève was estimated at more than 300,000 square yards."

MOTIONS OF CAMPHOR UPON WATER.

When small pieces of camphor are dropped on the surface of a glass of water, several curious phenomena may be observed. They immediately commence to rotate, and move about with remarkable energy; varying sometimes in rapidity, but usually conducting their gyrations in a strange and erratic manner. In order to obtain the best effects, some precautions are necessary: thus, the camphor should be tolerably pure, the piece employed should be cut and separated from the large lump with a perfectly clean instrument, and contact with the fingers should be scrupulously avoided. Moreover, the glass should be quite clean and the water pure. When these conditions are satisfied, the phenomena are very striking. In the *Annual of Sci. Dis.* for 1863, p. 131, the account of some operations by Mr. Tomlinson of London on this subject was published. The following additional memoranda of interest have recently been laid before the public by Mr. Lightfoot, another experimentalist. This latter gentleman states, that if instead of using a torn or cut fragment from a lump of camphor, one or two fine crystals are detached with a clean needle-point from the cork of a phial in which camphor is kept, and these are let fall on clean water, they at once begin to move about with wonderfully increased rapidity, darting away in various directions, as if shot from some miniature engine, or endowed with life and a will of their own; each crystal quivering and rocking on the water with an apparently high degree of indignation at its forced contact with the humid surface. This fury gradually diminishes, and a regular dance begins; the various particles select partners to some of which they will seem to cling with pertinacity; whilst others will either remain indifferent, or, if attracted, will only stay a very short time in embrace, and wander again in search of more congenial floating associates. The explanations which Mr. Lightfoot gives of these movements is the emanation of a vapor from the volatile camphor, which has a very low tension; the water upon which it floats being capable of dissolving and diffusing this vapor more readily in certain directions of the crystalline axes, thereby removes sufficient vapor pressure at those points for the opposite side to drive about (by recoil) the nicely-suspended particle. In certain positions two crystals of camphor will attract each other, whilst in other situations there is a mutual repulsion. It will sometimes happen that two crystals of camphor may be thrown on the water and not have any tendency to locomotion. When this is the case, a continual trembling or vibration will be noticed in the crystal. When two such stationary vibrating crystals come in contact by attraction, immediately an eccentric, irregular change of place occurs, as if the force agitating each previous to the grouping, produced a new resultant force, in obedience to which the combined crystals move.

As above stated, it is of essential importance that in separating and placing the camphor in water everything should be quite clean, and that the fingers should not touch the camphor in any stage. The reason of this is found in the circumstance that if camphor is actively moving on water, and the most minute particle of certain greasy substances touch the water, instantaneously, as if by some magic, the camphor is deprived of all motion. The scene of previous activity is changed into immobility. This curious property has been made use of by Mr. Lightfoot to detect grease in quantities so extremely minute as would appear almost fabulous, for camphor cannot be made to rotate on water containing the most infinitesimal portion of grease. Mr. Lightfoot has made use of this test in a most ingenious manner, to distinguish between the two different methods of dyeing cloth with madder and with garancine. It is difficult and often impossible for calico-printers and merchants to distinguish between the two; and as the garancine dye is more fugitive than the first, and also of less intrinsic worth, it is sometimes substituted for it. There is however, a slight difference in the process of manufacture, — madder-dyed goods are, in one stage of the process, passed through a solution of soap to fix the color, whilst in garancine-dyed goods the soap is replaced by hypochlorite of lime. By proceeding as follows, it is easy to distinguish between the two kinds of dye: Let camphor rotate on water in any glass vessel, as previously described, then immerse a small strip of the cloth to be tested. If the rotation stops, we infer the presence of soap, and conclude it to have been dyed with madder. But if, on plunging in the small piece of cloth, the rotation is not stopped, we then arrive at the conclusion that garancine was the dyeing material used. In like manner the purity of water may also, to a certain extent, be tested by dropping a fragment of camphor upon its surface.

CURIOUS ELECTRICAL PHENOMENA.

Prof. Tyndall publishes the following account of some curious electrical phenomena observed by Mr. R. Watson, and a party of tourists in ascending a portion of the *Jung frau* Mountain in Switzerland. Mr. W., in a letter to Prof. Tyndall says, On the 10th of July, 1863, I visited with a party of three, and two guides, the *Col de la Jung frau.* The early morning was bright, and gave promise of a fine day, but, as we approached the Col, clouds settled down upon it, and, on reaching it, we encountered so severe a storm of wind, snow, and hail, that we were unable to stay more than a few minutes. As we descended, the snow continued to fall so densely that we lost our way, and, for some time, we were wandering up the Lötsch Sattel. We had hardly discovered our mistake when a loud peal of thunder was heard, and shortly after, I observed that a strange singing sound, like that of a kettle, was issuing from my alpenstock. We halted, and, finding that all the axes and stocks emitted the same sound, stuck them into the snow. The guide from the hotel now pulled off his cap, shouting that his head burned; and his hair was seen to have a similar appearance to that which it would have presented had he been on an insulated stool, under a powerful electrical machine. We all of us experienced the sensation of pricking or burning in some part of the body, more especially in the head and face, my hair also standing on end in an uncomfortable but very amusing manner. The snow gave out a hissing, as though a heavy shower of hail were falling; the veil on the wide-awake of one of the party stood upright in the air, and on waving our hands, the singing sound issued loudly from the fingers. Whenever a peal of thunder was heard, the phenomena ceased, to be resumed before the echoes had died away. At these times, we felt shocks, more or less violent, in those portions of the body which were most affected. By one of these, my right arm was paralyzed so completely that I could neither use nor raise it for several minutes, and I suffered much pain in it at the shoulder-joint for several hours. At half-past twelve, the clouds began to pass away and the phenomena finally ceased, having lasted twenty-five minutes. We saw no light-ning, and were puzzled at first as to whether we should be afraid or amused.

INTERESTING ELECTRIC ILLUMINATION.

Prof. W. B. Rogers communicates to *Silliman's Journal* the follow-ing observations on a powerful electric illumination, exhibited in Bos-ton, August, 1863, by Mr. Ritchie, the well-known electrician, as a part of the display attendant on a public rejoicing. The battery in question, consisting of 250 Bunsen elements, having each an acting zinc surface of about eighty-five inches, and grouped in five battalions of fifty each, was arranged in the dome of the State House; and the carbon light, and the photometric apparatus prepared for the purpose were placed in line across the same apartment, commanding a range of fifty feet. Prof. Rogers says: —

In view of the immense power of the light, as observed in the pre-vious experiment, I substituted for the 20-candle gas burner, used at that time as the standard of comparison, a unit ten times as great, formed by the flame of a kerosene lamp placed in the focus of a small parabolic reflector, and throwing its concentrated light on a photomet-ric screen of prepared paper fixed in front of it at the distance of five feet. Before the observation, the lamp and reflector were so adjusted as to make the light cast on the near side of the screen equivalent by measure to the action of 200 candles.

This was done by the intervention of a kerosene lamp fitted up with a bridge of platinum wire for defining and restricting the height of the square flame. Such a lamp I find of frequent use in ordinary photome-try, as, when suitably adjusted, it gives the light of about eight stand-ard candles, and thus transfers the measurement in the photometer to the wider divisions of the scale. Being suspended in a balance of pe-culiar construction, its rate of consumption enables us to correct for any slight departure from the assigned illumination. The lamp thus regulated was placed with its flat flame twelve inches from the screen, while the lamp in the reflector was distant sixty inches, and the flame of the latter was adjusted until the effects on the screen were equalized.

A platform supporting the standard lamp and screen at the assigned distance was arranged to slide on a horizontal graduated bar, extend-ing directly toward the carbon points so that the screen should receive the rays from the electric light and from the reflector perpendicularly on its opposite faces, In making the observations, the platform was moved to and fro until the illumination on the opposite sides of the screen was judged to be equal, and then the measured distances of the two antagonizing lights from the screen gave by easy computation their relative illuminating power.

By a series of such observations, it was found that the carbon light had a force varying from 52 to 61 times that of the lamp with reflector, making it equivalent in illuminating power to the action of from 10,000 to 12,000 standard sperm candles, pouring their light from the same distance upon the surface of the screen. This, it will be remembered, is the effect of the unaided carbon-light sending its rays equally in all directions from the luminous centre, and falls vastly short of the illumin-ating force of the cone of collected rays which was seen stretching, like the tail of a comet from the surface of the great reflector. Judging from some recent experiments on the power of such a reflector to augment the intensity of the light emanating from its focus, there can be no doubt that, along the axes of the cone, when brought to its narrowest limits, the illuminating force of the carbon light as displayed on the State House could be rivalled only by that of several millions of candles shining unitedly along the same line.

In the above-described observations, a thick screen was necessary, on account of the great intensity of the lights to be antagonized. I need hardly say that the different color of the two lights added much to the difficulty of the measurements. But, by marking in each case the extreme limits on either side, it was practicable to adjust the screen pretty accurately to equality of illumination.

The only previous experiment, of precisely the same kind, which I can recall is that of Bunsen, cited in the books, which was made with a battery of forty-eight elements. In this, the photometric equivalent of the carbon light was estimated at 572 candles, or nearly twelve candles to the cell. My observations show a power more than three times as great, or about forty candles to the cell; a difference due no doubt largely to the more intensive battery at my disposal and the cumulative effect of its arrangement. I suspect, too, that the elements in Bunsen's observation were of inferior size, but on this point I am without definite information.

ELECTRICAL SUMMARY.

Electric Express. — M. Bonelli, the Italian electrician, suggests a new application of electricity for the transmission of letters, light parcels, &c. A series of coils of insulated wire are adjusted along the route, and through them runs a pair of rails upon which travels the wagon which carries the despatch-box. This wagon also carries an electric battery, and the end of the coils are so adjusted that the battery connection is made, by means of the wheels and rails, through the coil which it is just about to enter. As the wagon is of sheet-iron, it will be attracted to the centre of the coil, and the momentum which it acquires will carry it far enough to make the connection through the next coil, when the impulse is renewed.

This contrivance will make a very pretty philosophical toy, or piece of illustrative apparatus; but can it be economically applied on a practical scale? — *Cosmos.*

Efficacy of Lightning Conductors. — M. Quetelet, in commenting on a remarkable thunder-storm that raged over a considerable part of Belgium, in February, 1860, states that, in his statistics of the buildings or vessels struck by lightning, " he found that out of a hundred and sixty-eight cases in which lightning-conductors had been struck, only twenty-seven, by reason of grave defects in their formation, had failed to exercise a preservative power."

Influence of Heat on the Voltaic Battery. — M. Carlo Roberti, of Verona, in a note forwarded to the Academy of Sciences at Paris, states that, while pursuing some experimental researches with Gauss's apparatus, he was struck first with the irregularity and afterwards with the progressive periodical intensity of the pile he employed. He was soon led to attribute this to the variation of the temperature, due to the hourly advance of a solar ray which had penetrated his laboratory. He immediately conceived the idea of applying this fact to the electric telegraph and other purposes, and states that he is now engaged in vigorous experiments, with the view of arriving at the exact numbers which establish the advantages which may be derived from the phenomena.

Magnetism, Electricity, and Vegetation. — In his *Physique du Globe*, M. Quetelet tells us that on examining attentively the value of the monthly magnetic variation, it is found to be in direct relation with the force of vegetation. When the latter sleeps, which happens in the months of November, December, January, and February, the magnetic variation, at Brussels, is almost uniformly 5′ 28″, or scarcely half during the period of its full activity, that is to say, from April to September, when its mean is 10′ 15″. It reaches its plenitude in April, when the mean is 11′ 14″, for Brussels. In another passage, M. Quetelet states, that the electricity of the air is intimately connected with the action of vegetation, and that the two phenomena have a nearly parallel march. It is not pretended that one depends on the other, but that both arise from the same cause. The quantity of atmospheric electricity at noon is much greater in winter than in summer, the relation being about 10 to 1. This augmentation of electric force proceeds in a manner almost parallel with the number of days of frost and fog, and inversely as the number of days of thunder, of elevation of temperature, of actinic power.

Terrestrial Magnetism and Temperature. — At a recent meeting of the Royal Society, the Astronomer Royal mentioned that the remarkable change which had taken place in the phenomena of terrestrial magnetism, as observed at Greenwich since 1845, was such as might be expected to take place, were the climate of the northern hemisphere to become more wintry in its character, while that of the southern hemisphere remained unaltered. It is already on record that Sir John Herschel considers the climate of the earth to be undergoing a change due to some cosmical cause. Is there any connection between his conclusions and those of the Astronomer Royal? To those who take interest in the progress of terrestrial magnetism as a science, it will be gratifying to know that Mr. Airy expresses himself decidedly in favor of long-continued simultaneous observations in various parts of the globe. With series of observations extending over many years it becomes possible to institute comparisons, to note fluctuations and disturbances, and to discover something of their laws; while short and broken series baffle investigation, and harass the inquirer to no useful purpose. — *London Athenæum.*

Sun-spots and Auroras. — The *Comptes Rendus* contains a letter from M. R. Wolf to M. Remmont, in which the former says, " I find, in accordance with M. Fritz, that the frequency of solar spots corresponds exactly with that of auroras, so that we observe in the latter both the period of $11\frac{1}{9}$ years and the great period of 56 years, the existence of which I have demonstrated for solar spots."

Thunderstorms and the Moon. — M. Bernardin calls the attention of the Belgian Academy to the fact that many thunderstorms have occurred about the period of the new or full moon, and he invites inquiry for the purpose of ascertaining whether there is any connection between the movements of our satellite and the electrical condition of the atmosphere.

RESEARCHES IN ELECTRO-PHYSIOLOGY.

M. Matteucci has forwarded to the Academy of Sciences, at Paris, an analysis of his latest electric researches in relation to physiology, undertaken with the view of explaining one of the most remarkable yet obscure laws of the science. He began by proving that the passage of an electric current in a non-metallic body, which is, however, a conductor of electricity on account of the liquid which it has imbibed, acquires the property termed secondary polarity. By virtue of this property, if it be touched by the homogeneous ends of the galvanometer, it is found that this body is traversed by an electric current, directed in a way opposite to the voltaic current which has excited the polarity. Such is the case with a cotton wick moistened with water, a vegetable stem, a membrane, and a nerve, independently of its vitality. Among these different bodies a nerve is remarkable by the rapidity with which it is polarized in all its points, and by the intensity of its polarity.

Electricity of the Circulation of the Blood. — M. Scoutetten has reported to the Academy of Sciences at Paris an account of some experiments made upon horses which were previously made insensible to pain. He found that the electric positive sign, indicating the direction of the current, was constantly from the red, or arterial, to the black, or venous, blood. He concludes his memoir by saying that since it is demonstrated that the red blood and the black blood, in their contact through the walls of the vessels, which act as true porous vases, give stated electric reactions to the galvanometer, we must admit, that as all the parts of our body are traversed by sanguineous fluids, there must necessarily be a constant disengagement of electricity in the most relaxed tissues of our bodies. Thus each organic molecule is incessantly stimulated by the electric fluid, and thus under the influence of this excitement, all the functions of the body are performed. The oxygen contained in the red blood burns up the organic molecules with which it is in contact, and produces heat, without which life is impossible. Under the influence of electricity is effected, during digestion, the selection of the nutritive molecules and their assimilation. The same action takes place in respiration and in all the other functions. These facts perfectly agree with the electric phenomena of combustion. The carbon takes the negative electricity and the surrounding air the positive, or rather, the current is established between the carbon and the oxygen of the air. Now, the principal action of the red blood, by reason of the oxygen in it, is the producing a true combustion in our tissues.

Electric Conductivity of Muscle. — Ranke, a German physiologist, has published, among the results of his investigations into the phenomena of electric currents in the living muscle, the fact that dead muscle is a much better conductor of electricity than living muscle, because of the presence of certain products of decomposition which do not appear till after death. He concludes, further, that the conducting power of living muscle is three million times weaker than that of mercury, and one hundred and fifteen million times below that of copper.

ELECTRICITY BY FRICTION AND BY CONTACT DERIVED FROM ONE SOURCE.

H. Buff (*Ann. der Chem. u. Pharm.* Vol. 114) says: For electricity to be evolved by friction, it is essential that the two surfaces which are rubbed against each other, are different in character, and if traces of electricity do appear on rubbing together substances of similar kind, it is owing to their being really in some way modified, either at the beginning or while the friction is taking place. Chemical modifications in this connection exert a much stronger influence than changes depending on mechanical or physical causes.

The discharging force which makes its appearance at the point of contact between two conductors, and which is known as " electro-motory power," although first observed in conductors, is not wholly confined to them. On the contrary, it shows itself with equal constancy, wherever two bodies, be they conductors or not, but of different kind, come into contact, and it causes on one of these bodies the discharge of positive, and on the other that of negative electricity. In the moment of the separation of these bodies the fluida formed at their points of contact are set free in the form of electricity. The direction taken by the discharge is always the same for the same bodies, be they rubbed against each other or only brought into contact. The fluida, which are kept separated during actual contact, in the case of conductors and while they are thus separated, may be carried off in opposite directions ; on this principle depends the circulation of electricity in the Voltaic pile. Bad conductors offer resistance to this carrying away of the fluida ; on the other hand, they favor the accumulation of frictional electricity. The process of friction itself not only multiplies the points of contact, but aids their process of separation to penetrate still deeper. It, however, does not influence the direction of the discharge ; this depends upon the electro-motory force which again corresponds with or depends upon the difference between the bodies so treated.

THE NATURE OF THE FORCES PRODUCING THE GREATER MAGNETIC DISTURBANCES.

The following are the chief points of discourse on the above subject, delivered before the Royal Institution, London, by Prof. Balfour Stewart, of the *New Observatory* : — When a bar of steel is magnetized, it has acquired a tendency to assume a definite relation to our earth. Nothing in science is more mysterious than the cause of this. The earth, like a great magnet, acts upon a magnetized needle with nearly a directive force. At the present moment, a mariner's compass-needle points in a direction of about twenty-one and a half degrees west of true north, termed a declination to that extent, and at the same time dips downwards, making an angle of about sixty-eight degrees with the horizon. This declination and dip vary with time and place. But there are other changes which the magnet experiences when kept suspended in the same place. 1. The secular change, viz., during a great many years. 2. The annual variation. 3. The daily variation ; and 4, a change due to the moon. In addition to these are those curious and unaccountable changes termed magnetic disturbances, or storms. Atmospheric storms, even the greatest, are only local phenomena ; but magnetic storms are cosmical, as has been shown by Gauss and Sabine, and occur almost at the same moment all over the world. Hence many colonial observatories have been established. Mr. Stewart having explained the methods of observation, and referred to diagrams giving ːⁿ ː⁻⁻ showed that these magnetic disturbances are connected with the sun, inasmuch as they obey a daily law, and are moreover independent of the light of the sun. They have a yet still more mysterious relation with our luminary. Schwabe, of Dessau, having for nearly forty years watched and recorded the spots on its disc, saw that these spots exhibit a maximum and minimum nearly every ten years; and General Sabine having discovered that magnetic disturbances have also a ten years' period, fortunately thought of comparing the two periods, and found that they were precisely the same, having the same years of maximum and minimum. This brought us into the presence of some great cosmical bond, other than gravitation. On one occasion the sun was believed to be caught in the very act of causing a magnetic disturbance. On Sept. 1st, 1859, Messrs. Carrington and Hodgson, independently, observed a bright sun spot, and at the very same moment the magnets at Kew were found to be suddenly disturbed. It has also been proved that these disturbances are accompanied by auroras and also by electric earth-currents, in some cases interfering with the telegraph wires, both having a ten-yearly period. The nature of the bond by which these phenomena are allied is still a profound mystery. Mr. Stewart, however, with diagrams and models, endeavored to elucidate it by the application of the laws of induced primary and secondary electric currents, demonstrated by Faraday. The earth, being considered as the iron core of an electro-magnet, is no doubt excited by some primary current (probably in the sun), and, having a conductor in the upper and rarer strata of the atmosphere, and another conductor round it in the upper and moist crust of the earth, has also an insulator in the lower and denser strata of the atmosphere. Mr. Stewart considers that every time a small but rapid change takes place in the magnetism of the earth, it gives rise to a secondary or induced current in the two conductors; and this occasions the electric earth-currents and auroras, probably due to the inequality of the earth's surface. With regard to the spots on the sun's disc, Mr. Stewart suggests that, if that luminary, by causing magnetic disturbances, is capable of producing auroras in the earth's atmosphere, it is surely capable of producing similar phenomena in its own.

THE CAUSES OF FAILURE IN SUBMARINE TELEGRAPH CABLES.

A recent article in the *London Times* states several important facts in reference to the causes of failure in various submarine telegraph cables, and in respect also to the precautions now taken to prevent future similar disasters.

"Every operation in submarine telegraphy — even the great Atlantic line — has contributed its quota of valuable experience; for, though successfully laid by Sir Charles Bright and his assistant engineers, in spite of its imperfect construction, it was *destroyed by the injudicious electrical treatment it received after submersion.* This fact is now so well established that the cause of the failure of the Atlantic cable may be considered as set at rest forever. The insulation of that line was not very perfect, as may be imagined from the infancy of the science at that time, but yet the electrical power used was such as would infallibly break down even the most perfect cables manufactured at the present day. Of this our readers may judge when it is stated that the large induction coils first used in signalling between England and

America were probably equal in electrical power to 2000 battery cells, while now it is found inexpedient to use more than two or three cells in working the longest submarine lines in existence. Some of this great power was no doubt used in the vain hope of forcing signals through the line at a greater speed than the very slow and unremunerative rate at which it has alone been found possible to communicate through an unbroken length of 3000 miles. The result was disastrous, but the experience, though dearly bought, has proved of great value. It has taught electricians the value of moderating the power used in working lines, and above all has pointed out the imperative necessity of having no single section of a submarine line of more than six hundred miles in length. To lay long submarine cables in a continuous length without intermediate stations has been found to answer no other purpose than that of greatly diminishing the speed of working and multiplying every imaginable risk both of manufacture and submersion. The Indian Government, acting under the judicious counsel of their scientific advisers, have wisely determined to divide the Persian Gulf cable into three sections, though its total length will not exceed 1500 statute miles."

The Red Sea line was destroyed by faults of another character. Being laid without any allowance for slack, that the cable might conform the more readily to the irregularities of the bottom, the suspended portions became loaded with barnacles and coral, and crumbled from its own weight.

"To obviate this cause of danger, which in the above-mentioned lines has probably occasioned a loss of property to the value of over a million sterling, the Persian Gulf line is cased in twelve No. 7 gauge harddrawn iron wires, thickly galvanized, so as effectually to prevent their corrosion. But, in order to secure more effectually the permanent stability of the line, the whole finished cable is thickly coated with two servings of tarred hemp yarn, overlaid with two coatings of a patent composition invented by Sir Charles Bright and Mr. Latimer Clark. The composition consists of mineral pitch or asphalt, Stockholm tar, and powdered silica, mixed in certain proportions, and laid on in a melted state. While yet warm, it is passed between circular rollers, which give it a round, smooth surface. When quite cold this forms a massive covering of great strength and perfect flexibility, totally impervious to water, and incapable of being destroyed by the minute animalculæ which exist in such abundance in warm latitudes, and which, when the cable is not protected against their attacks, eat every atom of hemp, as in the case of the cable laid between Toulon and Algiers."

Another important fact is stated, that wire varies greatly — as much as fifty or sixty per cent. — in its capacity for conducting electricity. The cable for the Persian Gulf is so well selected, and so well protected by gutta percha and compound, that the loss by leakage is scarcely appreciable by the most delicate instruments. To such minute perfection has the system of testing adopted by the engineers been carried, that the loss of one thousand-millionth part of the current by leakage would be detected and estimated. The cost of this submarine section will exceed $1,500,000.

ON THE COMPARATIVE LIGHT OF THE SUN AND STARS.

The following interesting research is communicated to *Silliman's Journal* by Mr. Alvan Clark, the discoverer of the companion to Sirius:
" If we place a lens of known focal distance, one foot for instance, between the eye and a star of the first magnitude, or one of any considerable brightness, with conveniences for guiding its movement in distance, to any point where it may be needed, and find the star just visible, or reduced to a sixth magnitude, when the lens, if a convex, is eleven feet from the eye, it becomes clear that, since the star has undergone a reduction of ten diameters, it would be visible, if removed in space to ten times its present distance. This, however, is on the supposition that no absorbing or extinguishing medium exists in space. If a concave lens be employed, the measure must be commenced at the lens itself, but if convex, at the focal point; or once the focal distance must be subtracted from the measure, and the number of focal distances remaining corresponds to the number of reductions under which the object is viewed.

Castor is visible, when reduced, ...	10·3 times.
Pollux, ...	11 "
Procyon, ...	12 "
Sirius, ...	20 "
The full Moon, ...	3,000 "
The Sun, ...	1,200,000 "

I have actually seen the sun under such a reduction; attended by circumstances which have led me to believe that it is about the limit at which the naked human eye could ever perceive this great luminary.
I have an under-ground, dark chamber, two hundred and thirty feet in length, one end terminating in the cellar of my work-shop, and the other communicating with the surface of the ground by a vertical opening, one foot square, and five feet deep. In a movable partition, between this opening and the end of the chamber, a lens of such focal distance as I choose can be inserted. A twentieth of an inch focus I have employed, of the best finish possible ; its flat side cemented to one face of a prism with Canada balsam. No light whatever can enter the dark chamber, except through this little lens. A common, plane, silvered glass mirror, placed above-ground, over the vertical opening, receives the direct rays from the sun, and sends them down into the prism of total reflection, by which they are directed through the little lens into the chamber. An observer, in the cellar, two hundred and thirty feet distant, sees the sun reduced 55,200 times; and its light, in amount, varies but little from that of Sirius. Upon a little car, movable in either direction, by cords and a pulley, is mounted another lens, with a focal distance of six inches. The eye of the observer is brought into a line with the lenses, or so near it, that he sees the light through the six inch lens ; then, by the cord, he sends the car into the chamber, to the greatest distance at which he can see the light, like that from a star of the sixth or seventh magnitude. At noon, March 19th, with a perfectly clear sky, I found the sun visible through the six-inch lens, when it was removed to the distance of twelve feet from the eye. The distance between the lenses being two hundred and eighteen feet, the reduction by the small lens, if viewed from the point occupied by the six-

inch lens, would be 52,320times; and that again by the six-inch, distant from the eye twelve feet, or twenty-four times its focal distance, is reduced twenty-three times; making the total reduction 1,203,360 times.

It becomes now an important matter to ascertain, as nearly as possible, the proportion of light lost by and through the media above described — the looking-glass, the prism, and two lenses — though joining the little lens with balsam to the prism, it may be regarded as one piece. I have only investigated by experiments with artificial lights; but I find, when the mirror is placed at the angle which the sun requires at the date above given, the difference in the distance at which a direct light, and the same light reflected, are brought to a *minimum visible*, does not exceed one-eighth part of the entire distance, and could not reach one-seventh, when the prism and lenses were interposed.

Again: the image of the highly-illuminated atmosphere, for some degrees about the sun, is admitted with the sun's direct light, through the little lens, to the dark chamber; and the light, thus augmented, is observed in contrast with a darkness greater than that of a clear nocturnal sky. The entire loss by reflecting and absorbing is manifestly so small, and the light of the sky in the immediate vicinity of the sun, so great, that I can readily believe the waste, in effect, is fully made up; especially when considering the absolute blackness of the ground upon which the light in the dark chamber is projected; and I can find no reason to doubt that the sun would appear as a star of the sixth magnitude, or be only just visible to the unassisted human eye, even setting aside the idea of an extinguishing medium, if removed 1,200,000 times his present distance; and at 100,000 times his present distance, he would only rank as a pretty bright star, of the first magnitude; though his parallax would be double that imputed to any star in the whole heavens. If his intrinsic splendor generally proves to be less than that of those stars whose distances have been measured, we need not infer that it is less than the average of existing stars; for, in case of a diversity among them, bearing any proportion to that among organic bodies, on the face of the earth, or the planets of our system where the numbers are so comparatively small, the *visible* stars would, of course, exceed, upon the average, our sun; for, by the laws of perspective, the small ones would be lost to our view, at distances from which the brighter individuals would appear as conspicuous objects. Such would be the case with telescopic magnitudes, as well as with those visible to the naked eye. The number of stars visible, by aid of the more powerful telescopes, is far less, in proportion to the power of the instruments, than those visible to the unassisted eye, or with smaller telescopes. This fact has given rise to the doctrine of an extinguishing medium in space; which is accepted by the most able astronomers as the truth, and has been the foundation of much ingenious reasoning.

Plausible or probable, as this appears, I see no difficulty in understanding that an exceedingly great diversity in the intrinsic brightness of the stellar orbs, promiscuously scattered through space, *might* result in the same appearances as those on which this doctrine is founded. For, at the smaller distances, we should see the whole, both great and small, when using only moderate powers; but in the regions bounding the remotest reach of the great telescopes, though the great and the small might be there, it would be only the great that we should see; and those only as the most minute specks of light that can be imagined.

The vast number of smaller, or more moderate lights, like our sun, which may remain concealed among those of extraordinary splendor, yet so remote as only just sensibly to impress our vision when aided to the utmost that human skill can do, will be better understood when we consider the ratio in which an increase of radius increases the cubic contents of a sphere. Upon the outer limits of such a sphere as would embrace the great mass of telescopic stars, a moderate depth, extended round the whole, would afford an immense amount of room for stars of all imaginable sizes. I desire to be particularly understood, that it is in those very remote regions, or beyond where any telescope, now in use, can possibly show stars of the average, or smaller sizes, that we may look for the modification introduced, by such supposed diversities, into the investigation of this doctrine of an absorbing medium. Were all the stars in existence of one pattern, one uniform brightness, scattered broadcast through all space, I think the great telescopes would count up more nearly the numbers belonging theoretically to their powers than they now do. However, with these suggestions, I leave this interesting branch of my subject for the present.

The ratio, in which the light from a celestial object diminishes with an increase of distance, needs no explaining; and I will close by briefly giving, in tabular form, my own results, with those published by Mr. Bond of the Harvard College Observatory, and by Dr. Wollaston, in the *Transactions of the Royal Society of London*, of comparisons between the bright star *a* Lyræ and the sun.

To bring the magnitude of our sun to an equality with that of this star, his distance would require to be increased, according to

Wollaston, nearly	425,000 times.
Bond,	155,000 "
Clark,	102,000 "

The light received from these luminaries differs, according to

Wollaston, as	180,000,000,000 to 1
Bond, "	24,000,000,000 "
Clark, "	10,400,000,000 "

I have alluded to the light in the atmosphere about the sun, as giving an increase to his photometrical force, though I am aware that such must be the case with a star; and it must bear the same proportion to the star's light that it bears to the sun's light. The difference, in effect is here: we have several thousand stars playing into our atmosphere at once, but only one sun. If the distances imputed to several of the stars, from parallax, can be true, I am sure those having the taste, talent, and leisure, necessary for following up photometrical researches with efficiency, cannot fail to find our glorious luminary a very small star; and to the human understanding, thus enlightened, more than ever must the heavens declare the glory of God.

THE TENEBROSCOPE FOR PROVING THE INVISIBILITY OF LIGHT.

At the last meeting of the British Association, the Abbé Moigno exhibited and described an instrument invented by M. Soleil, of Paris, for illustrating the invisibility of light, and called the " Tenebroscope." It is well known to scientific men, although the general public do not sufficiently appreciate the fact, that light in itself is invisible unless the eye be so placed as to receive the rays as they approach it, or unless some object be placed in its course, from whose surface the light may be reflected to the eye, which will generally thus give notice of the presence of that object.   Thus, if a strong beam of sunlight be admitted into a darkened chamber through a small opening, and received on some blackened surface placed against the opposite wall, the entire chamber will remain in perfect darkness, and all the objects in it invisible, except in as far as small motes floating in the air mark the course of the sunbeam by reflecting portions of its light.   Upon projecting a fluid or small dust across the course of the beam its presence also becomes perceptible.   The instrument exhibited consisted of a tube with an opening at one end to be looked into, the other end closed, the inside well blackened, and a wide opening across the tube to admit strong light to pass only across.   On looking in, all is perfectly dark, but a small trigger raises at pleasure a small ivory ball into the course of the rays, and its presence instantly reveals the existence of the crossing beam by reflecting a portion of its light.

THE STAR CHROMATOSCOPE. BY M. CLAUDET.

The scintillation and change of colors observed in looking at the stars are so rapid that it is very difficult to judge of the separate lengths of their duration.   If we could increase on the retina the length of the sensations they produce, we should have the better means of examining them.   This can be done by taking advantage of the power by which the retina can retain the sensation of light during a fraction of time which has been found to be one-third of a second — a phenomenon which is exemplified by the curious experiment of a piece of incandescent charcoal revolving round a centre, and forming a continual circle of light.   It is obvious that if the incandescent charcoal, during its revolution, was evolving successively various rays, we could measure the length and duration of every ray by the angle each would subtend during its course.   This is precisely what can be done with the light of the star.   It can indeed be made to revolve like the incandescent charcoal, and form a complete circle on the retina.   When we look at a star with a telescope, we see it on a definite part of the field of the glass; but if with one hand we slightly move the telescope, the image of the star changes its position, and during that motion, on account of the persistence of sensation on the retina, instead of appearing like a spot, it assumes the shape of a continued line.   Now if, instead of moving the telescope in a straight line, we endeavor to move it in a circular direction, the star appears like a circle, but very irregular, on account of the unsteadiness of the movement communicated by the hand.   Such is the principle of the instrument employed by the author to communicate the perfect circular motion which it is impossible to impart by the hand.   The instrument consists of a conical tube, placed horizontally on a stand, and revolving on its own axis by means of wheels; inside this tube, a telescope or an opera-glass is placed, by which, by means of two opposite screws, the end of the object-glass can be placed in an eccentric position in various degrees according to the effect desired, while the eye-glass remains in the centre of the small end of the tube. Now, if we understand that when the machine makes the tube to revolve upon its axis, the telescope inside revolves in an eccentric direction, during the revolution the star seen through it must appear like a circle. This circle exhibits on its periphery the various rays emitted by the star, all following each other in spaces corresponding with their duration, showing also blank spaces between two contiguous rays which must correspond with the black lines of the spectrum. The instrument, in fact, is a kind of spectroscope, by which we can analyze the light of any star, study the cause of the scintillation, and compare its intensity in various climates or seasons and at different altitudes. — *Proc. "British Association,"* 1863.

SOME PHENOMENA PRODUCED BY THE REFRACTIVE POWER OF THE EYE.

In a paper read before the British Association, 1863, by Mr. A. Claudet, the author gave an explanation of several effects of the refraction of light through the eye; one of which is, that objects situated a little behind us are seen as if they were on a straight line from right to left. Another, that the pictures of external objects which are represented on the retina, are included in an angle much larger than one-half of the sphere at the centre of which the observer is placed; from this point of view a single glance encompasses a vast and splendid panorama extending to an angle of 200°. This is the result of the common law of refraction. All the rays of light passing through the cornea to the crystalline lens are more and more refracted in proportion to the angle at which they strike the spherical surface of the cornea. Consequently, the only objects which are seen in their true position are those entering the eye in the direction of the optic axis. By this refraction, the rays which enter the eye at an angle of 90° are bent at 10°, and appear to come from an angle of 80°. This phenomenon produces a very curious illusion. Where we are lighted by the sun, the moon, or any other light, if we endeavor to place ourselves in a line with the light and shadow of our body, we are surprised to find that the light and the shadow seem not to be connected at all, and that, instead of being in a line, they appear bent to an angle of 160° instead of 180°, so that we see both the light and the shadow a little before us, where they are not expected to be. The eye refracts the line formed by the ray of light, and the shadow and the effect is like that of the stick, one-half of which being immersed in water, appears crooked or bent into an angle at the point of immersion. This enlargement of the field of vision to an angle of 200°, is one of those innumerable and wonderful resources of nature by which the beauty of the effect is increased. Our attention is called to the various parts of the panorama which appear in any way a desirable point of observation, and we are warned of any danger from objects coming to us in the most oblique direction. These advantages are .

9*

particularly felt in our crowded towns, where we are obliged to be constantly on the lookout for all that is passing around us.

BREWSTERIAN LIGHT FIGURES.

Prof. von Kobell, of the University of Munich, has recently published an account of some interesting experiments similar to those made by Brewster in 1837, relating to the appearance of bright stars, elliptical colored rings, and various coruscant forms visible, at certain angles, in particular minerals and salts. Pliny was aware of this phenomenon, and mentions a stone that he calls Astreos, which showed a bright star reflected within it. The stone he alludes to is, however, believed to be no other than a sapphire, which presents the brilliance described.

For a long time, it was believed these appearances were only to be seen in sapphires and garnets, until about the same time as Brewster, Babinet and Volger discovered the incorrectness of that opinion.

Babinet found that the phenomenon was produced by numberless parallel grooves or furrows, whose sides were all situated at regular angles to each other; so that the light which fell on the crystal was reflected back from an infinitesimal number of such furrows' sides or little angular slopes. He therefore gave the forms of light thus produced the name of "trellis-work appearances;" and the more simple forms may be produced by engraving on a smooth copperplate the fitting parallel lines in close proximity to each other, and then, in a darkened room, holding the plate before a candle in such wise that the reflected light of the flame be transmitted from the plate to the eye. In this case, a streak of light is perceived on the spot where the lines are drawn; should, however, two sets of lines be drawn on the plate at right angles to (crossing) each other, a streak of light crossing the other bright streak at right angles will be seen. If the lines on the plate — the rows of little furrows rather — cross each other at an acute angle, then the lines of the bright cross, which becomes visible, are also at an acute angle to each other. Should the drawn lines all emanate from a common centre, then, if the light be transmitted at a certain angle, a parhelion is observed. This last appearance may often be seen in a small piece of glass rod about one-third of an inch thick, when the base of the portion thus cut off is ground smooth. Be it observed, however, that it is not *every* piece which shows it. By bringing this at a proper distance between the eye and a taper, as above described, a ring of light is seen, in the midst of whose periphery the flame of the candle will be placed. In crystals, a perfectly formed parhelion is very seldom seen.

Babinet attributed these appearances to the filamentous structure and the corresponding laminated transits of the crystal. Volger called attention to the fact, that very often it is the various faces of a twin formation which cause this coruscation, and that the star-like appearance in a ribbed or striped outer crystalline surface changes when the said surface is polished and then again looked through. "But," observes von Kobell, "neither of them makes any mention of the researches which Brewster, contemporaneously with Babinet, made in the matter, by experimenting with surfaces naturally corroded, as well as with those whose inner structure was made available for the purpose, either by a slight artificial corrosion or by roughening the surface of the crystals by means of friction."

Brewster observed, that when he used water, muriatic acid, nitric acid, etc., as a corrosive, the figures changed according to the corrosive used. When, however, the surface of the crystal was prepared, by rubbing on a stone or by means of a file, similar figures were produced, but not clearly and distinctly formed; and, what was most extraordinary they appeared in a position directly the reverse of those produced by corrosion.

Brewster examined minutely crystals of the cubic, pyramidal, and hexagonal systems only; with those of the rhombic and the klinic systems he could obtain no determined results by means of artificial corrosion.

It may be well here to give a few hints as to the method to be observed when experimenting with crystals whose surfaces are to be thus etched. An essential necessity is that such surfaces be smooth and polished, and that a beginning be made with only a *slightly* corroding power. For salts easily soluble in water, Prof. von Kobell adopted the following mode of procedure. He wetted a piece of woollen cloth (broadcloth) with water, leaving one part of it dry; then laying the crystal evenly on this dry part, he glided it forwards to the part which was damp and back again immediately. This was repeated according to circumstances. The crystal should be held by the thumb and forefinger of each hand close to the taper, and low down, in order that the rays may fall upon it as perpendicularly as possible. The eye is to be brought as close to it as may be, and the crystal then slowly turned till the appearance of the reflection of the light be clearly seen on its surface. It will be well to have a sheet of dark paper on the table, at the spot where you hold the crystal.

If the transparency of the crystal allows the observation of transmitted light, it may then be held between thumb and finger close to the eye, and the flame of the taper gazed at through it. A side-light is to be carefully guarded against; it may be remarked, too, that the bright figure is generally seen distinctly when you stand two or three or more steps distant from the candle. In judging of the figure thus seen, you must not forget to observe whether only *one* surface has been etched, or its parallel also; for the latter will often give the figure of the former reversed. Thus, for example, if three radiating lines of light are seen when one surface has undergone corrosion, a star with six rays would be observed, should the parallel surface have also been etched.

Such figures are most easily observed in, and produced by, alum. If a damp piece of cloth be passed once or twice over the smooth surface of an octahedron, and it then be wiped with a dry one, a three-rayed star at once appears. If wetted thus several times, then a change takes place in the central part, and three additional short lines of light appear in the space between the rays. The star, however, will be instantly turned into one with six rays of light, if the surface of the crystal be wetted in the manner described above, with a solution of muriatic or nitric acid. If again wetted with pure water and dried on a bit of cloth, the six-rayed star instantly changes back into one with three rays. Brewster also asserts that such an etched or corroded surface on which a number of little triangular forms are observed, may be restored to its original perfect state by dipping the crystal into a solution of alum.   To use his own words, " The singular fact in this experiment is the inconceivable rapidity with which the particles in the solution fly into their proper places upon the disintegrated surface, and become a permanent portion of the solid crystal."

Von Kobell made the above experiment, without, however, obtaining the same result as Brewster.   But the further he went in his investigations, the more wonderful and inexplicable were the revelations that unfolded themselves.   The existence of certain infinitesimal combinations became evident, which it is as impossible for the human mind even to comprehend, as it is for science to follow or to fathom.   In one such crystal is enlocked a world of wonders.   Subtle powers are there at work, elementary changes going on, of which, as yet, we have not the slightest, the remotest conception ; immutable laws are there governing, whose existence we have no knowledge of, and whose manifold bearings our bounded understanding would be quite inadequate to grasp. And the more we discover on this particular field, the more are we inclined to start back in bewilderment at the boundlessness of the horizon which opens before us.

Well may von Kobell observe, that " theoretic crystallography stands here, as it were, before a mirror, which shows all the difficulties and riddles which must be conquered and solved, — riddles which, as yet, it seems, will never be brought to a solution."   And he further quotes what Brewster once expressed when writing on the subject : " In whatever way crystallographers shall succeed in accounting for the various secondary forms of crystals, they are then only on the threshold of their subject.   The real constitution of crystals would be still unknown ; and though the examination of these bodies has been pretty diligently pursued, we can at this moment form no adequate idea of the complex and beautiful organization of these apparently simple structures."

One of the discoveries which Professor von Kobell made gives us some insight into the marvels of this organization ; not, however, explanatory of it, but showing us, behind newly-discovered wonders, others half-hidden, receding with systematic order into absolute infinity.

He discovered, namely, that the luminous appearances in calcareous spar are quite different when the surface of the crystal is disintegrated by means of nitric acid from those when muriatic acid is employed. And what is very extraordinary is, that when the corrosion is produced by muriatic acid, a shining figure is called into existence, regularly formed of *straight* lines ; but when nitric acid is used to corrode the polished face of the crystal, then it is *elliptic* figures — offshoots like tendrils — which show themselves.   Here then, we have, in addition to the final phenomena, the fact that the molecular construction of the crystal is affected by one acid only in one direction, and by another in a direction quite different.   How marvellous the combination of the atoms,—admitting now a channel between them, and now closing it hermetically against the intruding acid !   What a strange secret of affinities and alienation does this disclose of qualities and powers that we cannot even conceive of ?   On a hexagonal prism of calcareous spar, when the surface is subjected to the corrosive influence of muriatic acid, a luminous figure appears, resembling the hilt of an ancient sword.

Without going into further detail, what has been here described will sufficiently show how interesting the results are which have been obtained by the different experiments. Prof. von Kobell has named these beautiful luminous appearances after their first discoverer, our illustrious countryman, Brewster. He calls them "Brewster'sche Licht-figuren," which may most fitly be rendered by "Brewsterian Light Figures."

THE COMPOSITION OF LIGHT AND THE LAW OF HARMONIOUS COLORING.

In a work published some time since, on "Chromotography," by Mr. Field of London, the author has described an experiment by means of which he considers he has determined the proportion of colored rays which constitutes white or solar light. The problem, the solution of which Mr. Field has attempted, is admitted to be one of the most delicate and unmanageable in the domain of physical science, and philosophers who have instituted experiments and speculated on the subject — from Newton, in former days, to Brewster and Herschel, in our own time — have felt and confessed the difficulties which beset the inquiry. It is well known that Newton, from his famous experiment with the prism, concluded that white or solar light is composed of seven colors of different refrangibility, which he named violet, indigo, blue, green, yellow, orange, and red. He also measured the size of the variously-colored portions of the spectrum, in order to ascertain the amount of colored light in the sunbeam. Should we admit with Newton that white light is made up of no fewer than seven parts, still the difficulty of measuring the colored spaces of the spectrum is great, if, indeed, the task be not quite a hopeless one. It is hardly possible to find two persons who see so nearly alike that they can agree as to where one color ends and the next begins, and thus no two estimates of the colored spaces are likely to be the same. A notable instance of variance is afforded in the values assigned to the spaces by Newton and Fraunhofer. While they are at one in their opinion of the size of the orange and indigo spaces, the former finds the yellow and violet to be in the ratio of 40 and 80, whereas the latter assigns them the very different ratio of 27 and 109. No subsequent observer has ventured to alter either estimate, and no one who is familiar with the spectrum will put much faith in any measurement of it, by whomsoever or with what care soever it may have been made.

Another analysis of light was afterwards made by Dr. Wollaston, a high authority in optical questions. As he employed a narrow beam of light, he obtained a spectrum which consisted apparently of only four colors, namely, red, green, blue, and violet; and on dividing the space occupied by the spectrum into 100 equal parts, he found these colors to occupy respectively 16, 23, 36, and 25 of the divisions. A single narrow band of yellow, dividing the red from the green space, was all he could detect, and he hastily concluded that this color was merely a mixture of red and green, and consequently not a primary and important element in the composition of light. This statement of Wollaston's analysis shows how widely the observations of this observer differed from those of Newton.

An important step in the analysis of light was made by Sir David Brewster when he showed that, by looking at the spectrum through absorbing media of different colors, it is seen to consist neither of seven colors as Newton believed, nor of four as Wollaston alleged, but of three spectra — red, yellow, and blue, which have equal lengths but varying intensities, superposed on one another. Beyond this conclusion, however, Brewster did not go; and he certainly does not hazard an estimate of the *quanti'y* of red, yellow, and blue rays present in solar light. It is true that in accounting for the presence of the white light which becomes visible at any point of the spectrum when a sufficient amount of the colored light at that point has been absorbed, he conjectures that there is a combination of some definite proportion of red, yellow, and blue rays which forms the white light. He conjectures, for example, that if we admit the intensity of white light to be 10, this intensity may result from the combination of three rays of red, five yellow, and two of blue. These numbers are given, be it observed, merely by way of example; and the great master of experimental optics who gives them is too profoundly versed in his science to imagine for a moment that he has attained such knowledge of light as to express in numbers the amount of its constituent elements. The preceding hypothesis was given upwards of thirty years ago in more than one article on the New Analysis of Light, and that the author has not changed his views in the interim is proved by his employing, in the last edition of the *Encyclopædia Britannica*, precisely the same words in elucidating the subject.

A consideration of the difference in the views of Newton, Wollaston, and Brewster ought to convince every one of the extreme difficulty — to say the very least of it — of determining the amount of colored rays which compose the sunbeam. Mr. Field offers a solution of the question that professes an accuracy to which no one of the three now given lays any claim. His analysis so far agrees with that of Brewster as to give red, yellow, and blue as the constituents of light, but it differs from it inasmuch as it assigns definite numerical proportions to these colors. White light, Mr. Field says, is composed of red, yellow and blue colors, in the proportion of five, three, and eight respectively. This, it will be seen, differs wholly from the hypothesis of Brewster, in which is assigned a proportion of three, five, and two to the same rays.

Mr. Field's analysis of light does not appear to have found favor with scientists, but the practical art of ornamental coloring has very generally been inclined to adopt it. Thus Mr. Owen Jones, in his *Grammar of Ornament*, states his first law of importance, as follows, " The primary colors of equal intensities will harmonize with or neutralize each other in the proportion of three yellow, five red, and eight blue," etc. The same law is also given in the short handbook on Harmony of Color issued at the Kensington School of Art, — apparently with the sanction of government, — and widely circulated among the art-students of the Kingdom. — *London Athenæum.*

CURIOUS SPECULATIONS ON THE NATURE OF LIGHT.

The following curious speculations on the nature of light are put forth by Mr. B. S. Barnard, in the London *Photograph News* : —

" ' As white as fine linen,' ' as white as snow,' are frequent comparisons; but they are all dull examples as compared to many chemical precipitates. Precipitated chalk far outshines the natural varieties, and fine qualities of magnesia carbonate surpass this. Microscopic examination indicates that this latter consists of particles, clear and colorless, but very minute. White lead consists of particles equally minute and also transparent, but of a yellow-brown color by transmitted light; consequently, when seen in bulk it appears of a less pure white. But magnesia cannot be used as a pigment because it possesses no body; and the difference between the white lead and the magnesia in this respect depends upon the different refractive powers of the individual particles which compose the separate powders. They are both transparent in their individual particles, but the magnesia is more so. They are both bodies possessed of considerable refractive power, but the lead is more so. When air intervenes between their particles the reflective power of both so much exceeds that of air, that they are highly reflecting and very slightly transmitting; but the less absorbing power of the magnesia makes it the whitest, the more reflecting of the two. But when oil intervenes, as would be the case if they were used for pigments, the refractive power of the magnesia so nearly coincides with that of the oil, that much transmission and little reflection is the result, and this constitutes what painters call want of body. But the lead so greatly exceeds the oil in refracting power that its reflective property is not much interfered with, and even with its greater absorbing power it reflects much and transmits little light; and this is what painters call great body.

"The length of an undulation of violet light is seventeen millionths of an inch; the red undulation is twenty-six millionths; undulations longer or shorter than these not being visible. Again, the length of the light wave varies in the medium. An undulation in air measuring four will measure only two and a half when it enters glass, and will again elongate to its former measure on its exit. When an undulation passes from air into water, or into the humors of the eye, it likewise becomes shortened. If we say that luminous undulations, which in air measure twenty-two millionths of an inch, look yellow when they enter the eye (that being the wave length belonging to what we call yellow light), we must also remember that they measure one-third less in that organ in consequence of its refracting power. We then come to the singular conclusion that the blue sky is yellow, sunshine is red, and the rosy tints of evening are not luminous at all till they enter the eye. If the color depends upon the length of the light wave, and the length of the wave depends upon the refracting power of the medium through which it is passing, every beam of light changes color; red it may be on passing through the region of the stars, yellow or green it may be when it enters our earth's atmosphere, blue or violet when it enters water, non-luminous as it passes through glass. But if light, which we perceive as violet while it exists in the aqueous humor of the eye, was red originally, what color must that light be which we perceive is red? Its undulations in air must be too long to be luminous at all. This introduces us to the solemn thought that all this vast universe is dark! Light only exists in the eye. It is only a sensation, a perception of that which in nature exists as a force capable of producing a sensation."

NEW METHOD OF PROPAGATING LIGHT.

"A New Mode of Propagating Light" is the title of a note lately read by M. Babinet at a meeting of the Academy of Sciences at Paris, in which he treats of the regular luminous waves which result from a network or streaked surface placed in the path of a luminous band. From this proceed many spectra of great brilliancy, anterior and posterior, the origin of which cannot be derived either from propagation in a straight line, or from reflection, refraction, or diffraction. The very regular wave from the network borrows each of its elements from the waves which successively arrive at the network, and thereby obtains characters quite exclusive. The compensation in the celebrated experiment of Arago, which, according to Fresnel, prevents the influence of the motion of the earth from becoming sensible in the phenomena of the prism, has no place in regard to the network; and M. Babinet concludes that, by substituting the network for the prism, we shall be able to render sensible that influence, so long and so unsuccessfully sought for by Fresnel and himself.

COLOR OF WATER.

The color of water has been frequently discussed by physicists. Arago said, "The reflected color of water is blue, and the transmitted color is green;" and explained "the green color of the waves by considering them as prisms of water, of which one of the faces reflects white light, which is refracted by the following wave, and thus goes forth green." Bunsen asserts that water chemically pure is not colorless, but is of a pure blue color. M. Wettstein, after minute chemical researches, states that the green color is due to the presence of organic matters. M. Beetz has recently investigated the subject, and records his interesting observations in the *Bibliothèque Universelle* of Geneva, the results of which are opposed to the conclusion of Arago, and favor the opinion of Wettstein that the color is due to minute particles of matter suspended in the water, modified by the color of the sky and surrounding objects.

THE GREAT FOUCAULT TELESCOPE.

M. Léon Foucault has laid before the French Academy an account of the great telescope constructed upon his principle for the Observatory, at Paris. He observes that his efforts to obtain large instruments with reflectors of silvered glass could not be deemed completely successful until he had reached dimensions exceeding those of the largest achromatic objectives, and that it was only by way of establishing a claim to the recognition of his plans that he announced the formation of mirrors of 10, 20, and 40 centimetres in diameter. Now, he is able to speak of one nearly 80 centimetres in diameter, having a focal length of $4\frac{1}{2}$ metres,[1] which has been completed in the establishment of M. Secrétan. This mirror, mounted in a Newtonian telescope, has been at work for some months, at the Observatory, performing to the entire satisfaction of the director, M. Chacornac.

---

[1] The metre is 39.3779 inches; the centimetre 0.3937 of an inch.

CURIOUS OPTICAL ILLUSION — ARTIFICIAL GHOSTS.

An interesting optical phenomenon, namely, the production of spectral apparitions, or ghosts, has been recently devised by Professor Pepper, of the Polytechnic Institution, London, and most successfully and practically applied in theatrical exhibitions.

The manner in which the illusion is used for effect, in a theatrical play, may be stated as follows : —

An actor in the character of a murderer is seen asleep on a lounge in the rear of the stage, which is dimly lighted. Presently he rises in his sleep and begins to rave under the tortures of remorse for his crime. Instantly there appears at his side a bright image of a skeleton, so luminous that it sheds some light upon the obscurity around. Though startlingly distinct, it is seen to be only the image of a skeleton, as objects on the stage are visible directly through the bones. The murderer strikes his sword through the grizzly horror, but it is as impalpable as air. After a brief space the apparition vanishes as suddenly as it came. It makes no movement up or down or to either hand, but simply disappears, the whole effect being so perfect, that the spectator can hardly bring himself to realize that he is really the subject of a deception.

The scientific explanation of the phenomena may be thus stated : —

When any one looks into a glass or metallic mirror, he sees an image or ghost of himself. If his neighbor looks over his shoulder he, too, sees the same ghost. What gives this business of ghost-making its chief mystery is the plan of concealing adroitly the person or object who or which is to be ghostified, and showing only the image or ghost, and thus snapping the otherwise palpable connection between the true object, animate or inanimate, and its picture or representation. If a plain metallic or silvered glass mirror only were employed in producing the ghost, a child would not be startled at the effects produced, however completely the original object might be concealed from view ; but it is otherwise, and all are surprised, when an image or ghost is called up before the observer without any apparent connection with mirror action at all.

Now, without going into the questions in optical science respecting the reflection of light from plane surfaces, the formation of images by plane mirrors, or of multiple images formed by glass mirrors, we may remark that metallic mirrors have but one reflecting surface, giving only one image of an object. With glass mirrors this is different. They give rise to several images which are readily observed when the image of a candle is looked at obliquely in a common looking-glass. A very feeble image of a candle is seen, and then a very distinct one. Behind this there are several others, whose intensity or clearness gradually decreases until it disappears. This phenomenon or appearance arises from the looking-glass having two reflecting surfaces, — that of the face of the plate, and that of the layer of metal which covers the hinder surface of the glass. The greater feebleness of the image reflected from the glass than from the metal surface arises from the circumstance that metal reflects better than glass. It completely intercepts the light reflected from the original object, and throws it back to the eye.

In ghost-making, a plate of clear glass is placed between the observers and where the ghost is made to appear; and what is seen as the ghost is nothing more than the feeble image of a true object, produced by reflection from the surface of the plate. But the ghost, when well shown, is an intensely vivid image, the very reverse of feeble; and the question is, How is the intensification of an originally feeble image effected? It is effected by greatly reducing or extinguishing all other lights, and by concentrating an intense light on the original object, and thus greatly increasing the reflecting power of the clear glass plate, and by at the same time forming a dark background behind the plate, which further assists in throwing out the image or ghost to the eye of the spectator. All this is quite a common occurrence in the shop-windows along the streets, and perhaps still better shown in a lighted railway-carriage at night. The ghosts of the passengers in the carriage are shown through the carriage windows upon the apparent ground of the dark sky, and the carriage lamp, from its being the most luminous object, presents the most vivid ghost of all.

As applied to theatrical performances the arrangements for the representation of a ghost are substantially as follows: Upon the stage of the theatre is placed a large plate of glass, inclined at an angle toward the person or object that is to be "ghostified." The audience does not always perceive this, because the stage is darkened, and because objects behind the glass may be seen through it. In front of this glass is a large trap, opening beneath the stage, and forming a square enclosure; this is lined with black cloth. The person whose ghost is to be represented stands in a sloping position against the back of this place, and a strong light is thrown upon his figure from a lamp placed opposite. Now the image of the object is reflected from the glass plate to the audience, and this image is seen by them to be as far behind the plate as the true object is placed in advance of it. The light used to illuminate the person should be very powerful, as the "lime," or Drummond light, though a good argand burner with a reflector will answer. The ghost is seen to be illuminated from below up, and this comes of placing the lamp low and throwing the light on the true object upwards. A white, lustrous dress given to a female personating the ghost exalts the effect.

All the room-lights are in the mean time reduced, otherwise the audience also, as in the case of the passengers in the railway-carriage, would be converted into ghosts. As much light, and no more, is left on the stage as admits of the actors on it being seen. These performers see no ghost; all their movements are calculated as to place and time. The ghost placed on the stage, so far as the adaptations of this illusion have yet gone, is fixed; a hand or part of the body may be moved, but not the whole, beyond a very small distance.

Ghost-making, according to the above device of Prof. Pepper, can be applied for social, as well as theatrical entertainment, and the simplicity of the apparatus employed for the production of the many illusions of which this arrangement is capable will doubtless henceforth furnish a fruitful source of amusement.

The introduction in London of the above-described optical arrangement into theatrical performances, for the production of ghostly images, gave rise to a lawsuit of an interesting character. The device in question proving profitable as an adjunct to the theatre, a patent was applied for by Prof. Pepper; the issue of which was strenuously opposed by competing exhibitors; to compass their ends, the latter lodged objections against the issuing of the patent, just before it was to receive the Great Seal, and the provisional patentee was allowed one month to answer the objections. The trial of "the ghost" came off before the Lord Chancellor, and distinguished counsel appeared for both parties. Mr. Bower, for the objectors, against Prof. Pepper, put in several affidavits to the effect that "the ghost" was somewhat of an antiquated personage, that he was well known to several public characters, and could not be justly claimed as the exclusive property of Prof. Pepper. It was averred that a respectable spectre was shown in London in 1845, by Herr Dohler, the celebrated conjurer, and that it made the tour of the whole country with him. Other evidence of a similar nature was also produced; and in the course of the arguments on the subject, the Lord Chancellor himself stated that he had seen a ghost, fifty-five years before, exhibited by the celebrated Belzoni. Upon the other side, however, evidence was put in, from no less scientific personages than Prof. Wheatstone and Sir David Brewster, to the effect that the invention was new; and the Lord Chancellor hearing both sides fully, came to the conclusion that the ghost in question was a new ghost, and accordingly gave judgment for the defendant, Prof. Pepper.

That Prof. Pepper's plan of producing spectral appearances is, however, a very old affair, seems to be proved by the following extract from a work written by John Baptista de Porta, in 1558, upon "Natural Magick"; and translated into English in 1582.

It says: "How we may see in a chamber things that are not — I thought this an artifice not to be despised; for we may in any chamber, if a man look in, see those things which were never there; and there is no man so witty that will think he is mistaken: Wherefore to describe the matter. — Let there be a chamber whereinto no other light cometh unless by the door or window where the spectator looks in; let the whole window or part of it be of glass, as we used so to do to keep out the cold; but let one part be polished, that there may be a looking-glass on both sides, whence the spectator must look in; for the rest do nothing. Let pictures be set over against this window, marble statues and such like; for what is without will seem within, and what is behind the spectator's back he will think to be in the middle of the house, as far from the glass inward as they stand from it outwardly, and so clearly and certainly that he would think he sees nothing but truth. But lest the skill should be known, let the part be made so where the ornament is that the spectator may not see it, as above his head, that a pavement may not come between above his head; and, if an ingenious man do this, it is impossible that he should suppose that he is deceived."

PHOTOGRAPHY IN CONNECTION WITH ART.

The following is an abstract of a lecture on the above subject, recently read before the Cornwall Polytechnic Society, of England, by Col. Wortley: The lecturer began by alluding to photographic portraiture, as carried on in the present day; and asked his hearers to disabuse their minds of a common error into which most people fall, namely, that a photograph, because it is taken as it were by machinery, must necessarily be a likeness. He stated that this was not the case, and for the following reasons: "The photograph portrait lens is not a perfect instrument, and of necessity magnifies the objects that are nearest to it, and makes them out of proportion with those situated in a plane somewhat further from the instrument. To prove this, you have only to look over any collection of photographic portraits, and you will at once see that the hands or feet, or any object prominently brought forward, are larger than they should be, to be in due proportion. This defect, of course more visible in the case of a hand, foot, or other large object, alters the *proportion*, and indeed the *expression*, of a sitter's head and face. If, then, in posing a sitter, you allow the chin to be elevated, or brought forward, it is of course appreciably magnified; and the forehead and eyes, being thrown back at the same time, are diminished, and a coarse, foolish expression given to a face that may be full of intelligence and refinement of feature. This defect is of course much greater in a cheap, bad lens than in one by any of the best makers; though it is one that can easily be guarded against."

Entering on a wider field, the lecturer then alluded to the true difficulty in photographic portraiture, — that of being able to give a pleasing and natural *pose* to a sitter. "You have," said he, "probably the pictures of many ladies in your respective albums. Now, how many of those photographs do the ladies justice? Do any? Are not the majority atrocious libels? In how many of the positions selected by the photographer would a portrait-painter have placed his sitter? It appears singular that such an utter want of artistic feeling and taste should be shown in the majority of photographic portraits; but such is undeniably the case. It is not the want of color in a photograph that makes it so unsatisfactory. You must all of you have come across, occasionally, most charming portraits in monochrome, chalk, and crayon drawings, in sepia, and even with pencil and pen and ink, and occasionally a photograph." The lecturer then inquires why the good photograph is the exception and not the rule? "In many cases, the professional photographer has taken up photography as a profession, and so long as he makes it pay he is content. He does it by machinery. He has no knowledge of art, no feeling for the beautiful, and in many cases, as any one can see, is entirely ignorant of the optical properties of his lenses. And the amateur, — he takes to photography because it is so nice to be able to get pictures of all one's friends! He gets *photographs* of them certainly, but between photographs and pictures there is a wide chasm, bridged by a narrow plank, across which not many of our amateur portraitists have yet walked, and as few of our professionals."

The following counsel was then given as to portrait photography:— It was recommended to adopt the style of taking the head and shoulders only, making the head about the size of a shilling, and carefully vignetting it, using always a plain background, varying the color of the latter according to the color of the sitter's hair, dress, etc. Then, directing attention to landscape photography, — a branch of the art more practised by amateurs, but requiring on their part more knowledge of high art, more feeling for all that is beautiful and glorious in nature, and more perseverance and hard work before they can attain to eminence, — Col. Wortley said: "I maintain that the highest art, the purest taste, is shown in the most scrupulously faithful transcript from nature itself; because nothing, and no imaginary form or coloring, can equal, or, I might indeed say, approach in beauty what we, if we care to look for it, and know how to find it, can find for ourselves in nature. And it is preëminently this earnest desire to seek for and discover the beauties of nature, and the knowledge of how and where to find them that distinguish the artist from the mere painter or photographer. . . . If you aim at art in photography, you must study nature, and you must give as faithful a transcript of nature as you can.   Suppose a painter were to say, ' Well, I cannot be at the trouble to do skies or clouds to my landscapes; people must be content with carefully painted fore-grounds,' what should we think of that individual? who would look at his pictures? what would the photographer himself say to them? Then, what does he imagine artists, and all who have a feeling for and a love of nature, think of his photographs?   I hold all such productions to be unfaithful to nature and untrue to art.

" But in addition to the real feeling for the beautiful, some *knowledge* is desirable, some study of the works of celebrated painters, in order to know how to combine the various beauties of nature.   To give an illustration of my meaning:— A view may be very beautiful from a certain point, but it might happen that, by moving two or three yards one way or the other, you may make exactly the same view more available, as a picture, by including some object for the foreground, such as a mass of rock, an old gate, the trunk of a tree, or any object that may happen to be within reach.

" There are many other branches of photography to which I might call your attention, — the copying of pictures, photolithography and its various processes, and composition photography.   But I am anxious to confine myself to photography in connection with its claims to be considered as a fine art.   Composition photography, more than any other, shows how difficult it is to attain really artistic results in photography, and shows most forcibly the weak points of photography in its claims to the rank of a fine art.   Wonderful results may be achieved considering the means at our disposal, but the insurmountable difficulty of controlling the sitter's expression of face, not to mention other minor difficulties, will always prevent that class of photography from rising beyond a certain level, and will always remind us that photography has much that is mechanical, and that it is necessary to obtain far greater rapidity than any process at present possesses, before composition photography can worthily assist in claiming for photography in general the dignity of a fine art.   In conclusion I should strongly recommend an amateur to adopt a rapid process, so as never to have any difficulty in getting life into his pictures.   A man in the foreground, a cow, a wagon, and team, give life and reality to a photograph, and are often of the utmost value, and even necessity to the composition of a picture.   In the present state of photography, with the minutiæ of the processes carefully laid down by experienced photographers, two or three months' hard study should make any lover of nature and art an accomplished photographer; and if he knows somewhat of chemistry, or studies it a little at the same time, so much the better. . . . I am confident that, by photography, pictures are to be obtained far superior to anything else ever produced in monochrome; and any one can obtain these by study, always allowing that they have the feeling and taste for nature and art

10*

to begin with as a foundation; and people will soon begin to see that, in the rendering of the effects of nature, photography has in many cases no equal. Artists will take it up, and make it the handmaid to painting; and, with its truthful power and delicate sensitiveness, it can be of the greatest assistance to them; for whatever effects may be chosen as subjects for painting, nature, in the first instance, must be taken as the guide; photography can imitate nature as *truthfully* as it is possible without color, and truth is everything."

WHO DISCOVERED PHOTOGRAPHY?

The taking of permanent photographic pictures is generally considered to date back only to the year 1839, when Daguerre, in Paris, and Fox Talbot, in England, made public their results. Some recent investigations in England have, however, rendered it probable that the art was in fact discovered and practically applied by Mathew Boulton, (the partner of James Watt), and others, as long ago as the close of the last century, and was then allowed to fall into neglect and to become "lost." The circumstances of this discovery were thus related by Mr. Smith, curator of the Kensington Museum of Patents, at a late meeting of the London Photographic Society: —

For purposes connected with his department, Mr. Smith had occasion to visit an old house at Soho, near Birmingham, where the renowned engineering establishment of Watt and Boulton was originally founded. This house appears to have been occupied by Boulton, and it was also the place where a "secret" scientific society, called the "Lunar-Society," was accustomed to meet. This society included among its members the chief scientific men of its day, and was accustomed to meet on the night of every full moon, for discussion and experimentation. It may also be remarked, that experiments with a view of producing "sun-pictures" are no very modern affair. The camera was invented more than three hundred years ago, and the influence of light on the salts of silver was known as early as the sixteenth century. But those investigators who recorded the result of their labors, only chronicled a succession of failures in their endeavors to render permanent the pictures obtained; the latest confession of failures in the essential part of the process being that made by Davy, in 1802.

Boulton died in 1809, but his library and contents remained undisturbed in the old house at Soho, until very recently; when, in the course of clearing out, and whilst removing a vast collection of documents, there were found a number of crumpled and folded sheets of paper with pictures on them of the most puzzling kind. On smoothing out these pictures, they were found to consist of copies, on large sheets of very coarse paper, of certain well-known designs by Kauffmann — the porous water-marked paper being thickly coated with some varnish-like substance, on the surface of which the picture had been produced. All the sheets found in the library, as well as others subsequently discovered, presented the same characters, — a glossy surface with minute varnish-like cracks, the drawing of the figures most elaborately finished, the lights and shades so fully rendered as to give much the effect of a mezzotint, and an invariable reversal of the position of the figures, so that all the nymphs and cupids (Kauffmann's pet subjects) appeared to be left-handed. These paper pictures were sent to London and submitted to the best authorities on drawing and painting; and here the mystery about them begins; for they were pronounced to have been produced by some process entirely different from anything previously seen, and certainly not to have been done by hand. This led to immediate search being made for any more of the pictures that might exist, and also to inquiries among the oldest inhabitants, for any one who had lived at Soho in the time of Boulton, and could supply any information about them.

In a broker's shop were found several more of the pictures, which had been bought from the house at Soho as waste paper. One of these represented a large figure-picture by West, and was on two sheets of paper, each about two feet by eighteen inches, intricately cut at the joining-place so that the line of union might fall at the edge of a shadow, and not be perceived when the two halves were put together to form the complete picture. Further research at Soho also led to the discovery of a couple of silvered-metal plates, each about the size of a sheet of note-paper, precisely resembling in appearance those used by Daguerre in the early days of photography. On each of these plates was a faint image of the house at Soho, so unmistakably taken from nature, and so evidently produced by the aid of light, that all experts of any authority at once pronounced them to be photographed pictures taken directly by means of a camera. Attached to these plates was a memorandum stating that they were sun-pictures representing the house prior to certain alterations made in 1791. Following out their search as to the means by which these pictures were produced, the investigators learnt that there had once been found a camera in Boulton's library, answering in description to the kind of instrument required for plates of this size. Not very long ago, there was living an old man who had for many years been employed at Soho, and who related how the wise men used to come there at each full moon, and used to sit very late at night, and that he remembered Mr. Boulton and some of them once took a picture of the house, and had to go into a dark place during the process.

So far the evidence as to the metal plates, which, if substantiated, will go far to prove that the discoveries of Niepce and Daguerre were anticipated by Boulton. It may possibly prove more; for the resemblance between these plates and the productions of Daguerre is really marvellous if only accidental, and if no link be found to connect the two processes. But the further evidence already obtained as to the pictures on paper discovered at Soho presents quite a tangle of curious circumstances. From invoices and other office papers, all bearing date about the end of the last century, it is evident that these pictures, however produced, were actually sold at Soho in large quantities, and at low prices. The demand for them was great, and considerable pains appears to have been taken to prevent the method of their production becoming generally known. So there must exist a large number of them at the present time scattered through various collections and portfolios.

It appears that Sir William Beatty painted Boulton's portrait about 1794, the picture being subsequently exhibited at the Royal Academy. He was horrified on being shown a number of paper pictures similar to those recently discovered; and he got up a petition, signed by a number of artists, and presented either to or through the Lunar Society, entreating that the manufacture of these pictures might be stayed, as it would inevitably ruin the picture trade. A sort of foreman of Boulton's, named Edginton, appears to have superintended the production of these pictures, if he did not actually discover the process by which the transfer to paper was done. Several of his letters are extant referring to the subsequent coloring which some of the pictures underwent; none of them, however, afford any clew as to the original method of their production. But a little later, and after the alarm was taken by the artists, we find a talk of granting Edginton a government pension. This fell through because of a curious autograph letter of Matthew Boulton's which has been fortunately found. In this letter, officially addressed to the Minister, he claims for himself the discovery of the process on account of which Edginton's annuity had been contemplated; he intimates his knowledge that the grant was only intended to insure the discontinuance of the process, suggests that he could arrange this in a much more certain way, and concludes his letter with a strong hint that he is open to be dealt with. Whatever ensued as the result of this letter, it seems very clear that the production of the pictures was thenceforward discontinued.

Here the evidence comes to an end, so far as regards these curious paper pictures, and the silvered plates which the highest authorities refer to about the year 1791. In this same year, Thomas Wedgwood, son of the famous potter, was certainly at work on photography, as is shown by his bills and orders for apparatus and chemicals. At the meeting of the Photographic Society there was exhibited, side by side with the above-mentioned metal plates, a photograph of a neatly-laid breakfast-table taken upon paper by Wedgwood, and the information about it tended to the conclusion that it also was done in the year 1791.

Thus far, we have written the history of this curious discovery in accordance with the evidence laid before the Photographic Society; but still there are many links wanting before it can be taken as proved that the pictures found at Soho were produced by photography. If it shall be shown that they were so produced, then it will also be established that at that time photographic feats were done which we cannot nowadays accomplish. For it has been proved by chemical analysis that these pictures do not contain a trace of silver, and must therefore, if of photographic origin, have been produced by some process that has been lost to us. That an art promising such great results should have been suffered to die out, is in itself curious in these days of diffusion of knowledge; but still more remarkable is the double coincidence existing between the independently produced metal and paper photographs of Boulton and Wedgwood in 1791, and of Daguerre and Fox Talbot in 1839.

LUNAR PHOTOGRAPHS.

At a recent meeting of the New York Photographic Society, October, 1863, Dr. Henry Draper gave an account of some extensive arrangements made by him for the photographic delineation of celestial objects, and of the results he had already attained to in this department of science. He stated, that in the autumn of 1858, he " determined to make the largest reflecting telescope in America. Its construction, together with the various improvements successively added, has occupied me up to the present time, — more than five years. The instrument, which is nearly sixteen inches in aperture and thirteen feet in focal length, was intended to be devoted to celestial photography, and consequently contains many novelties especially fitting it for that purpose. It has now the largest silvered-reflector of any instrument in the world except that in the Observatory at Paris." " The reflecting telescope," said Dr. Draper, "is greatly superior to the achromatic for photographic purposes. In my instrument, a movement of the sensitive plate, one-hundredth of an inch on either side of the true focus, visibly injures the image. In the great achromatic at Cambridge, on the contrary, the position of the plate may be varied over an inch without any noticeable change. The difference is simply that, while by reflection the visual and chemical rays both converge to the same focus, by refraction they do not. A sensitive plate, put where the eye sees the image sharply, produces a fine result in a reflecting telescope, but does not in an achromatic. Besides this, more light is reflected by a large silver mirror than an achromatic of equal size can transmit.

" At first, I used speculum metal for my mirrors, but abandoned it at Sir John Herschell's suggestion in favor of silvered glass, the reflecting power of the latter being ninety-three per cent., while that of the former is at the best but seventy-five per cent. A large achromatic only transmits about seventy-five per cent. The glass mirror, too, weighs not more than one-eighth as much as the metal one, the one weighing sixteen pounds, the other one hundred and twenty-eight pounds. It is also greatly more permanent; for if the silver coating which covers the glass concave should by chance be injured, it can be dissolved off easily with nitric acid, and the mirror re-silvered in an afternoon; and this may be repeated indefinitely. A person making such a silvered glass reflector is content to take the greatest pains to produce a glass concave of the utmost perfection, for when once it is obtained it need never be lost. The thin sheet of silver deposited upon it, only one two-hundred thousandth of an inch thick, copies with the last degree of accuracy the glass beneath, and does not modify the figure of the surface, but only increases the reflecting power from two or three per cent. up to more than ninety. This silver coating is transparent, and shows bright objects, such as the sun, of a light blue tint by transmitted light.

" As regards the degree of excellence that can be reached by such telescopes, I can only say that mine can show every object that other instruments of similar size do, and more too. I can see the 18th magnitude pair near β Capricorni, discovered by Herschell's eighteen and a half inch speculum; and in tests for sharpness of definition, it will separate the blue component of Andromeda with a power of four hundred, and the instrument, on a favorable night, will bear three times that power. It must not be supposed, however, that so excellent a result was obtained without labor. I have ground and polished more than a hundred mirrors, of sizes varying from nineteen inches to one-quarter of an inch in diameter.

" The mirror is sustained in a walnut tube hooped with brass and supported in a frame which holds the tube at both ends. This is to avoid the tremulous motions so common in large instruments. The eye-piece, or, what is the same thing, the place of the photographic plate, is stationary at all altitudes, and an observer has never to strain himself by awkward positions, but always looks straight forward. When photographs of the moon are taken, the telescope is not driven by clock-work, but is allowed to come to rest completely. The sensitive-plate alone is moved in a direction and at a rate to correspond with the moon's motion. The difference is, that instead of having to carry more than half a ton, the clock has only one ounce to move. Of course, there is no comparison between the precision of movement possible in the two cases.

"The observatory where the above-described instrument is erected, is at Hastings, Westchester County, N. Y., and is a building twenty feet square and twenty-two feet high, and is one-half excavated out of the solid rock, so as to keep the reflector at a uniform low temperature, and at the same time give steadiness and immobility to the telescope. It stands on a hill two hundred and fifty feet above the level of the sea. The photographic laboratory is attached to the observatory on the western side, only a few feet intervening between the telescope and developing sink. It contains all the requisite conveniences for taking photographs up to three feet in diameter, and is furnished with a tank which holds a ton of rain-water. This supply is procured from the roof of the buildings, which are on this account painted with a stone paint so as not to contaminate the water.

"This instrument," said Dr. Draper, "has been in working order for eighteen months, but a large part of the time has been unused because of my absence with the Twelfth Regiment in Virginia, and on account of professional duties. I have, however, taken some fine photographs during the past summer. Some changes have been made in the photographic processes commonly used, in order to fit the pictures for bearing high magnifying powers. I have negatives which can be enlarged by a power of thirty-two without showing granulation or other defects to an offensive degree. The photograph which I show you to-night is nearly two feet in diameter, and is magnified to two hundred and ten times the size of the moon, as seen by the naked eye. I have now another, however, still larger in my observatory, — nearly three feet in diameter, — made under a power of three hundred and twenty. It represents the moon on a scale of seventy miles to the inch. In the picture before you, attention should be directed particularly to the Apennine Range, Copernicus, with his reflecting streams, the great groove from Tycho, the numerous craters, with an internal cone, the irregularities visible in the bottom of the Mare Imbrium. But it is useless to particularize; there is an almost inexhaustible supply of objects for study and admiration.

"The Society will see that, although celestial photography may be, as yet, only in its infancy, it is rapidly advancing. Every day is giving origin to improvements, and even now the limit of size in these pictures is rather owing to the great expense and difficulty of working such enormous plates than to any intrinsic defect of the images to be copied."

Upon the conclusion of his paper, Dr. Draper exhibited a photographic view of the moon's surface, the singular distinctness and beauty of which took the audience quite by surprise. It was a view of the moon when about half full, and presented a semicircle of nearly two feet in diameter. The whole of this surface was pictured with great vividness, covered with long ranges of mountains, or dotted with huge volcanic summits into the depths of which one could look down. From one of these central points, the lava streams could be traced for some eight inches, which, as an inch in length in the picture corresponds to a hundred miles upon the moon's surface, afforded ocular evidence of volcanic agency through a line of eight hundred miles. From another, vast fissures were seen to radiate, which displayed evidence of convulsions reaching through an area of half that diameter. When it is considered that the largest photographs hitherto obtained of the moon are not more than from four to six inches in diameter, it will be perceived how great a triumph has been achieved by the science and skill which have been requisite for so great an improvement as a picture of twenty-two inches across.

Foreign Lunar Photographs. — Mr. De la Rue, of London, who has long been successfully experimenting in lunar photographs, has also recently succeeded in obtaining two of these images of our satellite, 39 inches (3¼ feet) in diameter, which he has exhibited to the French Academy.

THE DIOPTRIC AND ACTINIC QUALITIES OF THE ATMOSPHERE AT HIGH ELEVATIONS.

In a paper on the above subject, read before the British Association, 1863, by Professor Piazzi Smyth, he stated, that the chief object of the astronomical experiment on the Peak of Teneriffe in 1856 was to ascertain the degree of improvement of telescopic vision, when both telescope and observer were raised some two miles vertically in the air. Distinct accounts have, therefore, already been rendered as to the majority of clouds being found far below the observer at that height, and to the air there being dry, and in so steady a state and homogeneous a condition, that stars, when viewed in a powerful telescope with a high magnifying power, almost always presented clear and well-defined minute discs, surrounded with regularly-formed rings, — a state of things which is the very rare exception at our observatories near the sea-level. Quite recently, however, the author had been engaged in magnifying some of the photographs which he took in Teneriffe in 1856, at various elevations, and he finds in them an effect depending on height, which adds a remarkably independent confirmation to his conclusions from direct telescopic observations. The nature of the proof is on this wise : at or near the sea-level a photograph could never be made to show the detail on the side of a distant hill, no matter how marked the detail might really be by rocks and cliffs illuminated by strong sunlight ; even the application of a microscope brought out no other feature than one broad, faint, and nearly-uniform tint. But on applying the microscope to photographs of distant hills taken at a high level in the atmosphere, an abundance of minute detail appeared, and each little separate " retama " bush could be distinguished on a hill-side four and a half miles from the camera. Specimens of these photographs thus magnified have been introduced into the newly-published volume of the Edinburgh Astronomical Observations.

HELIOCHROMY.

It is well known that M. Niepce Saint-Victor of Paris, has for a long time occupied himself with the very interesting subject of the reproduction of colors by photography. Some time since he announced to the scientific world his success in obtaining red, blue, and green; but, at the same time, he confessed that to obtain a yellow tint in combination with others was a matter of extreme difficulty, if not, at that time, practically impossible to him. Of course, there was nothing at all surprising in this, as every one knows that yellow is most troublesome even in ordinary photography. Within the past year, however, he has announced to the French Academy, that he has at last succeeded in reproducing yellow tints by preparing his silver plates in a bath composed of hyperchloride of soda instead of potash, and he produced specimens which are said to hold out great expectation of complete success. He has not yet, however, succeeded in absolutely fixing the colors; they remain perfect so long as the plate is kept in the dark, but soon disappear when exposed to the light. But in this respect, also, M. Niepce has made important progress; for, by the application of gum benjamin as a varnish to the plate, he has managed to retain the colors for three or four days even when exposed to the full glare of a July sun. The recent memoir read before the Academy by M. Niepce contains much interesting matter. Amongst other things, he has discovered that all compound colors are decomposed by the heliochromic process. The examples given are highly interesting, — for instance, if a natural green, such as that of the emerald, of arsenite of copper, of oxide of chromium, sulphate of nickel, or carbonate of copper, be presented, it is reproduced on the plate; but, if the green be a compound formed, for instance, of chrome yellow and Prussian blue, that of a textile fabric dyed with a mixture of the two latter colors, or that produced on glass in a similar manner, it produces a blue color in whatever manner it is treated. Moreover, when transparent blue and yellow glasses are used, so as to produce a green, it matters not whether the blue be before or behind or placed between two glasses of the other color, the effect is invariably the same; no matter how long they are exposed to the light, the product is always blue. An orange effect produced by the combination of red and yellow glasses produces invariably red. A red and blue glass together produce at first a violet, because the plate itself is red; but the result is blue. White paper colored green by means of the recently-discovered Chinese green, made from the juice of the buckthorn, has but a sluggish action upon the heliochromic plate; but, after a long exposure to the light, a blue-gray is produced; and the same effect is obtained from foliage of a grass-green color in the camera; but bluish-green foliage, such as that of the leaves of the dahlia, produces a tint that is almost positive blue. The eye of a peacock's feather is well rendered in the camera, the tints appearing to vary between blue and green. Apart from photographic purposes, the experiments of M. Niepce Saint-Victor promise to be of considerable assistance in the analysis of the solar spectrum, for it is evident that his attempts to fix the colors of nature on a heliochromic plate go far to confirm the new theory which recognizes the existence of three, but not of the seven primitive colors; namely, violet, indigo, blue, green, yellow, orange and red.

NOVELTIES IN PHOTOGRAPHY.

Permanency of Photographs. — The Paris correspondent of *The Photographic News* (London) states that, at a late meeting of the Paris Photographic Society, M. Davanne presented two photographic pictures, on paper, which had been submitted to the test of exposure in two exhibitions (1861 and 1862), and which showed no signs of fading or alteration whatever. This, then, may be accepted as a satisfactory proof that photographs, when carefully prepared, are permanent ; for the pictures in question were submitted to the severest test to which photographs are ever likely to be exposed, the conditions being every variation of light, heat, moisture, etc., and they remain as fresh and pure as at first. It was also remarked that photographs are more liable to change when kept in a portfolio than under glass exposed to luminous action. A sulphurized proof, if kept in a perfectly dry place, remains for a very long time without exhibiting any signs of alteration, while in a damp place, change is immediately evident. Thus, a photograph carefully framed is much better sheltered from humidity than when kept in a portfolio.

Photographic Engraving. — The London *Athenæum*, under date of November 14th, 1863, states that it has recently seen a beautiful specimen of photoglyphic engraving on steel, — in other words, a photographic picture on steel, — effected solely by the agency of light acting on certain chemicals. The specimen (it is stated by Mr. Fox Talbot) is quite untouched. It represents an exquisite scene in Java, — a ravine and rivulet fringed with banana-trees. Not the least wonderful circumstance connected with it is, that at least 5,000 copies can be taken before the plate deteriorates. Such a result, after so many years of labor, must be, for Mr. Fox Talbot, a genuine triumph.

New Photographic Fixing Agent. — To fix photographic pictures, a solution of the hyposulphite of soda has been the common agent employed. In this, the picture is treated, and is thus prevented from changing. The London *Photographic News* asserts that the days of this agent in photography are numbered, and that sulphocyanide of ammonium will take its place as a superior agent, by the use of which a faded positive picture will be unknown. The original source of the cyanide of ammonium is the thick, tarry liquid remaining after the separation of the free ammonia from gas liquor: this has long been known to contain large quantities of sulphocyanide of ammonium, but hitherto all attempts to separate it from the impurities which accompany it have failed.

Photo-Lithography. — A communication has been recently made to the French Academy, by M. Morvan, in which he describes a new method for obtaining photographic impressions upon stone, and which he can afterward print off. He first applies a coating, in the dark, of a varnish composed of albumen and bichromate of ammonia. Upon this he lays the right side of the image to be reproduced, whether it be on glass, canvas, or paper, provided it be somewhat transparent. This done, he exposes the whole to the action of light for a space of time, varying between thirty seconds and three minutes, if in the sun, and between ten and twenty-five minutes, if in the shade. He then takes off the original

11

image, and washes his stone, first with soap and water, and then with pure water only, and immediately after inks it with the usual inking-roller. The image is already fixed, for it begins to show itself in black on a white ground. He now applies gum-water, lets the stone dry, which is done in a few minutes, and the operation is complete ; copies may at once be struck off by the common lithographic process. The process may be explained thus : The varnish has been fixed and rendered insoluble by the action of light wherever it could penetrate ; but, on the contrary, all the parts of the varnish protected by the dark portions of the image still retain their solubility, and are, therefore, still liable to be acted upon by the soda and acid contained in the soap, of which they moreover retain a part of the substance. Hence the action produced on the stone is a combination of etching and lithography. The advantages of the process may be briefly summed up as follows : Simplicity and rapidity in the operation, exactness in reproducing the design, no need of negative impressions on glass or paper, the positive original comes out positive, the original design or model is not spoiled during the process, and the cost is trifling, owing to the cheapness of the substances.

Material for Photographic Lenses. — M. Gaudin states that rock-crystal is the best material for photographic lenses, on account of its permitting the passage of the largest quantity of actinic rays. The editor of *Cosmos* observes : " It is evident that a transparent substance which gives a passage of the greatest quantity of the violet and extra violet rays, would be best adapted to the construction of active lenses."

Photography for Book Illustration. — With the cheapening and perfecting of photographic processes, the use of photographs for embellishing and illustrating the text of books, etc., in the place of lithographic prints or engravings, is daily becoming more and more extensive. The following are some of the more important works which have been recently issued, in which photographs constitute a special feature.

Atlas of the Peripheral Nervous System of the Human Body by Ruedinger, photographed from nature by Joseph Albert, folio ; Cotta, Munich.

Atlas of the General Description of the Animal Tissues, published by Theodore von Hessling and Jul. Kollmann. Photographed from nature by J. Albert, Munich, 42 plates in 4 numbers ; Engelmann, Leipsic.

Heeger Ernst, an album of photographed microscopic representations from the kingdom of Zoölogy, 1 and 2 parts large Lex : (each containing 15 photographs and 18 pages of text) (Gerold's Son). Vienna.

Still later Cotta, in Stuttgart, has published a splendid edition of Schiller's Poems with photographs of original drawings by different artists. Besides these alluded to, photographic embellishments have been introduced into several journals ; as in a work by Baron Helfert on the exhibition of articles of instruction from Austria, as well as in the Vienna Journal of Fashion.

But it is not photography alone that has been thus applied ; we know now that lithographs are prepared directly from photographs and extensively applied to the illustration of works. Although photolithography can simply reproduce line drawings with accuracy, yet this branch can and will be applied in various ways in the copying of letters, as, for instance, in Schiller's Life, and in the reproduction of maps (in England and Austria).

In London, Scott's *Lady of the Lake* has also recently been published, with photograph illustrations from nature of many of the picturesque scenes alluded to in the poem.

TRANSFERRING PHOTOGRAPHIC PICTURES TO PORCELAIN AND GLASS.

The *Photographic News* gives the following account of a new method of transferring photographic pictures to glass, discovered by M. Grume, a Berlin chemist: "The paper (resembling ordinary albumenized) is silvered as usual, but very much over-printed from the negative; in fact, till the lights are quite gone, and the print appears lost. It is then washed, to free it from silver, and toned, and then rinsed. While rinsing, the print may be observed to be covered with blisters. These gradually increase in size until finally the delicate film of gelatine upon which the picture is splits off and floats into the water. It is then very carefully placed in hypo-sulphate of soda and then well washed, every washing appearing to render it more tough, till at last it may be handled with impunity. The glass, or porcelain, upon which it is to be placed is then passed under the film, and both lifted out of the water together. When dry it is trimmed and covered with transparent, hard varnish. Excite the paper as for albumenized paper. Dry. Print *very* deeply, — you can scarcely print too deep. Tone as albumenized paper; more care will be required, as the prints are over-printed, and the changes of tone are not so readily observed. Wash in water. A film now begins to leave the paper. Pass into the hypo-bath one part in five. The film now entirely separates from the paper, and the paper must be removed. Let the film remain in the hypo about ten minutes, and then carefully and thoroughly wash in water. The film is now very elastic. To transfer this film to any surface, clean the surface, and bring it under the film which is floating on pure water. Raise both out of the water together, pull the film into the desired position on the object and let it dry. Then varnish with a clear varnish. If the film should not adhere as closely as desired on round surfaces, wash it (without removing it from the object) with a mixture of one part acetic acid 32° and 6 of water. As soon as it becomes elastic, wash with water, and it will adhere well. As the manipulations thus described seem to present some difficulties, we were anxious, prior to bringing the process before our readers, to put it into practice. We have accordingly exposed half a dozen pictures and transferred them according to instructions. We have succeeded beyond our expectations, and have obtained, at the first attempt, some very pleasing transfers. The paper was excited on a sixty-grain bath and a couple of pieces exposed under a portrait negative, until the highest lights were of a lavender tint. This we subsequently found was not quite deep enough. The prints were washed and toned as usual, reaching a deep purple in the gold bath, which was one made after Parkinson's formula. On being transferred to a dish of water, and washed well, we did not observe either blistering or entire separation of the film as expected. We then transferred them to the hypo-bath, and allowed them to remain a quarter of an hour. A slight blistering was now apparent, which increased in the subsequent wash of water. But as the separation did not take place so speedily as we anticipated it, we added a trace of carbonate of soda to the water, and in a few minutes we saw the delicate transparent film separated from the paper, and floating in the water. After rinsing, we placed a piece of white enamel glass underneath the floating film, and by a little careful management lifted it from the water uninjured, and stretched flat upon the glass, where it dried, smooth, bright, and firm. We now exposed a couple more, and printed until the image was completely buried; after which, before toning, we trimmed the print to the shape we desired, as we found it was a difficult thing to shape the film when once detached from the paper. We toned this time in a bath containing a little carbonate of soda, and we observed in the subsequent rinsing that the blisters began to rise; these increased in the hypo bath, and in the course of the subsequent washings, the film readily separated and floated away from the paper. A subsequent couple were toned in the lime-bath, washed, and fixed. These also separated in the subsequent washing without any trouble; but a longer time was necessary, some hours elapsing before the film of albumen was quite detached. The attenuated film, as delicate as the wing of the smallest fly, at first sight seems quite unmanageable, curling, twisting, and folding itself with the slightest disturbance of the water; and if the object on which it is to be placed be brought under it, and both lifted out of the water without proper precaution, it will probably be found to have run up together into a shapeless mass, apparently beyond remedy. If it be carefully returned to the water, the probability is that it will gradually float straight out again, and present itself quite uninjured. A little care and patience will be required. The variety of ornamental purposes for such transfers will readily suggest themselves. When transferred to plain white enamel glass, the pictures acquire not only a beauty as transparencies, but also as positives, which they did not possess before. The pure white and fine surface seems to impart a wondrous charm of delicacy and brilliancy altogether unexpected, which, for locket and brooch portraits, will possess especial value. It is probable that the film so transferred to ivory will be of value to the miniature painter. As ornaments for vases of opal glass, etc., many very beautiful effects may be produced. In the art of diaphanie, and as an adjunct to the now fashionable art of decalcomanie, it will probably be found useful; and in a variety of ways which do not now occur to us. At present, the only protection is a hard varnish, but it is possible that by the use of an enamel powder fusing at a low temperature, a vitreous surface might be secured."

A NEW KIND OF MINIATURE POSSESSING APPARENT SOLIDITY BY MEANS OF A COMBINATION OF PRISMS.

A very ingenious and beautiful application of optical principles to the mounting of photographic miniatures has been recently made by Mr. Henry Swan, photographic artist of London. The effect of the new process is to exhibit the subject of the portraiture with life-like verisimilitude, and in natural relief, the image being apparently imbedded in the thickness of a small inclosed block of glass or crystal, thereby defining form and expression with a degree of accuracy unattainable in a flat portrait. The projection of the nose, the moulding of the lips, and all the gradations of contour, are as distinct as if an able sculptor had exercised his skill; while the hair and the flesh are of their proper tint, and the whole thing has a singularly vital and comfortable look. Indeed, were it not for the reduction in size, it would be difficult to avoid the belief that an actual man or woman, in ordinary dress, and with characteristic expression, was presented to your eye.

This curious and beautiful effect is produced by a new application of the principles of binocular vision employed in the ordinary stereoscope. Two portraits (taken at an angle suitable for the effect intended) are produced by the ordinary photographic means. To effect the combination of these, the block of glass or quadrangular prism, in the interior of which the solid image is to appear, is composed of two rectangular prisms ground to an angle of about 39° or 40°. These are placed together so as to form one solid quadrangular prism, divided lengthwise by a thin film of air. If one of the pictures be now placed at the back of this combination, and the other picture at the side, on attempting to look through the combination the two images will be superposed on each other (forming one solid image, apparently imbedded in the crystal), all the rays which fall on one side of a line perpendicular to the surface of the prism next the eye suffering total reflection at the inner oblique surface of that prism, while nearly all those rays which fall on the other side of this line will be transmitted, unaltered in direction, through the body of the combination. Thus one of the eyes only perceives the object at the back at the prisms, while to the other eye the picture at the side is alone visible, and that lying apparently at the back also, producing the perfect appearance of solidity. It is evident that, to produce these results, care must be taken, not only that the pictures are not misplaced so as to produce the pseudoscopic effect, but also that the picture which suffers reflection shall be reverted to compensate for the reversion occasioned in reflection.

All these portraits are viewed as transparencies; the photographs being printed from ordinary negatives on small mica plates which are affixed to the prisms.

THE VELOCITY OF LIGHT AND THE SUN'S DISTANCE.

From an article contributed to the *American Journal of Science* (Sept. 1863), by Prof. Lovering, of Cambridge, we derived the following interesting memoranda respecting the above subjects: Four methods have been devised for determining the velocity of light, two of which may be termed astronomical and two experimental. The results obtained from these determinations, although agreeing so essentially as to prove their comparative accuracy, yet differ slightly among themselves to an annoying and at present inexplicable extent. The first discovered method for obtaining the velocity of light, was by observations on the eclipses of Jupiter's Satellites, and the result obtained was 193,-350 statute miles per second. The second process which astronomy has supplied is through observations on the aberration of light, and the result obtained gives 191,513 miles as the velocity of light per second. The determination of the velocity of light, by the two methods of astronomy, differ therefore by 1837 miles; a small quantity comparatively, being only 1 *per cent.* of the whole velocity. It should be also stated that the velocity which aberration ascribes to light belongs to it at the earth's surface; that is, in the dense atmosphere; whereas the velocity discovered from the eclipses is that which extends from the

11*

planetary spaces. This distinction, however, will do little toward bringing the two results into greater accordance, as the theoretical difference of velocities is less than $\frac{1}{1000}$ of the whole, or less than 70 miles.

Compare with these conclusions of astronomy two experimental results on the same subject. The first attempt to obtain the velocity of light, by direct experiment and test, was made by the eminent French physicist, Fizeau, in 1849. The plan adopted by him for resolving this abstruse problem will be readily understood from the following description. If a wheel finely cut into teeth on its circumference is put in rapid rotation, a ray of light, which escapes between two consecutive teeth, will, after being reflected perpendicularly by a mirror, return to strike the wheel at a different point, and either be intercepted by a tooth or admitted at another interstice. Suppose the velocity of the wheel just sufficient to bring the adjacent tooth to the position whence the ray first started, in the time which the light occupies in going to the mirror and returning. In this time the wheel has moved over an angle found by dividing 360° by twice the number of teeth which the wheel contains. Therefore the time taken by light, in going over a line equal to twice the distance of the mirror, is that portion a second found by dividing unity by the product of the number of turns the wheel makes in a second, multiplied by double the number of teeth on the wheel; the velocity of the wheel being first made the smallest which will cause it to intercept the light. Such an experiment was made in 1849, by Fizeau, the wheel being placed in a tower at Suresne, near Paris, and the mirror upon a hill (Montmartre) at the distance of 8633 metres. As the wheel contained 720 teeth, and the slowest velocity which produced obscuration was 12.6 turns a second, it appeared that light required $\frac{1}{18144}$ of a second to go 8633 metres and return. Hence its velocity was 313,274,304 metres, or 194,667 miles a second.

Since then, M. Foucault has successfully achieved the measurement of the *absolute* velocity of light by an experiment which admits of being brought within the compass of a single room. The apparatus employed by him embodied substantially the principle of Fizeau's apparatus, but was much more complicated, and so accurately devised that Foucault states that the mean result of his experiments can be trusted to the fraction of $\frac{1}{500}$. This result gives for the velocity of light 185,-177 statute miles per second; which is less by 6336 miles than the velocity for light usually admitted into science, namely, the velocity obtained from the aberration of light. This discrepancy between the results of experiment and that of the astronomical determination, which comes nearest to it, is three times greater than the variation between the velocity deduced from aberration and that derived from eclipses. Now, neither the velocity by Foucault's experiment nor the value of aberration can be charged with a possible error of three per cent., or of any error approaching to this large discrepancy; and the question arises, how is the new velocity of light obtained by Foucault to be reconciled with the old value of aberration? It should be stated that aberration establishes only the *ratio* between the velocity of light and the velocity of the earth; but this ratio being established, the astronomer is enabled to assign the value of the one with all the accuracy which pertains to his knowledge of the other. Now if this ratio cannot be tampered with, and if one term of it (the velocity of light) must be diminished three per cent. to suit Foucault's experiment, then we must at the same time diminish the other term (the velocity of the earth) proportionally; and the old ratio will be preserved, and the value of aberration will be left unchanged. Is it possible, therefore, that there can be an uncertainty to the extent of three per cent. in the velocity of the earth? If so, the tables are turned; and, instead of employing the ratio which aberration supplies to calculate the velocity of light from the velocity of the earth, as the best known of the two, we henceforth must calculate the velocity of the earth from the velocity of light. For Foucault has found the latter by experiment more accurately than astronomy gives the former. If there is an error of three per cent. in the velocity of the earth, it is an error in space and not in time. To diminish the velocity of the earth sufficiently by a change of time would demand an increase in the length of the year amounting to eleven days nearly.

The only other way of reaching the velocity of the earth is by diminishing the circumference of the earth's orbit, and this, if diminished, changes proportionally the mean radius of the orbit; that is, the sun's mean distance. The question, therefore, resolves itself into this: Can the distance of the sun from the earth be considered uncertain to the extent of three per cent. of the whole distance?

The answer to this question leads to a discussion of the processes by which the sun's distance from the earth has been determined, and the limits of accuracy which belong to the received value. To know the sun's distance, the astronomer studies the solar parallax, which is the angle between the directions in which two astronomers, located at opposite extremities of the earth's diameter, point their telescopes when they are looking at the sun at the same moment.

As Kepler's third law establishes a relation between the distances of the different planets from the sun, and their periods of revolution, if the astronomer finds either distance by observation, the others can be computed from this law. As the solar parallax is only about eight seconds, and an error of one-tenth of a second includes an error of more than a million of miles in the sun's distance, he takes advantage of the law of Kepler, and selects a planet which comes occasionally nearer to the earth than the sun. The choice lies between Venus at inferior conjunction and Mars at opposition.

What are the results which have been obtained?

1. Only two transits of Venus have occurred since the time when the sagacious Dr. Halley invoked the attention of posterity to these rare, astronomical events, as pregnant with the grandest results to science, namely those of 1761 and 1769. The astronomers of the last century did not neglect the charge which Halley consigned to them. The transit of 1769 was eminently favorable, offering a chance which comes only once in a millennium; and whatever verdict posterity shall pronounce on the deductions from the observations then made, they will never, says Encke, reproach astronomers or governments with negligence or want of appreciation toward this golden opportunity. The solar parallax which Encke deduced from an elaborate discussion of all the observations, fifty years after they were made, is 8″.57116. This corresponds to a solar distance of 95,360,000 statute miles.

Although transits of Venus will take place in 1874 and 1882, and astronomers already begin to talk of preparing for them, Encke declares that, in comparison with that of 1769, the next two transits will be so unfavorable that nothing short of perfection in the construction of instruments, and in the art of observing, can compensate for the natural disadvantage ; so that the reduction of the possible error in the sun's parallax within the limit of one-hundredth of a second is hopeless for at least two centuries more.

2. The solar parallax may also be derived from the parallax of Mars, when this planet is in opposition.   In 1740, the French astronomer, Lacaille, was sent to the Cape of Good Hope, and from the parallactic angle observed between the direction of Mars as seen from that station and from the observatory of Paris (deduced from observations of declination), the horizontal parallax of Mars was computed, and consequently that of the sun.   The solar parallax thus found was $10'.20$, with a possible error not exceeding $0''.55$.   Henderson, by comparing his own observations of the declination of Mars at its opposition in 1832 with corresponding observations at Greenwich, Cambridge, and Altona, computed the solar parallax at $9''.028$.

The United States Naval Astronomical expedition to Chili, under the charge of Lieut. J. M. Gilliss, during the years 1849–1852, had for its object the advancement of our knowledge of the solar parallax, partly by observations of Mars at opposition, and partly by observations of Venus during the retrograde portion of her orbit, and especially at the stationary points, in conformity with a method suggested by Dr. Gerling; the whole to be compared with simultaneous observations at northern observatories.   Although the observations at Chili were made on two hundred and seventeen nights, covering a period of nearly three years, the coöperation of northern astronomers was so insufficient that only twenty-eight corresponding observations were made.   On this account, the second conjunction of Venus was useless : the other conjunction of Venus and the second opposition of Mars were of little value ; and even the first opposition of Mars led to no significant result.   Dr. B. A. Gould has computed the solar parallax from the first opposition of Mars, observed at Chili, at $8''.50$.

3. The solar parallax can also be computed from the law of universal gravitation.   The principle may be thus stated : the motion of the moon round the earth is disturbed by the unequal attraction of the sun on the two bodies.   The magnitude of the disturbance will be in some proportion to the distance of the disturber, when compared with the relative distance of the two disturbed bodies ; and this ratio of distances is the inverse ratio of the parallaxes of the sun and moon.   By selecting one of the perturbations in the moon's longitude, particularly adapted to this purpose, Mayer, as early as 1760, computed the solar parallax at $7''.8$.   In 1824, Burg calculated this parallax, from better observations, at $8''.62$.   Laplace gives it at $8''.61$.   Fontenelle had said that Newton, without getting out of his arm-chair, found the figure of the earth more accurately than others had done by going to the ends of the earth. Laplace makes a similar reflection on this new triumph of theory : " It is wonderful that an astronomer, without going out of his observatory, should be able to determine exactly the size and figure of the earth, and its distance from the sun and moon, simply by comparing his observations with analysis, the knowledge of which formerly demanded

long and laborious voyages into both hemispheres." The accordance of the results obtained by the two methods is one of the most striking proofs of universal gravitation. Pontecoulant makes the solar parallax, by this method, 8″.63. Lubboch, by combining Airy's empirical determination of the coefficient with the mass of the moon, as he finds it from the tides (viz., $\frac{1}{57}$) makes the solar parallax 8″.84. If the mass of $\frac{1}{78}$ is substituted, the parallax is changed to 8″.81. Finally Hansen, in his new *Tables of the Moon*, adopts 8″.8762 as the value of the solar parallax. Moreover, Leverrier, in his *Theory of the apparent motion of the Sun*, deduces a solar parallax of 8″.95 from the phenomena of precession and nutation.

The conclusions of this review are summed up in the following table ; in which the values of the solar parallax and of the sun's distance, by the three methods of astronomy, and by the experiment of Foucault, are placed in juxtaposition ; also the different velocities of light found by astronomical observations and by experiment.

Observer or Computer.	Method.	Parallax.	Distance.
Encke,	By Venus (1761),	8″.53	95141830 miles
Encke,	" " (1769),	8 .59	95820610
Lacaille,	By Mars,	10 .20	76927900
Henderson,	" "	9 .03	90164110
Gilliss and Gould,	" "	8 .50	96160,00
Mayer,	By Moon,	7 .80	104079100
Burg,	" "	8 .62	94802440
Laplace,	" "	8 .61	94915970
Pontecoulant,	" "	8 .63	94689710
Lubboch,	" "	8 .84	92313580
"	" "	8 .81	92652970
Hansen,	" "	8 .88	91861060
Leverrier,	" "	8 .95	91066350
Foucault,	By Light,	8 .86	92087342
Fizeau,	" "	8 .51	95117000
Velocity of Light,	By Eclipses,		193350
" "	" Aberration,		191513
" "	" Fizeau's experiment,		194667
" "	" Foucault's experiment,		185177

The three astronomical methods present solar distances, which, even if we select the most trustworthy decision of each, differ by three or four millions of miles ; that is, by three or four per cent. of the whole quantity. Though the best products of the first and third methods were at one time within a million of miles of each other, an increase of lunar observations, and especially improvements in the lunar tables, have now carried that difference up to four millions of miles. If Foucault's experiment were allowed to give the casting vote, it would decide in favor of the third method ; thus making the reflection of Laplace, already quoted, still more memorable.

In regard to the commonly received distance of the sun, which is based upon Encke's profound discussion of all the observations made at the last two transits of Venus, the case stands thus : Encke decides, from the weights of the observations, discussed in the light of the mathematical principle of *least squares*, that the probable error of the sun's distance, as given by the transits, does not exceed $\frac{1}{256}$ of the whole quantity.   Astronomers have also reason to believe that the adopted value of aberration is correct within $\frac{1}{1800}$ of the whole quantity.   Moreover, Foucault is confident of his determination of the velocity of light within $\frac{1}{500}$ of the whole quantity; nay, he expects to improve his instruments so as to banish all errors larger than $\frac{1}{5000}$ of the whole quantity.   Neither the velocity of light, aberration, nor the sun's distance can be suspected of an error to the extent of three or four per cent.; and yet one at least must be wrong to this degree, as the best values of the three elements are irreconcilable with each other. Which shall be changed ?

It may excite surprise in those who have heard of the *accuracy* of astronomy, without weighing the exact significance of the word as applied to so large a subject, that there should still be a lingering uncertainty, to the extent of three or four millions of miles, in the sun's distance from the earth.   But the error, whatever it is, is propagated from the solar system into the deepest spaces which the telescope has ever traversed.   The sun's distance is the measuring rod with which the astronomer metes out the distances of the fixed stars and the dimensions of stellar orbits.   An error of three per cent. in the sun's distance entails an error of three per cent. in all these other distances and dimensions.   Trifling as three per cent. may seem, the correction runs up to 600,000 millions of miles, in the distance of the nearest fixed star !

Additional Determinations of Solar Parallax. — Mr. Stone, principal assistant at the Greenwich Observatory, has been making a series of calculations on the mean horizontal parallax of the sun, deduced from observations made at Greenwich on the planet Mars at his recent opposition, compared with similar observations made in Australia.   The result is that the sun is found to be three millions of miles nearer to the earth than previous calculations have made it.   The Greenwich observations give 8″.97 for the sun's mean horizontal parallax. Dr. Winnecke, from observations on Mars made in Germany compared with others made at the Cape of Good Hope, obtains 8″.96 for this element. M. Leverrier, from planetary disturbances, suspected 8″.95 ! The close coincidence of these results, thus independently obtained, is not only remarkable as indicating extreme accuracy of observation, but as an additional confirmation of the firmness of grasp with which gravitation binds together the planetary Cosmos.

CURIOUS OBSERVATION ON THE REFRACTION OF LIGHT.

M. Babinet, the distinguished French physicist, states that the lunar eclipse of June 1st, 1863, presented a peculiarity not before noticed.   When the moon left the earth's shadow and formed a crescent, whose greatest breadth was equal to one-quarter of the moon's semidiameter, the eastern half was illuminated, while the western half remained in shade.   This appearance lasted so long as to leave no doubt that at the end of the eclipse the shadow of the earth extended further on the western than on the eastern side of the meridian of Paris.   M. Babinet explains the reason of this phenomenon as follows : He states that, at a pressure of seventy-six centimeters, the refraction of the atmosphere amounts to thirty-five minutes with regard to rays that reach us from the horizon, and seventy minutes for those solar rays which pass close to the earth's surface and traverse the atmosphere again before escaping behind the earth, and that thus the illumination of the atmosphere diminishes the earth's shadow by more than twice the diameter of the moon. The bent rays are the first to reach the moon as she emerges from the shadow. As the refraction is proportioned to the density of the air, those rays which traverse the atmosphere at a considerable elevation are less bent than those which pass close to the earth. On the 1st of June, the solar rays passed over the earth's surface in the middle of Greenland. In the western part of the circle of illumination, the rays traversed the air above glaciers which have an elevation of at least five hundred meters, while at the eastern part they traversed the air close to the open sea, and having a refractive power of seventy minutes, that of the air above the glaciers being refracted at least four minutes less. This accounts for light reaching one part of the lunar crescent before the other.

THE MOST RECENT SPECTRUM DISCOVERIES.

The following is an abstract of a lecture on the above subject, recently delivered before the Royal Institution, London, by Professor Miller, F. R. S. : —

Among the rays, emitted by the sun, there were three kinds, interesting as endowed with special action, — those which conveyed heat, light, and chemical action. With heat, he should have but little to do, on this occasion; about light, he had something to say; but he was now principally concerned with the rays which manifested themselves by producing chemical action. It was well known that transparent substances did not transmit all these rays with equal facility. Glass was only imperfectly transparent to the chemically active rays, which were found in the most refrangible rays of the spectrum, heat-rays being in the least refrangible portion, and light occupying the middle place. It had been found that rock-crystal was one of the few substances which perfectly transmitted those highly refrangible rays, which glass absorbed.

The professor then showed that some kinds of light were without chemical action, the light from a mixed air-gas flame possessing scarcely any, while that from an ordinary gas flame did possess a little. The oxy-hydrogen flame, while attended with intense heat, was endowed with very little chemical action. A prepared collodion plate exposed to this light for twenty seconds gave a very faint picture. But when the flame was thrown on lime, although the temperature was lower, the light had sufficient chemical activity to produce a strong picture on a similarly prepared plate, exposed for the same time. In the case of the chemically acting ray, the intensity, number, and position of the lines on the spectrum had been found to vary with the source of light. The most remarkable illustration of this was the different spectra produced by the electric spark of an induction coil between poles of different metals, and projected upon a photographic plate.

The spectrum produced by the spark from silver poles, for example, was found to be three times the length of the whole of the solar spectrum transmitted by quartz. In order to obtain views of this invisible spectrum, it was necessary to transmit the rays through a medium more transparent to chemical rays than glass, which, it had been said, was opaque to the higher rays of this kind, and various experiments had been made to ascertain what substance allowed them to pass most freely. The principal results attained to were as follows : —

Of the solids experimented with, rock-crystal, ice, rock-salt, iceland spar, and the diamond, in the order named, exhibited the greatest photographic transparency ; while thin glass, mica, iodide of potassium, and nitrate of potash, considerably affected the transmission of the photographic rays. The photographic transparency of different liquids may be indicated as follows : water, 74 ; alcohol, 63 ; chloroform, 26 ; oil of turpentine, 8 ; of gases, hydrogen, nitrogen, oxygen, and carbonic acid, have a photographic transparency indicated by the number 74 ; coal gas, 37 ; sulphurous acid, and sulphuretted hydrogen, 14 each. This remarkable fact was also noticed, namely, that solid bodies, when dissolved or melted, maintain exactly the same photographic transparency as when in the solid state. The same was the case when they were converted into vapor, which showed that this power was part of the nature of the substance.

The lecturer then described the phenomenon of fluorescence, and showed that the chemical rays of the spectrum corresponded with the rays of fluorescence, by taking a photograph in that part of the spectrum which, though otherwise invisible on the screen, lighted up a solution of æsculine. He then showed that all metals give characteristic photographic spectra, some of them bearing a strong family resemblance to each other, as in the cases of iron, cobalt, and nickel ; the last metal giving one of the longest spectra observed, and which extended to 190° of the scale. Arsenic, antimony, and tin showed as great differences in the invisible as visible part of the spectrum. The most interesting of the metals to study, in this respect, was magnesium, which opened a wide field for investigation. There were certain points of resemblance between the spectrum of magnesium and that of the sun, which led to the supposition that this metal existed in the solar atmosphere. The comparison of the spectrum of magnesium with that of the sun led also to some important considerations as to the temperature of the sun. It was known that the higher the temperature the more refrangible were the rays of light emitted by a body. We have no conception of the temperature of the electric spark. The heat of the strongest wind-furnace was estimated at 4500° F., and that of the oxy-hydrogen jet was supposed not to exceed 15,000° F. ; yet with neither of these could the same effects be produced as with the electric spark. The lines of the photographic spectrum of magnesium were not seen in photographs of the solar spectrum, and yet there was no doubt that this metal was present in the solar atmosphere. Kirchoff, had discovered that solids, when heated, give a continuous spectrum, but that bodies in the form of gas give rays of definite and limited refrangibility, each substance emitting light of a definite property. He had also noticed that light from a luminous mass, by passing through ignited vapor, which, *per se*, would give bright lines in the spectrum, became furrowed out in dark bands, occupying exactly the same position in the spectrum as the bright lines. Now, ignited magnesium vapor emitted green rays which were absolutely identical with the group of fixed lines *b* in the solar spectrum, and it was, therefore, certain that magnesium was a constituent of the sun. It was, moreover, probable that the heat of the sun was inferior to that of the electric spark, inasmuch as it was insufficient to bring out the highly refrangible lines observed in photographs of the magnesium spectrum.

There were thirteen bodies known on earth, which these researches lead us to suppose existed in the solar atmosphere. Nor are they limited merely to the sun. Fraünhofer, had examined the spectra of several stars, and found that, although they presented no similarity to that of the sun, nor to each other, yet that some general relationship between them was observable. Mr. Huggins and the lecturer had recently been investigating this subject, and had obtained very perfect maps of the visible spectra of several stars. They had also obtained a photograph of the spectrum of Sirius. This star is 130,000,000,000 of miles distant, and the light which produced the photograph must have left it twenty-one years ago.

A photograph of the spectrum of Capella, which is three times further distant than Sirius, had also been obtained, the light to produce which, the lecturer said, must have left that star when the oldest in the room was a little boy.

Spectrum Analysis applied to the Stars. — In a communication published in the *Intellectual Observer* (London), by Mr. W. Higgins F. R. S. who was associated with Prof. Miller in the foregoing described investigations, the author speaks more particularly respecting the results arrived at in respect to the spectra of the fixed stars. He says, " A single glance at the spectra afforded by Sirius, Aldebaran, and α Orionis, will show that the fixed stars have been created upon the same general plan as our sun, and yet that to this unity of plan is added variety of purpose in the different groupings of the elements composing each. In Aldebaran, α Orionis, Capella, Arcturus and other stars, the sodium line of the solar spectrum is so clearly defined, that the proof of the presence of this metal in the stellar atmospheres may be considered as conclusive. Amongst some fifty stars observed, a very large number, if not all, have lines *coinciding* with those proved to result from the presence of hydrogen. This would show that hydrogen — the element upon this earth, next to oxygen, perhaps, the most widely present, and equally essential with oxygen to the structure of everything that has life — is also very widely diffused through the universe. Magnesium and iron would seem to be present in a large number of stars."

Mr. Higgins and Prof. Miller considered the direct observation of the coincidence of stellar with metallic lines so important that they intend not to rely upon measures, but to compare the metals directly with the stars. This has already been done with some metals. Most of the star spectra appear to be as full of lines as is the solar spectrum. Other lines have been seen in Sirius, in the orange and in the green.

If these distant suns have thus an analogous constitution with our sun, may we not suppose that the planets, which, doubtless, they uphold and energize, are of like material structure? And if terrestrial elements, with their properties unchanged, be present, may we not further surmise, that life in forms not wholly dissimilar to those on this planet, and which these elements are so eminently adapted to subserve, may not be wanting? The spectrum of solar light reflected from the planets has also been observed. Numerous lines have been measured in the spectra of Venus, Jupiter, and the Moon. They have also been

12

recognized in Saturn and Mars. No addition or change of lines has been seen to indicate that the light has undergone any change by reflection from them. It is probable that, with the exception of the moon, we receive the light reflected from clouds or vapor in the atmosphere of the planets, and not from the true planetary surface. The light would not, under these circumstances, pass through so great a length of planetary atmosphere, and in the same proportion would it be less liable to have any modification impressed upon it.

At a recent meeting of the Astronomical Society, Prof. Airy, in an account of the observations on stellar spectra made at the Royal Observatory, stated that the line F of Fraünhofer indicating iron was seen in most stars, the sodium line D in two stars ; and a line nearly, but not quite coinciding with G in many. The star a Orionis appeared most like our sun, but generally the stars seemed not to be so complex in constitution.

Temperature of the Sun and Stars. — Besides the light of the sun, which, when spread out, forms the visible spectrum, the sun sheds upon us a large amount of energy invisible as light. Professor Stokes's investigations have shown that this invisible energy, when passed through a prism of quartz, is spread out like light, and contains lines or spaces where this energy is absent, similar to the dark lines in the visible spectrum. By the substitution of a collodion plate for the eye, Professor Miller has investigated the invisible spectra of metallic flames. These are as distinct and characteristic of each metal as is the light spectrum of each. Observation has shown that the length of these spectra of invisible energy and their lines are closely connected with the temperature of the source of heat. Thus, when photographs of the refrangible portion of the solar spectrum and that of the metal magnesium were compared, it was observed that that of the magnesium extended much beyond the solar, and it was especially noticeable, that there was a strong band in the magnesium spectrum just beyond the limits of the solar. Yet no metal has been proved to be present in the sun with more certainty than magnesium. Professor Miller regards this difference as an indication of the solar temperature. The magnesium spectrum was obtained by the electric spark. If, in place of this intensely high temperature, the oxy-hydrogen flame of only 15,000° F. be substituted, the magnesium spectrum is shortened, and does not extend beyond that of the sun. From this, Professor Miller infers that " the temperature of the sun may be approximately estimated to be not higher than that of the oxy-hydrogen flame. It certainly appears to be far below that of the electric spark." This seems to be scarcely in accordance with the known law of the decrease of radiant heat. This decreasing, inversely as the square of the distance, gives an intense amount of heat to the solar surface. Waterston, in a communication to the Royal Astronomical Society, in February, 1860, states that his experiments, founded upon the supposition that the difference between the temperature in the sun and the temperature in the shade is a function of the sun's absolute temperature, give above " ten million degrees, probably twelve million, Fahrenheit," to the solar surface.

Is it not possible that vapors may exist in the solar atmosphere which, as Professor Miller shows to be the case with sulphuretted hydrogen, are but imperfectly diactinic, and so arrest these extreme rays of energy? Not that sulphuretted hydrogen, or any compound body, can be supposed to exist upon the solar surface. The elements there must stand too much aloof, by the mutual hate of the fierce heat, to unite themselves in alliances with each other. It may be, however, that conditions unknown to us alter or modify the terrestrial law of decrease of heat.

It seemed, however, an object of great interest to know if similar photographic spectra could be obtained of the stars. Mr. IIiggins and Dr. Miller have already been successful in photographing the more refrangible portion of the spectra of Sirius and Capella.

New Observations on Spectral Analysis by Prof. Plucker. — The following new views respecting spectral analysis were presented to the British Association by Prof. Plucker : " It is generally admitted now," he said, " that every gaseous body rendered luminous by heat or electricity sends out a peculiar light, which, if examined by the prism, gives a well-defined and characteristic spectrum. By such a spectrum, by any one of its brilliant lines, whose position has been measured, you may recognize the examined gas. This way of proceeding constitutes what is called spectral analysis, to which we owe, until this day, the discovery of three new elementary bodies. In order to give to spectral analysis a true and certain basis, you want the spectrum of each elementary substance. Most recently, some eminent philosophers, in examining such spectra, met with unexpected difficulties, and doubts arose in their minds against the new doctrine. These doubts are unfounded. The fact is, that the molecular constitution of gases is much more complicated than it has been generally admitted to be till now. The spectra, therefore, always indicating the molecular constitution of gases, ought to be more complicated also, than it was thought at first. By these considerations, a new importance, a rather physical one, is given to spectral analysis. You may recognize by the spectrum of a gas, not only the chemical nature of the gas, but you may also obtain indications of its more intimate molecular structure — quite a new branch of science. Allow me now to select out of the results already obtained two instances only. Let me try to give what I may call the history of the spectra of two elementary bodies — of sulphur and nitrogen. In order to analyze by the prism the beautiful light produced by the electric current, if it pass through a rarefied gas, I gave to the tube in which the gas is included such a form that its middle part was capillary. Thus I got within this part of the tube a brilliant film of light, extremely fitted to be examined by the prism. After having provided myself with apparatus more suited to my purposes, I asked, about a year ago, my friend, Prof. Hittorf, of Munster, to join me in taking up my former researches. The very first results we obtained in operating on gases of a greater density opened to us an immense field of new investigation. We found that the very same elementary substance may have two, even three, absolutely different spectra, which only depend on temperature. In our experiments we made use of Ruhmkorff's induction coil, whose discharge was sent through our spectral tubes. In order to increase at other times the heating power of the discharge, we made use of a Leyden jar. Now, let us suppose a spectral tube, most highly exhausted by Geissler's mercury pump, contains a very small quantity of sulphur. The discharge of the coil will not pass through the tube if it do not meet with ponderable matter, either taken from the surface of the glass, or, if the discharge be very strong, by the chemical decomposition of the glass. In heating slowly the tube by means of a lamp, in order to transform a part of the sulphur into vapor, all accidental spectra, if there be any, will disappear, and you will get a pure and beautiful spectrum of sulphur. I supposed the Leyden jar not to have been interposed. If you now interpose it, the spectrum just spoken of will suddenly be replaced by a quite different one. We were generally led to distinguish two quite different classes of spectra. Spectra of the first class consist in a certain number of bands, variously shadowed by dark transversal lines. Spectra of the second class consist in a great number of most brilliant lines on a dark ground. Accordingly, sulphur has one spectrum of the first class and another one of the second class. You may as often as you like obtain each of these two spectra. In operating on a spectral tube, containing nitrogen at a tension of about 50 millimetres, you will, without the Leyden jar, get a most beautiful spectrum of the first class. After interposing the jar, a splendid spectrum of the second class will be seen. But here the case is more complicated yet. The above-mentioned spectrum of the first class is not a simple one, but it is produced by the superposition of two spectra of the same class. Ignited nitrogen, at the lowest temperature, has a most beautiful color of gold. When its temperature rises, its color suddenly changes into blue. In the first case, the corresponding spectrum is formed by the less refracted bands extended toward the violet part; in the second case, it is formed by the more refracted band of the painting extended toward the red. Nitrogen, therefore, has two spectra of the first class and one spectrum of the second class. The final conclusion, therefore, is, that sulphur has two, nitrogen three, different allotropic states. It may appear very strange that a gaseous body may have different allotropic states, i. e., different states of molecular equilibrium. It may not appear, perhaps, more strange that a substance, hitherto supposed to be an elementary one, may really be decomposed at an extremely high temperature. From spectral analysis there cannot be taken any objection that sulphur and nitrogen may be decomposed. Chloride of zinc (or cadmium), for instance, exhibits two different spectra. If heated like sulphur, and then ignited by the discharge of Ruhmkorff's coil, you will get a beautiful spectrum either of chlorine or of the metal, if either the Leyden jar be not interposed or be interposed. There is, in this case, a dissociation of the elements of the composed body in the highest temperature, and recomposition again at a lower temperature. You may consider the dissociation as an allotropic state, and, therefore, I may make use of this term as long as the decomposition be not proved by the separated elements.

Practical Application of the Spectrum Analysis. — A beautiful practical application of the principles of the spectrum analysis has recently been made in England in the casting of steel. In a newly-adopted process of melting the metal, it is important to know the exact moment at which to shut down the cover of the furnace; time must be allowed for the escape of the gaseous products which are injurious to the steel, but if that time be prolonged, an injurious effect of another kind is produced. To meet this contingency, it has been proposed to test the gases as they fly off, by means of the spectroscope ; and as soon as the particular color is observed, peculiar to the gas, which begins to escape at the moment the molten metal is in proper condition, the manufacturer will then have an infallible sign of the proper moment for closing the furnace.

RADIATION THROUGH THE EARTH'S ATMOSPHERE.

The following abstract of a lecture delivered during the past year, by Prof. Tyndall, before the Royal Institution, London, is a summary of the results and conclusions which this eminent physicist has arrived at in respect to the radiation of heat through the earth's atmosphere : —

When we speak of radiation through the atmosphere, we ought to be able to affix definite physical ideas to both the term atmosphere and the term radiation. It is well known that our atmosphere is mainly composed of the two elements, oxygen and nitrogen. These elementary atoms may be figured as small spheres scattered thickly in the space which surrounds the earth, and they constitute about 99½ per cent. of the atmosphere. Mixed with these atoms, we have others of a totally different character ; we have the molecules or atomic groups of carbonic acid, ammonia, and aqueous vapor. In these substances diverse atoms have coalesced to form little systems of atoms. The molecule of aqueous vapor, for example, consists of two atoms of hydrogen united to one of oxygen, and they mingle as little triads among the monads of oxygen and nitrogen which constitute the great mass of the atmosphere. These atoms and molecules are separate ; but in what sense? They are separate in the sense in which individual fishes of a shoal are separate. The shoal of fish is embraced by a common medium, which connects the different members of the shoal, and renders intercommunication between them possible. A medium also embraces our atoms. Within our atmosphere exists a second and a finer atmosphere in which the atoms of oxygen and nitrogen hang like suspended grains. This finer atmosphere unites not only atom with atom, but star with star ; and the light of all suns and of all stars is in reality a kind of music propagated through this interstellar air. This image must be clearly seized, and then we have to advance a step. We must not only figure our atoms suspended in this medium, but we must figure them vibrating in it. In this motion of the atoms consists what we call their heat. " What is heat in us," as Locke has perfectly expressed it, " is in the body heated nothing but motion." Well, we must figure this motion communicated to the medium in which the atoms swing, and sent in ripples through it with inconceivable velocity to the bounds of space. Motion in this form, unconnected with ordinary matter, but speeding through the interstellar medium, receives the name of radiant heat ; and, if competent to excite the nerves of vision, we call it light.

Aqueous vapor was defined to be an invisible gas. Vapor was permitted to issue horizontally with considerable force from a tube connected with a small boiler. The track of the cloud of condensed steam was vividly illuminated by the electric light. What was seen, however, was not vapor, but vapor condensed to water. Beyond the visible end of the jet, the cloud resolved itself into true vapor. A lamp was placed under the jet at various points; the cloud was cut sharply off at that point, and when the flame was placed near the efflux orifice, the cloud entirely disappeared. The heat of the lamp completely prevented precipitation.

This same vapor was condensed and congealed on the surface of a vessel containing a freezing mixture, from which it was scraped in quantities sufficient to form a small snow-ball. The beam of the electric lamp, moreover, was sent through a large receiver placed on an air-pump. A single stroke of the pump caused the precipitation of the aqueous vapor within, which became beautifully illuminated by the beam; while, upon a screen behind, a richly-colored halo, due to diffraction by the little cloud within the receiver, flashed forth.

The waves of heat speed from our earth, through our atmosphere, toward space. These waves dash in their passage against the atoms of oxygen and nitrogen, and against the molecules of aqueous vapor. Thinly scattered as these latter are, we might naturally think meanly of them as barriers to the waves of heat. We might imagine that the wide spaces between the vapor molecules would be an open door for the passage of the undulations; and that if those waves were at all intercepted, it would be by the substances which form 99½ per cent. of the whole atmosphere. Three or four years ago, however, it was found by the speaker that this small modicum of aqueous vapor intercepted fifteen times the quantity of heat stopped by the whole of the air in which it was diffused. It was afterwards found that the dry air then experimented with was not perfectly pure, and that the purer the air became, the more it approached the character of a vacuum, and the greater, by comparison, became the action of the aqueous vapor.[1] The vapor was found to act with thirty, forty, fifty, sixty, seventy times the energy of the air in which it was diffused; and no doubt was entertained that the aqueous vapor of the air which filled the Royal Institution Theatre, during the delivery of the discourse, absorbed ninety or one hundred times the quantity of radiant heat which was absorbed by the main body of the air of the room.

Looking at the single atoms, for every two hundred of oxygen and

[1] Melloni of Italy, who has been styled the "Newton of Heat," was the first to apply the thermo-electric pile to the investigation of dark, thermal radiations which are emitted from all bodies below a red heat, by the use of plates, lenses, and prisms of rock-salt (common salt in blocks), which is transparent to dark heat, Melloni first engaged in these researches, and in fact founded this branch of science. Prof. Tyndall, taking up the subject where Melloni left it, investigated the relations of radiant heat to gases and vapors in the following manner: He prepared a long glass tube, closed air-tight at its ends with plates of rock-salt, and which he could empty and fill with various gases at pleasure. At one end he placed his source of heat, — a canister of hot water, — and at the other the sensitive face of a thermo-electric pile. By exhausting the air and forming a vacuum, and then introducing various gaseous bodies, he determined how much dark heat passed through and also the different absorbing or intercepting powers of the various substances in the tube. It was found that the simple gases, oxygen, hydrogen, and nitrogen arrested hardly a trace of the passing heat, acting toward it as practical vacuum. On the contrary, other equally transparent gases, as ammonia, carburetted hydrogen, etc., stopped enormous numbers of the dark rays; in fact, were almost opaque to them. The small trace of ammonia, exhaled into an apartment by opening a lady's smelling-bottle arrested many times more of the dark heat rays than the nitrogen and oxygen gases which form the body of the atmosphere. Professor Tyndall found that perfectly pure air stopped an exceedingly minute portion of the heat, which he assumed as the unit for comparison of other bodies, and upon investigation it proved that the small amount of aqueous vapor contained in the air struck down sixty or seventy times as much heat as the gases of the air itself.

nitrogen there is about one of aqueous vapor. This one, then, is eighty times more powerful than the two hundred; and hence, comparing a single atom of oxygen or nitrogen with a single atom of aqueous vapor, we may infer that the action of the latter is 16,000 times that of the former. This was a very astonishing result, and it naturally excited opposition, based on the philosophic reluctance to accept a result so grave in consequences, before testing it to the uttermost. From such opposition, a discovery, if it be worth the name, emerges with its fibre strengthened; as the human character gathers force from the healthy antagonisms of active life. It was urged that the result was on the face of it improbable; that there were, moreover, many ways of accounting for it, without ascribing so enormous a comparative action to aqueous vapor. For example, the cylinder which contained the air in which these experiments were made was stopped at its ends by plates of rock-salt, on account of their transparency to radiant heat. Rock-salt is hygroscopic; it attracts the moisture of the atmosphere. Thus, a layer of brine readily forms on the surface of a plate of rock-salt; and it is well known that brine is very impervious to the rays of heat. Illuminating a polished plate of salt, by the electric lamp, and casting, by means of a lens, a magnified image of the plate upon a screen, the speaker breathed through a tube for a moment on the salt; brilliant colors of thin plates (soap-bubble colors) flashed forth immediately upon the screen, — these being caused by the film of moisture which overspread the salt. Such a film, it was contended, is formed when undried air is sent into the cylinder; it was, therefore, the absorption of a layer of brine which was measured, instead of the absorption of aqueous vapor.

This objection was met in two ways. First, by showing that the plates of salt, when subjected to the strictest examination, show no trace of a film of moisture. Secondly, by abolishing the plates of salt altogether, and obtaining the same results in a cylinder open at both ends.

It was next surmised that the effect was due to the impurity of the London air; and the suspended carbon particles were pointed to as the cause of the opacity to radiant heat. This objection was met by bringing air from Epsom Downs, a field near Newport, in the Isle of Wight, and a sea-beach. The aqueous vapor of the air from these localities intercepted at least seventy times the amount of radiant heat absorbed by the air in which the vapor was diffused. Experiments made with smoky air proved that the suspended smoke of the atmosphere of London, even when an east wind pours over it the smoke of the city, exerts only a fraction of the destructive powers exercised by the transparent and impalpable aqueous vapor diffused in the air.

The cylinder which contained the air through which the calorific rays passed was polished within, and the rays which struck the interior surface were reflected from it to the thermo-electric pile which measured the radiation. The following objection was raised: You permit moist air to enter your cylinder; a portion of this moisture is condensed as a liquid film upon the interior surface of your tube; its reflective power is thereby diminished; less heat therefore reaches the pile; and you incorrectly ascribe to the absorption of aqueous vapor an effect which is really due to diminished reflection of the interior surface of your cylinder. But why should the aqueous vapor so condense?

The tube within is warmer than the air without, and against its inner surface the rays of heat are impinging.   There can be no tendency to condensation under such circumstances.   Further, let five inches of undried air be sent into the tube — that is, one-sixth of the amount which it can contain.   These five inches produce their proportionate absorption.   The driest day on the driest portion of the earth's surface would make no approach to the dryness of our cylinder when it contains only five inches of air.   Make it ten, fifteen, twenty, twenty-five inches: you obtain an absorption exactly proportional to the quantity of vapor present.   It is next to a physical impossibility that this could be the case if the effect were due to condensation.   But lest a doubt should linger in the mind, not only were the plates of rock-salt abolished, but the cylinder itself was dispensed with.   Humid air was displaced by dry, and dry air by humid in the free atmosphere; the absorption of the aqueous vapor was here manifest, as in all the other cases.

No doubt, therefore, can exist of the extraordinary opacity of this substance to the rays of obscure heat ; and particularly such rays as are emitted by the earth after it has been warmed by the sun.   It is perfectly certain that more than ten per cent. of the terrestrial radiation from the soil of England is stopped within ten feet of the surface of the soil.   This one fact is sufficient to show the immense influence which this newly-discovered property of aqueous vapors must exert on the phenomena of meteorology.

This aqueous vapor is a blanket more necessary to vegetable life than clothing is to man.   Remove for a single summer-night the aqueous vapor from the air which overspreads this country, and you would assuredly destroy every plant capable of being destroyed by a freezing temperature.   The warmth of our fields and gardens would pour itself unrequited into space, and the sun would rise upon a land held fast in the iron grip of frost.   The aqueous vapor constitutes a local dam, by which the temperature at the earth's surface is deepened; the dam, however, finally overflows, and we give to space all that we receive from the sun.   The sun raises the vapors of the equatorial ocean ; they rise, but for a time a vapor screen spreads above and around them.   But the higher they rise, the more they come into the presence of pure space, and when, by their levity, they have penetrated the vapor screen, which lies close to the earth's surface, what must occur ?

It has been said that, compared atom for atom, the absorption of an atom of aqueous vapor is 16,000 times that of air.   Now the power to absorb and the power to radiate are perfectly reciprocal and proportional.   The atom of aqueous vapor will therefore radiate with 16,000 times the energy of an atom of air.   Imagine then this powerful radiant in the presence of space, and with no screen above it to check its radiation.   Into space it pours its heat, chills itself, condenses, and the tropical torrents are the consequence.   The expansion of the air, no doubt, also refrigerates it : but in accounting for those deluges, the chilling of the vapor by its own radiation must play a most important part.   The rain quits the ocean as vapor; it returns to it as water. How are the vast stores of heat set free by the change from the vaporous to the liquid condition disposed of ?   Doubtless, in great part they are wasted by radiation into space.   Similar remarks apply to the cumuli of our latitudes. The warmed air, charged with vapor, rises in columns, so as to penetrate the vapor screen which hugs the earth; in the presence of space, the head of each pillar wastes its heat by radiation, condenses to a cumulus, which constitutes the visible capital of an invisible column of saturated air.

Numberless other meteorological phenomena receive their solution, by reference to the radiant and absorbent properties of aqueous vapor. It is the absence of this screen, and the consequent copious waste of heat, that causes mountains to be so much chilled when the sun is withdrawn. Its absence in Central Asia renders the winter there almost unendurable; in Sahara the dryness of the air is sometimes such, that though during the day "the soil is fire and the wind is flame," the chill at night is painful to bear. In Australia, also, the thermometric range is enormous, on account of the absence of this qualifying agent. A clear day, and a dry day, moreover, are very different things. The atmosphere may possess great visual clearness, while it is charged with aqueous vapor, and on such occasions great chilling cannot occur by terrestrial radiation. Sir John Leslie and others have been perplexed by the varying indications of their instruments on days equally bright — but all these anomalies are completely accounted for by reference to this newly-discovered property of transparent aqueous vapor. Its presence would check the earth's loss; its absence, without sensibly altering the transparency of the air, would open wide a door for the escape of the earth's heat into infinitude.

DYNAMICAL THEORY OF HEAT.

Professor Frankland, in a recent lecture before the Royal Institution, London, presented the following points in reference to the dynamical theory of heat: The amount of heat necessary to raise the temperature of a body through a given number of degrees (e. g. from 32 deg. to 212 deg.) is termed "the specific heat" of that body, and that an atom of each solid element requires the same quantity of heat to raise its temperature through the same number of degrees. Hence, at any given temperature, the amount of heat-force associated with each solid elementary atom is the same; but the proportion of this force evolved during chemical combination differs in each element (which was shown experimentally in the case of heated balls of lead and iron placed on cakes of wax; the iron dissolving more wax than the lead). It was stated that the greater the amount of heat evolved during combination, the more difficult is the compound to decompose; and it was shown that even when atoms of the same kind are combined, heat is liberated. This occurs, also, whenever alcohol and water are mixed, when paper is moistened, etc. The heat-force associated with the atoms of matter exists as molecular motion. When two or more atoms unite or come into collision, a certain amount of this motion is destroyed and takes the form of heat. The greater the amplitude of the molecular motion of two bodies, in so-called contact with each other, the more imminent is the collision of their atoms. An augmentation of temperature increases the amplitude of this molecular motion; hence, heat usually promotes chemical combination. In some cases, the molecular motion of two bodies, at ordinary temperatures, is sufficient to bring them into collision; hence, what is termed "spontaneous combustion" (e. g., phosphorus burns in air, potassium in water, etc.). In regard to the spontaneous combustion of the human body, Professor Frankland showed that it was a physical impossibility, on account of the large amount of water in its constitution.

Gunnery and the Dynamical Theory of Heat. — In an address at the opening of the British Association, 1863, Sir W. Armstrong stated, "that the science of gunnery was intimately connected with the dynamical theory of heat. When gunpowder is exploded in a cannon, the immediate effect of the affinities, by which the materials of the powder are caused to enter into new combinations, is to liberate a force which first appears as heat, and then takes the form of mechanical power communicated in part to the shot and in part to the products of explosion which are also propelled from the gun. The mechanical force of the shot is reconverted into heat, when the motion is arrested by striking an object, and this heat is divided between the shot and the object struck, in the proportion of the work done or damage inflicted upon each. These considerations recently led me, in conjunction with Captain Noble, to determine experimentally, by the heat elicited in the shot, the loss of effect due to its crushing when fired against iron plates. Joule's law, and the known velocity of the shot, enable us to compute the number of dynamical units of heat representing the whole mechanical power in the projectile, and by ascertaining the number of units developed in it by impact, we arrived at the power which took effect upon the shot instead of the plate. These experiments showed an enormous absorption of power to be caused by the yielding nature of the materials of which projectiles are usually formed; but further experiments are required to complete the inquiry."

THE EFFECT OF INTENSE HEAT ON LIQUIDS.

At a recent meeting of the London Chemical Society, Mr. Grove, in a paper on the above subject, first called attention to the difference existing between the boiling of water, under ordinary circumstances, and that of sulphuric acid. He stated that the equable evolution of steam, when water is boiled in an open vessel, is caused by the presence of a certain amount of air dissolved in the water, and that boiling may be regarded as an evaporation into the liberated bubble of air set free by the elevated temperature. In an open vessel, a sufficient amount of air is continually reabsorbed, so that the ebullition goes on equally. On the contrary, when water is heated in a very long tube, it boils in the first instance evenly, but after the air is expelled it boils with the most violent concussions; during the regularly-recurring intervals between the sudden and violent emissions of steam, the temperature rises far above 212°, and then a sudden explosive production of steam occurs, almost resembling the discharge of gunpowder. By placing a portion of water in a flask under the vacuum of a good air-pump, and heating it by the transmission of a strong electric current, passed through a fine platinum wire contained in the water, Mr. Grove proved that the water did not boil at all, but that the whole burst up into violent concussions at regularly-recurring intervals. When the air was exhausted, ebullition occurred at intervals of about a minute, upon which a burst of vapor would almost eject the contents of the flask. On this action's increasing, the water would again become perfectly tranquil, and remain so for a minute, when another tumultuous ebullition would occur, to be succeeded by a period of rest; and the same phenomena would be repeated at such regular intervals that the apparatus might almost serve as an indicator of time. If a thermometer were placed in the flask, it would be found that the temperature alternately rose and fell some few degrees. Indeed, it could not be asserted that the boiling point of water was constant, for it depended upon the amount of air in solution ; and Mr. Grove believed that no one had yet succeeded in observing the boiling point of absolutely pure water.

Mr. Grove suggested that the phenomena of the Geysers, or intermittent explosive fountains of Iceland, would admit of a more satisfactory explanation by reference to these facts than on the supposition of the existence of complicated subterranean chambers.

In the course of his experiments, Mr. Grove ascertained that it was almost impossible to free water from gaseous bodies ; and, as a proof of this, he cited the following experiment : A long glass tube closed at one extremity, was bent in the middle to nearly a right angle ; the closed limb was then half-filled with water, from which, by long boiling, the air was supposed to have been expelled ; the remaining space in the tube was then completely filled with olive oil, and the open extremity was dipped into a small basin of the same. Heat was then applied to the tube until the water boiled, and this temperature was maintained for a considerable time. Each bubble of steam which left the surface of the water passed through the column of oil, becoming smaller and smaller during its ascent ; but it never condensed without leaving a microscopic bubble of gas, which at length accumulated to such an extent that it could be examined. It was found to consist of pure nitrogen ; and he had never succeeded in expelling the whole of this gas from the water. The evaporation of nineteen-twentieths of the water did not secure the remainder from being mixed with nitrogen. On boiling ordinary water, air containing a slightly-increased proportion of oxygen was first driven off, the oxygen gradually diminishing until pure nitrogen was expelled. The avidity with which such water again absorbs air is remarkable. In the expressive words of Mr. Grove, " it sucks it up again almost as a sponge takes up water." By a slight modification in the apparatus, the experiment was repeated with mercury, instead of oil, in contact with the boiling water. It furnished a similar result.

A number of facts regarding the solubility of gas in water were finally enumerated. The general conclusion drawn from the experiments, was to the effect that water had a very powerful affinity for the gases of the atmosphere ; that the oxygen could be eliminated by several processes, but the nitrogen resisted all attempts to expel it from solution ; so much so that it might be doubted whether chemically pure water (i. e., a compound of the two elements, oxygen and hydrogen, only), had ever been prepared ; and, further, that ebullition (as applied to water), under all circumstances, consisted merely in the production and disengagement of bubbles of aqueous vapor, formed upon a nucleus of permanent gas. The question, therefore, was raised as to whether nitrogen is so absolutely inert a body as had formerly been supposed.

JOULE'S NEW SENSITIVE THERMOMETER.

At a recent meeting of the Manchester Philosophical Society, Dr. Joule exhibited an exquisitely sensitive air thermometer, capable of being affected by the $\frac{1}{1000}$ of a centigrade degree of heat. The construction is thus described: A glass vessel in the shape of a tube, two feet long by four inches in diameter, is divided longitudinally by a blackened pasteboard diaphragm, leaving spaces at the top and bottom, each little over an inch. In the top space, a piece of magnetized sewing needle, furnished with a glass index, is suspended by a single filament of silk. It is evident that the arrangement is similar to that of a bratticed coal-pit shaft, and that the slightest excess of temperature on one side over that on the other must occasion a circulation of air, which will ascend on the heated side, and, after passing across the fine glass index, descend on the other side. It is also evident that the sensibility of the instrument may be increased to any required extent, by diminishing the directive force of the magnetic needle. I purpose to make several improvements in my present instrument; but in its present condition, the heat radiated by a small pan, containing a pint of water heated 30°, is quite perceptible at a distance of three yards. A further proof of the extreme sensibility of the instrument is obtained from the fact that it is able to detect the heat radiated by the moon. A beam of moonlight was admitted through a slit in the shutter. As the moon (nearly full) travelled from left to right, the beam passed gradually across the instrument, causing the index to be deflected several degrees, first to the left and then to the right. The effect showed, according to a very rough estimate, that the air in the instrument must have been heated by the moon's rays a few ten-thousandths of a degree, or by a quantity, no doubt the equivalent of the light absorbed by the blackened surface, on which the rays fell.

CHANGE OF FORM IN METALS BY IRREGULAR COOLING.

Colonel H. Clerk has communicated to the Royal Society some curious experiments on this subject. It appears that a wheel had to be shod with a hoop-tire, which was required to have a bevel of about $\frac{3}{8}$ths of an inch, and one of the workmen suggested that this could be accomplished by heating the tire red-hot, and immersing one-half its depth in cold water. This was done, with the predicted result; the part out of the water being reduced in diameter. A series of experiments followed, with similarity of action, the cylinders always exhibiting a contraction above the water-line, followed, if they were sufficiently high out of the water, by an expansion corresponding to that below the fluid. The explanation given is, that the parts under the water cooled quickly, and those above it slowly. If no cohesion had united the two parts, both would have obtained the same diameter, one first, and the other afterwards; but as the cohesive power of cast-iron, or other metal, is great, the under part tends to pull in the upper, and the upper to pull out the under. In this contest, the cooler metal, being the stronger, prevails, and so the upper part gets pulled in, a little above the water-line, while still hot. But it has still to contract in cooling, and this it will do to the full extent due to its temperature, except so far as it may be prevented by its connection with the rest. — *Proceedings of the Royal Society.*

IGNEOUS CONDITION OF MATTER.

In a recent work " *On Matter and Ether ;* or, *the Secret Laws of Physical Change,*" by Thomas Birks, M. A., Cambridge (England), 1862, the author, in a chapter entitled the " Igneous Condition of Matter," sets forth the following views: " According to the present theory of the laws of matter, there may be more truth than has latterly been recognized in the old arrangement of the four elements, which placed a fourth region of fire above the solid, liquid, and gaseous constituents of our globe. In fact, above the region where the air, though greatly rarefied, is still elastic, there must be a still higher stratum where elasticity has wholly ceased, and where the particles of matter, being very widely separated, condense around them the largest amount of ether. All sensible heat, in the collision or oscillation of neighboring atoms of matter, will thus have disappeared; but latent heat, in the quantity of condensed ether or repulsive force ready to be developed on the renewed approach of the atoms, will have reached its maximum, and may be capable of producing the most splendid igneous phenomena, like the northern lights, or tropical thunder-storms."

THE FORMATION OF SMOKE-RINGS.

Mr. W. B. Tegetemeir, in the London *Intellectual Observer*, in an article on the production of " smoke-rings," such as are produced by the spontaneous combustion of phosphuretted hydrogen, and by practised tobacco-smokers, describes an interesting method by which these rings can be produced at pleasure by mechanical means. He says, " If six ordinary, oblong cards, each about three inches by four, are taken and the ends folded down, after being partially cut through, so as to leave a central square, as here shown, they may with a little dexterity be combined into a very pretty cubical box. Previous to being put together, a circular hole about the size of a fourpenny-piece should be cut in one card. If the box so con- 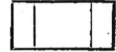 structed be filled with any dense smoke, such as that from a tobacco-pipe, or by allowing vapors of hydrochloric acid and ammonia to enter together, smoke-rings, in any number, and at any desired rate of succession, may be caused to issue from the hole in the box, by the slightest series of gentle taps on one of the sides. Their production in this manner is so facile, and so perfectly under control, that their formation constitutes — if the experiment be performed in a room in which the air is perfectly still — a very interesting and pretty experiment.

" So much for the mode of producing these rings. Now let us consider their construction. If the reader has ever observed an ascending column of smoke, on a perfectly calm day, he cannot fail to have been struck with the extreme beauty of its form, — rising, perhaps, from the summit of one of those tall factory chimneys, now, alas, so smokeless ! It ascends perpendicularly, spreading out as it rises, and gradually assuming the form of an elongated convolvulus, or, to use a less poetical and more homely comparison, that of a long funnel. This spreading out is due to the resistance of the air, which is greater, being more concentrated, toward the centre than at the outside.

" If the reader can imagine the emission of smoke to be intermittent, instead of continuous, it is obvious that this expanding column would be

13

broken up into rings, the constantly enlarging circular form of which would be due to the same cause as that which produces the enlargement of the column, namely, the greater pressure of the air in the centre. That this is the case will be evident on a close inspection of a single ring, when it will be found to consist of a vast number of rapidly rotating circles, arranged on a circular axis.   Let us imagine a number of common, circular, bone button-moulds, each with a single hole through its centre, strung on a piece of wire, which is then bent in a circular form.   This would give a correct idea of the structure of a smoke-ring; and if we imagine, further, each of these bone moulds rotating downward and inward, as the ring rises and expands, the resemblance would be still more complete."

PHENOMENA OF SOUND.

The following is an abstract of a recent lecture before the Royal Institution, London, by Prof. Tyndall, on the "phenomena of sound : "—

He began by showing how musical sounds can be produced by causing water to flow through small apertures, these sounds being probably due to the viscosity of the liquid, causing it to create tremors in the orifice.   He then proceeded to consider and exemplify the phenomena of resonance in open tubes, the cavity of the mouth being adduced as an instance, as in the case of the jewsharp, which thereby becomes a musical instrument.   The human voice, it was also stated, is produced by a reed instrument, the reeds being vibrating membranes, which can be tightened so as to vary the pitch (as has been made visible by Czermak's remarkable apparatus, the laryngoscope).   Vibrating reeds, or tongues, also produce the sound in the concertina and harmonica, and are also associated with organ pipes.   The latter part of the lecture was devoted to the consideration of the phenomena of interference, and discord or dissonance, in accordance with the following principles, based on the researches of Young, Wheatstone, Savart, and other philosophers.   The sonorous shocks communicated to the ear by two tuning-forks slightly out of unison are termed beats, which succeed each other more rapidly as the departure from perfect unison augments, — their number, in a given time, being equal to the difference in the number of vibrations executed in that time by the sounding bodies.   When the beats were slow, they could be counted with ease ; but when exceedingly rapid, they manifested themselves to the ear by the roughness which they impart to the sound ; the roughness is the cause of dissonance.   Professor Tyndall concluded his lecture by exhibiting some of Lissajous's remarkable acoustic experiments, by means of tuning-forks, mirrors, and the electric lamp.   It having been proved that a tuning-fork does not emit sound with the same intensity in all directions, and that the sounds of two tuning-forks which vibrate exactly at the same rate blend together so as to give the impression of a single sound, it was next shown that if one tuning-fork vibrate a little more rapidly than the other, at certain times both forks conspire to augment the sound, and at other times they act in opposition to each other.   The consequence being an intermittent effect, composed of successive periods of sound and silence.   When two sounds thus neutralize each other, the effect is technically called interference.   It was also shown how, by the stifling of a portion of the vibrations of a sounding disk, we can augment the sonorous intensity.

Propagation of Sound in the Air. — Newton was the first to study the propagation of motion in the atmosphere, and the solution which he gave still excites the admiration of geometers, and is termed by Laplace "a monument of his genius." Sometimes, however, it does not entirely agree with experience; for instance, it gives for the swiftness of propagation a value of about a sixth below that given by observation. Since his time Lagrange, Euler, Laplace, Poisson, and other geometers, have occupied themselves with this problem with the view of either establishing the true mathematical theory, or discovering the cause of the difference between calculation and experience. The subject has also been taken up by the eminent mathematician Duhamel, who has laid a memoir before his associates of the French Academy, giving his calculations, whereby he arrives at this singular consequence, — "that the theoretic swiftness of sound in the air, supposing that there is no elevation of temperature, is identical with that given by experience." The hypothesis of an elevation of temperature, which appears so probable, and which comes so conveniently to the assistance of the theory, becomes a difficulty, and we find ourselves compelled either to demonstrate that this hypothesis is not legitimate, or to find a new and hitherto unknown cause which shall neutralize the effect.

Transmission of Sound to a great Distance. — Dr. F. C. Robinson, of Greensburg, Westmoreland County, Pa., says that the report of artillery at the battle of Gettysburg, on the 3d of July, was distinctly heard at Greensburgh, a distance of one hundred and twenty-five miles from the seat of conflict; on lying down on the ground, jarring could be distinctly felt. Dr Robinson says, "That the whole neighborhood claim to have heard the firing. During Friday, the air was calm and the sky cloudless."

Function of the Ear. — Prof. Helmholz regards the snail-shell, or *cochlea*, as the special organ for transmitting musical sounds to the nerves, while noises affect other portions of the ear. The so-called "fibres of Corti," of which there are about three thousand, he considers each capable of being affected by a simple sound, while a compound sound acts upon several, and produces a corresponding impression on the nerves. Each filament of the acoustic nerve is united to an elastic filament, which he supposes to be thrown into vibration by appropriate sounds.

VIBRATING WATERFALLS.

The *American Journal of Science and Arts*, for November, 1863, contains an article, by Prof. E. Loomis, discussing anew the subject "*vibrating waterfalls,*" and detailing observations on three vibrating waterfalls, namely, in South Natick, Holyoke, and Lawrence, Mass. In 1843, Professor Loomis published an article on this same subject, in which he suggested that the dam itself was the vibrating body, and that the vibrations were analogous to those of a stretched cord. Prof. Snell, of Amherst, however, differed from such a conclusion, and in turn attributed the cause of the vibrations to a column of air behind the sheet of water falling from the dam. Prof. Loomis, after an extended series of observations, has apparently abandoned his original views, and arrived at conclusions similar to those of Prof. Snell. A series of careful observations were made, in 1862, by Mr. William Edwards, at the request of

Professor Loomis, on the vibrations of a dam at South Natick, Mass. These resulted in ascertaining that the time of a vibration, according to the depth of water on the edge of the dam, was a little less than the time in which a solid body would fall through a space equal to the depth of the water. Thus, when the depth of water was 5.06 inches, the time of one vibration was 0.138 of a second, while the time of a solid body falling through that depth was 0.162 of a second.

The dam across the Connecticut River, at Holyoke, Mass., is 1017 feet long, and 30 feet high. It is formed of square timbers inclined 22 degrees to the horizon. From the crest of the dam, the water descends along an apron about four feet in length, sloping downward at an angle of 22 degrees. The sheet of water falling over this dam exhibits three different rates of vibration, namely, about 256, 135, and 81 vibrations per minute, corresponding to depths of 16, 28, and 56 inches of water on the dam. The change from the first to the second rate of vibration takes place when the depth of water is from 23 to 26 inches; and the change from the second rate to the third takes place when the depth is from 35 to 47 inches. The vibrations are not noticed when the depth of water is less than about 12 inches, and they also disappear when the depth is as great as 80 inches.

At Lawrence, Mass., Mr. B. Coolidge, engineer, made a series of observations, as also did Prof. Loomis. In all these, the time of the vibrations was taken, and compared with the time which a solid body would occupy in falling from the same height; and the number of vibrations of a column of air of the depth behind the sheet of falling water has been calculated. Now, as to the conclusions, Prof. Loomis says, " I do not know of any theory which will enable us to compute the precise influence of a sheet of water of given dimensions; but at present, it seems probable that the vibratory motion originates in the column of air behind the sheet of water, and that the descending sheet serves merely as a load to retard the velocity of these vibrations." When the edge of the dam is uneven, and when the sheet of water is very thin, an opening will be left for the column of air behind the sheet, and no vibrations are produced. In reference to this point, Prof. Loomis says, " It is believed that most waterfalls exhibit some degree of vibratory motion, at certain stages of water; but in order that these vibrations may be powerful and long-continued, the edge of the dam must be horizontal, and quite smooth; otherwise, the thickness of the descending sheet will not be uniform; and the sheet will swell into ridges in some places, while other parts become thin. The sheet will divide in some places before reaching the bottom of the fall, and this leaves an opening in the enclosure which contains the column of vibrating air. This is probably the reason why many waterfalls never exhibit this phenomenon in a palpable manner; and why, in only a few cases, is the vibration so powerful as to cause any annoyance."

The answer to the question, Why the vibrations vary or disappear with variations in the height of the water is given as follows: " The descending sheet of water must have a thickness of several inches; otherwise, it is divided by the action of the air, and the column of air ceases to be enclosed on all sides. With a fall of nine feet, as at South Natick, a thickness of four or five inches is requisite; and with a fall of thirty feet, as at Holyoke, a thickness of nearly a foot is requisite.

At Lawrence, with a fall of thirty-four feet, the vibrations are not noticed when the depth of water is much less than three feet; but this seems to be owing to the inequalities on the top of the dam. The vibrations cease almost entirely when the water exceeds a certain height because the thickness of the sheet becomes too great in comparison with its height, and there being some cohesion between the particles of the liquid, the sheet partakes somewhat of the rigidity of a solid body. In order to produce a strong effect, the thickness of the sheet must not exceed about one-sixth or one-eighth of the height of the fall. At South Natick, with a fall of nine feet, which is somewhat diminished by the back-water at the time of a freshet, the vibrations cease when the depth of water much exceeds ten inches. At Holyoke, with a fall of thirty feet, which is also diminished by the back-water at the time of a freshet, the vibrations cease when the depth of water much exceeds five feet. At Lawrence, also, where the fall is a little greater than at Holyoke, the vibrations cease when the depth of water, on the crest of the dam, much exceeds five feet."

According to these views, all dams may be built so as to avoid jarring vibrations.

SCIENTIFIC BALLOON ASCENSIONS.

Under the auspices of the British Association, the balloon ascensions inaugurated in 1862, for scientific observation and experiment, have been continued during the past year by Mr. Glaisher the well-known British meteorologist, and the former aeronaut, (see *Annual Sci. Dis.* 1863, pp. 137–144.) At the last meeting of the Association, this gentleman gave the following *resumé* of the facts and deductions arrived at in his recent ascensions : —

On ascending with a cloudy sky, the temperature usually declines till the clouds are reached ; but on breaking through them, there is always an increase of several degrees of temperature ; and after this the decline of temperature usually continues, and would do so continuously if there were no disturbing causes in operation. On ascending with a clear sky, we start with a higher temperature than with a cloudy one as much higher as the loss of heat caused by the clouds; an approximate measure of which is that sudden increase of temperature in passing from cloud to a clear sky. In no instance have I met with the atmosphere in a normal state in respect to temperature ; at different elevations even up to four or five miles, warm currents of air have been met with. By warm, I mean that their temperature was higher than in the stratum beneath. These warm strata are variable in thickness, from 1,000 feet to 10,000 feet, and varying from 1° to 20° in excess. It is necessary, in considering the law of the decrease of temperature, to take into account the state of the sky, and to separate the experiments made in one state from those in the other. The results in the cloudy state do not at all confirm the theory of a decline of 1° of temperature in 300 feet. If we now consider the decrease at heights above the cloud plane, — the decrease of the temperature of the air, at heights exceeding 5,000 feet, — the results follow almost in sequence with those found with a partially clear sky, and show that an average change takes place of 1° of temperature in 139 feet near the earth and that for a change of 1° at the height of 30,000 feet, we have to pass through at

13*

least 1,000 feet. If we now take the whole decrease of temperature with elevation, we shall have the following results: From the ground to 1,000 feet 7.2°, or 1° in 139 feet. About 14,000, the average is the same as would be given by using the mean as found from observations on mountain-sides, namely 1° in 300 feet; but at heights less and greater than 14,000 feet the space is less or greater than 300 feet. It is certain, then, in any balloon ascent, between 8,000 and 20,000 feet, if the temperature on leaving the earth, and at the highest elevation, were only used, that the results, 1° in 254 feet in the former, and 1° in 355 in the latter, would have been looked upon as generally confirming the theory of a decline of 1° in 300 feet, and hence the necessity of noting the temperature on leaving the earth, as frequently as possible afterwards, and extending the observations to the highest point possible. It would appear from the results obtained that the decline of temperature is largest near the earth, smallest at the highest elevations, and intermediate with increasing spaces for the same decrease of temperature, in these respects agreeing, therefore, with the general law, as formed from the extreme high ascents. This law seems to me more natural and consistent than a uniform rate of decrease could be, received as a physical law, up even to moderate elevations. But I have reasons to believe that the amount of change is different at different seasons of the year, and I think it is different during the night from that during the day. And it seems certain that these laws will not hold good for all countries, although they probably will for very large tracts of country. I have reason to believe they will not hold good in India.

From all the experiments made in the year 1862, it was found that at the earth's surface there were upon the average very nearly five grains of water in a cubic foot of air, in the invisible shape of vapor, or 1-50th part of a cubic inch of water; or a cube of water whose sides were a quarter of an inch nearly. This value decreased gradually to one-half at the height of 5,000 feet, where there was only 1-100th of an inch of water in a cubic foot of air. At the height of 10,000 feet this amount was reduced to less than $1\frac{1}{4}$ grain; at 15,000 feet high there was only 9-10ths of a grain, or 1-280th part of a cubic inch; at 20,000 feet, this was reduced to half a grain; and at 25,000 feet to 1-10th only of a grain or to a drop of water, $=$ 1-2530th part of a cubic inch, being 1-50th part only of the water at the surface of the earth; in other words, about a drop of water but little more than 1-100th of an inch in diameter. But the actual amount met with on any ascent will most probably differ from these results, as, like the temperature of the air, the diffusion of water seems to be very rarely in a normal state. The amount of water in the air at the same height seems to be constantly varying, and to be affected with diurnal changes, so that on comparing the moisture shown at one ascent with that experienced in another, the time of day at which the experiments were made will have to be considered. I have been speaking of the amount of water actually present in the air. This information, without reference to temperature, gives no idea of the moisture of the atmosphere, since a capacity of air for moisture doubles itself for an increase of about 20° of temperature; a clearer idea of the relative moisture at different heights will be given, by considering that amount of water in the air which would saturate it as divided into 100 parts, and then ascertaining how many of these parts are present. From all the experiments treated in this way, the laws of moisture thus expressed are, with an overcast sky, almost uniform degree of humidity to the height of 3,000 feet — or 77 out of the 100 parts — then a rather sudden decrease to 80, and to 83 at 5,000 feet. With a partially clear sky, the laws of moisture show a humidity on the ground, with 15 out of 100 parts more than in partially clear skies, and of 14 at 5,000 feet. Above 5,000 feet, the humidity decreases to 10 at 25,000 ; that is, low as the temperature there is, 10, out of the 100 possible to be present, at the temperature, is all that is present. Higher than this, there would seem to be an almost entire absence of aqueous vapor. These seem to be the general laws; but, as I have before remarked, the regular dimensions are frequently interrupted, and strata of moist air may exist at great elevations.

As regards the *blue color of the sky*, Mr. Glaisher was inclined to attribute the phenomena to reflection of light from the molecules of air, and not, as some have supposed, to reflection from the thin pellicle of water forming the vesicles of vapor floating in the air ; inasmuch as the blue was found to be brightest at the greatest heights (six and seven miles) attained to by the aeronaut, where the air is almost deprived of moisture.

In an ascent made in a rain-storm on the 27th of July, Mr. Glaisher directed his attention particularly to observe whether there was a stratum of cloud at a certain elevation above that from which the raindrops fell ; and also as regards the size of the drops at different elevations. The conclusions arrived at were, that whenever rain is falling from an overcast sky, there is a second stratum above; but with an overcast sky and no rain, then the sun is shining on the upper surface of the clouds. In regard to the second point, he says, " The size of the rain-drops, as they fell on my note-book before starting, was fully as large as a four-penny piece ; they decreased in size on ascending ; but our upward movement was too quick, and we soon passed out of rain. On descending from above the clouds, we first encountered a dry and then a wet fog ; passed into that which may be described as damp air or exceedingly fine rain ; then experienced very fine but decided drops of rain, like pins' points, covering the note-book ; these increased in size on approaching the earth, but more rapidly when very near the earth. The drops of rain, on returning to the earth, were as large as those noted on leaving ; and rain had been falling heavily all the time we were in the balloon." Another curious fact elicited in these ascensions is that the action of the sun's rays upon " sensitized" photographic paper is much less at great altitudes than near the earth's surface. In an ascension made April 21st, 1863, Mr. Glaisher took with him slips of such paper, and arranged that similar slips should be exposed at Greenwich Observatory, and the amount of coloration noted simultaneously every five minutes. In his report, he states that the paper in the balloon was exposed to the full rays of the sun, with this extraordinary result, — that at three miles high the paper did not color so much in half an hour as in the grounds of the Royal Observatory in one minute ; — a fact which would seem to indicate that the chemical effects of light are largely due to its passage through the atmosphere, or at least to the density of the atmosphere through which it has recently passed."

In this same ascent, observations were made on *the solar spectrum,* especially upon the fixed lines of the spectrum. The number of lines visible seemed to be innumerable, and the conclusion arrived at is thus given: "The number of lines in the solar spectrum appear to be increased when viewed from a position above the clouds, and therefore none of the lines as viewed from the earth would seem to be atmospheric."

The most extraordinary ascent was made in the month of June 1863, of which Mr. Glaisher's record is as follows: —

"We left the earth at 1h. 5m. P. M.; at 1h. 9m. we were at the height of two thousand feet; at 1h. 15m. we passed above eight thousand feet; a height of eleven thousand feet was reached at 1h. 17m.; in nine minutes afterwards, we were fifteen thousand feet from the earth, and rose gradually to about four and a quarter miles at 1h. 55m.; on descending, at 2h., we were twenty thousand feet from the earth; at 2h. 13m. about fifteen thousand; at 2h. 17m. ten thousand; at 2h. 22m. five thousand; and on the ground 2h. 28m. Before starting, the temperature of the air was sixty-six degrees. It decreased rapidly on leaving the earth; it was fifty-four degrees at three thousand feet high, forty-nine degrees at four thousand feet, forty-one degrees at one mile, thirty degrees at two miles; and, up to this time, every succeeding reading was less than the preceding. But here the decrease was checked; and, while passing from two to three miles, the temperature at first increased to thirty-two degrees, then decreased to twenty-nine degrees. A second increase followed, and at the height of three and a quarter miles the temperature was thirty-five degrees. A rapid decrease then set in, and at three and a half miles the temperature was twenty-two degrees. From this time till the height of four miles was reached, the temperature varied frequently between twenty-two degrees and eighteen degrees, and at the height of four and a quarter miles, the lowest temperature took place — namely, seventeen degrees. On descending, the temperature increased to twenty-six degrees, at the height of twenty-three thousand feet, and then to thirty-two degrees, at the height of four miles; it then decreased nine degrees in one minute to twenty-three degrees. It continued at this value for some time, then increased slowly to twenty-nine degrees at nineteen thousand feet. It continued almost constant for a space of two thousand feet, then increased to thirty-two degrees at fifteen thousand feet; and was thirty-two degrees or thirty-three degrees, almost without variation, during a snow-storm which we experienced from thirteen thousand five hundred feet to ten thousand feet, where an increase set in; at five thousand feet, the temperature was forty-one degrees, and sixty-six degrees on the ground."

At a height of two miles the sighing or rather moaning of the wind was heard, as preceding a storm, and was the first instance in which Mr. Glaisher had heard such a sound at such a height. It was not owing to any movement of the cordage of the balloon above, but seemed to be below, as from conflicting currents beneath. "At the highest point reached, about four and a quarter miles, the sky was very much covered with cirrus clouds, and its color, as seen through the breaks in the clouds, was of a pale blue, such as is seen from the earth through a very moist atmosphere. We were above clouds, but there were no fine views or forms, — all was dirty-looking and confused, the atmosphere being thick and murky.

"At the height of three miles a train was heard, and at four miles another. These heights are the greatest at which sounds have ever been detected, and indicate the generally moist state of the atmosphere."

Mr. Glaisher concludes: "This ascent must rank amongst the most extraordinary ever made. The results were most unexpected. We met with at least three distinct layers of cloud on ascending, of different thicknesses, reaching up to four miles high, when here the atmosphere, instead of being light and clear as it always has been in preceding ascents, was thick and misty; but perhaps the most extraordinary and unexpected result in the month of June was meeting with snow and crystals of ice in the atmosphere at the height of three miles, and of nearly one mile in thickness."

ASCERTAINING THE HEIGHT OF CLOUDS.

At the British Association, 1863, Prof. Chevallier gave the following description of an instrument of his invention, designed to ascertain the height of clouds. It consisted, he said, of two jointed rulers, graduated from the centre of the joint, and one of them furnished with an upright sliding-piece, with an opening to allow the sun's light to pass, the edge of which is at a known distance by the scale from the ruler on which the piece slides. If, then, the distance in miles or yards at which the shadow of a cloud is cast upon the earth be known, by laying one branch of the ruler toward the shadow of the cloud and the other in the direction of the vertical line from the part of the cloud which casts the shadow directly on the earth beneath the cloud, and then moving the sliding-piece along this latter branch of the ruler until the shadow of the edge of the opening just reaches the middle of the rod laid in the direction of the shadow of the cloud, you have on the ruler and the sliding-piece an exact representation in miniature of the actual circumstances of the cloud, and a simple rule-of-three calculation gives the vertical height of the cloud above the earth. Thus, "multiply the distance of the shadow of the cloud (supposed to be known) by the height of the sliding-piece, and divide by the distance of the shadow of the sliding-piece from the angle of the rulers, and the quotient is the height of the cloud required."

OBSERVATIONS ON WINDS.

Prof. Dove, the celebrated meteorologist of Berlin, in the second edition of his *Law of Storms*, recently published by the Longmans, of London, thus explains his so-called "Laws of Gyration," or the rotation of the wind in relation to the rotation of the earth. He says, — "In the northern hemisphere, when polar and equatorial currents succeed each other, the wind veers in general in the direction S., W., N., E., S., round the compass. Exceptions to this rule are more common between S. and W. and between N. and E., than between W. and N. or between E. and S.

"In the southern hemisphere, when polar and equatorial currents succeed each other, the wind veers in general in the direction S., E., N., W., S., round the compass. Exceptions to this rule are more common between N. and W. and between S. and E., than between W. and S. or between E. and N.

"*This is the phenomenon which I have termed* THE LAW OF GYRATION."

The trade-winds and monsoons are special causes of this law. Professor Dove enters into a minute examination of the phenomena of the first, dividing what he calls the permanent winds into the under and upper trade-winds. Both, he is disposed to regard, as imperfectly developed monsoons, the word monsoon being as he shows, derived from the Arabic *mausim*, or season. This is confirmed by the fact that where monsoons exist, there are but two oscillatory movements of the atmosphere annually; monsoons being polar and equatorial currents, alternately, according to the season of the year; so that their directions in the northern hemisphere are N. E. and S. W., and in the southern S. E. and N. W. Violent as monsoons generally are, they are tame in comparison to cyclones, which are truly terrible. Fortunately, the area of these hurricanes is comparatively limited, being confined to the West Indian seas; their usual course being in a parabolic curve, having some point near Bermuda for its focus — originating in the Gulf of Florida — and running along the coast of the United States, following generally the course of the Gulf-stream. Cyclones, as their name imports, are strictly rotatory, and they never deviate from the following rules. Cyclones in the northern hemisphere possess a motion that is retrograde, or in the contrary direction to the hands of a watch, whereas, those occurring in the southern hemisphere have a converse motion. On the equator itself cyclones never occur. According to Professor Dove, they are —

" Most common in the district between the S. E. trade-wind and the N. W. monsoon, which is called the region of the ' variables.'

" The rotatory motion takes place in the direction from E. through S. toward W. and N. The intensity of the cyclone increases regularly toward its centre. At the centre itself there is a dead calm, and the greatest violence of the storm is experienced at the edge of this calm circle. The diameter of this circle is greatest when the storm is just commencing. If the rotatory motion increases in violence, the diameter of this circle is decreased to about ten or twelve English miles.

" The advance of the cyclone, up to lat. 20° S., is at the rate of 200 to 220 miles in the twenty-four hours. From that point it becomes less rapid up to the outer edge of the S. E. Trade. The direction of the advance is from lat. 10° S., near the Indian Archipelago, to lat. 28° or 30° on the east coast of Africa; first toward W. S. W., then toward S. W. by S., and lastly toward S. S. W.

" Throughout the whole of the cyclone, torrents of rain fall, which are more violent in front of it than behind it. The clouds are dark, massive, and lead-colored, as the centre is approaching. Electrical explosions are most frequent on that side of the cyclone which is nearest to the equator. The sea is disturbed irregularly to the distance of 300 or 400 miles during every such storm. The barometer falls rapidly as the centre of the cyclone approaches, but the lowest level appears to occur a little before it passes."

Direction of the Wind. — Professor Airy has observed some curious facts respecting the direction of the wind. It seems that there are only eight points of the compass from which the wind ever blows steadily for any length of time, namely, the S. S. W., the W. S. W. a point between the W. and N. W., another between the N. and E., another between E. and S. S. W., the N., the W., and the E. The wind never blows directly from the south.

PRESSURE OF THE ATMOSPHERE, OCEAN, ETC.

The following novel views respecting the pressure of the atmosphere, and of the waters of the ocean at varying depths have been communicated by Mr. C. E. Townsend, Esq., of Tompkinsville, N. Y. : —

According to the philosophy of the day, the pressure of the atmosphere at sea-level is calculated at fifteen pounds for every square inch, being equal to a column of water one inch broad and thirty-three feet in height, and every thirty-three feet descent into the ocean adds an additional fifteen pounds pressure, over every square inch, thus augmenting the density of parts beneath in proportion to the superincumbent pressure. Recent discoveries prove that a high order of radiate animals and fleshy inhabitants of shells, in vast numbers, are found living at the bottom of the ocean one and a half miles down.

In a paper from Dr. I. C. Wallack, in the *Scientific Annual* for 1862, page 344, Professor Agassiz, is made to say " that animals subject to such enormous pressure, to avoid being crushed by the weight, from depths at fifteen pounds for every thirty-three feet descent, must admit water very freely through their tissues." Surely such explanation must be unsatisfactory, for the animal tissues remaining, *they* could not possibly sink in a medium one and a half miles down, which, according to the old philosophy, is equal to two hundred and forty times the specific gravity of surface water. Wood, which is specifically a little heavier than surface water, is supposed to sink to the bottom, whatever that depth may be, and to enable it to do so, in accordance with the above estimates of increasing pressure, must have its bulk diminished 240 times to enable it to sink into the lower stratum, whose density is equal to 8600 pounds to the square inch. Thus a block of wood six inches square, would have to be reduced by successive pressures to a little less than one inch square, to reach the bottom. Animal life could not exist subject to such disorganizing pressures and survive on being brought to the surface, subject to a corresponding inflation, and yet we know animals do live at the bottom, and are brought to the surface alive. Indeed, according to this old philosophy, the shells must be subject to the same contraction and expansion, which is hardly a supposable case.

It is said that animal bodies, on the surface of the earth, support a pressure of fifteen pounds to every square inch, which is equal to 30,-000 pounds pressure for the average size of man ; and to enable him to bear this weight (for it is not supposed that his muscular power is equal to the task), it is contended that the pressure exists equally on all sides, pressing with equal force upwards, downwards, sideways, inwards and outwards, thus confessedly making such supposed weight a nullity. As this same pressure acts on the same principle throughout the mass of the earth, water and air, it is necessarily a nullity everywhere, and consequently only an imaginary philosophy. The true explanation is, we suggest, the existence of a molecular repulsion, as well as admitted attraction, operating throughout the mass of all solids, liquids, and gases, in their normal condition, which effectually prevents any considerable condensation from simple incumbent weight, and this molecular repulsion and attraction may be positive and negative electricity.

RESEARCHES ON THE FIGURE OF THE MOON.

Some interesting researches have recently been made respecting the figure of the moon, which suggest many interesting speculations. Prof. Hansen, the German astronomer, claims to have proved by investigation, that the hemisphere of our satellite, which alone is visible to us, is nothing but a mountain-range, raised twenty-nine miles above the average level of the moon's surface; or, to express the same thing more technically, that the centre of gravity of the moon is not her geometrical centre, but twenty-nine miles on the opposite side of her geometrical centre. That is, the more solid part of the moon would be on the far side from the earth, and all that we see of her would be a bulging hemisphere, comparatively much less dense and weighty, projecting twenty-nine miles beyond the surface which the moon ought to show to us if the density were equal throughout; and if the hemisphere on this side, therefore, were uniform in weight and form with the hemisphere on the other side, Prof. Hansen supposes, in fact,—and astronomers appear to think that he has proved his case,—that the moon turns a sort of tower of crusty, broken, porous, and therefore lighter, substance to the earth; so that we see only an exaggerated Alpine or Andes region, projecting nearly thirty miles beyond the average level of the lunar surface. If this be true, there are all sorts of provoking consequences. As we never get a glimpse of the other side of the moon, which keeps always facing about just so as to avoid showing us her other hemisphere, we never get a glimpse at the average level of the lunar surface. Hence, all our conclusions as to the uninhabitability of the moon, derived from a knowledge that no clouds and no atmosphere of any appreciable degree exist on *this* side of the moon, are untrustworthy. Twenty-nine miles above the average surface of the earth, the rarity of even our own atmosphere would be probably so great as to render it scarcely appreciable at all, even to astronomical instruments, and quite unequal to the support of any of the vegetable or animal life of our earth. Accordingly, conjecture may take full possession of this invisible side of the moon; and conjecture does, in fact, give it back the atmosphere which had been denied it, the outer margin of which is supposed so far to touch the mountain heights of this barren side, as to justify those astronomers who fancy they have seen proof of a very thin atmosphere in the refraction of stars just on the edge of the moon; and to confirm the assertion of the astronomer Schröter, that he had discovered traces of twilight there, which could, of course, only be due to an atmosphere of some kind. Thus much may certainly be granted, that if Prof. Hansen is correct, the lunar atmosphere, if it exist at all, would certainly be attracted to the opposite or heavy side, and might well fail to be sensible at an elevation of twenty-nine miles, even though quite dense enough to support terrestrial life and vegetation at the average level of the lunar surface. It gives no proof that such an atmosphere exists, but does give very good reasons why, if there be one, we have failed to detect it with any certainty.

ADDITIONAL RESEARCHES ON THE FIGURE OF THE MOON.

No one who has seen Mr. De la Rue's (London) stereoscopes of the full moon, in which the two images are obtained separately, but by one and the same optical instrumentality at the epochs of her extreme eastern and western librations in longitude, according to Mr. Wheatstone's ingenious suggestion, can fail to have been struck by the marked and undeniable deviation from the spherical form which the double picture suggests, standing out, as the convex surface does, in bold and full relief; exhibiting the most complete appearance of a round, projecting (vaguely speaking), *globular* figure. It is quite obvious, in a certain mode of presenting the images to the eyes, that, were it really a solid object so presented to our view, no one would hesitate to pronounce it rather egg-shaped than *spherical*. The apparent curvature of the surface under such circumstances is not that of a perfect sphere, alike throughout; but conveys the irresistible impression of an elongation in one direction, and that, not directly toward the eye, but forming a pretty considerable angle, with the visual ray joining the eye and the moon's centre. Nor does the form even present a perfect symmetry, as of a solid of revolution; but, on the contrary, somewhat distorted, or, as it were, skewed. The question which now arises is, how far any such appearances in a stereograph are to be received as evidence of a corresponding reality of conformation in the moon itself. And here we must at once reject any idea of explaining them by optical distortion, due to instrumental causes, or to photographic error, or subsequent distortion in procuring the positive impressions from the original negatives. The instrumental means at Mr. De la Rue's command preclude the one supposition, and the photographic process employed (collodion on glass, optically copied), the other.

Mr. Gussew, Director of the Imperial Observatory at Wilna, with a view to determine how far the whole or any part of this apparent anomaly of figure is real, has subjected each of the two pictures of a pair in his possession, given him by Mr. De la Rue, to careful and rigorous microscopic measurement, by selecting on each of the pictures a considerable number of sharply-defined, and securely identifiable points, identical in each, and by measuring with extreme precision, by the aid of an apparatus constructed for the purpose, their distances from the centres and several points in the circumferences of the pictures. From these measures (which under such circumstances must be regarded as fully entitled to all the confidence of micrometrical measures, astronomically taken at the telescope), on subjecting them to mathematical computation, and applying the necessary corrections for parallax and refraction as affecting the diameter of the moon, and the apparent figure of her disk, Mr. Gussew has been led to conclude that a real eccentricity of the figure actually does exist, and that, in point of fact, a portion of the moon's surface having its axis directed about five degre from the earth as seen from the moon at the epoch of her mean libr may be considered as belonging to a sphere of smaller radi

14

therefore, more convex) than the mean radius of the moon by about eighteen parts in 1,000, and, of which, the centre is situated nearer to the earth than that of the whole moon, by seventy-three thousandths of such mean radius (seventy-nine English miles). The portion of the moon, then, turned toward the earth may be considered as a continuous mountain mass, in the form of a meniscus lens, capping the sphere of the moon, and rising in its middle to a height of about seventy-nine English miles above the general level of its figure of equilibrium.

THE MATHEMATICS OF THE BEEHIVE.

In the *Annals of Natural History* (London), 1863, will be found an analysis of the mathematics of the beehive, by the Rev. S. Houghton, in which the theory of the bee's forming hexagonal cells is completely overthrown. Lord Brougham, in his treatise *Dialogues on Instinct*, remarks: "There is no bee in the world that ever made cylindrical cells;" and the fact of the existence of hexagonal cells in the honeycomb is generally quoted as a wonderful example of instinctive combination of means to ends in a low form of animal existence.· Mr. Houghton, however, shows that the bee makes only cylindrical cells, and that the hexagonal and rhomboidal cells are alike the result of pressure, and represent the angles of equilibrium between the pressure and the resistance, just as the orbits of the planets are the midway lines between centrifugal and centripetal forces; the bee is not, therefore, such a mathematician as has been generally supposed. The alleged economy of material resulting from the bee's method of working is also shown to be fallacious. Several mathematicians have carefully investigated the relation of expenditure of material to the mathematical requirements of connected cells of given dimensions, and of a form adapted to the uses to which they are to be put. L'Hullier, in 1781, arrived at the conclusion that the economy of wax referred to the total expenditure is $\frac{1}{51}$st, so that the bees can make fifty-one cells instead of fifty by the adoption of the rhombic dodecahedron. He also showed that mathematicians can make cells of the same form as those of the bees, which, instead of using only a *minimum* of wax, would use the *minimum minimorum*, so that five cells could be made of less wax than that which now makes only four, instead of fifty-one out of fifty. The humble-bee, moreover, in the construction of its cells, uses proportionably more than three times the amount of material that is used by the hive-bee.

SUBSTITUTE FOR WOOD-ENGRAVING.

The London *Art Journal* gives the following description of a process invented by Mr. Schulze, a German architect, for producing blocks for type-printing, to be used as a substitute for wood-engraving. "The material on which the drawing is to be made may be of glass or any other hard and smooth surface. The drawing is produced with a pen, and ink composed of pure gum-arabic dissolved in water, with the addition of sufficient sugar to prevent it cracking when dry; lamp-black, or any other color, is mixed with the gum solution to render the work visible. When the drawing is completed, it is covered with a coat of bees-wax, asphaltum, resin, and linseed oil. The thickness of the covering depends on the kind of work adopted by the artist; if the lines of the drawing are very close together, a thin coat will suffice. After this ground has been applied, the plate or glass has to be submerged in water for about ten or fifteen minutes ; then a strong stream of water is poured upon it, which will remove the waxy substance *above* the lines of the drawing, but will leave that *between* the lines undisturbed. In most cases, the grounding will be sufficiently high to insure a good electrotype for printing ; but where considerable height is required between lines far apart, this can readily be effected by applying wax according to the method now employed by stereotypists, or by adding asphaltum with the brush. Should the artist prefer to make his drawing on paper, the latter must first be rendered water-proof ; and after it has undergone this process, it should be attached, with a water-proof paste, to a hard and even plate before it is covered with the wax ; in all other respects, it is treated in the manner just described. Before taking the electro deposit the plate must be covered with alcoholic varnish, and when dry, black-lead — plumbago — is applied with a soft brush.

" The advantages of the process are stated by the inventor to be — The obtaining a perfect fac-simile of the artist's work ; the drawing has not to be reversed, as in the methods now in use for copying on the wood pictures or objects ; cheapness, and saving of time."

New Process of Engraving. — The following new process has been devised by M. Dalos, of Paris : A plate of copper is covered with a varnish of india-rubber and zinc-white. Lines are traced through this surface down to the metal by an ivory point. The plate is then plunged in a solution of hydrochlorate of ammonia, the positive electrode being a plate of iron in communication with the negative pole of the pile. Iron is deposited on all the parts of the copper exposed by the ivory point, but not on the varnish, which is removed by benzine. The plate is once more exposed to electric action in a bath of silver, and that metal is precipitated on the copper but not on the iron. It is then heated to 80° C., and an alloy, fusible at that temperature, is poured over it. The liquid moistens the silver and adheres to it, but not to the iron, which it does not moisten. When cold, the fusible alloy will be found standing on each side of every line, and forming a mould, from which a new plate, adapted to printing, is obtained by a galvanoplastic process.

DESIDERATA IN SCIENCE AND ART.

The London Society of Arts proposes annually a list of subjects for invention, discovery, or explanation, for the attainment of which it offers medals, or money premiums, varying in amount from $100 to $500. From the list proposed for this year, 1864, we copy such of the subjects as seem to us most important and suggestive, and as best illustrative of the more practical wants of the present epoch.

Goldsmith's Work. — For the best essay on ancient goldsmith's work.

Bronzes. — For the best essay on the manufacture and casting of bronzes, and on bronze washes.

Moulds for Metal Casting. — For the production of a material to be used in the formation of moulds for casting bronzes and other molten metals, so as to enable the casts to be produced without seams.

Pigments. — For an account of the various pigments used in the Fine Arts, with suggestions for the introduction of new and improved substances.

Substitute for Wood Blocks. — For the discovery of a substitute for the blocks used by wood-engravers, so as to supersede the necessity of uniting several pieces of wood.

Photographs on Enamel. — For the best portrait obtained photographically and burnt in in enamel.

Photographs on China. — For the production of a dessert or other service, in china or earthenware, ornamented by means of photography, and burnt in from an impression obtained either directly from the negative, or from a transfer from a metal plate obtained directly from the photograph.

Photographs on Windows. — For the production commercially of ornamental glass for windows by means of vitrified photographs.

Fluoric Acid. — For a substitute for fluoric acid, to be used for engraving on glass, which shall be free from noxious fumes.

Reproducing Designs for Printing. — For a rapid means of reproducing artistic designs or sketches, for surface-printing by machinery, such process to provide for lowering portions of the work to fit it for steam-printing.

Rollers for Calico-Printing. — For any important improvements for facilitating the production and economizing the cost of engraving rollers for printing calicoes and other fabrics.

Aniline Colors. — For a means of fixing upon cotton and other fabrics all the ordinary aniline colors, so that the dyed fabric will effectually resist the action of soap and water, or cold dilute alkalies.

Napthaline. — For a process for converting the napthaline of gasworks into alizarine or madder-red.

Chlorophyll. — For the manufacture of chlorophyll from grasses, suitable for dyeing silk and other fabrics of a green color.

Green Dyes. — For the manufacture of green dyes from coal, or wood-tar.

Paints for Carriages. — For the production of cheap purple and yellow lakes of good quality, suitable for carriage-builders, etc., and not liable to fade or change color.

New Scarlet Dye. — For the production of a scarlet dye for cotton.

Bleaching Wool. — For an account of any important improvements in the bleaching of wool.

Thickening Colors. — For the introduction of any substance, the use of which will essentially economize the cost of thickening the colors and sizes used in dyeing and dressing fabrics.

Substitute for Egg-Albumen. — For a thoroughly decolorized blood-albumen, or any economic and efficient substitute for egg-albumen in calico-printing.

Uses of Seaweed. — For the extraction from seaweed of any substance or preparation capable of extensive application as a dye, drug, thickening, tanning agent, or any other generally useful product. Also, for a means of rendering seaweeds generally available as a wholesome vegetable food on board ship.

Mining Machinery. — For improvements in the machinery for dressing poor ores of tin, lead, etc.

Regenerative Furnaces. — For the best account of the structure and application of regenerative furnaces to manufacturing purposes.

Melting Cast-Steel. — For an easy and cheap method of melting cast-steel in large masses.

Hydraulic Engine. — For a small, simple, cheap, and effective hydraulic engine, which, in connection with the ordinary water service of towns could be applied to lifts in warehouses, driving lathes, blowing the bellowses of organs, and many other purposes where steam cannot be made available.

Protecting Iron. — For the invention of an efficient method of protecting iron from the action of air and water, applicable to the various forms in which iron is used as a building material generally, and also to iron ships and armor-plated vessels.

Shoal Recorder. — For an instrument to indicate the depth of water under a ship's bottom, to prevent danger when at sea or nearing land.

Application of Electricity to Organs. — For the production of an organ in which, by the use of electricity or magnetism, tunes of greater length and variety than those ordinarily produced in barrel-organs may be performed mechanically.

Lace Machinery. — For a mechanical substitute for hand-labor in running in the outline to figures in machine-wrought lace.

Woven Garments. — For the production in the loom, and introduction into commerce, of woven garments, suited for soldiers, sailors, emigrants, operatives and others, so as to economize the cost of production, and reduce the amount of hand-labor.

Incombustible Paper. — For the production of an incombustible paper, so as to render the ledgers of commercial men, bankers, etc., indestructible by fire.

Dyeing and Dressing Leather. — For improvements in the method of dyeing or dressing morocco or calf-leather, in such manner as to prevent the surface from cracking in working, and to render it more fit to receive the gilding required in ornamenting books, furniture, and other articles.

Leather Cloth. — For improvements in the manufacture of leather-cloth, or artificial leather, especially in imparting strength and durability, so as to fit it for the purposes of saddlers, harnessmakers, trunk-makers, shoemakers, bookbinders and others.

New Gums. — For any new substance or compound which may be employed as a substitute for india-rubber or gutta-percha in the arts and manufactures.

New Gums or Oils. — For any new gums or oils, the produce of Africa, calculated to be useful in the arts and manufactures, and obtainable in quantity. Samples of not less than twenty-five pounds of gum, and fifty pounds of oil, to be transmitted to the Society.

Elastic Tubing. — For an elastic material for tubing, suited to the conveyance of gas, and not liable to be affected by alterations in temperature, or to be acted upon by the gas itself.

Color for Japanned Surfaces. — For the preparation of any color, applicable to the Japanned surfaces of *papier maché,* that shall be free from the brightness (or glare) of the varnished colors now used, but possess the same degree of hardness and durability.

14*

Color for Slate. — For the preparation of light colors to be used in enamelling or Japanning slate, which will stand the action of the heat from the fire without blistering or discoloration, and be sufficiently hard to resist scratches.

Electric Weaving. — To the manufacturer who practically applies electricity to the production commercially of figured fabrics in the loom.

Japanning Zinc. — For a process whereby the surface of articles manufactured in zinc may be economically japanned.

Coating Walls. — For the production of a cheap white enamel-like composition for the interior walls, etc., of houses, applicable to all ordinary surfaces, easily cleansed, not liable to crumble or chip, and capable of being tinted.

Substitute for Turpentine. — For a new and efficient substitute for turpentine, applicable to the manufacture of varnishes and to purposes for which turpentine is now ordinarily applied.

Substitute for Pitch. — For a cheap substitute for pitch, tar, &c., equally impervious to air and moisture, but not inflammable.

Paper Machinery. — For a portable machine for planing the bars of a rag-engine-roll true when the roll is in position.

Rollers for Printing Paper-Hangings. — For a composition for feeding rollers for printing paper-hangings by cylinder-machinery, similar in consistency and texture to the gelatine rollers used in letter-press printing, but adapted for working in water-colors.

Paper-Hangings Colored in the Pulp. — For the manufacture of papers from colored pulp, bearing upon them designs, either colored or white, discharged after the manner of calico-printing.

Green without Arsenic. — For the manufacture of a brilliant green color, not containing arsenic, copper, or other poisonous materials.

Improved Chemical Balance. — For the best chemical and assay balance, suitable for the use of students and experimentalists, which will (with 600 grains in each pan) show a difference of .005 or less. To be sold at a moderate price.

Cheap Spectroscope. — For the best and cheapest form of spectroscope.

Dialysing Apparatus. — For the best and cheapest form of dialysing apparatus, capable of being packed in a small compass, but of sufficient size to aid the country practitioner in the detection of poisons and adulterations, and in the preparation and purification of salts and drugs.

Incombustible Wick. — For the production of an incombustible wick, suitable for oil, spirit, and other lamps.

Cyanogen Compounds. — For the economical production of cyanogen compounds for employment in the arts, or as manures.

Oxygen Gas. — For a more economical process of obtaining oxygen gas than any in present use.

New Edible Roots. — For the discovery and introduction into this country of any new edible root, useful as food for man or cattle, and capable of extensive and improved cultivation.

Edible Seaweeds. — For a means of rendering seaweeds generally available as a wholesome vegetable food on board ship.

Colored Starches. — For the production of a series of colored starches, which can be applied to articles of dress, such as lace, etc., without injuring or staining the fabric, but at the same time give to them the required tints, and thus render them in harmony with other portions of dress.

Titanium. — For the best essay upon titanium, with suggestions for extracting and utilizing the metal.

Smelting Zinc. — For an account of the processes now in use for smelting zinc ores, with suggestions for their improvement.

Emigrants' Dwellings. — For the best essay (for the information of emigrants proceeding to new settlements), descriptive of the means of treating existing natural products in any locality, such as earths, shells, chalks, and limestones, woods, barks, grasses, etc., and applying them in the construction of dwellings. Diagrams and illustrations of the methods of applying materials should be given.

Dutch Prizes for Investigation. — The Dutch Society of Sciences have also recently issued a prize-list of subjects for scientific investigation, to which they invite answers to be sent in prior to January, 1865 ; and the following are some of the topics selected: A gold medal is offered for a paper on the Vertebrata (not including fishes) of the Indian Archipelago, particularly those of Borneo, Celebes, and the Moluccas, and above all those of New Guinea. In astronomy, a prize is offered for a determination, as exact as possible, of the errors of Hansen's Lunar Tables, by the occultations of the Pleiades, observed during the last revolution of the node of the lunar orbit. In electricity, the celebrated physicist, Ruhmkorff, has obtained sparks of extraordinary length, by the inductive machines which bear his name. Required: a determination, by experimental and theoretical researches, of the laws which govern the length and intensity of these sparks in machines of different sizes and construction. Other questions are, What difference is there between the perception of sounds with one and both ears ? Is fermentation, as indicated by the researches of Pasteur and others, due to the development of cryptogamia and infusoria ? and, if so, what is the exact description of these plants and animals and their mode of action ? Required: an investigation into the heat-conducting power of certain insulating, or non-conducting substances, as glass, marble, etc. Another is stated as follows: The researches of Gladstone and others have directed the attention of physicists to the changes which the indices of refraction of liquids undergo by a change of temperature. The Society attach great importance to a knowledge of the relation between the index of refraction and the temperature, convinced as they are that this knowledge would throw light on other very interesting points of the theory of light. They therefore invite a series of exact researches on these changes, in pure liquids and in solutions. The prizes are a gold medal worth 150 florins, and an equal amount in money.

CHEMICAL SCIENCE.

THE RECENT PROGRESS OF ORGANIC CHEMISTRY.

The following is an abstract of an address made to the chemical section of the British Association, 1863, by Professor Williamson, on assuming the Chair: —

One of the features of our science is the rate at which materials have been accumulating by the labors of chemists, in the so-called organic department of the science. The study of the transformation of organic bodies leads to the discovery of new acids, new bases, new alcohols, new ethers, and at a constantly increasing rate. Some of these new substances are found to possess properties which can at once be applied to practical manufacturing processes, such as dyeing, but the greater number of them remain in our laboratories and museums, and text-books. New discoveries are constantly coming in to fill up the gaps which still disfigure our growing system. In mineral, or in organic chemistry, there is not the same scope for discovery at present, inasmuch as the elements which belong to it do not combine in those numerous proportions which occur among the chief elements of organic bodies. But yet, mineral chemistry has not been standing still, for even the heavy metals, most remote in their properties from those volatile and unstable substances of organic chemistry, have been made in many instances to combine together, and the organic metallic bodies thus formed have not only proved most valuable and powerful agents of decomposition, but they have served as a connecting link between the two branches of chemical science. A system of classification of elements is now coming into use, in which the heavy metals arrange themselves harmoniously with the elements of organic bodies, and in accordance with the principles which were discovered by a study of organic compounds. It is now many years since the attention of chemists was directed by a French professor to some inconsistencies which had crept into our system of atomic weights. Gerhardt showed that the principles which were adopted in fixing the atomic weight of elementary bodies generally required us to adopt for oxygen, carbon, and sulphur, numbers twice as great as those generally in use for those elements. The logic of his arguments was unanswerable, and yet Gerhardt's conclusions gained but few adherents. It is to be observed, that for some years Gerhardt represented chemical reactions by so-called synoptic formulæ, which took no account of the existence of organic radicles. These synoptic formulæ represent in the simplest terms the result of a chemical reaction; but they give no physical image of the progress by which the reaction is brought about. The introduction, in this country, of the water-type in connection with poly-atomic as well as mon-atomic radicles, was found to satisfy the requirements of the synoptic formulæ. Gerhardt was the first to adopt them from us. He gave a system of organic chemistry on that plan, and his book has been of immense service to the development of our science. The extension of these principles to mineral chemistry had been commenced in the cases of the commonest acids and bases, but their general introduction met with difficulties, and sometimes seemed wanting to their complete success. It was reserved for Prof. Cannizzaro, of the University of Palermo, to show us how the remainder of the knot could be untied. He argued, upon physical as well as chemical grounds, that the atomic weight of many metals ought to be doubled, as well as those of oxygen, sulphur, and carbon. His conclusions are confirmed by the constitution of those organo-metallic bodies which I mentioned just now, and it certainly does seem to supply what was still wanting for the extension of our system of classification from the non-metallic elements to the heavy metals themselves. The elements are now arranged into two principal groups : — 1. Those of which each atom combines with an uneven number of atoms of chlorine or hydrogen. 2. Those of which each atom combines with an even number of atoms of chlorine or hydrogen. Like every classification founded upon nature this one draws no absolute line, as some elements belong to both classes. The first group includes the mon-atomic elements of the chlorine family, the tri-atomic elements of the nitrogen family, hydrogen, and the alkali metals, silver and gold, — in all about eighteen elements. The usual atomic weights of these are retained. The usual atomic weights of all the other elements, biatomic, tetratomic, etc., are doubled. This second group includes the oxygen family, carbon, silicon, and the alkaline earths, the metals zinc, iron, copper, lead, etc. Every step in our theoretical development of chemistry has served to consolidate and extend the atomic theory, but it is interesting to observe that the retention of that theory has involved the necessity of depriving it of the absolute character which it at first possessed. Organic compounds were long ago discovered, containing atoms of carbon, hydrogen, and oxygen in proportions far from simple ; and the atomic theory must have been abandoned, but for the discovery that the atomic, or rather molecular, weights of these compounds correspond invariably to entire numbers of the elementary atoms. We now use the term " molecule " for those groups which hold together during a variety of transformations, but which can be resolved into simpler constituents ; whilst we reserve the word " atom " for those particles which we cannot break up, and which there is no reason for believing that we ever shall break up.

RELATION OF SCIENTIFIC RESEARCH TO MEDICAL SCIENCE.

At the last meeting of the British Association, several examples were brought forward demonstrating the direct bearing of scientific researches upon the advance of medical science. No sooner is any new substance (whether an elementary body, such as thallium, or a compound) discovered, than experiments are made to investigate its physiological and therapeutical action on the living organisms of men and animals. In many cases, these experiments are made by the observers on their own bodies, and the records of science offer several examples of enthusiastic investigators whose lives have been perilled by the self-administration of dangerous reagents. As a rule, these investigations are made, in the first instance, on the lower animals ; but the results so obtained only give a very slight approximation to what would be the nature of the action of these bodies on the human frame.

We know absolutely nothing of the different constitutional powers in the different animals, so that our only means of acquiring a knowledge of the therapeutical action of remedies is by direct experiment in every case. For example, the goat and the sheep are so slightly different in structure and organization that it is difficult even to discover a well-defined specific distinction between the two animals. Nevertheless, many substances are fatal to the sheep that the goat eats with impunity. A goat will eat at a meal a sufficient quantity of laurel twigs (*Cerasus Lauro cerasus*) to destroy the life of a cow, a ruminating animal, whose organization closely resembles its own. In the same manner, tobacco — one of the most fatal of all poisons to the human frame — is eaten by goats and monkeys with great avidity, and without any apparent evil consequences. Sir Emerson Tennant, in his work on Ceylon, referring to the invulnerability of the mongoose to the bites of poisonous serpents, says, " Such exceptional provisions are not without precedent in the animal economy ; the hornbill feeds with impunity on the deadly fruit of the strychnos ; the milky juice of some species of euphorbia, which is harmless to oxen, is invariably fatal to the zebra ; and the tsetse fly, the pest of South Africa, whose bite is mortal to the ox, the dog, and the horse, is harmless to man and the untamed creatures of the forest."

Among the most important new remedies which science has bestowed upon medicine may be mentioned the preparations of the element bromine. This, as is well known, belongs to the same group of elements as chlorine, iodine, and fluorine ; each of these, though perfectly capable of replacing each other in chemical combinations, has a totally different action on the vital organism.

Chlorine is an essential to the life of all animals, and is supplied in the form of common salt, chloride of sodium. Iodine is, both when simple and in combination, a powerful stimulant, exciting the glandular system.

Fluorine, though never yet isolated, is in some of its combinations a powerful poison.

Bromine has been discovered by Dr. Gibb to possess, when administered in the form of bromide of ammonium, $Br\,N\,H_4$, a power of producing insensibility or even partial paralysis of the nerves going to the glottis and larynx, or organs situated at the top of the windpipe. This knowledge has been at once applied to practical medicine. The painful disease known as whooping-cough owes its chief danger and discomfort to spasm of the nerves going to the respiratory organs. It has been found that the administration of a few grains of bromide of ammonium three times a day has the effect of allaying this spasm, and so preventing the most dreaded symptoms of the disease.

Having alluded to the newly-discovered metal, thallium, it may be as well to mention that M. Lamy states that continued investigation into its properties has resulted in extreme lassitude and pain in the lower limbs. With a view of determining its real influence on the animal economy, he has administered it to the lower animals, and he mentions that a decigramme of the sulphate given to a dog has caused death in forty hours. Mr. Crookes, on the other hand, denies its power, and states that he has occasionally swallowed a few grains of its salts without injurious effect.

THE SYNTHETIC PRODUCTION OF ORGANIC SUBSTANCES.

A lecture was recently given before the French academy by M. Berthelot, " On Synthetic Methods in Organic Chemistry." It was an able *résumé* of the chief steps by which complex, organic substances have been built up from the elements carbon, hydrogen, oxygen, and nitrogen. Although no absolutely new facts were given, yet the treatment of the subject was such as to present some of the phenomena in a new light. It was illustrated by several experiments; the most interesting among these showed the first and most important synthetic step — the direct combination of carbon and hydrogen with formation of acetylene, $C_4 H_2$. The union was thus accomplished : a stream of hydrogen was conducted into a globe, in which the electric arc was shown between two carbon poles. The particles of carbon, transferred mechanically from one pole to the other, took no part in the chemical action, but the volatilized carbon combined, in the intense heat, with the hydrogen present. The acetylene thus produced was converted into a compound with copper; from this substance olefiant gas was prepared, and, finally, from olefiant gas, alcohol.

Prof. Franklin stated, in a recent lecture before the Royal Institution, London, that more than one thousand organic bodies can now be produced from these inorganic elements (oxygen, hydrogen, nitrogen, carbon, etc.) without the agency of vitality.

CONVERSION OF ALBUMEN INTO FIBRIN.

A paper by Mr. Alfred Suree, Jr., recently read before the Royal Society, appears, so far as can be judged at present, to have a bearing on physiological chemistry. In few words, the facts may be thus stated : Pass a stream of oxygen through a quantity of albumen, and portions of that albumen will be converted into fibrin. The albumen may be derived from the serum of blood, from eggs, or from the gluten of wheat ; the result is the same, — formation of fibrin. Taking the facts for granted, this is a very remarkable discovery ; and it is thought that it may throw some light on the phenomena of fibrinous diseases, — phthisis, peritonisis, and the like, — which are obscure in their origin. If a small quantity of potash be mixed with the albumen, there is then no formation of fibrin.

THE MOLECULAR MOBILITY OF GASES.

The following paper on the above subject by Prof. Graham, presented to the Royal Society, June, 1863, is a continuation of that eminent scientist's researches on dialysis, and is one of the most important contributions made to science during the past year : —

The molecular mobility of gases is here considered in reference chiefly to the passage of gases, under pressure, through a thin porous plate or septum, and to the partial separation of mixed gases, which can be effected, as will be shown, by such means. In the diffusiometer, as first constructed, a plain cylindrical glass tube, rather less than an inch in diameter and about ten inches in length, was simply closed at one end by a porous plate of plaster-of-paris, about one-third of an inch in thickness and thus converted into a gas-receiver. A superior material for the porous plate is now found in artificially compressed graphite, of the quality used for making writing-pencils. A circular dish of this graphite, reduced to the thickness of a wafer (one half a millimetre) is attached, by resinous cement to one end of the glass tube, above described, so as to close it and form a diffusiometer. The tube is filled with hydrogen gas over a mercurial trough, the porosity of the graphite plate being counteracted for the time by covering it tightly with a thin sheet of gutta-percha. On afterwards removing the latter, gaseous diffusion immediately takes place through the pores of the graphite. The whole hydrogen will leave the tube in forty minutes or an hour, and is replaced by a much smaller proportion of atmospheric air (about one-fourth) as is to be expected from the law of the diffusion of gases. During the process, the mercury will rise in the tube, if allowed, forming a column of several inches in height, — a fact which illustrates strikingly the intensity of the force with which the interpenetration of different gases is effected. The native or mineral graphite is of a lamellar structure, and appears to have little or no porosity. It cannot be substituted for the artificial graphite as a diffusion septum. Unglazed earthenware comes next in value to graphite for this purpose. The pores of artificial graphite appear to be really so minute that a gas *in mass* cannot penetrate the plate at all. It seems to be molecules only which can pass ; and these may be supposed to pass wholly unimpeded by friction ; for the smallest pores that can be imagined to exist in the graphite must be tunnels in magnitude, to the ultimate atoms of a gaseous body. The sole motive agency appears to be that intestine movement of molecules which is now generally recognized as an essential property of the gaseous condition of matter. According to the physical hypothesis now generally received, a gas is represented as consisting of solid and perfectly elastic spherical particles or atoms, which move in all directions, and are animated with different degrees of velocity in different gases. Confined in a vessel, the moving particles are constantly impinging against its sides, and occasionally against each other, and such collisions take place without any loss of motion, owing to the perfect elasticity of the particles. Now, if the containing vessel be porous, like a diffusiometer, then gas is projected through the open channels by the atomic motion described, and escapes. Simultaneously, the external air or gas, whatever it may be, is carried inwards in the same manner, and takes the place of the gas which leaves the vessel. To the same atomic or molecular movement is due the elastic force, with the power to resist compression, possessed by gases. The molecular movement is accelerated by heat and retarded by cold ; the tension of the gas being increased in the first instance and diminished in the second. Even when the same gas is present, both within and without the vessel, and is therefore in contact with both sides of the porous plate, the movement is sustained without abatement ; molecules continuing to enter and leave in equal numbers, although nothing of the kind is indicated by change of volume or otherwise. If the gases in communication be different, but possess sensibly the same specific gravity and molecular velocity, as nitrogen and carbonic oxide do, an interchange of molecules also takes place without any change in volume. With gases opposed of unequal density and molecular velocity, the amount of penetration ceases, of course, to be equal in both directions. These observations are preliminary to the consideration of the passage through a graphite plate in one direction only, of gas under pressure, or under the influence of its own elastic force. It is to be supposed that a vacuum is maintained on one side of the porous septum and that air or some other gas, under a constant pressure, is in contact with the other side. Now, a gas may pass into a vacuum in three different modes, or in two modes besides that immediately before us, 1st. The gas may enter the vacuum by passing through a minute aperture in a thin plate such as a puncture in platinum-foil, made by a fine steel point. The rate of passage of different gases is then regulated by their specific gravities, according to a pneumatic law, which was deduced by Prof. Robinson from Torricelli's well-known theorem of the velocity of efflux of fluids. A gas rushes into a vacuum with the velocity which a heavy body would acquire by falling from the height of an atmosphere composed of the gas in question, and supposed to be of uniform density throughout. The height of the uniform atmosphere will be inversely as the specific gravity of the gas ; the atmosphere of hydrogen for instance, sixteen times higher than that of oxygen. But as the velocity acquired by a heavy body in falling is not directly as the height, but as the square root of the height, the rate of flow of the different gases into a vacuum will be inversely as the square root of their respective densities. The velocity of oxygen being 1, that of hydrogen will be 4, the square root of 16. This law has been experimentally verified. The times of the effusion of gases, as I have spoken of it, are similar to those of the law of molecular diffusion ; but it is important to observe that the phenomena of effusion and diffusion are distinct and essentially different in their nature. The effusion movement affects masses of gas, the diffusion movement affects molecules ; and a gas is usually carried by the former kind of impulse with a velocity many thousand times greater than by the latter. The effusion velocity of air is the same as the velocity of sound. 2. If the aperture of efflux be in a plate of increased thickness, and so becomes a tube, the effusion rates of gases are disturbed. The rates of flow of different gases, however, assume again a constant ratio to each other when the capillary tube is considerably elongated, when the length exceeds the diameter at least 4,000 times. These new proportions of efflux are the rates of the " Capillary Transpiration of Gases." The rates were found to be the same in a capillary tube composed of copper as they are in a tube of glass, and appear to be independent of the material of the capillary. A film of gas, no doubt, adheres to the inner surface of the tube, and the friction is really that of gas upon gas, and is consequently unaffected by the nature of the tube-substance. The rates of transpiration are not governed by specific gravity, and are, indeed, singularly unlike the rates of effusion. The transpiration velocity of oxygen being 1, that of chlorine is 1.5, that of hydrogen 2.26 ; of nitrogen and carbonic oxide half the velocity of hydrogen ; of olefiant gas, ammonia and cyanogen 2, double, or nearly double, that of oxygen ; of carbonic acid 1.376. In the same gas, the transpirability of equal volumes increases with den-

15

sity, whether occasioned by cold or pressure. The transpiration ratios of gases appear to be in constant relation with no other known property of the same gases, and they form a class of phenomena remarkably isolated from all else at present known of gases. There is one property of transpiration immediately bearing upon the penetration of the graphite plate by gases. The capillary offers to the passage of gas a resistance analogous to that of friction, proportional to the surface, and consequently increasing as the tube or tubes are multiplied in number and diminished in diameter, with the area of discharge preserved constant. The resistance to the passage of a liquid through a capillary was observed by Poiseuille to be nearly as the fourth power of the diameter of the tube. In gases, the resistance also rapidly increases, but in what ratio has not been observed. The consequence, however, is certain that as the diameter of the capillaries may be diminished beyond any assignable limit, so the flow may be retarded indefinitely, and caused at last to become too small to be sensible. We may, therefore, have a mass of capillaries of which the passages form a large aggregate, but which are individually too small to permit a sensible flow of gas under pressure. A porous, solid mass may possess the same reduced penetrability as the congeries of capillary tubes. Indeed, the state of porosity described appears to be more or less closely approached by all loosely aggregated mineral masses, such as lime-plaster, stucco, chalk, baked clay, noncrystalline earthy powders, like hydrate of lime, or magnesia compacted by pressure, and in the highest degree perhaps by artificial graphite. 3. A plate of artificial graphite, although it appears to be practically impenetrable to gas by either of the two modes of passage previously described, is readily penetrated by the agency of the molecular or diffusive movement of gases. This appears on comparing the time required for the passage of equal volumes of different gases under a constant pressure. Of the following three gases, oxygen, hydrogen, and carbonic acid, the time required for the passage of an equal volume of each through a capillary glass tube, in similar circumstances as to pressure and temperature, was formerly observed to be as follows : —

	Time of capillary transpiration.
Oxygen	1
Carbonic Acid	0.72
Hydrogen	0.44

Through a plate of graphite, of half a millimetre in thickness, the same gases were now observed to pass, under a constant pressure of a column of mercury of 100 millimetres in height, in times which are as follows :

	Time of molecular passage.	Square root of density (oxygen 1).
Oxygen	1	1
Hydrogen	0.2472	0.2502
Carbonic acid	1.1886	1.1760

It appears, then, that the times of passage through the graphite plate have no relation to the capillary transpiration times of the same gases first quoted above. This penetration of the graphite plate by gases appears to be entirely due to their own proper molecular motion, quite unaided by transpiration. It seems to offer the simplest possible exhibition of the molecular or diffusive movement. This pure result is to be ascribed to the wonderfully fine porosity of the graphite. The interstitial spaces, or channels, appear to be sufficiently small to extinguish transpiration, or the passage of masses entirely. The graphite becomes a molecular sieve, allowing molecules only to pass through. With a plate of stucco, the penetration of gases under pressure is very rapid, and the volumes of air and hydrogen passing in equal times are as 1 to 2.891, which is a number for hydrogen intermediate between its transpiration volume 2.04 and diffusion volume 3.8; showing that the passage through stucco is a mixed result. The rate of passage of gas through graphite appeared also to be closely proportional to the pressure. Further, hydrogen was found to penetrate through a graphite plate into a vacuum, with sensibly the same absolute velocity as it diffused into air; establishing the important fact, that the impelling force is the same in both movements. The molecular mobility may therefore be spoken of as the diffusive movement of gases; the passage of gas through a porous plate into vacuum, as diffusion in one direction or single diffusion; and ordinary diffusion, or the passage of two gases in opposite directions, as double, compound or reciprocal diffusion.

Atmolysis. — A partial separation of mixed gases and vapors of unequal diffusibility can be effected by allowing the mixture to permeate through a graphite plate into a vacuum, as was to be expected from the preceding views. As this method of analysis has a practical character and admits of wide application, it may be convenient to distinguish it by a peculiar name. The amount of the separation is in proportion to the pressure, and attains its maximum when the gases pass into a nearly perfect vacuum. A variety of experiments were made on this subject, of which perhaps the most interesting were those upon the concentration of the oxygen in atmospheric air.. When a portion of air confined in a jar is allowed to penetrate into a vacuum, through graphite or unglazed earthenware, the nitrogen should pass more rapidly than the oxygen in the proportion of 1.0668 to 1; and the proportion of oxygen be proportionally increased in the air left behind in the jar. The increase in the oxygen actually observed when the air in the jar was reduced from 1 volume to 0.5 volume, was 0.48 per cent.; to 0.25 volume, was 0.98 per cent.; to 0.125 volume, was 1.54 per cent.; to 0.0625 volume, was 2.02 per cent.; or, the oxygen increased from 21 to 23.02 per cent. in the last sixteenth part of air left behind in the jar. The most remarkable effects of separation are produced by means of the *tube-atmolyser.* This is simply a narrow tube of unglazed earthenware, such as a tobacco-pipe stem two feet in length, which is placed within a shorter tube of glass and secured in its position by corks, so as to appear like a Liebig's condenser. The glass tube is placed in communication with an air-pump, and the annular space between the two tubes is maintained as nearly vacuous as possible. Air or any other mixed gas is then allowed to flow in a stream along the clay tube, and collected as it issues. The gas so atmolysed is, of course, reduced in volume, much gas penetrating through the pores of the clay tube into the air-pump vacuum; and the slower the gas is collected, the greater the proportional loss. In the gas collected, the denser constituent of the mixture is thus concentrated in an arithmetical ratio, while the volume of the gas is reduced in a geometrical ratio. In one experiment, the proportion of oxygen in the air after traversing the atmolyser was increased to 24.50 per cent., or 16.7 upon 100 oxygen originally

present in the air.   With gases differing so much in density and diffusibility as oxygen and hydrogen, the separation is, of course, much
more considerable.   The explosive mixture of two volumes of hydrogen
and one volume of oxygen gave oxygen containing only 9.3 per cent.
of hydrogen, in which a taper burned without explosion ; and with
equal volumes of oxygen and hydrogen, the proportion of the latter
was easily reduced from 50 to 5 per cent.

Speculative Ideas respecting the Constitution of Matter. — It is conceivable that the various kinds of matter, now recognized as different
elementary substances, may possess one and the same ultimate or
atomic molecule existing in different conditions of movement.   The
essential unity of matter is an hypothesis in harmony with the equal
action of gravity upon all bodies.   We know the anxiety with which
this point was investigated by Newton, and the care he took to ascertain that every kind of substance, " metals, stones, woods, grain, salts,
animal substances, etc.," are similarly accelerated in falling, and are
therefore equally heavy.   In the condition of gas, matter is deprived
of numerous and varying properties with which it appears invested
when in the form of a liquid or solid.   The gas exhibits only a few
grand and simple features.   These again may all be dependent upon
atomic and molecular mobility.   Let us imagine one kind of substance
only to exist, — ponderable matter ; and further, that matter is divisible
into ultimate atoms, uniform in size and weight.   We shall have one
substance and a common atom.   With the atom at rest the uniformity
of matter would be perfect.   But the atom possesses always more or
less motion, due, it must be assumed, to a primordial impulse.   This
motion gives rise to volume.   The more rapid the movement, the greater
the space occupied by the atom, somewhat as the orbit of a planet
widens with the degree of projectile velocity.   Matter is thus made to
differ only in being lighter or denser matter.   The specific motion of
an atom being inalienable, light matter is no longer convertible into
heavy matter.   In short, matter of different density forms different
substances, — different inconvertible elements as they have been considered.   What has already been said is not meant to apply to the
gaseous volumes which we have occasion to measure and practically
deal with, but to a lower order of molecules or atoms.   The combining
atoms, hitherto spoken of, are not therefore the molecules of which the
movement is sensibly affected by heat, with gaseous expansion as the
result.   The gaseous molecule must itself be viewed as composed of a
group or system of the preceding inferior atoms, following, as a unit,
laws similar to those which regulate its constituent atoms.   We have,
indeed, carried one step backward, and applied to the lower order of
atoms, ideas suggested by the gaseous molecule, as views derived from
the solar system are extended to the subordinate system of a planet
and its satellites.   The advance of science may further require an indefinite repetition of such steps of molecular division.   The gaseous
molecule is, then, a reproduction of the inferior atom on a higher scale.
The molecule or system is reached which is affected by heat, — the diffusive molecule, of which the movement is the subject of observation and
measurement.   The diffusive molecules are also to be supposed uniform
weight, but to vary in velocity of movement, in correspondence with
their constituent atoms.   Accordingly, the molecular volumes of differ-

ent elementary substances have the same relation to each other as the subordinate atomic volumes of the same substances. But further, these more and less mobile or light and heavy forms of matter have a singular relation connected with equality of volume. Equal volumes of two of them can coalesce together, unite their movement, and form a new atomic group, retaining the whole, the half, or some simple proportion of the original movement and consequent volume. This is chemical combination. It is directly an affair of volume, and only indirectly connected with weight. Combining weights are different, because the densities, atomic and molecular, are different. The volume of combination is uniform, but the fluids measured vary in density. This fixed combining measure — the *metron* of simple substances — weighs 1 for hydrogen, 16 for oxygen, and so on with the other " elements." To the preceding statements, respecting atomic and molecular mobility, it remains to be added, that the hypothesis admits of another expression. As in the theory of light we have the alternative hypothesis of emission and undulation, so in molecular mobility the motion may be assumed to reside either in separate atoms and molecules, or in a fluid medium caused to undulate. A special rate of vibration or pulsation originally imparted to a portion of the fluid medium enlivens that portion of matter with an individual existence, and constitutes it a distinct substance or element. With respect to the different states of gas, liquid and solid, it may be observed that there is no real incompatibility with each other in these physical conditions. They are often found together in the same substance. The liquid and the solid conditions supervene upon the gaseous condition rather than supersede it. Gay-Lussac made the remarkable observation, that the vapors emitted by ice and water, both at 0° Cent., are of exactly equal tension. The passage from the liquid to the solid state is not made apparent in the volatility of water. The liquid and solid conditions do not appear as the extinction or suppression of the gaseous condition, but something *superadded* to that condition. The three conditions (or constitution) probably always coexist in every liquid or solid substance, but one predominates over the others. In the general properties of matter we have, indeed, to include still further (1.) the remarkable loss of elasticity in vapors under great pressure, which is distinguished by Mr. Faraday as the Caignard-Latour state, after the name of its discoverer, and is now undergoing an investigation by Dr. Andrews, which may be expected to throw much light upon its nature ; (2.) the colloidal condition or constitution, which intervenes between the liquid and crystalline states, extending into both, and affecting probably all kinds of solid and liquid matter in a greater or less degree. The predominance of a certain physical state in a substance appears to be a distinction of a kind with those distinctions recognized in natural history as being produced by unequal development. Liquefaction or solidification may not, therefore, involve the suppression of either the atomic or the molecular movement, but only the restriction of its range. The hypothesis of atomic movement has been elsewhere assumed, irrespective of the gaseous condition, and is applied by Dr. Williamson to the elucidation of a remarkable class of chemical reactions which have their seat in a mixed liquid. Lastly, molecular or diffusive mobility has an obvious bearing upon the communication of heat to gases, by contact with liquid or solid surfaces. The impact of the gaseous molecule, upon a surface possessing a different temperature, appears to be the condition for the transference of heat, or the heat movement, from one to the other. The more rapid the molecular movement of the gas, the more frequent the contact, with consequent communication of heat. Hence, probably, the great cooling power of hydrogen gas as compared with air or oxygen. The gases named have the same specific heat for equal volumes, but a hot object placed in hydrogen is really *touched* 3.8 times more frequently than it would be if placed in air, and 4 times more frequently than it would be if placed in an atmosphere of oxygen gas. Dalton had already ascribed this peculiarity of hydrogen to the high "mobility" of that gas. The same molecular property of hydrogen recommends the application of that gas in the air-engine, where the object is to alternately heat and cool a confined volume of gas with rapidity.

THE NEW METALS.

Indium. — In the summer of 1863, thallium having been detected in minute quantities in many of the products of the smelting works at Freiberg, Saxony, F. Reich and Th. Richter, examined some of the ores, at the laboratories of the works, hoping to ascertain its source. These ores consisted of pyrites, mispickel, blende, and galena; with earthy matter, silica, manganese, copper, and minute quantities of tin and cadmium. The ores were roasted to expel the greater part of the sulphur and arsenic; then mixed with hydrochloric acid, evaporated to dryness and distilled. The impure chloride of zinc thus obtained was examined before the spectroscope for thallium. No thallium line was found; but, instead, an indigo blue line, entirely new, and different from that produced by any known substance. The experimenters succeeded in isolating the conjectural substance, necessarily in very minute quantity, partly in the form of chloride, partly as hydrated oxide, and partly in the metallic state. On submitting these, moistened with chlorhydric acid, to the spectroscope, the blue line was seen so brilliant, sharp, and persistent, that they did not hesitate to conclude that it belonged to a hitherto unrecognized metal, to which they accordingly gave the name *Indium.* Its chemical properties have not as yet been fully determined. Its chloride is not precipitated from an acid solution by sulphuretted hydrogen, but is precipitated from the same solution by ammonia, as a hydrated oxide. The oxide, fused on charcoal with soda, yields a lead-gray globule of metal, very soft and ductile; while the metal heated alone on charcoal gives a yellow coating, which, upon being moistened with nitrate of cobalt, gives no characteristic reaction.

Rubidium and Cæsium. — M. Seybel, an Austrian chemist, has recently prepared five ounces of the chlorides of rubidium and cæsium, in a state of perfect purity, from 800 lbs. of the mica of Finnwald, in Bohemia. This mica contains nearly 3 per cent. of the oxides of these two metals, which is a more considerable proportion than is known at present in any other substance. M. Seybel is engaged in making arrangements for the production of these interesting substances in larger quantities, so as to render them accessible to all interested in chemical pursuits. Prof Bunsen, of Heidelberg, also announces, that he has met with a kind of lepidolite which contains three per cent. of rubidium; and that Mr. O. Struve, manufacturing chemist at Leipzig, is ready to deliver a raw salt containing twenty per cent. of chloride of rubidium at the comparatively moderate price of 23 francs the kilogramme.

The Properties of Rubidium. — Bunsen, who has succeeded in reducing rubidium to a metallic state, thus enumerates its properties: As a metal, it is very brilliant, like silver, white, with a scarcely perceptible tinge of yellow. In the air it oxidizes instantly to bluish-gray suboxide, and takes fire, after a few minutes, much more easily than potassium. At −10° C. it is still as soft as iron: it melts at 58°.5 C., and below a red heat is converted into a blue vapor with a shade of green. According to Bunsen, the true fusing point of sodium is 95°.6 C., and that of potassium 62°.5 C.; the latter does *not* pass through an intermediate pasty condition in fusing. The density of rubidium is about 1.52. It is considerably more electro-positive than potassium, takes fire upon water, and burns with a flame which cannot be distinguished from that of potassium by the eye. Rubidium burns with brilliancy in chlorine, and in the vapor of bromine, iodine, sulphur, and arsenic.

Additional Facts Respecting Thallium. — This new metal, which was first publicly shown at the London International Exhibition, 1863, has since that time been produced in comparatively large quantities. At the meeting of the British Association, 1863, Mr. Crookes, its discoverer, exhibited a mass weighing upwards of a quarter of a hundred-weight, and demonstrated its more obvious properties. It is the softest of the new alkaline metals, being easily scratched by a point of lead. When obtained, in larger quantity, thallium will doubtless be employed to furnish a magnificent green flame. Eight parts of chlorite of thallium, two parts of calomel, and one of resin, yields a splendid light on being ignited, and a very little reduction in price would enable it to be used for ship-signals; its extraordinary intensity and monochromatic character enabling it to penetrate through a hazy atmosphere, which alters altogether the color of the ordinary green lights produced by the salts of baryta.

Mr. Crookes finds, in testing for thallium in the fine dust which accumulates in the flues of furnaces burning iron pyrites, that the spectrum analysis is comparatively useless from its extreme delicacy; $\frac{1}{1000}$ part of thallium in a mass being indicated as strongly and vividly as the pure metal itself. Mr. Crookes has been experimenting upon several tons of this dust. The most ready method of extraction he finds to consist in washing it with pure water, acidulating the liquid with hydrochloric acid, so as to convert the thallium into chloride. In this manner, he has obtained from three tons of flue-dust sixty-eight pounds of impure chloride, which was afterwards converted into sulphate by heating with sulphuric acid; this conversion into chloride and reconversion into sulphate being repeated, in order to get rid of impurities. Finally, the sulphate was reduced to the metallic state by fusing with black flux or with cyanide of potassium. Thallium melts at 550° Fahr., and can consequently be easily fused over a gas jet, its surface being protected from the air by a stream of coal-gas. Mr. Crookes also detailed the following circumstances connected with the discovery of this new metal: About three years ago he was engaged in the examination of a residue from a sulphuric acid manufactory at

Tilkerode. Many of the chemical properties of this substance induced him to believe that the rare metal tellurium was present; but all attempts at a separation of this metal by chemical means failed. Still unsatisfied of its absence, he then had recourse to the most recent method of chemical analysis by means of the spectroscope. In the spectrum obtained, there was no evidence of tellurium, but a magnificent green band was observed, which had never been noticed in the spectrum of any known element. It was this that convinced Mr. Crookes that he had in the substance under examination a body endowed with properties distinct from those of any other, and in course of time led him to the isolation of the new metal. He pointed out a curious parallelism between the history of the discovery of thallium and of selenium. The great Swedish chemist Berzelius, a little more than half a century ago, was engaged on the examination of a residue from a sulphuric acid manufactory, similar to that Mr. Crookes examined. Berzelius, too, was looking for tellurium. He failed to find it; but in the course of his examination he discovered selenium, a body belonging to the sulphur group of elements. Had Berzelius been acquainted with spectrum analysis, Mr. Crookes remarked, it is very probable he would have discovered thallium also, since the new metal gives the simplest and best-defined spectrum hitherto observed. Mr. Crookes first succeeded in isolating thallium by the use of voltaic electricity in September, 1861. It is precipitated from its solutions by this means, like lead and tin; but, if the precipitation be carefully conducted, the metal crystallizes out in elegant tufts, which spread out in branches resembling some of the delicate seaweeds. This was beautifully shown on a screen by means of the electric light. When precipitated more rapidly, it comes down in a spongy state, and can then be easily pressed into an ingot.

Report of the French Academy on Thallium. — A committee of the French Academy, instructed to report on the subject of the new metal, in a paper presented to them during the past year, remarks, " That its discovery forms an epoch in the history of chemistry, on account of the astonishing contrast between its chemical and physical characters — and they call it the " ornithorynchus of metals." It has nearly the same appearance as lead, may be cut in a similar manner, and leaves a similar trace on paper. It has, moreover, the same density, nearly the same fusing point, and the same specific heat. Its solutions, like those of lead, yield a black precipitate with sulphuretted hydrogen, a yellow one with iodides and chromates, and a white one with chlorides. But it indubitably belongs to the family of alkaline metals, which recent discoveries have doubled in number. In this list thallium stands, as regards the weight of its equivalent, at the opposite extremity of the scale to lithium, the numbers being, lithium, 7; sodium, 23; potassium, 39; rubidium, 85; cœsium, 120; thallium, 204. The commission remark that the equivalent of sodium is exactly the mean between that of potassium and lithium; that if double the atomic weight of sodium is added to that of potassium, the equivalent of rubidium is obtained; that adding double the weight of sodium to double that of potassium gives very nearly that of cœsium; and that adding double the weight of sodium to four times the weight of potassium, gives nearly that of thallium. The equivalents of all the alkaline metals, thallium included, must be halved to make them fit Dulong and Petit's law concerning the relation of atomic weight to specific heat. The commissioners further observe that the alkaline metal series contains one, lithium, whose atomic weight is so light as to place it near hydrogen, and another, thallium, so heavy as to rank with bismuth whose equivalent is the heaviest known."

Thallium in American Furnace Products. — Mr. W. T. Roepper, in a communication published in *Silliman's Journal*, states that he has detected thallium in the dust deposited on the boilers of the Bethlehem Iron Works, of Penn., and in similar dust from a furnace on the Lehigh. He considers it not unlikely "that it is a common product of the anthracite furnaces, and is perhaps derived from the pyrites accompanying the coal." Mr. Roepper states, however, that he has not been able as yet to detect it in the ashes of anthracite from a common stove.

PREPARATION OF MAGNESIUM.

At a recent meeting at the Royal Institution, London, Mr. Tegetmeier exhibited a mass of magnesium which had been prepared by Mr. E. Sonstadt, who has recently patented a process whereby this metal may be obtained in quantity. Mr. Faraday called the attention of the members to the remarkable properties of this metal. Its whiteness, resembling that of silver, and high metallic brilliancy, were shown by means of the electric lamp. A wire of the metal was ignited in the flame of a candle, when it burnt with a white light of such dazzling intensity as totally to obscure the ordinary illuminating agents, such as gas and candles, and to rival the brilliancy of the electric light. Mr. Faraday stated that notwithstanding its strong attraction for oxygen, it was preserved from change, when in a mass, by the thin film of oxide covering and protecting the exterior surface from the exposure of the air.

Mr. Sonstadt's process for preparing magnesium on a manufacturing scale consists in decomposing a mixture of fused chlorides of magnesium and sodium by means of metallic sodium, and in the employment of iron vessels to effect the decomposition. It is found that the magnesium acts on the silica of earthenware crucibles, decomposing it, and uniting with the silicon; nor can platinum crucibles be employed, as the magnesium alloys with that metal, causing it to become fusible at a moderate temperature. The chloride of magnesium employed is best obtained from the mother liquor, left after evaporating sea-water for its salt. Mr. Faraday stated that as every ton of sea-water contained above two pounds of magnesium, in the form of chloride, the entire ocean would contain 160,000 cubic miles of magnesium. This would form a solid block fifty-four miles cube. The specific gravity of magnesium is 1 75, resembling in its lightness the analogous metal aluminum. Now that magnesium is capable of being obtained quickly, there is no doubt that important applications of its singular properties will present themselves. The metallic bases of the earths are in so much greater abundance than the ordinary metals, that any attempt to isolate them for economic and practical purposes must be regarded with great interest, as bearing strongly on the advance of not only the scientific arts, but also of those having reference to daily life and advancing civilization.

CHEMISTRY OF STEEL.

M. Caron, in a communication made to the French Academy of Sciences, attributes the combination of iron with carbon or other elements of the same family, by which tempered steel is formed, to the sudden shrinking of the mass, which he considers as analogous to the instantaneous compression produced by hammering. In illustration of this point, he found that by hammering a bar of iron heated to a bright redness, on an anvil covered with powdered charcoal, the face of the bar in contact with the charcoal, was, in spots, converted into steel, and made capable of resisting the file. His researches also confirm the results of previous experiments, that the density of steel is decreased by tempering. In one specimen, after thirty successive temperings, the density was reduced from 7.817 to 7.743.

BESSEMER'S PROCESS FOR THE PRODUCTION OF IRON AND STEEL.

This method of converting pig-iron into steel and bar-iron (described in former numbers of the *Annual Sci. Dis*).; is constantly increasing in favor among European ironmasters, and thousands of hundred-weight of Bessemer steel and iron are now annually produced in England and Sweden and it has become an article of commerce; while large works are also being erected for the employment of the method in France. Whenever the proper raw material is used, Bessemer's process gives steel, which in all respects is fully equal to the best varieties of cast-steel; and iron of as good quality as the best forge iron. The loss in converting pig-iron into steel, by this method, is twelve to fifteen per cent., and in making bar-iron eighteen to twenty-two per cent. In five to ten minutes, fifteen to twenty cwt. of fluid pig-iron are converted into steel or bar-iron with scarcely any cost for fuel, and without hand labor. The pressure of blast used is from one-half to one one-half atmospheres, and the amount is 800 to 1200 cubic feet of cold air of the ordinary atmospheric density. Only good charcoal-iron is adapted for conversion by this method, and the reason of the failure of the earlier experiments was the employment of improper and inferior raw-material. Swedish pig-iron is now always used in England for the production of the best sorts of steel and iron. In some of the new iron works, attempts have been made to improve the quality of English pig-iron which has been carried to the point of conversion by adding to it melted Swedish pig-iron; manganese compounds have also been used for the same purpose. But the separation of the deleterious substances associated with carbon in pig-iron still remains an unsolved problem. For the success of this method, a good quality of pig-iron is therefore indispensable, and further a high temperature; this last is attained by converting large quantities of iron in a single operation. In Sweden, fifteen cwt. for a charge is the minimum quantity used, and if sixty to one-hundred cwt. be employed, the result would be still more favorable. In converting large quantities at one operation, the cost is proportionally diminished, and the product may also be made more uniform.

One great advantage of Bessemer's process is that so much larger quantities of material can be operated upon at one charge than in the ordinary methods of refining, and this quantity is not restricted within narrow limits, as in puddling and hearth refining. For the production of the proper temperature, the relative amount of blast to the pig-iron operated upon should be carefully regulated. If too little, the process goes on slowly, and much heat is lost by radiation ; on the other hand, if too much blast is used, there is also a loss from the heat carried off by the air which is forced through the iron before it has effected the desired decomposition. The pressure of the blast must, at all events, be greater than that of the column of iron in the furnace, in order that the bath of molten iron shall be thoroughly penetrated and the whole melted mass set in violent agitation. In Sweden, the pressure of half an atmosphere has in most cases been found sufficient, while in England a pressure equal to one one-half atmospheres has been used.

Prof. Tanner, a German scientist, places particular emphasis on the employment of a high pressure with hot blast. He says that if the blast were to be heated to 200 – 300° C., or perhaps even to 500 – 600° C., the conversion would unquestionably proceed with great regularity and completeness, and the difficulties in the manufacture of soft bar-iron and steel would be overcome. Further, it is to be borne in mind, that, in order to produce a given variety of steel or iron, the process of conversion must be interrupted whenever the refining has reached the desired point ; this last is determined by observing the character of the gases and sparks which escape from the furnace, very much as is the case in hearth refining ; practice is of course required to be able to determine this point with accuracy. The fracture of the metal serves as a control in sorting the different qualities. The cost for furnace-repairs is much less than was at first anticipated, but the waste product in conversion (equal to 20-30 per cent., when the iron is made into bars) demands consideration, especially as no use has yet been found for this more or less impure product. If, however, we take into consideration the length of time that has been necessary to bring the puddling process to its present perfection, while on the other hand Bessemer's process has accomplished so much in so short a time, we have every reason to hope that the day is not far distant when the still remaining difficulties in this process will be reduced to a minimum. — *Polytechnisches Journal*, clxvi. 447. [A wide field is open for the application of Bessemer's process in this country, where pure iron ores, fully equal in quality to those of Sweden and Norway, occur in such abundance.] — *Silliman's Journal*.

A NEW COMPOUND OF SILICON SENSITIVE TO LIGHT.

The addition of a new member to a class of bodies is always of interest, but the discovery of a new and very sensitive photographic body is of especial value, more particularly, if entirely new ground is opened out by it, and the stranger comes before us as the representative of a new series of elementary bodies hitherto unsuspected of the slightest tendency to photographic change. If we had had to hazard a prediction as to the body whence the next photographically sensitive compound would be derived, certainly the last substance which would have suggested itself would have been common flint or silica. Until the last few years, silicium, the basis of this, was about the most uninteresting substance in chemistry ; but now, through the researches of Wöhler, it bids fair to rival any of the other elements in the number and interest of its compounds. This chemist has recently discovered several new compounds of silicium which are of the highest importance. The starting-point of them all is a curious, metallic-looking alloy of silicium and calcium, which is easily prepared by fusing together silicium, chloride of calcium, and sodium, with certain precautions. The silicide of calcium is then obtained in a button of a lead gray color and perfect metallic lustre. In water, this slowly disintegrates, forming a mass of lustrous scales like graphite, some impurities being extracted from it by this solvent. Strong nitric acid does not attack the silicide, and this acid affords the best means of obtaining it free from impurities. The most remarkable action of the silicide of calcium is its behavior with hydrochloric acid, by which it is changed into an orange-yellow substance, a brisk evolution of hydrogen taking place. This yellow body is called by the discoverer *silicon*, an inappropriate name ; as the metallic basis of silica, *silicium*, is often called silicon, and is generally known under that name in chemical books. Silicon is prepared in the following way : The silicide of calcium, purified as above, is treated with concentrated hydrochloric acid. An evolution of hydrogen soon takes place, and the silicide is gradually transformed into silicon. The mixture is then diluted with six or eight times its volume of water, the silicon filtered off, carefully protected from the light, well washed, and finally dried in a vacuum over sulphuric acid, the bell-glass being covered with a black cloth. Silicon is of a bright orange-yellow color. It is composed of transparent yellow laminæ. It is insoluble in water, alcohol, and other solvents ; when heated, it becomes of a dark orange yellow. On applying a stronger heat, it takes fire with a faint deflagration and some sparkling, leaving a residue of silicic acid.

" The behavior of silicon when exposed to the light is very remarkable. In the dark, even when moist, it remains quite unchanged. In diffused light it becomes paler ; but in direct sunlight it, in a short time, becomes perfectly white, and hydrogen is given off. When placed under water in sunlight, hydrogen begins to be evolved immediately, and continues like a fermentation until the silicon has become quite white. The purer the substance, the more quickly does the change take place, and several grammes are transformed in a few hours. If, however, it has not been perfectly protected from the light in the course of preparation, it is much longer before the whole is altered in sunlight. The formula of silicon is not accurately settled ; but it contains silicium, hydrogen, and oxygen, and is supposed to resemble an organic body, in which silicium replaces the carbon. Professor Wöhler, indeed, suggests that it may, perhaps, be the type of an entire series of similar bodies, and it would then open the prospect of a special chemistry of silicium as of carbon.

" The behavior of silicon with metallic salts is curious. In the presence of an alkali, even of dilute ammonia, it is gradually changed into silicic acid, with evolution of hydrogen. When mixed with an alkali whilst this decomposition is going forward, it acts as a powerful reducing agent on the salts of the heavy metals. Solutions of copper or silver salts soon become black, and gold solutions brown. A solution of lead in caustic soda is precipitated in the metallic state as a gray mass. The reducing agent, in all these cases, is evidently the hydrogen in a nascent condition. When silicon is thoroughly acted on by light, it is converted into a white body, to which the name Leukon has been given. The composition of this is also a matter of doubt, but it is a body of a somewhat similar composition to silicon, and in the presence of alkalies it behaves in the same way with some metallic salts. The mode of formation of leukon from silicon, under the influence of light, is also obscure; the most probable theory is that four atoms of water are decomposed, four of oxygen and one of hydrogen uniting to the silicon, and the other three of hydrogen being set free."

MANUFACTURE OF ALCOHOL BY ILLUMINATING GAS.

The French correspondent of *Silliman's Journal* thus describes a process of manufacturing alcohol at a very low cost from common illuminating gas which has been devised in France, and which has of late attracted attention; a quantity of alcohol so prepared being one of the principal curiosities at the last London Exhibition. To carry out this invention, the patent for which has been issued to a French chemist, by the name of Cotelle, a company has been organized at St. Quention, France. "The patent," says the correspondent of the *Journal*, "is founded upon the experiment by means of which Berthelot, in 1855, accomplished the synthesis of alcohol, by causing the absorption of olefiant gas, $C^4 H^4$, by sulphuric acid, thus converting it into sulpho-vinic acid, a compound readily turned into alcohol by processes long since known. This experiment, made known by Hennell, thirty years ago, has now been repeated with $C^4 H^4$ prepared from alcohol. Mr. Cotelle employs mostly illuminating gas, which, as we know, contains from four to twelve per cent. of $C^4 H^4$. Separating this, by means of sulphuric acid, there remains a gaseous mixture, composed of $C^2 H^4$, CO, H, &c., very suitable for burning, so that this first material ought to cost very little, especially if the manufacture be undertaken at the mines, so as to take advantage of the gas which issues from the coke furnaces.

"To produce one hectolitre of alcohol of ninety per cent., Mr. Cotelle uses not more than forty cubic metres of $C^4 H^4$, which corresponds to about two tons of the northern coal used at St. Quentin. But the difficulty is not solely in the production of $C^4 H^4$; there is also needed a large amount of concentrated sulphuric acid, (ten parts of $HO SO^3$ to one of alcohol). This, used at 66° of Beaume's areometer, remains, after the completion of the work, at from 20° to 25°. It is necessary, then, either to concentrate it again for a new process, or to utilize it in its diluted state; from this, we see the necessity for either concentrating apparatus or leaden chambers; for a hectolitre of alcohol requires for its production 1500 kilometres of sulphuric acid at 66°. Thus we perceive a series of difficulties which are not yet overcome, but which are vanishing, day by day. Still, Cotelle's process is interesting, and we will give it in a few words. Starting with the purification of gas, we free it from sulphydric acid and ammonia, then desiccate it by passing it over $HO SO^3$. Drawn along by suction like that of a pump, the dry gas is directed to a column of glass or sandstone furnished with trays or diaphragms pierced with small holes, from which descends $HO SO^3$ in a finely divided state, to meet and dissolve the $C^4 H^4$. This solution takes place slowly, so that the apparatus needs as many as forty trays to distribute enough sulphuric acid to absorb the gas and be saturated with it. The sulpho-vinic acid thus obtained is next treated with

five times its volume of water, and the mixture submitted to the action
of a stream of vapor which carries over the alcoholic product.   The
vapors are condensed ; the alcoholic liquid thus obtained is re-distilled
over a little lime, to separate any sulphuric acid which may have distilled over, and the liquid condensed from this distillation is rectified to
produce alcohol of 90°.   The residue of this operation is, as we have
seen, sulphuric acid of 20° to 25°, and a gaseous mixture representing
the gas from ordinary coal less II S, N H^3, and $C^4 H^4$; this latter can
be advantageously used for fuel."

PASTEUR'S RESEARCHES ON FERMENTATION AND PUTREFACTION.

For some years past, M. Pasteur, a distinguished French chemist,
has been engaged in investigating the phenomena of fermentation and
putrefaction, and the results attained to by him constitute some of the
most important contributions made to chemical science during the past
few years.   In the report of researches heretofore published, (see Annual of Scientific Discovery, 1861, p. 228 ; 1862, p. 237, and 1863, 237.)
M. Pasteur claims to have proved that the effects hitherto attributed
to the atmosphere of oxidizing and thus consuming dead organic matter, are really dependent on the growth of infusorial animalculæ.   In a
recent paper submitted to the French academy, M. Pasteur says, —
" We must banish from science those preconceived views which consisted in the supposition that a whole class of organic substances — the
nitrogenous — could acquire, by the hypothetical influence of direct
oxidation, an occult force characterized by an internal movement,
ready to communicate itself to organic substances pretended to be
slightly stable."   And further, " the slow combustion of organic matter
after death, though real, is scarcely perceptible if the air is deprived of
the germs of the lower organisms.   It becomes rapid if the organic matter is permitted to cover itself with moulds, mildews, bacteriums, and
monads.   .   .   .   The intermediate principles of organized beings
would be, in some sort, indestructible, if we were able to suppress
altogether those beings which God has made so extremely small, so useless in appearance, and life would become impossible, because the return to the atmosphere and to the mineral kingdom of that which had
ceased to live would be entirely suspended."

M. Pasteur's latest researches have led to the opinion that all fermentation, properly so-called, as well as the phenomena of putrefaction,
is due to the presence of infusorial animalcules, which are able to live,
(and do in fact live) and multiply without the presence of free oxygen
gas, and without any contact with air.   These animalcules belong to
the genus vibrio, a genus which according to Ehrenberg contains six
species.   Why they should thus act as ferments, M. Pasteur does not
undertake to explain, but he calls attention to this interesting fact;
namely, " That while the ordinary actions of vegetables and animals
upon the principles (substances) which nourish them, is not associated
with fermentation, properly so-called ; " we have, in the case of these
animalcules, " the fact of nutrition accompanied by fermentation, and a
nutrition without the consumption of free oxygen."

M. Pasteur's latest paper presented to the French Academy dis-
cusses especially the phenomena of putrefaction, and it contains so many
points of interest, that we give from the Comptes Rendus a full abstract
of it.   He says, —

"In every case in which animal or vegetable matter undergoes spontaneous alteration and develops fetid gases, putrefaction is said to occur. We shall perceive in the course of our examination that this definition has two opposite defects. It is too general, because it brings together phenomena that are essentially distinct; and it is too restricted, because it separates others which have the same nature and origin. The interest and utility of an exact study of putrefaction has never been misunderstood. Long ago it was hoped it might lead to practical consequences in the treatment of maladies which the old physicians termed *putrid*. Unfortunately the disgust inseparable from labors of this kind, joined to their evident complication, has hitherto arrested the majority of experimenters, so that nearly everything has still to be done. My researches on fermentation have naturally conducted me toward this study; and to the general conclusion that putrefaction is determined by organic ferments of the genus *vibrio*.

"The conditions under which putrefaction is manifested may vary considerably. Suppose, in the first instance, the case of a liquid, that is to say of a putrescible substance, of which all the parts have been exposed to contact with the air. Either this liquid may be shut up in a close vessel, or it may be placed in an open vessel, having an aperture more or less large. I will examine in succession what happens in the two cases.

"It is commonly known that putrefaction takes a certain time to manifest itself, and that this time varies according to temperature, neutrality, acidity, or alkalinity of the liquid. Under the most favorable circumstances a minimum of about twenty-four hours is necessary before the phenomenon begins to be manifested by external signs. During this first period the liquid is agitated by an internal movement, the effect of which is to deprive of its oxygen the air which is in solution, and to replace it by carbonic acid gas. The total disappearance of the oxygen when the liquid is neutral or slightly alkaline is due, in general, to the development of the smallest of the infusoria, the *Monas crepusculum* and *Bacterium termo*. A very slight agitation occurs as these little beings travel in all directions. When this first action of exhausting the oxygen in solution is accomplished, they perish and fall to the bottom of the vessel like a precipitate; and if by chance the liquid contains no fecund germs of the ferments I have spoken of, it remains indefinitely in this condition without putrefaction — without fermenting in any way. This is rare, but I have met with several examples. Most frequently when the oxygen in solution has disappeared, the vibrion-ferments, which have no need of this gas, begin to appear, and putrefaction immediately sets in. Gradually it accelerates itself, following the progressive march of the development of the vibrions. The putridity becomes so intense that the microscopic examination of a single drop is very unpleasant. The fetid odor depends chiefly on the proportion of sulphur the substance contains. The odor is scarcely sensible if the matter is not sulphuretted, as, for example, in the fermentation of the albumenoid matter which water can carry away from the yeast of beer. The same is the case with butyric fermentation; and after my experiments butyric fermentation must, from the nature of its ferment, be considered as a phenomenon of exactly the same order as putrefaction properly so-called. Thus we see what happens when putrefaction is in some sort restrained. It results from what precedes, that contact with air is not necessary to the development of putrefaction, but that, on the contrary, if the oxygen, dissolved in a putrescible liquid, is not removed by the action of special beings, putrefaction will not occur, as the oxygen would cause the vibrions to perish if they tried to develop themselves.

" I shall now examine the case of free putrefaction in contact with air. That which I have already said might make it appear that it could not take place under such circumstances, as oxygen kills the vibrions which excite it. Notwithstanding this, I shall demonstrate that putrefaction in contact with air is more complete than when it is effected under shelter from air. Let us go back to our aerated liquid, this time exposed to contact with air in a wide-mouthed vessel. The removal of the oxygen takes place as previously described. The difference is that the bacteriums, etc., do not perish, but propagate themselves to infinitude at the surface of the liquid which is in contact with the air. They form a thin pellicle, which gradually thickens, falls into rags to the bottom of the vessel, is formed again, and so forth. This pellicle, with which is usually associated divers mucors and mucedines, prevents the solution of oxygen gas in the liquid, and thus permits the development of the vibrio-ferments. For them the vessel is as if closed against the introduction of air. They can even multiply in the pellicle at the surface, because they find themselves protected by the bacteriums and mucors against too direct an action of the atmospheric air.

" The putrescible liquid thus becomes the seat of two kinds of action, very distinct, and which are in relation to the physiological functions of the two kinds of beings that nourish themselves in it. The vibrions, on one hand, living without the aid of atmospheric oxygen, determine, in the interior of the liquid, acts of fermentation — that is to say, they transform nitrogenous substances into more simple, though still complex, products. The bacteriums or the mucors burn these same products, and bring them back to the simple condition of binary compounds, water, ammonia, and carbonic acid.

" We have yet to distinguish the very remarkable case in which the putrescible liquid forms a layer of slight thickness with easy access to atmospheric air. •I shall demonstrate experimentally that both putrefaction and fermentation may be absolutely prevented, and that the organic matter will yield only to the operation of combustion.

" Such are the results of putrefaction effected with free contact with the atmosphere. On the contrary, in the case of putrefaction under shelter from the air, the products of the doubling [1] of the putrescible matter remain unchanged. This is what I meant when I said that putrefaction in contact with air is a phenomenon, if not always more rapid, at least more complete, more destructive of organic matter, than putrefaction under shelter from air. In order to be better understood, I shall cite some examples. Let us putrefy — I employ the word designedly in this instance as a synonym of ferment, — let us putrefy lactate of lime sheltered from air. The vibrion-ferments will transform the lactate into several products, one of which is always butyrate of

[1] " *De doublement de la matière putrescible.*" Pasteur means the products of the putrefactive fermentation, which he has described as complex, though more simple than the original substances.

lime. This new compound, indecomposable by the vibrio which provoked its formation, will remain indefinitely in the liquid without any change. But repeat the operation in contact with air. As fast as the vibrion-ferments act in the interior of the liquid, the pellicle on the surface gradually and completely burns the butyrate. If the fermentation is very active, this combustion is arrested, but entirely because the carbonic acid that is disengaged hinders the arrival of atmospheric air. The phenomenon recommences as soon as the fermentation is finished or lessened in rapidity. It is precisely the same, if we cause a naturally sweet liquid to ferment under shelter from air; the liquid is charged with alcohol almost indestructible; while if we operate with contact of air, the alcohol, after being acetified is burnt and transformed entirely into water and carbonic acid. Then the vibrions appear, and in their suite putrefaction, when the liquid only contains water and nitrogenous matter. At length, in their turn, the vibrions and the products of putrefaction are burnt by the bacteriums or the mucors, of which the last survivors incite the combustion of their predecessors, and thus is accomplished the return of the organized matter to the atmosphere and to the mineral kingdom.

" Let us now consider the putrefaction of solid bodies. I have recently shown that the body of an animal is, under ordinary circumstances, shut against the introduction of the germs of inferior beings; consequently putrefaction begins first at the surface, and afterwards reaches the interior of a solid mass. If a whole animal is left after death either in contact with, or sheltered from air, its surface is covered with germs of inferior organism which the atmosphere has conveyed. Its intestinal canal in which fæcal matters are formed is filled not only with germs, but with fully-developed vibrions, as Leewenhoek perceived. These vibrions are much in advance of those on the surface of the body. They are adult individuals, deprived of air, bathed in liquids, and in process of multiplication and function-performance. It is by their aid the putrefaction of the body begins, which has only been preserved up to that time by life and the nutrition of its organs."

After a few observations, M. Pasteur declares his conviction that " neither in their origin nor in their nature is there any resemblance between putrefaction and gangrene," and he adds, " instead of being a putrefaction, properly so-called, gangrene appears to be that condition of an organ in which one part is preserved in spite of death from putrefaction, and in which the liquids and solids act and react chemically and physically beyond the normal actions of nutrition."

We shall only remark upon this very important and interesting paper that few English microscopists adhere to Ehrenberg's notion, which is adopted by M. Pasteur, that vibrions are *animals*. On the contrary, most authorities, agree that they belong to the vegetable kingdom, and are in many cases transitional forms of Algæ.

FERMENTATION AS A CAUSE OF DISEASE.

M. Polli, of Milan, Italy, has recently published a treatise " *on fermentation as the cause of various diseases.*" He states that there exists a great analogy between the processes of fermentation and many organic metamorphoses, which occur in some diseases; and he has made experiments by injecting substances into the blood-vessels of animals,

16*

which have acted as ferments, and have produced a state of action resembling natural diseases. By injecting purulent putrid matter into the veins of animals, diseases presenting all the characteristics of typhoid fever were produced. Contagious diseases, such as glanders, which is produced by the injection of glanderous humors, are facts which prove that a general affection may be induced by the simple introduction into the blood of a substance capable of acting as a ferment. M. Polli also believes that he has proved, by a series of experiments, that it is possible to neutralize morbific ferments in the blood of animals, by chemical substances which do not act in a manner incompatible with life; and it is by these substances that he hopes to treat successfully those diseases of which fermentation is the primary cause. It is well known that sulphuric acid gas prevents alcoholic and acetic fermentation, and also the fermentation of animal substances and organic matters in general. Thus, it arrests, if it be already begun, the fermentation produced by saliva and diastase in contact with starch. M. Polli has proved that alkaline or earthy sulphites possess the same antiseptic properties.

From a number of experiments made upon dogs, and alluded to in his memoir, he has determined the safe and efficacious dose of sulphites for internal administration, the changes which they undergo in the organization, and their curative action in the affections produced by the injection of putrid or contagious matters into the blood. The following is an account of some of his experiments : —

Ten grammes of sulphite of soda were given to a dog during a period of five days, then one gramme of pus was injected into the femoral vein. The animal became dull, and refused the food which it was offered, but the next day its spirits returned and it ate willingly. Two days after, the same experiment was repeated, and was followed by the same results. At the end of a few days, the animal was perfectly cured.

One gramme of pus was injected in two portions into the veins of a dog, of a more robust nature than that operated upon in the preceding experiment. The animal became spiritless, but the next day took some food ; the following day it was very low, it breathed with difficulty, its wounds were sanious, its left leg and foot swollen, and it died ten days afterward.

An equal quantity of putrid blood was injected into the veins of three dogs ; one died five hours after the infection, another after five days of illness, and the third, to which some sulphite of soda had been administered, after having experienced some trifling symptoms of illness, rapidly recovered.

Numerous other experiments made with putrid blood and morbific mucus proved that the animal died with all the symptoms of a general infection, whenever sulphite of soda was not administered, and that, on the contrary, they speedily recovered under its influence.

In a communication, on essentially the same subject as the above, made to the British Association, 1863, by Dr. G. Robinson, the author alluded to the circumstance of the analogy between many of the phenomena of fevers and other zymotic diseases, and the ordinary process of fermentation having been perceived and recognized by Hippocrates and the oldest writers on medicine. Their idea was, that a poisonous ferment existing in the atmosphere entered the mass of the blood, and induced in it a series of changes, which gave rise to the excessive heat and other peculiarities of that class of diseases. At the present time, this doctrine, modified by the discoveries of Liebig and other chemists, has been adopted by most physicians, and forms the basis of the classification of disease framed by Dr. Farr, and used by the registrar-general. It thus supposes living germs to exist in the atmosphere, which, when introduced into the body, give rise to a specific and regular series of morbid actions, pursuing a definite course in a definite time, as in small-pox, — those germs being disclosed and multiplied, and producing others capable of reproducing in other bodies the same succession of changes. Other pathologists have supposed that the atmospheric poison acts on the blood chemically, by giving rise to what may be termed catalytic actions; while the author is disposed to believe, from what he saw during the cholera epidemic in Newcastle, in 1853, that some of these volatile organic matters in the atmosphere are capable of acting on the human body as direct poisons ; and that this inanimate, volatile, poisonous matter also furnishes nutrition to the organic germs suspended in the air. After these preliminary remarks, he proceeded to refer briefly to a number of scattered facts, which seemed to him to indicate the existence of a great principle, which might hereafter be found applicable to the prevention or mitigation of epidemic diseases, by the direct use of substances capable of arresting the process of morbific fermentation. He mentioned the following facts as converging to this conclusion : — 1. Antiseptic substances, ranging from simple, innocuous matters, such as sugar, up to the powerful metallic poisons, such as corrosive sublimate, and forming a very numerous and diversified group, have been long known to be capable of arresting the putrefaction of animal and vegetable structures. 2. The same substances prevent the formation of fungi, as is seen in the use of solutions of metallic salts in taxidermy, in the prevention of dry-rot, etc. 3. Many of those agents are also known to arrest at once the process of fermentation, — as, for instance, sulphurous acid ; and Emi and other chemists have observed under the microscope the rapid stoppage of the vitality of the yeast-plant when a solution of arsenious acid was added to the fermenting liquor. 4. The formation of the fungus in and on the plant, which causes the vine disease, is prevented by applying sulphur to the affected vines. 5. In Cornwall, it is believed that the arsenical fumes from the tin-calcining furnaces exercised an influence over the potato-plants in the neighborhood, which preserved them from the disease then affecting other parts of the same county. [A statement to this effect, signed by Capt. Charles Thomas, sen., of Dolwath, and sixteen cottagers was here read.] 6. It has been found, that when a species of fermentation has taken place in the human stomach, resulting in the development in large quantities of a minute organism (the *sarcina ventriculi*), this morbid action can be controlled and stopped by the direct anti-zymotic influence of certain salts, such as sulphate of soda, in doses perfectly compatible with the patient's safety. 7. In different parts of the world, among different races, a belief has long existed that certain antiseptic substances, of which arsenic may be taken as the type, are capable of acting as antidotes or preservative and curative agencies against atmospheric and other poisons; and in some cases that popular belief has proved to be well-founded. The experience of the multitude discovered the value of arsenic as a cure for ague long before it was recognized as such by physicians. The arsenical fumes of certain works in Cornwall were stated by the late Dr. Paris to have stopped the ague, previously endemic there. More recently it has been stated, that the arsenic eaters of Styria are peculiarly exempt from fevers and other epidemic diseases ; and in India the natives have long used arsenic as an antidote to the poison of snakes. Dr. Robinson concluded by expressing a belief that these scattered observations were not only sufficient to justify and necessitate further inquiries in this direction, but seemed in themselves to shadow forth the outline of a great law, which might at some future time be productive of immense benefit to mankind.

PESTILENCE IN INDIA.

The following is extracted from the Calcutta correspondence of the *London Times*, dated April 9th, 1863 : "The country of Jessore, on the confines of which the Ganges loses itself in those innumerable creeks which constitute the rich Sonderbund marshes, is well known as the source of that cholera which in 1817 infected Lord Hastings' army, and then became, for the first time, the scourge of Europe. In the same country, a pestilence like the Egyptian plague, generally preceded by cholera, has long been endemic, and during the last three years — since June, 1860 — has spread all round Calcutta and along the line of the East Indian Railway to Burdwan. It has slain no less than 40,000 victims, or sixty per cent. of the whole population affected. By dispensaries and native doctors, Government, always benevolent, in vain attempted to arrest it, but in November, '62, with the last fall of rain, it spent its fury. For miles whole villages are abandoned, and there were none left to bury or burn the dead, whose corpses still pollute the air. The report of Dr. Elliott, appointed to investigate the epidemic, reveals horrors which even the technical language of the medical man does not modify. All is attributed to malaria, and water so filled with decaying organisms that an oily scum floats on its surface. A Bengalee village is always covered with the densest vegetation, for the sake of privacy and fruit, and is destitute of the simplest means of conservancy. Orders have gone forth for the clearance of jungle and the filling up of pestilential pools, but the people are apathetic and hate cleanliness, and probably the next rainy season, in June, will see a recurrence of the plague, described as a remittent, congestive fever, which carries off the victim in periods of from five hours to fifteen days. Fortunately for the tropics, where vegetation is so dense, the great heat destroys or checks malaria ; but the four months of rain are deadly."

SOLVENT FOR SILK.

M. Persoz, the eminent French chemist, has recently discovered that when silk is exposed to the action of a neutral solution of chloride of zinc (concentrated to about 60° of the areometer), it is converted at first into a gummy mass, preserving the threads of the tissue, then gradually changes into transparent clots, and finally becomes completely dissolved. In fact, the process of solution is very similar to that of dissolving gun-cotton in alcoholized-ether. The solution of silk in chloride of zinc, of the above strength, takes place gradually at ordinary temperature ; but if heat is applied to the solvent, the solution is rapidly effected, becoming viscous and capable of being drawn into threads like thick syrup. It then resembles a strong solution of gum-arabic. By employing Mr. Graham's method of dialysis, the silk can now be entirely separated from the chloride of zinc, used as its solvent, and obtained in a pulpy or gelatinous state, resembling golden-yellow varnish. M. Ozanam, another French chemist, taking advantage of this fact, informs the Academy of Sciences that he is experimenting as to the possibility of manufacturing silk without the trouble of spinning or weaving. The silkworm produces a soft, gummy thread which gradually hardens, and the proposal is to imitate nature and to draw out the silk into threads of any length and of any thickness, and thus avoid the trouble of spinning, by a process similar to wire-drawing. Or silk cloth might be produced, either by a process of pouring out and rolling, or in endless lengths, after the manner of paper-makers. Other applications suggest themselves; and if the silk-pulp can be hardened on drying, it might be manufactured into ornamental and useful articles for which gutta-percha is now used. And with this capability of reduction to the gelatinous condition, we have the means for reconverting old waste silk, woven or twisted, refuse cocoons and floss, to a useful and valuable article of commerce.

M. Persoz's discovery has also suggested a method for detecting tricks of trade as practised by silk-manufacturers. Much of the woven silk contains a large proportion of wool or cotton, sometimes of both. Now, as above stated, chloride of zinc dissolves the silk, but leaves untouched the wool and cotton; the wool in turn is dissolved by an aqueous solution of caustic potash, which leaves the cotton uninjured. M. Ozanam, in a recent communication to the French Academy, also carries the question a step further, by showing that the several operations may be accomplished in one single bath of ammoniuret of copper. Let the piece of cloth be plunged into this, and in a short time the cotton disappears; at the end of three, six, or twelve hours, according to the strength of the bath, the silk is dissolved, leaving the wool intact. Thus the quality and proportions of the materials of the warp and weft may be easily determined.

Extent of the Silk Trade of Europe. — The importance of the silk-trade may be judged of by a few particulars concerning the produce of Europe only. In an ordinary year, the silk-crop of Italy, including Southern Tyrol and the canton of Ticino, amounts to more than 100,-000,000 pounds' weight, worth, according to quality, from fifteen-pence to half a crown a pound. The total value is thus seen to be of great importance; and from that a notion may be formed of the loss arising from the silkworm disease, a disease for which no effectual cure has yet been discovered. In an average year, Lombardy alone produces 30,-000,000 pounds of silk.

IMPROVEMENTS IN THE MANUFACTURE OF ILLUMINATING GAS.

Mr. William Armstrong, in his address before the British Association, 1863, thus alludes to some recent improvements in the manufacture of illuminating gas : " In this connection," he says, " it may be proper for me to notice a recent discovery by Berthelot of a new form of carburetted hydrogen possessing twice the illuminating power of ordinary coal-gas (see *Annual Sci. Dis.*, 1863, p. 197). Berthelot succeeded in procuring this gas by passing hydrogen between the carbon electrodes of a powerful battery. Dr. Oddling has since shown that the same gas may be produced by mixing carbonic oxide with an equal volume of light carburetted hydrogen, and exposing the mixture in a porcelain tube to an intense heat. Still more recently, Mr. Siemnes has detected the same gas in the highly-heated regenerators of his furnaces, and there is now every reason to believe that the new gas will become practically available for illuminating purposes. Thus it is that discoveries which in the first instance interest the philosopher only, almost invariably initiate a rapid series of steps leading to results of great practical importance to mankind."

A correspondent of the N. Y. *Tribune*, under date of Oct. 24, 1863, also describes some improvements in the manufacture of gas, recently effected by Dr. W. Elmer, of New York. These improvements, he says, are based upon the general fact that all the materials it is desirable to convert into illuminating gases have in them an *excess* of carbon over even the requirements of the richest gas that can be ordinarily burned; — still more, over what the common or coal-gas process can convert. All those materials have in them *some hydrogen*, but none of them enough to render all their carbon available. In the first place, then, the new method obtains from an extraneous source an abundant supply of the simple element hydrogen, adequate to the needs of any of the crude materials operated on ; and it regulates this supply so as to afford to each of the sorts of materials just the percentage of hydrogen required, in view of its composition and that of the gas to be generated.

This additional supply of hydrogen, it is proposed to obtain, by decomposing the vapor of water, by bringing steam in contact with metallic zinc at a high temperature, — oxide of zinc and free hydrogen being the resultant products. This oxide of zinc, in the form of zinc-white, it is claimed, has a higher value as a pigment than the metallic zinc originally employed ; and, therefore, the cost of hydrogen, liberated through its agency, is comparatively trifling. The hydrogen, as above produced, is, by means of an appropriate apparatus, intermixed, at or near the moment of its liberation, with hydro-carbon vapors containing an excess of carbon, and obtained by the distillation of bituminous coals, shales, peat, resin, or other similar substances ; the effect of which, it is stated, is to produce a mixture containing any desired percentage of carbon, or such a one as will have the greatest illuminating property. Illuminating gas, thus produced, is claimed to be more economical in its production and uses than that manufactured by any other process.

Purifying Gas. — An important improvement in purifying coal-gas, having for its main object the removal of sulphur, has been lately made by the Rev. Mr. Bowditch, of England. All gas that is purified in the common way contains certain quantities of sulphur in the form of bisulphide of carbon, and probably also in that of sulphur-organic compounds. The gas may be passed in the usual manner over lime or the peroxide of iron ; but, this operation does not, in the slightest degree, affect the sulphur compounds in question. During the combustion of the gas, however, the sulphur is converted into sulphurous acid, which diffuses itself in the apartment in which it is burned, and a great deal of the discomfort of which many complain in the use of gas is due to this cause. Mr. Bowditch discovered that though cold hydrate of lime will not remove these impurities, they are, to a great extent, got rid of by heating the hydrate of lime to a temperature varying from the boiling point of water up to 400° or 500° Fah.; a temperature of 400° being probably the most convenient for the development of the effects of his process. This process has been found by repeated experiments to remove all but about 2 or 3 grains of sulphur per 100 cubic feet of gas, the quantity of sulphur originally contained in the gas varying from 5 or 6 grains up to as much as 40 or 50 grains per 100 feet.

CHEMICAL MEMORANDA.

Remarkable Chemical Terms. — The production of numerous new organic bodies in chemical research, which are the derivatives of several prior derivatives, have led chemists to the coining of terms, which although expressive, are in some instances absurdly complicated and unpronounceable. Thus, Messrs. Perkin and Church, English chemists, who are devoting themselves to the preparation and practical application of the various dyes and other derivatives of coal-tar, announce in a recent communication to the London Chemical Society, that they have discovered a new organic base, to which they have applied the name " Azodinapthyldiamine; " and to a derivative of the base, a new organic acid, they give the still more remarkable name of " Azodinapthyldicitraconanaic."

Mercuric Methyl. — This name is given to a remarkable substance discovered by Dr. Frankland, of London. It is formed by allowing iodide of methyl to act upon sodium amalgam, in the presence of acetic ether. When purified it forms a colorless, highly-refracting liquid, of the specific gravity 3.069, being in fact the heaviest known liquid, with the exception of mercury itself. So dense is it that a piece of heavy glass will float upon it. Dr. Frankland states that in the event of this organo-mercuric compound being required in quantity, no difficulty would be experienced. Upon seeing the specimen of mercuric methyl handed round at a late meeting of the Chemical Society, London, the idea occurred to a correspondent of the *Chemical News* to apply this liquid to the manufacture of prisms. At present, the only liquid suitable for this purpose is bisulphide of carbon, which is not above half the density, besides being objectionable from its offensive odor, its great volatility and the ease with which it ignites. The mercuric methyl appears to be superior to the bisulphide of carbon in all these respects. Besides its use for prisms, this liquid might be advantageously employed in the manufacture of lenses. Formerly, compound lenses, in which one of the constituents was a fluid held between outer meniscus lenses, were somewhat in vogue, but were abandoned owing to the advantages of their construction not being sufficiently great to counterbalance the difficulties.

New Source of Oxygen for the Animal Organism. — At a recent meeting of the Munich Academy of Sciences, Baron Liebig announced what he considered as a very important discovery. The atmospheric air has hitherto been regarded as the chief or only source of the oxygen employed in the processes of nutrition and metamorphosis within the animal organism. By the aid of an apparatus, for which the King of Bavaria provided 7,000 florins from his private purse, it has now been shown that within the bodies of carnivora, a very considerable amount of oxygen is produced from water; and that, under given circumstances, a powerful process of decomposition is set up, resolving the water into its constituent parts, its oxygen serving for the formation of carbonic acid, and the hydrogen (which often exceeds the volume of the animal in quantity) being discharged by expiration.

Microscopic Use of Magenta Dye. — Magenta dye can be employed in microscopic research to great advantage, to tinge blood-globules or animal cells. It causes nuclear structures to be distinctly displayed.

Pigments from Coal Tar Colors. — The practical application of the beautiful colors extracted from coal-tar has recently received a further extension, in the discovery, by a French chemist, of a method whereby pigments can be prepared from the dyes suitable for use in oil painting. The process consists essentially in mixing a solution of the coal-tar color in an alcoholic solvent, with a solution of pure white soap in hot water. To this is added alumina in a gelatinous state (prepared from alum), when the colors are precipitated in connection with the alumina. By these means, and especially by the assistance of an animal matter in a soapy state, the colors are rendered solid and durable, and are applicable for painting. When the blue and yellow products are combined, a fine green is obtained, and the mixture of red and yellow produces an orange color; and, by the mixture of the different colors, all varieties of tints can be procured. The richness of these colors is unequalled; and it is claimed that they remain unchanged when exposed to light.

Poisoning by Nitro-Benzole. — By a paper communicated to the Royal Society (G. B.) by Dr. Letheby, it appears that if a dose of nitro-benzole be not too large, its poisonous action will not be immediately apparent, but it may " destroy life by a lingering illness, which shall not only defy the skill of the physician, but shall also baffle the researches of the jurist." After death, the blood of animals so killed is black and turbid, and the large organs congested, and no nitro-benzole can be discovered, if sufficient time has elapsed, as it will then be converted into aniline. Such facts show the necessity of having medical men well trained in chemistry. Aniline produces symptoms very similar to nitro-benzole. The conversion of the latter into the former takes place in a dead stomach, or by contact with putrid flesh for several hours.

Effects of Suppressed Action of Skin. — Edenhuizen has performed some experiments on rabbits, sheep, a dog, and other animals, for the purpose of ascertaining what changes take place in the organism when the action of the skin is suppressed. When one-eighth to one-sixth of the skin of an animal was covered with glue, oil-color, varnish, gum, tar, etc., it was sure to die of the effects. Edenhuizen infers from his researches that in the healthy state, a small quantity of nitrogen in a gaseous form is given off by the skin, and that this function being suppressed, the nitrogen is retained in the blood in the form of ammonia, which is then deposited as triple-phosphate in the subcutaneous areolar tissue, and in the peritoneum. The nitrogenous compound retained in the blood acts as an irritant to the nervous system, producing rigors, palsies, cramps, and tetanic attacks.

Secretion of Urea and Chloride of Sodium. — Dr. Emil Becher, assistant-surgeon army medical staff, took advantage of a voyage to China to make a series of observations on the relation between air temperature and the secretions above mentioned, as carried on in his own person. He found a constant increase of the secretions with the rising temperature from 50° to 70°, and an equally constant falling off, with the further rise of temperature from 70° to 90°. — From *Proceedings of the Royal Society.*

Causes of Coagulation of the Blood.—Prof. Lister observes, " that the coagulation of the blood is in no way connected with the evolution of ammonia any more than with the influence of oxygen or of rest. The real cause of the coagulation of the blood, when shed from the body, is the influence exerted upon it by ordinary matter, the contact of which for a very brief period effects a change in the blood, inducing a mutual reaction between its solid and fluid constituents, in which the corpuscles impart to the *liquor sanguinis* a disposition to coagulate."— *Proceedings of the Royal Society.*

The Effect of Petroleum upon Health has lately been made the subject of investigation. A memorial was sent to the Liverpool Health Committee, signed by several hundred citizens, and complaining of the storage of petroleum in their neighborhood as " a nuisance and prejudicial to health." The question was referred to Dr. French, the medical officer of the Board of Health; and, after a very thorough personal examination of the case, he reported that, while he had no hesitation in pronouncing the oil a nuisance on account of its strong, offensive smell, his investigation satisfied him that petroleum was not prejudicial to health. In order to make a full investigation, he visited 153 houses in the vicinity of the oil stores, and found no cases of sickness arising from the petroleum. ·

New Application of Chloroform. — M. Graw, a French physician, proposes to destroy the taste of intensely-bitter medicines, by mixing chloroform with them in certain proportions. He claims that the taste and odor even of assafœtida can be annihilated.

New Substitute for Albumen. — In consequence of a prize having been offered in France, for the invention of a substitute for albumen prepared from hens' eggs, an albumen equal in quality and much cheaper has been discovered, which is made from fish-roe.

Artificial Manufacture of Ice. — M. Nickles, in his correspondence with *Silliman's Journal*, states that an invention by M. Carré's for the artificial production of ice is finding its way into various branches of French industry. Brewers use it to freeze the wort of beer destined to undergo fermentation; coffee-house keepers for making ices and sherbets; vine-growers to concentrate wine, etc. The principle of this apparatus is based upon the great quantity of heat which ammonia, liquefied by condensation absorbs in becoming again gaseous, as this body contains an immense amount of latent heat.

Ammonia in the gaseous state is readily obtained, as is well known, by boiling the ammoniacal liquid known in commerce as " volatile alkali," to reproduce which it is only necessary to expose ammonia in the presence of water : to liquefy the gas, simple pressure is adequate. As it so readily takes the gaseous form, it is sufficient simply to remove the pressure which retains it as a liquid, and as this change of state is possible only on the condition that the liquefied ammonia retakes the

17

heat lost in its liquefaction, we perceive that it will rapidly cool the vessel which contains it and, consequently, the neighboring material. To undertake the method of putting these principles in operation, we have only to suppose an apparatus composed of two retorts soldered together by the necks, the whole perfectly close and without communication with the outer air. In the larger of these retorts, we place a concentrated solution of ammonia in water and heat it. Driven off by the heat, the gaseous ammonia cannot escape without becoming liquefied in the small retort.

Reduction of Chloride of Silver. — MM. Millon and Commaille have communicated to the French Academy of Sciences an extremely elegant reaction, by which absolutely pure metallic silver may be precipitated from its ammoniacal combinations, with all the accuracy necessary for rigid analysis, and in such a division as to render it available in the arts.

The reagent employed is ammonio-subchloride of copper. When this substance is added to ammonio-nitrate or ammonio-chloride of silver, the whole of the silver is at once thrown down in the metallic state as a gray amorphous precipitate. The precipitate readily assumes a metallic lustre under the burnisher, and may be applied to the surfaces of wood, stone, etc. The reaction takes place so perfectly that it may be employed either for the estimation of silver, or for the analysis of a mixture of sub and protosalt of copper ; every atom of silver thrown down representing one atom of sub-chloride of copper. It is, however, especially valuable for reducing the chloride of silver residues of the laboratory. These are dissolved in ammonia, and the ammoniacal subchloride of copper added, when the metallic silver is at once obtained in its purity. Moreover, it is only necessary to digest the filtrate with a little powdered zinc in a closed flask, in order to reduce again the copper salt, and it is ready for a fresh operation. In this way, the same quantity of copper solution suffices for an indefinite number of precipitations.

Tinned Lead Pipes, etc. — At a late meeting of the Liverpool Chemists' Association, specimens of lead pipe and sheet-lead, electro-plated with tin, were exhibited by Mr. Holt, and some discussion ensued respecting the use of lead coated in this manner for water cisterns and pipes. It appeared to be the opinion of the meeting that a coating of tin, instead of preserving the lead, was far more likely to ensure its more rapid corrosion ; for if the coating of tin by any means happened to be scratched off, even to the slightest extent, galvanic action would take place, and the lead would be destroyed very quickly. Dr. Nevins and Dr. Edwards stated that their experiments had proved that such would undoubtedly be the case ; Dr. Edwards remarking that in one case which he had examined, a cistern made of lead, in which was an accidental admixture of tin, was eaten out by well-water in six months, the lead being rapidly precipitated in the form of sulphate, etc.

Use of Dead-Sea Water. — M. Roux has laid before the French Academy an analysis of this water, which shows that, in addition to considerable quantities of chlorides of magnesium, sodium, calcium, and potassium, it contains bromide of magnesium to the extent of 0.364 grammes in 100,000 grammes. M. Roux considers that it may prove a very valuable medicine in scrofulous, syphilitic, and many other affections. Shall we have this locality converted into a fashionable watering-place, and find Dead-Sea water figuring amongst the articles of import trade ? It is evident that if bromides come into greater demand for photographic, medical, and other purposes, they might be economically prepared on this spot, at least to the extent of evaporating the water in shallow basins by natural heat, and sending the solid residue to our laboratories for future manipulation.

Interesting Application of Dialysis. — Already an economical application of Mr. Graham's ingenious process of dialysis has been discovered, and tried, with an interesting result, in the utilization of brine. In the curing of meat, there commonly remains a quantity of waste brine ; but Dr. Marcet, by dialysing this refuse liquor, separates the salt from the juice of the meat, and the latter remains fit for use as an article of diet. Separated in quantities on a great scale, it might be converted into soup for prisons and penitentiaries, or for half-starved cotton-spinners in Lancashire. From this beginning it would, perhaps, be safe to predict that dialysis will prove as valuable to commerce as to science.

Cement of Casein.—Dr. Wagner, in *The Technologist,* recommends the employment of a cold saturated solution of borax or of silicate of soda, to dissolve casein. The solution of casein by borax, is a clear liquid, of viscid consistence, more adhesive than gum, and able to replace in many cases strong glue. Stuffs of linen and cotton impregnated with this solution can be treated with tannic acid or acetate of alumina and rendered impermeable.

Non-Inflammable Fabrics. — A French chemist recommends the following simple method of rendering muslins and all other light stuffs incombustible ; it is merely necessary to mix with the starch used in making them up the half of its weight of carbonate of lime, commonly called Spanish chalk or Spanish white. The muslin or other stuff is then ironed as usual. The chalk thus added in no respect injures either the appearance, the quality, or the whiteness of the stuff. — *Times.*

M. Lauvageon, a French investigator, has also discovered that cotton cloth which has been exposed for a certain time to the vapor of burning sulphur assumes such an amount of incombustibility that although it will char and become brittle when held over the flame of a spirit lamp, it cannot be made to take fire, while under like conditions similar cloth, but unprepared in this way, inflamed immediately. If the alleged facts be borne out in practice, the problem is solved ; for the simplest domestic means may be devised for subjecting, after being washed, all white clothing to the vapor of sulphur, which will tend to make it still whiter. Moreover, it may not prove necessary to repeat the exposure so often.

Coffee Crushed vs. *Coffee Ground.* — It is not generally known that coffee which has been beaten is better than that which has been ground. Such, however, is the fact ; and in his brief article on the subject, Savarin gives what he considers the reasons for the difference. As he remarks, a mere decoction of green coffee is a most insipid drink, but carbonization develops the aroma, and an oil, which is the peculiarity of the coffee we drink. He agrees with other writers that the Turks excel in this. They employ no mills, but beat the berry with wooden pestles in mortars. When long used, these pestles become precious and bring great prices. He determined by actual experiment which of the two methods was the best. He burned carefully a pound of good Mocha, and separated it into two equal portions. The one was passed through the mill, the other beaten, after the Turkish fashion, in a mortar. He made coffee of each. Taking equal weights of each, and pouring on an equal weight of boiling water, he treated them both precisely alike. He tasted the coffee himself, and caused other competent judges to do so. The unanimous opinion was, that coffee beaten in a mortar was far better than that ground in a mill. And after mentioning that any may repeat the experiment, he tells a strange anecdote of the influence of one or the other kind of manipulation, namely: "Monsieur," said Napoleon, one day, to Laplace, "how comes it that a glass of water into which I put a lump of loaf sugar tastes more pleasantly than if I had put in the same quantity of crushed sugar?" "Sir," said the philosophical senator, "there are three substances, the constituents of which are identical — sugar, gum, and starch; they differ only in certain conditions, the secret of which nature has preserved. I think it possible that in the effect produced by the pestle, some saccharine particles become either gum or amidon, and cause the difference." — *Boston Transcript.*

THE DISSOCIATION OF WATER.

This term will seem strange to English ears, but perhaps not more so than its equivalent, "*la dissociation de l'eau*" to the French, and at any rate it seems most advisable to preserve the name given by M. H. St. Claire Deville to the very interesting phenomena described by him to the French Academy, in a paper of which we proceed to give an account.

M. Deville commences by stating that if a tolerably rapid current of hydrogen is made to traverse a porous earthen tube and the gas which escapes is collected, it is found to be, not hydrogen, but in round numbers, oxygen twenty-one, and nitrogen seventy-nine. "Thus the hydrogen is dispersed through the atmosphere, and air is absorbed by the porous tube in virtue of endosmose, and in spite of the pressure of some centimetres of water, or mercury, into which the abducting tube is plunged, and which is maintained in the interior of the apparatus." If the porous tube is introduced into an impermeable porcelain tube, shorter than itself, and closed at each end with a cork, through which the porous tube is inserted, a space is enclosed into which any kind of gas can be admitted. For this purpose, the corks are pierced so as to admit an exit and entrance tube of glass. The porous tube is similarly provided, and if a current of carbonic acid gas is made to traverse the space between the porous tube and the porcelain tube, while hydrogen is driven through the former, the hydrogen changes its place, and may be inflamed at the exit where the carbonic acid might have been expected, while the porous tube allows nearly pure carbonic acid to escape. These facts, observes M. Deville, are in accordance with the observations of Professor Graham and M. Jamin.

If the preceding apparatus is placed in a furnace supplied with dense fuel, affording a heat of 1100° to 1300° (C.), it will suffice to demonstrate the spontaneous decomposition of water, a phenomenon which M. Deville terms *dissociation.* To accomplish this, vapor of water is passed through the porous tube, instead of the hydrogen in the former experiment, while carbonic acid gas traverses the space between the two tubes. The gases that emerge are collected over a bath containing potash, to absorb the carbonic acid, and received in small glass jars. When the furnace is in activity, the tubes yield an explosive mixture of oxygen and hydrogen — the elements of water.

Thus it appears that part of the water is decomposed or " dissociated " in the porous tube. " The hydrogen, attracted (*appelé*) by the carbonic acid in the annular interspace, has traversed the walls of the porous tube, and separated itself by the simple action of a filter from the oxygen which remains in the interior tube. A considerable quantity of carbonic acid is attracted in a contrary direction, according to the rule established in the preceding experiments, and mingles with the oxygen." This is the broad explanation which M. Deville gives, but he remarks that the action is in reality more complicated; as, when the hydrogen comes in contact with the heated carbonic acid, some carbonic oxide is formed, and a certain quantity of the latter gas is found to replace the hydrogen. It is also difficult to avoid the escape of some hydrogen, which leaves the oxygen in excess, and the water contains enough air to effect the result. " The carbonic acid determines the separation of the gases by endosmose; but it may also act mechanically."

In explanation of these facts, M. Deville states, that the temperature of the combustion of hydrogen in oxygen is not equal to 2500° C., at which point the volume of the gases, estimated at 0° C., is multiplied tenfold, and beyond which the complete decomposition of water takes place. " But this decomposition is accompanied by a considerable absorption of latent heat, to the extent required to keep the molecules of oxygen and hydrogen at a distance beyond the radius of the sphere of their affinity. Thus the decomposition of a body resembles the ebullition of a liquid, the principal characteristic of which is invariableness of temperature under the same pressure." Admitting the comparison between decomposition and ebullition, M. Deville regards "dissociation," or partial decomposition at a temperature below the decomposing point, as resembling the evaporation of liquids below their boiling point. " If," he observes, " you shut up some water in a small vessel, at ordinary temperature, the evaporation is slight, on account of the tension that is produced when vapor is formed ; but, if you introduce a piece of chloride of calcium, the water evaporates until that substance is saturated, the tension remaining constant all the time." He imagines the carbonic acid to carry off the dissociated gases just as the chloride of calcium absorbs the vapor, and then the process of dissociation, like that of evaporation, is enabled to go on.

Porosity of Platinum. — In prosecuting further experiments in regard to the above subject, some interesting facts relative to the porosity of platinum and its endosmotic action were elicited. They caused a platinum tube to be drawn out of one piece, so as to be free from all solder, and to present a uniform and unbroken surface. This platinum tube was introduced into a porcelain one, so that an empty cylindrical space was left all round between the two, properly stopped at each end. Through this space, a constant current of hydrogen was made to pass, by means of two glass tubes inserted at the extremities, so as not

17*

to allow of the slightest communication with the platinum tube, which was filled with dry air.   On exposing this tube to a high temperature, the air by degrees lost its oxygen, and water was formed; a circumstance which could only be explained by admitting that hydrogen had penetrated through the pores of the platinum tube ; and, on the temperature being further raised, a considerable quantity of free hydrogen was found to issue from that tube.   This shows that platinum, at a high temperature, is capable of producing the phenomena of endosmosis with gases.

CONCENTRATION OF MINERAL WATERS.

Sea-water, in freezing, forms flakes of ice consisting of nearly pure water, and an extremely saline liquid which in northern countries is utilized in the production of marine salt.   Very recently, Dr. Robinet, a physician of Paris, has discovered that the same process can be applied in the purification of fresh water.   In freezing water from the Seine, from wells, and from springs, he found the ice produced to be so entirely free from the salts of lime and magnesia which were contained in the water, that, thus purified, it may be considered as nearly equal to distilled water.   So it is now proposed to procure water on board ships, no longer by distillation but by congelation.

The same fact is made use of in the concentration of mineral waters, a problem which has offered itself for a long time, but which the employment of heat could not solve, on account of the gas originally in solution which the heat expelled.   Cold works better.   Dr. Ossian Henry, of Paris, has experimented with forty different varieties of water, and finds that it is possible, by congelation, to reduce mineral waters to one-eighth, one-tenth, one-fifteenth, or even one-twentieth of their original volume, without producing any alteration in the gases contained in them.   100 litres of mineral water can thus be reduced to 5, giving great economy to transportation; moreover, the ice itself is also valuable.   But we do not believe that the therapeutic properties of the extract will be identical with those of the water in its original state, because of the changes which manifestly take place in the contained salts, changes so evident that Mr. Balard has been able to base upon them a manufacture of sulphate of soda, by exposing to a temperature sufficiently low the water containing $NaCl$ and MgO, SO^3, which result from the manufacture of sea-salt by the evaporation of sea-water.

The publication of this process has given occasion for a protest on the part of Mr. Tichon, an apothecary of Aix les Bains (Savoy), according to which the same process has been used since 1856, by him and a Mr. Melsens, who was staying at Aix for his health.   The mineral water which he drank here, and which is sulphurous, proving disagreeable to his taste, he undertook to remove part of the odor by submitting it to a freezing mixture.   In this way, he was able, not only to mask the disagreeable odor, but also to concentrate the mineral ingredients.   Mr. Tichon adds that congelation will not suit all mineral waters, inasmuch as it alters the organic matter therein dissolved.

FORM OF A DROP.

Without examination, of a close and careful character, we are apt to assume that a drop of any known fluid has one form. It is round : and whether it be a drop of oil, a drop of water, a drop of ether, or any other of the innumerable fluids which are known, they all appear to be round. Prof. Tomlinson, of King's College, London, finds, however, if we examine drops of different liquids under certain conditions, that each drop assumes a form peculiar to its own kind of liquid, by which it may be known and identified. A drop of otto of lavender puts on one shape, a drop of turpentine another. Drops of sperm-oil, olive-oil, colza-oil, naptha, creosote — indeed, each individual drop, be the fluid what it may — can be easily recognized by its form. In order to test any of these forms or shapes, we have but to place a drop of the fluid under examination upon water. For this purpose, we must employ a glass to hold the water, taking the greatest care that it is quite clean ; it must even be rinsed after being wiped, lest there be the least dust from the cloth adhering to the vessel. The glass being then filled with distilled or clean filtered river water, we let fall upon it a drop of the fluid, and watch the shape or form it puts on. A very little practice will show how easy it is thus to distinguish a drop of one fluid from that of another. Even more ; if one fluid be mixed with another, for any sinister motive or design, we can thus detect the mixture, because we can see each fluid in one drop of the mixture. Thus, by the examination of one drop of sperm-oil adulterated with one-twentieth of colza-oil, the mixture is instantly discovered. So, if turpentine be mixed with otto of lemons, or otto of lavender, we have now a ready mode of discovering the cheat. — *Scientific American.*

SUBSTITUTION OF SOLUBLE GLASS FOR THE RESINOUS SOAP USED IN THE MANUFACTURE OF ORDINARY SOAP.

In many countries, but especially America, enormous quantities of colophony have long been used in making hard brown or yellow soap. These compound soaps are very useful, and in point of cheapness no other soap can compete with resinous soap. The civil war in America, by causing the blockade of the ports of the Slave States, whence most of the resin is derived, has induced an extraordinary rise in the price of colophony, so that the further manufacture of cheap soaps seemed for the time arrested.

To meet this difficulty, the attention of soap-makers has been directed to the preparation of soaps containing silicate of soda, or the so-called " soluble glass." This idea is by no means new, and has been for some time practically introduced in England ; but the process lately introduced into the United States differs notably from those previously in use, by making use of a product rich in silica, capable of forming a hard and comparatively neutral soap, instead of extremely alkaline mixtures, as in England.

The American process commences in preparing, by the dry way, a silicate of soda containing five equivalents of silica and two of soda, which is dissolved by prolonged boiling in water. The solution is sometimes hastened by pressure. The limpid solution, freed from all insoluble impurities, is decanted and concentrated to about 35° B. ;

1.32 specific gravity being the state in which it is sold.   After preparing, by the usual process, a certain quantity of pure soap with tallow, oil, or other kind of grease, and when the boiling is just finished, it is poured, while still hot and in a fluid state, into forms or moulds, and the desired quantity of concentrated solution of silicate of soda, either cold or heated, is added at the same instant.   To incorporate the silicate thoroughly, the mass is stirred until the cooling renders this operation difficult.   It is then left to harden.   By this process, the silicate of soda becomes so perfectly incorporated with the soap that as much as sixty per cent. of this solution at 35° B. may be added, and yet yield a soap of adequate consistency.   But generally not more than from twenty-five to forty per cent. of silicate is added to the soap. It is this power of adding so large a proportion of alkaline silicate, thoroughly saturated with silica, which forms one of the great advantages of the American process.

Soap prepared by the American process differs materially from ordinary resin soap neither in appearance or action.   It has passed satisfactorily through the trial of a great demand, and appears to serve perfectly well for all the uses to which ordinary soap is applied.   The American government has already bought large quantities of it for the use of the army at a much lower price than was formerly given for resinous soaps, and it has undergone all the tests exacted by its agents.

It may also be remarked, that a mixture of silicate of soda and ordinary soap has been preferably used for some time in washing woollen fabrics in one of the largest establishments of the United States.

Silicate of soda is useful to soap-makers for several qualities not possessed by resin ; for instance, the addition of a large quantity of silicate of soda imparts to the soap neither that disagreeable odor nor the glueiness which too great a proportion of resin communicates.   It may be introduced into soap in much larger proportions than resin without in any way injuring the sale of the product.

It is not probable that resin will ever resume its former importance to the soap-maker.   It will still be used conjointly with the silicate of soda, since a little resin serves to correct the nauseating odors of inferior fats, and because, according to some makers, it augments the detersive action of the soap.

The use of soluble glass in hard soaps should not be confounded with the use, as detergents, of simple solutions of silicate of soda.   The latter are simply alkaline solutions, similar to those of alkaline carbonates. They act chiefly, if not wholly, by their chemical nature, for they do not lather, and in that and other respects are unlike real soaps ; while the silicate of soda soap, owing to the portion of fatty acid it contains, lathers abundantly, and behaves like ordinary soap, the mechanical and chemical conditions required by a good soap being fulfilled.

It should be borne in mind that silicate of soda soap is distinct from siliciferous soaps formerly prepared by the mechanical addition of silica or of some insoluble silicate, such as silicate of alumina, which is simply a useless adulteration, while in soaps containing soluble glass a portion of fatty acid, so to speak, is replaced by a weak, mineral acid, equally efficacious in modifying the causticity of the alkali.

The introduction of soluble glass for the manufacture of soap constitutes another example of the rapidity with which one industrial process displaces another, previously preferred, but whose further development is impeded by circumstances.

THE COLORING MATTER OF THE RED SEA.

To Ehrenberg is due the merit of having first described (in 1826) the nature of the organism from which this coloring matter is derived. He found it in the Bay of Tor, and called it Trichodesmium Erythraeum, which another writer, Montagne, advisedly changed to T. Ehrenbergii. " No one," says Mr. Carter, " who has read the memoir of M. Danste on this subject, can doubt that this is not the only organism which colors the sea red in different parts of the world." In June, 1862, Mr. Carter himself had an opportunity of seeing the color of the Red Sea, on which he gives a few observations. When approaching Aden, on May 31, he passed through large areas of a yellowish-brown oily-looking scum on the surface of the sea; and on June 2, when off the Arabian side of the first island sighted in the lower part of the Red Sea, after leaving Aden, it again appeared, and he frequently passed through large areas of it. Only once, he saw a portion of brilliant red and one of intense green together in the midst of the yellow. The odor which came from this scum was like that of putrid chlorophyll or like that from water in which green vegetables have been boiled. He drew up some of this scum, and found it to be composed of little short-cut bundles of filaments, like oscillatona. On examining the specimens, microscopically, in January, 1863, he found the little bundles, which were still just visible to the naked eye, like so much sawdust. Their color was still faint ·yellowish to the naked eye; but the filaments under the microscope were faintly green. After referring to the evidence of other observers, Mr. Carter considers that the occurrence of Trichodesmuim Ehrenbergii in the Red Sea, in the Gulf of Aden, the Indian Ocean and the Sea of Onan is so far substantiated; and as the yellow color, in all instances, probably passes into red, we have apparently the explanation of the whole of these seas having been called by the Greeks, Erythraean (red). Next to the yellow color, red is most prevalent and green least of all. Although Mr. Carter adds many other interesting particulars, he concludes by saying that much yet remains to complete the history of this little plant, which unfortunately, can only be obtained by watching it long and narrowly in its habitat. — *Annals of Natural History.*

THE NUTRITION OF PLANTS.

One of the vexed questions in vegetable nutrition has long turned upon the source from which plants derive their nitrogen. As this gas is so abundant in atmospheric air, the early speculators naturally assumed that plants derived their nitrogen from the air, by the simple process of direct absorption. This was, however, subsequently shown to be eminently improbable, and the very chemists who propounded the hypothesis, retracted it. The denial has for many years been stereotyped in text-books, and M. Dumas felt some hesitation in bringing forward the recent discovery of a young chemist, M. Jobin, which proves that the Confervæ — if no other plants — really *are* capable of the direct absorption of nitrogen, instead of receiving it by a decomposition of nitrates. His experiments consist in placing Confervæ where they can receive no nitrogen except that which is in the air, the rest of their food being furnished from simple carbonates, such as sugar, glycerine, etc. Under such conditions, they grow and develop perfectly; and as growth is impossible without a supply of nitrogen, the conclusion is irresistible. Moreover, M. Jobin finds, that at the moment of the absorption of the nitrogen by the plant, the hydrogen thus released combines with the nascent oxygen given off by the plant, and thus forms water. — *Proc. French Academy.*

THE CAPABILITIES OF SOILS.

Prof. Voelcker, the well-known agricultural chemist, in a recent lecture before the Royal Institution, London, on the " soils of England," advocated several views opposed to the general belief of agriculturists. He stated that the fertility of land was not capable of being permanently decreased by bad management, whereas, by good management the poorest land may be made to yield large and remunerative crops, as evidenced by the success of Flemish agriculture. Formerly the influence of the mechanical properties of the soil were much overrated, and at the present time too much influence is ascribed to the chemical properties. When potash or ammonia salts pass through soils the basic portion is retained, the acids passing away in conjunction with the lime of the soil. Soda, which is of less importance to plants, is not retained, whereas potash and ammonia are absorbed both by clay or silicate of alumina, and by hydrated oxide of iron, and retained in spite of repeated washings. The sesquioxides, of which those of iron ($Fe^2 O^3$) and aluminum ($Al^2 O^3$) are taken as types, may be regarded as weak acids, retaining the alkalies in the soil. Prof. Voelcker mentioned that so far from the soil of England being in the process of exhaustion, that its fertility was being greatly augmented, in good farm practice the restoration being in advance of the exhaustion. As a proof of this he stated that in Norfolk the average produce of wheat was — in 1773 = 15 bushels per acre. In 1796 = 28 bushels per acre. In 1862 = 32 to 36 bushels per acre. The increase being due to drainage, tillage, and to the growth of improved varieties.

NEW RESEARCHES ON OZONE.

In a communication to the *Annales de Chimie*, M. De Luna states that, — 1. Every time that chemical reaction takes place in atmospheric air the oxygen in the air is ozonized. 2. The ozonoscopic paper made blue by the ozone is decolorized in an atmosphere of hydrogen. The coloration and decoloration of the paper can thus be produced nearly indefinitely, by plunging the paper alternately in ozonized air and hydrogen. The following is the mode of operation: In an empty flask, perfectly dry, is placed a tube terminating with a funnel, by which sulphuric acid may be so poured in that the extremity of the tube may rest in it, the tube having a piece of ozonoscopic paper twisted round it. While the flask is dry, no change takes place; but if the flask be made damp, when the sulphuric acid is poured in, the combination of the latter with the water ozonizes the air, and the paper becomes blue. Ozonification takes place when chemical action is set up by putting fragments of soda or potash into the dry flask. M. De Luna also easily prepares ozone by adding to a flask of oxygen a concentrated solution of caustic potash and a little sulphuric acid. As soon as the ozonoscopic paper becomes blue, the odor of ozone is perceived, and the gas may be removed by the ordinary modes.

The Composition of Ozone. — *Comptes Rendus,* No. 14, 1863, contains an important paper on ozone, by M. J. L. Soret, presented to the French Academy by M. Regnault, in which, amongst other facts, he states that if ozone is destroyed by heat, by bringing a platina spiral, passed up into a globe containing ozonized oxygen, to a dull red heat, the volume of oxygen is considerably increased, while a very slight increase takes place in oxygen that has not been ozonized. For this and other reasons, the writer regards ozone as composed of more than two atoms of oxygen. M. Soret observes that many chemists regard oxygen in its ordinary gaseous state as composed of two atoms, oo, and he says we may conceive molecules of ozone to consist of three atoms of oxygen, ooo, and to constitute a binoxide of oxygen. He thinks it may contain *more* than three atoms of oxygen, but to determine the exact number its density should be known.

Ozone as a Disinfectant. — Dr. Delabrousse recommends the manufacture of ozone in the wards of hospitals, for the purpose of their disinfection. " What we want is," he says, " a proper supply of ozone — that is, of a body which is capable of decomposing, and so of neutralizing, the miasms constantly arising in hospital wards, and which at the same time is not hurtful to the patients " And thus, he tells us, the problem is solved. Ozone is such a body, and may be thus used. A spiral platinum wire is placed beneath an inverted funnel, and is rendered incandescent by means of Bunsen's pile. Hereupon the characteristic smell of ozone is perceived in the heated air circulating above the funnel ; and its presence is shown by the test paper. Thus may we obtain a ready and practical supply of ozone, and so insure the disinfecting of our hospital wards. — *British Med. Jour.*

ABSORPTION OF GASES BY CHARCOAL.

The absorption of gases by charcoal is the subject of a paper by Dr. R. Angus Smith (so eminent for his method of testing the purity of the atmosphere), in a recent number of the *Proceedings of the Royal Society.* His observations show that — 1. Charcoal absorbs oxygen so as to separate it from common air, or from its mixtures of hydrogen and nitrogen, at common temperatures ; and, 2, that charcoal continues this absorption for at least a month, although the chief amount is absorbed in a few hours, sometimes in a few seconds, according to the quality of the charcoal. 3. It does not absorb hydrogen, nitrogen, or carbonic acid for the same period. 4. Although the amount absorbed is somewhat in the relation of the condensability of the gases by pressure, this is not the only quality regulating the absorption of oxygen at least. 5. When it is sought to remove the oxygen from charcoal by warmth, carbonic acid is formed, even at the temperature of boiling water, and slowly even at lower temperatures. 6. Charcoals differ extremely in absorbing power and in the capacity of uniting with oxygen, animal charcoal possessing the latter property in a greater degree than wood charcoal. 7. Nitrogen and hydrogen, when absorbed by charcoal, diffuse into the atmosphere of another gas with such force as to depress the mercury three-quarters of an inch. 8. Water expels mercury from the pores of charcoal by an instantaneous action. 9. The action of porous bodies is not indiscriminate, but elective. Dr. R. Smith, in his " Theoretical Considerations," says, " The elective nature of porous bodies may be closely allied to three properties, — the condensability of the gases, the attraction and perhaps inclination to combine, and the capacity of combination. Chemical affinity is supposed to involve an attraction which is purely chemical. We have no proof of any such attraction as a separate power; we have only a proof of the combination. Attraction may exist without the power of combining chemically, or without, in other terms, chemical affinity, which is only known by combination. The previous attraction has never yet been shown to be of two kinds; and it seems more in accordance with nature to diminish than increase the number of original powers."

THE QUALITY OF WATER IN RELATION TO THE ARTS AND MEDICINE.

The quality of water in relation to the arts and to medicine has been very fully considered by M. E. Chevreul in his " Chemical Researches on Dyeing," the thirteenth and fourteenth memoirs of which have just been laid before the French Academy of Sciences. Although the employment of distilled water in dyeing has been found to possess many advantages over well-water and river-water, such as that of the Seine (e. g., the first with salts of copper giving an azure tint, which the other will not), yet it is found that, when woollen stuff is passed through steam, the sulphur that is contained in the wool will form with the salts of copper the reddest color that would have succeeded to the azure-tinted whiteness of the wool. In accordance with the results of many of the researches of the present day, M. Chevreul says that his experiments prove the grave inconveniences of the " absolute " in our judgments. In regard to medicinal waters, he considers that we have been indebted to empiricism for our knowledge of the diverse actions of sulphurous, ferruginous, and alkaline waters in the animal economy. He exemplifies the necessity of accurate analyses by pointing out the errors which have ensued in the preparation of artificial mineral waters. For instance, it has only lately been discovered that some mineral waters contain arsenic. How, then, can a water be prepared without fully comprehending the effect which this ingredient has upon the human system, one which almost certainly would be lost in the imitation. To determine the true action of medicinal waters, M. Chevreul requires that we should know — 1, The definite matters or chemical species contained in the water; 2, The influence of the climate in which the water is taken by the sick persons; 3, The change in their habits consequent upon their removal from home ; and, 4, The influence of their respective idiosyncrasies (their physical and mental peculiarities).

Water for Domestic Purposes. — At a late meeting of the London Chemical Society, Dr. Woods read a paper on the character of the water which should be used for drinking and domestic purposes. He insisted that organic matter in water was injurious to health, and it was as much the duty of a physician to prevent as to cure disease. He stated that his attention was pointedly directed to this subject by the case of two French ships that had been dispatched simultaneously with troops from Algiers to France, and under similar circumstances excepting the water with which they had been furnished. The water of one was obtained from a marshy place where the ague was prevalent ; that of the other from an elevated position where the ague did not prevail. Soon after sailing, the troops on board of the vessel supplied with water from the marsh spring were seized with remittent fever, while not a case occurred on board of the other vessel. Dr. A. Smee, who was present, stated as his opinion that as a rule all animal excreta in water should be considered poisonous to animals of the same class, and all organic matter of a decomposable character in water was highly prejudicial to health.

DEODORIZATION OF SEWAGE.

A late number of the London *Journal of Gas-Lighting and Sanitary Improvement* contains a report of Dr. Letheby, on the deodorization of sewage at Northampton, England, where there is an establishment for the purpose. About 100,000 gallons of drainings from the sewers are received at the works daily. Lime and the chloride of iron are used for defecation ; ten bushels of the former and sixty pounds of the latter are used for 100,000 gallons of sewage. The two substances are mixed with water in separate tanks, and the solutions flow over in graduated quantities, into a common discharge pipe, whence they pass into the sewage as it flows from the outfall of the town into the subsiding tanks. Here the solid matter precipitates, and the comparatively clear water runs away by an overflow at the opposite end of the tank, into the outfall-ditch. After working continuously in this manner for about a fortnight or three weeks, the solid matter, in a slushy condition, is drawn up from the bottom of the tanks, and run into prepared pits, where it is mixed with about its own bulk of ashes. This gives consistence to the material, and converts it into a solid compost, which is sold for manure. Respecting this mode of deodorizing the sewage, Dr. Letheby says, —

" The chloride of iron should be dissolved in water, and allowed to run by a graduated stream into the sewage before it reaches the lime. A contrivance should also be used for effecting a perfect mixture of the iron solution with the sewage. This having been accomplished, the sewage should then receive its dose of lime-liquor, and be again well agitated, so as to be thoroughly mixed. In this manner, a heavy, clotty precipitate will be produced, which will rapidly fall in the subsiding tanks, and leave the supernatant liquor clear, and perfectly inoffensive. The proportion of chloride of iron and lime should be about 4 or 5 grains of the former; and 14 or 15 of the latter to a gallon of sewage. The total for a day's working with 100,000 gallons of sewage would be about 64 pounds of the former, and about 200 pounds of the latter. The quantities should be so regulated that the supernatant liquor at the outfall should be clear, colorless, and but faintly alkaline. With this modification of the process, I am of opinion that the sewage works may be conducted and managed so as not to be at all offensive or injurious to those who reside in the neighborhood."

SUGAR AS FOOD.

Mr. Bridges Adams, the English physiologist, in a recent paper on the " Uses of sugar in assisting assimilation of food," says, " I know
18

by experience the difference in nutritious effect produced by the flesh of tired cattle on a march, and those slain in a condition arising from abundant food and healthy exercise. In a former case any amount might be eaten without the satisfaction of hunger, whilst in the latter a smaller amount removed hunger. But I discovered that certain other food of a different quality, such as grape-sugar and fruit, would help the tired meat to assimilate, and thus to remove hunger." Puddings and fruit-tarts are not, therefore, simply flatteries of the palate, but digestive agents; provided, always, they are not themselues made of rebelliously indigestible materials. The reviewer alludes to the fondness of artisans for confectionery, and of patients just discharged from the hospital asking for " sweets" in preference to " good substantial food," as examples of a correct instinct. There is no doubt that in children, in whom the requirements of growth call for a rapid and efficient transformation of food into tissue, the demand for sweets is very imperious; and parents should understand that the jampot will diminish the butcher's bill, and increase the amount of nutrition extracted from beef and mutton.

THE CHEMISTRY OF DIGESTION, BY DR. MARCET.

Until very recently, but little attention had been bestowed by chemists on those changes which go on under the influence of organic life, and, in consequence, many vague speculations had been entertained and published concerning this most interesting department of science : of late years, however, many able investigators had taken the subject in hand, and much progress had already been made. Many obstacles attended these inquiries, on account of the difficulty of observing the conditions of the immediate principles during life ; the term " immediate principles" being applied to those substances produced by organic life from which no less complex body could be obtained without a complete destruction of the substance in question. As an example of the power possessed by organic substances of preventing ordinary chemical reactions, the influence of albumen or the serum of blood on lactate of iron was shown. A mixture of this salt with white of egg gave no color with ferrocyanide of potassium, although the lactate itself furnished the ordinary blue precipitate. With respect more especially to the chemistry of digestion, it appeared that after a long fast the contents of the stomach were alkaline, and very small in quantity : as soon, however, as food was introduced, the gastric juice was secreted in quantity, and an acid reaction was perceptible. The object of the action of the gastric juice was, no doubt, to render the food capable of absorption ; and accordingly it was found that albuminous, gelatinous and other similar matters introduced into the stomach, became converted into a substance called " peptone," which, according to Lehmann, might be viewed as the same body, whatever nitrogenous food was employed ; it had been shown, however, that the peptones resulting from the digestion of cartilage and the mucous membranes rotated the plane of polarization of light, whereas peptones from albumen had not this power. The gastric juice, which was at first abundant, gradually diminished in quantity and became more acid, probably in order that it might act on the less masticated or less easily digestible portions of the food. Besides the conversion of the albuminous matter into peptone another important change took place in the stomach, namely, the decomposition of the neutral fats and setting free of the fatty acids; this was an important decomposition, for the bile would form an emulsion with a fatty acid, but not with a neutral fat; some of the fat sometimes escaped decomposition, but the pancreatic secretion formed an emulsion with this portion. The formation of an emulsion seemed to depend on the incrustation of each globule with a layer of soap, which prevented the globules from coalescing, and increased their specific gravity, so that they remained for a long time suspended in the liquid. Dr. Marcet considered that in experiments on digestion it was always better to employ gastric juice obtained directly from the stomach of an animal, instead of an artificial compound, such as was employed by some physiologists. There was some dispute as to the nature of the free acid existing in the gastric juice, — some supposed it consisted of hydrochloric acid, while others imagined that other free acids, especially lactic acids, were present; since quantitative determinations of the amount of hydrochloric acid and of the bases present in the gastric juice showed that there was more hydrochloric acid than was sufficient to combine with all the base, it was evident that there must be some free hydrochloric acid present; it was highly probable, however, that other acids were present in a free state; for on placing some gastric juice in a dialyzer and leaving it until all the hydrochloric acid had passed away, the remaining matter was found to be still acid. It had been supposed that the soda introduced in the shape of common salt with the hydrochloric acid of the gastric juice was employed in the formation of bile; but it appeared from the interesting researches of Dr. Bence Jones that this was not exactly the case, for healthy blood was always alkaline, but appeared to have an incessant tendency to become acid; the acid was, however, as rapidly removed by the secreting organs; and it had been found that when the secretion of gastric juice was active, the urine became less acid, and it gradually increased in acidity as the gastric secretion was moderated, so that the two actions balanced one another. It appeared that if no salt were supplied with the food eaten, the hydrochloric acid secreted was totally absorbed again with the food, furnishing an example of that wonderful power of adaptation to circumstances which enabled animal life to continue under varying external conditions. The only materials of the food that passed through the stomach and intestines undigested were such substances as hair, horns, etc.; together with these, however, a small quantity of excrementitious matter, obtained from the various secretions poured into the intestines, was always present, and a crystalline matter of definite chemical composition, and bearing some analogy to cholesterine, might be extracted from it.

LIEBIG'S THEORY OF FOOD.

After having for many years enjoyed an almost uncontested approval from physiologists and chemists — after having been the universal doctrine taught in class-rooms and text-books — and after having been put to the test by cattle-breeders — Liebig's theory of food is now becoming less and less accepted among real investigators; that is to say, among men who, loyal to fact, are able to resist the seduction of a facile formula which seems to explain the mystery, but really leaves it untouched.   The latest opponent we have to name is Mr. Savory, who recently presented a paper before the Royal Society, entitled, *Experiments on Food ; its Destination and Uses.*

Liebig's theory may be briefly stated thus : — Animals require food to build up the *fabric*, and keep up the *temperature* of their bodies. The plastic, or tissue-making food, is furnished by certain organic substances which contain nitrogen, and only by these ; it is therefore called, indifferently, either nitrogenous, or tissue-making food.   The heat-making food is furnished by certain organic substances destitute of nitrogen ; it is therefore called, indifferently, either non-nitrogenous or calorifacient food.   Albuminous substances, rich in nitrogen, form the animal fabric ; carbonaceous substances, — fats, oils, starch, sugars, alcohol, etc., are quite incapable of forming any part of the animal fabric, and are used as so much fuel, which is burned in the body to keep up the temperature.

The theory is thus here re-stated, simply with a view to enable our readers to better appreciate the experimental results arrived at by Mr. Savory.   He fed animals upon different diets, taking particular note of the weight, temperature, and general condition of the animals. In one class, they were fed on a non-nitrogenous diet, consisting of equal parts, by weight, of arrow-root, sago, tapioca, lard, and suet ; in this mixture there was only a slight fraction of nitrogen, (.22 per cent.) In another class, the diet was nitrogenous, with only a small amount of fat, (1.55 per cent.)   In the third class, the diet was mixed.   What were the results?   These :—

Nitrogenous materials are not only heat-making, but, under some circumstances, suffice alone to maintain the requisite temperature. [This is in perfect accordance with the results obtained by Bischoff and Voit.]

It is in the highest degree probable, that under certain circumstances, nitrogenous materials may prove directly heat-making, without previously forming tissue.   Although life cannot be maintained without nitrogenous food, no matter how abundantly the other kinds are supplied, life, and even health and the normal temperature, can be maintained upon a diet almost exclusively nitrogenous.

Finally, " in these experiments the significant fact appeared, that while the weight, strength, and general condition of the animals varied very widely under the different diets to which they were subjected, *no considerable fluctuation was observed in their temperature.*   Even the slight variation from time to time recorded, seemed rather to result from other causes, than to depend directly on the food."

It is unnecessary to point out the irreconcilable contradiction between Liebig's theory, and such facts.   We will only add in conclusion, that Liebig's theory was not founded on any precise investigations, but was simply a deduction from certain chemical premises, supported by random facts drawn from the reports of travellers, the observation of a few countries, and such-like sources.   The theory had so plausible an air that the illustrative facts seemed merely required to render it popularly intelligible, and not to serve as proofs.   But a rigorous scrutiny of the theory detects its initial mistake, a rigorous confrontation with facts exposes its want of solid basis.

GEOLOGY.

THE EARTH'S CLIMATE IN PALEOZOIC TIMES.

The following interesting suggestion relative to the climate that prevailed upon our earth during the paleozoic epoch, is communicated to the *American Journal of Science* by Prof. T. S. Hunt.

The late researches of Tyndall on the relation of gases and vapors to radiant heat are important in their bearing upon the temperature of the earth's surface in former geological periods. He has shown that heat, from whatever source, passes through hydrogen, oxygen and nitrogen gases, or through dry air, with nearly the same facility as through a vacuum. These gases are thus to radiant heat what rock-salt is among solids. Glass and some other solid substances, which are readily permeable to light and to solar heat, offer, as is well-known, great obstacles to the passage of radiant heat from non-luminous bodies; and Tyndall has recently shown that many colorless vapors and gases have a similar effect, intercepting the heat from such sources, by which they become warmed, and in their turn radiate heat. Thus while for a vacuum the absorption of heat from a body at 212° F. is represented by 0, and that for dry air is 1, the absorption by an atmosphere of carbonic acid gas equals 90, by marsh gas 403, by olefiant gas 970, and by ammonia 1195. The diffusion of olefiant gas of one-inch tension in a vacuum produces an absorption of 90, and the same amount of carbonic acid gas, an absorption of 5.6. The small quantities of ozone present in electrolytic oxygen were found to raise its absorptive power from 1 to 85, and even to 136; and the watery vapor present in the air at ordinary temperatures in like manner produces an absorption of heat represented by 70 or 80. Air saturated with moisture at the ordinary temperature absorbs more than five-hundredths of the heat radiated from a metallic vessel filled with boiling water, and Tyndall calculates that, of the heat radiated from the earth's surface warmed by the sun's rays, one-tenth is intercepted by the aqueous vapor within ten feet of the surface. Hence the powerful influence of moist air upon the climate of the globe. Like a covering of glass, it allows the sun's rays to reach the earth, but prevents to a great extent the loss by radiation of the heat thus communicated.

When, however, the supply of heat from the sun is interrupted during long nights, the radiation which goes on into space causes the precipitation of a great part of the watery vapor from the air, and the earth, thus deprived of this protecting shield, becomes more and more rapidly cooled. If now we could suppose the atmosphere to be mingled with some permanent gas, which should possess an absorptive power like that of the vapor of water, this cooling process would be in a great measure arrested, and an effect would be produced similar to

18*   209 that of a screen of glass ; which keeps up the temperature beneath it, directly, by preventing the escape of radiant heat, and indirectly by hindering the condensation of the aqueous vapor in the air confined beneath.

Now, we have only to bear in mind that there are the best of reasons for believing that, during the earlier geological periods, all of the carbon since deposited in the forms of limestone and of mineral coal existed in the atmosphere in the state of carbonic acid, and we see at once an agency which must have added greatly to produce the elevated temperature that prevailed at the earth's surface in former geological periods. Without doubt, the great extent of sea, and the absence or rarity of high mountains, contributed much to the mild climate of the Carboniferous age, for example, when a vegetation as luxuriant as that now found in the tropics flourished within the frigid zones ; but to these causes must be added the influence of the whole of the carbon which was afterwards condensed in the forms of coal and carbonate of lime, and which then existed in the condition of a transparent and permanent gas, mingled with the atmosphere, surrounding the earth, and protecting it like a dome of glass ; To this effect of carbonic acid it is possible that other gases may have contributed. The ozone, which is mingled with the oxygen set free from growing plants, and the marsh gas, which is now evolved from decomposing vegetation under conditions similar to those then presented by the coal-fields, may, by their great absorptive power, have very well aided to maintain at the earth's surface that high temperature the cause of which has been one of the enigmas of geology.

SECULAR COOLING OF THE EARTH.

Professor William Thomson, in a communication to the Royal Society of Edinburgh, says, " The fact that the temperature of the earth increases with the depth below the surface implies a continual loss of heat from the interior by conduction outwards, through, or into the upper crust. Since the upper crust does not become hotter from year to year, there must, therefore, be a secular loss of heat from the whole earth. It is possible that no cooling may result from this loss of heat, but only exhaustion of potential energy, which, in this case, could scarcely be other than chemical affinity between substances forming part of the earth's mass. But it is certain that either the earth is becoming, on the whole, cooler from age to age, or that the heat conducted out is generated in the interior by temporary dynamical action (such as chemical combination). To suppose, as Lyell has done, that the substances combining together, according to the chemical hypothesis of terrestrial heat, may be again separated electrolytically by thermo-electric currents, due to the heat generated by their combination, and thus the chemical action and its heat continued in an endless cycle, violates the first principles of natural philosophy, in exactly the same manner and to the same degree as to believe that a clock constructed with a self-winding movement may fulfil the expectations of its ingenious inventor by going forever.

"Adopting as the more probable, the simpler hypothesis that the earth merely a heated body cooling, and not, on the whole, influenced to sensible degree by interior chemical action, the author applies

Fourier's theory of the conduction of heat to trace the earth's thermal history backwards. From data regarding the specific heat and thermal conductivity of the earth's substance, he investigates the time that must elapse from an epoch of any given uniform high temperature throughout the interior, until the present condition of underground temperature could be reached. Taking into account the very uncertain character of the data when high temperatures are concerned, he infers that most probably either the whole earth must have been incandescent at some time from 50,000,000 to 500,000,000 years ago, or that at some less ancient date, but still anterior to the earliest human history, there must have been up to the surface a temperature above the boiling point of water. Either alternative — or indeed any theory whatever consistent with the principles of natural philosophy regarding previous conditions of the earth — is as decisive against the views of those naturalists who acknowledge no creation of life on the earth within fathomable periods of time, as the plainest elements of dynamics are against those who maintain that we have no evidence in nature of an end." — *Edinburgh New Philosophical Journal.*

THE FORMS OF STRATIFIED ROCKS.

The following is a report of a lecture, embodying some curious and original views, delivered before the Royal Institution, London, by Mr. J. Ruskin, the well-known writer on art. The purpose of the discourse was to trace some of the influences which have produced the present external forms of the stratified mountains of Savoy, and the probable extent and results of the future operation of such influences. The subject was arranged under three heads, — 1. The Materials of the Savoy Alps. 2. The Mode of their Formation. 3. The Mode of their subsequent Sculpture. 1. *Their Materials.* The investigation was limited to those Alps which consist, in whole or in part, either of Jura limestone, of Neocomian beds, or of the Hippurite limestone, and include no important masses of other formations. All these rocks are marine deposits; and the first question to be considered, with respect to the development of mountains out of them is the kind of change they must undergo in being dried. Whether prolonged through vast periods of time, or hastened by heat and pressure, the drying and solidification of such rocks involved their contraction, and usually, in consequence, their being traversed throughout by minute fissures. Under certain conditions of pressure, these fissures take the aspect of slaty cleavage; under others, they become irregular cracks, dividing all the substance of the stone. If these are not filled, the rock would become a mere heap of *debris*, and be incapable of establishing itself in any bold form. This is provided against by a metamorphic action, which either arranges the particles of the rock, throughout, in new and more crystalline conditions, or else causes some of them to separate from the rest, to traverse the body of the rock, and arrange themselves in its fissures; thus forming a cement, usually of finer and purer substance than the rest of the stone. In either case, the action tends continually to the purification and segregation of the elements of the stone. The energy of such action depends on accidental circumstances. First, on the attractions of the component elements among themselves; secondly, on every change of external temperature and relation. So that mountains are at different periods in different stages of health (so to call it) or disease. We have mountains of a languid temperament. mountains with checked circulations. mountains in nervous fevers, mountains in atrophy and decline. This change in the structure of existing rocks is traceable through continuous gradations, so that a black mud or calcareous slime is imperceptibly modified into a magnificently hard and crystalline substance, enclosing nests of beryl, topaz, and sapphire, and veined with gold. But it cannot be determined how far, or in what localities, these changes are yet arrested; in the plurality of instances, they are evidently yet in progress. It appears rational to suppose that as each rock approaches to its perfect type the change becomes slower; its perfection being continually neared, but never reached; its change being liable also to interruption or reversal by new geological phenomena. In the process of this change, rocks expand or contract: and, in portions, their multitudinous fissures give them a ductility or viscosity like that of glacier-ice on a larger scale. So that many formations are best to be conceived as glaciers, or frozen fields of crag, whose depth is to be measured in miles instead of fathoms; whose crevasses are filled with solvent flame, with vapor, with gelatinous flint, or with crystallizing elements of mingled natures; the whole mass changing its dimensions and flowing into new channels, though by gradations which cannot be measured, and in periods of time of which human life forms no appreciable unit.

2. *Formation.* Mountains are to be arranged, with respect to their structure, under two great classes, — those which are cut out of the beds of which they are composed, and those which are formed by the convolution or contortion of the beds themselves. The Savoy Mountains are chiefly of this latter class. When stratified formations are contorted, it is usually either by pressure from below, which raises one part of the formation above the rest; or by lateral pressure, which reduces the whole formation into a series of waves. The ascending pressure may be limited in its sphere of operation; the lateral one necessarily affects extensive tracts of country, and the eminences it produces vanish only by degrees, like the waves left in the wake of a ship. The Savoy Mountains have undergone both these kinds of violence in very complex modes and at different periods, so that it becomes almost impossible to trace separately and completely the operation of any given force at a given point. The speaker's intention was to have analyzed as far as possible, the action of the forming forces in one wave of simple elevation, the Mont Salève; and in another of lateral compression, the Mont Brezon; but the investigation of the Mont Salève had presented unexpected difficulty. Its facade had been always considered to be formed by vertical beds, raised into that position during the tertiary periods; the speaker's investigations had, on the contrary, led him to conclude that the appearance of vertical beds was owing to a peculiarly sharp and distinct cleavage, at right angles with the beds, but nearly parallel to their strike, elsewhere similarly manifested in the Jurassic series of Savoy, and showing itself on the fronts of most of the precipices formed of that rock. The attention of geologists was invited to the determination of this question. The compressed wave of the Brezon, more complex in arrangement, was more clearly defined. A section of it was given, showing the reversed position of the Hippurite

limestone in the summit and lower precipices. This limestone wave was shown to be one of a great series, running parallel with the Alps, and constituting an undulatory district, chiefly composed of chalk beds, separated from the higher limestone district of the Jura and lias by a long trench or moat, filled with members of the tertiary series —chiefly nummulite, limestones, and flysch. On the north side of this trench, the chalk beds were often vertical, or cast into repeated folds, of which the escarpments were mostly turned away from the Alps; but on the south side of the trench, the Jurassic, Triassic, and Carboniferous beds, though much distorted, showed a prevailing tendency to lean toward the Alps, and turn their escarpments to the central chain. Both these systems of mountains are intersected by transverse valleys, owing their origin, in the first instance, to a series of transverse curvilinear fractures, which affect the forms even of every minor ridge, and produce its principal ravines and boldest rocks, even where no distinctly excavated valleys exist. Thus, the Mont Vergi and the Aiguilles of Salouvre are only fragmentary remains of a range of horizontal beds, once continuous, but broken by this transverse system of curvilinear cleavage, and worn or weathered into separate summits. The means of this ultimate sculpture or weathering were lastly to be considered.

3. *Sculpture.* The final reductions of mountain form are owing either to disintegration, or to the action of water, in the condition of rain, rivers, or ice, aided by frost and other circumstances of temperature and atmosphere. All important existing forms are owing to disintegration, or the action of water. That of ice had been curiously overrated. As an instrument of sculpture, ice is much less powerful than water; the apparently energetic effects of it being merely the exponents of disintegration. A glacier did not produce its moraine, but sustained and exposed the fragments which fell on its surface, pulverizing these by keeping them in motion, but producing very unimportant effects on the rock below; the roundings and striation produced by ice were superficial; while a torrent penetrated into every angle and cranny, undermining and wearing continually, and carrying stones, at the lowest estimate, six hundred thousand times as fast as the glacier. Had the quantity of rain which has fallen on Mont Blanc in the form of snow (and descended in the ravines as ice), fallen as rain, and descended in torrents, the ravines would have been much deeper than they are now, and the glacier may so far be considered as exercising a protective influence. But its carriage is unlimited, and when masses of earth or rock are once loosened, the glacier carries them away, and exposes fresh surfaces. Generally, the work of water and ice is, in mountain surgery, like that of lancet and sponge, — one for incision, the other for ablution. No excavation by ice was possible on a large scale, any more than by a stream of honey; and its various actions, with their limitations, were only to be understood by keeping always clearly in view the great law of its motion as a viscous substance, determined by Prof. James Forbes. The existing forms of the Alps are, therefore, traceable chiefly to denudation as they rose from the sea, followed by more or less violent aqueous action, partly arrested during the glacial periods, while the produced diluvium was carried away into the valley of the Rhine or into the North Sea. One very important result of denudation had not yet been sufficiently re-

garded; namely, that when portions of a thick bed had been entirely removed, the weight of the remaining masses, pressing unequally on the inferior beds, would, when these were soft, press them up into arched conditions, like those of the floors of coal-mines in what the miners called " creeps." More complex forms of harder rock were wrought by the streams and rains into fantastic outlines : and the transverse gorges were cut deep where they had been first traced by fault or distortion. The analysis of this aqueous action would alone require a series of discourses ; but the sum of the facts was, that the best and most interesting portions of the mountains were just those which were finally left, the centres and joints as it were of the Alpine anatomy. Immeasurable periods of time would be required to wear these away ; and to all appearances, during the process of their destruction, others were rising to take their place, and forms of perhaps far more nobly-organized mountains would witness the collateral progress of humanity.

THE FORMS AND WASTE OF ALPINE PEAKS.

Mr. Whymper, a well-known Alpine explorer, in a letter to Prof. Tyndall, thus describes his observations respecting the causes which give form to, and at the same time tend to degrade, the prominent peaks of the Alps. He says, The manner in which the peak of the Matterhorn has been produced has given rise to much speculation amongst geologists and others, but hardly any theory which has been advanced can be regarded as satisfactory, while the simple agency of frost does not seem to have been taken into sufficient consideration. The enormous power brought into play by the action of frost, and its influence in forming the outlines of mountains, more particularly the Matterhorn, are subjects which recurred to me on this expedition on many occasions. It was, indeed, impossible not to think about them. Whence come these avalanches of rocks which fall continually, day and night ? They fall from two causes : the first, and least powerful, is the action of the sun, which detaches small stones or masses of rock which have been arrested on ledges, and bound together by snow or ice. Many times, when the sun has risen high, I have seen such released, fall gently at first, gather strength, and at last grow into a shower of stones. The second, and by far the most powerful, is the freezing of the water which has trickled during the day into the clefts and crannies of the rock. This agency is, of course, most active in the night, and then, or during very cold weather, the greatest falls take place. It is not too much to say that I have, on several occasions, seen *hundreds of tons* of rocks careering down one particular part of the Matterhorn well known to all those who have attempted to ascend the mountain. During seven nights which I have passed on it, at heights varying from 11,500 to nearly 13,000 feet, the rocks have fallen incessantly in showers and avalanches. The greatest fall I have heard or seen was at midnight in 1861. I was dozing in a blanket-bag, when from high aloft there came a tremendous report, followed by a second of perfect quiet. Then, mass after mass poured over the precipices, the great rocks in advance, and as they descended toward the place where we lay in safety, we could hear them smiting each other, bounding and rebounding from cliff to cliff, making a hurricane of sound, — the more impressive as the cause was invisible. It seemed to me, at the time, as if the entire face of a cliff had fallen outwards, producing the first great crash, and had afterwards rolled over as I have described. This action of the frost does not cease in winter, inasmuch as it is impossible for the Matterhorn to be entirely covered with snow. Less precipitous mountains may be entirely covered during winter, and if they do not then actually gain height, the wear and tear at least is suspended in their case. It is impossible that agencies so powerful as these can be continually at work without producing some visible alteration in the form of the mountain, and I was not surprised on the last attempt to find many places very much changed. The ledges, for instance, which are traversed below the Col are becoming difficult from breaking away, and in many other places I noticed great alterations. We arrive, therefore, at the conclusion that, although such snow peaks as Mont Blanc *may* in the course of ages grow higher, the Matterhorn must decrease in height. Whether the action of frost is sufficient to account *entirely* for the separation of the peak of the Matterhorn from the ranges of which it is part, may be doubtful; it is, however, a fact worthy of notice, that the southern *arêtes* of the mountain, those on which the combined action of the sun in melting and cold in freezing is most powerful, are crenellated in a most extraordinary manner, while the northern faces are comparatively smooth and unworn. Not only is it so in the case of the Matterhorn, but also in that of the Dent d'Erron, and many other rocky peaks among the first-class mountains of the Alps.

CONFORMATION OF THE ALPS.

Prof. Tyndall, in a paper in the *Philosophical Magazine*, No. 161, arrives at the following conclusions, after having, during the last seven summers, viewed the Alps from many commanding points: —

It is, then, perfectly certain that all this mountain region was held by ice, enormous as to mass, and in incessant motion. That such an agent was competent to plough out the Alpine valleys cannot, I think, be doubted; while the fact that during the ages which must have elapsed since its disappearance the ordinary denuding action of the atmosphere has been unable, in most cases, to obliterate even the superficial traces of the glaciers, suggests the incompetence of that action to produce the same effect. That the glaciers have been the real excavators, seems to me far more probable than the supposition that they merely filled valleys which had been previously formed by water denudation. Indeed, the choice lies between these two suppositions: shall we assume that the glaciers filled valleys which were previously formed by what would undoubtedly be a weaker agent? or shall we conclude that they have been the excavators which have furrowed the uplifted land with the valleys which now intersect it? I do not hesitate to accept the latter view; and this view will carry us still further. According to it the glacier is essentially self-destructive. The more deeply it ploughs the surface of the earth, the more must it retreat. Let the present Alpine valleys be filled to the level of the adjacent ridges, and vast glaciers would again start into existence; but every one of these valleys is a kind of furnace which sends draughts of hot air up to the heights, and thus effectually prevents the formation of ice. While standing on the summit of the Grauhaupt a week or two ago, I was perfectly astonished at the force with which these gusts of heated air rose vertically from the Val du Lys. Marked by the precipitated vapors which chanced to be afloat at the time, the vertical gusts were often as violent as the draught from a factory chimney. Thus, given the uplifted land, and we have a glacial epoch; let the ice work down the earth, every foot it sinks necessitates its own diminution; the glaciers shrink as the valleys deepen; and finally we have a state of things in which the ice has dwindled to limits which barely serve as a key to the stupendous operations of a bygone geologic age. To account for a glacial epoch, then, we need not resort to the hard hypothesis of a change in the amount of solar emission, or of a change in the temperature of space traversed by our system. Elevations of the land, which would naturally accompany the gradual cooling of the earth, are quite competent to account for such an epoch; and the ice itself, in the absence of any other agency, would be competent to destroy the conditions which gave it birth.

STRUCTURAL ORIGIN OF ROCKS.

It has long been known that pressure has an important effect on the solubility of salts. Mr. Sorby, the well-known English geologist and microscopist, has recently found, that by filling the tubes with which he experiments, at a very low temperature, and placing them afterwards in proper situations, he is enabled to keep the solutions which they contain, under a pressure of from 2,000 to 3,000 pounds to the square inch, for weeks or months continuously, and to watch the results. The pressure is measured and indicated by a capillary tube enclosed within the principal one. The researches of Mr. Hopkins and Prof. W. Thomson have made us acquainted with the effects of pressure on fusion and freezing, and there appears to be an intimate connection between them and the experiments here under notice. Mr. Sorby has proved that if a salt *contract* in dissolving it is *more* soluble under pressure, and that if it *expand* it is *less* soluble. The law, as might be anticipated, varies with the nature of the salt. For common salt it may be stated thus: the extra quantity dissolved varies directly and simply as the pressure. On comparing sulphate of copper with ferricyanide of potassium under the same pressure, it is found that one quantity dissolved of the former is ten times that of the latter; and there is a still greater variation of the mechanical equivalents. Reasoning upon the interesting facts brought out by this investigation, Mr. Sorby concludes that the experiments "indicate that in some cases pressure causes a slower and in others a quicker chemical action. And I think it probable," he continues, "that further research will show that pressure weakens or strengthens chemical affinity according as it acts in opposition to or in favor of the change in volume, as though chemical action were directly convertible into mechanical force, or mechanical force into chemical action, in definite equivalents, according to well-defined general laws, without its being necessary that they should be connected by means of heat or electricity." Apply these principles, and it seems easy to explain peculiarities in the structure of metamorphic rocks, to account for slaty cleavage, for some of the phenomena of crystallization, that is, the direction in which the crystals are formed, and for the impressions made by one limestone-pebble in another, as seen in the "Nagelflue," — the latter a much-debated question amongst the geologists of Switzerland, Germany, and France.— *Proc. Royal Society.*

GLACIAL MUMMIES.

In the year 1844, a man of the commune of Passy, situated between Chamounix and Sallenches, went on a pilgrimage of devotion to the celebrated hospice of St. Bernard. He accomplished his journey, paid his devotions at the perilous shrine, and returned by the mountain road to Martigny, where he purchased at the fair then holding there a large roll of cloth, which he intended to smuggle into Savoy, then belonging to Sardinia, while Martigny was, as now, in the canton of Valais, in Switzerland. But the pilgrim of St. Bernard never reached his home in Passy. His wife mourned his absence, the villagers wondered for a few days, and gradually, as years glided along, he was comparatively forgotten, and his memory began to be lost in obscurity.

During the last week of August, 1863, however, a hunter crossing the *glacier de Buet*, while leaping a crevasse, had his attention attracted by a dark object below, and peering down into the chasm, he saw, beneath a transparent sheet of pale blue ice, a human form laid as in an icy sarcophagus! The features were ruddy and natural, though in horrid contrast to this were the eyeless sockets, whence the eyes had fallen away. The astonished hunter hastened to inform the village authorities of Chamounix of his discovery; and on extricating the body it was readily recognized as that of the long-lost merchant of Passy, and more certainly identified by the roll of cloth bought nineteen years before at the Martigny fair, and which was lying near the glacier-preserved corpse. It was evident that the smuggling mountaineer, in trying to avoid the frontier authorities and regain his home by circuitous Alpine passes, had fallen into some crevasse, and the slow motion of the great glacier had gradually brought the lifeless, frozen body down the slope of Mt. Blanc, to the point where it was discovered.

In the *Annual of Scientific Discovery* for 1862, page 306, an account was given of the discovery of a portion of the body of one of the three guides who perished in 1820, while attempting the ascent of Mt. Blanc with Dr. Hammel, a Russian scientist. This body in 1861, after an entombment of forty years in the ice, was, by the movement of the *glacier des Boissons*, thrown out near its base, in a state of remarkable preservation, though mutilated. During the past summer, additional remains of one of these guides have been ejected by the moving glacier, namely, a foot covered with flesh and adhering by the nerves to a dried up thigh-bone. By the side of the foot was found a compass, probably that of the doctor, and carried by the guide Auguste Tairraz, as stated by the surviving guides, which fact leaves but little doubt of the identity of the limb now found. Strange to say, it was the grandson of Tairraz who discovered it. A shirt-sleeve of one of the victims was found in a crevasse, but the arm which it once protected, being a thicker and larger substance, will, it is predicted, not be recovered for two or three years yet. All the remains above referred to were buried at Chamounix, with appropriate religious services. In this connection, the following account, published by Dr. Hammel in 1820, of

19

the disaster, which resulted in the death of his guides, while attempting the ascent of Mt. Blanc, will be read with interest. He says:—

"When near the Rochers Rouges, my companion H—— and three of the guides passed me, so that I was now the sixth in the line and the centre man. H—— was next before me, and as it was the first time we had been so circumstanced during the whole morning, he remarked it, and said we ought to have one guide at least between us in case of accident. This I overruled by referring him to the absence of all appearance of danger at that part of our march, to which he assented. I did not then attempt to recover my place in front, though the wish more than once crossed my mind, finding, perhaps, that my present one was less laborious. To this apparently trivial circumstance I owe my life. A few minutes after the above conversation, my veil being still up, and my eyes at intervals turned toward the summit of the mountain, which was on the right, as we were crossing obliquely the long slope above described, which was to conduct us to the Mont Maudit, the snow suddenly gave way beneath our feet, beginning at the head of the line, and carried us all down the slope to our left. I was instantly thrown off my feet, but was still on my knees and endeavoring to regain my footing, when, in a few seconds, the snow on our right, which was, of course, above us, rushed into the gap thus suddenly made, and completed the catastrophe by burying us all at once in its mass, and hurrying us downward toward two crevasses about a furlong below us, and nearly parallel to the line of our march. The accumulation of snow instantly threw me backwards, and I was carried down, in spite of all my struggles. In less than a minute I emerged, partly from my own exertions, and partly because the velocity of the falling mass had subsided from its own friction. I was obliged to resign my pole in the struggle, feeling it forced out of my hand. A short time afterwards I found it on the very brink of the crevasse. This had hitherto escaped my notice, from its being so far below us, and it was not until some time after the snow had settled that I perceived it. At the moment of my emerging, I was so far from being alive to the danger of our situation, that on seeing my two companions at some distance below me, up to the waist in snow, and sitting motionless and silent, a jest was rising to my lips, till a second glance showed me that, with the exception of Mathieu Balmat, they were the only remnants of the party visible. Two more, however, being those in the interval between myself and the rear of the party, having quickly reappeared, I was still inclined to treat the affair rather as a perplexing though ludicrous delay, in having sent us down so many hundred feet lower, rather than in the light of a serious accident, when Mathieu Balmat cried out that some of the party were lost, and pointed to the crevasse, which had hitherto escaped our notice, into which he said they had fallen. A nearer view convinced us all of the sad truth. The three front guides, Pierre Carrier, Pierre Balmat and August Tairraz, being where the slope was somewhat steeper, had been carried down with greater rapidity, and to a greater distance, and had thus been hurried into the crevasse, with an immense mass of snow on them, which rose nearly to the brink. Mathieu Balmat, who was fourth in the line, being a man of great muscular strength as well as presence of mind, had suddenly thrust his pole into the firm snow beneath, which certainly checked the force of his fall. The two guides, Julien Devassoux and Joseph Marie Coutet, soon appeared. It was long before we could convince ourselves that the others were past hope, and we exhausted ourselves fruitlessly for some time in fathoming the loose snow with our poles. We ventured in the crevasse, on the snow which had fallen therein. Happily it did not give way beneath our weight. Here we continued above a quarter of an hour to make every exertion for the recovery of our poor comrades. After thrusting the poles in to their full length, we knelt down and applied our mouths to the end, shouting along them, and then listening for an answer, in the fond hope that they might be still alive, sheltered by some projection of the icy walls of the crevasse; but, alas! all was silent as the grave."

This calamity, of course, resulted in the abandonment of Dr. Hammel's enterprise, and served for a time as a check to other attempts to reach the summit of Mont Blanc.

DISCOVERY OF GIGANTIC ANIMALS IN SIBERIAN ICE.

An effort has recently been set on foot, by the Imperial Academy of St. Petersburg, for promoting the further discovery of the congealed remains of gigantic mammalia in Siberia. Since the discovery, in 1771, of the rhinoceros imbedded in ice at Wiljui (lat. 64°), of which hardly any portion was preserved; and that of the mammoth at the mouth of the Lena, in 1806, of which the preservation of such remains as still exist was owing to the purely accidental circumstance of the failure of a Russian embassy to China, one of whose members, happening to be on the spot, succeeded in obtaining and preserving those precious relics, but with little or no information as to the circumstances of the locality, and with the loss of by far the larger portion of the carcass — a third of a century elapsed, when another of these gigantic mummies, thus wonderfully preserved, came to light. Three years, however, were allowed to elapse before any effective steps were taken to obtain possession of what then remained, which by that time was reduced to an undistinguishable mass. What could be collected was indeed despatched to St. Petersburg, but without so much as any precise information as to the place of the discovery, or any circumstances beyond the fact of the discovery having been made. Since that time, nothing has been done in the way of further research. It cannot, however, be doubted that many other such relics must exist, similarly preserved, and susceptible of detection by active and systematic research. During the last two centuries, it is computed that, at the very least, 20,000 mammoths, and probably twice or thrice that number, have been washed out of the ice and soil in which they have been imbedded by the action of the spring floods, and among them the occurrence of perfect skeletons is far from infrequent. The tusks only, however, have been made an object of conservation, from their commercial value as ivory.

THE GLACIERS OF THE HIMALAYAS.

An interesting communication on the glaciers of the Himalayas has recently been made to the Asiatic Society of Bengal, by Capt. Montgomery, chief of the staff of the Trigonometrical Survey of India, now in the course of prosecution by the British Government.

In one part of his communication, he tells us of "a continuous river of ice, running sixty-four miles in an almost straight line, and without any break in its continuity beyond those of the ordinary crevasses of glaciers. The Biafo glacier is supplied in a great measure from a vast dome of ice and snow about 180 square miles in area, in the whole of which only a few projecting points of wall are visible. Further west, the Holi Valley produces a fine glacier sixteen miles in length. The Báshá Valley contains the Kero glacier, eleven miles in length, besides many branches and minor glaciers. The Braldo and Báshá, in fact, contain such a galaxy of glaciers as can be shown in no other part of the globe, except it be within the Arctic Circle. Captain Montgomery pointed out that the Baltoro, with its main glacier thirty-six miles in length, and its fourteen large tributary glaciers of from three to ten miles in length, would form a study in itself, and give employment for several summers before it could be properly examined. It takes its rise from underneath a peak 28,287 feet high. The crevasses in the ice of these glaciers were of great breadth, and of the most formidable description. An attempt was made to measure the thickness of the ice by sounding one of these yawning chasms, but a line of 100 feet in length failed to reach the bottom of it. Observation made at the end of the glaciers gave a thickness of 300 or 400 feet, but doubtless higher up a still greater thickness of ice will be found.

REMARKABLE DEPOSIT OF ROCK SALT IN LOUISIANA.

One of the facts of scientific interest brought to light during the pending civil war is the discovery of an important deposit of rock salt, of remarkable purity, on the island of *Petite Anse*, in Vermillion Bay, on the Gulf coast of Louisiana. The island is a body of very productive land in every part, of undulating surface, growing rich crops of sugar-cane, corn, forest trees, shrubbery, etc., and rises to a height of about 170 feet, in the midst of a wide-spreading sea swamp, and is about two and a half miles long from north to south, and about one and a half miles wide. The soil of the island is an umber-colored argillaceous loam, capable of forming good bricks. The salt deposit is found near the southwesterly border of the island, under dry forest ground, which ground is only about fifteen feet above the level of the tide-water in the bayou. The salt quarry consists of a whitish or cream-colored solid smooth rock, underlying the earth, within a space, so far as yet ascertained, of about forty-five acres, and on an average of nineteen and a half feet below the surface of the earth, and about four and a half feet below the surface of the bayou or tide-water.

There is no water or brine moisture within the salt deposit. The rock is hard, compact, and perfectly dry. The only moisture attending it is contained in the earthy soil above the rock.

The salt was discovered as follows: salt-springs were recognized on the island as far back as 1791, and from time to time subsequently. Salt was manufactured from their water by evaporation. In May, 1862, the proprietor endeavored to improve one of the springs, and if possible to find a better supply of brine by digging much lower into the earth; and when only about thirteen feet below the surface, the pickaxe man at the bottom struck upon, as he thought, a cake of ice, but this, upon being examined, proved to be nearly pure rock salt.

A writer in the New Orleans *Era*, describes the appearance of the mine as follows : " As we neared the saline bed, we could see through the scattered trees and bushes white heaps of the quarried rock salt, stacked up in piles ten to fifteen feet high, and short distances apart ; giving evidence of the wells or shafts excavated within the earth below, and adjacent to these several piles of quarried blocks of salt.

" The wells or shafts for the blasting and excavating this rock deposit are about twelve in number, of different sizes, and located within a radius of about four hundred feet. They consist of a square or oblong excavation down from the surface into the earth — a depth on the average of about nineteen and a half feet below the surface — to the hard, smooth, rock salt deposit below. From all of these pits there has been excavated more or less salt, down into the rock to a depth of from ten to thirty-five feet below its surface. The salt is so compact as to require a drill and powder blast for its excavation ; the quantity appears to be inexhaustible. An analysis of the *Petite Anse* salt by Dr. Riddell, of New Orleans, gives the following composition : — Chloride of sodium, 98.88 ; sulphate of lime, 0.76 ; chloride of magnesium, 0.23 ; chloride of calcium, 0.13, = 100. From this analysis, the salt would appear to be the purest natural salt yet discovered.

THE GOLDEN PARALLELS.

From a summary of interesting facts respecting the two great gold fields of the world, — Australia and California, — given in a recent number of the *Edinburgh Review* we derive the following. The gold fields of New South Wales and Victoria extend without any interruption along the slopes of the great mountain range which separates the eastern seaboard of Australia from the interior of the continent, and the gold fields of California and British Columbia occur without interruption along the western slopes of the Rocky Mountains. Thus there are presented two great gold-bearing regions, extending along two widely distant elevations, and probably " owing their auriferous character to some influence connected with the upheaval." The possibility of establishing a connection between these two gold-bearing regions will be understood after a little consideration of their characteristics. The American gold fields, under various names, run along the eastern seaboard of the Pacific, almost from pole to pole — from Behring's Straits in the north to Cape Horn in the south. Throughout this vast region, large quantities of the precious metal are found. " From Chili, in the south, to the British Possessions, in the north, its slopes, spurs, and subordinate ranges are now yielding gold. From Chili we mount through Bolivia, Peru, Ecuador, New Granada, all still continuing to yield the precious metal, after some three centuries of gold mining. Thence, after we pass the Isthmus, we find the gold miner at work through Mexico, California, Oregon, Washington, until at length we come to the British Possessions, stretching to the shores of the Arctic Ocean." Such is a brief description of the gold-bearing system of America. Turning now to that of Australia, there is found a coast-range running from the extreme northern point of the continent to the extreme southern point. But this range neither begins nor terminates in Australia. It extends across Bass' Straits, on the one hand, and beyond Cape York on the other ; in which direction the chain of

19*

rocks forms at intervals numerous islands, such as New Guinea, the Carolines, the Ladrones, and others, until Japan, with its gold-bearing rocks, is reached. Thus, in accordance with this theory, the basin of the Pacific has on each side a continuous elevation of volcanic origin. At intervals, on both sides, gold is now found, from Behring's Straits to New Zealand; and it is stated that at the "beach diggings" in California, a bluish sand, not unlike the pipe clay of Ballarat, is frequently thrown up by the waves, and is found to contain gold in considerable quantities.

The conclusion arrived at by this reasoning is, that the great gold fields of the world, as at present known, are included in the vast system of volcanic rocks which surround the Pacific. This chain, though broken here and there, is said to be traceable between Australia and America, and to be easy of identification on both sides of the ocean. Such a continuous and well-marked line of volcanic elevation has often received the attention of geologists. Humboldt's view, which is the one generally accepted on the subject, is that the bed of the Pacific attained its present depth at a comparatively late period; that its unbroken crust, forced down on the molten mass underneath, caused a quantity of it to rush toward the line of fracture at the edges, and that this disturbed matter found vent in the elevations which are now connected with the gold fields of America and Australia. So far, these considerations, as bearing on the science of geology, are highly important; but it has to be shown in what way gold is to be connected with volcanic shocks in some places, and not in others. On this point it is laid down by Sir Roderick Murchison, that the rocks which are the most auriferous are of the Silurian age, and that a certain geological zone only in the crust of the globe is auriferous at all. Gold, he states, has never been found in any stratified formations composed of secondary or tertiary deposits, but only in crystalline and paleozoic rocks, or in the drift from those rocks. The most usual original position of the metal is in quartzose vein-stones that traverse altered Silurian slates, frequently near their junction with eruptive rocks. Sometimes, however, it is partially diffused through the body of rocks of igneous origin. From this it appears that volcanic eruptions, in connection with Silurian rocks, are to be regarded as the origin of gold formations.

INTERESTING OBSERVATIONS ON EARTHQUAKES.

It is well known to the scientific world that the subject of earthquake phenomena has for some years been made a specialty of investigation by Mr. Robert Mallet, of England, and that several valuable reports by this gentleman have been published by the British Association and Royal Society, — including a descriptive catalogue of seven thousand earthquakes. When the intelligence of the great Neapolitan earthquake of December, 1857, reached England, Mr. Mallet was despatched, under the auspices of the Royal Society, to examine the district affected, with a view of reporting on the phenomena in question. This report has recently been laid before the public, and from it we derive the following information : —

The great Neapolitan earthquake of 1857 occurred in December, thus adding another proof to the remarkable fact that earthquakes are more prevalent and violent in winter than during summer. Taking the whole of Europe, the preponderance of earthquakes during winter is very marked ; the earthquake catalogue to which we have alluded shows that during fifteen centuries and a half 857 earthquakes occurred during spring and summer, and 1157 during autumn and winter. And with respect to Italy it is recorded that generally but little alarm has been felt in summer when signs portended coming earthquakes, whereas those in winter have always inspired the greatest terror.

Mr. Mallet arrived on the scene of the catastrophe in February, 1858, and although the weather was very inclement, he worked on steadily until he had examined the entire area. This was about 200 miles long by 160 miles broad, and embraced the peninsula of Calabria Ultra, south of a line from Cape Suvero to Cape Colonna. The seismic force greatly varied throughout the region.

The general direction of the earth-waves, southeast of Naples, appears to have been from north to south, crossed, however, not unfrequently, by other waves from east to west. In both cases the waves recoiled, producing the terrible *replica*, or return shock, which whelms every object within its influence in immediate ruin. Saponara, a town of eight thousand inhabitants, was absolutely reduced to ruins in a few minutes, its destruction being so absolute that it is not at all probable that it will ever be rebuilt. Beneath its ruins hundreds of human beings and animals lie entombed, with fragments of every household utensil, personal and domestic ornaments, and innumerable records of human art ; yet such is the vitalizing property of the Italian climate that in a few years verdure and luxurious vegetation will mantle the heaps where once stood a city, and after but a few generations the terrible fate of its inhabitants, nay, its very site, will have become a tradition as dim as that of the neighboring Grumentum.

Although the earthquake was not felt sensibly at Rome, the disturbance evinced by several delicate instruments in the observatory of that city led the director of that establishment to conclude that a faint earthquake wave passed beneath that city. Mr. Mallet traced it distinctly north of Naples, until the effects of it became lost in the alluvium near Terracina.

Having next ascertained the locality of the greatest seismic force, he proceeded to investigate its depth from the earth's surface. This he found to be about five geographical miles, and he believes that the greatest probable depth of origin of any earthquake impulse occurring in our planet is limited to 30.64 geographical miles, and therefore only just touches the depth which, upon received notions as to the movement of hypogeal temperature, is supposed to form the upper surface of the imaginary ocean of liquid lava of the earth's interior. Mr. Mallet, we observe, doubts the existence of a general increment of temperature as we descend from the surface of the earth. His speculations on volcanic heat in connection with this subject are very interesting : —

" When on Vesuvius, on the occasion of this report, I feel satisfied that I could have so measured the temperature of the minor mouth, then in powerful action, to the depth of several hundred feet, had I possessed the instrumental means at hand. To this smaller mouth it was then possible, by wrapping the face in a wet cloth, to approach so near upon the hard and sharply-defined (though thin and dangerous) crust of lava, through which it had broken, as to see its walls for quite 150 feet down by estimation. They were glowing hot to the very lips, although constantly evolving a torrent of rushing steam with varying velocity. Accustomed as I have been, by profession, for years to judge of temperatures in large furnaces by the eye, I estimated the temperature of this mouth, by the appearance of its heated walls, at the lowest visible depths; they were there of a pretty bright red, visible in bright winter sunlight overhead. I have no doubt, then, that the temperature of the shaft at from 300 to 500 feet down was sufficient to melt copper, or from 1900° to 2000° of Fahrenheit. From the extremely bad conducting power of the walls of a volcanic shaft, there is scarcely any loss of heat from any cause except its enormous absorption in the latent heat of the prodigious volume of dry steam which is constantly being evolved. It is perfectly transparent for several yards above the orifice of the shaft, and is not only perfectly dry steam, but also superheated; and although this steam may be at the mouth very much below the highest temperature of the hottest point, the temperature of the shaft or duct that carries it off will be very nearly at all depths the same, to probably within a very short distance of the point of the greatest incandescence. In the absence, at present, of better information, we may suppose the temperature of volcanic cavities in this region (where Vesuvius is the most 'glaring instance') to be about 2000° Fah. This would give a superior limit of temperature for the interior of our seismic focal cavity, two and one-fifth times as great as the maximum arrived at, by applying the supposed law of hypogeal increment, and would raise the tension of the contained steam (admitting that we know anything about the state of water at such temperatures and pressures) to much more than that due to fired gunpowder. The capability of producing an earthquake impulse depends greatly, however, upon the suddenness with which the steam is flashed off, and its tension brought to bear upon the walls of the cavity; and this is not most rapid at the highest temperature of the evaporating surface, unless, indeed, intense pressure, by bringing the fluid more completely into contact with the walls of the heated cavity, may modify the effects of the spheroidal state. On the other hand, the experiments of Boutigny and others indicate that the most sudden production possible of steam would take place from the walls of a focal cavity heated to about 500° or 550°, which is but a few degrees below that of the mean focal depth as ascertained, namely, 582° Fah."

The rate at which earthquake-waves travel has always been a subject of great interest and doubt. Mr. Mallet's investigations have, however, so far decided the question, that we may safely assume the following data to be correct. The extreme velocities of the Neapolitan earthquake-waves he found to be 1000 feet per second through substances highly adapted to transmit the waves without much opposition, and 700 feet per second through bad transmitting materials. It is essential to remark, that these velocities represent the transit of the wave upon the surface. The velocity of the wave at its maximum, or that of the wave of *shock*, is considerably less. Mr. Mallet found it to average twelve feet per second, which also agrees with the Holyhead experiments. Indeed, calculating from the data published by Humboldt of the celebrated Riobamba earthquake, probably the most violent of which we have authentic records, — when the bodies of many of the inhabitants were thrown upon a hillside several hundred feet at the other side of the river, — the greatest velocity of the shock on that occasion did not exceed eighty feet per second. This Mr. Mallet considers to be the maximum force at present possible upon our earth; it is nearly as great as that with which the body of a man falling from the top of the Duke of York's Column would strike the pavement.

The latter portion of Mr. Mallet's work is occupied by discussing the curious and mysterious phenomenon attaching to earthquakes, called their secular motion. Humboldt pointed out long ago that the mighty seismic force which periodically desolates vast districts in South America is continually changing position; and it is equally certain that the centre of seismic intensity is not constant in the Italian peninsula. Since the last century it has continued to move steadily northward of Calabria, and in Sicily it is moving westward : —

"These facts distinctly point toward some great conclusions. They indicate that the same forces, whatever they may be, that develop themselves as volcanic vents and as earthquakes, are operative everywhere along the lines of the seismic bands, — that is to say, along the axial lines of nearly all the great mountain-ranges upon our globe, — but that the intensity of these forces is greater by much at some points along these axial lines than at others; that the intensity remains constant nowhere, but shows itself paramount at certain points for immense periods of historic time; that it wanes and again waxes powerful at the same point (Vesuvius in volcanoes, Antioch in earthquakes, for example, both long in repose, again long in intense action); and that the points of greatest intensity at any given time have been found to shift along the axial lines, now most active here, then further on, but slowly moving, and in the same direction (or expanding in both directions, as Humboldt says of the New Madrid band), in the same cycle of time. Can we possibly, with these facts before us, rest in the commonly-received vague notion that volcanic and seismic action have their common origin in an all-pervading and perfectly uniformly-distributed planetary temperature, increasing everywhere alike by a uniform hypogeal increment? Can we remain satisfied with the pompous but almost empty phrase, although sanctioned by a Humboldt, that 'they are due to the reaction of the interior of our planet upon its exterior,' if the only meaning that we are to attach to the phrase is that the reaction is that of a universal ocean of heated or of molten matter, everywhere to be reached within some certain limit of depth? Do not the facts rather all point toward some cause that has been long present, and is so now, and still in action wherever mountain-ranges have been elevated, as well as wherever volcanic vents are thrown or are throwing up their lines of cones, but whose nature must be such as is called locally and spasmodically into action, now most energetically at one point, now at another of the same line, but yet is never exhausted at any? The discovery of the real nature of this cause will be the key to all true knowledge, both of volcanic action, which is only its symptom, and of all the forces that have produced and do produce the elevations, or, to speak more correctly, the changes of level of the surface of our own and that of other planets. Earthquakes, then, demand to be regarded not as themselves agents of permanent elevation of the land, which they cannot be at all, and with respect to which even the great-est volcanic efforts (accumulated cones) upon our globe are mere skin-deep phenomena. We must regard seismic and volcanic phenomena as both unequal effects and local evidences of a wide-spread and con-stantly but unequally acting yet always active force, resulting in ele-vation, whi·h is not evidenced indifferently all over the surface of the globe, but is mainly confined to broad bands conforming to its moun-tain-ranges."

We observe that Mr. Mallet dissents entirely from the doctrine that earthquakes are agents of permanent elevation of the earth's surface. All his investigations and researches point, he maintains, to a totally opposite conclusion. Earthquake waves may, he observes, and un-doubtedly do elevate the ground, but only for a moment ; for when the shock is over, the surface returns to its normal condition. His investi-gations, however, indorse the doctrine that seismic force generally fol-lows the lines of elevation of the globe, such as mountain chains and ridges, while, on the other hand, the areas of the smallest or of no known seismic disturbance are the great oceanic or terra-oceanic basins or saucers, and the great islands existing in shallow seas. Earthquake energy may, however, become sensible at any point of the earth's sur-face, its efforts being always more frequent as the great volcanic lines of activity are approached.

NEW SUBMARINE VOLCANO IN THE MEDITERRANEAN.

During the month of July, 1863, a submarine volcanic eruption ac-companied by the formation of a new island, took place off the coast of Sicily in the Mediterranean, near the island of Pantillaria, and about twenty-five miles from the shore. There is a report that a volcano ex-isted here in the year 1701, and on an old chart there is a reef laid down precisely on the spot where the volcano now is. It was first seen by smoke rising from the sea, about the 12th of July. This grad-ually increased in volume for several days, till fire was seen, and even-tually a *small island* was thrown up above the surface, about eighty or ninety yards long and twenty or thirty feet high, composed of cin-ders. In the centre of this is a crater, which at the time when the ac-count from whence we derive our information was written (July 30th), was in a constant state of eruption, ejecting great volumes of steam and smoke, as well as cinders and large stones. It is noticeable that the appearance of this volcano was nearly coincident with the occur-rence of an earthquake in the island of Lamos.

A correspondent of the *London Times*, writing from Malta, thus describes the appearance of the volcano as seen on the 19th of August, 1863. He says, " when first seen, the volcano appeared like a low black line, higher at each end than in the middle, with a column of white smoke rising from the southeast end of it. Running our vessel within a mile and a half, we landed in boats. The beach, which ap-peared to be a mixture of ashes and sand reduced to powder, was as hard as the firmest sand ; but very few yards from the water side the surface was extremely rough, composed of loose cinders of all sizes heaped lightly together, and very hot to the touch. The summit of the island we estimated to be about 200 feet above the sea-level. The crater was at a less elevation, about thirty or forty yards in diameter, with water in it standing some twenty feet befow the highest edge. This water was much discolored and boiling strongly, throwing up quantities of white steam, with sulphurous vapor which much annoyed us. There was apparently an underground rush of boiling water from the southeast side into the sea, which might be traced a long way by its dark color, as well as by the white vapors emitted. Nothing can be more singular than the appearance of this mass of ashes in the middle of the sea. You may form some idea of the force of the fire that must have been required to form it by considering that it is, as near as could be guessed, three quarters of a mile round, and that, where it now stands, former charts give soundings in one hundred and thirty fathoms, and from the soundings lately made it seems to stand on a large base."

CURIOSITIES OF COAL MINING.

From the last volume of the *Transactions of the North of England Institute of Mining Engineers* we derive the following interesting information relative to what may properly be termed the "curiosities of coal-mining."

"What is called Murton Pit, not far from Durham, is remarkable for the difficulties overcome in sinking to the coal. In the process of excavation, the sinkers encountered probably the largest body of water ever met with in any one mining adventure. The estimated quantities seem incredible. No less than nine thousand three hundred gallons of water were lifted every minute from a bed of quicksand which lay at a depth of five hundred and forty feet from the surface. This bed was forty feet in thickness, and for its whole extent thoroughly saturated with water. Any person may conceive of the difficulty of sinking through such a quicksand. To encounter and defeat not far short of ten thousand gallons of flooding springs, minute after minute and day after day, might well have appalled any engineer. But the engineer fought the floods with their own weapons: he made use of the vapor generated from water — steam — and added horse-power to horse-power, until, in all, he placed steam engines around that one pit to the extent of no less than one thousand five hundred and eighty-four horse-power. Night and day those pumping-engines were at work in pumping up the floods; cranks, 'crabs' and all kinds of requisite engineering were added, and the water was obliged to give in, or, rather, to come out. Murton Colliery is now a thriving concern, and sends up tubs of coal instead of gallons of water every minute to the surface. But at what cost was this water pumped out? At an expenditure of no less than $2,000,000.

"It is remarkable that in another sinking for coal, about a couple of miles from the same locality, the same enemy was again encountered, and in a continuation of the same bed of quicksand. The colliery-viewer, however, conducted his campaign so adroitly that he was able to insulate each separate 'feeder' of water as it was met with in each stratum of sand and limestone; so that, while an aggregate amount of upwards of five thousand gallons of water per minute was met with in passing through the various beds, so cleverly was the whole passage accomplished that at no time were there more than five hundred gallons in one minute to pump away. This, indeed, was a quantity sufficient to frighten some ; but in comparison with the nine thousand and odd gallons at Murton it was nothing.

"There are pits where, long after coal has been for many years extracted from them, the waters break in and flood the mine. In these instances, again, great enterprise is manifested. In the case of the 'drowned' colliery at Jarrow, an attempt was made a few years ago to draw off the water and to resume ordinary operations. But the sum of one hundred and ten thousand dollars was spent fruitlessly in this attempt, and it was ultimately abandoned without drawing up a single ton of coal.

" Whence all this subterranean water comes is an interesting question, but scarcely capable of receiving a satisfactory reply. Its amount must be immense to afford nearly ten thousand gallons per minute at one sinking, and probably it is the accumulation of numberless centuries of surface-waters which have percolated through the porous strata. It is always threatening, and never materially diminished, as respects its vast aggregate, by any efforts of man ; on the contrary, it is always gaining on man and filling up his excavations. No less than thirty-six collieries near the river Tyne have been, in mining phrase, ' drowned out,' or rendered unworkable by an irresistible irruption of water, after the best main Wallsend seam had been nearly exhausted. These stand in the coal district like closed factories in the cotton towns, with this difference, that the cotton factories may be reopened and busily at work again, while the drowned collieries are probably drowned for all future time."

Exhaustion of the British Coal Mines. — The subject of the possible exhaustion of the British coal mines formed a leading topic of consideration in the address of the President of the British Association for 1863, Sir W. Armstrong. "If we contemplate," he says, " the rate at which we are expending those seams of coal which yield the best quality of fuel, and can be worked at least expense, we shall find much cause for anxiety. We have already drawn from our choicest mines a far larger quantity of coal than has been raised in all other parts of the world put together, and the time is not remote when we shall have to encounter the disadvantages of increased cost of working and diminished value of produce. The estimates which have been made at various periods as to the time requisite to produce complete exhaustion of all the accessible coal in the British Islands, are extremely discordant: but the discrepancies arise, not from any important disagreement as to the available quantity of coal, but from the enormous differences in the rate of consumption, at the various dates when the calculations were made, and from different estimates of the probable increase of consumption in the future. The annual product of the British coal mines has almost trebled within the last twenty years, and has probably increased tenfold since the commencement of the present century ; but as this increase has taken place pending the introduction of steam navigation and railway transit, and under exceptional conditions of manufacturing development, it would be too much to assume that it continue to advance with equal rapidity. The statistics collected Hunt, of the Mining Records Office, show that at the end of e quantity of coal raised in the United Kingdom had reached rmous total of 86 millions of tons, and that the average annual increase of the eight preceding years amounted to two and three-fourths millions of tons. Let us inquire, then, what will be the duration of our coal-fields if this more moderate rate of increase be maintained.

" By combining the known thickness of the various workable seams of coal, and computing the area of the surface under which they lie, it is easy to arrive at an estimate of the total quantity comprised in our coal-bearing strata. Assuming 4,000 feet as the greatest depth at which it will ever be possible to carry on mining operations, and rejecting all seams of less than two feet in thickness, the entire quantity of available coal existing in these islands has been calculated to amount to about 80,000 millions of tons, which, at the present rate of consumption, would be exhausted in 930 years, but, with a continued yearly increase of two and three-fourths millions of tons, would only last 212 years. It is clear that long before complete exhaustion takes place, England will have ceased' to be a coal-producing country on an extensive scale. Other nations, and especially the United States of America, which possess coal-fields thirty-seven times more extensive than ours,•will then be working more accessible beds at a smaller cost, and will be able to displace the English coal from every market. The question is, not how long our coal will endure before absolute exhaustion is effected, but how long will those particular coal-seams last which yield coal of a quality and at a price to enable this country to maintain her present supremacy in manufacturing industry. So far as this particular district is concerned, it is generally admitted that 200 years will be sufficient to exhaust the principal seams even at the present rate of working. If the production should continue to increase, as it is now doing, the duration of those seams will not reach half that period. How the case may stand in other coal-mining districts I have not the means of ascertaining ; but as the best and most accessible coal will always be worked in preference to any other, I fear the same rapid exhaustion of our most valuable seams is everywhere taking place. Were we reaping the full advantage of all the coal we burnt, no objection could be made to the largeness of the quantity, but we are using it wastefully and extravagantly in all its applications. It is probable that fully one-fourth of the entire quantity of coal raised from our mines is used in the production of heat for motive power ; but much as we are in the habit of admiring the powers of the steam-engine, our present knowledge of the mechanical energy of heat shows that we realize in that engine only a small part of the thermic effect of the fuel. That a pound of coal should, in our best engines, produce an effect equal to raising a weight of a million pounds a foot high is a result which bears the character of the marvellous, and seems to defy all further improvement. Yet the investigations of recent years have demonstrated the fact that the mechanical energy resident in a pound of coal, and liberated by its combustion, is capable of raising to the same height ten times that weight. But although the power of our most economical steam-engines has reached, or perhaps somewhat exceeded, the limit of a million pounds raised a foot high per pound of coal, yet, if we take the average effect obtained from steam-engines of the various constructions now in use, we shall not be justified in assuming it at more than one-third of that amount. It follows, therefore,

20

that the average quantity of coal which we expend in realizing a given effect by means of the steam-engines is about thirty times greater than would be requisite with an absolutely perfect heat-engine.

" The causes which render the application of heat so uneconomic in the steam-engine have been brought to light by the discovery of the dynamical theory of heat ; and it now remains for mechanicians, guided by the light they have thus received, to devise improved practical methods of converting the heat of combustion into available power.

" I have hitherto spoken of coal only as a source of mechanical power, but it is also extensively used for the kindred purpose of relaxing those cohesive forces which resist our efforts to give new forms and conditions to solid substances. In these applications, which are generally of a metallurgical nature, the same wasteful expenditure of fuel is everywhere observable. In an ordinary furnace employed to fuse or soften any solid substance, it is the excess of the heat of combustion over that of the body heated which alone is rendered available for the purpose intended. The rest of the heat, which in many instances constitutes by far the greater proportion of the whole, is allowed to escape uselessly into the chimney. The combustion also in common furnaces is so imperfect that clouds of powdered carbon, in the form of smoke, envelope our manufacturing towns, and gases which ought to be completely oxygenized in the fire pass into the air with two-thirds of their heating power undeveloped."

" Some remedy for this state of things, we may hope, is at hand, in the gas regenerative furnaces recently introduced by Mr. Siemens. In these furnaces the rejected heat is arrested by a so-called " regenerator," as in Stirling's air-engine, and is communicated to the new fuel before it enters the furnace. The fuel, however, is not solid coal, but gas previously evolved from coal. A stream of this gas, raised to a high temperature by the rejected heat of combustion, is admitted into the furnace, and there meets a stream of atmospheric air also raised to a high temperature by the same agency. In the combination which then ensues, the heat evolved by the combustion is superadded to the heat previously acquired by the gases. Thus, in addition to the advantage of economy, a greater intensity of heat is attained than by the combustion of unheated fuel. In fact, as the heat evolved in the furnace, or so much of it as is not communicated to the bodies exposed to its action, continually returns to augment the effect of the new fuel, there appears to be no limit to the temperature attainable, except the powers of resistance in the materials of which the furnace is composed.

" With regard to smoke, which is at once a waste and a nuisance, I can state with perfect confidence that, so far as the raising of steam is concerned, the production of smoke is unnecessary and inexcusable. The experiments to which I refer proved beyond a doubt, that, by an easy method of firing, combined with a due admission of air and a proper arrangement of firegrate, not involving any complexity, the emission of smoke might be perfectly avoided, and that the prevention of the smoke increased the economic value of the fuel and the evaporative power of the boiler. As a rule, there is more smoke evolved from the fires of steam-engines than from any others, and it is in these fires that it may be most easily prevented. But in the furnaces used for most manufacturing operations the prevention of smoke is much more difficult, and will probably not be effected until a radical change is made in the system of applying fuel for such operations."

DEEP SEA PRESSURE.

Some interesting experiments have recently been tried in England, in reference to the effect of deep sea pressure, and especially with a view of experimentally ascertaining the effect of pressure upon a submarine cable submerged to a depth of $2\frac{1}{4}$ miles. The experiments were made in a large hydraulic press capable of resisting a pressure of above 10,000 lbs. on the square inch. The specimen of cable used is known as the Persian gulf standard, having a coating of gutta-percha $\frac{3}{8}$ of an inch in diameter. It was subjected to a pressure equal to two miles and one-quarter of a mile deep, and the pressure kept on for one hour. An opinion had been expressed by some experts that this enormous pressure — about 5,000 lbs. on the square inch — would force the water into the copper core, and by this means deteriorate the cable, if not quite destroy it, but this theory was not sustained; on the contrary, the condition of the cable, when the pressure was removed, was, so far as electric conductivity was concerned, decidedly improved, and materially had sustained no damage.

The occasion of testing the cable was taken advantage of by several gentlemen present, to test the truth of stories current among sailors to this effect; 1st, that when a bottle of wine securely corked, is sunk to great depths in the ocean, and then raised to the surface, the wine is replaced by salt-water; and 2d, that if you take an empty bottle, securely corked, and sink it to a great depth, it will come up filled with salt-water, while the cork remains undisturbed.

In order to test the first of these theories, bottles of ale, lemonade, and ginger beer were securely corked, wired down, and the corks covered with capsules, and then submerged. To test the second theory, one empty bottle was securely corked and wired down; one was corked after the manner of a champagne bottle, with a large knob left on the upper part of the cork, to prevent its being driven in; while a third bottle had a cylinder of wood put inside, resting on the bottom, and reaching the cork, to give another form of resistance to the cork. The pressure was the same as before, and the time under pressure the same, namely, one hour.

The results were as follows : — The ale, lemonade and beer came out sound and unimpaired; the small space, however, left by the bottler between the cork and the liquor was filled up. With this exception all was the same. The first empty bottle the cork was driven in, and as a matter of course the bottle came up filled with water. The second bottle with the large knob was also driven in, and the bottle came up full. The third, that had the wooden cylinder inside, on which the cork rested, was driven in to a certain extent, but not entirely, and this bottle came up also full, showing that at great depths, no corking, however secure, will prevent the water from getting into an empty bottle, but that when you send the bottle down filled and well corked, there is no danger of the liquor's making its escape and being replaced by salt-water.

Another interesting experiment was tried to test the accuracy of Dr. Wallich's statements as regards living creatures at great depths in the ocean.   Some live fish, lobsters, eels, etc., were enclosed in a cylinder, and subjected to the same pressure as above, and for the same time, i. e., one hour.   At the expiration of this time the pressure was removed, when the fish, etc., were found to have all perished; thus indicating that Dr. Wallich's statement needs additional confirmation.

NEW FACTS RESPECTING THE ANTIQUITY OF MAN;—DISCOVERY OF HUMAN REMAINS IN THE DRIFT.

At the commencement of the year ·1863, notwithstanding the discovery of some thousands of flint implements, knives, arrow-heads, etc., in the drift-sand, and gravel of the north of France, and in similar deposits in England, no fragment of a human skeleton, not even a tooth, had been detected in connection with these ancient evidences of man's existence.   At the same time, in these same formations, and in close contiguity with the worked flints, the bones of mammalia belonging to living and extinct species, occur in considerable abundance.   On the 28th of March, 1863, M. Boucher de Perthes, the French geologist, who has so greatly distinguished himself during the last few years by his investigations into the antiquity of man (see *Annual Sci. Dis.*, 1861, p. 331, and 1863, p. 276), discovered and extracted from a bed of gravel, four and a half metres below the surface at Moulin-Quignon, (a suburb of the town of Abbeville), France, the half of a human jawbone, containing a molar tooth.   The bed of gravel from which this jaw was extracted contains the osseous remains of the mammoth and the (extinct) rhinoceros; and at a short distance from the spot where the jaw was found, a flint hatchet was also at the same time disinterred. Attention having been immediately drawn to this discovery, numbers of scientific men visited Abbeville, among whom were M. Quatrefages, of Paris, and Drs. Carpenter and Falconer, of London; and these gentlemen, after examining the locality in question, concluded that it was an undisturbed deposit, and that the fragmentary jaw was undoubtedly fossil.   On the 15th of April, M. Perthes discovered in the sand of the same bank, 3½ metres below the surface, (or one metre above the line of deposit from whence the jaw was excavated), the fragments of the tooth of a mammoth.

A number of English geologists and paleontologists having, however, in communications to the London *Times* and otherwise, expressed doubts on the authenticity of the alleged human fossil, a sort of international congress was proposed to discuss the whole matter; and such a meeting convened in Paris on the 10th of May, 1863.   The English deputies consisted of Mr. Prestwich, Dr. Falconer, Dr. Carpenter, and Mr. Busk.   The French members were M. Milne Edwards, the eminent zoologist, who acted as president of the meeting, M. de Quatrefages, M. Lartet, M. Delesse, and M. Desnoyers.   Numerous other scientists were also present at the conference.   Three days were occupied in discussing the question of the flint *hatchets* and in the examination of the jaw, the latter of which was taken up on the third day. No decisive result was arrived at.   The English members of the Commission maintained the unauthentic character of all the flint *hatchets* which were yielded by the diluvial bank at Abbeville, and nothing was established on the other side to shake their convictions.   The jaw was sawn up and washed; a black coating, derived from oxides of iron and manganese associated with the sand and gravel which surrounded the jaw, was removed from it with the utmost facility; there was no infiltration of metallic matter through the walls of the bone, and the section was comparatively fresh-looking. The tooth was in every respect remarkably fresh-looking also. The confidence of some of the French members of the Commission was seriously shaken by the characters yielded by the jaw, which, so far as internal evidence went, was wanting in every appearance which commonly distinguishes fossil bones, and especially those found elsewhere in the deposits near Abbeville. Had the conference been closed at Paris, it is not improbable that the result might have been the Scotch verdict of Not proven, but, at the suggestion of the President, the Commission adjourned to Abbeville on the 12th, when the complexion of the case was at once altered.

Here, after taking great care to prevent any deception, they made new excavations, and, at the depth of four metres, in a bed apparently identical with that from which the jaw had been extracted, found many hatchets of flint every way similar to those previously examined, whose authenticity had been doubted by the English savants. Direct testimony as to the actual finding and occurrence of the jaw in the gravel-bed was also brought forward; so that the Commission unanimously agreed as to the following facts: — 1st, that the worked flints in the form of hatchets excavated from the gravel were authentic; 2d, that the jaw was found where it was represented to have been, and that it had not been introduced into the quarry surreptitiously. The majority of the Commission also agreed that the age of the jaw, of the flints, and of the gravel deposit, enclosing them, was substantially the same. Dr. Falconer and Mr. Busk, however, dissented from this, and gave in writing an opinion to this effect, " that the finding of the jaw was authentic, but that the characters which it presents, i. e., the internal condition of the bone, etc., are irreconcilable with an antiquity equal to that assigned to the deposits at which it was found. From all this, it will be seen that the question of the relative antiquity of the relic is left open to discussion. It is manifest that the evidence was very conflicting; that it is in some respects of an incompatible character; and that a great deal still remains to be cleared up before the scientific world can arrive at a definite judgment on the case. The subject having subsequently come up before the French Academy, M. de Beaumont, the distinguished and veteran French geologist gave it as his opinion, that the gravel deposit of Moulin-Quignon did not belong to the Quaternary or Diluvian age at all, but that it was a member of the *terrains meubles* of the *actual* or *modern* period, in which he would not be in the least surprised if human bones were found; adding, moreover, that he did not believe in the asserted existence of man as a contemporary of the extinct elephants, rhinoceroses, etc. of the Quaternary period! M. Milne Edwards, however, at the same time, expressed his opinion most decidedly, that the jaw from Abbeville was contemporary with the fossil bones obtained from the same locality.

THE ANTIQUITY OF MAN.

The following is an extract of a paper read before the British Association at its last meeting, on the above subject, by Mr. J. Crawford,

20*

the well-known British ethnologist. He commences by saying, "that it is my conviction that the evidence which has of late years been adduced, giving to the presence of man on the earth an antiquity far beyond the usual estimate of it, is already satisfactorily established. There can, I think, now be no question that man was a contemporary of animals, such as lions, hyænas, elephants, and rhinoceroses, extinct far beyond the reach of human record. But among the evidences brought forward to prove the antiquity of man, the paucity of relics of his own person, compared with the abundance of those the unquestionable work of his hands, has attracted especial notice. Thus, in the valley of the Somme and other places, where flint implements have been found in abundance in the same drift with the bones of the extinct elephant and rhinoceros, not a single bone of a human skeleton has yet been discovered. The scarcity of human remains, compared with those of the lower animals, may, I think, be to some extent accounted for. In the savage state, man is ever few in number compared with the wild animals; and when he first appeared on earth, — when naked, unarmed, without language, and even before he had acquired the art of kindling a fire, — the disparity must have been still greater. In that condition, he would have to contend for life and food with ferocious beasts of prey, with nothing to depend upon but a superior brain and the capacity of wielding a club. In such circumstances, the wonder is, not that he should be few in number, but that he should have been able to maintain existence at all. Sir C. Lyell adopts the theory of the unity of the human race, but neither Mr. Lyell nor any one else has ventured to point out the primordial stock from which the many varieties which exist proceeded. The Ethiopian represented on Egyptian paintings four thousand years old is exactly the Ethiopian of the present day. The skeleton of an Egyptian mummy of the same date does not differ from that of a modern Copt. A Persian colony settled in Western India one thousand years ago, and which have rigorously refrained from intermixture with the black inhabitants, are not now to be distinguished from the descendants of their common progenitors in the parent country. For three centuries, Africans and Europeans have been planted in almost every climate of the New World and its islands; and, as long as the races have been preserved pure and unmixed, there is no appreciable difference between them and the descendants of their common forefathers. In the same manner, the human skeletons found in the pile buildings of the Swiss lakes, and computed by some to be twelve thousand years old, differ in no respect from those of the present inhabitants of Switzerland. If the existing races of man proceeded from a single stock, either the great changes which have taken place must have been effected in the locality of each race, or occurred after migration. Now, distant migration was impossible, in the earliest period of man's existence. Man must have acquired a considerable measure of civilization, — that is, he must have domesticated some animals for food and transport, have cultivated some kind of corn, and have provided himself with arms of offence and defence, — to enable him to undertake even long land journeys, while the physical geography of the world forbids the possibility of distant sea voyages, which would imply the possession of strong boats or ships, with some skill in navigation, and therefore a still greater advance in civilization. With the exception of a few inconsiderable islands, every region has, within the historical period, been found peopled, and usually with a race peculiar to itself. The peopling of these countries by migration must have taken place in very rude times; and in such times nothing short of a great miracle could have brought it about. It is only within the last three centuries and a half that the existence of half the inhabitants of the world became known to the other half. But for one race of men more highly endowed than the rest, the different races of mankind would now have been unknown to each other. It is this superior race which still keeps them in mutual acquaintance, or at least in intercommunication. I conclude, then, that there is no shadow of evidence for the unity of the human race, and none for its having undergone any appreciable change of form. If one thousand years, or four thousand, or one hundred thousand, — supposing this last to be the age of the skeletons of the Belgian race contemporary with the mammoth, — have effected no appreciable change, it is reasonable to believe that multiplying any of these sums by a million of years would yield nothing but the same cipher.

Mr. Lyell has adopted the Aryan theory of language, and fancies he finds in it an illustration of the hypothesis of the transmutation of species by natural selection. The Aryan or Indo-European theory, which had its origin and its chief supporters in Germany, is briefly as follows: In the most elevated table-land of Central Asia there existed, in times far beyond the reach of history or tradition, a country, to which, on very slender grounds, the name of Aryana has been given, the people and their language taking their name from the country, The nation, a nomadic one, for some unknown cause betook itself to distant migrations, — one section of it proceeding in a southeastern direction across the snows and glaciers of the Himalayas, to people Hindústan, and another in a northwesterly direction, to people Western Asia and Europe, as far as Spain and Britain. "Before that time," says Prof. Max Müller, the most recent expounder of the theory, "the soil of Europe had not been trodden by either Celts, Germans, Sclavonians, Romans, or Greeks," — an assertion which can be interpreted to signify only that Europe at least was, before the supposed migration, uninhabited. According to the theory, the human skeletons found in the caverns near Liége must have belonged to the nomadic wanderers from Central Asia or their descendants; and so the era of the imaginary migration carries us back to a time when man was a contemporary of the extinct mammoth, the cave-lion, and rhinoceros.

The entire fabric is founded on the detection of words, in a mutilated form, common to most, but not to all, of the languages of Western Asia and Europe, a discovery, no doubt sufficiently remarkable, but clearly pointing only to an antiquity in the history of man far beyond the reach of history or tradition. A language which the theorists have been pleased to call the Aryan is the presumed source of the many languages referred to. But the Aryan is but a language of the imagination, of the existence of which no proof ever has been, or ever can be adduced. The object of the theory would seem to be to prove that the many languages called the Aryan, or Indo-European, sprang all of them from a single source. The doctrine is extended to all the other languages of the earth, with the hope of reducing ther

from thousands to a very small number.   The Aryan theory proceeds
on the principle that all languages are to be traced to a certain residuum called " Roots."   Some languages either are so, or are made to be so
by grammarians.   The copious Sanskrit is said to be traceable to some
1,900 roots, all monosyllables.   The languages to which I have myself
given special attention are certainly not traceable to any such roots.
In their simplest form, a few of the words of these languages are monosyllables, but the great majority are dissyllabic or trissyllabic, without
any recondite sense whatever.   But were the Aryan, or Indo-European, hypothesis as true as I believe it to be baseless, I cannot see
how it illustrates, or, indeed, can have any possible bearing at all on
the theory of the transmutation of species by natural selection, the
progress of which is so slow — if, indeed, there be any progress at all,
— that no satisfactory evidence of it has yet been produced.   The
changes in language, on the contrary, are due to forces in unceasing
and active operation, and the evidences are patent and abundant.
They consist of social progress, and of the intermixture of languages
through conquest, commercial intercourse, and religious conversions.
Sir Charles Lyell attaches more value than I can do to the fact, that
philologists have not agreed as to what constitutes a language and
what a dialect.   Following the philosophers of Germany, his object
would seem to be to reduce all languages to a small number of primordial ones, in the same manner as the authors of the theory of the
transmutation of species would reduce all species to a few monads.   If
there were any truth in the Aryan theory, which is here again advocated, it would of necessity follow that there would be no language at
all in Western Asia or Europe, ancient or modern, and that Sanskrit,
Greek, Latin, with all the modern languages, would be reduced to the
rank of mere dialects or subdivisions of one primordial tongue, — the
airy, fabulous Aryan, the mere creature of Teutonic imagination.   I
cannot give my belief to so monstrous a fiction, or see how it can be a
parallel to the transmutation of species by natural selection.   Changes
in language are the exclusive work of man ; those in species by natural selection, if they have any existence at all, the spontaneous work
of nature, unaided by man, and in operation long before he was created.   I come now to offer a few remarks on the work of Prof. Huxley.   The professor compares man with the apes, placing them anatomically and physiologically in the same category ; and here I must
premise that the views which I have to offer are more of a popular
than scientific character.   To begin with the brain : even if there were
no material structural difference between the brain of man and that
of the most man-like ape, what would be the practical value of
the resemblance, when the working of the two brains is of a nature so
utterly different, — less an affair of degree than of absolute quality?
The brains of the dog and elephant bear no resemblance to the brain
of man or ape, or even to those of each other ; yet the dog and elephant are equal, if not, indeed, superior in sagacity, to the most man-
like ape.   The brain of the wolf is anatomically the same with that
of the dog ; but what a vast difference in the working of the two
brains !   The common hog is an animal of great intelligence, and
wants only a pair of hands like the ape's to enable him to make a display of it equal if not superior to that of the most anthropoid monkey.

Sheep and goats have brains not distinguishable; yet the goat is a very clever animal, and the sheep a very stupid one. In the dentition of man and the apes there is certainly a singular accord. The digestive organs also agree. Yet with this similarity, man is an omnivorous, and the monkey a frugivorous animal, seemingly resorting to worms and insects only from necessity. The teeth of the monkeys are more powerful, proportionally, than those of man, to enable them to crush the hard-rinded fruits on which they mainly subsist, as well as to serve as weapons of defence, for they have no other. Prof. Huxley has very satisfactorily shown that the designation of "quadrumane," or four-handed, is incorrectly applied to the family of monkeys. Their feet are real feet, although prehensile ones; but the upper limbs are true hands, and it is in the possession of these, far more than in a similarity of brain, that the ape approaches the nearest to man. Notwithstanding his seemingly dexterous hands, the monkey can neither fashion nor use an implement or weapon. It is his brain, anatomically so like that of a man, but psychologically so unlike, that hinders him from performing this seemingly simple achievement. All the different races of man intermix to the production of fertile offspring. No intercourse at all takes place between the different species of monkeys. Man, of one variety or another, exists and multiplies in every climate. The monkeys are chiefly found within the tropics, and seldom above a few degrees beyond them. The natural abode of man is the level earth; that of the monkeys, the forest. Man came into the world naked and houseless, and had to provide himself with clothing and dwelling by the exercise of superior brain and hands. The monkeys are furnished by nature with a clothing like the rest of the lower animals, and their dwellings are not superior to those of the wild boar. Man has the faculty of storing knowledge for his own use and that of all future generations; in this respect, every generation of monkeys resembles that which has preceded it, and so, no doubt, has it been from the first creation of the family. The special prerogative of man is language, and no race of men, however meanly endowed, has ever been found that had not the capacity of framing one. In this matter, the monkey is hardly on a level with the parrot or the magpie. But is it true that the anthropoid apes come nearest to man in intelligence? They ought to do so, if they be the nearest grade to man in the progress of transmutation by natural selection. Prof. Huxley has fully and faithfully described four of these anthropoids; and it appears to me that, among them, those which anatomically approach the nearest to man are the least like to him in intelligence. At the top of the list is the gorilla; and all we know about him is, that he is ferocious and untamable. The orang-utan, or mias, seems to me to be the nearest in form to man; but he is described as a slow, sluggish, dull, and melancholy animal. The other two species, the gibbon and chimpanzee, seem to me incomparably more lively, playful, and intelligent than the more anthropoid. If, adopting the theory of the transmutation of species by natural selection, we believe the gorilla to be the next step to man in the progress of change, it must be taken for granted that the transmutation must have proceeded from the lower to the higher monkeys. Exclusive of the lemurs, there are some two hundred distinct species. Which species is at the bottom of the long scale implied by this num-

ber? and has any naturalist ever ventured to describe the long gradation from it till we reach the gorilla? How are the tailed and tailless
monkeys to be classed? and how are we to place the monkeys of the
New World, with their four supernumerary teeth? In America there
is no anthropoid monkey at all; every one has a long tail, often a prehensile one. Between man and the apes, then, in so far, at least, as
America is concerned, one great link is absent. The monkeys, then,
have an outward and even a structural resemblance to man beyond
all other animals, and that is all; but why Nature has bestowed upon
them this similarity is a mystery beyond our understanding.

THE EXTINCTION OF RACES.

The following is an abstract of a paper on the above subject, read to
the British Association, 1863, by Mr. R. Lee : The author said that
the rapid disappearance of aboriginal tribes before the advance of
civilization, was one of the many remarkable incidents of the age. In
every new country, from America to New Zealand, this seemed to be
the result of an approximation of different races, peculiar, however, in
degree at least, to this portion of the world's history. Such circumstances have not always been the result even of enduring oppression,
still less of civilization. Two millions of the Coptic race still testify
to the inability of the ancient Eastern powers to destroy all remnants
of the people they subdued. Egypt numbers a vast crowd of the lineal
descendants of the men who fell before the Persian tyrant 2,000 years
ago; and to come nearer home, the Celts, Britons, and Gauls have a
large host of worthy representatives upon their own soil. The author
then referred to the disappearance of the aboriginal inhabitants in
Tasmania and New Zealand. In 1815, the aborigines of Van Diemen's
Land were estimated at 5,000. Five years later, this number was
reduced to 340; of whom 160 were females. In 1831, when they
were invited to place themselves under the protection of the local
authorities, there were but 196. In 1847, the party were removed
from Flinders Island — the station which had been assigned to them
— to an old convict station on the shores of D'Entrecasteaux's Channel, and there were then only forty-seven. In 1855, there were only
sixteen. A similar process of extinction was now taking place in New
Zealand. From these facts it was evident that there were causes in
operation to produce an extinction of race which at present could not
be clearly defined. The average mortality among them was greater
than among more civilized nations, and there was also an inequality of
the sexes. Out of several tribes the proportion of males to females
under fourteen was as 5.974 to 4.860; and above fourteen, as 16.443
to 11.989. The introduction among aboriginal races of some European
diseases and of injurious habits, intemperance and the like, as well as
an increasing mortality owing to the antagonism between the white
and native races, were among the artificial causes of this extinction ;
but none of these causes would account for the paradox that exists in
respect to the inequality of the sexes, the unusual diminution of females, and the increase to such an enormous extent of unproductive
marriages. For an explanation of all this, we must look deeper, and
is more than a question whether at the present time anything like a
factory explanation can be offered. As an almost abstract ques-

tion for discussion, it might be suggested whether the disappearance of the aboriginal tribes might be taken as a type of what might happen at a future period of the world's history, when the present population shall have given place to an order of beings superior to the now dominant race of mankind. Europe was now the centre from which this flood of civilized life was overspreading the globe, and our own Anglo-Saxon race contributed one of the chief elements of that civilization. It might be the lot of nations now springing into existence at the antipodes to outstrip her in the pursuit of knowledge, and, when ages shall have passed away, to supply a nobler race and a more perfect humanity to the lands which now rank foremost in civilization. To speculate upon this, however, was of little value. Viewed as a bare fact, and taking it in connection with what we knew of the previous history of man, there was nothing in the extinction of races to justify us in regarding it as a type of anything to follow at some future period. The man who now wanders free through the unknown wilds of Australia had not only not advanced in moral development since the formation of his species, but he had actually retrograded. We must, therefore, regard this extinction of races rather as an illustration of humanity in its crudest form shrinking and passing away before a race endowed with superior intelligence.

FOSSIL EAR-BONES OF FISHES.

The fossil ear-bones, or as they are technically termed *otoliths*, of fishes, have generally escaped the notice of fossil collectors; but attention has been recently called to them by Mr. W. W. Stoddard in a communication to the *Intellectual Observer*, (England.) He states that although these remarkable little fossils are not described in any work on geology hitherto published, they are to be obtained in great numbers from some strata. Since 1859, when Mr. Stoddard's notice was first drawn to the subject, he has successfully determined the fossil otoliths of the cod, whiting, whiting-pout, power-cod, pollack, flying fish, and also of many of the Pleuronectidæ. They have been principally found in the Crag of Suffolk, the Eocene beds of Sussex, Hampshire, and Isle of Wight.

In order to ascertain the species of fish to which the several ear-bones belong, it is necessary to dissect an immense number of heads; for a most striking fact has been demonstrated, and one without analogy in natural history, namely, *that a characteristic form is more peculiar to the species than the genus or family.* That is to say, the ear-bones of a species have invariably a configuration peculiar to itself. But no form has yet been observed that will point out a genus, family, or tribe; for example, the same general form is equally found in the ear-bones of the Clupeidæ and Scrombidæ, but still there is no difficulty in determining, with the greatest confidence, the specific name of a mackerel or a herring by the markings on their ear-bones, because they are always constant, and never the same in two species.

With all these interesting relations, and the frequency of their occurrence, it is very remarkable that the fossil otoliths have not been noticed before. Mr. Stoddard states, however. his collection even now contains more than forty species of fossil otoliths, all distinct, and many of fish hitherto unknown in the fossil state.

Otoliths occur in the tertiary beds much more abundantly than any other parts of fishes, and much more so than the teeth. This fact at first sight may appear startling to the collector from the palæozoic rocks, when the commonest remains are the teeth, spinous defences, and scales. But a little reflection will easily solve the apparent riddle. In the Silurian, carboniferous, etc., seas, the principal inhabitants were cartilaginous fishes, and the hardest and most indestructible portions of their bodies were the teeth and spines; whereas in the later tertiary beds the osseous fishes predominated, which do not possess the fin-spines or solid crushing teeth. Of them the hardest parts are the ear-bones in question.

The appearance of the otoliths is very different in appearance from the bones of the fish; they have a porcellaneous appearance, and quite distinct from the semi-transparent bones of the cranium. The otoliths of the fresh-water are much more rounded and globose than those of the marine fishes. As objects for the binocular microscope, none are more beautiful than these bodies; among them may be recommended those of the sprat, brill, smelt, anchovy, and gray mullet.

GEOLOGICAL SUMMARY.

The Origin of the Granites. — At a recent meeting of the London Geologists' Association, Mr. Tomlinson, after adverting to the close resemblance or identity of the slags and dross of iron-furnaces with naturally formed volcanic rocks — as lavas, pitch-stones, etc., stated, that while we may regard the plutonic origin of *such* rocks as certain, it should be borne in mind, that volcanic rocks formed but a very small proportion only of the rocks termed plutonic or fire-formed. All granites and certain porphyries were generally regarded as having been fused by such action at great depths. But as many of these plutonic rocks contained magnetic iron-ore they could not be the results of fusion, else their composition would be that of a vitreous instead of crystalline rock. In cooling, quartz and iron would not separate, the oxides having a strong affinity for silica. Another difficulty which presented itself to the mind of the plutonist was that fossil forms were occasionally met with in magnetic iron-ore, as the Devonian brachiopod, *Spirifer speciosus*, which was thus found, in a quartz rock, mixed with iron-pyrites. Such facts pointed more to a neptunistic than a plutonic origin for granite, quartz, and the allied rocks.

Professor Morris commented at considerable length upon the subjects touched upon in Mr. Tomlinson's paper. He described the evidences, chemical, mineralogical, and dynamical, which favored the conclusion to which most geologists had now come — that granite and the allied rocks were formed under conditions dissimilar from those which obtained at or near the surface of the earth. Water at a high temperature was probably an important feature in these metamorphisms; indeed, so important was it deemed by Professor Haughton, that he had proposed to divide the granites into hydro- and pyro-metamorphic groups.

The Origin and Subsequent Alteration of Mica-Schist. — Mr. H. C. Sorby, in a paper on this subject, recently presented to the London Geological Society, stated, that when ripples are formed whilst material is being deposited, a structure is generated which is termed "ripple-drift." This structure may frequently be seen in polished sections of clay-slates, and also, in a form modified through metamorphism, in many mica-schists. From a consideration of the facts revealed by an examination of those rocks, the author concluded that mica-schist is of sedimentary origin, metamorphosed after deposition, and sometimes after the production of cleavage and other physical changes, and that the bands of different minerals represent the planes of original deposition.

Origin of Flint Nodules in Chalk. — In a recent discussion on this subject in the London Chemical Society, Dr. Church claimed that the flints in chalk could be traced to water holding silica in solution. During the percolation of such water through beds of chalk, the silica became separated, and the carbonate of lime took its place in the water thus deprived of its silica. An interesting example of the deposition of silica in the form of chalcedony took place within a comparatively recent date, geologically speaking. About the year 1400, a basket of hen's eggs had been left in a chalk pit at Winchester, England, and this basket was lately found covered up with broken chalk. The organic matter and the shell of the eggs had entirely disappeared and their places were occupied with the semi-transparent variety of silica, chalcedony. Silica was also deposited upon the willow twigs composing the basket, forming a crust of silica.

The Progressive Development of Organic Life. — At a meeting of the British Association, 1863, Professor Harkness stated, that the remains of reptiles, and the impressions of feet discovered within the last few years in the sandstones of the northeast of Scotland, afforded evidence of forms belonging to a period far more remote than any of which palæontology had as yet taken cognizance; upon this, Sir C. Lyell remarked, that if the facts put forward were true, one of the greatest blows had been struck at the theory of development, as generally understood, that could possibly have been dealt. There had been too great an inclination on the part of geological discoverers to assume that any given form of animal entered into this planet at the period of the rock in which it happened to be found; and the warning he had constantly given against this tendency had been interpreted as a much stronger protest against the doctrine of progression than it ought to have been. When the first of these telerpetons, being a new form, was announced to be found in a rock, reported on good authority to be Devonian, or, at any rate, palæozoic, he did feel a pleasure in the rebuke such a fact gave to the doctrine that no reptiles existed at that period. It always appeared to him unphilosophical, merely because we knew nothing of the vertebrate life of that period, to assume, therefore, that no reptiles existed older than the trias. But afterwards, when it was discovered that the Stagonolepis, a supposed fish, was a crocodilian reptile, and that some of the other forms were the same as those of the crocodiles now living in the Ganges, he began seriously to doubt whether his friends had assigned a true position in the geological series to these beds. Now, he saw clearly from the investigations that these must be admitted to be a consecutive regular series from unquestionably Lower Red beds containing the well-known fishes of the Old Red forms that were known to be carboniferous up to the beds containing those reptiles.

21

Succession of Strata. — Prof. Ramsay in the anniversary address 1863, before the British Geological Society, adduced evidence to show that the epochs in the palæozoic formations not stratigraphically represented in the British Islands were of longer duration than those which are so represented. From these premises, the professor argued that the apparent breaks in the succession of living forms were to be accounted for by the incompleteness of the record, and not by theories of violent destructions and new creations, which were not borne out by known facts. Nor was it just to assume that we saw the dawn of life in the earliest British strata, especially as older corals have been discovered in Canada.

Prof. Ramsay likewise adverted to the question of whether similar formations in distant countries were contemporaneous, and stated his opinion that in many cases the length of time occupied in the disposition of palæozoic strata was so enormous as to have rendered a very wide migration of species possible, and to make it probable that similarity of organic remains indicated an approximation of date.

New Views Respecting Stratification. — Certain French geologists are trying to account for the arrangement of geological strata by referring it either to the earth's annual revolution or daily rotation. In one or the other of these movements, they find an explanation of certain phenomena of stratification which are not easy to explain on any other known theory, among which are the appearances of stratification observable in embankments when cut through a few years after their formation.

Submergence of the British Islands during the Drift Period. — At the British Association, 1863, Sir C. Lyell, referring to certain shells which had been found in Wales, said it was proved to demonstration that the whole of Snowdonia, the highest mountains in Wales, were islands at the time the shells existed. The changes that must have taken place in the earth's crust to produce this permanent upheaval were really most astonishing; and it was proved how the study of the living species of shells, which Mr. Jeffreys had so successfully cultivated, opened up wonderful geological inferences in regard to the changes that had taken place in the earth in modern times.

The Divisions of the Tertiary System. — At a recent meeting of the Boston Society of Natural History, Prof. Agassiz gave an account of the conclusions at which he had arrived by the study of tertiary fossils in reference to the division of the strata in which they occur. He was satisfied that the primary divisions given by Lyell were natural, although the subdivisions are much more numerous, and the basis upon which the larger groups had been founded was erroneous; the relations of one group of beds to another being correctly based upon a percentage of species, representative of, rather than identical with, those now living. He was further satisfied that the principles upon which fossiliferous deposits of distant regions had been synchronized, namely, by the similarity of their organic forms, was entirely erroneous, since such fossils, even when unquestionably contemporaneous, showed frequently, when compared together, greater differences than the fossils from successive horizons in the same country.

The Tertiary Shells and Corals of Jamaica. — At a recent meeting of the British Geological Society, Mr. J. C. Moore communicated the result of an examination of seventy-one species of tertiary mollusca from Jamaica, showing that twelve are still living, and that twenty-eight are common to the tertiary beds of Jamaica and St. Domingo. The same relation between those deposits had been found to exist by Dr. Duncan through a comparison of the corals. The " Pacific " affinity of many of these shells and corals was noticed as confirmatory of a conclusion arrived at by the author in a former paper ; and it was shown, from the occurrence of tertiary beds on the Panama Isthmus at a height of 250 feet above the sea, that the complete separation of the Atlantic and Pacific Oceans did not take place until after the commencement of the tertiary period.

Formation of Coral Islands. — M. de Rochas announces to the French Academy the result of his inspection of coral islands in various parts of the globe, as not in harmony with the accepted theory on this subject. That theory assumes that the polyps which build up the earthy substance of these islands cease to build when the edifice reaches the low-tide mark ; and that the subsequent deposits, from the waves dashing over its surface, completes the elevation. M. de Rochas thinks that the first part of this statement is correct ; the second part is incorrect. He attributes the elevation above the surface of the water to volcanic agency. " No coral island without an upheaval, which pushes above the surface of the water the coral abandoned by the polyps ; " that is the formula of his experience. He finds the surface free from the attrition and fractures which would result from the throwing over them of pebbles and sand by the waves ; and he also finds the coral, in many places, where no upheaval has raised it above the surface, remaining in precisely the same position in which it was observed long ago, with no accumulation of *débris* on its surface.

Height of Mount Shasta, California. — A careful and elaborate series of barometrical observations recently made by the State Geological Corps of California has fixed the elevation of Mount Shasta at 14,440 feet. Previous to this the height of Shasta had been variously estimated. Fremont's estimate was 15,000 ; Williamson's, in the Pacific Railroad Survey, 18,000 ; and Wilkes, 14,350.

The Mineral Statistics of Great Britain for 1862, as given by Mr. Hunt of the School of Mines, are as follows : — the quantity of gold extracted was 5,209 ounces ; silver, 686,123 ounces ; tin, 8,476 tons ; copper, 14,843 tons ; lead, 69,031 tons ; zinc, 2,151 tons ; coal, 81,638,-338 tons ; representing a total value of £34,691,037.

Tin Ore in Maine, — At a recent meeting of the Boston Society of Natural History, Mr. A. E. Verrill called attention to the circumstance, that tin ore (cassiterite) has now been found at three localities in Oxford Co., Maine, in similar situations ; in each case, in a vein consisting in great part of albite, passing through granite ; and in two of the localities at least, it is intimately associated with these small crystals of zircon, both often being seen in the same specimen. At the locality in Greenwood that he had discovered a few years ago, the associated minerals were zircon, pyrochlore and magnetite, all in small crystals like the tin ore itself. At Mount Mica, in Paris, so well-known for its rare minerals, he had found the ore in 1854 in a mass weighing about five pounds, and also in small crystals. Specimens from this locality had already been exhibited to the Society. At this place the

principal associated minerals are the red, green, blue and black tour-
malines, lepidolite in large masses, mica, beryl, amblygonite yttrocerite,
brookite and zircon.   These all occur disseminated through a wide
vein of albite and feldspar, with some other more common minerals.   In
Hebron, about eight miles from this locality, there is another vein containing nearly the same minerals, except perhaps the last three, which
have not yet been noticed; and, in addition, mispickel.   Tin ore was
found here by Prof. Brush in small crystals.   These localities will perhaps serve as an indication of the manner in which this ore may occur
at other places in New England.   •

   Cryolite. — This interesting mineral, which a few years since was
only looked upon as a mineralogical rarity, has now become an important article in commerce.   Aside from its use as a source of aluminum
as suggested by Percy and H. Rose, we learn from recent articles in
Dingler's Polytechnisches Journal, that it is now extensively employed
in chemical works at Copenhagen and Harburg for the production of
caustic soda and salts of alumina.

   J. Thomsen claims to have discovered in 1850 that cryolite could be
decomposed by lime and lime salts ; and after perfecting his process, he
commenced the manufacture of soda in 1857, and in 1858 erected large
works at Copenhagen which now use 40,000 cwt. of cryolite annually.
The exploration of the cryolite deposit in Greenland has become so extended that another large manufactory has been erected at Harburg,
and others are being put up at Prague, Selicie and Mannheim.   It is
estimated that these manufactories will consume from 120,000 to 150,-
000 cwt. (6000 to 7500 tons) of cryolite annually.   Cryolite is delivered at Harburg for about two dollars per cwt. — *Silliman's Journal.*

   Natural Formation of Carbonate of Soda. — Prof. R. Haines, of
Bombay, has communicated to the London *Pharmaceutical Journal* a
note relating to a substance found all along the coast to the east of
Aden, to an extent of perhaps ten miles, and in quantity, practically,
unlimited.   It is usually obtained in hollows behind or beyond high-
water mark, to which sea-water has access by percolation.   The only
use made of it was to mix with snuff to give it pungency, and also, but
rarely, to wash clothes.   Prof. Haines describes this substance as consisting of " irregular, nearly colorless, partly crystalline masses, of a
greasy feel, and rather strong, soapy odor, very similar to that of crude
borax.   The chemical analysis gave — neutral carbonate of soda,
51.05 ; common salt, with traces of sulphate of soda and chloride of
magnesium, 24.94 ; water and organic matter, 19.66 ; sand, 4.35.   A
writer in a later number of the *Pharmaceutical Journal* also adds : —
From a paper recently published by Mr. H. J. Carter in the Transactions of the Royal Asiatic Society, on the geology of Arabia, it appears
that the whole of the southeast coast of Arabia is capped with num-
mulitic limestone, pierced at frequent intervals with basaltic effusions,
and in many places elevated so as to form lofty and abrupt cliffs, in
which, beneath the limestone, other formations are visible.   As a result of this formation, the shingle on the coast consists mainly of limestone ; and although no specific description of the coast immediately
to the east of Aden has been given, there is no reason to doubt that
the same peculiarities prevail there.   It is then to the percolation of

sea-water through a stratum of fragments of limestone that we must attribute the production of the carbonate of soda, by which percolation, probably, a partial interchange of elements has been effected between the chloride of sodium and the carbonate of lime, giving rise to the formation of chloride of calcium and carbonate of soda. It has been long suspected that the natural production of carbonate of soda was dependent on the presence of carbonate of lime, and was brought about somewhat in this way ; but what the conditions are under which the separation of the carbonate of soda from the chloride of calcium is effected, without allowing the former to exert its ordinary converse action upon the lime-salt and reproducing carbonate of lime, is a question that would form a very interesting subject of scientific inquiry. This is, I believe, the first time that the natural production of alkali from sea-water itself, without organic agency, has been observed.

Odor of Precious Stones. — Fournet discovered that many precious stones owed their colors to carburets of hydrogen. In 1855, J. Schneider, by analysis confirmed this discovery. In a note recently inserted in *Poggendorff's Annalen*, Schneider calls the attention of mineralogists to the empyreumatic odor which certain forms of quartz and granite give forth when rubbed. He thereby perceives the indication of the presence of organic matter or a carburet of hydrogen. — *Cosmos.*

Cavities in Precious Stones. — Sir David Brewster, in a paper recently read before the Royal Society of Edinburgh, gives a brief account of the various phenomena of fluid and gaseous cavities which he has discovered in diamond, topaz, beryl, and other minerals. He describes : —

1. Cavities with two immiscible fluids, the most expansible of which has received the name of *Brewstolyne*, and the most dense that of *Cryptolyne*, from the American and French mineralogists. 2. Cavities containing only one of these fluids. 3. Cavities containing the two fluids, and also crystals of various primitive forms, some of which melt by heat and recrystallize in cooling. 4. Cavities containing gas and vapor.

The author states that the first class of cavities exist in thousands, forming strata, plane and curved, and intersecting one another at various angles, but having no relation to the primitive and secondary planes of the crystal. From these facts, he draws the conclusion that the minerals which contain them are of igneous origin ; and he considers this conclusion as demonstrated by the existence of what he calls *pressure cavities*, which are never found in crystals of aqueous origin. These microscopic cavities, which are numerous in diamond, exist also in topaz and beryl. The gas which fills them has compressed by its elastic force the substance of the mineral around the cavities, as shown by four sectors or quadrants of light which it polarizes ; consequently the mineral must have been in a soft or plastic state by fusion when it thus yielded to the pressure of the included gas.

Localities of Primoidial Fossils. — The localities of primoidial fossils in Europe, according to Mr. Marcou, are restricted to two places in Bohemia. In this country they have been found at Braintree, Mass., St. Mary's Bay (Newfoundland), Georgia, Highgate, and Swanton Vt., the vicinity of Quebec, and in Tennessee. In Vermont he had r

21*

cently discovered a species of *Ampyx*, the first ever found in America, which had been named *A. Halli*.

Interesting Fossils. — Dr. Burmeister, the curator of the National Museum of Buenos Ayres, S. A., has recently in a voyage to the Solado River secured a most unrivalled collection of the fossil remains of the animals peculiar to South America during the tertiary period. Among them he mentions skeletons, in a fine state of preservation, of the *Megatherium*, *native horse* (now extinct), *Mylodon*, *Mylodon Robustus*, *Glyptodon*, *Toxodon*, and *Seclidotherium*.

On a minute vertebrate lower jaw. — In the *Annual Sci. Dis.*, 1863, p. 229, notice was given of a jaw-like object $\frac{1}{100}$ of an inch in length, dredged up by Dr. Wallich near St. Helena, which he considered as "evidence of the existence of a vertebrate animal measuring only $\frac{1}{20}$ inch in length!" This has excited much discussion, several papers having since been written upon the subject, and although its vertebrate character has been fully disproved, there is much diversity of opinion in regard to the true character of the object. C. Spence Bate (*Ann. and Mag.*, Dec., 1862) thinks it to be the claw of an amphipod. It has also been suggested that it may be part of the lingual ribbon of a gasteropod; or part of the manducatory apparatus of a Rotifer. Mr. Busk, in an illustrated paper in the *Quarterly Journal of Microscopical Science*, for Jan., 1863, has given the most probable solution : — that the jaw figured by Dr. Wallich is one of the valves or jaws of a pedicellaria of an Echinoderm, allied to *Amphidotus*.

The Flying Lizards of the Mesozoic Period. — Mr. H. Woodward, an English palæontologist of note, states that up to the present time, thirty-seven species of pterodactyles have been identified and described from the strata of the Mesozoic Period ; how many individuals have been discovered is not known. There is every reason, however, to believe that they were very abundant ; but we are not justified in supposing that they *altogether* took the place of birds. The largest species of pterodactyles,— P. Sedgwickii,— is supposed, from careful measurement and fitting of its bones, to have been upborne on an expanse of wings, not less than twenty-two feet from tip to tip.

The Solenhofen Fossil. — At a recent meeting of the Boston Society of Natural History, Prof. Agassiz made a few remarks about the enigmatic fossil which has been lately discovered at Solenhofen (see *Annual of Scientific Discovery*, 1863, p. 274) ; and, after passing in review the opinions of Owen, of Meyer and of Wagner concerning the nature of the animal, he inclined to the belief that this was but an additional case of a synthetic type such as he had at first pointed out among fishes, where there were fishes with reptilian characters. In this case it was a synthetic type of a higher class — a reptile with bird characters.

The Remains of a Fossil Tortoise, of a new species, discovered by M. Lennier, of Havre, were described by M. Valenciennes at a recent meeting of the Academy of Sciences at Paris. A remarkable distinction in this tortoise is its possessing nine ribs, all those hitherto known having but eight.

Fossil Egg. — A fossil egg has been found in the guano of the Isles of Chinchas, at a depth of about forty feet. It was about the size of a goose's egg, and weighed 252 grammes. Its texture was crystalline ; but the silky brilliancy of the fracture was lost on its exposure to the

air. This egg was truly metamorphic, since it contained scarcely anything of its original constituents. It contained in 100 parts — sulphate of potash, 70.59; sulphate of ammonia, 26.55; chloride of ammonium, 1.25; chloride of sodium, 0.65; and organic matter, .06. It is remarkable that it contained no lime or phosphoric acid, two substances which never fail in the eggs of birds. The shell had undergone great modification; yet there remained in 100 parts — phosphate of lime, 77.82; silica, 0.45; potash, 2.33; and organic matter, 2.07.

The Dinornis of New Zealand. — Mr. Haast, President of the Philosophical Society of New Zealand, in a recent inaugural address at Canterbury, N. Z., states that two species of the Dinornis, new to science, have recently been described. And to quote his own description, " another still larger Kiwi, provisionally named *Apteryx maxima,* and called Roa by the natives, still exists in the western mountains of the island. Living specimens of this bird, which is as large as a turkey, have not yet been procured; though," adds Mr. Haast, " I observed its tracks in the fresh-fallen snow, and heard its call during the night." A still larger Kiwi, *Palapteryx ingens,* is believed from " auricular evidence " to be in existence in the great beech forests which cover for many miles the slopes of the New Zealand Alps.

Source of the Pennsylvania Petroleum. — A recent number of the *Journal of the Franklin Institute* contains a report on the oil district of " Oil Creek," Penn., by Mr. T. S. Ridgeway, mining engineer and geologist, who has carefully surveyed the whole oil region.

He states that at one place there is a mass of oil-bearing strata 1,200 feet in thickness. The oil-bearing strata is broken up in huge cakes of sandstones and shales, having fissures between the strata extending to a great depth, and these are generally filled with gravel and pebbles. These openings are numerous in Oil Creek, and are the cause of much perplexity to drillers in search of oil. In one case, a pipe was sunk 160 feet below the surface before the permanent rock was reached, while at a few yards distant the rock was struck at a depth of thirty feet. At a distance of about 530 feet from the surface there appears to be a great oil pool below, and for a distance of seven miles down to the mouth of Oil Creek the flowing wells rise from it. Stones taken out of the oil-bearing rocks are employed in several places for buildings, and the petroleum may still be noticed sometimes trickling from their surfaces. Mr. Ridgeway, from his examinations, is convinced that the petroleum is not produced from the coal-fields, because in that case it would-have had to flow up hill into the oil basin. He says : — " Petroleum found in bituminous coal basins, no doubt, originates from beds of coal, but it is my opinion that the petroleum of the Oil Creek valley is the result of the decomposition of marine plants. The plants which produced the oil in the rock existed and flourished at a long period of time before the vegetation which now forms coalbeds ; they are unlike the vegetable impressions found in the accompanying shales and clays associated with beds of coal ; and they grew where the flag-stones and shales of Oil Creek were laid down by saltwater currents. The climate was so hot, during this age of marine vegetation, and the growth of plants so rapid and rank, caused by the supposed large amount of carbonic acid and hydrogen then composing the atmosphere, that these conditions on the face of the earth produce plants containing more hydrogen and less carbon than the plants which produced coal-beds, and hence their fermentation produced the petroleum."

The Petroleum Trade of the United States for 1863. — The export of petroleum from the United States for the year 1863, is estimated at not less than 28,000,000 gallons. As an illustration of the unexampled rapidity with which the trade in this article has developed, we give the total export of petroleum for the years 1861 and 1862. They were as follows: 1861, 1,112,476 gallons; 1862, 10,887,000 gallons; the quantity exported in 1863 amounted to 252,000 tons' weight, and engaged no less than 252 ships of 1,000 tons' burden each, to carry it. The amount of money derived from its sale is estimated at $12,000,000.

NOTES ON METEORITES.

From numerous reports of eleven large meteors which passed over England in the two years 1861–63, collected from the British Association, the heights of appearance were found to vary from thirty to 196 miles above the earth, and of disappearance from fifteen to sixty-five miles above the earth. Their velocities were from twenty-three to sixty miles in a second.

Referring to some recent experiments by Deville, of Paris, and Plücker of Bonn, in which, by great heat, oxygen has been dissociated from hydrogen in steam, and carbonic acid and other chemical compounds had been decomposed, Herschel has conjectured that the violent heat of a fire-ball is sufficient to destroy the chemical affinities in the meteoric surface, and to cause the glowing sparks and phosphorescent streaks, which follow the flame, by the gradual recombustion, in the rear, of the reduced metals and elements in the track of the meteor's flight.

Meteoric Iron from Tucson, Arizona. — A mass of meteoric iron from Tucson has been presented to the city of San Francisco by General Carleton. In a recent letter, Prof. Whitney states that this iron is four feet one inch long, and weighs 632 lbs. It was found at or near Tucson, Arizona, by Gen. Carleton's California column on their march through that region, and has evidently been used for an anvil, although it is not the one figured by Bartlett as having served that purpose.

A specimen of this meteorite analyzed by Prof. Bush, of Yale College, gave the following result: — Iron, 81.56; nickel, 9.17; cobalt, 0.44; copper, 0.08; phosphorus, 0.49; silica, 3.63; protoxide of iron with a trace of alumina, 0.12; lime, 1.10; magnesia, 2.43; chlorine, sulphur, chromium, minute traces. The composition of this meteorite corresponds very closely with another meteoric iron from Tucson, discovered by Mr. Bartlett, and described by Prof. J. Lawrence Smith, in the *Am. Journ. of Science*, 2d ser., vol. xix. page 161.

Molecular Structure of Meteorites. — Mr. Sorby, the well-known English geologist and microscopist, has recently turned his microscope upon meteorites, or rather upon sections of these exotic minerals, with a view to ascertain their origin by close examination of their microscopical structure. The evidence thus far appears to be strong in favor of the conclusion that they are formed by the aggregation of smaller fragments or minute particles, in which particular they are most nearly resembled, among terrestrial rocks, by consolidated volcanic ashes. Is there anything in this fact of aggregation which touches the nebular hypothesis?

PRODUCTION OF CRYSTALLINE LIMESTONES.

In the *Annual Sci. Dis.* 1862, p. 289, an account is given of experiments made by Rosé of Berlin, tending to show that chalk or compact limestone *cannot* be converted into crystalline limestone (or calc spar) by exposure to high temperature in close vessels; and that the experiments made some years since by Sir James Hall, tending to prove the affirmative of the proposition, were eroneous. Recently, however, Rosé has repeated his investigations on the subject, and has now obtained results which differ entirely from those he formerly published, and which fully confirms the correctness of Sir James Hall's conclusion, that marble can be produced by exposing massive carbonate of lime to a high temperature under great pressure. The experiments were made with aragonite from Bilin, in Bohemia, and with lithographic limestone. In one case, the mineral was heated in a wrought-iron cylinder, and in the other, in a porcelain bottle, special precautions being taken to exclude the air, and make the vessels as near air-tight as possible. These were exposed to a white heat for half an hour, and, on cooling, both the aragonite and the lithographic limestone were found to be converted into crystalline limestone, the former very much resembling Carrara marble, and the latter a grayish-white granular limestone. The change took place without any material decomposition, the resulting marble containing a trifle less carbonic acid than the lithographic limestone from which it was produced. — *Silliman's Journal.*

THE FLORA OF THE DEVONIAN PERIOD.

Prof. Dawson, of Montreal, communicates to the Journal of the Geological Society (London), the following general conclusion arrived at by him, from a careful study of the " Flora of the Devonian Period in North Eastern America." 1st. In its general character, the Devonian Flora resembles that of the Carboniferous Period, in the prevalence of Gymnosperms and Cryptogams; and, with few exceptions, the generic types of the two periods are the same. Some genera are, however, relatively much better represented in the Devonian than in the Carboniferous deposits, and several Carboniferous genera are wanting in the Devonian.

2d. Some species, which appear early in the Devonian Period, continue to its close without entering the Carboniferous; and the great majority of the species, even of the Upper Devonian, do not reappear in the Carboniferous Period; but a few species extend from the Upper Devonian into the Lower Carboniferous, and thus establish a real passage from the earlier to the later Flora. The connection thus established between the Upper Devonian and the Lower Carboniferous is much less intimate than that which subsists between the latter and the true Coal-measures. Another way of stating this is, that there is a constant gain in number of genera and species from the Lower to the Upper Devonian, but that at the close of the Devonian many species and some genera disappear. In the Lower Carboniferous, the Flora is again poor, though retaining some of the Devonian species; and it goes on increasing up to the period of the Middle Coal-measures, and this by the addition of species quite distinct from those of the Devonian Period.

3d. A large part of the difference between the Devonian and Carboniferous Floras is probably related to different geographical conditions. The wide, swampy flats of the Coal Period do not seem to have existed in the Devonian era. The land was probably less extensive and more of an upland character. On the other hand, moreover, it is to be observed that, when in the Middle Devonian we find beds similar to the underclays of the Coal-measures, they are filled, not with *Stigmaria*, but with rhizomes of *Psilophyton*; and it is only in the Upper Devonian that we find such stations occupied, as in the Coal-measures, by *Sigillaria* and *Calamites*.

4th. Though the area to which this paper relates is probably equal to any other in the world in the richness of its Devonian Flora, still it is apparent that the conditions were less favorable to the preservation of plants than those of the Coal Period. The facts that so large a proportion of the plants occur in marine beds, and that so many stipes of Ferns occur in deposits that have afforded no perfect fronds, show that our knowledge of the Devonian Flora is relatively far less complete than our knowledge of that of the Coal-formation.

5th. The Devonian Flora was not of lower grade than that of the Coal Period. On the contrary, in the little ·that we know of it, we find more points of resemblance to the Floras of the Mesozoic Period, and of modern tropical and austral islands, than in that of the true Coal-formation. We may infer from this, in connection with the preceding general statement, that, in the progress of discovery, very large and interesting additions will be made to our knowledge of this Flora, and that we may possibly also learn something of a land Fauna contemporaneous with it.

6th. The *facies* of the Devonian Flora in America is very similar to that of the same period in Europe, yet the number of identical species does not seem to be so great as in the coal-fields of the two continents. This may be connected with the different geographical conditions in these two periods; but the facts are not yet sufficiently numerous to prove this.

7th. The above general conclusions are not materially different from those arrived at by Gœppert, Unger, and Broun, from a consideration of the Devonian Flora of Europe.

PROGRESSIVE CHANGES IN THE CHARACTER OF THE PRAIRIES OF SOUTHERN ILLINOIS.

Prof. Engelmann of the State Geological Survey of Illinois communicates to the *American Journal of Science*, some interesting observations on the progressive changes which are taking place in the character of the prairie country of Southern Illinois. He says : — In this district, the prairie growth is undergoing a considerable spontaneous change with the progressing settlement and cultivation of the country. Since the prairie grass is no longer burnt off annually, as it used to be by the Indians and early settlers, whereby all but the hardiest grasses were destroyed, and those especially remained which propagate by throwing out suckers from the roots, and since the grass is continually cropped close and tramped down by cattle, the former vegetation of the prairies has gradually given way to softer and shorter grasses, the rank prairie and barren grasses dying out. At many points also timber is encroaching spontaneously upon land formerly occupied by tall grasses; while, on the contrary, old forests yield to the axe and the ploughshare. The effect of these changes upon the climate, especially in decreasing the humidity of the country, must be powerful, and may be compared to the change of sensation which we experience, on a clear summer evening, in coming from a sheltered damp creek bottom to the airy top of a dry hill. The effect is similar to that produced in other countries by the clearing of extensive forests. The growth of dense tall grasses, of which untold generations have died and rotted upon the same spot, not only protects the soil from the warming rays of the sun and thus checks evaporation, but it actually increases the precipitation of moisture, especially in the form of dew, by the low degree of temperature consequent upon the humidity of the surface and upon the powerful radiation of heat from the spears and leaves of the grass waving in the night air, which, as can be easily proved by experiment, grow much colder than the bare soil. The grasses also check the surface drainage effectually. With their disappearance, the above effects cease, the soil becomes more exposed to the direct rays of the sun and to the drying breezes, while the succeeding growth does not favor the precipitation of dew nearly as much as the grass. The natural impediments to the speedy abduction of the falling rains are also lessened to a considerable degree, and thus the soil is rendered dryer. The artificial works of drainage, and even the cuts and ruts of the roads do their share also. The breaking up of the sward and deep cultivation of the soil facilitate the sinking of the water, and expose a greater surface of soil to the desiccating influence of the sun and winds. Every old settler can bear witness to the remarkable and rapid change in the conditions of moisture of the prairies, which is also manifested by the gradual failing of the wells at numerous points. It is a common observation, that they must be dug much deeper now than formerly in the same vicinity. The healthiness of the country has thereby improved, and the farmer is enabled to plant much earlier, and at points which were formerly too wet; his loss by the freezing out of the winter crops is much reduced. The droughts in summer and fall are perhaps also more severe at present, but an advantage can seldom be gained without some sacrifice, and a remedy is accessible if only we will apply it. This is "thorough cultivation and underdraining." Where these are practised, the roots are enabled to strike deeper, beyond the direct influence of the sun's rays; a much larger quantity of nourishment is presented to them; the humidity of the soil is equalized; its absorbing power for moisture and gases is vastly increased; and the growth of the plants is consequently much invigorated and placed beyond the reach of sudden changes of the weather.

THE DISTRIBUTION OF ARCTIC PLANTS.

Dr. Hooker, of the Kew Botanic Gardens, has published a memoir on this subject in the *Linnean Society's Transactions*, which will be fully appreciated by geographical botanists. The Arctic flora forms a circumpolar belt of ten to fourteen degrees. There is no abrupt break or chain in the vegetation anywhere along this belt except in the meridian of Baffin's Bay, where the opposite shores present a sudden change from an almost purely European flora on the east coast to one with a large admixture of American plants on the west. The number of flowering plants is estimated at 762; of cryptogamia at 925; total, 1687. Regarded as a whole, Dr. Hooker considers the Arctic flora to be decidedly Scandinavian; for Lapland, though a very small tract, contains by far the richest Arctic flora, amounting to three-fourths of the whole. Of the five districts into which Dr. Hooker divides the Arctic belt, Greenland is the most remarkable; since, although so favorably situated for harboring an Arcto-American vegetation, it presents but little trace thereof, and has an almost absolute identity with that of Europe. This, he considers, cannot be accounted for except by admitting Mr. Darwin's hypothesis of the great geological antiquity of the Scandinavian flora; its subsequent migration southward in every latitude during the glacial period, and even across the tropics into the south temperate zone; and the ascent of the mountains of the warmer zone by many species at the commencement of the warmth of the present epoch.

HIGHEST MOUNTAINS IN THE UNITED STATES.

Professor J. D. Whitney, the Superintendent of the California Geological Survey, in an article in the *Proceedings of the California Academy*," announces his conclusion, that Mount Shasta, 14,400 feet high, probably overtops all other peaks within the limits of the United States. Mount Hood, sometimes called the loftiest peak of the Cascade Range, is probably not so high as Mounts Shasta, Rainier or Adams, and by no means entitled to the supremacy of the chain, although one of the highest points in it. Trigonometrical measurements of Mount Hood, in 1860, give its height as 11,934 feet.

Mount St. Elias, in the Russian Possessions, has generally been considered the highest mountain in North America, on the authority of Malespina's manuscripts, discovered by Humboldt in the archives of Mexico, which assign to it an elevation of 17,854 feet. Mr. Whitney, however, thinks this estimate erroneous, and the estimate given on the British Hydrographical charts of Captain Denham, of 14,970, more nearly correct. Mount Brown and Mount Hooker, in British Columbia, have assigned to them a height of 16,000 and 16,750 feet respectively. But the highest mountain on the North American continent is, beyond all doubt, the Mexican volcano of *Popocatapetl*, which rises to the well-ascertained height of 17,783 feet.

ZOÖLOGY.

THE most satisfactory progress made in zoölogy of late years, has been in the study and classification of the lower forms of life. The aquarium and the microscope have given an impetus to the study of the invertebrata, and such immense additions have been made to the knowledge of this great section, that the mere weight of facts threatens to separate it from the hitherto recognized connection with the vertebrates, and so to constitute in zoölogy two distinct sciences, the future paths of which will be separate though parallel. It is in this section that we have most striking evidence of the abundance of life in every region of the globe. The recent researches on the subject of deep sea life, have enlarged immensely the geographical limits and the physical conditions known to be favorable to the production of animal existence.

In that still lower department of the Infusoria, the magnificent work of Pritchard offers another example of the splitting up of old divisional arrangements through the accumulation of facts indicative of distinctive characteristics.

But if we ever feel astonished at the abundance of life on the globe, it is also pretty certain that some of its forms are fast passing away from us, and that, not very far in the future, the zoölogist will pay as much attention to mammals recently extinct, as we do to certain fossil forms, because they fill up gaps in our classified system of transitions. That the dodo is utterly extinct there can be no reasonable doubt, for the region it inhabited has not only been thoroughly explored, but is now densely populated. The kiwi or apteryx is fast going in the same direction, and as the interior of New Zealand becomes a home for the white man, that and other feræ must of necessity disappear. The last dinornis has probably long since perished; yet it could not be long since there were at least eight species of dinornis, varying in size, from that of the bustard upwards; *D. giganteus* being vastly superior to the ostrich in magnitude. The great quadrumana will probably be the next to disappear, for civilization will not tolerate the existence of anthropoid apes, and the mere savagery of what is called "sport" will extinguish them. The gorilla evidently occupies but a limited range of country, and that near the coast, and the tendency of civilization is to people the coasts everywhere with colonies of Anglo-Saxons, French, and Portuguese, respecting whom it is not easy to say which are the most active in the destruction of indigenous fauna. The beaver still holds a few secluded weirs in the North of Europe, but no one can say when it became extinct in Britain. The otter is so scarce in Great Britain that the sport of hunting it is almost obsolete. Of the *Falconidæ* there are few living examples left in the British Islands, and the eyrie of an eagle is as rare in England as the nest of a thrush in France, where the most melodious of songsters is valued only for its flavor in a pasty by a people who make great pretensions to the culture of the sentimental. The noble blackcock and the ignoble black rat appear to have vanished almost simultaneously from the British fauna, and the fox is probably following the wolf in full conviction that its mission is accomplished. Indeed the fiercest war maintained by man against animal races, is waged against the carnivora and the raptorial birds. In the Biblical narrative, there are numerous evidences of the abundance of beasts of prey in Palestine and Phœnicia, where there is now scarce anything more rapacious than a fox to be found. David's adventure with the lion and bear could not now be repeated by any brave shepherd within a hundred miles of Jerusalem, and the traveller on the Euphrates and Tigris need entertain but little fear of those hungry lions which figure so conspicuously on the hunting friezes of Nineveh. Man not only lays the whole animal kingdom under tribute to furnish him with meat and labor and entertainment and knowledge, but he busies himself to disturb the balances. The relations of Sir Emerson Tennent and Dr. Livingstone make it pretty evident that the "half-reasoning elephant" is fast passing from the face of the earth to be numbered among the extinct animals by the naturalists of a century hence. When we read of the wanton slaughter of thousands of elephants, with no object but the gratification of the passion for destruction, we are tempted to lament that man possesses such complete dominion to subjugate, and such unlimited power to destroy. "Had the motive," says Sir Emerson Tennent, "that invites to the destruction of the elephant in Africa and India prevailed in Ceylon, that is, had the elephants there been provided with tusks, they would long since have been annihilated for the sake of their ivory. But it is a curious fact that, whilst in Africa and India both sexes have tusks, with some slight disproportion in the size of those of the females, not one elephant in a hundred is found with tusks in Ceylon, and the few that possess them are exclusively males." In Africa the hunger for meat and ivory causes the destruction of the elephant to an extent which threatens soon to extinguish the large-eared species altogether, but with neither of these incitements, it is perhaps being extinguished with still greater speed in Ceylon and India. There is a saving clause in the fact now established, that elephants will breed in captivity, but against it must be set the fact that in captivity it does not pay for its keep, and is scarcely worth the attention of those who employ it either for burden or draught. The elephant has too much character, too high a reasoning faculty, to be perfect as a servant; it has too many whims, too many eccentricities of temper, and consumes far more food than it earns in harness. Thus economically regarded, everything is against its preservation, and when the wild herds disappear, there will probably remain but few in a domesticated state, for unlike the horse, ox, ass, and sheep, it is both unprofitable and unmanageable.

Zoölogy has been somewhat restricted in aim, spite of its own breadth ᴀ a science and the liberality of its leading cultivators. It owes most of its advance in recent times, in the absorption into its circle of the facts of past biological history, to Prof. Owen, whose " Palæontology" is a sort of panorama of extinct forms, placed side by side with their existing congeners and representatives. Australia and New Zealand have not only furnished innumerable subjects of anomalous kinds for the consideration of system-makers, but they have opened the way for rays of light to fall on the present direct from the past, by their illustrations of geological eras. Nothing more strikingly exemplifies the relationship that subsists between all departments of knowledge, than the aid which zoölogy and geology respectively offer to each other. The existing fauna of Ceylon, as analyzed by Sir Emerson Tennent, affords very satisfactory indications that the island is, in no geological or zoölogical sense, an outlier of the vast Indian continent, but a site *sui generis* like Australia, detached not only in its geography from the neighboring continent, but in its chronology also, and in all its organic productions. On the other hand, geology does more than whisper of the connection that once subsisted between England and the Continent of Europe by way of the straits of Dover; for it furnishes all the evidence requisite to establish the conclusion that the separation was effected not very long antecedent to the commencement of the historic era. Zoölogy does not touch the chronology of the question, but it affixes the general conclusion; and we begin to discover that, however valuable are the floras and faunas of Britain, they tell but half their proper story unless considered in connection with the floras and faunas of the Continent. — *Intellectual Observer.*

ANIMAL AND VEGETABLE CHARACTERISTICS OF ASIA AND AUSTRALIA.

Mr. Wallace, the well-known English naturalist, in a recent paper before the British Geographical Society stated that while Asia and Australia were more widely distinct in their animal and vegetable productions than any two portions of the earth, it could be shown that these peculiarities extended on each side into the adjacent islands, so that when you came to the little islands of Bàly and Lombock, separated only by a strait 15 miles wide, you have the production of two continents brought into close contact without intermingling; the birds, for example, being almost totally different in the two islands, and not the species merely, but even the genera and families of the one not extending into the other.

NEW CLASSIFICATION OF THE ANIMAL KINGDOM.

At a recent meeting of the French Academy, M. Chevreul explained a plan devised by him for a new classification of the animal kingdom. His principle may be briefly stated as follows: Under the present system, in which the physical organization of the animal is taken for a guide, it often happens that its intellectual development is at variance with its physiological state. Thus, the quadrumana precede the carnivora in the present system, the organization of the former being superior to that of the latter. Now, if we take the ourang outang, chimpanzee, and gorilla, as types of the quadrumana, both their organization and intellectual faculties will induce us to place them immediately after man. But the makis, which are also quadrumanous, and therefore precede the carnivora, are far below some of them, such as the dog and phoca, as regards their intellectual faculties. To obviate the inconvenience resulting from this discrepancy between the physical and intellectual qualities of animals, M. Chevreul proposes to classify them by shelves instead of columns, as is now the case. Let us suppose the centre of the upper shelf to be occupied by man ; then describing a circle from that centre, that the ourang outang, chimpanzee and gorilla be placed at equal distances on the circumference, and other inferior species of quadrumana further off from the centre, but on the same shelf. Now let the lower shelf be devoted to the carnivora, and let the centre be occupied by the best species, namely : the dog, phoca, bear, and cat ; then the inferior species will be arranged further and further from the centre, according to the degree of their intellectual faculties. The advantage of this arrangement will be that the dog, being inferior to the most perfect kinds of quadrumana, will stand below them on the second shelf ; but being superior in sagacity to the makis, this circumstance is denoted by his being at the centre, and the makis at a distance from it, though on the upper shelf. In the same way other shelves may be arranged for the orders immediately inferior to the carnivora in point of sagacity, and from this succession of shelves new relations may be discovered between species belonging to different genera and orders.

ON THE PHENOMENA CONNECTED WITH DEATH.

Mr. Savory, in a recent lecture before the Royal Institution, London, on the above subject, drew a broad distinction between what he termed general death, and special, or molecular death. The latter occurs sometime after the last breath has been drawn, since several functions of the body, such as digestion, muscular contraction, and the circulation of the body, may go on for some time after the change, we term death has taken place. In this aspect, the more important functions of animal life are suspended much sooner than those relating to our organic life. So also, cold-blooded animals, and those with very simple organization, such as polyps and worms, retain vitality of various degrees under circumstances fatal to such complex organisms as ours. In commenting on the various modes of dying, and the causes, whether arising from the suspension of the action of either of the three great organs termed the " tripods of life," the heart, the lungs, and the brain, — Mr. Savory expressed his own conviction, that death was primarily occasioned by either the sudden or gradual stoppage of the supply of blood to the nervous centres. He also expressed his concurrence with the statement of the late Sir Benjamin Brodie, that, in almost all cases, the point of death is free from physical suffering. He duly described and analyzed the signs of death, namely, loss of heat, the muscular contraction, termed " rigor mortis," the coagulation of the blood, and finally, decomposition. The last, he said, is always going on in life, but is then accompanied by renewal ; this ceases after death. The body then becomes subject to chemical and physical forces, and is resolved into its component elements, to be taken up again for the constitution of new organisms. Death, then, is a condition of life.

Essential Features of Life. — Mr. Savory in the same lecture also defined the essential features of life, when reduced to its simplest terms, as a state of dynamic equilibrium — a continual succession of waste and repair; the former being the consequence of every act of mind or body, the latter the result of the various processes of nutrition carried on during repose. In a human body weighing 140 lbs. about a ton of various matters, solid, liquid, and gaseous, are received and assimilated during a year; yet the body appears exactly the same. Some organs, however, such as the teeth and hair, have a limited existence. This may be compared to the metamorphoses of insects. Life is maintained in a normal state when demand and supply are perfectly adjusted, consumption being ever proportional to the total energy exercised. A seed of a plant is in a state of dormant vitality, which the hibernation of certain animals closely resembles. The blood which we have in three stages or conditions — that of to-day in its perfect state, that of yesterday in its used state, and that of to-morrow in its preparatory stage — is the important agent in the nutrition or repair of wasted tissues. Its great organ, the heart, has also its due periods of work and rest or repair. The same is the case with the organs of respiration. In health an increased demand for power meets with increased supply. Hence the large size of the muscles of the arm of a blacksmith, and the greater development of the brain when the mental power is raised by education. The mutual sympathy existing between all the organs of the body is maintained by means of the blood and the nervous system; and by the action of the nerves on the blood-vessels, the varied phenomena of the countenance (pallor, blushing, &c.) are produced. In conclusion, Mr. Savory proposed to reduce the seven ages of man to three : — Growth or development, when supply of nutrition to the tissues exceeds the demand; maturity, when the two are balanced; and decline, when supply falls short of the demand, and decay ensues.

NATURE OF THE VITAL FORCE.

The following is an abstract of a discussion before the British Association, on the nature of the so-called " vital force."— Dr. Daubeny was quite ready to allow that the term " vital force" was conditional. At the same time, he felt that some of the phenomena of plant-life could not be explained by physical causes. Such, he thought, was the power plants had of selecting one kind of food rather than another, and the power the leaves possessed of decomposing carbonic acid. — Prof. Williamson expressed his conviction that the processes of life did not depend on physical causes. There were always causes acting in the life of plants and animals that no physical principles with which we were acquainted could explain. He instanced the fact of a hydra taking one of its own tentacles into its stomach with an animalcule. It digested the animalcule, but its tentacle suffered no harm. Mineral bodies were subject to no decay as organic bodies were; and it was this death that showed the existence of a departed vital force from the dead plant or animal. Mr. Lubbock thought the danger of using the term " vital " force or principle was, that persons who employed it thought it explained the phenomena, which in no instance was the case. He thought that the death of marine animals in fresh water, and of fresh-water animals in salt water, was an instance of how physical circumstances influenced life. Dr. Lankester said, that the term " vital force " had been used in various senses, and Dr. Daubeny only

22*

accepted it as a provisional term. What he wished to point out was, that in the sense in which it was employed by Dr. Daubeny, it was only equivalent, as Dr. Jepen had stated, to the "crystallizing force" of minerals, which exercised the same selecting power in crystallizing as the roots of plants did in growing. The only phenomena in plants for which we had really no physical explanation were, the movements of the protoplasm in the interior of the cells of plants, and the locomotive power of unicellular plants and their cilia. These movements were similar to the muscular contractility and nervous sensibility of the highest animals. These movements were, however, dependent on physical causes, and the chemical decomposition of the sugar and protein of our food was necessary for their development. As to death's not occurring in the mineral world, this was but another name in animals and plants for change; and change occurred in crystals and in all the physical phenomena of the universe, as much as in organic bodies.

PHYSIOLOGY OF REPRODUCTION.

The student of nature wonders the more, and is astonished the less, the more conversant he becomes with her operations; but of all the perennial miracles she offers to his inspection, perhaps the most worthy of admiration is the development of a plant or an animal from its embryo. Examine the recently laid egg of some animal, such as a salamander or a newt. It is a minute spheroid in which the best microscope will reveal nothing but a structureless sac, enclosing a glairy fluid, holding granules in suspension. But strange possibilities lie dormant in that semi-fluid globule. Let a moderate supply of warmth reach its watery cradle, and the plastic matter undergoes changes so steady and purpose-like in their succession, that one can only compare them to those operated by a skilful modeller upon a formless lump of clay. As with an invisible trowel, the mass is divided and subdivided into smaller and smaller portions until it is reduced to an aggregation of granules not too large to build withal the finest fabrics of the nascent organism. And, then, it is as if a delicate finger traced out the line to be occupied by the spinal column, and moulded the contour of the body; pinching up the head at one end, the tail at the other, and fashioning flank and limb into due salamandrine proportions, in so artistic a way that, after watching the process hour by hour, one is almost involuntarily possessed by the notion that some more subtle aid to vision than an achromatic glass would show the hidden artist, with his plan before him, striving with skilful manipulation to perfect his work.

As life advances, and the young amphibian ranges the waters, the terror of his insect contemporaries, not only are nutritious particles supplied by its prey, by the addition of which to its frame growth takes place, laid down, each in its proper spot, and in such due proportion to the rest, as to reproduce the form, the color, and the size characteristic of the parental stock; but even the wonderful powers of reproducing lost parts possessed by these animals are controlled by the same governing tendency. Cut off the legs, the tail, the jaws — separately or all together — and, as Spallanzan showed long ago, these parts not only grow again, but the redintegrated limb is formed on the same type as those which were lost. The new jaw or leg is a newt's, and never by any accident more like that of a frog. What is true of the newt is true of every animal and plant; the acorn tends to build itself up again into a woodland giant such as that from whose twig it fell; the spore of the humblest lichen reproduces the green or brown incrustation which gave it birth; and at the other end of the scale of life, the child that resembled neither the paternal nor the maternal side of the house would be regarded as a kind of monster. So that the one end to which, in all living beings, the formative impulse is tending — the one scheme which the Archæus of the old speculators strives to carry out — seems to be to mould the offspring into the likeness of the parent. It is the first great law of reproduction that the offspring tends to resemble its parent or parents more closely than anything else. — *Westminster Review.*

INFLUENCE OF THE NURSE UPON THE NURSLING.

In general, people are wholly unaware of the fact that bones grow and waste with great rapidity. Bone is composed chiefly of earthy matters, and we should as soon expect a mile-stone to increase and decrease with the changing hours, as this inorganic-looking bone. Nevertheless, it is a fact, that bones are always in an active state of waste and repair, and no tissue in the body is so rapidly and successfully repaired after injury, or after portions have been cut away, as the bony tissue. Some years ago, M. Flourens hit upon the ingenious device of tracing the growth of bone, by giving animals madder in their food. The madder colored all the new deposits, so that, after a time, every bone in the body was of a deep red. If, of two animals thus fed, one were deprived of madder at a certain period, the tale was told by the layers of uncolored bone which covered those that were colored, and in time, the whole of the colored bone would disappear. M. Flourens has since made valuable and varied use of his discovery. He has employed it to show the influence of the mother upon her offspring. Taking a sow with young, and freely administering madder with her food, he found the little pigs all born with colored bones. That the reader may fairly understand the surprising nature of this result, he should know that the communication between parent and offspring is of an extremely *indirect* kind. It is only through the blood; and that blood does not simply flow from her arteries into the arteries of the offspring, but circulates in a system of *closed* vessels, which lie side by side with the closed vessels of the young one, and through the *walls* of both these vessels, certain constituents of the blood ooze, and among these constituents, apparently, the coloring matter.

Nor do the marvels end here. M. Flourens has recently submitted to the *Academie des Sciences* the result of his experiments on "nursing mothers." These are so important in their suggestions to human mothers, especially to those who suffer their children to be brought up by wet nurses, or "by hand," that we deem it right to give it not only publicity, but all the emphasis we can command. Let the facts first be stated. The litter of a sow was kept carefully separated from her, except during the moments of sucking. She was fed on food with which madder had been mingled. In a fortnight or three weeks, all the bones of the little pigs were reddened. Remember that the milk of such a sow is to the eye as white as that of any other sow; nothing reveals the presence of the madder, save the remarkable effects on the osseous tissues of mother and offspring. The doubt thus raised helps to strengthen the idea that probably it was not through the milk, that these little pigs received the coloring matter, but in some more direct way. This doubt M. Flourens very wisely considered. He observed that when the sow was admitted to her young ones, she had her snout covered with the remains of the food in which she had plunged it, and this the little ones began to lick greedily enough. He therefore chose other animals with whom he could be certain of no such possible source of error. He chose white rats and rabbits. The rats are born blind and naked; they never eat during the first few days after birth, they only suck; and they quit the nest when between two and three weeks old. Rabbits also are born blind and naked, and quit the nest on the twenty-fifth or thirtieth day, and only suck at first. Here were all the conditions for an unexceptionable experiment. M. Flourens began to feed a rat with madder directly after she had produced her young, and examining the young on the eleventh day, every part of their osseous tissue was red. It was the same with rabbits on the ninth day. He carefully examined, in each case, the mouth, throat, stomach, and intestines of these animals, without finding a trace of the madder.

The conclusion is inevitable. The milk of the mother affects the organism of the child, and whatever the mother eats or drinks affects her milk. It has long been known, that medicines administered to the nurse affect the nursling, that if the nurse indulge in alcohol, the nursling suffers for it. But it is now clear that influences less obvious than these, influences which do not betray themselves by such easily recognized effects, must also affect the milk, and through the milk, the nursling. Although the organism, by its marvellous chemistry, transmutes the most various substances of food into the few organic compounds, *assimilating* them, as we say, so that the herbage of the meadow is converted into bone, muscle, membrane, and nerve, not distinguishable from those got out of beef-steak, there are, nevertheless, very many substances which resist this transmutaiton, which cannot be assimilated, and which act, therefore, for good or evil, like strange bodies.

MENTAL CONDITION OF BABIES.

A writer in the *Cornhill Magazine*, (May, 1863,) after discussing at some length the interesting question, " What is the mental condition of very young infants? " considers that the following conclusions are substantiated by recent scientific experiment and investigation. He says, " We cannot escape the conclusion that, from the first, a baby manifests the special sensibilities which are, as it were, the *pabulum* of the mind, and through which it gains its knowledge of the external world. Not only are the senses active, but desire, will, and expression, also manifest themselves, and all these are manifested in such varying degrees as to indicate marked individuality in several infants. Thus far science leads us. If we wish to penetrate further, and learn the condition of the " higher faculties," we are left without our experimental guide, and must rely on inference. Up to this point we have had some means of testing our inferences. The organs of sense, when stimulated, respond in the baby very much as in the adult. The emotions find their well-known expressions. This language we can interpret. But how are we to interpret the language of the higher faculties, supposing them to be in action? What can we know of the baby's imagination, abstraction, or comparison? We may warrantably reject the old notion, of the mind's being from the first well furnished with truths of wide generality, — " innate ideas," as they were called ; but the advance of psychology, founded on physiology, has made it pretty certain that if not furnished with ready-made truths, if not enriched with innate ideas, the mind is from the first furnished with hereditary tendencies and aptitudes, even in directions purely intellectual. Inasmuch as memory presupposes the experiences which are remembered, abstraction presupposes the experiences which furnish the materials, and ratiocination presupposes the experiences which furnish the propositions, we are forced to conclude that these actions of the soul emerge gradually ; but the various epochs of their emergence and development are necessarily hidden from us. According to the platonic theory, the intellectual condition of the baby is transcendentally superior to that of the philosopher, for he has just quitted the higher world of existences, and has descended amid the shadows,— the phenomena. If he is conscious of the previous state of existence, what a mist of vanishing and futile shadows must *this* world appear to him.

MARRIAGES OF CONSANGUINITY.

A recent writer in the *Westminster Review*, after discussing the evidence *pro* and *con*, relative to the injurious effects of marriages between blood-relations, thus finally expresses himself as led to the following conclusions : —

On the whole evidence before us, we cannot conclude otherwise than that the very general opinion, that there is some special law of nature which close-breeding infringes, is founded rather on a kind of superstition than on any really scientific considerations. If we look upon the question as one of science, we find that the facts given as evidence in favor of this opinion, can for the most part without difficulty be reduced under the ordinary laws of inheritance. On the other hand, the known facts brought to light by investigation among the lower animals and plants, are such as positively to disprove this hypothesis, as regards them ; and it would require much more stringent proof than any one has ever yet attempted to bring forward, in order to justify us in believing that man is under the action of physiological laws differing from those which obtain in the rest of the animal kingdom. The aspect of the question before us from the practical point of view is, however, somewhat different. Here further evidence is still required, and will, no doubt, be collected. It is, of course, conceivable, whether probable or not, that there may exist at the present time, in civilized communities, so few families really free from all taint of disease or imperfection, as to render intermarriage of blood-relations unsafe by the action of the ordinary laws of inheritance. We are ourselves strongly disposed to disbelieve, in the absence of strict evidence, in any such degenerate condition as the normal state of modern humanity ; but it is this point, and nothing further, which observation and statistics are capable of deciding ; and in order even to do this, the observations must be more careful, and the statistics far more extensive, than any which have yet been recorded.

THE DEAF AND DUMB.

In a paper recently presented to the French Academy, Dr. Boudin gives the following curious statistics: Marriages of blood-relations form about two per cent. of all marriages in France; the deaf and dumb offspring, by birth, of consanguineous marriages are in proportion to the deaf and dumb born in ordinary wedlock; at Lyons, at least twenty-five per cent; at Paris, at least twenty-eight per cent; at Bordeaux, at least thirty per cent.   2. The proportions of the deaf and dumb, by birth, increase with the degree of blood-relationship.   If the danger of having a deaf and dumb child in ordinary marriage, represented by figures, is one, there will be eighteen in marriages between first cousins; thirty-seven in marriages between uncles and nieces; seventy in marriages between nephews and aunts.   3. At Berlin we find thirty-one deaf and dumb on ten thousand Catholics, six deaf and dumb on ten thousand Protestants, twenty-seven deaf and dumb on ten thousand Jews.   In other words, the proportions of the deaf and dumb born grow with the facility religion affords to consanguinity in marriage.   4. In 1848, twenty-three deaf and dumb born of ten thousand whites were counted in the territory of Iowa (U. S.), and two hundred and twelve deaf and dumb among ten thousand slaves; a shocking proof how little our social, moral and religious laws are considered valid for the slaves.   5. The misfortune of being born deaf and dumb falls not always directly from parents wedded in consanguinity; it appears sometimes indirectly from marriages in which one of the parents issued from wedlock between blood-relations.   6. The most healthy parents, but related in blood, may have deaf and dumb children; while deaf and dumb parents, but not blood-related, very rarely beget deaf and dumb children.   7. The number of deaf and dumb born increases formidably in places where natural obstacles stand in the way of cross-marriages. Thus we have the proportion of the deaf and dumb, which in France in general is six upon ten thousand inhabitants; in Corsica, fourteen on ten thousand; in the High Alps, twenty-three on ten thousand; in Iceland, eleven; in the Canton of Berne, twenty-eight.   8. The number of the deaf and dumb in Europe may be reckoned at about 250,000.

WHY THE STOMACH DOES NOT DIGEST ITSELF.

At a late meeting of the Royal Society, England, Dr. Pavy, in a communication discussing the "Immunity enjoyed by the stomach from being digested by its own secretion during life," after stating that the "living principle" suggested by John Hunter, as the protecting agency, did not stand the test of experiment, for it had been shown that the tissues of living animals might be dissolved by the stomach secretion, said that the prevailing notion of the mucous lining of the organ serving as its source of protection by its susceptibility of constant renewal during life was equally untenable; for he had found by experiment that a patch of entire mucous membrane might be removed, and food would afterwards be digested in the stomach without the stomach itself presenting the slightest sign of attack.   The view propounded by Dr.

Pavy was one dependent on chemical principles. The existence of acidity was an absolutely essential condition for the accomplishment of the act of digestion. Now, the walls of the stomach being permeated so freely as they are during life by a current of alkaline blood, would render it impossible that their digestive solution could occur. After death, however, the blood being stagnant, there would not be the resistance to the penetration of the digestive menstruum with the retention of its acid properties that existed during the occurrence of a circulation, and thus the stomach became attacked when death took place during the digestive process, notwithstanding it had previously been maintained in so perfect a state of security. Dr. Pavy, in advocating this view, brought forward experiments which showed that digestion of the stomach might be made to take place during life. Whenever the circumstances were such that an acid liquid in the stomach could retain its acid properties whilst tending to permeate the walls of the organ, gastric solution was observed. The question of result resolved itself into degree of power between acidity within the stomach and alkalinity around. It did not appear that the digestion of living frogs' legs and the extremity of a living rabbit's ear introduced through a fistulous opening into the stomach offered any valid objection to his view. In the case of the frogs' legs, it might be fairly taken that the amount of blood possessed by the animal would be inadequate to furnish the required means of resistance. In the case of the rabbit's ear, the vascularity of it being so much less than that of the walls of the stomach, there was nothing unreasonable in conceiving that whilst the one received, the other might fail to receive protection from the circulating current, on account of the disparity of power that must belong to the two.

THE BEATING OF THE HEART.

About ten years ago, M. A. Bernard discovered a fact of very high importance, — the influence of certain nerves on the local circulation. In his first researches, this eminent physiologist demonstrated that the great sympathetic nerve was connected with the contractility of the arterial terminations; and further, the existence of nervous filaments antagonistic to the preceding, which appeared to regulate the relaxation of the vessels. These experiments, repeated by all modern physiologists, have been extended to other nerves, and show that the circulation of the blood is accelerated or retarded by nervous influences in a manner which was formerly only vaguely suspected. M. Marcy has recently studied the subject in relation to the beating of the heart, and its connection with muscular exercise, fever, and the violent emotions of anger, fear, joy, &c., all of which exercise a direct action on the peripheric circulation. He does not consider variation in the beating of the heart to be due to any change in the activity of the heart alone. Without delivering himself to any hypothesis on the subject, he says that it is certain that changes in the general circulation take place under the influence of moral emotions, the face reddens, or pales, etc. These changes must entail variations in the frequency of the beatings of the heart, so that the power which moderates or accelerates the contractions of the heart, he thinks, can be no other than the contractility of the vessels of the whole body by nervous agency.

MECHANISM EMPLOYED IN THE CIRCULATION OF THE BLOOD.

In a recent lecture on the above subject before the Royal Institution, London, Professor Marshall attributed the heart's rhythmical movements to the alternate contraction and expansion of the auricles and ventricles, — its slight rotary movement, its two peculiar sounds, one long and soft, due to the closure of large valves; the other, sharp and abrupt, due to the closing of the small, semilunar valves. The pulse was attributed to the pulsations or waves of the mass of blood, caused by the elongation and distension of the elastic walls of the arteries, and said to be simultaneous with, but distinct from, the onward flow of the blood. By means of an ingeniously-contrived apparatus, these pulsations have been measured in a number of animals. They are found to increase as the size of the animal diminishes, — e. g., the average pulse of a horse is fifty-five beats in a second; of a man, seventy-two; of a dog, ninety-six; of a rabbit, two hundred and twenty; of a squirrel, three hundred. Yet it is found that, whatever be the size of the animal, the number of beats required to complete the circulation through the whole body averages twenty-seven, and the proportion of the weight of the blood to that of the whole averages one twelfth. While in health we are perfectly unconscious of the existence of the complicated mechanism employed in the circulation of our blood; this is due to the position of the heart, and its relation to the nervous system.

INFLUENCE OF EFFORTS OF INSPIRATION ON THE HEART.

Dr. Brown-Séquard has communicated to the Royal Society his " Experimental Researches on the Influence of Efforts of Inspiration on the Movements of the Heart."

A very interesting fact, of which many circumstances have been carefully investigated by Professor Donders and Dr. S. W. Mitchell, has received a wrong explanation from those physiologists. This fact consists in a diminution of either the strength or the frequency of the beatings of the heart when an energetic effort at breathing is made and maintained for half a minute or a little more. Professor Donders thinks that this influence of inspiration on the heart is due to a mechanical agency of the dilated lungs on this organ. Dr. Brown-Séquard continues. —

It is admitted that the state of the lungs has a great influence on the heart, but the principal cause of the diminution in the movements of this organ is very different from what has been supposed by Professor Donders, by Professor J. Müller, and others. It is known that when the *medulla oblongata* or the *par vagum* is excited (either by galvanism, as the Brothers Weber have discovered, or by other means, such as a mere compression, or a sudden wound, as I have found), the heart's beatings diminish or cease entirely. Whether this stoppage be due to the cause I have attributed it to or not is indifferent to my present object. What is important is that in these cases an irritation on the origin of the *par vagum* acts through it on the heart to diminish or to destroy its action. I thought that it would be interesting to decide, if, at the time that there is an effort at inspiration, there is not also an influence of the *medulla oblongata* on the *par vagum*, more or similar to that which exists when we galvanize or otherwise irritate the *medulla oblongata*. To ascertain if it is so, I have made experiments on newly-born animals, and on birds. As I have already published some of the results of my researches on newly-born animals, and as these results are not so completely decisive as those of my experiments made on birds, I will merely give here a summary of what I have seen in these last animals. I have found the same facts in ducks, geese, and pigeons; but as I have repeated the experiments more frequently on the last-mentioned animals, I will speak of them only. When their abdomen has been widely opened and their heart exposed to sight, pigeons may live, as it is well known, for a long while. I wait until they are almost dying, having only one, two, or three inspirations in a minute, and then, if the weather is cold, and if the animal has lost many degrees of its temperature, I find that, at each effort it makes to inspire, the heart either almost suddenly stops, or beats much less quickly.

I have frequently seen the heart completely arrested for five or ten seconds, and twice for twenty or twenty-five seconds, in cases where there was only one respiration in two minutes. This stoppage of the heart's movements was the more remarkable, as they were at the rate of more than two hundred in a minute when the effort at inspiration took place. To decide that it was in consequence of an influence of the *par vagum* that this occurred, I divided this nerve in the neck, and then found that there was no more influence of the inspiration on the heart, or if there was, it consisted in an augmentation of the frequency of the movement of this organ; an augmentation due to the shaking of the heart when the chest dilated.

Sometimes, when the heart was very irritable, and when the efforts at inspiration were still frequent and not energetic (the *par vagum* being undivided), these efforts were accompanied, or rather immediately followed, by an increase in the strength of the heart's movements, probably caused by the shaking. But always when the inspiratory efforts were energetic and rare, they coexisted with a diminution or a momentary cessation of the heart's contractions; and always in these cases the section of the *par vagum* has destroyed the diminishing influence of the respiratory efforts on the heart. It would be easy to show that the influence of the inspiratory effort on the central organ of circulation is comparable to the change taking place in the pupil when the globe of the eye is drawn inward; it is an associated action.

From the facts I have found in the case of newly-born animals and birds, and from the facts observed in man by Professors J. Müller, Donders, and others, it results that, during efforts at inspiration, a nervous influence passes along the *par vagum* from the *medulla oblongata* to the heart, diminishing the movements of this organ. And, as by an action of our will we may inspire with energy, it follows that we can by an influence of our will diminish the action of our heart, just as we can contract our pupil by drawing our eyes inwards.

CIRCULATION OF POISONS IN THE SYSTEM.

A London physiologist, Mr. Blake, has lately developed some interesting results, by experiments in regard to the rapidity with which the various poisons disseminate themselves through the system, and prove fatal. We must not be understood, however, to suppose that these

23

processes are always synonymous, many poisons proving fatal without any dissemination at all.

Mr. Blake observed the following method : Having provided a delicate measure of the condition of the circulating system, by inserting into the femoral artery of the animal to be experimented on Poiseulle's hæmadynamometer (an instrument for measuring the rapidity of the circulation), he proceeded to ascertain the time required for the passage of the poisons from one part of the system to the other. This he effected chiefly by introducing various substances, previously known to paralyze the heart, directly into the vessels, and, by means of the instrument, noting the instant of time at which the first effects of the poison manifested themselves, and at which the heart ceased to beat. Without entering into a minute account of the experiments themselves, it may suffice to state that, in the dog, the time required for a poison to pass from the jugular vein to the lungs was four seconds, or from four to six seconds ; from the jugular vein to the coronary arteries of the heart, seven seconds; from the jugular vein to the carotid artery, five to seven seconds, and from the aorta to the capillaries, four seconds. A poison introduced into the jugular vein was distributed through the whole body in nine seconds. In the horse, the time required for the completion of the circulation was from twelve to twenty seconds, or somewhat less than the time (twenty-five seconds) deduced by Hering, of Stuttgardt, from his experiment. These experiments are in harmony with the more recent case of M. Claude Bernard. A saturated solution of sulphuretted hydrogen, introduced into the jugular vein of a dog, began to be eliminated from the lungs in three seconds ; and when injected into the femoral vein of the same dog, in six seconds.

ARE THE NERVES EXCITORS OR CONTROLLERS?

Owing to the excessive complexity of the vital mechanism, our ingenuity is severely taxed in every attempt to arrive at the precise function of each organ in its relation to others. The observation which to-day seems conclusive, may become dubious to-morrow, and rejected the day after, when more accurate experiments reveal the source of fallacy. This being so, we hear with little surprise that the most brilliant physiologist of the day, Claude Bernard, has been led to doubt the truth of what has been considered indubitable ever since the nervous system has been systematically investigated, namely, that nerves are *excitors*, their functions being to excite the activity of the muscles and glands to which they are distributed. His words are these : " May it not be, that we have formed false ideas relative to the influence of nerves in provoking the activity of organs? Instead of being excitors, nerves are only bridles; the organs, whose functional power is in some sort idio-organic, can only manifest that power at the moment when the nervous influence is suspended." It is certain that a perfectly quiescent muscle is thrown into activity by a stimulus applied to its nerve. M. Bernard, perhaps, means his remarks to refer only to glands, since he makes no mention of the activity of muscles.

ABSORBING POWER OF THE HUMAN SKIN.

Dr. Murray Thompson observes: "For the last sixty years physi ological and other authors have been maintaining two very opposite views in regard to the absorption by the skin of substances dissolved in the water of baths. Some authors holding that such salts as iodide of potassium readily reach the blood through the skin, when applied in the form of a bath containing that salt; while others hold that absorption, under such circumstances, never takes place.

" My experiments were all made on my own person at various intervals during the last two years. Six of them were made on as many successive nights, so as to try if frequency of bathing rendered the skin more permeable. The general method of making the trials was this: Into an ordinary bath a measured quantity of warm water was let, the temperature of which was recorded. Means were taken to keep the heat constant during the experiment. The temperatures ranged usually from 90° to 98°. The salt to be tried was then dissolved and mixed with the water. The time in the bath was noted; it varied from half an hour to one hour and a quarter. The whole body was immersed, excepting the head and neck. All the urine voided in twenty-four hours after each bath was collected and concentrated, then tested for the substances experimented on. Six baths were taken, in which iodide of potassium was dissolved. The quantity of the salt varied from 200 to 1300 grains. Five baths, in which quantities of ferro-cyanide of potassium, varying from 1400 to 5000 grains, were dissolved. Four baths were taken, the water of which was rendered strongly alkaline by soda. The result of these fifteen experiments was, that I could not find that any of the substances in the baths passed through the skin into the blood, so as to be found in the urine; the soda baths did not render it alkaline, nor could I detect the other salts in it; and it is to be noted that the tests for them were extremely delicate.

" The general conclusion which my experiments lead me to are, — 1. That though not denying that absorption by the skin of aqueous solution does take place, yet it seems to be the exception and not the rule. 2. That medicated warm baths, whether natural or artificial, do not appear to owe any virtue they may have to the substances dissolved in them reaching the blood through the skin. At the same time, as there are other ways by which one can conceive such baths to operate on the system, it is not to be concluded that, because absorption may not take place, such baths are useless as therapeutic agents." —*Proc. Royal Soc. Edinburgh.*

ACTION OF DIFFERENT MEDICINES ON THE MENTAL FACULTIES.

" All stimulant and exciting medicines increase the quantity of blood that is sent to the brain. If this quantity exceeds a certain amount, then most of the faculties of the mind become over-excited. Nevertheless, the degree of this action is observed to vary a good deal in different cerebral organizations; and it is also found that certain stimulants exercise a peculiar and characteristic influence upon special or individual faculties. Thus ammonia and its preparations, as well as musk, castor, wine, and ether, unquestionably enliven the imaginative powers, and thus serve to render the mind more fertile and creative. The empyreumatic oils are apt to induce a tendency to melancholy and mental hallucinations. Phosphorus acts on the instinct of propagation, and increases sexual desire; hence it has often been recommended in cases of impotence. Iodine seems to have a somewhat analogous influence; but then it often diminishes, at the same time, the energy of the intellectual powers. Cantharides, it is well known, are a direct stimulant of the sexual organs; while camphor tends to moderate and lull the irritability of these parts.

" Of the metals, arsenic has a tendency to induce lowness and depression of the spirits; while the preparations of gold serve to elevate and excite them. Mercury is exceeding apt to bring on a morbid sensibility, and an inaptitude for all active occupation.

"Of narcotics, opium is found to augment the erotic propensities, as well as the general powers of the intellect, but more especially the imagination. In smaller doses it enlivens the ideas and induces various hallucinations, so that it may be truly said that, during the stupor which it induces, the mind continues to be awake while the body is asleep. In some persons opium excites inordinate loquacity. Dr. Gregory says that this effect is observed more especially after the use of the muriate of morphia. He noticed this effect in numerous patients; and he then tried the experiment on himself with a similar result. He felt, he tells us, while under the operation, an invincible desire to speak, and possessed, moreover, an unusual fluency of language. Hence he recommends its use to those who may be called upon to address any public assembly, and who have not sufficient confidence in their own unassisted powers.

" Other narcotics are observed to act very differently on the brain and its faculties from opium. Belladonna usually impairs the intellectual energies; hyoscyamus renders the person violent, impetuous, and ill-mannered. Conium dulls and deadens the intellect, and digitalis is decidedly anti-aphrodisiac. Hemp will often induce an inextinguishable gayety of spirits. Tobacco acts in a very similar manner with opium, even in those persons who are accustomed to its use; almost all smokers assert that it stimulates the powers of the imagination.

" If the psychological action of medicines were better known, medical men might be able to vary their exhibition, according to the characters and mental peculiarities of their patients. The treatment of different kinds of monomaniacal derangement also might be much improved; and it is not improbable but that even a favorable change might be wrought on certain vicious and perverse dispositions, which unfortunately resist all attempts at reformation, whether in the way of admonition, reproof, or even of correction." — *Prof. Otto, Medico-Chirurgical Review.*

IS FRESH AIR NECESSARY DURING SLEEP?

Most readers will be surprised that such a question should be asked; to ask it, they would say, is to answer it. An eminent French physiologist, M. Delbruck, however, has recently doubted the affirmative of the above proposition, in a paper of some merit, presented to the French Academy, in which he propounds a difficulty, arising out of the consideration of some very familiar facts. He thinks that the calculations of physiologists are erroneously exaggerated, and that very much less air (or, what comes to the same thing, air of less purity) is needed during sleep. He first appeals to animals. The lion, bear, or tiger retires into his lair to sleep, quitting the open air, and excluding it as much as possible. The dog seeks his kennel or corner, curls himself up, and buries his head beneath his paws or body. Even birds, those aërial creatures, who perish so rapidly when confined under a bell-glass, and therefore seem peculiarly dependent upon fresh air, when sleep approaches, hide their heads under their wings, the beak covered with the soft down. Hibernating animals, as is well known, never pass into their long sleep but when sheltered from the air. All this is very true, but what about man? Acting upon instinct, man imitates the animals; upon science, he does the very reverse. The schoolboy, if he is cold, or if he cannot sleep, hides his head under the bedclothes much as the bird hides its head under a wing. The unenlightened man or woman carefully draws the curtains round the bed. The enlightened physician or nurse tears those curtains down. Soldiers and travellers " camping out" are obliged to cover their heads if they wish to sleep; and railway travellers at night, although six or eight may be in one carriage. always finish by closing the windows.

These, and other facts of similar significance, require to be well considered. The suggestion of M. Delbruck does not, we confess, present a very acceptable aspect to us. He supposes that since plants, during the night, absorb the oxygen which they exhale during the day, " analogy would lead to the conclusion that animals at night absorb some of the carbonic acid which they exhale during the day." Analogy is a treacherous guide ; and in the present case, a more comprehensive acquaintance with the physiological facts would have recognized the imperfection of the analogy. It is true, that plants absorb oxygen during the night ; but it is only the woody parts, and *these absorb it also during the day*, although the quantities are so small as to be almost inappreciable. It is the green parts which absorb carbonic acid during the day, and these requiring the stimulus of sunlight, are inactive at night.— Nothing of the kind takes place in the animal organism. The blood refuses to absorb carbonic acid from the atmosphere, at all times, and under all conditions.

What, then, is our explanation of the paradox? Why, if the fresh air is so indispensable to the waking organism, is it less so to the sleeping organism? In other words, why can we sleep with a very moderate supply of oxygen? Physiology furnishes an answer. Sleep is a condition during which the *vital functions are all depressed.* It, therefore, is incompatible with any excitement of the functions ; as we see in the sleeplessness which succeeds over-fatigue or over-excitement, (and which, by the way, suggests that the proverb, " After supper walk a mile," must not be stretched to, "After supper walk five miles.") Hence, the stimulating effect of oxygen too freely administered, is instinctively avoided by man and beast, in order that sleep may be placid and undisturbed. Sleep requires diminished activity of the circulation, and *external* warmth to compensate for this diminished activity. Hence an atmosphere that is at once highly oxygenated and cold prevents sleep.

No rational reader will push these suggestions to absurd extreme
23*

because there may have been an oversight in the popular opinion, respecting the beneficial effect of well-ventilated dormitories, we are not to conclude that ventilation even in dormitories is useless. Far from it. The question is a question of degree. That amount of fresh air which permits prolonged sleep is the standard we must aim at, but better to have impure air than cold."— *Cornhill Magazine.*

WHY ANIMALS TO BE EATEN MUST BE KILLED.

It is universally understood that animals which die from disease are not fitted for our markets. It is also understood, that when cattle have been over-driven, their meat is notably inferior to that of healthy animals, unless they are permitted to recover their exhausted energies before being slaughtered. Why is this? The first and most natural supposition respecting those which die from disease is that their flesh is tainted; but it has been found that prolonged agony or exhaustion is quite as injurious, though in these cases there is no taint of disease. M. Claude Bernard propounds the following explanation: In all healthy animals, no matter to what class they belong, or on what food they subsist, he finds a peculiar substance, analogous to vegetable starch, existing in their tissues, and especially in their liver. This substance he calls *glycogène, i. e.* the sugar-former. It is abundant in proportion to the vigor and youth of the animal, and disappears entirely under the prolonged suffering of pain or disease. This disappearance is singularly rapid in fish; and is always observed in the spontaneous death of animals. But when the death is sudden none of it disappears. He finds that a rabbit, for example, which is killed after suffering pain for five or six hours, exhibits no trace whatever of this sugar-forming substance: and its flesh has a marked difference in flavor. The same remark applies to exhausted over-driven animals; their muscles are nearly deficient in *glycogène,* and yield in water a far larger proportion of soluble principles than the same muscles in a normal condition. M. Bernard finds, moreover, that animals which are suffocated lose more of the sugar-forming substance than similar animals killed in the slaughter-house. To this let us add the fact, that the blood of over-driven animals will not coagulate, or coagulates very slowly and imperfectly; and we shall see good reason for exercising some circumspection over the practices of our meat markets.

CHANGES IN THE HABITS OF FISH.

At a recent meeting of the Boston Society of Natural History, Capt. Atwood, of Provincetown, Mass., gave an account of the changes the fisheries of the New England coast had undergone; and of the variable habits of many species of fish. Early accounts state, that up to 1764, blue-fish (*Tennodon saltator* Cuv.) were very common north of Cape Cod; after which date they disappeared. Having had an experience of forty years in connection with the fisheries, he could say that none had been seen north of Cape Cod, until twenty-five years ago, when he saw his first blue-fish. Those found at that time were invariably small, the largest weighing about two pounds. In 1839, they were caught off Nantucket, weighing eight to ten pounds; in two or three years more those coming north of Cape Cod were larger, and ~ve away the mackerel and smaller fishes, and completely filled

Provincetown Harbor. They are found now in great abundance. They make their appearance in June, coming into the harbors all at once, and driving away the mackerel entirely. On one occasion they came on the 22d of June; the day previous 8,000 mackerel were caught in the harbor; on the 22d, not one was to be found. They leave the coast with the appearance of the first cold northeast storm, about the last of September, though two or three individuals were taken in Provincetown, December, 1862. They have only recently come into the market, for several years ago scarcely any were sold; but during the past season, he alone had brought to the market 45,000 pounds weight.

Since their great increase, the lobsters (*Homarus americanus* Dekay) had multiplied four-fold, for the natural enemies of their young had been driven away by the blue-fish. Formerly these fish appeared in large shoals near the surface, constantly " flouncing out " of the water, and they were caught in sweep seines and by the hook; now, though they come in large quantities, they seem to prefer the deeper waters.

Mackerel (*Scomber vernalis* Mitch.) also had changed their habits much. The former method used in catching them was by dragging hooks on lines twenty fathoms long, and constantly raising and lowering them; now they are caught at the surface with bait, large quantities of it being strewn alongside to attract them. The bait used is generally the poorer mackerel, ground up. The former method of obtaining them has now entirely failed.

The Cod (*Morrhua americana*) upon the Banks of Newfoundland seem also to have changed their habits. Formerly, all the fish were caught on board of the vessels while lying at anchor. The vessels take a crew of eight men, each using two lines; when the fish were abundant, all the men would fish, but usually not more than half the crew; at times, when no fish could be taken, all the lines but one would be drawn in, and then they would begin to be taken abundantly; but let two or more men begin to drop their lines, and not an individual would be taken; while, should all the lines but one be again taken in, the captures would once more be frequent. This suggested the idea of carrying small boats with them, so that each man could fish apart from the others, and in this they met with perfect success: and, generally, when all the fishermen in the boats would catch them plentifully, few or none could be taken from on board the vessel. Capt. Atwood thought that the cause was the different motion of the small boats from the vessel, as there is constantly an agitation of the waves upon the Banks.

THE HEARING OF FISHES.

Fishes can do no more than be sensible of a noise. They cannot distinguish modulations or differences of tone.

One is reluctant to destroy a pet idea, however poetical and pretty, yet the searcher into scientific truths is often compelled to do so. It is so in this instance, for truth compels the assertion of the impossibility of the supposed fact that fishes delight in musical sounds, or come to be fed by the attraction of a whistle. The true explanation is, that the vibration of the footstep, not of the whistle, is the source of attraction This may be proved by a walk along the margin of any canal or pon·

Every one must have noticed that a footstep will instantly startle any of the finny tribe that may be lurking under the grassy margin.   On the other hand, if the observer be standing still, he may talk or whistle almost as loud as he likes, without the fishes' taking the slightest notice, provided he keeps himself and his shadow out of sight. — *W. W. Stoddard On the Auditory Organs of the Lower Animals. — London Intellectual Observer.*

How Whales Hear. — Had aquatic animals the ears of aerial ones, they would, owing to the superior conduction of sound by water than by air, be stunned by what we should call a slight noise.   The whale, then, being a true warm-blood mammal, and at the same time living the life of a fish, how can it hear?   The truth is, that the cetacean ear is a very wonderful combination of the ichthyic and mammalian organ.   It hears, as it were, backwards; for the Eustachian tube opens into the blowhole, while the external orifice is nearly closed.   The petrotympanic bone acts as a true otolith, while the mammalian ossicula and tympanic membrane are also present.   When, therefore, the cetacean comes to the surface for air, it hears aërial vibrations through the Eustachian tube, while at the same time the otolithic ear is immersed, and cognizant of aquatic sounds. — *Ibid.*

THE EYE OF THE SPERM WHALE.

At a recent meeting of the Boston Society of Natural History, Dr. Jeffries Wyman gave the following account of a dissection of an eye of the sperm whale and the parts surrounding it : —

On examining the region of the eye, an enormous development of the muscles was immediately observed.   The sclerotic coat of the eye was very thick, and likewise formed a very thick sheath around the optic nerve, imbedding the bloodvessels, and almost as hard as bone.   It was found, however, to contain no ossific matter, and to be simply very dense, fibrous tissue.   Behind the globe of the eye, and occupying a large space, was a large venous plexus.   The eyelids were thick, and the conjunctiva folded back in such a manner as to permit the eye to recede in the socket.   The globe of the eye, together with the optic nerve, weighed three and a half ounces.   The powerful retractor muscle, analogous to that of ruminants, weighed five and a half ounces. The other muscles seemed only indirectly connected with the globe, and their use seemed rather to be to open the lid than to move the globe.   The muscles which were attached to the lids were of great size, and together weighed one and a half pounds.   The object of such muscular power he could not divine.   The vascular plexus distended would tend somewhat to force forward the eye, and a sphincter muscle behind the eye would have a similar effect ; but these do not seem to demand such extensive muscular power.

ANIMAL EPIDEMICS.

Don Ramon Paez, in his recent work "*Life in the Llanos, Venezuela,*" South America, states, that at certain seasons, nature appears to interfere most actively for the prevention of a superabundance of animal life on the banks and in the waters of the great rivers, which flow through the dense forests and over the Llanos, or luxuriant plains of Venezuela ; — a circumstance which has a bearing on the extinction of species, which is known to have occurred in geological periods. This is effected through the prevalence of an epidemic disease, which apparently has its origin in the decomposition of vegetable detritus, at or near the river's head waters. Its ravages are thus described as witnessed on the river *Apure*, in Venezuela : —

" The first symptoms of the epidemic appeared among the crocodiles, whose hideous carcasses might then be seen floating down the stream in such prodigious numbers, that both the waters and air of that fine region were tainted with their effluvium. It was observed that they were first seized with a violent fit of coughing, followed by a black vomit which compelled them to quit their watery home, and finally find a grave amongst the thickets on the river banks. The disease next attacked the fish and other inhabitants of the water, with equal violence, until it was feared the streams would be depopulated. The fearful mortality among them can be better estimated from the fact that, for more than a month, the rippling waves of that noble river, the Apure, were constantly washing down masses of putrefaction, its placid surface being by them actually hidden from view for several weeks. The next victims were the pachidermata of the swamps; and it was a pitiable sight to see the sluggish *chigüires* (capyvaras), and the grizzly wild-boars dragging their paralyzed hind-quarters after them ; hence the name of *derrengadera* applied to this disease. Not even monkeys in their aërial retreats escaped the contagion, and their melancholy cries resounded day and night through the woods like wailings of the eternally lost. It is a singular fact, that while the scourge did not spare any of the countless droves of horses roaming the savannas of the Apure and adjacent plains, donkeys, and horned cattle were seldom, if ever attacked, so that, by their aid, the owners of cattle-farms were enabled to prevent the entire dispersion of their herds."

Some of the Venezuelian rivers are infested with a peculiarly ferocious and blood-thirsty fish known as the *caribe*, which, though not larger than a perch, is one of the most formidable creatures that man or beast can have the misfortune to encounter. Their sharp, triangular teeth, arranged in the same manner as those of the shark, are so strong, that neither copper, steel, nor twine can withstand them, and hence the angler stands no chance of sport where the *caribe* is found. " The sight of any red substance," says Don Ramon, " blood especially, seems to rouse their sanguinary appetite ; and as they usually go in swarms, it is extremely dangerous for man or beast to enter the water with even a scratch upon their bodies. Horses wounded with the spur are particularly exposed to their attacks, and so rapid is the work of destruction, that unless immediate assistance is rendered, the fish soon penetrate the abdomen of the animal, and speedily reduce it to a skeleton." This cannibal fish is as beautiful in aspect as it is fierce in nature. " Large spots of a brilliant orange hue cover a great portion of its body, especially the belly, fins, and tail. Toward the back, it is of a bluish-ash color, with a slight tint of olive-green, the intermediate spaces being of a pearly white, while the gill-covers are tinged with red." This fish, however, suffers from a special and constantly recurring visitation ; being subject to a yearly mortality during the heat of summer when the water is deprived of a portion of the air it hold‹ in solution. " Their carcasses," says Don Raymon, " may then l seen floating on the water by thousands, while the beach is strewn with their bones, especially their bristling jaws, which render walking barefoot on the borders of lagoons extremely dangerous."

MARINE LIFE AT GREAT DEPTHS.

At a recent meeting of the Boston Society of Natural History, Mr. Marcou observed, in regard to deep sea-soundings, that a Norwegian naturalist had recently obtained, — by means of the same instruments used by Capt. McClintock and Dr. Wallich, — between Cape North and Spitzbergen, living animals from a depth of 8400 feet (more than a mile and a half;) at this depth, where the temperature was only three-tenths of a degree centigrade (nearly the freezing point), were found living polyps, mussels, tunicata, annelides, and bright-colored crustaceans. The same naturalist had found ammonites (probably Jurassic), and leaves resembling those of the palmetto (probably miocene), at Spitzbergen.

Mr. M. also referred to some animals which had been drawn up by the broken telegraphic cable between Africa and Marseilles. The Mediterranean is very deep along some portions of this line, even three or four miles; living acephala, very rare on the coasts, echinoderms of a very beautiful red color, had been drawn up from a depth of two miles, where, probably, no light penetrates. From this and similar instances, previously alluded to, he was led to the opinion that we know very little about the downward extension of submarine animal life.

Dr. Gould observed that the deep living animals are red or bright colored, while those most exposed to the light, like the clam, are white. He did not think it proved that this cable had ever reached the bottom or the depth indicated; and we know comparatively little that is certain in regard to the penetration of light to great depths; still, facts are constantly coming to notice, showing that the range of animals in the marine depths is much greater than was till recently admitted.

Prof. Agassiz alluded to the beautiful variety of color in the liver of fishes, the color being even characteristic of genera, though he was unable to state upon what structure or secretion the color depended; the color of the bile has a remarkable uniformity in the class. He stated that, according to Oersted, different rays of light penetrate to different depths in water, — green the least and red the deepest.

Mr. Marcou said that the fact of the more extended distribution in depth of marine animals would have important geological bearings, as changing the views of paleontologists in regard to the necessity of a shore line for many fossil species.

Dr. Pickering remarked that the clearness of the water made a great difference in the depth to which light will penetrate, though it will certainly penetrate to a considerable depth even in turbid water. Fishes were obtained by Risso from great depths in the basin of Nice, even from 3000 feet, which had the eyes very large.

BREEDING OF OYSTERS.

The sowing and breeding of oysters has recently been undertaken by the French Government, upon an extensive scale. The place chosen for experimenting is a part of the Bay of St. Brieuc, at a locality where the bottom is a shelly sand, slightly mixed with clay or mud.

The tide, which there runs from N. W. to S. W., and from S. W. to N. W., at the rate of about three miles an hour, keeps the water constantly renewed, and carries off all unhealthy deposits, and contracts, by breaking against the rocks on the shore, the necessary vivifying properties. The immersion of the breeding oysters was commenced in March, and concluded about the end of April, during which time about 3,000,000 of oysters, taken some from the sea, were distributed in ten longitudinal beds in different parts of the bay, forming together a superficies of 1000 hectares. The position for these banks had been traced out beforehand on a chart, and floating flags were placed to direct the movement of the vessels engaged in the operation. In order that the immersion of the oysters should be made with perfect regularity, and that the female oysters should not be injured by lying too thickly one over the other, two steamers, towing boats laden with oysters, proceeded from one end of the bank marked out to the other, letting down the oysters as they went, and then, when reaching the other end, turning round and retracing their way, thus distributing the fish with as much regularity as a plough could turn up a furrow in a field. After having laid down the oysters in conditions most favorable for their multiplication, it was necessary to organize around and over them prompt means for collecting the spawn, and constraining it to fix itself on the spot. One of the plans adopted to accomplish this object was to cover the bottom of the new bed with old oyster shells, so that not a single embryo could fall without finding a solid body to fix itself to. The second plan, as already stated in a former report, was to place long lines of boughs of trees, arranged like fascines, from one extremity of each bed to the other. These fascines were ballasted by a weight placed at the bottom, and the tops of them when fixed in their position, stood about eighteen or twenty inches above the bed of oysters, and thus prevented any of the spawn from being carried away by the current. These fascines were placed by men with diving dresses. As the cords with which the fascines were at first fastened would soon wear out, the report states that they may hereafter be replaced by small chains of galvanized iron, manufactured for the purpose in the arsenals of the State. The most exact indications have been made on the chart of the bay, so that the fascines may be taken up as regularly, in order that the oysters attached to them may be collected, as a farmer could pick the fruit from his trees. The report then goes on to say that, although six months have scarcely elapsed since the operations were performed, the result has exceeded the most sanguine expectations. The fascines have on their branches such clumps of oysters that they resemble trees in an orchard, the boughs of which are in the spring hidden by the exuberance of the blossoms.

INSECT VISION.

The following article is communicated to the *Intellectual Observer*, by Hon. Richard Hill, of Jamaica: In setting up a collection of crickets, locusts, and grasshoppers, we see that there is a prevailing color, as marked and as intense in the eyes as in the body; thus, locusts are red; grasshoppers green; and crickets black; and their eyes are of similar decided hues. Are we to infer that objects to them have the same tint as these hues of the choroid? Are they colored ι we see landscapes to be when we look through a window of painted glass ? Through the red, are objects beheld as if they were blazing in a fiery furnace ; or do they appear as frigid as a snow scene in blue eyes — as through the blue glass ? Some purpose is served by the relation.

In the solar spectrum, there are rays independent of those of light, which impart a sensation of heat. These calorific rays are most abundant a little beyond the red verge of the spectrum, and diminish gradually toward the violet. When it was observed, in the Conservatory at Kew, that plants suffered from the scorching influence of the calorific rays through the glass covering, a series of experiments were pursued to ascertain the possibility of cutting off the heat-imparting rays by means of tinted glass. A glass tinted of a pale yellow-green prevented the permeation of the heat rays to the maximum of the calorific action. The pinky hue of the light was modified, and the scorching influence subdued. What they sought to accomplish was effected. They obtained a properly moderated heat.

White is the simultaneous sensation of all the prismatic colors. By suppressing red, we obtain a bluish-green hue ; by suppressing the blue and the green, we obtain an excess of yellow and red. The purest air, or clearest water, gradually extinguishes, by absorption, the rays passing through it. The natural stimulus of the retina is the action of the luminous rays. Modifications are essential where the activity of perception may be allied to the conditions of diseased sight. " Many are the waves and coruscations, the fiery clouds and flaming spectra which haunt the amaurotic when certain morbid complications exist," and when the optic nerve is peculiarly influenced, a compensatory modification of the peculiarity in regard to tint is made by the adoption of colored glasses for the sight. We may presume that what is in excess in the locust is modified by the red pigment of the eye, and what is superabundant in the grasshopper by the yellow and the blue.

The eyes of insects are what are called facetted eyes. They are cut in hexagonal compartments, and have the appearance and the power of multiplying glasses. The outer coat is composed of a thin plate, resembling horn. It is stiff but flexible, and compact but transparent. Immediately beneath each corneule or hexagonal compartment, that is, beneath the facets of the outer covering of the eye, is a layer of color. It covers the whole of the inner surface of the corneules, excepting only in the centre of each where a minute aperture is seen, admitting light by the iris. Between the iris and the end of the cornea is a space, flattened and convex, filled with an aqueous humor. Each convex lens corresponds with each facet. The rays of light passing through them fall upon a transparent space occupied by a vitreous humor. The choroid in the eyes of insects, like the choroid in the vertebrata, is the proper vascular structure of the organ of vision. The pigment of the choroid is subject to much variety of color in different insects. In some it is nearly black, in others dark blue, violet, green, purple, brown, and yellow, and in some, two or three layers of pigment are of different colors. The usual arrangement of these variegated pigments is, first, a dark-colored portion near the bulb of the optic nerve, then a lighter color, and lastly, again, a darker near the cornea.

Puget adjusted the eye of a flea (*Pulex irritans*) in such a way as to see objects through it. On applying the microscope to the multitude of mirrors, nothing could exceed the singularity of what was seen. "A soldier appeared like an army of pigmies; for what it multiplied it diminished; the arch of a bridge exhibited a spectacle more magnificent than any edifice erected by human skill; and the flame of a candle seemed the illumination of a thousand lamps." The minute regularity of the objects in each of the facets, so disposed as to converge to a central ganglion, make but a single picture in perception. The great optic nerve uniting into a focal point the coincidence of what Dr. Wells designates "*the visual direction*," impresses an image intensely concentrated. The perception of each impression being confined to that of the object immediately in a line with the axis of vision, the impacted lights and shadows of a thousand representations of one and the same form — the visual product of a thousand facets — give a stereoscopic representation under a thousand adjustments, and render the small organ of the small animal, in power and concentration, a microscope. The successive zones in the insect eye modify the rays that penetrate the sight, passing by each facet, and by the centre of each converging cylinder radiating to the optic ganglion. The layer of pigment does nothing but diminish the quantity of light, and adjust it. It is found in most if not all *diurnal insects*, and the iris being perforated with as many holes as there are facets in the cornea, it is subjected to multiplied modifications. As might be expected, this pigment is not met with in any of the *nocturnal insects*.

Insects that fly require an ample field of vision. The combined corneules become one large pupil. The multiplied facets render superfluous eyelids and muscles to move the eye. In consequence of the vision being directed to the whole circumference, it comprehends, by relative adjustment, all objects around. A simpler eye occurs in the grovelling insects that see only what is near with distinctness. In insects which fly by night, like the moths, there is, in place of the black or colored pigment, a substance of a resplendent green, or silvery color, serving not to absorb, but to reflect the rays of light, and enabling them to see by a more obscure illumination than that of daylight. The eyes of moths look always luminous, and appear as if they were phosphorescent, from this reflecting power. This organization gives a solution to the reason why moths fly to the candle. They lose all discernment in the blaze of radiance that overwhelms them by reflection; and they perish in the flame into which they rush.

I requested a friend to verify for me Puget's examination of the facetted eye of an insect, by an inspection of the organ under a large microscope. He complied with my request, and sent me the following letter: —

"My Dear Sir, — I have taken a dragon-fly (*Libellula*) as the study of the eye of an insect.

"The eye was first simply removed from the head of the dragon-fly and examined under a good lens; seen thus, it seemed as if it were covered with intensely small drops of water, something like dew. The eye was next immersed in solvents, and cleaned with a fine camel's-hair brush, leaving nothing behind but the cornea. This to the naked eye had the appearance of a white, transparent, horny substance, hav-

24

ing the form of a shallow cup. It was now placed under a microscope with a power of 250 diameters, or magnifying 62,500 times.

" Under this power the bead-like appearance, noticed with the simple lens, resolved itself into a definite form, resembling precisely the cells of the honeycomb as they appear on the broad plane. Like these cells, each division was hexagonal. The substance of each division was convex exteriorly. We are reminded that this is the form which economizes space the most, and that it is also the form always taken by the *equal* sized round bodies when *equally* pressed together. This law we see exemplified in the cellular tissue of plants, and we account for the elongated form of the cells of the fibrous tissue, by *unequal* pressure. We see this law in the formation of the cells of the honeycomb, as equally sized globular cells equally pressed *laterally*, and forming hexagonal cells. We see it again, though imperfectly, it is true, in soap-bubbles. Might we not, therefore, infer that this peculiar form is the natural effect of a known law, and that it could not assume any other form? But to remove all doubt, we must prove our premises, that is, if the facets of an insect's eye, composed originally of an immense number of spheres of equal size, equally pressed, laterally, pass into the hexagonal form, or suffer any other modification. That they are of equal size is manifest from simple inspection.

" We will now see if experiments prove they are, or have been, spheres; but I must first speak of some further examination of the cornea. I counted the number of facets, or faces, by the micrometer, and found in each eye 12,500, but I think they are somewhat more numerous. Around each facet I found a fringe of fine hairs which seem to fulfil the purpose of eyelashes.

" I now placed the cornea in such a manner, that, in looking through the microscope, and *through* the cornea, I could see the flame of a candle. I then saw, not one flame, but an immense number of flames ; in fact, an illumination of candles on a large scale, which arrangement quite corresponded with the hexagonal form of the facets ; thus there was a row of flames, and above this another row, not one flame above another, but intermediate flames in intermediate rows, and so on one row with another. Each facet is then a distinct eye, producing a distinct image in each facet.

"An ordinary observer might infer that the insect saw not one object, but a multitude of objects ; not one flower, but thousands, producing a complete ' *embarras de richesses*,' most confusing to the poor fly. It is natural that we should be led to such a conclusion. But, on the other hand, we are taught by analogy that ' Order is Nature's first law.' To help us to the clue of this second point, or of this apparent confusion, we will continue our experiments. Taking for granted that spheres were upon the disk, I severed them with a needle and found one end of the several pieces circular, and the other pointed ; in fact, each separate ocellus, or eye, had the form of a cone, the basis forming the facet, and the apex converging to a centre. Each was imbedded in a mass of pigment, — in plain terms, black paint; with each apex receiving a filament of the optic nerve. Each separate ocellus, therefore, has a separate power of vision. Each facet, cone, and filament being separated from all other facets, cones, and filaments by a layer of pigment, forms a separate ocellus, so circumstanced that no ray of light received by one passes into another, and all the filaments being severed from each other by the pigment, they in no way interfere with one another.

" We now see, by experiment, that as each ocellus takes up a distinct picture, each picture is, necessarily, slightly altered in perspective. The images, by the direction of the facetted mirrors severally, are each slightly varied; but being united on the central ganglion, they form one perception of one object, or one scene. This is only a multiplication of the incidents of our own vision with two eyes. If we close one eye, we see an object in a certain perspective ; if we close that eye that was open, and open that which was shut, we see the same object in another perspective ; yet if we open both eyes we do not see two images of the same object in different perspectives, but only one object in proper visual union by coincident perception.

" The movable eyes in ourselves, and the immovable eyes in the insect, do not affect this analogy. The multitude of facets accommodate the immovable eyes to a whole panorama. The stereoscope will illustrate all the facts in both circumstances of vision. In the stereoscope we have exhibited to us two representations of the same object in different perspectives : — the difference corresponds with the distance between the two lenses through which we are looking ; they are both immovable, but visually combined, they are but one perception of one and the same object. In the same way insects, with their multiplied incidents of vision, see by coincidence but one representation from a multitude of eyes."

THE SLEEP OF INSECTS — BY RICHARD HILL.

The ocelli, or secondary eyes of insects, which Linnæus regarded as a kind of coronet, and called *stemmata*, and which Reaumur conceived were designed for that near vision, which the primary eyes, by their immovable structure, could not accomplish with proper distinctness, have, I have but little doubt, by the experiments which have been made on vision, and on the excitement of sleep, a very important influence in determining somnolency in insects. The vast field of objects commanded in vision, without the concentration of attention, is one of variety, but not of accuracy. In insects there is no dilation or contraction of a pupil to accommodate the sight to the circumstances of light and darkness. By attention we are conscious of perception. If the attention be limited to one point of a landscape, it sees only the objects *there*, and though there be visual impressions, there are no visual perceptions, where the mind is not attentively absorbed on what it is looking at. It is without the consciousness of seeing.

How do insects, with their great orbicular eyes always exposed to external stimulants, sleep ? Sleep, like the inclination for food, is periodical. The habit in the lower animals is the alternation of light and darkness, in the degree in which one indicates day and the other night; for in a total eclipse birds retire to roost, and the diurnal insects resort to repose, and the nocturnal awake.[1] The influence that tends to

---

[1] Lyon Playfair, in his lectures on the application of physiology to the rearing of cattle, gives a very remarkable illustration of the influence of rapid alternations of light and darkness, without reference to the diurnal revolutions of the earth, in inducing sleep and inclination for food, in the Italian mode of rapidly fattening orto-

wakefulness or to slumber is the condition of the nervous system. If its functional activity be protracted, the vision gives way under the exhaustion of the nervous powers. If the action of the mind be purely intellectual, if the feelings be not excited under that action, the waste sensorially suffered is to be repaired by sleep, and the sensation of slumber becomes uncontrollable. The demand for sleep is the desire to have it; and whether the absence of sensorial impressions results from the settling of the mind to rest, or whether it be that darkness cuts off all stimulation from light, or silence conduces to repose, sleep is induced by the cessation of all visual or emotional excitement. If the mind be withdrawn from the consciousness of its own operations, or if it be acted upon by a monotony that either wearies attention, or, distracting it, leaves the sensorial image without perceptive impression, the result is slumber, or the nervous relaxation of sleep.

When the mind divides itself between the thoughts and the emotions, mental activity being unsuspended, and the feelings unappeased, the restlessness of anxiety becomes the inquietude of wakefulness; and, though there be weariness of both heart and soul, tired nature remains ungratified by the restoration of sleep.

Having thus indicated the circumstances under which beings slumber that combine an intelligent nature with a sensational one, let us examine *how* insects sleep. When the senses are blunted to external impressions, under the lessened excitability of the mind, and our ideas, more confused than vivid, are carried beyond ourselves in time and place, we instinctively lie down to repose. All the creatures organized with eyelids close the eyes against the influence of light. The temperature of the body sinks, owing to diminished nervous energy, and we seek with soft things to rest upon, warm things to cherish us with heat, and then we go to sleep. The lower animals instinctively do what we do, though each accommodates itself differently. The horse will sleep standing in the warm shelter of the stable, though it lies down in the pasture; the bird reposes perching, but with its head buried in the feathers of the wing; the serpent coils itself in a circle, or folds itself into the smallest possible space; the fish screens itself in the weeds, or buries itself in the sand or in the mud of the stream; the insect withdraws from the scenes of its ordinary activity, and is in a state of somnolent rest, when it remains motionless. As the insect has no eyelids, no external closure of the eye gives evidence of sleep.

As all the physiological facts of sleep in the vertebrate animal coincide with effects exhibited by the heart and brain, and as insects have neither of these organic centres, then sleep cannot be induced by any

lane. At a certain hour in the morning, the keeper of the birds places a lantern in the orifice of the wall, made for the special purpose of darkening and illumining the room. The dim light thrown by the lantern on the floor of the apartment induces the ortolans to believe that the sun is about to rise, and they wake and greedily consume the food upon the floor. The lantern is withdrawn, and the succeeding darkness acting as an actual night, the ortolans fall asleep. During sleep, little of the food being expended in the production of force, most of it goes to the formation of flesh and fat. After the birds have been allowed to repose for one or two hours, to carry on digestion and assimilation, the keeper again exhibits the lantern through ●c aperture. The mimic daylight awakes the birds again; again they rise and feed; again darkness ensues, and again they sleep. The representative ●unshine is made to shed its rays four or five times every day, and as many nights ●ow its transitory beams. The ortolans thus treated become like balls of fat in ● days.

peculiar change, either in lessening or quickening the flow of blood from one extremity to the other, but must result solely from the quietude of the senses, and from electrical incidents externally. Cabanis, in his *Rapports du Physique et Moral*, has observed in man that some of the members and senses go to sleep sooner than others. He assigns the soporific influence sensationally to fatigue. The part first feels drowsy in which the flow of the blood is affected. Among the senses, the eye is the first that goes to sleep; after it the smell, taste, hearing, and touch become successively drowsy. The touch is never entirely insensitive. The sight is more difficult to awaken than the hearing; a slight noise will rouse a sleep-walker who had suffered light upon his unshut eyes without any apparent influence; but insects, if affected at all internally, are very little affected in this way.

The insect world are acutely acted upon by atmospheric circumstances. Rain or cloudy weather operates upon them like a continuance or recurrence of night. It is not the warmth or the dryness of the air, its humid state or its coldness; it is the electrical condition that affects them. The constant alternations of sleep and waking, in whatever way they may be induced by repose, or affected by functional activity, are regulated as periodical recurrences by the electrical laws of the seasons, by the reiteration of day and night, by the daily variations of the barometer, and by the conditions that move the magnetic needle from east to west at stated hours every day. Extreme weariness will prevent sleep if fatigue is unaccompanied by powerless attention, and unsettled sensation. Let us see how these known facts may serve to explain the sleep of insects.

We shall comprehend some of the physiological incidents of slumber by attending to the processes of mesmeric sleep, as developed by Mr. Braid in his work on Neurypnology, or the *rationale* of nervous sleep, in relation with animal magnetism. I would be brief with my extract, and yet I can scarcely venture to abridge his language. He says he induced cataleptic sleep, which he designates hypnotism, by keeping the eyes fixed on an object, and the mind riveted on the idea of *that* one object. He so regulated the distance of it from the sight as to produce the greatest possible strain upon the eyes and eyelids. "It will be observed," he says, "that, owing to the consensual adjustment of the eyes, the pupils will be at first contracted; they will shortly begin to dilate; and after they have done so to a considerable extent, and have assumed a wavy motion, the eyes will close involuntarily, with perceptible vibrations. Ten or fifteen minutes elapse, and the arms and legs are found disposed to be retained in the position in which they are placed. If the patient has not been so intensely affected as this implies, then, if he be spoken to in a soft tone of voice, and desired to retain the limbs in that, or in an extended position, the pulse will speedily become greatly accelerated, and the limbs involuntarily fixed. It will now be found that all the organs of special sense, excepting sight, including heat and cold, and muscular motion and resistance, and certain mental faculties, are at first prodigiously exalted. It is such an exaltation as happens with regard to the primary effects of opium, wine, and spirits. After a certain point, however, this exaltation of function is followed by a state of depression far greater than the torpor of *natural* sleep. From the state of the most profound torpor of the organs of

24*

special sense, and tonic rigidity of the muscles, they may at this stage be *instantly* restored to the *opposite* condition of extreme mobility and exalted sensibility, by directing a current of air against the organ or organs we wish to render limber, and which had been in the cataleptiform state. By mere repose, the senses will speedily merge into the original condition again." Now, none of these processes, in inducing sleep, would be applicable to insects whose eyes are immovable, if the provision for seeing was confined to the two large globular eyes on each side of the head; but being provided with ocelli, or auxiliary eyes, placed on the vertex of the head, these facts illustrate the drowsy insect. The structure of these auxiliary organs is just that of one of the lenses of the compound eye; but being so placed that they can be set close to what they examine, and can concentrate the attention to the exclusion of the objects that occupy the globular facetted eyes, it is possible that such visual concentration, when the insect retires to repose, induces just that perceptive vibration described in cataleptic sleep by which slumber can be brought on.

An insect composes itself to sleep with its antennæ folded. Some of the beetles adjust them to their breast; the butterfly seeks some particular aspect of a tree, and folds vertically its wings, throws back the antennæ, and remains motionless and insensible to all external circumstances. When caterpillars, which are insatiable feeders, are observed resting immovable with their heads bent down, they are asleep. The geometers may be remarked stretched out for hours projected from a twig resembling the angular stem of those trees they are feeding upon, and the processionary caterpillars, whose night marches, in marshalled communities, are regulated with such remarkable exactness that they resemble battalions platooning over a field, in " strict love of fellowship combined" in passing the day in inaction, spend it in repose.

Whatever may be the controlling cause that renders some insects diurnal feeders and flyers, and some noctu nal and crepuscular movers, frolicking or feasting in the twilight, the solution must be sought in the adaptive differences that regulate the " *sleep of plants.*" Some plants repose by night; others expand in the darkened hours, and slumber under the stimulation of light. Whether the closing of the flower be at nightfall, or its opening be as soon as daylight fades, or whether it be the reversal of this order, the differences are precisely the same as in those animals that sleep through the day and awake at night, or that awaken in light and slumber in darkness. The regular intervals that lead to sleeping or waking are the recurrences of those *electrical* incidents that attend the interchanges of day and night in the atmosphere.

THE EYES OF BEES.

Men never knew what the eyes of bees really were, until the greatly-improved microscopes of the present day, in effect, gave us another eye to gaze upon those of bees. They have simple eyes, three in number, and disposed in a triangle between the two compound eyes. The latter are wonderful objects under a microscope. The compound eye of a bee, particularly of a drone, is one of the most exquisitely constructed instruments of nature's handiwork. One of the leaves of chaff that surround a grain of wheat may represent its appearance; but the piece of chaff shows only a uniform glazed surface, whilst in the eye of the bee, which is much darker in color, though alike externally glazed, the brightness arises from the presence of about 3,500 small but perfectly hexagonal lenses, fitting closely together, and disposed in regular rows over the whole circumference. This structure, then, may be likened to a bundle of 3,500 telescopes, so grouped that the large terminal lenses present an extensive convex surface, whilst, in consequence of the decreasing diameter of the instruments, their narrow ends meet, and form a smaller concentric curve. Could we look through all these telescopes at one glance, and obtain a stereoscopic effect, we might be able to form some conception of the operation of vision in this insect.

Even one of these 3,500 lenses would occupy us long in a complete examination of it. Each of the eyelets, which, when aggregated, constitute the compound eye of the bee, is itself a perfect instrument of vision, consisting of two remarkably formed lenses — an outer *corneal* and an inner *conical* lens. The corneal lens is a six-sided prism, and the assemblage of these prisms forms the *cornea* of the compound eye. If the whole or a portion of this cornea be peeled off, and placed under a microscope, the beautiful grouping of the lenses becomes distinctly visible. On a close and careful examination, the corneal lens of the eyelet is perceived to be not a simple but a compound lens, composed of two plano-convex lenses of different densities or refracting powers. The plane surface of these lenses being adherent, it follows that the prismatic corneal lens is a compound double convex lens, as was discovered by Dr. Hicks. The effect of this arrangement is, that if there should be any aberration or divergence of the rays of light during their passage through one portion of the lens, it is rectified in its transit through the other. It is nothing very new to find lenses of different densities in an animal's eye, but where is there another instance in which one compound lens consists of two adherent lenses of this description?

Yet the wonder does not end here. Man has been unconsciously groping his way in the formation of his most perfect microscopic lens to an imitation of the bee's eye. His aim has been to correct the aberration of light, which caused his lenses to color and distort the objects under investigation, and he attained this end by employing compound lenses of varying densities. When, after long study, he obtained an achromatic lens, he had but equalled the little bee; and how striking the thought, that, by the use of his own achromatic lens, man first distinctly perceived that of the bee! The little insect had used it for thousands of years perhaps, before man trod the earth. By its wonderful lenses and numerous facets, it gains light in the dim cups of flowers. Into those floral hollows it carries, as it were, thousands of light collectors and reflectors, capable of forming a single picture by the means of a great number of smaller images. Into the dark hive it bears the same optical apparatus, and thereby economizes every particle of straggling or slanting light. If bees, as one alleges, always work in the dark, has not each one of them three or four thousand illuminators? And if we reflect upon the many thousands of these, all in optical operation throughout the hive, how can it be said that these creatures work in the dark? — *The Honey Bee; its Natural History, Anatomy etc., by James Samuelson, and Dr. J. B. Hicks, London.*

THE AYE-AYE *(Chiromys Madagascariensis).*

This curious animal, which has recently been brought anew to the attention of naturalists, by a monograph by Prof. Owen, of England, was first noticed in Madagascar by Souverat, in 1780, and owes its name to an exclamation of astonishment uttered by the natives of the east coast, to whom, it is said, he exhibited it for the first time. Souverat brought home with him a stuffed skin and a cranium, which have since remained in the museum of the Garden of Plants, the only representatives of the species in European cabinets. Zoölogists have been puzzled as to the true affinities of the Aye-Aye, some placing it among the Rodents, and others among the Quadrumana. A specimen preserved in spirits, recently forwarded by Dr. Sandwith to Prof. Owen, has, however, enabled him to determine definitely its position among the Lemuridæ. But remarkable as the mingling of Rodent and Quadrumanous characters may be in the Aye-Aye, they are surpassed in the correlations of physical structure and strange habits. " The wide openings of the eyelids, the large cornea and expansile iris, the subglobular lens and tapetum, are arrangements for admittting to the retina and absorbing the utmost amount of light which may pervade the forest, at sunset, dawn, or moonlight. Thus the Aye-Aye is able to guide itself among the branches in quest of its hidden food. To detect this, however, another sense had need to be developed to great perfection. The large ears are to catch and concentrate, and the large acoustic nerve and its ministering ' flocculus ' seem designed to appreciate any feeble vibration that might reach the tympanum from the recess in the hard timber, through which the wood-boring larva may be tunnelling its way by repeated scoopings and scrapings of its hard mandibles." The food of this nocturnal animal, to whose strange physiognomy the eyes and ears add so much, consists mostly of wood-boring grubs. To extract these, there are, united with the common Lemurine characters, chisel-shaped incisors, resembling those of Rodents, and a most remarkable modification of the middle finger, which is not only used for eliciting by percussion the hollow sound from the bored limb, but as a hook for extracting the grub. All the fingers are of somewhat unusual length, but the middle one " has been ordained to grow in length, but not in thickness with the other digits; it remains slender as a probe, and is provided at the end with a small pad and a hook-like claw." The use made of this part will be best learned from the very interesting letter to Prof. Owen by Dr. Sandwith, in which his own observations on the habits of the Aye-Aye are recorded.

" In a cage where a fine male healthy adult Aye-Aye was confined, were placed a large number of branches, bored in all directions, by a large and destructive grub, called the Montouk. Just at sunset, the Aye-Aye crept from under his blanket, yawned, stretched, and betook himself to his tree, where his movements are lively and graceful, though by no means so quick as those of a squirrel. Presently he came to one of the worm-eaten branches, which he began to examine most attentively ; and bending forward his ears and applying his nose close to the bark, he rapidly tapped the surface with the curious second digit, as a woodpecker taps a tree, though with much less noise, from time to time inserting the end of the slender finger into the worm-holes, as a surgeon would a probe. At length he came to a part of a branch which evidently gave out an interesting sound, for he began to tear it with his strong teeth, rapidly stripped off the bark, cut into the wood, and exposed the nest of a grub, which he daintily picked out of its bed with the slender tapping finger, and conveyed the luscious morsel to his mouth. I watched these proceedings with intense interest, and was much struck with the marvellous adaptation of the creature to its habits, shown by his acute hearing, which enables him aptly to distinguish the different tones emitted from the wood by his gentle tapping; his evidently acute sense of smell, aiding him in his search; his secure footsteps on the slender branches, to which he firmly clung with his quadrumanous members; his strong, rodent teeth, enabling him to tear through the wood; and lastly, by the curious slender finger, unlike that of any other animal, and which he used alternately as a pleximeter, a probe, and a scoop. But I was yet to learn another peculiarity. I gave him water to drink in a saucer, on which he stretched out a hand, dipped a finger into it, and drew it obliquely through his open mouth; this he repeated so rapidly that the water seemed to flow into his mouth. After a while, he lapped like a cat; but his first mode of drinking appeared to me to be his way of reaching water in the deep clefts of the trees."

ON THE ORIGIN OF SPECIES.

At the conclusion of a monograph, recently published by Prof. Owen, of England, on the "Aye-Aye," this eminent naturalist takes occasion to express his views in regard to that most interesting question of the day, namely, " *The Origin of Species*," and the following notice and critique of the opinions thus and there put forth, is derived from the pages of Silliman's journal.

Those who have joined in the issue involved in this question — the origin of species — may be arranged in one of two classes; 1st, comprising those who maintain that the present condition of the animal and vegetable kingdom was reached by a series of " progressive creations;" each species being created and suddenly introduced upon the surface of the earth, and the first-formed individuals having the same specific characters as all the successors; 2d, those who deny the preceding view, and assert that all animals and plants are the result of " progressive development," " deviation," or " transmutation" of species, the first created forms being of the simplest kind, or at all events of a simpler kind than those of the present day, and in the course of time transformed into them. How the changes from simple to complex forms were effected, or how specific characters were modified, has been very differently explained. Lamarck says by a " *besoin*," Darwin by " natural selection " and " the struggle for existence," and Owen " by the ordained potentiality of second causes," and by transmutation " under law."

We do not propose to enter into a discussion of these different theories, but, before citing Prof. Owen's views, we will merely remark that, if the progressive-creation hypothesis is adopted, we should be glad to see a better answer than has yet been made to the question, How, and in what condition did the first forms make their appearance ? When a mammal was created, did the oxygen, hydrogen, nitrogen, and carbon of the air, and the lime, soda, phosphorus, potash, water, etc., from the earth, come together, and on the instant combine into a completely formed horse, lion, elephant, or other animal? If this question is answered in the affirmative, it will be easily seen that the answer is entirely opposed by the observed analogies of nature. In the practical study of the history of the earth and the changes which it has undergone, of the development of individual animals and plants, the " order of nature " points in one direction, namely, to the process of differentiation. The one-celled plant and the tree, the polyp and man, and all organic forms intermediate between these extremes, pass from the homogeneous to the heterogeneous, from the nucleated cell, or even from what is more simple still, from plasma to the adult individual consisting of organs more or less complex, according to the position in the series. We nowhere see plants or animals reach maturity in any other way than by development or growth.

At the same time, we must not lose sight of the fact that what is true of the successive stages of individual organisms may not necessarily prove true with regard to the history of the races; that while, from the earliest embryonic condition of each individual to the last there is a connected series of observed changes or differentiations, and no break in the organic continuity, there are no observations whatever to prove a like organic continuity in the races. In the absence of such direct proof, we have no other alternative than to look to the analogies of nature and the geological record. The direction in which the former point is obvious; the testimony of the latter is thus far negative, but is it complete enough to be a safe guide?

In view of the difficulties met with, in explaining the first introduction of living forms, Agassiz has put forth the hypothesis of the creation of eggs. " I then would ask, is it probable that the circumstances under which animals and plants originated for the first time can be much simpler, or even as simple as the conditions necessary for their reproduction only, after they have been once created? Preliminary then to their first appearance, conditions necessary for their growth must have been provided for; for, if, as I believe, they were created as eggs, the conditions must have been conformable to those in which the living representatives first introduced now reproduce themselves. If it were observed that they originated in a more advanced stage of life, the difficulty would be still greater, as a moment's consideration cannot fail to show, especially if it is remembered how complicated the structure of some of the animals was, who are known to have been among the first inhabitants of our globe."— *Contrib. Nat. Hist. of U. States,* i. 12.

This hypothesis would answer very well for spawning fishes and reptiles, whose eggs may be trusted to the effects of physical agents. But does it help us with regard to viviparous reptiles and mammals? To take the case of the mammals, what " conditions conformable to those in which the living representatives first introduced now reproduce themselves" would answer the purpose for the development of the young, except a uterus, or something analogous to a uterus, and for its nourishment after birth, except a mammary gland, or something analogous to one? And how could there be a uterus or a mammary and without organs of nourishment, locomotion, etc.; in other words, bre creating the egg, it would be necessary to create some kind of an organism for the egg to live in. If such organism offered the same conditions with those of the individuals now living, why create the egg at all? Rather than this, it would seem to be a simpler matter to create the whole animal capable of producing eggs to begin with. If it be asserted that the conditions were not the same, this assertion would seem to be equivalent to the admission of variation, inasmuch as the first egg would be capable of being developed under different circumstances from the later ones.

How Prof. Owen meets this difficulty with regard to the first introduction of species may be inferred from the following quoted passages:

" But the conception of the origin of species by a continuously operative secondary cause or law is one thing ; the knowledge of the nature and mode of operation of that law is another thing. One physiologist may accept, another refute or reject, a transmutational or natural-selective hypothesis, and both may equally hold the idea of the successive coming-in of species by law."

" What I have termed the ' derivative hypothesis' of organisms, for example, holds that there are coming into being, by aggregation of organic atoms, at all times and in all places, under the simplest unicellular condition, with differences of character as many as are the various circumstances, conditions, and combinations of the causes educing them, —one form appearing in mud at the bottom of the ocean, another in the pond or the heath, a third in the sawdust of the cellar, a fourth on the surface of the mountain rock, etc., but all by the combination and arrangement of organic atoms through forces and conditions acting according to predetermined law. The disposition to vary in form and structure, according to the variation of surrounding conditions, is greatest in these first formed beings ; and from them, or such as them, are and have been derived all other and higher forms of organisms on this planet. And thus it is that we now find, energizing in fair proportions, every grade of organization from man to the monad." . . . .

" Now the foregoing hypothesis is at present based on so narrow and, as regards the origin of life, so uncertain a foundation of ascertained facts, that it can be regarded only as a kind of vantage-ground, artificially raised to expand the view of the outlooker for the road to truth, and perhaps as supporting sign-posts directing where that road may most likely be fallen in with." . . . .

" And herein is one main distinction between it (origin of species by natural selection) and the ' derivative hypothesis' which maintains that single-celled organisms, so diversified as to be relegated to distinct orders and classes of *Protozoa*, are now, as heretofore, in course of creation or formation, by the ordained potentiality of second causes; with innate capacities of variation and development, giving rise in a long course of generations to such differentiated beings as may be distinguished by the term ' plant' and ' animal'; from which all higher animals and plants have, through like influences, ascended and are being ascensively derived. This, as the naturalist knows, is mere hypothesis, at present destitute of proof. But it is more consistent with the phenomena of life about us, with the ever-recurring appearance of mould and monads, and with the coexistence, at the present time, of all grades of life rising therefrom up to man, than is the notion of the origin of life which is propounded in Mr. Darwin's book, ' On the Origin of Species by Natural Selection.' " . . . . .

"That organic species are the result of still operating powers and influences is probable from the great paleontological fact of the succession of such so-called species from their first appearance in the oldest fossiliferous strata; it is more probable from the kind and degree of similitude between the species that succeeds and the species that disappears never to return as such; the similitude being in the main of a nature expressed by the terms of 'progressive departure from a general to a special type.' Creation by law is suggested by the many instances of retention of structures in Paleozoic species, which are embryonal and transitory in later species of the same order or class; and the suggestion acquires force by considering the analogies which the transitory embryonal stages in the higher species bear to the mature forms of the lower species. Every new instance of structures which does not obviously and without straining, receive a teleological explanation, especially the great series of anatomical facts expressed by the 'law of vegetative or irrelative repetition,'—all congenital varieties, deformities, monstrosities — opposes itself to the hypothesis of the origin of species by a primary or immediate and never repeated act of adaptive construction."

If we correctly understand Prof. Owen's views, as expressed in the above paragraphs, he inclines to, in fact adopts, though cautiously, the hypothesis of the origin of species by "transmutation" or "deviation;" these transmutations being in no accordance with a pre-arranged plan, but carried out under the influence of second causes. The first organisms were unicellular, brought into existence by spontaneous generation "under law," and, by a slow and orderly transmutation, ascensively differentiated into the highest vegetable and animal organisms. For the precise mode of bringing about the individual changes, he offers no conjecture, whatever.

We leave it for the advocates of progressive creation to answer these views, and will conclude with expressing the belief, that there is no just ground for taking, and that we arrive at no reasonable theory which takes, a position intermediate between the two extremes. We must either assume, on the one hand, that living organisms commenced their existence fully formed, and by processes not in accordance with the usual order of nature, as it is revealed to human minds, or, on the other hand, that each species become such by progressive development or transmutation; that, as in the individual so in the aggregate of races, the simple forms were not only the precursors, but the progenitors of the complex ones, and that thus the order of Nature, as commonly manifest in her works, was maintained.

AGASSIZ ON THE TRANSMUTATION OF SPECIES.

Prof. Agassiz, in the preface to his recently published work, "*Methods of Study in Natural History*," takes occasion thus to define his views in regard to the hypothesis of the origin of species by transmutation. "I wish to enter my earnest protest against the transmutation theory, revived of late with so much ability, and so generally received. It is my belief that naturalists are chasing a phantom, in their search after some material gradation among created beings, by which the whole Animal Kingdom may have been derived by successive development from a single germ, or from a few germs. It would seem, from the frequency with which this notion is revived,— ever returning upon us with hydra-headed tenacity of life, and presenting itself under a new form as soon as the preceding one has been exploded and set aside,— that it has a certain fascination for the human mind. This arises, perhaps, from the desire to explain the secret of our own existence,— to have some simple and easy solution of the fact that we live.

"I confess that there seems to me to be a repulsive poverty in this material explanation that is contradicted by the intellectual grandeur of the universe ; the resources of the Deity cannot be so meagre that, in order to create a human being endowed with reason, he must change a monkey into a man. This is, however, merely a personal opinion, and has no weight as an argument ; nor am I so uncandid as to assume that another may not hold an opinion diametrically opposed to mine in a spirit quite as reverential as my own. But I nevertheless insist, that this theory is opposed to the processes of Nature, as far as we have been able to apprehend them ; that it is contradicted by the facts of Embryology and Paleontology, the former showing us forms of development as distinct and persistent for each group as are the fossil types of each period revealed to us by the latter ; and that the experiments upon domesticated animals and cultivated plants, on which its adherents base their views, are entirely foreign to the matter in hand, since the varieties thus brought about by the fostering care of man are of an entirely different character from those observed among wild species. And while their positive evidence is inapplicable, their negative evidence is equally unsatisfactory, since, however long and frequent the breaks in the geological series may be in which they would fain bury their transition types, there are many points in the succession where the connection is perfectly distinct and unbroken, and it is just at these points that new organic groups are introduced without any intermediate forms to link them with the preceding ones."

PHYSIOLOGICAL DIFFERENCES BETWEEN TYPICAL RACES OF MEN..

In a paper on the above subject, recently read to the British Ethnological Society, Mr. Robert Dunn maintained that the genus *homo* was distinctly defined, on the ground that in man's moral and religious attributes the inferior animals do not participate, and it was this that constituted the difference between him and them. The barrier was thus, he considered, impassable between man and the chimpanzee and gorilla ; and that wherever man, with his erect attitude and with his articulate voice, is found, his claims to our common humanity must be immediately acknowledged, however debased the type may be. His conviction was that there was proof of a general unity exhibited in all the races of the great family of man, inasmuch that they were all endowed with the same intellectual faculties and mental activities, however much they may vary in degree. It had, he thought, been fairly argued that all the races of the human family form but one species, from the physiological fact that they are all capable of fruitful union.. Believing the brain to be the material organ of the mind, the author considered the study of the cerebral organization and development in the various typical races as one of the most effectual means of better understanding and elucidating the psychological differences which characterize them. This subject, however, was one that yet required

25

to be worked out; and ethnic psychology was still a desideratum. The author then reviewed what had been done by anatomists and ethnologists, and pointed out that the lower savage races, such as the Sandwich islanders, made progress in the early part of their education, and were so far as apt and quick as the children of civilized Europeans; but at this point they stopped, and seemed incapable of acquiring the higher branches of knowledge. The Sandwich islanders have excellent memories, and learn by rote with wonderful rapidity, but will not exercise the thinking faculties; they receive simple ideas, but not complex ones. In like manner, it was found practically that negro children could not be educated with white children. In all these cases, as well as in the minor ones continually occurring amongst ourselves, of inability to understand subjects and reasonings of a certain order, the true explanation is that the cognate faculties have not reached a complexity equal to the complexity of the relations to be perceived; as moreover it is not only so with purely intellectual cognitions, but it is the same with *moral* cognitions. In the Australian language there are no words answering to justice, sin, guilt. Amongst many of the lower races of man, acts of generosity or mercy are utterly incomprehensible; that is to say, the most complex relations of human action in its social bearings are not cognizable. This the author thought was in accordance with what à *priori* might have been expected to have resulted from organic differences in the instruments of the higher psychical activities — or, in other words, in the nervous apparatus of perceptive and intellectual consciousness. The leading characters of the various races of mankind were simply representatives of particular stages in the development of the highest Caucasian type. The negro exhibits permanently the imperfect brow, projecting lower jaw, and slender bent limbs of a Caucasian child some considerable time before the period of its birth. The aboriginal American represents the same child nearer birth; the Mongolian the same child newly born.

ZOOLOGICAL SUMMARY.

Brains of Man and Animals. — Facts developed in a paper on the anatomy of the chimpanzee, read before the British Association, 1863, by Dr. Emberton, strongly corroborated the position heretofore taken by Prof. Huxley and other comparative anatomists, that the brain of the chimpanzee differs only in degree — that is, in the smaller size and extent of its parts — from that of man; and that, with this difference, essentially the same structures, without any exception, exist in both brains.

Dr. Crawford maintained in a subsequent paper that the consideration of the material structure of the brain was of far less value than a consideration of its working or living action, and that probably there exist subtle differences between the brain of man and those of the lower animals that anatomy has not, and probably never will, detect.

Thus the brain of the wolf is anatomically the same as that of the dog, one being an untamable glutton, the other the friend and companion of man. The Australian savages tame the young of the wild dogs, and use them in the chase, whereas the young of the wolf are not capable of complete or useful domestication. Again, the hog, with its low organized brain, is equal in intelligence to the most anthro-

poid monkey. The sheep and the goat have brains identical in structure, the one being a stupid, the other an intelligent, animal.

Smallest Human Brain on Record. — Dr. Gore has furnished the Anthropological Society an account of the smallest adult human brain on
record. The brain of the adult male averages forty-nine ounces; in
females, the average is forty-three and a half ounces. The female
whose brain was described was forty-two years of age, and without
any symptom of disease. She was five feet high, and her intellect
was infantile. The brain without the membranes weighed ten ounces
five grains, being the smallest mature brain on record.

Brain of Man and Apes. — At a recent meeting of the London
Anthropological Society, Prof. Owen, in commenting upon a paper
presented " On the Brain of a Female Idiot," observed, that as the
brain of man is more complex in its organization than the brain of
inferior animals, it is more subject to injury, and more liable to experience the want of perfect development. Instances of idiocy occur
among all races of mankind. Extreme smallness of the skull indicated
in all cases want of intellect approaching to idiocy. Alluding to the
attempts that have been made to find a link of connection between
man and apes, he remarked that it was possible that an idiot with an
imperfectly developed brain might wander into some cave, and there
die, and in two or three hundred years his bones might be covered with mud, or be imbedded in stalagmite, and when discovered,
such a skull might be adduced as affording the looked-for link connecting man with the inferior animals; but the brain of such an idiot,
as the female whose skull was exhibited, is distinctly different from
that of the anthropoid apes; and he expressed an opinion that the
difference is too wide to be bridged over by the skull of any creature
yet discovered.

Wounds of the Brain. — M. Flourens has presented to the Academy
of Sciences a note of a series of experiments performed by him for
the purpose of showing the curability of wounds of the brain, and,
what is more, the facility with which they are cured. He trepanned
the skulls of dogs and rabbits, made a small opening through the dura
mater and into the substance of the brain, and then put bullets into
the wound. These bullets gradually penetrated through the cerebral matter by their own weight. When the ball was small, he found
that the whole thickness of the lobe of the brain or of the cerebellum
might be traversed by it without occasioning any symptom of accident or disturbance of functions. The fissure made by the passage
of the ball remains for some time as a canal; it then closes up and
cicatrizes. In one case of a rabbit, a ball was placed on the posterior
part of the cerebellum, immediately above the vital point (Flourens's
nœud vital). When the ball had reached that part and had exercised
a certain degree of pressure, the animal died.

On the Physical Characteristics of the Andaman Islanders. — At a
recent meeting of the British Geographical Society, Prof. Owen made
some observations on the skeleton of a native of the Andaman Islands; the only one yet received in Europe, (See *Ann. Sci. Dis.*
1862, p. 14). He stated that he had found it to be that of an adult
male in the prime of life, showing evidence, in the texture of the
bones and the development of their parts, of having belonged to an

individual who, though small of stature, must yet have been of accurate proportion. He had been most interested in the examination of the cranium, which he had expected to find allied to the Papuan or to the negro variety. He had found, however, that the skull exhibited none of the characteristic peculiarities of the Papuan, and still less of those of the negro; that it had no affinity with the Malay or the Mongolian type of cranium; in fact, that, with the exception of the prognathous jaw-bones, in its classic oval, and in its general proportions, it was most nearly allied to the skull of a Caucasian. In the course of his investigations, some suggestions had presented themselves to him. Why is it necessary that, in determining the race to which the inhabitants of detached groups of islands belong, we should expect to find invariably that they are connected with the inhabitants of conterminous continents? In the case of many of these islands, particularly of Ceylon, it had been shown that the geological age of the island was much earlier than that of the adjacent mainland. Why, then, might not the inhabitants of such groups of islands be the descendants of races who had peopled continents which no longer exist, but of which these islands are the remains, and in comparison with which the present continents in the *eons* of geologic history are of very recent date?

Novelty in Cattle-Breeding.   Production of Sexes at Will. — The *Archives des Sciences* for Sept. 1863, contains a communication from a Swiss agriculturist, stating that in February, 1861, he received from Professor Thury, of Geneva, a letter containing confidential instructions, which he was to carry out for the purpose of experimentally verifying an assumed law regulating the production of the sexes among animals. The result was that in twenty-two successive cases, females were obtained, according to desire. The animals bred from were Swiss cows and a Durham bull. M. Cornaz then purchased a Durham cow, and desired to procure, by breeding, a Durham bull, in which he succeeded. He also desired to breed six bulls, crossed between Durham and Schwitz, and by selecting cows of the color and height he wanted, he was again successful, and regards Prof Thury's method as of the highest importance to breeders of cattle.

The law enunciated by Prof. Thury, and confirmed by M. Cornaz, is that sex depends on the degree of maturation of the egg at the moment of fecundation. In uniparous animals, fecundation at the commencement of the rutting period gives females, at its termination, males. In multiparous creatures, the first eggs that descend from the ovary generally give females, the last, males; but M. Thury says, that in a second generative period that succeeds the first, circumstances are considerably changed, and the last eggs give females. Many of our rural readers, engaged in agriculture, will be able to verify these curious statements, which may have an important influence on the profits of farming.

Inoculation for Pleuro-Pneumonia, or Cattle-Disease. — M. Lengleri describes to the French Academy the success of inoculation as a preservative against the above disease. In the first place, he obtained the virus from the lung of an ox that was affected; but subsequently he obtained the matter in a milder form from the tails of the inoculated animals, portions of which became diseased and were cut off by the operator. At the time of writing his paper, he was employing virus which had passed through twenty-five individuals.

Instinct in Infusoria. — Mr H. J. Carlter mentions in the *Annals of Natural History* (British) the following curious observation. He watched an actinophorus rhizopod extracting starch grains from a ruptured cell, looking like a spore; the creature then retired some distance off, and then returned, and although no more starch grains were protruding, he contrived to extract some from the interior. "This," he says, "was repeated several times, showing that the actinophys instinctively knew that these were nutritious grains, and that they were contained in this cell, and that although each time, after incepting a grain, it went away to some distance, it knew how to find its way back." He likewise mentions the cunning of an amœba, which crawled up the stem of an acincta, and placed itself round the ovarian aperture, so as to receive an infant as soon as it was born. He observes, "that these facts evince an amount of instinct and determination of purpose which could hardly have been anticipated in a being so low in the scale of organic development."

Material of Humming-Birds' Nests. — It has long been a matter of doubt as to what is the material of which the nest is made. It is soft, white, cottony, homogeneous, and shingled on the outside with lichens; though evidently of vegetable origin, the precise material was not known. In the Massachusetts nest, it proves to be the down which protects the buds of the oak-tree in spring, and in this instance of the red oak; in the Georgia nest it was of a coarser character, but probably obtained from a similar Southern oak.— *Dr. Brewer, Boston Nat. History Society's Proceedings.*

Mechanism of Locomotion. — Prof. Marshall, in a recent lecture on the above subject, before the Royal Institution, London, gave the following as the possible rates of animal locomotion per hour: shark and salmon, sixteen and seventeen miles; flies, four to six miles; eider-duck, ninety miles; hawk, one hundred and fifty miles; worms, thirty feet; race-horse, forty to sixty miles; man walking, four to five miles, running, twelve to fifteen miles. Especial attention was also directed to the advantage of the atmospheric pressure on the joints, amounting in the knee, where so much flexibility is required, to sixty pounds, and in the hip-joint, to twenty-six pounds.

Curious Observation respecting Yellow Fever. — The late Major E. B. Hunt, U. S. A., communicated to *Silliman's Journal* the following curious observation respecting yellow fever, made at Key West : —

" On two separate occasions. when there were cases of yellow fever in the U. S. Marine Hospital, which building I passed daily and saw almost habitually, I have seen a flock of buzzards, circling over and near the roof of the hospital by the hour together, and continuing this day after day. I have never seen them do this except when there were yellow fever cases in progress under the roof. So marked is this fact as to have produced a common belief in town, that they only hover over the hospital when there is yellow fever there. I am quite persuaded that such is the fact, and can only interpret what I have myself seen as indicating that an odor is then thrown out on the air which the keen scent of the scavenger bird detects from afar. The material particles, whose diffusion is thus testified to, seem likely t

25*

afford the means of transporting the disease on the air, in a manner quite agreeing with the facts of its propagation. The hint, thus afforded by the keen-scented buzzards, may have value in assisting to comprehend the mode of conveying and diffusing this fatal malady, and the particles scented may indeed be the actual *fomites* so much talked of and so little understood, in discussing the controverted questions of contagion and communication."

A proposed Plan for prolonging Life. — M. Robin, an eminent French chemist, in a memoir recently presented to the French Academy, expresses a belief that the period of human life may be greatly prolonged, and enters into an argument to show that his opinion is based upon sound reasoning. He also gives the result of his personal observations on this subject, and proposes to demonstrate the truthfulness of his position by actual experiments upon animals whose lives are of short duration. His argument is, that the mineral matter which constitutes an ingredient in most of our food, after the combustion, is left in our systems to incrust and stiffen the different parts of the body, and to render imperfect many of the vital processes. He compares human beings to furnaces which are always kindled ; life exists only in combustion, but the combustion which occurs in our bodies, like that which takes place in our chimneys, leaves a detritus or residue which is fatal to life. To remove this, he would administer lactic acid with ordinary food. This acid is known to possess the power of removing or dissolving the incrustations which form on the arteries, cartilages and valves of the heart. As buttermilk abounds in this acid, and is, moreover, an agreeable kind of food, its habitual use, it is urged, will free the system from these causes, which inevitably cause death between the seventy-fifth and one hundredth year.

Abnormal Lactation. — Dr. J. Adamson stated, at the British Association, 1859, that a female greyhound which had never had offspring suckled a kitten until it had grown to a considerable size. If the kitten was removed, the greyhound was as disconsolate as the kitten's own parent would have been, under similar circumstances, and her equanimity was only restored when the kitten was given back to her.

Dr. Ogilvie said the occurrence is not uncommon in the human female, and that lactation has often been carried on successfully by the human male. He remarked also, that it is common in Western Africa for young females who have never had children to be regularly employed in nursing the children of others, — a secretion of milk being excited by stimulating the breast to secrete milk by the application of the juice of one of the Euphorbiaceæ.

Peculiarities of Ants. — At a recent meeting of the British Entomological Society, Mr. Saunders called attention to a statement, in *Froebel's Travels in Central America*, that certain species of ants in New Mexico construct their nests exclusively of small stones, of the same material, chosen by the insects from the various components of the sand of the steppes and deserts ; in one part of the Colorado Desert, their heaps were formed of small fragments of crystallized feldspar, and in another, imperfect crystals of red, transparent garnets were the materials of which the ant-hills were built, and any quantity of them might be obtained.

Insections. — A committee was some time since appointed by the

Fren :h Government to investigate and report on the expediency of " Vivisections," or the dissection of animals alive,— a plan of late years much followed by French physiologists. The report of this commission was read to the Academy of Sciences on the 4th of August. It arrives at the following conclusions : —

" 1. Vivisection is indispensable to the study of physiology, and of operative veterinary surgery.

" 2. It ought, nevertheless, to be employed sparingly, and all appearances of cruelty should be avoided.

" 3. The experimenter should always have the real progress of science in view.

" 4. Students should not be permitted to perform vivisection except in public, and in the presence of experienced professors.

" 5. All means for alleviating pain compatible with the object in view should be employed."

. *Leaden Bullets injured by Insects.* — In 1857, the French Minister of War sent to the Academy of Sciences several cartouches which had been attacked in the wooden boxes in which they had been packed by the larvæ of insects of the order Hymenoptera. A similar fact has recently occurred at Grenoble, where several of these insects have been found with the deteriorated bullets in the cartouches. Specimens of these also have been forwarded to the Academy by Marshal Valliant, who is now united with the eminent naturalists, Milne Edwards and Quatrefages in a commission to inquire into the nature and labors of these remarkable insects.

Vocal Fishes. — Dr. Dufosse has communicated to the French Academy an account of certain researches into the vocal powers of certain fish, most of his observations being made upon species of *Trigla* and *Zeus* (gurnards and dories). He states the sounds to be produced by the vibration of the muscles belonging to the air-bladder, and that large gurnards may be heard at a distance of six or seven yards. Out of five or six hundred individuals, of the species mentioned, their voices were comprised between si_2 and re_5 inclusive. The sounds were instantaneous, or prolonged for several minutes, sometimes as long as seven or eight minutes. The pitch often varies during a single " sonorous emission." The finest vocal performers appear to belong to the species *Morrude*, who surpass all their congeners in producing a great number of completely distinct sounds. " They sustain the simple sounds better, and modulate better the compound sounds; they render more distinctly long successions of sounds different in tone and pitch ; in fine, there is less dissonance in the sonorous vibrations they produce. Other species, however, beat them in intensity.

The Rattle of the Rattlesnake. — At a recent meeting of the Boston Society of Natural History, Prof. Wyman made a communication on the mode of formation of the rattle of the rattlesnake.

In a fœtal specimen examined, the scales cease toward the end of the tail, and the unscaled portion is covered by thickened cuticle, the rudiment of a rattle, which must fall off; as the animal grows, the last three vertebræ are covered with hardened cuticle arranged in ridges; as growth continues, this covering is displaced, a new layer forming underneath it, and the old slipped backward over one ridge in a manner not well determined ; this is in turn displaced by a new layer beneath pushed backward over a single ridge, and so on indefinitely. An interesting point yet to be settled is whether the cuticular caudal rings are set free at the time of moulting. That there is no definite relation between the age of the animal and the number of rattles, he said, was shown by specimens over six feet long having only two rattles, and others of eighteen inches with six or seven.

Cause of Death by Drowning. — Death in cases of drowning has been attributed to various causes, — the introduction of air into the stomach, into the bronchial tubes, closure of the epiglottis, syncope, and asphyxia. M. Beau, of France, believes that the cause of death is asphyxia from want of respirable air; but that the small quantity of water which enters the bronchial tubes requires to be explained. Is it that, in drowning, there is an arrest of the respiratory movements? To the solution of this question, M. Beau has applied himself, and has endeavored to show by experiments, that death takes place in drowning from an irresistible horror of the water inducing an arrest of the movements of respiration and closure of the respiratory orifices; and that this takes place irrespectively of the actual introduction of a small quantity of water into the air-tubes at the moment of submersion. There is, then, in the words of M. Beau, a *hydrophobia of inspiration* in the drowning analogous to the *hydrophobia of deglutition* in persons bitten by rabid animals. The last class of experiments show that death in these cases is comparable to that which arises from strangulation.

M. Flourens on Respiration. — In a warm-blooded vertebrate animal, respiratory movements are instantly arrested if the medulla oblongata is divided "in the centre of the V of the gray matter," and the creature dies immediately. In a frog, pulmonary respiration ceases on making a similar division, but the animal continues to live through its cutaneous respiration. The respiration of a fish ceases if the medulla oblongata is divided by a section which passes just behind the cerebellum, and the animal dies more or less quickly, according to the species. M. Flourens observes, "The lobes, or cerebral hemispheres, minister to intelligence, and that only; the cerebellum is devoted to the coördination of the movements of locomotion, and there is a point in the medulla oblongata which presides over the movements of respiration."

PLASTICITY OF BLOOD CORPUSCLES.

Dr. Sharpy says, "The plasticity of the blood corpuscle is unrivalled by any other physical body. It will assume all sorts of protean shapes under the slightest influences. Elongating to a mere thread, it will pass through a narrow chink; it will wrap itself round an acute, projecting angle, or protrude feelers and tails under the influence of currents. In its natural state, it possesses sufficient elasticity to resume its original shape on the cessation of the modifying influences; but when gum or gelatine has been added, or when the plasma has been permitted to thicken spontaneously, the corpuscle retains any form it may have assumed till again altered by fresh influence." — *Proceedings of the Royal Society*, No. 52.

FERTILITY OF FISH.

Mr. Frank Buckland, of England, who has given much attention to artificial culture of fish, has recently ascertained the amount of ova in several species of fish, by counting the number in a given weight, say ten or twenty grains, and then weighing the entire roe. The following are the results: —

Salmon, to each pound the fish weighs, about	. . .	1,000 ova.
Trout of one pound weight	. . . .	1,008 "
Herring of half-pound weight	. . . . . .	19,840 "
Perch of half-pound weight	. . . . . .	20,592 "
Mackerel of one pound weight	. . . . . .	86,220 "
Turbot of eight pounds' weight	. . . . .	385,200 "
Roach of three-quarters of a pound weight	. . . .	480,000 "
Cod of fifteen pounds' weight	. . . . . .	4,872,000 "

THE STRUCTURE OF THE ELEPHANT.

A curious statement appears in the London *Veterinarian*, on the relative weight of the body and of the viscera of the elephant, by Dr. E. Crisp. The stuffed specimen in the Crystal Palace was originally in Wombwell's Menagerie ; it was 22 years of age and 10 feet in height. The weight of the body was stated to be 3 tons ; the relative proportion of the viscera is as follows (omitting fractions) : Brain, 12lb. ; lungs, 47lb. 8oz. ; heart, 17lb. 9oz. ; liver, 33lb. 12oz. ; spleen, 6lb. 9oz. ; right kidney, 7lb. 2oz. ; left kidney, 5lb. 10oz. ; the length of the alimentary canal 106 feet. A female which died last year at the Zoölogical Gardens from fright produced by a thunder-storm was about 30 years of age, and had been there 18 years. The weight of the various parts of the body was as follows : The skin, 683lb. ; flesh and bones, 3642lb. ; supposed loss, 200lb. ; viscera, 700lb., making a total of 5225lb., or 2 tons 5cwt. 73lb. The proportions were as follows (again omitting fractions) : Heart, 25lb. ; lungs, much congested, 107lb. ; liver, 50lb. ; spleen, 9lb. ; kidney, 8lb. ; alimentary canal, 123 feet ; the large intestines, about 35 feet in length, would probably hold about 150 gallons of water. A curious circumstance is the absence of fat generally in the elephant. In the male there was none, in the female, about 50lb. was found, not deposited in large masses, but dispersed over the body in thin layers, and evidently containing a large quantity of stearine.

THE AILANTHUS SILKWORM.

Many of our readers may be aware that there has recently been introduced to France a new species of silkworm, which promises to rival, if not supersede, that which has been so long the sole producer of all the silk of commerce. Unlike the old species, which is known to be of delicate and tender constitution, and has of late been subject to a disease which has produced great mortality in the silk-producing districts, the ailanthus worm, (so called from the circumstance that it feeds on the leaves of the ailanthus tree), is said to be much more hardy, and more easy of cultivation. It was first brought from China to Turin, Italy, in 1857, and was introduced into France, in 1858.

From a statement recently made to the French Academy, by M. Guérin-Meneville, it appears that the cocoons, which at first had to be carded, have been successfully unwound, but by what process he does not mention. This last discovery adds most materially to the value of this silk ; and the ease with which the ailanthus can be cultivated upon the poorest soils, together with the comparatively small amount of labor required in raising the worms, which, when a few days old, are placed upon the hedges in the open air, and require scarcely any further attention, renders this culture particularly worthy of attention. This worm has also recently been introduced into this country by Dr. Stewardson, of Philadelphia, who, in a recent communication to the Philadelphia Academy, states, that his experiments satisfy him, that our climate is well adapted to raising it, and that in the latitude of the Middle States, two crops of silk can be obtained in a season. Worms placed upon ailanthus trees, in a private garden in Philadelphia, exposed without care to all the mutations of the season, came to maturity during the summer and spun their cocoons most perfectly.

THE SENSES OF SMELL AND TASTE.

The following is an abstract of an essay on the above subject by Norton Folsom, Esq., for which a prize was awarded by the Boylston (Mass.) Medical Society.

These senses are so mingled in action that their separate offices are at first difficult to determine; and even the exact locality of the perceptions which constitute the two senses can hardly be pointed out without careful observation. We instinctively know that we smell odoriferous substances when they are presented to the nose, and that we taste sapid substances in the mouth, but more than this we can only derive from experiment.

When a substance to be tasted is placed in the mouth, we press it with the upper surface of the tongue against the palate, and thus force its particles in every direction, the saliva, poured in by its glands responsive to the stimulus, aids in dissolving and disseminating the particles over the mouth. When the substance reaches the fauces, and as it is swallowed, a current of air escapes from the glottis, and carries any volatile portion to the posterior nares, where it is liable to affect the sense of smell. Plainly, therefore, in order to separate the two sensations, we must either shut off the cavity of the nose during the tasting, which can be done by most persons voluntarily, by breathing through the mouth and applying the soft palate to the back of the pharynx, or we must interrupt the current of air through the nares, which can be done by holding the nose with the fingers. .

We recognize two classes of impressions made by articles of food, — one of *savors*, of which salt affords an example; the other of flavors, as that of vanilla. Most substances have both properties; thus a strawberry has an acid and a sweet taste, besides its own delicious flavor.

The distinction between these two classes has not, indeed, been fully made by physiologists until of late; and still less has the fact been recognized, that *all flavors are perceived by the organ of smell only*, reducing the number of impressions which the organ of *taste* is capable of receiving to four only, namely, sweet, sour, salt, and bitter. This can, however, be easily and certainly demonstrated. Let the nose be closed by the fingers, or let the posterior nares be shut off by the soft palate, and a solution of vanilla be taken into the mouth and swallowed. It cannot be distinguished from water. Soup, nutmeg, cheese, pineapple, and assafœtida are alike entirely *flavorless* under similar conditions, though the *ordinary sensibility* of the mucous membrane, and the perception of the four savors above mentioned, may enable us to apprehend certain *other* qualities which distinguish these substances. The common practice of holding a child's nose while it swallows disagreeable medicine has its origin in this peculiar relation of these two senses.

We have now to consider the exact locality of the sensations produced by these four classes of stimuli. Experiments have been tried by various physiologists with entirely different results, which may be attributed to want of care and to not recognizing the fact that all *flavors* should be excluded from the investigation. All agree, however, in this — that, to be tasted, a substance must be brought to the sensitive part *in solution*, inasmuch as insoluble substances have no taste. In the experiments performed by the writer, solutions of white sugar, tartaric acid, common salt, and sulphate of quinine, were carefully applied to various parts of the mouth and fauces by means of a camel's-hair pencil, pains being taken that no excess of fluid should be used, which might diffuse itself over other parts than that directly under observation. The following results were uniformly obtained on six different individuals, they all being unaware of the substances used in each experiment.

1. The upper surface, tip, and edges of the tongue, as far back as to include the circumvallate papillæ, are the *only* parts concerned in the sense of taste; the hard and soft palate, tonsils, pharynx, lips, gums, and under surface of the tongue, being entirely destitute of this sense.

2. The circumvallate papillæ are far the most sensitive portion of the organ. They perceive, at once, very minute quantities of any one of the four substances used, and are particularly sensitive to bitter. Irritation of these papillæ by pressure, or placing a drop of cold water on them, excites decided sensations of bitterness.

3. The central portion of the dorsum of the tongue, to within half an inch of the edge, is the least sensitive portion. Substances are distinguished with difficulty, or not at all, when applied to it.

4. The edges and tip of the tongue are quite sensitive, the edges becoming less so as we come forward. They recognize all the four classes of substances. The tip detects bitter with great difficulty, but is particularly sensitive to sweet. A sweet sensation, sometimes mingled with sour or salt, is produced by gently tapping it with any insipid soft substance.

The tongue possesses *ordinary sensibility* to a marked degree, especially at its tip, and in this way detects the size, shape, and texture of substances. It is in the same way that the qualities of pungency and astringency are perceived, which fact is proved by their being nearly as perceptible to the conjunctiva, or any other mucous membrane possessing ordinary sensibility, as to the mouth. A solution of tannin, applied to the circumvallate papillæ, gives the sensation of extreme bitterness, while at the tip it produces a slight sweetish taste, especially after it has been washed off by the saliva. These sensations are entirely distinct from the puckering, which, as just said, is perceived by other mucous membranes. The application of a solution of potass gives nearly the same result, proving that there is no such thing as a distinct alkaline taste.

Certain substances have been observed to produce sensations, painful or otherwise, when applied to perfectly sound teeth. As it has been ascertained that fluids are readily and rapidly absorbed by the tubules of the dental structure, and conveyed to the pulp cavity, it is highly probable that the sensation is excited at the latter organ.

The sense of smell is entirely performed by the olfactory nerve. This is proved by the corresponding increase of the relative size of the nerve in those animals which are known to possess a particularly acute power of scent, and also by the fact that in paralysis of the trifacial the sense remains unimpaired. The branches of the trifacial, which are distributed to the mucous membrane of the lower and anterior parts of the nasal cavity, endow it with a high degree of *common sensibility*, so as to guard the more delicate part of the organ from injury, by giving warning if we attempt to inhale any irritating vapor. This common sensibility appreciates the pungency of substances in the same way as in the case of any other mucous membrane. Many substances possess pungency beside odor, as ammonia and mustard, for example. These affect the conjunctiva almost as readily as the nose.

The organ of smell is affected by substances only when they are in the form of vapor; hence non-volatile substances have no smell. Vapors reach the organ in two ways. In the first place, a current of air may be drawn, by a forcible inspiration, so as to be directed by the external nose to the upper part of its cavity, and impinge upon the filaments of the olfactory nerve. If this air contains particles of any volatile substance, it gives rise to the sensation which we call *odor*. In the second place, if any volatile substance is taken into the mouth, and carried to the fauces, or swallowed, and a puff of air is allowed to escape from the larynx, it will be directed by the walls of the pharynx, so as to carry the particles of the substance directly to the upper part of the nares, where it produces what we describe as *flavor*. We unconsciously emit this current of air, immediately after swallowing, and when we are trying to taste anything. Thus we see that " scent and flavor are the same impression on the same nerve at the same part."

Flavors are connected, in a great majority of instances, with food. This is the reason that the smell of roast meat so strongly excites the appetite of a hungry man. The exercise of the sense of taste is simultaneous with that of smell in the act of eating, which accounts for the difficulty of distinguishing between them.

We can only classify these perceptions so far as to say that they are agreeable or disagreeable. Even this distinction cannot always be made ; thus the faint smell of putrid urine closely resembles that of sandal-wood. What is offensive to one person may be pleasant to another. The desire for certain flavors is entirely acquired, and the infant will reject with loathing what may become its favorite food in after-life. An agreeable flavor or odor sometimes becomes disagreeable by long continuance. The odors of substances which are similar in other respects are generally alike, so that we may attempt to classify them according to the sources from which they are derived. The smells of plants are nearly, if not quite, all derived from essential oils. The various ethers have kindred odors.

Substances differ as to the intensity of their odor without reference to their volatility. Thus the smell of musk is more intense than that of ether.

In man, this sense only serves the purpose of giving him pleasure, and guides him to a slight extent in the choice of food ; but with the lower animals, it not only becomes necessary in the detection and selection of food, but warns of the approach of friends or enemies, and performs numerous other duties, sometimes attaining a delicacy which renders it nearly equal in rank to sight and hearing. The hunting-dog and the antelope are well-known examples of this. The sexual appetite is frequently excited through this sense. But in man, this sense is not commonly developed to its fullest possible extent. It is well known that the senses possess a certain sort of compensating power; that is, if one is lost, the others become more acute. The capabilities of this sense in the human being are well exemplified by the case of James Mitchell, who was blind, deaf, and dumb from birth, and distinguished between persons principally by smell. It enabled him to detect the entrance of a stranger at once. It is recorded of the wine-tasters of Spain, that they can distinguish between five hundred different kinds of wine; and instances are familiar to every one, of the faculty of telling several kinds of wine, or several varieties of the same kind, many times in succession, with the eyes covered. The tea-tasters, to be found in great commercial cities, acquire very nice discriminating powers, frequently determining the investment of large sums of money by merely tasting a specimen of tea.

Persons accustomed to the use of tobacco can at once distinguish the variety brought from Havana, and even in some instances, the particular plantation from which it comes.

The French cultivate the olfactory sense to a much greater extent than most other nations, not only in the art of perfumery, but in cookery, which becomes almost a fine art with them; and there seems to be no reason why the imagination should not be reached through this organ as well as through the eye and the ear. The scent of the freshly-opened rose, or the flavor of the strawberry, has as valid a claim to the notice of the poet as the song of the lark, or the beauty of sunset. At all events, much pleasure and practical advantage might be gained by its systematic cultivation, even if we should never rival the powers of "the Monk of Prague, mentioned in the *Journal of the Learned* of the year 1684."

"He not only knew different persons by the smell, but, what is much more singular, could, we are told, distinguish a chaste woman, married or unmarried, from one that was not so. This Religious had begun to write a new treatise on odors, when he died, very much lamented by the gentlemen who record this story of him. For my part, I do not know whether a man of such talents would not have been dangerous to society."

THE PHYSIQUE OF FEDERAL SOLDIERS.

At a recent meeting of the Geographical and Statistical Society, N. Y. City, Dr. W. H. Thompson, State Examining Surgeon of New York, read a paper upon the "Physique of different Nationalities as indicated by the inspection of recruits for the Federal armies." Dr. Thompson stated that he had examined nearly 9,000 men, about half of whom were natives, and had, therefore, an excellent opportunity to make comparisons. Some of the most important results arrived at through these comparisons are detailed as follows:—

"The first subject which naturally presented itself was the bodily stratum and general physical appearance of the various recruits. In stature, the American born ranked the highest, the English next, the Irish next, the Germans next, and the French last. I found it at first somewhat difficult to lay down many different rules of classification, and I therefore adopted a very general division into four classes, which were respectively termed, prime, good, indifferent, and bad. Under the head ' prime' I included, first, those who had a well-proportioned osseous system (the groundwork of the personal figure), as shown by the shape of the skull, the bones of the thorax and fibres, and the lines of the extremities. The shape of the joints, the shape of feet and hands, and the condition of the ligaments was especially noted. Secondly came a good development of the muscular system, especially those of the lower extremities, as the most reliable indication of the vigor of spinal nutrition. Under the term ' good' were classed those who were then apparently healthy and strong, with more especially a good muscular development, but who did not equal the prime in the development of the osseous system, from lack of lateral symmetry, bow legs, large joints, flat feet, etc. Under the head of ' indifferent' might be found good forms and tolerable muscular development, but who had tendencies to constitutional diseases, as well as a good many who may have had good constitutions originally, but had become deteriorated from various causes. Under the head ' bad' were such as had never been good, nor ever would be so, from an originally vicious conformation.

" Of American-born recruits 47.5 per cent. had a prime physique ; the Irish 35 per cent., and the Germans 40.75 per cent. The percentage of good physique was, Americans 36, Irish 38, Germans 38.5. The percentage of indifferent was, Americans 13.5, Irish 19.5, Germans 19. The percentage of bad, Americans 3, Irish 7.5, Germans 3. From this it will be perceived that the Americans show the highest rate of prime physique, the Germans next, and the Irish last. Of good, the Irish and Germans are nearly equal, and four per cent. more than the Americans, but this is owing to the excess of the latter in prime. Of indifferent, the Irish are one-half higher than the Germans, which last are five and one-half per cent. higher than the Americans. Of the bad, the Irish are more than double the Americans and Germans, who in this respect stand alike. So far, therefore, these figures seem favorable to the American born ; but there are several considerations to be taken into account, which will, to a certain extent, modify the inferences to be drawn from them. In the first place, the Americans were largely from classes of society who from youth have been able to command better facilities in food, clothing and shelter, than the classes from whom the immigrant population is derived. What an influence this must exert on physical development is sadly illustrated by the mortality returns of New York City, which show that though the American population is not exceeded by the foreign, yet that seven children of foreign-born parents die in a year to one American child. Besides, more than half the Americans were born and reared in country districts, and the difference which this fact causes may be shown by comparing among them the city and country recruits. Thus the proportion of prime among city Americans was forty-two per cent., country fifty-eight per cent.; of good, city forty per cent., country twenty-nine per cent.; of indifferent, city fourteen per cent., country twelve per cent.; of bad, city four per cent., country one per cent. Another reason why the Irish are double the Americans in bad physique, seemed to be that they were often recruited, for several Irish regiments, almost exclusively from the sixth ward, one of the most active recruiting stations being the Tombs prison itself.

"Still these considerations do not affect the actual standing of the American recruits, for whatever the causes may be that have aided them, I feel safe in voting their physical development as of the highest order, and I have seen specimens of the armies of nearly all European, as well as eastern nations. With the exception of a general loss of fat, I do not believe that there is another race that can show a larger proportion in the average population of excellent osseous and muscular development. This I would ascribe almost wholly to the widely diffused blessings of meat and drink, and to comforts of life possessed by nearly all. Least of all would I set it down to the score of race, for it is doubtful if there is such a thing as an unmixed race in America. No sooner does one nationality reach this shore, where all the political, social, and religious distinctions of the Old World fail to survive the sea voyage, than it rapidly merges into another, and all the rare elements of Europe soon become utterly dissolved in a well-stirred mixture of Anglo-Saxons, Hollanders, Celts, Germans, and Norwegians."

BOTANY.

THE EXISTENCE OF MUSCLES IN PLANTS.

A recent discovery, by M. Cohn, a German naturalist, of a contract-ile tissue in plants, identical in properties with the muscular tissue of animals, adds one more striking fact to the accumulated evidence of identity between the vegetable and animal organizations. Well-informed biologists, have for some time past been agreed on the impos-sibility of drawing any absolute lines of demarcation between the two. Instead of the marked opposition, which may still be read in popular hand-books, thrown into the form of tabulated contrasts, we have learned that the physical, chemical, and physiological characters, by which the plant and animal were supposed to be separated, are une-quivocally characteristic of both. It is impossible to deny that plants have mobility, and some of them even locomotion. If we deny them sensibility, it is on grounds which will equally exclude many classes of animals; and these grounds are anatomical. It is because we fail to detect the *mechanism* of sensibility, that we endeavor to interpret the phenomena as physical. It is because we associate sensibility and contractility with peculiar nervous and muscular structures, that we deny that certain phenomena observed in plants are what we should consider them to be, if we could discover nerves and muscles. Take the case of the sensitive plant *Dionœa Muscipula*, or fly-trap. The edges of its leaf are fringed with hairs, like an eyelid. On the in-side of the leaf, six delicate hairs are arranged in such an order that it would be difficult for an insect to traverse the leaf without touching one of these hairs. No sooner is a hair touched, than the two sides of the leaf suddenly close; just as the two eyelids close when an insect, or bit of dust, touches the sensitive surface. The leaf entraps the in-sect — the fringe of hairs on the edges interlacing like fingers of oppo-site hands. If the insect be not speedily liberated, it is soon *digested*; as it would be in the stomach of an animal. It should be borne in mind, that this "sensitiveness" is not the property of the whole leaf, but is localized in the delicate hairs of the centre, precisely as sensi-tiveness is localized in the nervous mechanism of animals. Now, com-paring the *phenomena* observed in the plant with phenomena observed in animals, it seems impossible to discern any marked distinction; if the eyelid's closing on an insect proves sensibility, — if the arms of a polyp closing on an insect proves sensibility, — then the closing of the *Dionœa* proves it. But, the *mechanism* in the three cases is different. In the eyelid, we find nerves and muscles; in the polyp, we find mus-cles, and no nerves; in the plant, neither nerves nor muscles. This difficulty may be turned by considering all three cases as cases of *con-tractility* only; and the first, as contractility *stimulated* by sensibility.

If this view were adopted, we should have to cut off many classes of animals from the possession of sensibility, and by so doing, bring them into still closer connection with plants. But then arises the question, Whence the contractility of plants? It is here that Cohn's admirable memoir [1] throws a flood of light. He has discovered, that in at least one portion of a plant, — the stamen of the *Centaurea*, — there exists a tissue which presides over the phenomena of contractility; and he naturally infers that in all other supposed cases of plant-contractility a similar tissue will be present.

We cannot pretend here to condense the numerous observations and rigorously-conducted experiments by which he establishes his results. Curious readers must consult the original. We give the results. The stamen of the *Centaurea* is excited by the mechanical, chemical, and electrical stimuli which excite muscles; when excited, it contracts in the same way as a muscle, describing the same curve, when, after reaching its maximum, it begins to relax again. Like the muscle, it becomes tired by contraction, and recovers its exhausted force only by repose. Like a muscle, it is excited by a weak galvanic current, and rendered tetanic by a strong current. Like a muscle, it exhibits three properties, — first, that of being *excited* by stimuli; secondly, that of *changing its form* on being excited; thirdly, that of *transmitting* every stimulus — under its correlate as motor-force — to neighboring parts.

The importance of this discovery will not be overlooked. If, as one can only infer, the phenomena observed in other plants should be found equally reducible to a similar tissue of contractile cells, we shall have a beautiful explanation of many biological phenomena now very obscure. The reader will remark that we have, throughout, for certain purposes of our own, spoken of the " muscular tissue" where Cohn uses the term " contractile tissue." It is true, to remove any misconception, which might arise from this use of the term, by muscular tissue must not be understood the special organs named " muscles " in animals, which are formed of muscular tissue, *and* several other tissues. Nor, even, must it be understood as indicating a tissue of muscular fibres, such as we find in the higher animals; but simply a tissue of contractile cells. It will prevent any misconception, if we remember that what are called muscles, or muscular tissue in the simpler animals, are nothing but contractile cells; and a diagram of the muscles in a fresh-water polyp would differ very little from a diagram of a cellular tissue in plants.

THE DESTRUCTION OF NOXIOUS INSECTS BY MEANS OF THE PYRETHRUM (PERSIAN INSECT POWDER).

M. Willemot, of France, has recently published, in the *Technologist*, an interesting paper, on the cultivation and use of the Pyrethrum (*P. carneum*), of which the celebrated Persian powder for the destruction of insects is prepared. This powder was first introduced into France in 1850, and came exclusively from districts of Persia and the Caucasus. Within a few years, however, the plant itself has been introduced into France, and at the present date is cultivated successfully and in large quantities. It is described as a small perennial shrub, from twelve to

[1] F. Cohn; *Contractile Gewebe in Pflanzenreiche*, Breslau, 1862.
26*

fifteen inches in height, bearing flowers an inch and a half in diameter, and resembling those of the ox-eye daisy (*Chrysanthemum Leucanthemum*). Its cultivation is easy, and its appearance quite ornamental. It flowers from June to September, and may be propagated by layers as well as by seed.

The parts of the plants from which the powder is made are the dried flower-heads, gathered when ripe, on fine days, and dried by exposure to the sun. In the process of desiccation they lose about 90 per cent. When perfectly dried, they are reduced to powder.

A quantity of these plants grown upon eighteen square rods is estimated to furnish one hundred pounds of powder, which is best preserved in sealed vessels of glass. The application is made either as a powder or as an infusion, though in the latter form it is more beneficial, especially when intended for the destruction of insects on plants. The powder may be employed directly to the insects themselves, or in the places which they frequent. They are attracted by its smell, become stupefied, and immediately die. This substance may be employed without injury to the larger animals, or to man. It is intimated that the amount of this powder consumed annually in Russia alone is about 500 tons.

The principal insects to which the powder of the Pyrethrum is destructive, may be arranged under four classes, — first, insects injurious to agriculture and horticulture ; second, insects obnoxious to man and his habitation ; third, insects destructive to certain substances, as wool, furs, feathers ; and, fourth, insects injurious to museums of animal and vegetable products, and collections of natural history. We do not pretend to enumerate all the insects to which the powder is destructive ; it will suffice to mention a few instances, which will sufficiently show what applications may be made of it. Our domestic animals, — dogs, cats, fowls, pigeons, etc., — are subject to annoyance from insects, which cannot withstand the effects of this powder. Of the numerous insects injurious to agriculture and horticulture we may mention the following which have been destroyed by it : the weevil, bark-beetle, wheat-fly, maggots, cocci, aphides, earwigs, spiders, ants, etc. It is evident that not only the perfectly developed insects are destroyed, but also the larvæ, which in some cases do greater injury than the insects themselves. Large depots where military stores or navy supplies are kept, and especially extensive bakeries, may use the powder with great advantage for the destruction of weevils, midges, crickets, cockroaches, etc., the great plague of those establishments. The powder is equally efficacious in destroying insects which are a constant source of annoyance to the inhabitants of cities and the country. Gnats and mosquitoes are banished ; bugs, fleas, and flies disappear from houses under its influence.

The powder of the Pyrethrum applied to furs, feathers, woolens, objects of natural history and botanical herbariums, acts also as a complete protection against insect ravages, while as regards the human subject it is perfectly innocuous. In using the powder, says M. Willemot, it must be applied carefully and in sufficient quantity, otherwise the result will be unsatisfactory, especially if used against some of the hardy or very resisting species of insects. Occasionally the powder, by being exposed to the air or moisture, will have lost its destructive properties, so as to render the result doubtful and wholly inefficient; at others the result has been unsatisfactory, because the most favorable moment for the operation has been overlooked. A rainy or wet day, for instance, always lessens the destructive efficacy, because the powder, containing a very volatile essential oil, renders the conservation of this principle extremely difficult. Of all the methods for applying the powder to plants attacked by insects, including the vine, the bellows will best accomplish the object. As there is only a small quantity of powder thrown at once, the loss will be very small, whilst in any other way a good deal of it will fall upon the ground. The powder should be directly applied to the parts operated on, and with care and precaution it may be made to penetrate into the most inaccessible parts of a plant. If, for instance, a plant has been attacked by plant lice, which are often hidden or masked by thick foliage, it will become necessary to turn aside this foliage, so as to have the insects exposed, and the powder directly brought into contact with them. In all cases these operations should take place on a warm day, the morning being always preferable. A slight moisture arising from the morning dew will make the powder more easily adhere to the spots where it is applied, and maintain its properties long enough to cause the death of the insects. The insufflation should be renewed several times according to the nature and number of insects to be destroyed. The first operation generally stupefies them, while at the second or third application they lose their strength, fall to the ground, and die sooner or later.

M. Willemot also states, that by mixing the Pyrethrum powder with wheat, in the proportion of two ounces to two or three bushels previous to sowing the grain, the ravages of the wheat-midge may be entirely prevented.

IMPROVEMENT OF WHEAT.

Mr. Hallett, an English agriculturist, has recently published the result of some interesting experiments on the improvement of the wheat plant, whereby he has obtained a superior wheat, both in productiveness and weight. He commenced experimenting with what is known in England as "nursery wheat," and details the course pursued as follows: —

"A grain produces a stool, consisting of many ears. I plant the grains from these ears in such a manner that each ear occupies a row by itself, each of its grains occupying a hole in this row; the holes being twelve inches apart every way. At harvest, after the most careful study and comparison of the stool from all these grains, I select the finest one, which I accept as a proof that its parent grain was the best of all, under the peculiar circumstances of the season.

"This process is repeated annually, starting every year with the proved best grain, although the verification of this superiority is not obtained until the following harvest." The following table gives the result at the end of the fifth year from the original sowing: —

Year.	Length in Inches.	No. Grains.	Number of ears on Stool.
1857, Original ear	4 3–8	45	
1858, Finest ear	6 1–4	79	10
1859, Ditto	7 3–4	91	22
1860, Ears imperfect from wet season			39
1861, Finest ear	8 3–4	123	52

Mr. Hallett also states, that the improvement in the sixth generation was even greater than in any of the others. " Thus," he continues, " by means of repeated selection alone, the length of the ears has been doubled, their contents nearly trebled, and the tillering power of the seed increased five-fold." By " tillering," we should perhaps mention, is meant the horizontal growth of the wheat-plant, which takes place before the vertical stems are thrown up, and upon the extent of which, therefore, depends in a great degree the number of ears which the single plant produces.

" During my investigations," says Mr. H., " no single circumstance has struck me as more forcibly illustrating the necessity for repeated selection than the fact that of the grains in the same year one is found greatly to excel all others in vital power. Thus, the original two ears contained together eighty-seven grains; these were all planted singly. One of these produced ten ears, containing 688 grains; and not only could the produce of no other single grain compare with them, but the finest ten ears that could be collected from the produce of the whole of the other 86 grains contained only 598 grains. Yet, supposing that this superior grain grew in the smaller of the two original ears, and that this contained but 40 grains, there must still have been 39 of these 86 grains which grew in the same ear.

" Let us now consider whether pedigree in wheat, combined with a natural mode of cultivating it (as above), can produce a number of ears equal to that usually grown per acre under the present system. In order to ascertain this we ought to know the number of ears ordinarily grown from seven or eight pecks of seed; but there are really no data upon this point. It has, however, been considered as about equal to the number of grains in a bushel, or under eight hundred thousand, which is about one ear for every two grains sown. I will then compare the numbers grown in 1861 upon two pieces of land, only separated by a hedge, where the two systems were fairly tried, the same ' pedigree wheat ' being employed as seed in both cases. In the one instance, six pecks of seed per acre were drilled November 20th, 1860, and the crop, resulting in fifty-four bushels per acre, consisted, at its thickest part, of 934,120 ears per acre. In the other instance, 4½ pints per acre were planted in September, in single grains, one foot apart every way, and the number of ears produced per acre was 1,001,-880, or 67,760 ears in excess of those produced on the other side of the hedge, from more than twenty-one times the seed here employed. Now, as an area of a square foot is more than amply sufficient for the development of a single grain, it is clear that thin seeding is not necessarily attended by a thin crop."

It would appear from this, that thin seeding and early sowing are both beneficial; and that an immense saving may be made in the quantity of wheat used annually for seed. It is reported further, that the wheat, when thinly sown or planted, grows so strong in the straw, that while his neighbors' wheat was laid down by a heavy storm of wind and rain, Mr. Hallett's stood up as strong as before the storm.

TRANSMUTATION OF " SPECIES " IN THE VEGETABLE WORLD.

It has been repeatedly asserted that oats have been converted into rye, barley, and even wheat; but the " fact " has been always scoffed out of countenance, because it was inconsistent with preconceived theories. Now, however, there would appear to be no doubt about it. The *Mark-lane Express* vouches for the respectability of a gentleman who states that he carefully planted some picked oat grains in his garden in June ; and as the tillers sprang up to about a foot in height, he cut them down to within an inch of the root. This process was three times repeated that year, and some of the roots died ; but others survived ; and next year they yielded, — not oats, but perfect barley, rather thin, but by no means of a bad type. This barley, in the following spring, yielded a good return of better barley, approved by the maltster ; and of the produce of subsequent years the editor says he has seen a sample. It is remarkable that the grower did not look for barley, but rye, which he had been told had thus been obtained. The editor is of opinion that oats are a " spurt " or sport from other grain, — not *vice versa ;* as wheat and barley have been known for 4000 years, but not oats.

It is said that the transmutation of oats into barley is by no means infrequent in Norway and Sweden, which, by the way, geologists have found to be a notable centre of plant distribution.

A letter from Mr. William Cowper, of Wappenham, near Towcester, appears in the *Berkshire Chronicle*, stating that he has for ten years grown both wheat and barley from Dutch oats. Black oats, he adds, will produce rye in the same way.

If any one imagines, however, that when such facts can no longer be denied, we will be any nearer to an admission that one species of plant can be transmuted into another species, he will probably be mistaken ; for when the fact can be no longer resisted, it will only be seized hold of as proof positive that oats, rye, barley, and wheat are *not* distinct species at all ; so that the transmutations of species will be as far off as ever, and thus may well be deemed impossible. — *London Builder.*

ARTIFICIAL FECUNDATION OF PLANTS.

The following process devised by M. Hooibrenck for increasing the fertility of cereal and other plants, has excited considerable attention in France. When the grain is in flower, he passes over it an apparatus consisting of a string set with tufts of wool, close together, and having small lead weights between them. He repeats this brushing of the flowers three times, at intervals of two days. Espalier fruit trees he deals with in another fashion. First, he touches the stigmata with a finger carrying a little honey, and then brushes the flowers lightly with a powder-puff. By this means, pollen is brought into contact with the honey, and adheres. Larger trees he reaches with a sort of brush, composed of tufts of wool. A commission appointed by the Minister of Agriculture reports very favorably upon these processes, as increasing the yield of corn, and they observe, that the fruit trees operated on produced an abundant crop, but they could not so easily satisfy themselves as to what cause it was due.

MUMMY WHEAT.

The *Presse Scientifique des Deux Mondes* contains a description of a series of experiments made in Egypt by Figari-Bey on the wheat found in the ancient sepulchres of that country. A long dispute occurred a few years ago, as to what truth there might be in the popular belief, according to which this ancient wheat will not only germinate after the lapse of three thousand years, but produce ears of extraordinary size and beauty. The question was left undecided ; but Figari-Bey's paper, addressed to the Egyptian Institute at Alexandria, contains some facts which appear much in favor of a negative solution. One kind of wheat which Figari-Bey employed for his experiments had been found in Upper Egypt, at the bottom of a tomb at Medinet-Aboo. There were two varieties of it, both pertaining to those still cultivated in Egypt. The form of the grains had not changed ; but their color, both within and without, had become reddish, as if they had been exposed to smoke. On being sown in moist ground, under the usual pressure of the atmosphere, and at a temperature of 25 degrees (Reaumur), the grains became soft, and swelled a little during the first four days ; on the seventh day their tumefaction became more apparent with an appearance of maceration and decomposition ; and on the ninth day this decomposition was complete. No trace of germination could be discovered during all this time. Figari-Bey obtained similar negative results from grains of wheat found in other sepulchres, and also on barley proceeding from the same source ; so that there is every reason to believe that the ears hitherto ostensibly obtained from mummy wheat proceeded from grain accidentally contained in the mould into which the former was sown.

THE CONICAL GROWTH OF TREES.

If we look at the stem and branches of a tree in winter, when deprived of its summer leaves, we shall see at once that it is constructed on the principle of a cone ; for the main stem of the tree is broadest at the base, and gradually decreases in thickness toward the extremities of its branches. Any branch in the place where a side-branch originates, is thicker than the side-branch ; so also this side-branch is thicker than the branchlet which it produces, and in this manner the thickness of the main stem steps, as it were, away by degrees from branch to branch, until at length it loses itself in the fine branches of the youngest generation of shoots, or the most recent growths. It is well known that the cone is the stablest structure in nature, and the tree may be very properly regarded as an arborescent cone.

If a transverse section of a young beech-tree is examined, it will be found to consist of a number of concentrical and almost circular beds or layers of wood, ensheathing one another about a common centre, which is occupied by a canal of pith, the whole being covered by the bark formed on the outside of the stem. The longitudinal section, on the contrary, shows that the stem is composed of a series of superposed and hollow elongated cones, the old conical growth, or woody layers of the last and previous seasons, forming a firm foundation for the new conical layers of the next and succeeding years.

The conical growth of the tree is the result of the conical formation of the first year's shoot, which is the foundation of the subsequent annual additions of wood and bark ; for as these are deposited in strata which lie parallel with the wood and bark of the first year's shoot, the conical form of the superposed layers is necessarily retained.

Growth in length and growth in thickness must therefore be regarded as the result of one and the same vegetative cause, namely, the formation each year of a new conical layer or enveloping mantle of wood and bark, which extends from the top to the bottom of the tree. The following law will express the relation subsisting between the two dimensions of length and breadth: *the branches are more cylindrical the longer they are, and more conical in proportion as they are shorter.*

As examples of well-marked conical growths, we may mention those extremely abbreviated shoots called thorns, of which the blackthorn and the American cockspur thorn furnish us with good examples. That thorns are only abortive shoots or branches, is proved by the wild plum-tree ; this tree when planted in a good soil changes its thorns in-to branches.

In the case of the Weeping Willow, on the contrary, we have an instance of branches which tend more to a cylindrical than to a coni-cal form. In consequence of this peculiarity, the branches of this tree are long and pendulous, their waterfall-like curvature is extremely graceful, and as they wave backward and forward in the wind, the tree presents one of the most beautiful and picturesque of objects.

But the conical growth of trees is sometimes strikingly apparent in their landscape character, or general outline when viewed from a dis-tance. This is the case in the great natural order *Coniferæ*, or the cone-bearing family. The trees belonging to this order, such as the Juniper, the Red Cedar, the Norway Spruce Fir, and the celebrated Norfolk Island Pine, when seen from a distance, are clearly conical in their outline ; and this is the case with all the other members of this family. The leaves of these trees are excessively narrow and small, the blade being reduced to an abortive condition. They have been called by the German botanists with some propriety needle-leaved trees. These leaves are quite as capable of forming wood as those which possess a true lamina or blade, for they make up by their im-mense number and their persistent nature for their want of surface. The branches of the fir and yew have always on them the foliage of five or six summers, their leaves remaining usually that length of time attached to them.

The conical form is, in fact, more or less the original form of all trees during the earlier portion of their life ; for " at first, growth takes place in the direction of the main stem," and the growth of the branch-es is consequently greatly restricted ; but after a certain number of years, the stem obtains its greatest height, and growth is " diverted to its leading branches," which lose their conical figure or outline consid-ered collectively, and, spreading out on all sides, form a dome-shaped or hemispherical top or crown. This is particularly grand in the horse-chestnut, the lime-tree, and the elm, which make for this reason a fine appearance on a lawn or in a park, in addition to the recommendation of the perfect shade which they afford. At this second stage in the life of the tree, the main stem is no longer distinguishable from the other branches, because they have made with it an equally powerful growth. In the Coniferæ, however, development is not carried so far, for the tree stops at the first stage, and therefore retains permanently its cone-like appearance. For this reason, as well as on account of the simplicity of their leaves and flowers, and their high geological antiquity, coniferous trees may be regarded as of a low type of organi-zation.

This discussion of the conical growth of trees leads us necessarily to the investigation of the source from whence they derive their elaborated formative material. *This is undoubtedly the leaf.* Now, this law is plainly apparent in the single shoot, the figure of which depends on the manner in which the leaves are disposed about its surface ; for as the wood is formed by the leaves, when these are placed in regular order over every part of the circumference of the shoot, as in the beech and lime, the shoot is always necessarily cylindrical, for the woody matter proceeding from the leaves is then distributed equally on all its sides. On the contrary, when the leaves on the single shoot are opposite, or in pairs, placed at right angles to each other, as in the spindle-tree and maple, the descent of nourishing matter from them is necessarily limited to that portion of the stem immediately below them, and consequently the young shoots and branches of these trees are square.

But not only the form of the single shoot, but also the extent to which it is conical, depends on the leaves. If the vital activity of the leaves is too enfeebled to form wood, if they remain crowded together into clusters at the top of the shoot without separating, the shoot may increase in length, but there is no increase in breadth. Two shoots of the horse-chestnut are now lying before me, placed side by side for comparison, and the contrast between their figure is not only very perceptible, but also highly instructive. The shoot in the one case is conical; in the other, cylindrical. The conical shoot is the growth of a single year ; the cylindrical shoot is the growth of ten years ; yet both are nearly the same size. As the elaborated woody matter forming the substance of these shoots was derived from the leaves with which they were clothed, and as, in the case of the ten years' shoot, very little was supplied, that shoot is cylindrical, not conical, like the one year's shoot.

It follows, too, that the breadth of the wood-rings formed annually, and which are visible on the transverse section of the stem, must also correspond with the amount of active leaf-surface which is put forth into the atmosphere during the vegetative season. In order to verify this truth, it is only necessary to select branches, the leaves of whose side-shoots are annually put forth as leaf-clusters, and which therefore take a minimum of development, and consequently exercise the smallest possible amount of physiological influence on the branch, and where powerful growths are suddenly succeeded by growths greatly retarded. One such branch now lies before me, seven years old, whose main stem is eighteen inches long, and whose side-shoots are abortive in their growth. It grew the first three years five inches annually, or altogether fifteen inches ; but in the last four years the growth stagnated, or averaged only nine lines (a line is the twelfth part of an inch) annually ; and the cross section of the branch actually shows the three inner rings or woody layers, formed by the leaves of the first three years, to be much broader than the four outer rings, the leaf-deposits of the last four years.

These investigations and others lead irresistibly to the conclusion, that the breadth of the wood-rings is determined not only by the activity of the leaves of the terminal shoot of the main stem, but that the leaves of the side-shoots or of the whole system of shoots coöperate ; and therefore that the leafage of each season forms a common source, whence is derived not only the nutriment forming the new layer or covering of each individual branch or system of shoots, but of the main stem or support of the whole of them. The leaves are therefore the sources of the elaborated formative material which proceeds from them to the shoots, from the shoots to the branchlets, and from the branchlets to the branches, whose union forms the main stem of the tree, just as a thousand little streamlets pour together their tributary waters, which, united, form the broad river that rolls on to the ocean.

CHINESE ART OF DWARFING TREES.

" The art of dwarfing trees, as commonly practised both in China and Japan, is in reality very simple and easily understood. It is based upon one of the commonest principles of vegetable physiology. Anything which has a tendency to check or retard the flow of the sap in trees, also prevents, to a certain extent, the formation of wood and leaves. This may be done by grafting, by confining the roots in a small space, by withholding water, by bending the branches, and in a hundred other ways, which all proceed upon the same principle. This principle is perfectly understood by the Japanese, and they take advantage of it to make nature subservient to this particular whim of theirs. They are said to select the smallest seeds from the smallest plants, which I think is not at all unlikely. I have frequently seen Chinese gardeners selecting suckers for this purpose from the plants of their gardens. Stunted varieties were generally chosen, particularly · if they had the branches opposite or regular, for much depends upon this ; a one-sided dwarf-tree is of no value in the eyes of the Chinese or Japanese. The main stem was then, in most cases, twisted in a zigzag form, which process checked the flow of the sap, and at the same time encouraged the production of side-branches at those parts of the stem where they were most desired. The pots in which they were planted were narrow and shallow, so that they held but a small quantity of soil compared with the wants of the plants, and no more water was given than was actually necessary to keep them alive. When new branches were in the act of formation, they were tied down and twisted in various ways ; the points of the leaders and strong-growing ones were generally nipped out, and every means was taken to discourage the production of young shoots possessing any degree of vigor. ·Nature generally struggles against this treatment for a while, until her powers seem to be in a great measure exhausted, when she quietly yields to the power of Art. The artist, however, must be ever on the watch ; for should the roots of his plants get through the pots into the ground, or happen to receive a liberal supply of moisture, or should the young shoots be allowed to grow in their natural position for a time, the vigor of the plant, which has so long been lost, will be restored, and the fairest specimens of Oriental dwarfing destroyed. It is a curious fact that when plants, from any cause, become stunted or unhealthy, they almost invariably produce flowers and fruit, and thus endeavor to propagate and perpetuate their kind. This principle is of great value in dwarfing trees. Flowering trees — such, for ex· ample, as peaches and plums — produce their blossoms most profusely under the treatment I have described ; and as they expend their energies in this way, they have little inclination to make vigorous growth." — *Fortune's China and Japan.*

27

THE ORDEAL BEAN OF CALABAR.

At a recent scientific meeting in London, Prof. Harley exhibited specimens of the bean employed by the King of Calabar as a poisonous ordeal to determine the guilt or innocence of accused persons. The plant yielding this bean is kept secret from the natives generally, and the seeds are consequently to be obtained only with great difficulty. The name that has been given to the plant is *Physostigma venenosum,* or *Calabar ordeal bean.* It belongs to the leguminous tribe, having distinct papilionaceous flowers succeeded by pods six inches in length, each containing four or five seeds, having white cotyledons, resembling in taste the seeds of the common haricot, *Phaseolus vulgaris.* Taken internally, the beans, unless rejected by vomiting, produce fatal paralysis. In some experiments made in this country it has been found that twelve grains have produced partial paralysis, threatening to be serious in its results. In the course of investigation into its properties, it has been ascertained that the extract of the bean possesses a most extraordinary power over the iris, a few minims of its solution dropped into the eye causing contraction of the pupil to such an extent that the aperture becomes entirely obliterated, and the eye possesses the appearance of having an imperforate iris. In order to demonstrate this action more fully, and to contrast it with the opposite effect of a solution of belladonna, a cat was exhibited, to one eye of which belladonna had been applied several days previously, causing dilatation of the pupil to such an extent that the iris was scarcely visible; to the other eye a solution of the ordeal bean had been applied, which caused obliteration of the pupil. The contrast between the two eyes of the animal was of the most marked character, and imparted a strange weird expression to the face. In the course of the evening the pupil dilated somewhat — the effect of the Physostigma passing away gradually in the course of about twenty-four hours, whereas that of the belladonna persists for many days. Specimens of the plant have been raised in England from the imported seeds.

OZONE EXHALED BY PLANTS.

In an elaborate memoir presented to the Academy of Sciences, at Paris, M. Kosmann gives an account of a series of experiments in regard to this subject, carried on at his own house in the middle of Strasburg, in the Botanic Garden of that city, and in a spacious garden above thirty miles from it: these three places seeming to offer the differences which should characterize vegetation in the midst of towns and that of the country in various degrees. He made use of Schönbein's ozonometric scale and ozonoscopic bands, fixed on the plants. For details we must refer to the *Comptes Rendus.* He gives the following as the results of his observations from July 29 to Sept. 14 last. (He proposes to resume his studies in the spring.) — " 1. Plants give off ozonized oxygen from the midst of their leaves and green parts. 2. Their leaves give off during the day ozonized oxygen in ponderable quantity, much greater than that which exists in the surrounding air. 3. During the night this difference disappears where vegetables are own sparingly; but where there is an accumulation of plants, and ey grow vigorously, even in the night the ozone observed in the plants is greater than in the air, which is, doubtless, explained by supposing that the ozone disengaged during the day continues to surround the plants during the night when the weather is calm. 4. Plants in the country give off more ozone than those in the town during the day, — probably due to vegetative life being more active, — the former also reducing more carbonic acid. 5. Hence we may infer that the air of the country and that of habitations surrounded by vast gardens, forests, etc., is more vivifying than that of towns. 6. In the midst of towns and a concentrated population, the ozone of the air at night is more considerable than the ozone of the air by day. If we go away a little from this concentration of men, and enter into that of plants, the excess of the ozone of the night above that of the day diminishes; and if we advance further into the country, where plants are more numerous than men, the ozone of the day becomes more considerable than that of the night. 7. The interior of the corollas gives off no ozonized oxygen. 8. In dwelling-rooms oxygen does not generally exist in the ozonized state."

PHOSPHORUS IN VEGETATION.

M. Benjamin Corenwinder has lately contributed a voluminous paper to the French Academy describing experiments which shed much light on the manner in which phosphorus exerts such a beneficial effect on vegetation. The results that he arrives at are. — 1. That plants when young always yield ashes rich in phosphoric acid, but that after the plant has produced its seed or fruit, the stem or leaves contain very little of that principle. 2. That phosphoric acid exists in plants in close combination with nitrogenous matter. 3. That the organs of plants, not containing any nitrogen, and ill-adapted for food, contain no phosphates. 4. That the exudations of plants, such as manna and gum-arabic, do not generally contain phosphoric acid. 5. That if the skeleton of a young plant be separated from the pulpy matter, all the phosphoric acid remains in the latter; so that, unlike the skeletons of animals, those of plants do not owe their solidity to any phosphates. 6. That marine plants, growing on rocks, contain a large quantity of phosphates, as also the pollen of flowers, and the spores of cryptogamous plants.

ASTRONOMY AND METEOROLOGY.

NEW PLANETS AND COMETS.

The discovery of three new asteroidal planets has been announced during the past year, making the whole number now recognized *seventy-nine*. The seventy-seventh asteroid was discovered November 12, 1862, by Dr. C. H. F. Peters, at the Hamilton College Observatory N. Y.

The seventy-eighth asteroid was discovered March 15th, 1863, by Dr. Luther of Bilk, Germany. It has received the name *Diana*, and is of the tenth magnitude.

The seventy-ninth asteroid was discovered September 14th, by Prof. James C. W. tson, of the observatory of Ann-Arbor, Michigan; and has received the name *Eurynome*.

New Comets. — Six comets, which are believed to have not before been recognized, have been discovered during the past year. None of them, however, exhibited features of special interest. On the 21st of November, 1863, a comet was discovered with the naked eye by D. M. Covey, of Southville, N. Y., whose elements so closely correspond with the comet of 1810 that there can be but very little doubt of the identity of the two. Whether this is the first return to the perihelion since 1810, or whether it has returned several times unperceived, must be decided by subsequent observations.

Intra-Mercurial Planet. — In the *Monthly Notices* of the Royal Astronomical Society, Mr. Carrington has printed a letter from Dr. Von Littrow, of which we give a portion. The latter says that in the *Vienna Times* of April 27, 1820, he finds the statement, probably communicated by his father, that " M. Steinheibel, who, for the last four years has daily observed the sun, and recorded his spots and faculæ with care in a diary, on February 12, 1820, at 10h. 45m. in the morning, observed a spot which was distinguished from all the rest by its well-defined circular form, by its equally circular atmosphere, by its orange-red color, and especially by its unusual motion, completing the diameter of the sun in nearly five hours." This note is very interesting as confirmatory of M. Lescarbault's discovery of Vulcan in 1859, which, however, has never been seen again.

MORE COMPANIONS OF SIRIUS: — PLANETARY SYSTEMS AMONG THE STARS.

The assertion so frequently made and so generally accepted that our sun is one of the fixed stars, is of course incapable of demonstration. Its probability seems to rest chiefly upon two arguments, — that the ht of the stars is evidently of the same intrinsic and self-developed character with that of the sun, and that the sun, if viewed at a distance equal to that of the stars, would undoubtedly appear no otherwise than as one of them; and since no more direct proof can be obtained, we are willing to receive these as sufficient. But this point once admitted, it is evidently consistent with all analogy to proceed a step further, and to suppose that these other suns, or at least the insulated ones, may be, as our own, the centres of light and heat and gravity, and electrical and chemical influences to groups of surrounding worlds. The idea is a magnificent one, and in full accordance with every other declaration of the glory of God in the heavens, and it would be no matter of surprise at any time if observation were to give us direct evidence of its truth. Nor would it necessarily follow that the highest class of instruments would be required for the detection of these planetary systems, though so wonderfully remote in the depths of space. Analogy may point the way in many cases where it ought not to interpose a check, and the diminutive size of our planets in comparison with their ruler affords no adequate inference that in other systems a very different arrangement may not obtain. And thus, although planets no larger than our own might ever remain invisible at the distance of the fixed stars, it is not merely possible, but may be even probable, that bodies of a similar nature may be connected with other suns, of sufficient magnitude to be visible with our instruments, especially in their modern state of improvement. The idea was thrown out by Sir J. Herschel, many years ago, that certain very minute points, closely associated with larger stars, may be visible by reflected or planetary light; and he specified among others, ι Ursæ Majoris, γ Hydræ, κ Geminorum, and the *comites* of a^2 Cancri and a^2 Capricorni; but it does not appear that these suspicions have been verified, or that the matter has been subsequently investigated, notwithstanding its obvious interest and importance.

The subject, however, has been brought afresh before us by M. Goldschmidt's recent assertion that with an object-glass of little more than four inches aperture, he has not merely perceived Alvan Clark's companion of Sirius, which has hitherto been supposed to be reserved for the largest and most perfect instruments, but has detected five additional companions of the same character, at somewhat greater distances, varying from 15″ to 1′; and, in announcing this discovery, he suggests an inquiry as to whether the object discovered by A. Clark may shine by native or reflected light, which may of course be extended to the rest. It seems remarkable that the colossal telescopes of Clark, Bond, Lassell, and Chacornac, in which the nearest of these alleged attendants has been perceived, should have given no indication, as far as has hitherto been stated, of the other five; but M. Goldschmidt is so distinguished as an observer, that not a shadow of a suspicion can be attached either to his eye or his judgment. It is, however, possible that some source of deception may exist in his instrument, such as appears to have given rise to the supposed satellite of Venus in the last century. We shall soon, at any rate, know more about it. Should the existence of these minute points be established, the most natural supposition, of course, will be, that Sirius is accidentally projected on a background of small stars at an incalculably greater distance; and this idea would not be negatived by any appar-

27*

ent general displacement, which would be referred to the proper motion of the large star.   Should, however, any mutual change of position be detected among the *comites*, a wide field would be opened for
research among the fortunate possessors of competent telescopes.   The
question of native or reflected light would, of course, be a difficult one
to deal with, — its solution would, in fact, be impossible in the case of
orbits highly inclined to our line of vision ; but if bodies exist whose
revolutions carry them from side to side, or nearly so, with respect to
the central luminary, any periodical variation of light connected with
their positions in their orbits would, as indicating the existence of pha-
ses resulting from reflection, give sufficient evidence of their planetary nature.

Since the announcement of M. Goldschmidt, referred to above, M.
Secchi, of Rome, states that he has succeeded in seeing the satellite of
Sirius, with several contiguous luminous points; but in reference to
these last, he asks, " Are they realities or illusions ? "   One he noticed at 5″ distance, and about 180° angle of position.   He says he
mentions these observations to show the goodness of the telescope ; but
M. Goldschmidt's observations show that a much smaller instrument
will suffice when the air is favorable.

On the Observed Motions of the Companion of Sirius. — Mr. T. H.
Safford, of the Cambridge Observatory, has recently published the results of an inquiry into the observed motions of the companion of Sirius,
with a view of ascertaining whether it is in reality the disturbing body
which theory requires should exist.   " That the companion of Sirius,"
says Mr. Safford, " may produce the disturbances recognized, the faint
object barely visible in the largest class of telescopes must have a mass
nearly *two-thirds* that of Sirius itself.   It is difficult to believe this ;
but as the evidence of this year (1863) shows, we may be compelled
to do so."

" There are three hypotheses logically possible with respect to the
new star.   It may be either unconnected with the system of Sirius, or,
secondly, a satellite, but not the disturbing body, or, thirdly, the disturbing body itself."   Opposed to the first hypothesis is the improbable supposition, " that the small star can partake in the great proper
motion of Sirius without being physically connected with it ; " and if we
adopt the second hypothesis, the disturbing body, judging from the
feeble light of the companion recognized, must have less light, or be
absolutely invisible.   " *It is, therefore,*" concludes Mr. Safford, " *highly
probable that the disturbing body has been actually found ; and that what
was predicted by theory has been confirmed by sight.*   The importance
of continued observations on Sirius cannot be too highly felt.   The
companion must be measured the coming year, and for several years ;
while Sirius itself should be reobserved with meridian instruments."

VARIABILITY OF NEBULÆ.

In the *Annual of Scientific Discovery*, 1863, pp. 317–18, an account
was given of the discovery of the disappearance of a nebula in the con-
stellation *Taurus*, toward the close of October, 1861.   During the past
year the announcement is made that the nebula in question has reap-
ared, without change of place, but materially fainter than when first
rved.   In addition to this interesting statement, another still more
rkable has also been recently brought out.

Mr. Eyre B. Powell, an astronomer, resident at Madras, to whom we owe many valuable observations of double stars, and computations of their orbits, states that while engaged in making a series of microscopical measures of the stars, in the great nebula surrounding the remarkably variable star η Argus (the largest and finest nebula in the southern hemisphere), he was led to notice a most extraordinary change in its configuration. Close adjoining to the bright star Eta (η) is a very singular oval vacuity, quite devoid of nebula, of a shape somewhat resembling the figure 8, only with its two compartments communicating; and having its longer axis nearly in a meridian. According to the elaborate delineation made by Sir John Herschel, during his residence at the Cape of Good Hope, of which an engraving is published in the " Results " of his Cape observations, both ends of this oval were then (1835-1838) completely closed, the southern especially, being bounded by a strongly-marked and definite outline, as if cut out of paper. At present, this oval, we are informed by Mr. Powell, is *decidedly open* at the south end. The phenomenon, thus stated, is perhaps the most startling thing which has yet occurred in sidereal astronomy, and coupled with the capricious variability of Argus itself, is calculated to open a field for the wildest speculation.

PARALLAX OF MINUTE STARS.

It was long and naturally supposed that the most conspicuous fixed stars were also the nearest, and that their brightness was, at least in a general sense, dependent upon their situation with respect to ourselves. It is now capable of demonstration that this is a fallacy. As far back as the year 1826, Sir John Herschel stated that there were " plausible grounds for a belief that, in situations remote from the Milky Way, minuteness, on the average, is not the effect of distance;" and this belief may now be said to have ripened into confidence. It may still be doubtful whether such an assertion may be applicable to the *average* of stars in any portion of the heavens; but it is no longer a question whether, in many instances, it may not be capable of direct proof. A fair presumption would arise from the admitted fact, that the proper motions by which many of the stars are steadily changing their positions are by no means always the largest in the brightest individuals; still, this presumption would not amount to actual demonstration. This could only be attained in one of two ways: — either by showing that great differences of magnitude exist between the components of binary systems, or by the most direct mode of all — that of the detection of an annual parallax; in other words, an apparent change in the star's place resulting from an actual change in the position of the observer's eye, as our annual orbit carries us round the sun. It has been for some time known that the parallaxes of several of the brightest stars are, if not absolutely insensible, as Peters found with regard to α Cygni, and as Airy has suspected in the case of α Lyræ, yet much smaller than that of 61 Cygni, a star of only the 6th magnitude, which, according to Sir W. Herschel's estimate, would have been about twelve times more distant ; but it has been reserved to the present day to carry onward this demonstration to a much greater extent by applying it to stars of a far inferior order. This interesting result has been obtained by means of the excellent heliometer at Bonn, in the hands of M. Krüger. A star of the 8.9 mag., No. 21,258 of La-lande's Catalogue, and another of the 9. mag., No. 17,415-6 in the Cata-logue of Oeltzen, had been pointed out by Argelander as remarkable from their large amount of proper motion, in the latter case amounting to 1″.2 annually. Thirty-six comparisons of the former with two other suitably placed stars yielded an amount of parallax = 0″.260, with a probable error of 0″.020. The latter star, from a mean of forty-five similar comparisons, showed a parallax = 0″.247, with a probable error of 0″.021. This, if confirmed by future measures, would bring these inconspicuous objects actually nearer to us than Polaris, Arcturus, or even the magnificent Sirius himself, and must suggest very remarkable speculations as to the probable structure of the Universe. — *London Intellectual Observer.*

VISIBILITY OF STARS IN THE PLEIADES.

In a late number of the *Notices of the Royal Astronomical Society* the Astronomer Royal, Mr. G. Airy writes as follows: — To the greater number of star-gazers, with what are commonly called good eyes, I believe that Ovid's remark as to the visible number of Pleiades still applies: — 'Quæ septem dici, sex tamen esse solent' (which are wont to be called seven, yet are but six.) I find, however, that one of my family habitually sees seven, and on rarer occasions twelve." On the clear evening of Feb. 15th, 1863, a map of the visible stars was drawn from ocular view, and, on comparing it with a map drawn from Bessel's measures, Mr. Airy had no difficulty in identifying the stars with six numbered by Bessel.

THE PHENOMENA OF COMETS.

The great difficulty which confronts us in every attempt to investi-gate the nature of comets is the absence of all satisfactory analogy. No one can have watched an opposition of Mars without being con-vinced of a general similarity between the constitution of that globe and our own; and even in Jupiter and Saturn, though belonging to another planetary type, the evident and complete control of gravity, the provision for day and night, and the existence of an atmosphere of varying transparency and constant mobility, form points of contact, so to speak, of considerable significance. But in the case of comets, with the sole exception of the influence of gravity over the denser portions of the mass, analogy breaks down altogether, and direct observation has hitherto, for the most part, brought out nothing more than a series of marvellous and unaccountable facts, maintaining obstinately the se-cret of the law, which no doubt unites them into a harmonious and beautiful whole. We have not as yet any adequate information as to the composition of the nucleus; whether, even in the most brilliant comets, it ever attains a state of actual solidity, or whether all may not be as unsubstantial as one of our own clouds, which, at an equal dis-tance and under suitable illumination, would no doubt reflect a very vivid light; in fact, as to the real nature of the material of comets, be-yond that extraordinary attenuation of mass which makes their attrac-tion imperceptible, even in their closest known appulses to other bod-ies, we have not a single idea. That they are ponderable is certain, or they would not obey the attraction of the sun; but when we would trace their effect upon the balance of our system, we entirely fail. It appears from the experiments of Secchi upon the late comet with the polariscope, that the light of the nucleus and the brighter part of the "aigrettes" or jets, was never polarized, excepting very feebly on the last day of possible observation, while that of the surrounding nebulosity was strongly so, and the extremities of the jets exhibited an intermediate condition. But even this very interesting result, confirmed to a great extent by that of the great comet of 1861, in which the same observer found the polarization of the light of the tail and the rays near the nucleus very powerful, but no trace of it in the nucleus till July 3 and the following days, when it was strongly indicated, gives no distinct intimation as to the nature of the light. Secchi thinks that the condition of the nucleus may have resembled that of terrestrial clouds, which have no polarizing effect, while the coma and tail may have been in a gaseous state; but it is obvious on how slight a foundation such a conjecture as to a totally unknown material is raised; and though this great and justly celebrated observer says that if we continue to make as much progress with future comets as we have done with the last three conspicuous ones, our knowledge of their nature will be speedily complete, one cannot help thinking that "the wish was father to the thought." In fact, there would be no greater difficulty in maintaining the converse proposition, that we shall never obtain any satisfactory idea as to their composition, unless we should get actually involved in their extent. There was, indeed, reason to suppose that the edge of the tail swept over us in 1861, but from the imperceptible passage of those very attenuated streams it would be hazardous to infer the results of immediate contact with a glowing nucleus. Up to the present time, the simple question cannot be considered to be decided, whether comets shine by native or reflected light, or by a combination of both; even forms which have been considered to be of constant occurrence, such as the curvature of the tail backwards from the direction of its motion, and the superior density and distinctness of its convex edge, have been shown by the recent comet to be less universal than had been supposed. Few, indeed, are the points which we can consider adequately established. From the fixity, or limited movement of the jets issuing from it, it may be considered certain that the nucleus does not revolve; a rotatory motion of the whole tail round its axis has indeed been suspected, from the reciprocating form of its branches in 1769, 1811, and 1825, and thought not impossible by Secchi in 1860; but even should this be admitted in some instances, in others it would be quite incompatible with observation.

It is evident that the whole mass is vehemently acted upon by some influence emanating from the sun, the continuation and accumulation of which, after the perihelion passage, seems to point to a calorific rather than a more instantaneous electric or magnetic action; and it would appear as though the nucleus — even if translucent to light, and reflecting it alike, as Sir J. Herschel suggests, from its interior part and from its surface, and therefore having no shadow or dark side — were not equally permeable by that solar influence, whatever it may be; since the formation of fans and envelopes takes place only on the side exposed to the sun, while the opposite side is comparatively undisturbed, and as it were in a sheltered state. An intermittent or discontinuous process of development is frequently conspicuous, even when no regular period can be established; this was made very evident in the succession of envelopes raised from the nucleus of Donati's comet, as described by several observers, and more especially by Bond; it was again manifest in the marvellous alternations of brightness exhibited by Comet III. 1860; and reappeared strikingly in the aspect of the brilliant comet of the fall of 1862. As remote as most of these phenomena are from all our terrestrial analogies, a still wider deviation is to be found in the tendency of cometary matter to repulsion, expansion, and ultimate dispersion. In the formation of the jets and envelopes, in the emission of the tail, in its irreclaimable projection to uncontrolled distances, and in the actual disruption of the main mass, — to which there seemed a slight tendency in "the Donati," more in III. 1860, still more in I. 1860, and of which Biela's comet, in 1846, appeared to offer a perfect example, — we see indications of a process very foreign to our own experience, but remarkably characteristic of cometary matter. This brief and imperfect enumeration of some of the points, which we may look upon as "vantage ground" in such inquiries, may be useful in assisting amateurs to prepare for the next opportunity of further research, which, though it may be expected to confirm some of these deductions, may probably at the same time surprise us with unforeseen anomalies; for it is an interesting fact that as there is a broad family likeness, so to speak, among the whole class, so each individual (of any considerable magnitude) is apt to be distinguished by such peculiarities as imply most curious variations in composition; even in the same individual, diversities of color, or want of symmetry in form, give rise to the idea of a combination of various materials, all, to us, equally unknown. What can more strongly impress upon our minds the extent of our own ignorance, or the vastness and complexity of the work of the great Creator! — *Intellectual Inquirer.*

PROGRESS IN OBSERVING SOLAR PHENOMENA.

At the recent meeting of the British Association, Prof Phillips described a most ingenious invention of the English optician, Cooke, by which he has succeeded in separating the heat of the solar rays from the luminous portion before their arrival at the focus. The eye-piece constructed by him has a prism of 45° and a right angle, with one of its faces presented to receive the light after leaving the object-glass; the luminous rays are then received on the back of the prism at a larger angle than that of total reflection, so that fully ninety-five per cent. of them are reflected and pass on to the eye-piece; but the heating rays, from their having a smaller refractive index, are for the most part permitted to pass out at the back of the prism and are not reflected to the eye-piece, so that at least ninety-five per cent. of them are thus got rid of. By this simple contrivance the utmost comfort is secured to the observer engaged in examining the sun.

Dr. Lee, in remarking upon the increased facility which the above and other inventions have afforded to astronomers for investigating solar phenomena and their effects, said, " That their origin as yet remains unfathomable, like the question, Whence come the perpetual beams of light and heat of the orb itself? Yet these particulars, the ᵐe of endless plausible cogitations and ingenious suggestions without proof, though still among the unrevealed mysteries of nature, may finally submit to unremitting researches. For instance, the solar spots can now be safely pronounced to be no longer an object of idle curiosity, like the casual clouds of our atmosphere. The few land-marks hitherto recorded begin to indicate a regular progress of position in them, with periodical maxima and minima in their amount. Thus, in the years 1845–46, the groups of solar spots extended to about 40° north of the equator, and to 30° south of it, leaving a central blank band from 8° north to 5° south. This state of arrangement is now recurring, with the exception that the preponderance is at present on the south side of the equator. In 1853 and 1854, the spots were distributed from 20° north to about 20° south, decreasing in number till early in the year 1856, when there was a decided minimum, and the equatorial region remained clear; but spots appeared in both hemispheres from 20° to 40°. Their parallels are already again contracting. So much for their *position*, and now for their *motion*. Their daily drift in longitude reveals a general equatorial current 30° in breadth, in the direction of the rotation, and a reverse current of nearly the same breadth is perceptible beyond it, in each hemisphere. The observations of Gen. Sabine have also established a correspondence between solar and terrestrial magnetic disturbances extending through a decennial period, and also another connected with the earth's orbit. M. Dawes has also noticed the rotation of a remarkable spot on the sun's disc, to an extent of an arc of 100° in six days.

Distribution of Heat on the Sun's surface, and the Currents in his atmosphere. — Secchi, of Rome, has ascertained that the sun's equator is sensibly hotter than its poles. That this should be the case, follows from the meteoric theory of solar heat. The asteroids which revolve round the sun and are supposed to fall into its atmosphere as meteors, probably occupy, like the entire solar system, a lenticular space having its greatest diameter nearly coincident with the sun's equator, and if so, a greater number of meteors must fall on the equatorial than on the polar regions of the sun, making the former the hottest. The meteoric theory will also account for the currents in the sun's atmosphere observed by Mr. Carrington. He finds that the spots in the lowest latitudes drift most rapidly from W. to E. Were the sun's atmosphere, like the earth's, acted on by no other motive power than the one equal heating of different latitudes, the relative direction of the currents would be the reverse of this, in virtue of the well-known principles of the trade-winds and " counter-trades," and this would be true at all depths in the sun's atmosphere. But if meteors are constantly falling into the sun's atmosphere, moving from west to east with a velocity scarcely less than that of a planet at the sun's surface, and in greatest number in its equatorial regions, there is a motive power which is adequate to drive its atmosphere round it from west to east, and with greatest velocity at the equator. The intensely bright meteor-like bodies which Mr. Carrington and another observer simultaneously saw traverse the sun's disc, moved from west to east, and they were almost certainly asteroids falling into the sun.

Daily Photographs of the Sun's Disk. — At the Kew Observatory, England, two photographs of the sun's disk are taken daily (atmospheric conditions permitting), one to the east and the other to the west of the meridian. Four positive copies are made regularly from each negative, one of which it is proposed to retain at Kew, and it is in contemplation to distribute the others.

Resumé of recent investigations respecting the Sun. — Sir W. Armstrong, in his address as President of the British Association for 1863, thus reviews some of the most interesting of recent discoveries and speculations respecting the sun : —

" The spectrum researches of Bunsen and Kirchoff have enabled us not only to test the materials of which the sun is made, and to prove their identity, in part at least, with those of our planet, but they have corroborated previous conjectures as to the luminous envelope of the sun. I would here also advert to Mr. Nasmyth's remarkable discovery, that the bright surface of the sun is composed of an aggregation of apparently solid forms, shaped like willow-leaves or some well-known forms of Diatomaceæ, and interlacing one another in every direction. The forms are so regular in size and shape, as to have led to a suggestion from one of our profoundest philosophers of their being organisms, possibly even partaking of the nature of life, but at all events closely connected with the heating and vivifying influences of the sun. These mysterious objects, which, since Mr. Nasmyth discovered them, have been seen by other observers as well, are computed to be each not less than 1000 miles in length and about 100 miles in breadth. The enormous chasms in the sun's photosphere, to which we apply the diminutive term " spots," exhibit the extremities of these leaf-like bodies pointing inwards, and fringing the sides of the cavern far down into the abyss. Sometimes they form a sort of rope or bridge across the chasm, and appear to adhere to one another by lateral attraction. I can imagine nothing more deserving of the scrutiny of observers than these extraordinary forms. The sympathy, also, which appears to exist between forces operating in the sun and magnetic forces belonging to the earth, merits a continuance of that close attention which it has already received from the British Association. I may here notice that most remarkable phenomenon which was seen by independent observers at two different places on the 1st of September, 1859. A sudden outburst of light, far exceeding the brightness of the sun's surface, was seen to take place, and sweep like a drifting cloud over a portion of the solar face. This was attended with magnetic disturbances of unusual intensity and with exhibitions of aurora of extraordinary brilliancy. The identical instant at which the effusion of light was observed was recorded by an abrupt and strongly-marked deflection in the self-registering instruments at Kew. The phenomenon as seen was probably only part of what actually took place, for the magnetic storm in the midst of which it occurred commenced before and continued after the event. If conjecture be allowable in such a case, we may suppose that this remarkable event had some connection with the means by which the sun's heat is renovated. It is a reasonable supposition that the sun was at that time in the act of receiving a more than usual accession of new energy ; and the theory which assigns the maintenance of its power to cosmical matter plunging into it with that prodigious velocity which gravitation would impress upon it as it approached to actual contact with the solar orb, would afford an explanation of this sudden exhibition of intensified light in harmony with the knowledge we have now attained that arrested motion is represented by equivalent heat. Telescopic observations will probably add new facts to guide our judgment on this subject, and, taken in connection with observations on terrestrial magnetism, may enlarge and correct our views respecting the nature of heat, light and electricity. Much as we have yet to learn respecting these agencies, we know sufficient to infer that they cannot be transmitted from the sun to the earth except by communication from particle to particle of intervening matter. Not that I speak of particles in the sense of the atomist. Whatever our views may be of the nature of particles, we must conceive them as centres invested with surrounding forces. We have no evidence, either from our senses or otherwise, of these centres being occupied by solid cores of indivisible incompressible matter essentially distinct from force. Dr. Young has shown that even in so dense a body as water, these nuclei, if they exist at all, must be so small in relation to the intervening spaces, that a hundred men distributed at equal distances over the whole surface of England would represent their relative magnitude and distance. What then must be these relative dimensions in highly rarefied matter? But why encumber our conceptions of material forces by this unnecessary imagining of a central molecule? If we retain the forces and reject the molecule, we shall still have every property we can recognize in matter by the use of our senses or by the aid of our reason. Viewed in this light, matter is not merely a thing subject to force, but is itself composed and constituted of force."

Connection between Sun-spots and Planetary Configurations. — At the British Association, 1863, Mr. B. Stewart stated, that in the course of some recent investigations, as to whether there was any determinable connection between sun-spots and planetary configurations, he was led to observe the changes with regard to size which take place in sun-spots, from a remark by Mr. Beckley, of Kew Observatory, that, during a certain period, he did not observe any spots *break out* on the visible disk of our luminary. Besides about six months' records of these phenomena, made by means of the Kew photoheliograph at the Kew Observatory, the author has had the opportunity of investigating a year's records made by the same instrument at Mr. De La Rue's private Observatory at Cranford. All of these are collodion negatives, and, besides embracing a few months in the end of 1859, they give an almost continuous record of the state of the sun's disk between February, 1862, and the present date. There is little difficulty in finding from these, by means of a comparison of two or three consecutive pictures, approximately, at what portion of the sun's disk any spot ceases to increase and begins to wane, or, on the other hand, breaks out into a visible appearance. Now it appears to be a law nearly universal, that if we divide the disk of the sun roughly into longitude by vertical diameters, and if there be a number of spots on the surface of the sun, these will all behave in the same manner as they cross the same longitude ; that is to say, if one spot decreases, another will decrease also, and so on. This law can, of course, be only approximately ascertained by means of a preliminary examination of this nature ; but the impression produced upon the author is very strong, that if one spot decreases before coming to the central line, another does the same ; if, on the other hand, one spot breaks out on the right half and increases up

28

the border, another will do the same. The author thinks, moreover, that he has noticed a connection between this behavior of sun-spots and the configuration of the nearer planets, Mercury and Venus, and it would seem to be of this nature: Remembering that all motions are from left to right, let us suppose that Mercury and Venus are both in a line considerably to the left of the Earth; then spots will decrease as they come round from the left-hand side, and before they reach the centre of the disk. On the other hand, if these two planets are considerably to the right of the Earth, there will be a tendency for spots to form on the right half of the disk, and to increase up to the border. The author would, however, guard himself against the supposition that he attributes all the phenomena of spots to the agency of these two planets.

RESEARCHES ON THE PLANET MARS.

Mars, though not absolutely the nearest of our planetary neighbors, is certainly — of course, excluding the Moon, which is in many respects a world far more different in physical condition from the Earth than the proper planets — more within our range of observation than any other attendant of the sun. Venus, the next of the planets to the Earth going sunwards, is often nearer to the Earth than Mars, whose orbit envelops our own, can ever be; but the difficulty of observing a planet which is so bright that all the imperfections of our instruments are exaggerated, and which, when at its nearest point to us, must usually be observed at a low altitude, are so great, that we know less about Venus than about almost any other of the planets except Mercury. Mars, which can be observed, and has quite recently been closely observed by Mr. Lockyer, of England, within the very moderate distance of about fifty millions of miles, is at present the only planet into the secrets of whose physical, as distinguished from purely mechanical, structure we can at present hope to peep. We know all about it that we know of any other planet, and a good deal more as well. We know that the day and night of all the four planets, Mercury, Venus, Earth, and Mars, are nearly of equal length, and considerably more than *double* the days and nights of the more distant and more elaborately moonlit (or ringlit) planets. We know that they are, all four, much heavier, bulk for bulk, than the bigger planets, the little Mercury being much the heaviest in material of the four; we know that they all have atmospheres of greater or less density; and we know very little more about any of them except Mars. But of Mars the observations of Messrs. Beer and Madler, in 1830, 1837, and 1841, had already given us a good deal of fresh knowledge, which Mr. Lockyer's drawings, from observations made during the autumn of 1862, have partly confirmed and partly supplemented. A recent astronomer has asserted that " water would not remain fluid even at the Martial equator, and alcohol would freeze at the temperate zones." Probably no assertion was ever less well grounded. The calculation is made on the principle that Mars is so much farther from the sun that the intensity of his rays is there only four-ninths of their intensity here. That is true. But then so much more depends on the collecting effect of a thick atmosphere than on the mere intensity of the sun's rays, that water will freeze on Mont Blanc, where the mere rays are certainly much intenser, while it is summer heat in the valleys below. Accordingly, if the Martial atmosphere be only slightly denser than our own, the diminution in intensity would be in great measure compensated. So much for *à priori* reasoning. Now what is the fact? The polar snows of Mars can be distinctly seen. A white spot of excessive brilliancy at the pole, which diminishes as the summer draws on, and enlarges again with winter, has been observed by many astronomers in Mars. How is this compatible with water's freezing at its equator and alcohol at its temperate zone? Mr. Lockyer watched the south pole of Mars throughout last autumn. Early in August, the southern hemisphere of Mars would be entering on the season which corresponds with us to our May. In about a month's time, between August and September, he saw the white spot at the southern pole of Mars dwindle from about twenty degrees to ten degrees. In other words, the snow melted — for that this phenomenon is caused by the melting of the snow is scarcely doubted — from about eighty degrees south latitude up to ninety degrees south latitude, as the summer heat came on. The white spot was stationary, if not beginning to extend again before the observations ceased, nearly three months after the polar snow had begun to dwindle. This is a very remarkable confirmation and even extension of Beer and Madler's observations. They noted the decrease, but no decrease so rapid as that observed by Mr. Lockyer.

Mr. Lockyer's observations are also very interesting on the forms of what we may fairly call the oceans and inland seas of the southern hemisphere and equatorial regions of Mars. The observations are so clearly defined, and agree so well in general outline with all that have been made for the last thirty years that it is at least quite certain that they are permanent features of the planet, and not merely bands of clouds. It is assumed that the permanent dark surfaces — many of which, of exceedingly remarkable shapes, have now been verified again and again by successive observers — represent either seas, or permanent rifts and chasms in the planet, — seas, of course, being much the more likely, — while the brighter regions indicate the more perfect reflection of light from the surface of continents or land, — the permanently dazzling spots being confined to the polar snows. If this be so, we can assert that several very remarkable seas — including inland seas, some of them connected and some not connected by straits with still larger seas — are now defined in the southern hemisphere, in which (as is the case also with the Earth) water seems to be much more widely spread than in the northern hemisphere. There is, for example, a southern sea exceedingly like our Baltic in shape. And there is another and still more remarkable sea, now defined by the observations of many successive observers, near the equator,— a long straggling arm, twisting almost in the shape of an S laid on its back from east to west, which is at least a thousand miles in length and a hundred in breadth, as if a channel as wide as that between England and Ireland existed in equatorial Africa, and ran inland for a thousand miles or more. The masses of land in Mars appear to be less unbroken in the northern hemisphere; but it is long since we have had any good opportunity of observing the northern hemisphere of Mars, as its year is so nearly equivalent to two earthly years that it continually returns into proximity with the Earth, with the same southern pole toward us. The improved instruments of the last generation have therefore been employed as yet successfully only on the southern hemisphere.

There is every reason, then, to think that human life on Mars might be very much like human life on the Earth. The light cannot be so bright, but the organs of sight may be so much more susceptible as to make the vision quite as good. The heat is probably less, as the polar snows certainly extend further ; but by no means less in proportion to the lessened power of the solar rays. The density of the rocks and geological strata is very nearly the same, and the peculiar red color of the planet has sometimes been ascribed to a preponderance of red sandstone.

Additional Observations on Mars. — An account of some recent carefully conducted observations on Mars have also been laid before the Royal Society, by Professor J. Phillips, of Oxford. He states that the position of the planet in the autumn of 1862 was so favorable "that the entire circle of snow around the South Pole could be distinctly seen, and with such a well-defined edge as to have led to the conclusion that it terminates in a cliff. The equatorial region is occupied by a broad greenish belt fringed with deep bays and inlets, which may perhaps be water. In one place it is relieved by an island which exhibits the same ruddy color as the hemispheres on each side of the central belt.

During the past year, Mr. Nasmyth, of England, has also announced that his observations on Mars tend to confirm the existence of an island in the supposed sea of that planet.

RESEARCHES ON THE MOON.

During the last few years the surface of the Moon has been mapped and measured by several observers, and its features laid down with as much exactness as if the subject of delineation was some mountainous region of our own planet. The moon's surface presents a wondrous scene of lofty isolated heights, craters of enormous volcanoes, ramparts, and broad plains that look like the beds of former seas, and present a remarkable contrast to the rugged character of the rest of the surface. That what we look upon are really mountains and mountainous ranges is sufficiently evident from the fact that the shadows they cast have the exact proportion as to length which they ought to have from the inclination of the sun's rays to their position on the moon's surface.

The convex outline of the moon, as turned toward the sun, is always circular, and nearly smooth ; but the opposite border of the enlightened part, instead of being an exact and sharply defined ellipse, is always observed to be extremely rugged, and indented with deep recesses and prominent points. The mountains near the border cast long black shadows, as they should evidently do, inasmuch as the sun is rising or setting to those parts of the moon. But as the enlightened edge gradually advances beyond them, or, in other words, as the sun to them gains altitude, their shadows shorten ; and at the full moon, when all the light falls in our line of sight, no shadows are seen. By micrometrical measurement of the length of the shadows, the heights of the more conspicuous mountains can be calculated. Before the year 1850, the heights of no fewer than one thousand and ninety-five lunar mountains had been computed, and amongst them occur all degrees of altitude up to nearly twenty-three thousand feet — a height exceeding, by more than a thousand feet, that of Chimborazo in the Andes. It is a remarkable circumstance that the range of lunar Apennines, as they have been called, presents a long slope on one side, and precipices on the other, as in the Himalaya Mountains. During the increase of the moon, its mountains appear as small points or islands of light beyond the extreme edge of the enlightened part, those points being the summits illuminated by the sunbeams before the intermediate plain ; but gradually, as the light advances, they connect themselves with it, and appear as prominences detached from the dark border.

The moon, unlike the earth, has many isolated mountains, that is to say, mountains not connected with a group or chain, — the mountain named Tycho, which has the appearance of a sugar-loaf, is an example of this. The uniformity of aspect which the lunar mountains, for the most part, present is a singular and striking feature. They are wonderfully numerous, especially toward the southern portion of the disk, occupying quite the larger part of the moon's surface, and are, as Sir John Herschel remarks, almost universally of an exactly circular or cup-shaped form, foreshortened, however, into ellipses towards the limb. The larger of these elevations have, for the most part, flat plains within, from which a small steep conical hill rises centrally. They offer, indeed, the very type of the true volcanic character, as it may be seen in the crater of Vesuvius, and in a map of the volcanic districts of the Campi Phlegræi or the Puy de Dome, but with the remarkable peculiarity, that the bottom of the crater is in many instances very deeply depressed below the general surface of the moon, the internal depth being often twice or three times the external height. It has been computed that profound cavities, regarded as craters, occupy two-fifths of the surface of the moon. One of the most remarkable of these formations is fifty-five miles in diameter ; and, to give some idea of its magnitude, the late Professor Nichol used to say that, could a visitor approach it, he would see rising before him a wall of rock twelve hundred feet high ; and on mounting this height, would look down a declivity or slope of thirteen thousand feet, to a ledge or terrace, and below this would see a lower deep of four thousand feet more ; a cavity exceeding, therefore, the height of Mont Blanc, and large enough to hold that mountain besides Chimborazo and Teneriffe. Again, the lunar crater, called Saussure, is ten thousand feet in depth. These astounding calculations are founded on the observation of the sun's light falling on the edge, and illuminating the side of these gigantic depths. The Dead Sea, the greatest known depression on the earth, is thirteen hundred and forty feet below the level of the Mediterranean.

Striæ or lines of light, which appear like ridges, radiate from many of these enormous craters, and might be taken for lava-currents, streaming outwards as they do in all directions, like rays. The ridges that stream from the mountain called Tycho seem to be formed of matter that has greater power of reflecting light than the rock around it ; the crater named Copernicus is equally distinguished by these rays. The ridges, in some instances, cross like a wall both valleys and elevations, and traverse the plains as well as the rocky slopes of the lunar moun-

28*

tains; from which fact, and from the great distances they extend, it would seem that they are not such lava-streams as have flowed, for example, from Etna. It has been supposed that a force acting, as it were, centrifugally or explosively, and therefore differently from the force to which we attribute the upheaval of mountain-chains upon the earth, has formed the lunar craters, and overspread the adjacent surface with the ridges or rays in question.

In Professor Phillips' recent contributions to a Report of the Physical Aspect of the Moon, he notices another class of phenomena, — certain remarkable rills in the mountains mapped as Aristarchus, Archimedes, and Plato. The last exhibits a large crater; and a bold rock which juts into the interior has been seen during the morning illumination to glow in the sunshine like molten silver, casting a well-defined shadow eastward. The object known as the Stag's-horn Rill, east of the mountain Thebit, appears to be what geologists call a fault or dyke, one side being elevated above the other. Professor Phillips mentions a group of parallel rills about Campanus and Hippalus, and he traces a rill across and through the old crater of the latter mountain. All the rills appear to be rifts or deep fissures resembling crevasses of a glacier; they cast strong shadows from oblique light, and even acquire brightness on one edge of the cavity. Their breadth appears to be only a few hundred feet or yards. The mountain Gassendi is remarkable for rough terraces and ridges within the rings which form the crater. In the interior area there are central elevations of rocky character, which are brought into view by the gradual change in the direction of the incident solar rays as the lunar day advances. In Lord Rosse's magnificent reflecting telescope, the flat bottom of the crater, called Albategnius, is seen to be strewed with blocks not visible in inferior telescopes; while the exterior of another volcanic mountain (Aristillus) is scored all over with deep gullies radiating towards its centre.

The reader need not be reminded that our knowledge is limited to one hemisphere or face of the moon, in consequence of the period of its rotation upon its axis corresponding with the period of its revolution round the earth.

Depressions in the Moon's Disk. — These have long been recognized. Mr. Key, in a paper recently presented to the Royal Astronomical Society (G. B.), records his observations of certain large depressions in the western limit of our satellite, not of comparatively small gullies lying between elevated ranges, but of vast tracts, the general level of which lies very considerably beneath the mean level of the moon's surface. On the 20th of September last, while observing with a twelve-inch glass speculum the moon, then a few hours past her first quarter, he was astounded at observing that the limb of the moon was entirely out of shape; that it was in fact irregularly polygonal, as if several large segments had been cut off the spherical limb. Since then other astronomers had verified this observation. Rev. Mr. Webb, of the Hardwick Observatory, had also measured these depressions with a micrometer, and proved that they were actually flat.

Lunar Mountains. — At the last meeting of the British Association, Professor Phillips gave a detailed account of his examination of the moon's surface through an equatorial with an object-glass of six inches.

He desired, he said, to call attention particularly to the variations in the central masses of the lunar mountains, and their physical bearings. Many smaller mountains are simply like cups set in saucers, while others contain only one central or several dispersed cups. But in the centre of many of the larger mountains, as Copernicus, Gassendi, and Theophilus, is a large mass of broken rocky country, 5,000 or 6,000 feet high with buttresses passing off into collateral ridges, or an undulated surface of low ridges and hollows. The most remarkable object of this kind which the author has yet observed with attention is in Theophilus, in which the central mass, seen under powers of from 200 to 300, appears as a large conical mass of rocks about fifteen miles in diameter, and divided by deep chasms radiating from the centre. The rock-masses between these deep clefts are bright and shining, the clefts widen toward the centre, the eastern side is more diversified than the western, and like the southern side has long excurrent buttresses. As the light grows on the mountain, point after point of the mass on the eastern side comes out of the shade, and the whole figure resembles an uplifted mass which broke with radiating cracks in the act of elevation. Excepting in steepness, this resembles the theoretical Mount d'Or of De Beaumont; and as there is no mark of cups or craters in this mass of broken ground, the author is disposed to regard its origin as really due to the displacement of a solidified part of the moon's crust. On the whole, the author is confirmed in the opinion he has elsewhere expressed, that on the moon's face are features more strongly marked than on our own globe, which, rightly studied, may lead to a knowledge of volcanic action under grander and simpler conditions than have prevailed on the earth during the period of subaerial volcanoes. Professor Hennessy inquired whether Professor Phillips had met with any instances during his researches regarding the surface of the moon where the fissures, instead of being narrow at the lower part and growing wider toward the top, were on the contrary narrow above and grew wider toward the lower part. Fissures of this latter description were met with in Java, and indicated a formation arising from external causes, as those described by Professor Phillips were manifestly caused by internal disruptive forces. Professor Phillips replied, that he had not met with any instances of fissures of the class spoken of by Professor Hennessy. Any member of the Section who went to see the process of extracting the silver from lead ore would have an opportunity of witnessing, on a small scale, causes in operation producing exactly similar effects to those observed on the surface of the moon. After the process was completed, and the litharge all blown off from the pure silver, the observer would be very apt to go away, having seen all he could; but if he waited for a short time, as the mass of pure silver cooled, be would soon see its surface torn up by explosions from within, caused, as he (Professor Phillips) believed, by the extrication of oxygen gas, producing elevations and fissures exactly resembling those on the surface of the moon.

NEW BAROMETRICAL OBSERVATIONS.

Lately, a large barometer has been erected in the National Astronomical Observatory of Santiago de Chili. By this instrument has been observed a singular phenomenon, new to science. We know, particularly through the observation of Humboldt, that the barometer rises and falls during the day in a peculiar manner ; being at its maximum height at 10 A. M. and at 10 P. M., whilst the lowest readings are between 4 P. M. and 4 A. M. The regularity of this periodical movement within the tropics is such, during the year, that Humboldt could tell the time within fifteen minutes. This movement has been observed with much regularity in Santiago de Chili during the winter and summer months ; but in the month of February the movement entirely ceases, showing then only the extraordinary maximum and minimum heights in the twenty-four hours.

Senor Mœsta has tried to explain this occurrence, and has demonstrated mathemetically that the oscillatory movement of the barometer is produced by the sun's power, analogous to that of gravitation, and that the said movement ought to disappear in the month of February, in consequence of the great variation of temperature during the course of the day. Thus the interesting result has been arrived at, that, by virtue of the sun's power, a movement is manifested in the atmosphere analogous to the action of the tides ; and it is this that causes the rise and fall of the barometrical column in Santiago, about " 1.3 of a millimetre." — *Comercio de Lima*, 8 *January*, 1863.

FORMATION OF HAIL.

M. Sanna-Solaro contests the idea that hail-stones are formed by successive concretions. On the contrary, he affirms the congelation to begin from without, and the so-called nucleus to be the result of pressure. He says that when the external surface begins to freeze, the air bubbles are driven toward the centre, and give rise to a pressure under which the crust yields, " The shock determines the congelation of a fresh layer, which is formed of two distinct parts, one deprived of air and transparent, the other opaque, in consequence of its included air-bubbles." This phenomenon is reproduced at each successive congelation, and if the hail-stones reach the ground before the congelation is complete, their central portion may contain bubbles of air, water, and crystals of ice. Pyramidal stones he ascribes to the action of violent congelation, which causes the contained fluid to split the crust. He states that he has imitated hail-stones by freezing water in transparent envelopes of caoutchouc. He likewise adduces reasons, to show that hail-stones are formed instantaneously. Further details will be found in *Comptes Rendus*, 27*th April*, 1863.

LIFE IN THE ATMOSPHERE.

The following is an abstract of a paper on the above subject, presented to the British Association, 1863, by Mr. J. Samuelson. No subject in natural history except the allied one, the origin of species, had of late excited greater interest in the scientific world than the origin of the lowest types of living beings on the globe ; and although the problem was far from being solved, yet, the investigations that had accompanied the discussion had already served the useful purpose of throwing new light on the anatomy and life history of the mysterious little forms of which it treated. It was rather with the latter object, than in the expectation of being able to assist in the solution of the general question, that he ventured to lay before the Association the results of investigations recently made. He had, for example, taken rags imported from various countries, and shaken the dust from them into distilled water, which he then exposed to the atmosphere; and after describing generally the character of the living forms he had discovered in this pure water, he stated in detail the forms of life found in each kind of dust, and among these were some new species of Rhizopoda and Infusoria, and an interesting ciliated, worm-shaped form, which he believed to be a collection of the larvæ of some other Infusoria. The general result of the microscopical examination of these fluids was as follows: In the dust of Egypt, Japan, Melbourne, and Trieste, life was the most abundant, and the development of the different forms was rapid. In conclusion, he observed that if he was correct in supposing the germs of the living forms that he had described to be present in the dust conveyed by the atmosphere, and in distilled water, it was worthy of notice that these germs retain vitality for a long period, of which he could not pretend to define the limit. In his experiments they outlived the heat of a tropical sun, and the dryness of a warm room during the whole winter; but in Dr. Pouchet's case they retained their life 2,000 years, for he obtained his from the interior of the pyramids of Egypt, and they survived an ordeal of 400° of heat. A main purpose which Mr. Samuelson had in view, was to disprove the theory of spontaneous generation; and he suggested whether the great rapidity with which these germs are multiplied, might not account for the spread of epidemic diseases. He did not profess to have any acquaintance with such diseases; but might it not be desirable to subject the atmosphere of hospitals to the microscopic test?

Dust in the Atmosphere. — Professor J. Wyman, of Cambridge, has recently published an account of some observations made by him, on the different kinds of bodies found in the dust deposited from or floating in the atmosphere. The dust was obtained either from the floor of an unoccupied attic, or from plates of glass covered with glycerine and exposed to currents of air. The organic matter detected by the aid of the microscope consisted of various minute fragments of vegetable tissues, such as woody-tissue, spiral-ducts, hairs, pollen, etc. A few starch granules, resembling those of wheat, and giving the usual reaction with iodine, were occasionally found. In the dust from an attic over a frequently occupied college recitation-room, human cuticle and epithelium scales from the mouth were detected. The lecture-room and attic communicated freely by a ventilator. There were also found, less frequently, however, various spherical bodies; some of them spores of cryptogamous plants, and others resembling the eggs of some of the smaller invertebrate animals. Professor Wyman was unable to identify the bodies in question, except that in one instance he detected the spores of a confervoid plant. As these were found before the conferva were beginning to be developed, it is probable that they came from plants of the preceding year, and had been carried about by the winds after the drying up of the stagnant pools, in the latter part of summer or autumn. Some of the egg-like bodies appeared to contain an embryo, which could not be referred to any particular species. One of the spores detected was especially interesting from its resemblance to pus and mucous corpuscules; so close was the resemblance that one might be readily mistaken for the other. The fact is important, when considered in connection with the recent attempts made in Germany to establish the presence of pus in the atmosphere, and in this manner explain the transmission of certain forms of disease. The existence in the atmosphere of a large number of the spores of cryptogamia, gives a probable explanation of the transmission of certain of the algæ and fungi, which infest the bodies of men and animals.

In dust collected after a winter's snow-storm on plates of glass covered with glycerine, Professor Wyman detected, in addition to particles of mineral dust, probably that of coal ashes and of soot, spores of cryptogams, starch granules, and pollen. Fragments of coniferous and other woods were also found. The objects most unexpected at this season of the year were the grains of pollen. It was suggested whether these might have been derived from the trees, where they may have been lodged in the crevices of the bark, or other irregularities of the surface, and from ti ne to time detached by the wind.

GEOGRAPHY AND ANTIQUITIES.

DISCOVERY OF THE SOURCE OF THE NILE.

The great geographical event of the year, and we may add with propriety, of the century, has been the solution of that long-discussed problem, the source of the Nile. The details of this discovery, in brief, are substantially as follows. As early as 1852, Sir Roderick Murchison suggested that, instead of the interior of Africa being a barren desert, as men had been wont to consider it, it was probably an elevated basin and well-watered; an hypothesis fully confirmed a few years later by the researches of Livingstone and Burton. In 1858, Captains Burton and Speke, while engaged in African exploration, discovered the head of a great fresh-water lake, about 3° south of the equator and at an elevation of about 4000 feet above the sea-level. The name given by the natives to this lake, was *Nyanza*, and its position and extent impressed Captain Speke with the idea that it constituted the long-sought for source of the river Nile. Prevented for the time, from verifying his supposition, he returned to England, and under the patronage of the London Geographical Society, organized, with a Captain Grant, a new expedition, which had for its chief object the determination of this specific question. This expedition reached Zanz-ibor in the fall of 1860, and left the east coast of Africa itself, on the 1st of October, at a point about 7° south of the equator.

For twelve months they did not advance far, owing to the fierce intertribal wars of the natives. On the 1st of January, 1862, however, they reached the capital of a kingdom called Karagwe, on the southwest shore of the great Lake of Nyanza, discovered in 1858. The king of this country assisted them much. Thence they proceeded through the next kingdom of Uganda, which comprises the west and north shores of the same lake. Here toil was forgotten in triumph ; for here they achieved the main object of their journey and conclusively determined that the principal source of the Nile was, as had been anticipated, the Lake Nyanza.

It appears that the part of Africa in which the Nile rises is a tableland, gradually rising from the sea — to use Captain Speke's illustration — like an inverted dish (though of a very different shape), to a height of near 4,000 feet above the sea-level. One hill reaches 5,148 feet, and another 4,090, but the level, which is apparently of enormous extent, is between 3,000 and 4,000. The equator passes right through this tract of country, and for five degrees of latitude on each side the soil is extremely fertile, gradually decreasing in fertility as the distance from the equator increases. The climate is healthy, and the heat by no means excessive. Captain Speke says — " The general temperature of the atmosphere is very pleasant, as I found from experience ; for I walked every inch of the journey dressed in thick woollen clothes, and slept every night between blankets." About 1,000 miles west of the Indian Ocean, and fifty miles south of the equator, and in thirty degrees east longitude, lies a range of mountains, some of the peaks of which are said to be 10,000 feet high. Their form is semicircular; and from these mountains and the other high grounds the water drains east and north — and, indeed, west and north from the other side of the table-land — into three great lakes. One of these — a round piece of water about fifty miles by thirty — is said to lie in the semicircle formed by the Mountains of the Moon. Some distance south of this lies a much larger one, between three and four hundred miles long, and varying in width from thirty to sixty miles. It is pear-shaped, the larger end being at the south, and the direction nearly due north and south. The twentieth parallel of longitude runs along it for a considerable distance. The third and most important of the three lakes is the Nyanza. Its level is 3,740 feet above the sea, and its shape is very nearly that of an equilateral triangle of which each side is about two hundred miles in length. The lines are, of course, a little irregular; but if the north side were represented by a straight line, that straight line would be furnished by the equator. The best possible notion of the lake will be obtained by taking two hundred miles of the equator, and describing upon it an equilateral triangle with the point to the south. At the east corner of that triangle there is another long and somewhat irregular body of water imperfectly known. The Nile flows out of the north side of the lake in three separate channels. Two of them appear to be rather swamps or (as Captain Speke calls them) rush drains than rivers, but the third is a noble stream, and flows out of an arm of the Nyanza, and over a fall about twelve feet high and four or five hundred feet wide. The Nile is thus one of the very few rivers to which a definite beginning can be assigned, for from this point it pursues an independent course of upwards of 2,000 miles to the sea, having on its way only three or four tributaries, none of which can be compared to it in importance. No other river in the world has such a splendid individual career. The American rivers are the outlet of a thousand streams, and the same may be said of the great rivers of India and China ; but the Nile is the Nile from its source to the Mediterranean. Capt. Speke describes the stream as six or seven hundred yards wide, some way further down, and the banks as fertile and beautifully wooded, populous, and abounding in animal life.

Besides the Nyanza, which he actually saw, and to a great extent explored, Captain Speke obtained information of two other remarkable lakes. One of these is a very large one, called Lake Uniamesi, and said to lie east and somewhat to the south of the Nyanza; the other is a singular lake, called the Luta Nzige, said to be about two hundred miles long, and fifty broad, running from S. to N. E., which communicates with the Nile at its northeastern extremity. It is supposed by Captain Speke to be a mere backwater which the Nile fills by its overflow when the Nyanza receives an extra supply of water from the mountains. He supposes (as we understand him) that, when this reservoir is filled, and the Nile begins to fall, the water runs back into the Nile, and produces the floods down to Egypt.

The discoverers traced the course of the river to the second degree of north latitude, where it turns to the west and forms a bend. They crossed the channel of this bend for seventy miles, and when they again fell in with the river it had sunk in level almost a thousand feet. Here they met with some Turkish ivory traders, and bore them company to Gondokoro, on the White Nile 5° N. L., at which place they found a fellow-countryman, advancing to meet them with supplies.

As regards the population of the countries traversed, Captain Grant, in his address before the Geographical Society, London, says, "Looking back on the many tribes we had passed through, one apparently identical race of negro overspreads the entire land from the coast to Gondokoro, and onwards down the Nile, — that is to say, if you leave out their tribal marks, their dress and their dialect, it would, I believe, be impossible to distinguish the natives of one part from those of another. As regards the general populousness of the countries we have passed through, I may state that throughout the whole journey there were but three or four places where we had to carry our provisions for more than six days; we almost invariably got provisions from day to day. The country was too populous to admit of any large amount of game. Those mixtures of species and herds, as seen by Dr. Livingstone and other South African travellers, were seldom or never seen, and in many forests we might range from morn till noon and only see two or three antelopes."

"Much of the country passed through was exceedingly pleasant. Each head of an ordinary negro family cultivates sweet potato, pulse, Indian corn, and other tropical products for his own family's consumption only. No plough or beast of burden is in the country. Everything is done, after the rains have softened the soil, by means of a long or short handled hoe. Women are oftener seen at this work than men, whose duty it is, in the Land of the Moon, to thresh the corn with long rackets. Most of the tribes are purely pastoral, subsisting chiefly on milk, covering themselves with butter, dressing in cows' skins, seldom touching any grain; but they drink and get noisy on the banana wine, while meat some amongst them will merely suck, never swallowing it. They smoke tobacco universally. Crime, such as theft, is rarer than in England. Never had we a lock on one of our boxes or goods.

"Many of the chieftains have bands and musical instruments in many varieties, more remarkable for noise than harmony. As shooters with bows and arrows, they can put an arrow into a leaf at thirty or forty yards, and they can send an arrow to a distance of one hundred and fifty yards. Iron is smelted in small quantities all over the country, and the natives are also familiar with copper.

"Weaving is very backward ; one loom in every eighth village was all that was observed in the lower provinces. The clothes made are of the coarsest and heaviest material, all of cotton. Bark-cloths and deer-skins, sewn beautifully together, are prized very much more. The needles used are of iron, but differently made from ours. Silver and gold, coal and limestone, are unknown in the countries traversed. Pottery is made by the hand, the potter's wheel being unknown. Some races can glaze the ware. Wicker, grass, or bamboo baskets, trays, drinking-cups, etc., are made everywhere over the country, the patterns varying."

One of the most curious things in Captain Speke's published report is a small map of the Nyanza district printed in blue and red. The blue represents the actual state of things. The red represents the same country as depicted in certain ancient Hindoo documents, first published in Europe in 1801. It is impossible to look at them without seeing that the Hindoos had excellent information upon the geography of the country. The same "Mountains of the Moon" is taken from the Hindoo Map, and the situation of the mountains so-called is laid down not incorrectly, while the lake-system of the country is represented, not by three lakes, but by one large one, which is called the Lake of the Gods, and which might naturally be supposed to exist by any one acquainted with the Nyanza. Captain Speke supposes that in very ancient times there was a considerable trade between Hindostan and the interior of Africa, and that this was the source from which the authors of the map in question derived their information. That they had such information somehow, no one who looks at the two maps can possibly doubt.

THE PHYSICAL GEOGRAPHY OF THE MALAY ARCHIPELAGO.

The following is an abstract of a paper on the above topic, read before the British Association, 1863, by Mr. A. R. Wallace, well known from his travels and natural history investigations in Southern Asia:

It first becomes necessary to define accurately the limits of the Archipelago, pointing out exactly what islands we include within it; for, though "all the islands between southeastern Asia and Australia" seem pretty definite, yet to the eastward this region blends insensibly into the vast extent of the Pacific Islands. According to my views, the Malay — or, as I should prefer to name it, the Indo-Australian — Archipelago extends from the Nicobar Islands on the northwest to St. Christoval, one of the Solomon Islands, on the southeast, and from Luzon on the north to Rotte, near Timor, on the south. The eastern boundary is drawn at this particular point for reasons which will be explained further on. Though not geographically correct to include any part of a continent in an archipelago, it is necessary for our purpose to consider the Malay peninsula as not only almost but quite an island, since it cannot be physically separated from the region of which we are now treating. Thus limited, the archipelago is of a somewhat triangular form, with an extreme length of about 5,000, and breadth of rather more than 2,000 English miles. The mere statement of these dimensions, however, will give but an imperfect idea of the extent and geographical importance of this region, which, owing to its peculiar position, is worse represented on maps than any other on the globe. In many atlases of great pretension there is no map of the whole archipelago. A small portion of it generally comes in with Asia, and another piece with the Pacific Islands; but in order to ascertain its form and extent as a whole, we are almost always obliged to turn to the map of the Eastern Hemisphere. It thus happens that, seldom seeing this region, except on a diminutive scale, its real form and dimensions, and the size, situations, and names of its component islands, are, perhaps, less familiar to educated persons than those of an other countries of equal importance. They can hardly bring themselves to imagine that this sea of islands is really in many respects comparable with the great continents of the earth. The traveller, however, soon acquires different ideas. He finds himself sailing for days or even for weeks along the shores of one of these great islands, often so great that the inhabitants believe it to be a boundless continent. He finds that voyages among these islands are commonly reckoned by weeks and months, and that the inhabitants of the eastern and western portions of the archipelago are as mutually unknown to each other as are the native races of North and South America. On visiting the coasts of one of the larger islands, he hears of the distinct kingdoms which lie along its shores, of the remote north or east or south, of which he can obtain little definite information, and of the wild and inaccessible interior, inhabited by cannibals and demons, the haunt of the charmed deer which bears a precious jewel in its forehead, and of the primæval men who have not yet lost their tails. The traveller, therefore, soon looks upon this region as one altogether apart. He finds it possesses its own races of men and its own aspects of nature. It is an island-world, with insular ideas and feelings, customs, and modes of speech; altogether cut off from the great continents into which we are accustomed to divide the globe, and quite incapable of being classed with any of them. Its dimensions, too, are continental. You may travel as many thousand miles across it, in various directions, occupying as many weeks and months as would be necessary to explore any of the so-called quarters of the globe. It contains as much variety in its climate, in its physical phenomena, its animate and inanimate life, and its races of mankind, as some of those regions exhibit. If, therefore, the claim of Australia to be a fifth division of the globe is admitted, I would ask for this great archipelago (at least on the present occasion) to be considered a sixth. Looking at a map on which the volcanic regions of the archipelago are marked out — those which are subject to earthquakes, which are of volcanic origin, and which abound more or less in extinct as well as active volcanoes — we see at a glance that the great islands of Borneo and Celebes form the central mass around which the volcanic islands are distributed, so as rudely to follow their outline and embrace them on every side but one in a vast fiery girdle. Along this great volcanic band (about 5,000 miles in length) at least fifty mountains are continually active, visibly emitting smoke or vapor; a much larger number are known to have been in eruption during the last three hundred years; while the number which are so decidedly of volcanic origin that they may at any moment burst forth again, must be reckoned by hundreds. It is not now my object to describe the many fearful eruptions that have taken place in this region. In the amount of injury to life and property, and in the magnitude of their effects, they have not been surpassed by any upon record. Forty villages were destroyed by the eruption of Papandayang in Java, where the whole mountain was blown up by repeated explosions, and a large lake left in its place. By the great eruption of Tomboro, in Sumbawa, 12,000 people were destroyed, and the ashes darkened the air, and fell thick upon the earth and sea for three hundred miles around. Even quite recently, since I quitted the country, a mountain which has been quiescent for more than two hundred years suddenly burst into activity. The island of Makian, one of the Moluccas, was rent open in 1646 by a violent eruption which left a huge chasm on one side, extending into the heart of the mountain. It was

when I last visited it, clothed with vegetation to the summit, and contained twelve populous Malay villages. On the 29th of December,
1862, after 215 years of perfect inaction, it again suddenly burst forth,
blowing up and completely altering the appearance of the mountain,
destroying the greater part of the inhabitants, and sending forth such
volumes of ashes as to darken the air at Ternate, forty miles off, and
almost entirely to destroy the growing crops on that and the surrounding islands. The island of Java contains more volcanoes, active and
extinct, than any other known district of equal extent. They are
about forty-five in number, and many of them exhibit most beautiful
examples of the volcanic cone on a large scale, single or double, with
entire or truncated summits, and averaging 10,000 feet high. It is now
well ascertained that almost all volcanoes have been slowly built up by
the accumulation of the matter — mud, ashes, and lava — ejected by
themselves. The openings or craters, however, frequently shift their
position ; so that a country may be covered with a more or less irregular series of hills in chains and masses, only here and there rising into
lofty cones, and yet the whole may be produced by true volcanic action. In this manner the greater part of Java has been formed. The
great island of Sumatra exhibits, in proportion to its extent, a much
smaller number of volcanoes ; and a considerable portion of it has had,
probably, a non-volcanic origin. Going northward, Amboyna, a part
of Bouru, and the west end of Ceram, the north part of Gilolo, and all
the small islands around it, the northern extremity of Celebes, and the
islands of Siau and Sauguir are wholly volcanic. The Philippine
Archipelago contains many active and extinct volcanoes. In striking
contrast with this region of subterranean fires, the island of Celebes in
all its southern peninsulas, the great mass of Borneo, and the Malay
peninsula, are not known to contain a single volcano, active or extinct.
To the east of the volcanic band is another quiescent area of 1,000
miles wide, the great island of New Guinea being free from volcanoes
and earthquakes. Toward its eastern extremity, however, these reappear in some small islands off its coast, and in New Britain, New Ireland, and the Solomon Islands, which contain active volcanoes. The
contrasts of vegetation and of climate in the archipelago may be best
considered together, the one being to some extent dependent on the
other. Placed immediately upon the equator, and surrounded by extensive oceans, it is not surprising that the various islands of the archipelago should be almost always clothed with a forest vegetation, from
the level of the sea to the summits of the loftiest mountains. This is
the general rule. Sumatra, New Guinea, Borneo, the Philippines, and
the Moluccas, and the uncultivated parts of Java and Celebes, are all
forest countries, except a few small and unimportant tracts, due, perhaps, in some cases, to ancient cultivation or accidental fires. To this,
however, there is one important exception in the island of Timor, and
all the smaller islands opposite, in which there is absolutely no forest
such as exists in the other islands, and this character extends in a lesser
degree to Flores, Sumbawa, Lombock, and Bali. The changes of the
monsoons, and of the wet and dry seasons in some parts of the archipelago are very puzzling ; and an accurate series of observations in
nerous localities is required to elucidate them. Speaking generally,
the southwestern part of the Archipelago, including the whole

range of islands from Sumatra to Timor, with the larger half of Borneo and the southern peninsula of Celebes, have a dry season from April to November, with the southeast monsoon. This same wind, however, bends round Borneo, becoming the southwest monsoon in the China Sea, and bringing the rainy season to Northern Borneo and the Philippines. In the Moluccas and New Guinea, the seasons are most uncertain. In the southeast monsoon, from April to November, it is often stormy at sea, while on the islands it is very fine weather. There is generally not more than two or three months' dry, hot weather about August and September. This is the case in the northern extremity of Celebes and in Bouru, whereas in Amboyna, July and August are the worst months in the year. In Ternate, where I resided at intervals for three years, I never could find out which was the wet and which the dry season. The same is the case at Banda, and a similar uncertainty prevails in Menado, showing probably that the proximity of active volcanoes has a great disturbing meteorological influence. In New Guinea, a great amount of rain falls more or less all the year round. On the whole, the only general statement we can make seems to be that the countries within about three degrees on each side of the equator have much rain and not very strongly contrasted seasons; while those with more south or north latitude have daily rains during about four months in the year, while for five or six months there is almost always a cloudless sky and a continual drought." The author next considered the Malayan Archipelago in its geological and zoological relations to Asia and to Australia, mentioning the well-established fact that one portion of it is almost as much Asiatic in its organic productions as the British isles are European, while the remainder bears the same relation to Australia that the West India Islands do to America.

THE ORIGIN OF THE GIPSIES.

The following paper on the above subject was read to the British Association, 1863, by Mr. Crawford, the well known ethnologist.

" The origin, as our old English has it, of the ' outlandish persons calling themselves Egyptians or Gipsies,' and constituting ' a strange kind of commonwealth among themselves of wandering impostors and jugglers,' is, at least, a subject of great curiosity, not to say of etymological import. Although their first appearance in Europe be coeval with the century which witnessed the discovery of the New World and the new passage to the Indies, no one thought of ascribing to them a Hindú origin, and this hypothesis, the truth of which I now propose to examine, is but of very recent date. Their Hindú origin was not for a long time even suspected; it has of late years, however, received general credence, and I think, justly. The arguments for it consist in the physical form of the people, in their language, and in the history of their migration. The evidence yielded by physical form will certainly not prove the gipsies to be of Hindú origin. The Hindús are all more or less black; and assuredly no nation or tribe of Hindús now exists, or is even known to have ever existed, as fair as the gipsies of Europe. It is on language chiefly that we must rely for evidence of the Hindú origin of the gipsies, and even this is neither very full nor satisfactory. The dialects spoken by the different tribes of this people, although agreeing in several words, differ very materially from each

29*

other.   Besides the genuine Indian words to be found in the language
of the gipsies, they all contain a large intermixture of foreign tongues,
consisting of words of the languages of the people they dwell or have
dwelt amongst, — of Persian, of Arabic, of Turkish, of Greek, of Hun-
garian, and of various Sclavonian tongues ; these being, in some cases,
— as, for example, in the Persian, — more numerous than the Hindú
words.   This is what was to be looked for from four hundred years'
residence in Europe, and their sojourn among Oriental nations in their
necessarily slow journey westward.   The Indian words which exist in
the language of the gipsies are by no means so numerous as the Latin
ones which are found in the Welsh and Armorican, or in the Irish and
Gaelic, and there will be found wanting in the gipsy language classes
of words which are indispensable toward proving it of Indian parent-
age.   Of the migration of the gipsies from India, there is assuredly no
record in Indian history, neither have we of their arrival in any Asiatic country before they reached Europe.   In both France and Italy
their first appearance was in an inland city, in both of which they began at once to tell fortunes ; a fact which supposes, of course, some acquaintance with the language of the people whose fortunes they pretended to predict.   From these two facts, it may be inferred that the
gipsies were in France and Italy for some time before their appearance
in Paris and Bologna.   Most probably they came to Italy from Wal-
lachia, through Servia, Bosnia, and Dalmatia, crossing the Adriatic ;
but what internal commotion led to their adventure is unknown.
From Italy, where they were seen five years before they reached
France, they probably found their way into the latter country.   If the
gipsies were originally an Indian people (and there is no other evidence of their having been so than a few words of an Indian language),
they were most probably captives, carried off by some western invader
with the hope of peopling his own desert lands.   I must come to the
conclusion that the gipsies, when above four centuries ago they first
appeared in Western Europe, were already composed of a mixture of
many different races, and that the present gipsies are still more mon-
grel.   In the Asiatic portion of their lineage, there is probably a small
infusion of Hindú blood ; but this, I think, is the utmost that can be
predicated of their Indian pedigree.   Strictly speaking, they are not
more Hindús in lineage than they are Persians, Turks, Wallachians, or
Europeans ; for they are a mixture of all these, and that in proportions impossible to be ascertained."

OBITUARY

OF MEN EMINENT IN SCIENCE, 1863.

Alger, Francis, of Boston, a distinguished American mineralogist.

Bell, Luther V., an American physician, distinguished for his researches on insanity.

Bourmann, Moritz Von, an African explorer, murdered by the Sultan of Waddi.

Blyth, Prof. M. N., an eminent Norwegian botanist.

Bravais, August, a French physicist.

Borgnis, Signor De, an eminent Italian engineer.

Cartwright, Dr. Samuel, a naturalist of New Orleans.

Chilton, James R., an American chemist.

Clapp, Dr. Asahel, of Indiana, an American botanist.

Darlington, Dr. William, a distinguished American botanist.

Despretz, Cèsar Mansuète, the eminent French chemist.

Emmons, Dr. Ebenezer, one of the most eminent of American geologists; author of the "Taconic System."

Fitz, Henry, a distinguished American optician.

Green, Benjamin D., of Boston, an American botanist.

Grimm, Jacob, the well-known German philologist.

Hall, Samuel, a distinguished English engineer and inventor.

Hildreth, Dr. Samuel P., of Ohio, eminent as a geologist and naturalist.

Hubbard, Prof. J. S., an American astronomer.

Hunt, E. B., Maj. U. S. A., a distinguished American physicist, killed while experimenting upon ordnance.

Kieser, Dr. Von, late president of the German Society of naturalists.

Kinahan, Dr. John R., Prof. Zoölogy, Gov. School of Mines, G. B.

Leavenworth, Dr. Melines C., U. S. A., an eminent American botanist.

Lehmann, Prof., the eminent German physiological chemist.

Lewis, Sir G. Cornwall, author of the "Astronomy of the Ancients," &c.

Masterman, Stillman, an American astronomer.

Mitscherlich, Eilhard, Prof. of Berlin; — one of the first chemists of the age.

Moquin-tandon M., Prof. of Botany to the Faculty of Medicine, Paris.

Pike, Benjamin, an eminent American optician and mechanician.

Short, Dr. Charles Wilkyns, an eminent American botanist.

Stansbury, Maj. Howard, U. S. A.; the explorer of the Great Salt Lake of Utah.

Studner, Dr. Henry, an explorer of Central Africa; died in service.

Thornton, Richard, geologist to Livingstone's expedition to Central Africa.

Weale, John, an eminent publisher of English scientific works; "Weale's Series," &c.

Weisse, Maximilian Von, director of Observatory at Cracow, Poland.

Whipple, A. W., Gen. U. S. A.; distinguished for his exploration in connection with the Pacific Railroad; killed in battle.

AMERICAN SCIENTIFIC BIBLIOGRAPHY.

˙ 1863.

Agassiz, L. Methods of Study in Natural History. 12mo. pp. 320. Ticknor & Fields, Boston.

Almanac, American Nautical for 1864 and 1865. Bureau of Navigation, Washington, D. C.

Almanac, National, for 1863. pp. 698. Philadelphia, G. W. Childs.

American Annual Encyclopedia. Events of the Year 1862. D. Appleton & Co., N. Y.

Annals Observatory, Harvard College. Vol. IV. Part 1. Catalogue of Polar and Clock Stars. Cambridge. 1863.

Bache, A. D. Standard Mean Right-Ascensions, and Circumpolar and Time Stars, prepared for the use of the U. S. Coast Survey. Washington.

Binney, W. G. Bibliography of N. American Conchology, previous to 1860. Smithsonian Publications. Washington, D. C.

Brace, C. L. The Races of the Old World; a manual of Ethnology. C. Scribner, N. Y. 12mo. pp. 540.

Brand and Taylor's Chemistry. American reprint. Blanchard & Lea, Philadelphia. pp. 696.

Burgess, N. G. The Photographic Manual, a Practical Treatise on Photographic Operating. D. Appleton & Co., N. Y.

Campin, F. A Practical Treatise on Mechanical Engineering, comprising Metallurgy, Moulding, Casting, Forging, etc., etc. 8vo. $6. Baird, Philadelphia.

Canada, Geological Survey of. Report of Progress from its Commencement to 1863. 8vo. pp. 983. N. Y., Balliere & Co. $9.00.

Caswell, Alexis. Meteorological Observations made at Providence, R. I., from December, 1831, to May, 1860. Smithsonian Publications.

Chauvenet, William. Manual of Spherical and Practical Astronomy. Lippincott & Co., Philadelphia. 8vo., pp. 708, 632.

Dana, Jas. D. A Text-book of Geology, for Schools and Academies. 356 pp., 12mo. $1.75. Philadelphia, Peck & Bliss.

Dussauce, H. Treatise on the Coloring Matters derived from Coal-tar, and their Practical Applications in Dyeing. 12mo. $3. Baird, Philadelphia.

Folsom, Norton. Essay on the Senses of Smell and Taste. Pamphlet. Boston.

Gilmore, Q. A. Gen. Practical Treatise on Limes, Cements, and Mortars. N. Y. Van Nostrand. 8vo. pp. 333.

Gœsemann, Dr. C. A. Report on the Brines of Onondaga, N. Y.

Hammond, W. A. Surgeon-Gen. U. S. A. Physiological Memoirs. Lippincott & Co., Philadelphia. 8vo. pp. 348.

Hammond, W. A. A Treatise on Hygiene, with special reference to Military Service. Lippincott & Co., Philadelphia.

Hooker, Dr. W. Science for the School and Family: Natural Philosophy; Chemistry. Harpers, N. Y.

Huxley, Thos. H. On the Origin of Species. Appleton & Co., N. Y.

Isherwood, B. F. Experimental Researches in Steam Engineering, with plates and tables. 4to. pp. 355. $10.00.

Kustel, Guido. Processes of Silver and Gold Extraction, for General Use, and especially for the Mining Public of California and Nevada. 8vo. pp. 327. Illus. Carlton, San Francisco.

Liebig, Justus von. The Natural Laws of Husbandry. N. Y. Appleton.

Lyell, Sir C. The Geological Evidences of the Antiquity of Man. 8vo. pp. G. W. Childs, Philadelphia.

Mc Farlane, Thos. On the Extraction of Cobalt Oxide. 8vo. pamph. Philadelphia.

Maine, Second Annual Report on the Natural History and Geology of. 8vo. pp. 448. Augusta. Contents: Report on Fishes, Dr. E. Holmes; do. Mammals, I. G. Rich; do. Reptiles and Amphibions, Dr. B. F. Fogg; do. Insects, A. S. Packard, Sr.; do. Geology, C. H. Hitchcock.

Mitchel, O. M. The Astronomy of the Bible. Blakeman & Mason, N. Y.

Müller, Max. Lectures on the Science of Language. 8vo. pp. 416. Scribner, N. Y.

Nystrom's Pocket-Book of Mechanical Laws. Lippincott & Co., Philadelphia.

Nystroms, J. W. Treatise on the Parabolic Construction of Ships, and other Marine Engineering Subjects. Lippincott & Co. Philadelphia.

Packard, A. S. Jr. On Synthetic Types in Insects. Pamphlet. Boston.

Peirce, Benj. Report on the Determination of the Longitude of America and Europe from the Solar Eclipse of July 28th, 1851.

Peterson, R. E. Familiar Science; or, the Scientific Explanation of Common Things: to which is added Scientific Amusements for Young People. By Prof. Pepper. Philadelphia, G. W. Childs. 12mo. 150 illus.

Pharmacopeia of the United States. Fourth decennial revision. 12mo. pp. 339. Lippincott & Co., Philadelphia.

Porter, C. H. Medico-Legal Contributions on Arsenic. Pamph. Albany, N. Y.

Reizenstein, L. Von. Catalogue of the Lepidoptera of New Orleans and its Vicinity. 1863. New Orleans.

Report of Committee for 1862 on the Observatory of Harvard College; with Annual Report of the Director.

Report of the Commissioner of Agriculture for the Year 1862. Washington, 1863. Pub. Doc.

Report of the Regents of the University of the State of New York on the Longitudes of the Dudley Observatory, the Hamilton College Observatory, the City of Buffalo, and the City of Syracuse. Albany. 1862.

Ritter, Carl. Geographical Studies; translated by Rev. W. L. Gage; with a Sketch of the Author's Life. 12mo. $1.25. Gould & Lincoln, Boston.

Safford, T. H. The Observed Motions of the Companion of Sirius, considered with reference to the disturbing body indicated by theory. Cambridge, Mass. Pamph.

Scudder, S. H. List of the Butterflies of New England. 8vo. pamph.

Scudder, S. H. Materials for a Monograph of the N. American Orthoptera. 8vo. pamph. Cambridge, Mass.

Scudder, S. H. Remarks on the Insect Fauna of the White Mountains. Cambridge, Mass. Pamph.

Storer, Frank H. First Outlines of a Dictionary of the Solubilities of Chemical Substances. Sever & Francis, Cambridge, Mass.

Smithsonian Contributions to Knowledge. Discussion of the Magnetic and Meteorological Observations made at the Girard College Observatory, Philadelphia, in 1841–1845. Part II. Investigation of the Solar Diurnal Variation in the Magnetic Declination, and its Annual Inequality; by A. D. Bache.

The same. Part III. Investigation of the Influence of the Moon on the Magnetic Declination; by A. D Bache, LL.D. Washington. 1862.

Thoughts on some Natural Phenomena, bearing chiefly on the Primary Cause of the Succession of Species and the Unity of Force. Pamphlet. New York, Everdell, Publisher.

Transactions Illinois Natural History Society. Vol. I. 194. pp. 8vo. Springfield Illinois. Edited by C. D. Wilder, Secretary.

Treadwell, Daniel. On the Construction of Improved Ordnance. Cambridge, Mass. Pamph.

Tyndall, John, Prof. Heat considered as a Mode of Motion. Am. reprint. 12mo. pp. 480. D. Appleton & Co., N. Y.

Ure's Dictionary of Arts, Manufactures, and Mines, Supplement. Edited by Robert Hunt. Am. reprint. pp. 1096. Appleton & Co., N. Y.

Wells, D. A. Annual of Scientific Discovery for 1863. Gould & Lincoln, Boston.

Wetherill, C. M. Report on the Chemical Analysis of Grapes, submitted to the Department of Agriculture. Washington, D. C.

Whittlesey, Chas. Ancient mining of the shores of Lake Superior. Smithsonian Publications. 1863.

The Penokie Mineral Range, Wisconsin. Pamphlet. Boston.

Winchell, Alex. Description of Fossils from the Marshall and Huron Groups of Michigan. 8vo. pamph.

Youmans, E. L. A Class-Book of Chemistry, with 300 illust. N. Y., D. Appleton & Co.

INDEX.